T0212159

Lecture Notes in Artificial Intelligence 11691

Subseries of Lecture Notes in Computer Science

More information about this series at http://www.springer.com/series/1244

Jinchang Ren · Amir Hussain · Huimin Zhao ·
Kaizhu Huang · Jiangbin Zheng · Jun Cai ·
Rongjun Chen · Yinyin Xiao (Eds.)

Advances in Brain Inspired Cognitive Systems

10th International Conference, BICS 2019
Guangzhou, China, July 13–14, 2019
Proceedings

Editors
Jinchang Ren
University of Strathclyde
Glasgow, UK

Amir Hussain
Edinburgh Napier University
Edinburgh, UK

Huimin Zhao
Guangdong Polytechnic Normal University
Guangzhou, China

Kaizhu Huang
Xi'an Jiaotong-Liverpool University
Suzhou, China

Jiangbin Zheng
Northwestern Polytechnical University
Xi'an, China

Jun Cai
Guangdong Polytechnic Normal University
Guangzhou, China

Rongjun Chen
Guangdong Polytechnic Normal University
Guangzhou, China

Yinyin Xiao
Guangdong Polytechnic Normal University
Guangzhou, China

ISSN 0302-9743 ISSN 1611-3349 (electronic)
Lecture Notes in Artificial Intelligence
ISBN 978-3-030-39430-1 ISBN 978-3-030-39431-8 (eBook)
https://doi.org/10.1007/978-3-030-39431-8

LNCS Sublibrary: SL7 – Artificial Intelligence

This Springer imprint is published by the registered company Springer Nature Switzerland AG
The registered company address is: Gewerbestrasse 11, 6330 Cham, Switzerland

Preface

Welcome to the proceedings of BICS 2019 – the 10th International Conference on Brain Inspired Cognitive Systems. BICS has now become a well-established conference series on brain-inspired cognitive systems around the world, with growing popularity and increasing quality. BICS 2019 followed on from BICS 2004 (Stirling, Scotland, UK), BICS 2006 (Island of Lesvos, Greece), BICS 2008 (Sao Luis, Brazil), BICS 2010 (Madrid, Spain), BICS 2012 (Shenyang, China), BICS 2013 (Beijing, China), BICS 2015 (Hefei, China), BICS 2016 (Beijing, China), and BICS 2018 (Xi'an, China).

Geographically located at the south of China, Guangzhou is one of China's main industrial centers, covering an area of 7,434 square kilometers. It has a history of 2,200 years, and was historically the main port of the Maritime Silk Road. The city has always been the political, economic, and cultural center of South China for more than 2,000 years. Guangzhou was honored as a city of heroes, and now is famous for the diversity of the foods.

BICS 2019 aimed to provide a high-level international forum for scientists, engineers, and educators to present the state of the art of brain inspired cognitive systems research and applications in diverse fields. The conference featured plenary lectures given by world renowned scholars, regular sessions with broad coverage, and some special sessions and workshops focusing on popular and timely topics.

The BICS 2019 conference proceedings are published as part of the Springer LNAI series and indexed by EI. Selected best papers were recommended to SCI Journals including Cognitive Computation (Impact Factor 4.279). Selected papers were also recommended to several journal special issues including Journal of the Franklin Institute, Discrete Dynamics in Nature and Society (Hindawi), and others.

The BICS 2019 conference was primarily hosted by Guangdong Polytechnic Normal University (GPNU) and Guangdong Society of Image and Graphics (GSIG). Many organizations and volunteers made great contributions toward the success of this event. We are grateful for the great support from the University of Strathclyde, Edinburgh Napier University, Northwestern Polytechnical University, Sun Yat-sen University, and Guangdong University of Technology. We would also like to sincerely thank all the committee members for their great efforts and time in organizing the event. Special thanks go to the Program Committee members and reviewers whose insightful reviews and timely feedback ensured the high quality of the accepted papers and the smooth flow of the conference. We would also like to thank the publisher, Springer. Finally, we would like to thank all the speakers, authors, and participants for their support.

July 2019

Huimin Zhao
Amir Hussain
Jinchang Ren
Jun Cai
Jiangbin Zheng
Rongjun Chen

Organization

General Co-chairs

Huimin Zhao	Guangdong Polytechnic Normal University, China
Amir Hussain	Edinburgh Napier University, UK
Jiangbin Zheng	Northwestern Polytechnical University, China
Jinchang Ren	University of Strathclyde, UK
Jun Cai	Guangdong Polytechnic Normal University, China
Rongjun Chen	Guangdong Polytechnic Normal University, China

Honorary Co-chairs

David Feng	The University of Sydney, Australia
Derong Liu	University of Illinois, USA
Igor Aleksander	Imperial College London, UK
Tariq Tariq S. Durrani	University of Strathclyde, UK
Tieniu Tan	Chinese Academy of Sciences, China

Program Chairs

Cheng-Lin Liu	Chinese Academy of Sciences, China
Jiangqun Ni	Sun Yat-sen University, China
Bin Luo	Anhui University, China
Kaizhu Huang	Xi'an Jiaotong Liverpool University, China
Jin Zhan	Guangdong Polytechnic Normal University, China

Workshop Co-chairs

Chunmei Qing	South China University of Technology, China
Erfu Yang	University of Strathclyde, UK
Zheng Wang	Tianjin University, China
Zhijing Yang	Guangdong University of Technology, China

Publication Chairs

Fangyuan Lei	Guangdong Polytechnic Normal University, China
Yijun Yan	University of Strathclyde, UK
Jamie Zabalza	University of Strathclyde, UK

Publicity Chairs

Haibo He	University of Rhode Island, USA
Newton Howard	Massachusetts Institute of Technology, USA
El-Sayed El-Alfy	King Fahd University of Petroleum and Minerals, Saudi Arabia
Mohamed Chetouani	Pierre and Marie Curie University, France
Anna Esposito	Second University of Naples, Italy
Giacomo Indiveri	University of Zurich and ETH Zurich, Switzerland
Stefan Wermter	University of Hamburg, Germany
Erik Cambria	Nanyang Technological University, Singapore
Jonathon Wu	University of Windsor, Canada

Finance Chairs

Sophia Zhao	University of Strathclyde, UK
Yinyin Xiao	Guangdong Polytechnic Normal University, China

Registrations and Local Arrangements Chairs

Jin Zhan	Guangdong Polytechnic Normal University, China
Jujian Lv	Guangdong Polytechnic Normal University, China
Guoliang Xie	University of Strathclyde, UK

Organization Committee

Huimin Zhao	Guangdong Polytechnic Normal University, China
Jinchang Ren	University of Strathclyde, UK
Rongjun Chen	Guangdong Polytechnic Normal University, China
Yinyin Xiao	Guangdong Polytechnic Normal University, China
Jujian Lv	Guangdong Polytechnic Normal University, China
Jin Zhan	Guangdong Polytechnic Normal University, China
Leijun Wang	Guangdong Polytechnic Normal University, China
Weijian Li	Guangdong Polytechnic Normal University, China
Guoliang Xie	University of Strathclyde, UK

Academic Committee

Wei Huang	Chair of the Committee for Master's Degree of Education of Guangdong Polytechnical Normal University, China
Wenxin Deng	Director of Development Planning Department of Guangdong Polytechnical Normal University, China

Program Committee

Andrew Abel	Xi'an Jiaotong Liverpool University, China
Peter Andras	Keele University, UK
Xiang Bai	Huazhong University of Science and Technology, China
Vladimir Bajic	KAUST, Saudi Arabia
Yanchao Bi	Beijing Normal University, China
Erik Cambria	Nanyang Technological University, Singapore
Lihong Cao	Communication University of China, China
Chun-I Philip Chen	California State University, USA
Mingming Cheng	Nankai University, China
Dazheng Feng	Xidian University, China
David Yushan Fong	CITS Group, USA
Marcos Faundez	Zanuy Tecnocampus, Spain
Fei Gao	Beihang University, China
Alexander Gelbukh	CIC IPN, Mexico
Hugo Gravato	Marques ETH Zurich, Switzerland
Claudius Gros	Goethe University of Frankfurt, Germany
Junwei Han	Northwestern Polytechnical University, China
Xiangjian He	University of Technology Sydney, Australia
Bingliang Hu	Xi'an Institute of Optics and Precision Mechanics, Chinese Academy of Sciences, China
Xiaolin Hu	Tsinghua University, China
Kaizhu Huang	Xi'an Jiaotong Liverpool University, China
Tiejun Huang	Peking University, China
Amir Hussain	Edinburgh Napier University, UK
Rongrong Ji	Xiamen University, China
Zejun Jiang	Northwestern Polytechnical University, China
Donemei Jiang	Northwestern Polytechnical University, China
Yi Jiang	Institute of Psychology, Chinese Academy of Sciences, China
Jingpeng Li	University of Stirling, UK
Yongjie Li	University of Electronic Science and Technology of China, China
Cheng-Lin Liu	Institute of Automation, Chinese Academy of Sciences, China
Huaping Liu	Tsinghua University, China
Weifeng Liu	China University of Petroleum, China
Iman Yi Liao	University of Nottingham Malaysia Campus, Malaysia
Xiaoqiang Lu	Xi'an Institute of Optics and Precision Mechanics, Chinese Academy of Sciences, China
Xuelong Li	Xi'an Institute of Optics and Precision Mechanics, Chinese Academy of Sciences, China
Bin Luo	Anhui University, China
Mufti Mahmud	University of Padova, Italy

Zeeshan Malik	University of Stirling, UK
Deyu Meng	Xi'an Jiaotong University, China
Tomas Henrique Maul	University of Nottingham Malaysia Campus, Malaysia
Junaid Qadir	National University of Sciences and Technology, Pakistan
Jinchang Ren	University of Strathclyde, UK
Simone Scardapane	University of Rome, Italy
Bailu Si	Shenyang Institute of Automation, Chinese Academy of Sciences, China
Mingli Song	Zhejiang University, China
Genyun Sun	China University of Petroleum, China
Meijun Sun	Tianjin University, China
Walid Taha	Halmstad University, Sweden
Dacheng Tao	University of Technology Sydney, Australia
Yonghong Tian	Peking University, China
Isabel Trancoso	INESC-ID, Portugal
Stefano Vassanelli	University of Padua, Italy
Liang Wang	Institute of Psychology, Chinese Academy of Sciences, China
Zheng Wang	Tianjin University, China
Zhijiang Wang	Institute of Mental Health, Peking University, China
Qi Wang	Northwestern Polytechnical University, China
Hui Wei	Fudan University, China
Jonathan Wu	University of Windsor, Canada
Qiang Wu	University of Technology Sydney, Australia
Min Xu	University of Technology Sydney, Australia
Lei Xie	Northwestern Polytechnical University, China
Yong Xia	Northwestern Polytechnical University, China
Erfu Yang	University of Strathclyde, UK
Tianming Yang	Institute of Neuroscience, China
Zhijing Yang	Guangdong University of Technology, China
Jin Zhan	Guangdong Polytechnic Normal University, China
Aizhu Zhang	China University of Petroleum, China
Bing Zhang	Chinese Academy of Sciences, China
Daoqiang Zhang	Nanjing University of Aeronautics and Astronautics, China
Li Zhang	University of Birmingham, UK
Yanning Zhang	Northwestern Polytechnical University, China
Yifeng Zhang	Institute of Neuroscience, China
Jianbiao Zhang	Beijing University of Technology, China
Huimin Zhao	Guangdong Polytechnic Normal University, China
Xinbo Zhao	Northwestern Polytechnical University, China
Jiangbin Zheng	Northwestern Polytechnical University, China
Bing J. Zhou	Sam Houston State University, USA
Jun Zhu	Tsinghua University, China

Contents

Neural Computation

Biologically Inspired Systems

Data Analysis and Natural Language Processing

Neural Computation

Improving Image Caption Performance with Linguistic Context

Yupeng Cao, Qiu-Feng Wang(✉), Kaizhu Huang, and Rui Zhang

Xi'an Jiaotong-Liverpool University,
No. 111 Renai Road, Suzhou 215123, People's Republic of China
Yupeng.Cao17@student.xjtlu.edu.cn,
{Qiufeng.Wang,Kaizhu.Huang,Rui.Zhang02}@xjtlu.edu.cn

Abstract. Image caption aims to generate a description of an image by using techniques of computer vision and natural language processing, where the framework of Convolutional Neural Networks (CNN) followed by Recurrent Neural Networks (RNN) or particularly LSTM, is widely used. In recent years, the attention-based CNN-LSTM networks attain the significant progress due to their ability of modelling global context. However, CNN-LSTMs do not consider the linguistic context explicitly, which is very useful in further boosting the performance. To overcome this issue, we proposed a method that integrate a n-gram model in the attention-based image caption framework, managing to model the word transition probability in the decoding process for enhancing the linguistic context of translation results. We evaluated the performance of BLEU on the benchmark dataset of MSCOCO 2014. Experimental results show the effectiveness of the proposed method. Specifically, the performance of BLEU-1, BLEU-2, BLEU-3 BLEU-4, and METEOR is improved by 0.2%, 0.7%, 0.6%, 0.5%, and 0.1, respectively.

Keywords: Image caption · Linguistic context · CNN · Long-short term memory · Attention-base model

1 Introduction

As the saying goes "A picture is worth a thousand words", image caption aims to describe the image using natural words to represent its contents. With a high demand in web image searching, image caption has attracted much attention [1–4].

Inspired by the development of deep neural network and large image data growth, great progress has been made in some traditional tasks, such as image classification, object detection, sample generation and video analysis [5–9]. Image caption also gets the insights from these trends and achieves better results by combining Convolutional Neural Networks (CNNs) and Recurrent Neural Networks (RNNs) [3]. In order to avoid the clutter information and improve the captioning performance, recent mainstream approaches introduced the attention mechanism into the encode-decode framework (CNN-RNN) in which the

J. Ren et al. (Eds.): BICS 2019, LNAI 11691, pp. 3–11, 2020.
https://doi.org/10.1007/978-3-030-39431-8_1

model can capture the salient features from raw input images. However, the caption results obtained by the attention weight calculation describe global context, where the decoding part does not focus the explicitly linguistic relationship between different words or word group. In addition, RNN is difficult to capture the semantic relationships between two further words, hence probably ignoring previous information in decoding process [1,10].

To overcome this problem, we propose to integrate an n-gram model in the attention-based encode-decode framework for improving the captioning performance. Our approach models the word transition probability information and then embed this probability into the decoding process. Although the single generation word of RNN is obtained based on probability distribution (calculated from the attention weight), it may be affected by some clutter parts in feature image. In contrast to the internal probability information, our proposed method constructs the word probability matrix directly from raw reference sentences. Then this information is integrated into each decoding step of the baseline framework. We evaluate the performance of the proposed method in the dataset of MSCOCO 2014 [11]. Experimental results show the effectiveness of our proposed method. Furthermore, the proposed method can be easily integrated in different attention based models.

2 Related Work

In this section, we review some related works on image caption generation briefly. Prior to using the neural network based encode-decode framework, early image caption aims to build the corresponding relationship between visual information and the descriptive words [2,12]. Then, traditional object detection algorithms were involved in image caption to generate caption templates [13,14]. After that, RNN model was usually used to generate sentences behind the outputs of object detection [15].

Most recent methods followed the Google's Neural Image Caption (NIC) encode-decode framework, where the CNN models are used to extract a feature map from the input image and RNN models are exploited to translate the feature map to words [3]. Inspired by the progress of the attention model in machine translation, a lot of tasks in computer vision get significant improvement, especially the encode-decode framework incorporate the attention mechanism in the decoder part [1,16]. Every decoding step utilized the previous results to recalculate which part should be focused at current step. Following the achievement of the attention-base network, the adaptive attention method was proposed to reduce the disturbance from non-visual information results, such as, "a/an" and "the" [4]. Based on the attention-based image caption framework, our proposed method try to integrate the linguistic context explicitly.

3 Attention-Based Framework

In this section, we first describe the basic encode-decode pipeline for image caption. Then we explain the work principle of the attention mechanism in decoding process.

Encoder. In the encoder, we use CNN to extract features from the input image, which is divided to a sequence of frames. The encoder obtains the feature vector from the low level feature map of each frame of the input image. Since we do not use the CNN to classify the image, we engage as the feature vectors the output generated by the layer prior to the fully connect layer. Finally, the extracted feature vectors of the L frames of the input image can be defined by

$$V = \{v_1, \dots v_i, \dots, v_L\}, v_i \in R^D, \tag{1}$$

where v_i represents the i-th feature vector for the input image I and the size of V is L $\times$ D. It is noted that this is a straightforward parallel computation, requiring very little computation.

Decoder. We exploit the LSTM to generate the caption word sequence based on feature vectors [17] in the decoder, where each step includes a hidden state and generates a conditional probability as follows

$$\log p(y_t|y_1, \dots, y_{t-1}) = f(h_t, c_t). \tag{2}$$

In the above, h_t is the current hidden state, c_t represents the t-th visual information vector, and f is a nonlinear function to calculate the probability for y_t. In the decoder, the hidden state h_t will be updated by the LSTM model as follows

$$h_t = \text{LSTM}(V, h_{t-1}, \text{Gates}). \tag{3}$$

The LSTM includes four types of gates (i.e., input, forget, memory, and output gate) to enhance the relationship between the current result and previous generation word. It is able to reduce the occurrence of gradient disappearance in backpropagation process.

Attention Mechanism. When we use the attention mechanism into the decode, the focused area in the feature map at the current step will be recalculated. So the vector c_t will be updated as

$$c_t = \phi(\{v_i\}, \{\partial_i\}), \tag{4}$$

where ∂ describes the dynamic weights calculated by the following two equations:

$$e_{ti} = f_{att}(v_i, h_{t-1}), \tag{5}$$

and

$$\partial_{ti} = \frac{exp(e_{ti})}{\sum_{k=1}^{L} exp(e_{tk})}. \tag{6}$$

In Eq. (4), the function ϕ is determined by which attention mechanisms is used. In our work, we use the soft-attention, where it feeds in a mask ∂ into the corresponding feature map v_i. Finally, c_t is easily updated by

$$c_t = \sum_{i=1}^{L} \partial_{t,i} \cdot v_i. \tag{7}$$

Compared to the hard-attention, the soft-attention calculation process is differentiable. So the learning process is end-to-end and the parameters can be updated by back-propagation [1,18].

4 Attention-Based Network with Linguistic Context

Although the LSTM based method can model the context information in the sequence, it only captures the linguistic context implicitly from the large-scale the training data set of image caption. During the generation process, we find that each prediction word is only dependent on the last state, where the local linguistic context among the adjacent words are not explicitly considered. We hence consider the probability of occurrence for each word in the prepared large corpus as the local probability information in the decode of the attention based framework.

Figure 1 shows the system diagram of the proposed method, which is based on the encode-decode framework for image caption. During the decode process, we integrate the local linguistic context explicitly in the attention calculation. In the following, we will introduce the linguistic context and its integration in details.

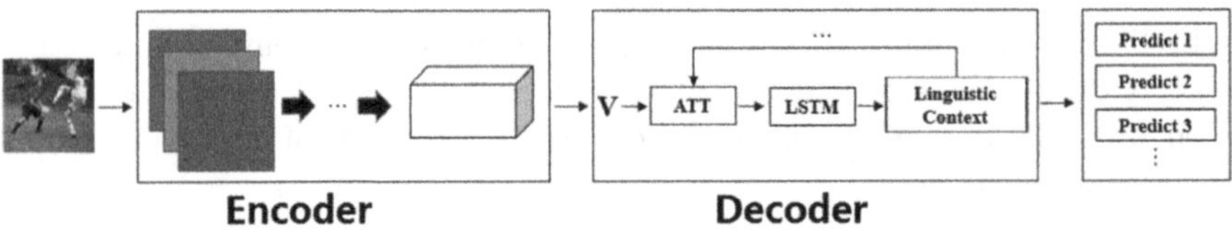

Fig. 1. System diagram of the proposed method.

Linguistic Context. Linguistic context is widely used in the natural language [19]. In the tasks similar to natural language processing (e.g., handwriting recognition [20,21], social text annotation [22] and speech recognition [23]), a statistical language model is usually used to estimate the probability of the sequence of the words, where the n-gram model is widely used due to its simplicity and efficiency [24].

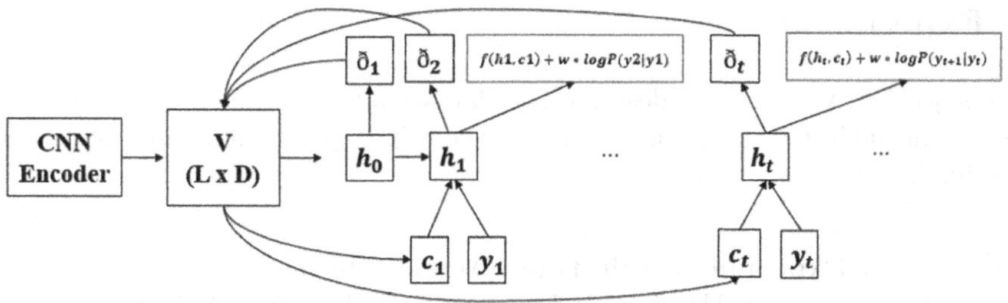

Fig. 2. Framework of integrating the linguistic context in decode process.

In our work, we merely consider the bi-gram model to represent the local linguistic context, which can be formulated by

$$P(y_i|y_1, y_2, ..., y_{i-1}) = P(y_i|y_{i-1}), \tag{8}$$

and the probability of each bi-gram can be obtained from a large-size linguistic corpus by

$$P(y_2|y_1) = \frac{P(y_2, y_1)}{P(y_1)}. \tag{9}$$

Moreover, all of the bi-grams construct a bi-gram probability matrix, which is constructed by the following algorithm.

Algorithm 1. Construct bi-gram probability matrix

```
for each annotation do
    Load Annotation. ["a cat is on a mat"]
    Split the sentence to signal word. ["a","cat","is","on","a","mat"]
    Append List
end for
Calculate bi-gram Probability. P("cat"|"a"), P("is"|"cat"), and so on.
Store calculate in the bi-gram probability matrix.
```

Integration of Linguistic Context. In this subsection, we will introduce how to integrate the linguistic context by using the probability matrix into the decode process, and Fig. 2 shows the illustrated integration procedure. In LSTM, the predicted probability of the next work is decided by $f(h_t, c_t)$ in Eq. (2), where we add the bi-gram probability to supplement the local linguistic context.

In this work, we use the log-linear combination for the integration of linguistic context, which is defined by

$$\log p(y_{t+1}|y_1, \ldots, y_t) = f(h_t, c_t) + \omega * \log(P(y_{t+1}|y_t)). \tag{10}$$

Here, $f(h_t, c_t)$ is the output by the LSTM decoder, and $P(y_t|y_{t-1})$ is the bi-gram probability obtained from the word transition probability matrix, and ω is a weight parameter to balance the two probabilities, which is empirically selected with a validation data set.

5 Experiment

In this section, we will first describe the dataset and experimental setting. We then detail the implementation. Finally, we show the quantitative analysis of the experimental results.

Dataset and Experimental Setting. We evaluate the proposed method on the benchmark dataset MSCOCO2014, consisting of complicated scene images with common objects in their natural context. COCO2014 has 82, 783 images for training, 40, 504 images for validation, 40, 775 images for test. COCO2014 provides the annotation to image, and every image has five referenced sentences. In the LSTM, we use the one-hot embedding method to represent each word [25].

Based on the annotation, we build the vocabulary list by using Python and summarize the appearance frequency for each single word. Overall,we have 361,257 sentences with the average length of 7 words. Finally, we get more than 2, 000, 000 words from the COCO2014 training dataset. Then, we calculate the transition probability for each word and store the result in the matrix with the size of $5,000 \times 5,000$.

Implementation Details. In the encoder, we first test both VGG and ResNet [26,27] and empirically we find that ResNet50 performs slightly better. We hence use ResNet50 in our experiments, with the pre-training on ImageNet. Each raw image can be divided into 2,048 frames, and each frame has a feature map with the size of 7×7. So the size of the final feature vector V after the ResNet model is $49 \times 2,048$, which will be input to the decoder. In decoder, we set every hidden layer to 512 units and we also specify the RNN length to 20 determined by the max sequence length. The embedding dimension of the word is fixed to 512. We also exploit the two-layer LSTM, meaning that there are two hidden layers in each longitudinal direction. In optimization, we utilize the cross entropy function as the loss function to measure the cost. The method of Adam is chosen to learn the parameters [28]. The learning rate is initialized at 0.0001, and the decay value is 0.9 for every 100, 000 steps. When LSTM generates prediction words, we take the beam search as the generation strategy with the higher probability. The beam width is set to 3 by following the previous work [4,10].

Results. In this subsection, we show several quantitative metrics on COCO 2014, including the BLEU standard from 1 to 4, METEOR, and CIDEr [29,30]. All of these metrics are popular in the evaluation of image caption.

Table 1 shows different metric values for the three methods, include the popular Google NIC method [3], the soft-attention based as baseline method [1], and the proposed method based on the soft-attention model. We can see that our proposed method improves the performance on all of the metrics.[1] Specifically,

[1] we get a higher score of CIDEr, but no results were reported on the other two methods in the literature.

Table 1. Experimental results of the proposed method on MSCOCO2014 dataset

Dataset	Model	BLEU-1	BLEU-2	BLEU-3	BLEU-4	METEOR	CIDEr
MS COCO	Google NIC [3]	63	41	27	\	\	\
	SoftAttention [1]	70.7	51.6	37.8	27.6	23.90	\
	Proposed method	70.9	52.2	38.4	28.1	24.00	81.8

the values of BLEU-1, BLEU-2, BLEU-3, BLEU-4 and METEOR are improved by 0.2%, 0.7%, 0.6%, 0.5%, and 0.1%, respectively. Comparing the four BLEU improvements, we can find that the improvement of BLEU-1 is the smallest, since BLEU-1 evaluates the single word between the prediction result and the annotation sentence, which include no sufficient linguistic information. On the other hand, we observe that the improvement of BLEU-2 is the largest, since we integrates the bi-gram probability, which appears to best match the BLEU-2 metric.

From Sect. 4, we can see the integration of linguistic context does not depend on the specific attention method. We hence evaluate the proposed method in another attention mechanism, e.g., adaptive attention. In adaptive attention, "visual sentinel" is used to determine whether a context vector is visual information or non-visual information where it can remove some words not corresponding visual part in raw image. These cases include "a" "an" and "the" [4]. By integrating the proposed linguistic context, we compare the experimental results in Table 2. We can see that the baseline method of the adaptive attention is much better than the soft-attention as seen in Table 1. The integration of the linguistic context also improves the performance, e.g., the BLEU-2, BLEU-4 and CIDEr are improved by 0.2%, 0.2%, and 1, respectively. This once again shows the effectiveness of the proposed method.

Table 2. Performance of the proposed method in the adaptive attention model on MSCOCO2014

Dataset	Model	BLEU-1	BLEU-2	BLEU-3	BLEU-4	METEOR	CIDEr
COCO2014	Adaptive attention	74.8	58.2	43.9	32.7	25.5	102
	Proposed method	74.8	58.5	43.9	32.9	25.5	103

6 Conclusion

The linguistic context plays an important role in many tasks of computer vision and machine learning. In this paper, we propose to integrate the linguistic context explicitly for image caption, where the n-gram probability is integrated in the attention based LSTM decoder. We evaluate the proposed method on benchmark data. Extensive experimental results show that our proposed model can consistently improve the performance. In future, we will consider to integrate much advanced language models (e.g., BERT [31]) in image caption.

Acknowledgements. The work was partially supported by the following: CCF-Tencent Open Research Fund RAGR20180109, National Natural Science Foundation of China under no. 61876155, and 61876154; The Natural Science Foundation of the Jiangsu Higher Education Institutions of China under no. 17KJD520010; Suzhou Science and Technology Program under no. SYG201712, SZS201613; Natural Science Foundation of Jiangsu Province BK20181189 and BK20181190; Key Program Special Fund in XJTLU under no. KSF-A-01, KSF-P-02, KSF-E-26, and KSF-A-10; XJTLU Research Development Fund RDF-16-02-49.

References

1. Xu, K., et al.: Show, attend and tell: neural image caption generation with visual attention. In: International Conference on Machine Learning, pp. 2048–2057 (2015)
2. Farhadi, A., et al.: Every picture tells a story: generating sentences from images. In: Daniilidis, K., Maragos, P., Paragios, N. (eds.) ECCV 2010. LNCS, vol. 6314, pp. 15–29. Springer, Heidelberg (2010). https://doi.org/10.1007/978-3-642-15561-1_2
3. Vinyals, O., Toshev, A., Bengio, S., Erhan, D.: Show and tell: a neural image caption generator. In: Proceedings of the IEEE Conference on Computer Vision and Pattern Recognition, pp. 3156–3164 (2015)
4. Lu, J., Xiong, C., Parikh, D., Socher, R.: Knowing when to look: adaptive attention via a visual sentinel for image captioning. In: Proceedings of the IEEE Conference on Computer Vision and Pattern Recognition, pp. 375–383 (2017)
5. Krizhevsky, A., Sutskever, I., Hinton, G.E.: ImageNet classification with deep convolutional neural networks. In: Advances in Neural Information Processing Systems, pp. 1097–1105 (2012)
6. Girshick, R., Donahue, J., Darrell, T., Malik, J.: Rich feature hierarchies for accurate object detection and semantic segmentation. In: Proceedings of the IEEE Conference on Computer Vision and Pattern Recognition, pp. 580–587 (2014)
7. Han, J., Zhang, D., Hu, X., et al.: Background prior-based salient object detection via deep reconstruction residual. IEEE Trans. Circ. Syst. Video Technol. **25**(8), 1309–1321 (2014)
8. Yang, X., Huang, K., Zhang, R., et al.: A novel deep density model for unsupervised learning. Cogn. Comput. **11**(6), 778–788 (2018)
9. Wang, Z., Ren, J., Zhang, D., et al.: A deep-learning based feature hybrid framework for spatiotemporal saliency detection inside videos. Neurocomputing **287**, 68–83 (2018)
10. Chen, H., Ding, G., Lin, Z., Guo, Y., Han, J.: Attend to knowledge: memory-enhanced attention network for image captioning. In: Ren, J., et al. (eds.) BICS 2018. LNCS (LNAI), vol. 10989, pp. 161–171. Springer, Cham (2018). https://doi.org/10.1007/978-3-030-00563-4_16
11. Lin, T.-Y., et al.: Microsoft COCO: common objects in context. In: Fleet, D., Pajdla, T., Schiele, B., Tuytelaars, T. (eds.) ECCV 2014. LNCS, vol. 8693, pp. 740–755. Springer, Cham (2014). https://doi.org/10.1007/978-3-319-10602-1_48
12. Barnard, K., Duygulu, P., Forsyth, D., de Freitas, N., Blei, D.M., Jordan, M.I.: Matching words and pictures. J. Mach. Learn. Res. **3**(Feb), 1107–1135 (2003)
13. Kulkarni, G., Premraj, V., Ordonez, V., et al.: BabyTalk: understanding and generating simple image descriptions. IEEE Trans. Pattern Anal. Mach. Intell. **35**(12), 2891–2903 (2013)

14. Yang, Y., Teo, C.L., Daum III, H., Aloimonos, Y.: Corpus-guided sentence generation of natural images. In: Proceedings of the Conference on Empirical Methods in Natural Language Processing, pp. 444–454. Association for Computational Linguistics, July 2011
15. Karpathy, A., Fei-Fei, L.: Deep visual-semantic alignments for generating image descriptions. In: The IEEE Conference on Computer Vision and Pattern Recognition, June 2015
16. Yan, Y., Ren, J., Sun, G., et al.: Unsupervised image saliency detection with Gestalt-laws guided optimization and visual attention based refinement. Pattern Recogn. **79**, 65–78 (2018)
17. Hochreiter, S., Schmidhuber, J.: Long short-term memory. Neural Comput. **9**(8), 1735–1780 (1997)
18. LeCun, Y., Bottou, L., Bengio, Y., et al.: Gradient-based learning applied to document recognition. Proc. IEEE **86**(11), 2278–2324 (1998)
19. Ellis, N.C.: Frequency effects in language processing: a review with implications for theories of implicit and explicit language acquisition. Stud. Second. Lang. Acquis. **24**(2), 143–188 (2002)
20. Wang, Q.-F., Yin, F., Liu, C.-L.: Integrating language model in handwritten Chinese text recognition. In: Proceedings of the 10th ICDAR, pp. 1036–1040 (2009)
21. Wang, Q.F., Yin, F., Liu, C.L.: Handwritten Chinese text recognition by integrating multiple contexts. IEEE Trans. Pattern Anal. Mach. Intell. **34**(8), 1469–1481 (2011)
22. Dong, H., Wang, W., Huang, K., et al.: Joint multi-label attention networks for social text annotation. In: Proceedings of the 2019 Conference of the North American Chapter of the Association for Computational Linguistics: Human Language Technologies, Volume 1 (Long and Short Papers), pp. 1348–1354 (2019)
23. Jurafsky, D., Martin, J.H.: Speech and Language Processing, 2nd edn. Pearson Prentice Hall, Upper Saddle River (2008)
24. Goodman, J.T.: A bit of progress in language modeling: extended version. Technical report MSR-TR-2001-72, Microsoft Research (2001)
25. Turian, J., Ratinov, L., Bengio, Y.: Word representations: a simple and general method for semi-supervised learning. In: Proceedings of the 48th Annual Meeting of the Association for Computational Linguistics. Association for Computational Linguistics, pp. 384–394 (2010)
26. Simonyan, K., Zisserman, A.: Very deep convolutional networks for large-scale image recognition. arXiv preprint arXiv:1409.1556 (2014)
27. He, K., Zhang, X., Ren, S., Sun, J.: Deep residual learning for image recognition. In: Proceedings of the IEEE Conference on Computer Vision and Pattern Recognition, pp. 770–778 (2016)
28. Kingma, D.P., Ba, J.: Adam: a method for stochastic optimization. arXiv preprint arXiv:1412.6980 (2014)
29. Banerjee, S., Lavie, A.: METEOR: an automatic metric for MT evaluation with improved correlation with human judgments. In: Proceedings of the ACL Workshop on Intrinsic and Extrinsic Evaluation Measures for Machine Translation and/or Summarization, pp. 65–72 (2005)
30. Vedantam, R., Lawrence Zitnick, C., Parikh, D.: CIDEr: consensus-based image description evaluation. In: Proceedings of the IEEE Conference on Computer Vision and Pattern Recognition, pp. 4566–4575 (2015)
31. Devlin, J., Chang, M.W., Lee, K., et al.: BERT: pre-training of deep bidirectional transformers for language understanding. arXiv preprint arXiv:1810.04805 (2018)

Self-focus Deep Embedding Model for Coarse-Grained Zero-Shot Classification

Guanyu Yang[1,2], Kaizhu Huang[1(✉)], Rui Zhang[1], John Y. Goulermas[2], and Amir Hussain[3]

[1] Xi'an Jiaotong-Liverpool University, SIP, Suzhou 215123, China
{Guanyu.Yang,Kaizhu.Huang,Rui.Zhang02}@xjtlu.edu.cn
[2] Department of Computer Science, University of Liverpool, Liverpool L69 3BX, UK
J.Y.Goulermas@liv.ac.uk
[3] School of Computing, Edinburgh Napier University, Edinburgh EH11 4BN, UK
A.Hussain@napier.ac.uk

Abstract. Zero-shot learning (ZSL), i.e. classifying patterns where there is a lack of labeled training data, is a challenging yet important research topic. One of the most common ideas for ZSL is to map the data (e.g., images) and semantic attributes to the same embedding space. However, for coarse-grained classification tasks, the samples of each class tend to be unevenly distributed. This leads to the possibility of learned embedding function mapping the attributes to an inappropriate location, and hence limiting the classification performance. In this paper, we propose a novel regularized deep embedding model for ZSL in which a self-focus mechanism, is constructed to constrain the learning of the embedding function. During the training process, the distances of different dimensions in the embedding space will be focused conditioned on the class. Thereby, locations of the prototype mapped from the attributes can be adjusted according to the distribution of the samples for each class. Moreover, over-fitting of the embedding function to known classes will also be mitigated. A series of experiments on four commonly used zero-shot databases show that our proposed method can attain significant improvement in coarse-grained data sets.

Keywords: Generalized Zero-Shot Learning · Coarse-grained · Class-level over-fitting

1 Introduction

In the field of computer vision, the deep learning methods have made great achievements in tasks such as image classification [7,23,26] and object detection [15,20]. Zero-shot learning (ZSL), as an active research topic in deep learning [4,18,22,24], aims to imitate the powerful ability of human that learns new

J. Ren et al. (Eds.): BICS 2019, LNAI 11691, pp. 12–22, 2020.
https://doi.org/10.1007/978-3-030-39431-8_2

categories only through some descriptive side information based on the experience. Specifically, in the zero-shot image classification task, semantic description attributes are commonly used as the side information [14]. By learning the correlation between the samples and the attributes of each category, the zero-shot model can simply construct concepts of new categories, also called unseen categories, based on the corresponding attributes instead of a large number of samples for those classes.

In order to improve the robustness of models, generalized relations between samples and attributes should be learned. To achieve this goal, one optional idea is to train the classifier after generating pseudo samples for unseen categories [2,10,22]. However, due to the special architectures of this kind of methods, unlabeled samples or semantic attributes in the test set are usually required during training, and the tasks become transductive ZSL or semantic transductive ZSL which violate the unseen principle. Table 1 shows the schematic diagrams of the data splits for different ZSL tasks. For the test process, conventional zero-shot learning (CZSL) simply assumes that all the test instances are from the new (unseen) classes, and as a more generalized setting, generalized zero-shot learning (GZSL) assumes that the test instances come from both of the seen and unseen classes [3,21].

Table 1. Schematic diagrams of data splits for several types of ZSL

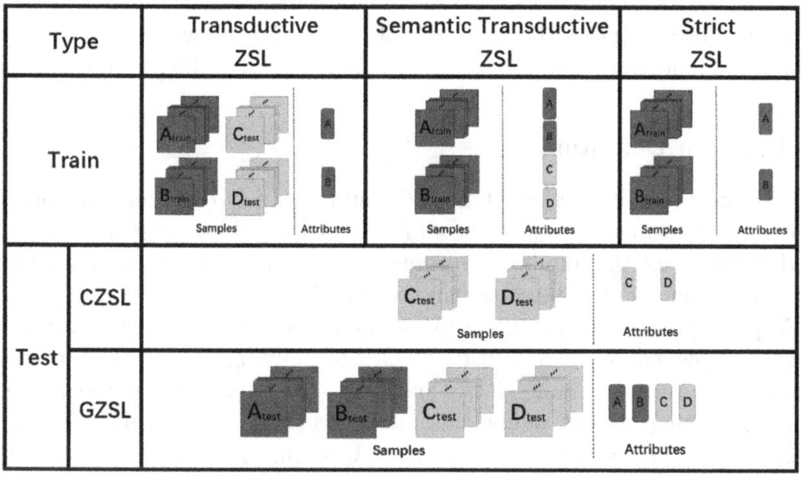

Type		Transductive ZSL	Semantic Transductive ZSL	Strict ZSL
Train		Samples: A_{train}, B_{train}, C_{test}, D_{test}; Attributes: A, B	Samples: A_{train}, B_{train}; Attributes: A, B, C, D	Samples: A_{train}, B_{train}; Attributes: A, B
Test	CZSL	Samples: C_{test}, D_{test}; Attributes: C, D		
	GZSL	Samples: A_{test}, B_{test}, C_{test}, D_{test}; Attributes: A, B, C, D		

For the strict ZSL, one of the most common ideas is to learn a metric space for label identification [9,12,17,24,25]. Based on this idea, the measurement of the distance and the generalization of the embedding function become the keys to improve the robustness. Some early models mapped the visual instances to the semantic information space to determine their corresponding categories [13]. However, this mapping direction will aggravate the hubness problem for ridge regression methods [5,16]. Inspired by this thought, the opposite direction embedding using deep neural network was applied in [25], and the distance in the reverse mapped space was used as a regularization term in [9]. Moreover, many other ideas were proposed to learn a better embedding space, such as, learning prototypes from samples to support training [12], preserving similarities between semantic attributes in the visual space [1], and pushing the inter-class distances via orthogonal mapping [24] or a learned similarity metric [18].

In this paper, we propose a self-focused deep embedding model using the visual feature space as the metric space. A self-focus mechanism, constructed as a 1-layer neural network with $softmax$, is connected behind the embedding module to calculate a focus-ratio vector for each dimension. Training the embedding function based on these focus-ratios, the correlation between the attribute and the importance of dimensions will be considered which leads the learned embedding function becomes more generalized, especially when samples are distributed unevenly with large intra-class distances. Our proposed framework can achieve outstanding performance on coarse-grained zero-shot classification tasks, which are validated later in the experimental section. Particularly, a series of experiments show that the proposed self-focus mechanism as a kind of neural network based regularization can effectively alleviate the class-level over-fitting problem.

2 Methodology

In order to better explain the structure of our model, we will first describe the zero-shot classification task. Here, we only focus on strict CZSL and GZSL.

2.1 Problem Definition

Let $X = \{x_1, x_2, ..., x_N\}$, $Y = \{1, 2, ..., C\}$ and $A = \{a_1, a_2, ..., a_C\}$ denote data sets of visual features, class number and semantic attributes respectively, where N and C represent the numbers of samples and categories respectively. Then a training set (seen set) can be settled in terms of 3-tuple as $D_s = \{(x_i, y_i, a_{y_i}), i = 1, ..., N_s\}$, where $y_i \in \{1, 2, ..., C_s\}$ represents the label of the corresponding class for each sample x_i, $N_s < N$ and $C_s < C$. Specially, $y_m = y_n$ $(m \neq n)$ means x_m and x_n are from the same class, thus, $a_{y_m} = a_{y_n}$ due to the correspondence. Under this setting, we can define the unseen set as $X_u \times Y_u \times A_u$ where $X_u = \{x_{N_s+1}, ..., X_N\}$, $Y_u = \{C_s + 1, ..., C\}$ and $A_u = \{a_{C_s+1}, ..., a_C\}$ which does not overlap with the seen set. Given a test sample set $X_t = X_u$, the aim of zero-shot classification is to predict labels of X_t from Y_t based on A_t, where $Y_t = Y_u$, $A_t = A_u$ for CZSL and $Y_t = Y$, $A_t = A$ for GZSL.

2.2 Model Architecture

To avoid the promotion of the hubness problem mentioned in [16], we selected deep embedding model (DEM) [25] as the baseline to project semantic attributes into the visual feature space. The structure of the proposed model is shown

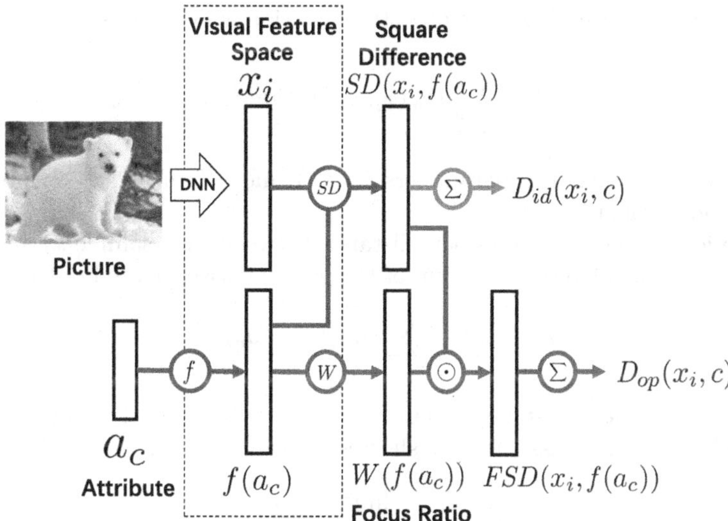

Fig. 1. The structure of the proposed self-focus deep embedding model. Paths in purple represent the embedding process, paths in red represent the optimization process and paths in blue represent the identification process. (Color figure online)

in Fig. 1, the paths in three colors represent the operations required for three process: embedding, optimization, and identification, respectively.

In the embedding process, each sample x_i denotes a d_v-dimensional feature vector extracted by a pre-trained DNN, and each attribute a_c denotes a d_a-dimensional vector containing the semantic information. $f(a_c)$ denotes the prototype of class c in the visual space projected by a learnable embedding function $f(\cdot)$, where $f(\cdot)$ is a fully connected deep neural network with input size d_a, output size d_v and activation function *relu*. Then the squared difference for each dimension between the prototype $f(a_c)$ and sample x_i is calculated as

$$SD_k(x_i, f(a_c)) = (x_{ik} - f(a_c)_k)^2, \tag{1}$$

where subscript $k \in \{1, 2, ..., d_v\}$ represents the dimension number.

In the optimization process, a focus-ratio vector is calculated as $W(f(a_c))$ based on the projected prototype, where $W(\cdot)$ is a 1-layer fully connected neural network with activation function *sigmoid* and followed by *softmax* operation. Then the focused square difference for each dimension is calculated as

$$FSD_k(x_i, f(a_c)) = SD_k(x_i, f(a_c)) \cdot W(f(a_c))_k, \tag{2}$$

and the distance between sample x_i and prototype $f(a_c)$ used for optimization is defined as the sum

$$D_{op}(x_i, c) = \sum_k FSD_k(x_i, f(a_c)). \tag{3}$$

By setting $c = y_i$ for each x_i, the objective function is defined as

$$\mathbb{L} = \sum_{i=1}^{N_s} D_{op}(x_i, y_i) + \lambda \|\boldsymbol{\theta}\|^2, \tag{4}$$

where $\boldsymbol{\theta}$ represents all the parameters in $f(\cdot)$ and $W(\cdot)$, and λ denotes the regularization weight.

In the identification process, the distance between each sample x_i and prototype $f(a_c)$ is calculated as the sum of the element-wise squared differences:

$$D_{id}(x_i, c) = \sum_k SD_k(x_i, f(a_c)), \tag{5}$$

which is the Euclidean distance. Therefore, the predicted label $\hat{y}_i$ can be calculated by choosing the class with the shortest distance to x_i as

$$\hat{y}_i = \arg\min_{c \in Y_t} D_{id}(x_i, c) \tag{6}$$

3 Experiments

To illustrate the effectiveness of the proposed model, we first compared the embedding results with the baseline, and then provided the results of comparisons between the proposed model and the state-of-art methods.

3.1 Datasets

Three coarse-grained and one fine-grained ZSL benchmarks were selected, which are AwA1 [11], AwA2 [21], aPY [6], and CUB [19], respectively. In order to avoid overlapping of categories in the test sets and sets for training feature extraction networks, we follow the GBU setting proposed in [21] for attributes, deep extracted visual features and training/test splits.

Table 2. Statistics for AwA1, AwA2, aPY, and CUB in terms of granularity, class size, sample size and sample divergence.

Dataset	Granularity	Class size		Sample size			Sample divergence	
		train(seen)	unseen	train	test$_{seen}$	test$_{unseen}$	avg$_{range}$	avg$_{var}$
AwA1	Coarse	40	10	19832	4958	5685	4.16	0.39
AwA2	Coarse	40	10	23527	5882	7913	3.88	0.36
aPY	Coarse	20	12	5932	1483	7924	3.96	0.44
CUB	Fine	150	50	7057	1764	2967	1.78	0.21

As the definition of each category is broad in coarse-grained datasets, the intra-class distances between samples would be larger compared with that of fine-grained datasets. To numerically illustrate this, we calculate the range and variance of the samples for each dimension in each class, and then calculate the average values of these ranges and variances over all the classes and dimensions, respectively. The details for each dataset are summarised in Table 2, where the average range and variance of the fine-grained database is roughly half of the values in coarse-grained databases.

3.2 Embedding Results

In the target mapping space, the correlations between the focus-ratios and positions of prototypes are concerned, due to the proposed self-focus mechanism. Figure 2 shows the mapping results for some dimensions, which visually indicated that the self-focus mechanism makes the mapping position biased compared with the baseline.

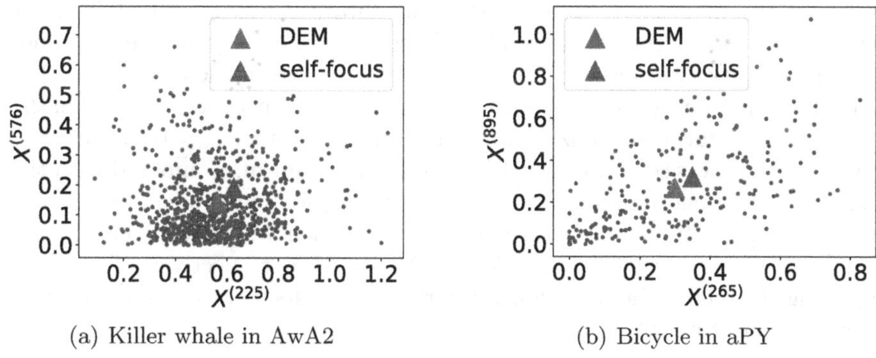

(a) Killer whale in AwA2

(b) Bicycle in aPY

Fig. 2. 2D plot of chosen dimensions and classes in AwA2 and aPY, where the subscript represents the dimension number.

The class-level over-fitting (CO) problem proposed in [24] describes the situation that models are not well generalized to the test sets due to $Y_t \cap Y_s = \emptyset$. For most of the embedding models, the CO problem mainly occurs in the learning process of embedding functions. Figure 3 provides an intuitive description of the CO problem when mapping the semantic attributes to visual space. Due to the samples of class A are available in the training process, the model excessively maps large areas in attribute space to the vicinity of the prototype of class A in visual space.

According to this description, the minimum value of the inter-class Euclidean distances from each unseen attribute to the seen attributes in the target space can be regarded as a representative criterion to illustrate the CO problem. In Table 3, the average of these minimum values for the baseline and the proposed method are provided, where subscript s_s denotes the distances between the seen attributes and their nearest seen attributes, u_s denotes the distances between

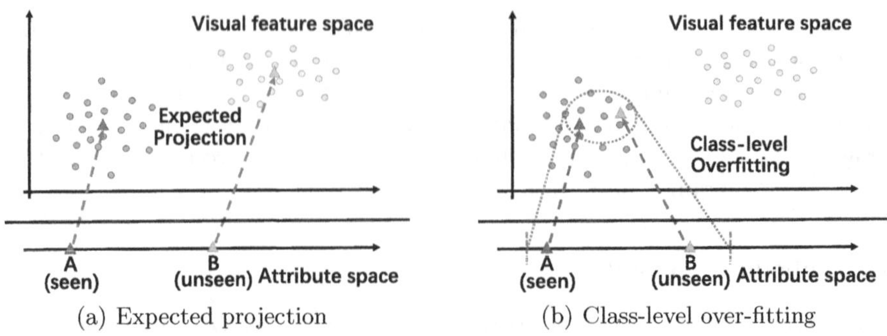

(a) Expected projection

(b) Class-level over-fitting

Fig. 3. The intuitive description of the CO problem: (a): The expected projection; (b): The undesirable projection caused by class-level over-fitting.

the unseen attributes and their nearest seen attributes and N_{zero_d} denotes the number of the dimensions whose values are always 0 during embedding. For fairness, when calculating the inter-class distances, the dimensions with 0 values for each method were excluded first and then the means of the distances in the rest of the dimensions were used. Since different distance measures are used in the proposed model during optimization and identification process, part of the class-level over-fitting was separated by the self-focus mechanism. Compared with the baseline, the average minimum inter-class distance for our model is obviously increased. Especially for coarse-grained datasets, such values are increased by 22.82%, 36.86% and 38.06% for AwA1, AwA2 and aPY, respectively. Therefore, optimizing the embedding function supported by the focus-ratios is an effective way to alleviate the CO problem.

Table 3. Evaluation of class-level over-fitting problem of the proposed model compared with the baseline DEM [25].

Dataset	$avgmin_{s\_s}$		$avgmin_{u\_s}$		N_{zero_d}	
	DEM	Self-focus	DEM	Self-focus	DEM	Self-focus
AwA1	0.1201	0.136	0.0746	0.0916	829	831
AwA2	0.1475	0.1844	0.0925	0.1266	978	1297
aPY	0.1476	0.19	0.0349	0.0481	38	23
CUB	0.0116	0.0123	0.0101	0.0115	135	308

3.3 Zero-Shot Recognition

Following the protocol in [21], the performance is evaluated using per-class average Top-1 accuracy. Moreover, GZSL evaluates the results of testing images from seen (s) and unseen (u) classes separately. We also use H to denote the harmonic mean of the seen and unseen accuracies $H = \frac{2 \times s \times u}{s+u}$.

Table 4. Comparison results of DEM, deeper DEM and the proposed self-focus model.

AwA1	CZSL	GZSL		
		s	u	H
DEM*(2-layer)	68.4	**84.7**	32.8	47.3
DEM(2-layer)	68.1	83.6	34.8	49.1
DEM_deeper(3-layer)	65.4	83.3	31.7	45.9
self-focus(2-layer)	**70.4**	83.2	**39.1**	**53.2**

AwA2	CZSL	GZSL		
		s	u	H
DEM*(2-layer)	67.1	**86.4**	30.5	45.1
DEM(2-layer)	67.1	85.9	32.0	46.6
DEM_deeper(3-layer)	65.3	86.0	31.8	46.4
self-focus(2-layer)	**68.1**	84.5	**39.0**	**53.4**

aPY	CZSL	GZSL		
		s	u	H
DEM*(2-layer)	35.0	75.1	11.1	19.3
DEM(2-layer)	35.2	76.4	12.7	21.8
DEM_deeper(6-layer)	38.8	**80.0**	23.3	36.1
DEM_deeper(7-layer)	**38.9**	78.1	24.6	37.4
self-focus(6-layer)	38.3	78.5	**26.2**	**39.3**

CUB	CZSL	GZSL		
		s	u	H
DEM*(2-layer)	**51.7**	**57.9**	19.6	29.2
DEM(2-layer)	49.2	48.6	21.5	29.8
DEM_deeper(3-layer)	46.2	42.3	19.1	26.3
self-focus(2-layer)	48.6	47.5	**21.9**	**30.0**

Our model has the same embedding structure as the DEM [25], but has one more fully connected layer in the self-focus module. In order to verify that the improvement of our model is not simply due to the increasing in the total number of layers, we also considered a deeper DEM as the baseline whose embedding neural network is one layer deeper.

Table 5. Experiment setup for each dataset.

Dataset	Embedding neural network		Learning rate	Regularization weight λ	Batch size
	Number of layers	Layer structures			
AwA1	2	85-1600-2048	0.0001	0.001	64
AwA2	2	85-1600-2048	0.0001	0.001	64
aPY	6	64-1600-2048-2048-2048-2048	0.0001	0.0001	64
CUB	2	312-1200-2048	0.00001	0.01	100

Table 4 lists the zero-shot comparison results between the proposed model and the baselines, where DEM* denotes the reported results on GitHub,[1] the rest of the results were obtained by our own implementations and the total numbers of layers in embedding modules are listed in brackets. On the aPY dataset, since the original structure was not deep enough to achieve the best performance, we did the comparison under a deeper network structure. When the embedding network is deep enough, the proposed self-focus mechanism can significantly increase the accuracies of the unseen classes with an acceptable reduction in accuracies of seen classes in the three coarse-grained datasets. However, simply

[1] Available at https://github.com/lzrobots/DeepEmbeddingModel_ZSL.

increasing the number of layers in the embedding module cannot achieve the same effect on aPY, and even makes the results worse on AwA1 and AwA2. On the CUB dataset, though we cannot achieve the reported performance, we show that the proposed self-focus mechanism has no obvious negative impact on the fine-grained zero-shot task. Therefore, the comparison demonstrates that the self-focus module benefits the coarse-grained zero-shot task due to its own structure.

Table 6. Comparison with state-of-the-art methods on CZSL and GZSL.

Method	AwA1				AwA2				aPY				CUB			
	CZSL	GZSL			CZSL	GZSL			CZSL	GZSL			CZSL	GZSL		
		u	s	H		u	s	H		u	s	H		u	s	H
SAE [9]	53.0	1.8	77.1	3.5	54.1	1.1	82.2	2.2	8.3	0.4	**80.9**	0.9	33.3	7.8	54.0	13.6
DEM [25]	68.4	32.8	84.7	47.3	67.1	30.5	86.4	45.1	35.0	11.1	75.1	19.4	51.7	19.6	57.9	29.2
DEM*	68.1	34.8	83.6	49.1	67.1	32.0	85.9	46.6	**38.9**	24.6	78.1	37.4	49.2	21.5	48.6	29.8
Relation Net [18]	68.2	31.4	**91.3**	46.7	64.2	30.0	**93.4**	45.3	–	–	–	–	55.6	**38.1**	61.1	**47.0**
Triple Verification Net [24]	68.8	27.0	67.9	38.6	–	–	–	–	41.3	16.1	66.9	25.9	**58.1**	26.5	**62.3**	37.2
Proposed	**70.4**	**39.1**	83.2	**53.2**	**68.1**	**39.0**	84.5	**53.4**	38.3	**26.2**	78.5	**39.3**	48.6	21.9	47.5	30.0

Moreover, during the training process, our model is initialized with random weights, and Adam [8] is selected as the optimizer for all of our experiments. Detailed experiment setup for each dataset is listed in Table 5 and the results of comparison with the state-of-the-art methods can be found in Table 6. The best performance are marked in bold, and our model obviously outperformed the others on coarse-grain zero shot datasets. Although for fine-grained databases, the methods whose objective functions are designed explicitly pushing the inter-class distances performed much more outstanding, it is not the goal in this paper.

4 Conclusion

In this paper, a deep embedding model with a novel self-focus mechanism is proposed for coarse-grained zero-shot learning. Specifically, a self-focus mechanism is designed to calculate focus-ratios for each dimension in the embedding space. By optimizing the embedding function based on these ratios, the relationships between location and dimensional importance in the embedding space are considered. Since the proposed mechanism can constrain the learned embedding function based on the distribution of samples for each class, it can also be regarded as a regularization operation during the training process. Furthermore, the class-level over-fitting problem can be effectively alleviated by the proposed mechanism. Extensive experiments on coarse-grained zero-shot benchmarks demonstrate both the effectiveness and outstanding performance of our approach.

Acknowledgements. The work was partially supported by National Natural Science Foundation of China under no. 61876155, and 61876154; The Natural Science Foundation of the Jiangsu Higher Education Institutions of China under no. 17KJD520010; Suzhou Science and Technology Program under no. SYG201712, SZS201613; Natural Science Foundation of Jiangsu Province BK20181189 and BK20181190; Key Program Special Fund in XJTLU under no. KSF-A-01, KSF-P-02, KSF-E-26, and KSF-A-10; XJTLU Research Development Fund RDF-16-02-49.

References

1. Annadani, Y., Biswas, S.: Preserving semantic relations for zero-shot learning. In: Proceedings of the IEEE Conference on Computer Vision and Pattern Recognition, pp. 7603–7612 (2018)
2. Bucher, M., Herbin, S., Jurie, F.: Generating visual representations for zero-shot classification. In: International Conference on Computer Vision Workshops: Transferring and Adapting Source Knowledge in Computer Vision (2017)
3. Chao, W.-L., Changpinyo, S., Gong, B., Sha, F.: An empirical study and analysis of generalized zero-shot learning for object recognition in the wild. In: Leibe, B., Matas, J., Sebe, N., Welling, M. (eds.) ECCV 2016. LNCS, vol. 9906, pp. 52–68. Springer, Cham (2016). https://doi.org/10.1007/978-3-319-46475-6_4
4. Ding, Z., Shao, M., Fu, Y.: Generative zero-shot learning via low-rank embedded semantic dictionary. IEEE Trans. Pattern Anal. Mach. Intell. **41**(12), 2861–2874 (2019)
5. Dinu, G., Lazaridou, A., Baroni, M.: Improving zero-shot learning by mitigating the hubness problem. In: International Conference on Learning Representations, Workshop on Track Proceedings (2015)
6. Farhadi, A., Endres, I., Hoiem, D., Forsyth, D.: Describing objects by their attributes. In: IEEE Conference on Computer Vision and Pattern Recognition, pp. 1778–1785 (2009)
7. Huang, G., Liu, Z., Van Der Maaten, L., Weinberger, K.Q.: Densely connected convolutional networks. In: IEEE Conference on Computer Vision and Pattern Recognition, pp. 4700–4708 (2017)
8. Kingma, D.P., Ba, J.: Adam: a method for stochastic optimization. In: International Conference on Learning Representations (2015)
9. Kodirov, E., Xiang, T., Gong, S.: Semantic autoencoder for zero-shot learning. In: IEEE Conference on Computer Vision and Pattern Recognition, pp. 3174–3183 (2017)
10. Kumar Verma, V., Arora, G., Mishra, A., Rai, P.: Generalized zero-shot learning via synthesized examples. In: IEEE Conference on Computer Vision and Pattern Recognition, pp. 4281–4289 (2018)
11. Lampert, C.H., Nickisch, H., Harmeling, S.: Attribute-based classification for zero-shot visual object categorization. IEEE Trans. Pattern Anal. Mach. Intell. **36**(3), 453–465 (2014)
12. Luo, C., Li, Z., Huang, K., Feng, J., Wang, M.: Zero-shot learning via attribute regression and class prototype rectification. IEEE Trans. Image Process. **27**(2), 637–648 (2018)
13. Mikolov, T., Le, Q.V., Sutskever, I.: Exploiting similarities among languages for machine translation. arXiv preprint arXiv:1309.4168 (2013)
14. Parikh, D., Grauman, K.: Relative attributes. In: IEEE International Conference on Computer Vision, pp. 503–510 (2011)

15. Ren, S., He, K., Girshick, R., Sun, J.: Faster R-CNN: towards real-time object detection with region proposal networks. In: Advances in Neural Information Processing Systems, pp. 91–99 (2015)
16. Shigeto, Y., Suzuki, I., Hara, K., Shimbo, M., Matsumoto, Y.: Ridge regression, hubness, and zero-shot learning. In: Appice, A., Rodrigues, P.P., Santos Costa, V., Soares, C., Gama, J., Jorge, A. (eds.) ECML PKDD 2015. LNCS (LNAI), vol. 9284, pp. 135–151. Springer, Cham (2015). https://doi.org/10.1007/978-3-319-23528-8_9
17. Snell, J., Swersky, K., Zemel, R.: Prototypical networks for few-shot learning. In: Advances in Neural Information Processing Systems, pp. 4077–4087 (2017)
18. Sung, F., Yang, Y., Zhang, L., Xiang, T., Torr, P.H., Hospedales, T.M.: Learning to compare: relation network for few-shot learning. In: IEEE Conference on Computer Vision and Pattern Recognition, pp. 1199–1208 (2018)
19. Wah, C., Branson, S., Welinder, P., Perona, P., Belongie, S.: The caltech-ucsd birds-200-2011 dataset (2011)
20. Wang, Z., Ren, J., Zhang, D., Sun, M., Jiang, J.: A deep-learning based feature hybrid framework for spatiotemporal saliency detection inside videos. Neurocomputing **287**, 68–83 (2018)
21. Xian, Y., Lampert, C.H., Schiele, B., Akata, Z.: Zero-shot learning-a comprehensive evaluation of the good, the bad and the ugly. IEEE Trans. Pattern Anal. Mach. Intell. **41**(9), 2251–2265 (2019)
22. Xian, Y., Lorenz, T., Schiele, B., Akata, Z.: Feature generating networks for zero-shot learning. In: IEEE Conference on Computer Vision and Pattern Recognition, pp. 5542–5551 (2018)
23. Yang, X., Huang, K., Zhang, R., Hussain, A.: Introduction to deep density models with latent variables. In: Huang, K., Hussain, A., Wang, Q.F., Zhang, R. (eds.) Deep Learning: Fundamentals, Theory and Applications. COCT, vol. 2, pp. 1–29. Springer, Cham (2019). https://doi.org/10.1007/978-3-030-06073-2_1
24. Zhang, H., Long, Y., Guan, Y., Shao, L.: Triple verification network for generalized zero-shot learning. IEEE Trans. Image Process. **28**(1), 506–517 (2019)
25. Zhang, L., Xiang, T., Gong, S.: Learning a deep embedding model for zero-shot learning. In: IEEE Conference on Computer Vision and Pattern Recognition, pp. 2021–2030 (2017)
26. Zhang, S., Huang, K., Zhang, R., Hussain, A.: Learning from few samples with memory network. Cogn. Comput. **10**(1), 15–22 (2018)

A Multi-view Images Classification Based on Shallow Convolutional Neural Network

Fangyuan Lei[1(✉)], Xun Liu[1], Qingyun Dai[1], Huimin Zhao[2], Lin Wang[1], and Rongfu Zhou[1]

[1] School of Electronic and Information, Guangdong Polytechnic Normal University, Guangzhou 510640, China
Leify@126.com

[2] School of Computer, Guangdong Polytechnic Normal University, Guangzhou 510640, China

Abstract. Multi-view images represent the target object from multiple perspectives. Learning the target object information from different viewpoints helps to improve the accuracy of multi-view images classification. We propose a multi-view recognition method (SCNN-a) based on shallow convolutional neural network. In order to improve the generalization capability and classification performance of model, we develop a new multi-view images classification method (SCNN), which adds Dropout (after each max-pooling layer) technology to SCNN-a. SCNN-a and SCNN regard the images from predefined views as latent variables, and extract the high-order features of multi-view images with two convolutional layers. Experimental results show that SCNN achieves similar accuracy to the state-of-the-art result of [7] with less layers and time complexity.

Keywords: Convolutional neural network · Shallow convolutional neural network · Multi-view images classification · Dropout · Latent variables

1 Introduction

Convolutional neural networks (CNNs) have been widely applied to single-view images, such as medical image segmentation [23], human pose assessment [3], and image retrieval [21]. However, describing the object images from various perspectives can get more and richer information of the images. Therefore, researchers focus on how to efficiently learn multi-view representations of target objects.

Currently, multi-view descriptors can be classified into the following four categories. (1) Voxel-based multi-view descriptors [2,14,15,25,27]. These descriptors directly learn the characteristics of 3D multi-view images and extract the features with 3D convolution. The input data of this method is high dimensional. For example, the input of [25] is $64 \times 64 \times 64$, which contains all spatial structure information of the 3D images. The descriptors are directed to the processing of regular grid data. However, there are many irregular graph-structured

J. Ren et al. (Eds.): BICS 2019, LNAI 11691, pp. 23–33, 2020.
https://doi.org/10.1007/978-3-030-39431-8_3

data such as point cloud data. (2) 3D point cloud based descriptors [6,16]. These descriptors directly process unordered 3D point cloud. However, they extract the features without the local features and structural constraints of point clouds. (3) Graph CNN-based descriptors [5,19]. These descriptors can deal with arbitrary graph-structured data. Compared to (2) descriptors, the descriptors are better in terms of local characterization of data. The graph CNN has a particularly high time complexity. Other than those above descriptors, Multi-view descriptors based on 2D images have recently attracted much interest. (4) Multi-view descriptors based on 2D images [1,22,29]. The descriptors fuse the features of 2D images from different views of target images, which have excellent performance in terms of accuracy and time complexity. We propose two new shallow CNNs, which effectively learn the multi-view representations of multi-view images. The networks take multi-view images as input, outputting a category likelihood matrix.

The main contributions of this paper are as follows.

(1) We propose two new shallow convolutional neural networks (SCNN-a and SCNN) with 2 convolutional layers, which fast learn the features of multi-view images.
(2) We introduce Dropout (after each max-pooling layer) strategy to improve generalization capability and classification precision.
(3) Compared to the 224×224 pixels of [7], the size of our input images is only 32×32, which saves valuable time and computing resources.
(4) SCNN can achieve higher accuracy than [5], with 26% relative improvement for multi-view images classification.

2 Related Works

Looking at a target image from different angles may obtain different information of the image. The information of the image should include a set of images from various viewpoints. Multi-view representation of a target image has become a hot spot. The common multi-view descriptors are as follows.

(1) Voxel-based multi-view descriptors. In [25], the author proposes a 3D-GAN, which combines general-adversarial modeling and volumetric convolutional networks to generate high-quality 3D objects. In [2], the author develops a residual network to improve accuracy for volumetric image classification. In [15], the author develops two novel losses, which obtains stable results from different domains. However, the approach cannot be applied to non-Euclidean domains such as 3D point cloud.
(2) 3D point cloud-based multi-view descriptors. In [6], the author proposes a new 3D convolution model to process 3D point clouds. In [16], the author develops a novel 3D point cloud network framework, which uses 3D spatial transformation matrix to align data. The framework fuses the feature by 3 layer perception with 64, 128, and 1024 neurons respectively. However, the approach does not consider the local features and structural constraints of data.

(3) Graph CNN-based multi-view descriptors. In [5], the author constructs the exact mesh data, and utilizes a graph convolutional neural network to learn multi-view images. In [19], the author proposes a dynamic graph convolutional neural model, which can deal with an arbitrary graph of varying size and connectivity. The filter weights vary according to the connected edge labels. However, training the network requires high amount of calculation.
(4) 2D image-based multi-view descriptors. In order to solve the problem of graph CNN-based descriptors, 2D image-based multi-view descriptors are applied to multi-view images. In [22], the author utilizes pooling strategy to combine the feature information of pre-defined 2D images. In [29], the author proposes a new method for 3D shapes classification, which builds a set of 6 depth maps of 3D shapes. In [1], the author designs a method, which generates 3D images by 2D images of different views. In [7], the author develops a novel approach by combining VGG19 [20] with RNN models, which can achieve the state-of-the-art precision of 94.05%.

3 Method

3.1 Dropout to Improve Accuracy

In CNN model, if the parameters of the model are too many whereas the training samples are too few, the model is prone to over-fitting. To solve the over-fitting problem, an effective approach is to perform k times cross-validation. However, it takes much time to train. In order to address the above issues, Dropout technology is applied to the networks of [8,10]. In [8,10], the authors just use dropout (after fully connected layer) trick to prevent over-fitting. However, the features extracted by convolution are redundant, which may lead to over-fitting of network. To further prevent over-fitting of model, we propose a new network model using Dropout trick after each max-pooling layer. The Dropout-based model reduces the dependency of local features, forcing the model to learn more robust features. We use Dropout trick (each max-pooling layer and after fully connected layer) to prevent over-fitting and improve precision.

3.2 SCNN-a and SCNN Model

We propose two shallow CNNs models with two convolutional layers. The models are shown in Figs. 1 and 2. (1) SCNN-a model (Fig. 1). We propose a shallow CNN model (SCNN-a) without Dropout (after each max-pooling). SCNN-a first extracts low-order features by the former convolutional layer with 32 filters. Then the convolutional layer followed by Relu to increase the nonlinearity of the model. Next 2×2 max-pooling is used to reduce data dimension and computation. After first max-pooling layer, SCNN-a extracts depth characteristics by using the latter convolutional layer with 64 filters. Then the latter convolution followed by Relu to enhance learning ability of the model. Next the second max-pooling layer with the size of 2×2 is applied to further reduce data redundancy and computation.

After the second max-pooling layer, a fully connected layer with 1280 neurons is introduced to fuse the extracted features. Then Relu is used to make the model non-linear. Next Dropout is introduced to reduce over-fitting and improve the generalization ability of the model. Finally, softmax output layer to achieve multi-classification.

(2) SCNN model (Fig. 2). We develop a shallow CNN model (SCNN), which the Dropout (after each max-pooling) trick is introduced to SCNN-a to get more accuracy. See Sect. 3.1 for details on Dropout.

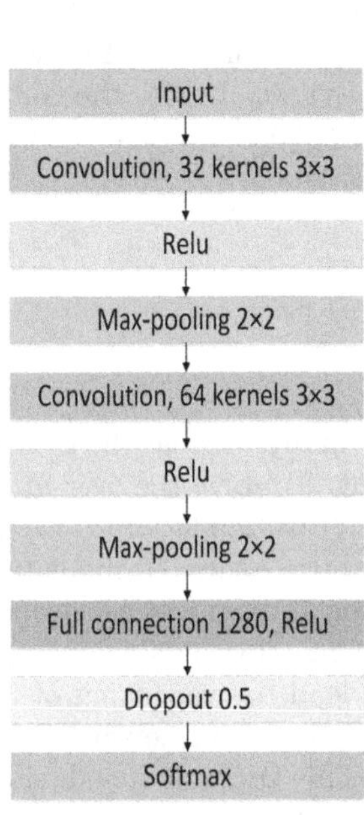

Fig. 1. SCNN-a model.

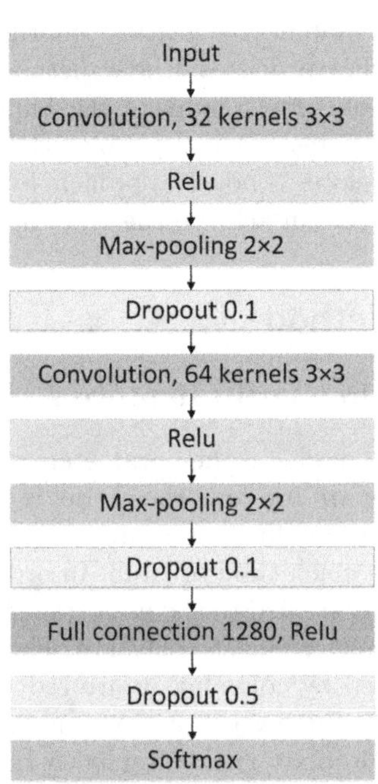

Fig. 2. SCNN model.

3.3 Training and Testing Process with $SCNN-a$ and $SCNN$

Since SCNN-a and SCNN have the same training and testing process, we introduce SCNN as an example to analyze the training and testing process of the model. The process of SCNN inspired by [9]. The training process of SCNN is mainly to maximize Eq. (3).

$$\max_{SCNN,\{v_k\}_{k=1}^{M}} \sum_{k=1}^{M} (\log p_{v_k,y}^{(k)} + \sum_{j \neq v_k} \log p_{j,N+1}^{(k)}) \tag{1}$$

$$= \max_{SCNN,\{v_k\}_{k=1}^{M}} \sum_{k=1}^{M} (\log p_{v_k,y}^{(k)} + \sum_{j=1}^{M} \log p_{j,N+1}^{(k)} - \log p_{v_k,N+1}^{(k)}) \tag{2}$$

$$= \max_{SCNN,\{v_k\}_{k=1}^{M}} \prod_{k=1}^{M} \frac{p_{v_k,y}^{(k)}}{p_{v_k,N+1}^{(k)}}. \tag{3}$$

where $\{x_k\}_{k=1}^{M}$ and $y \in \{1, 2, ..., N\}$ denote the object images from M views and its labels. $N+1$ is incorrect category label. Where $p_{v_k,y}^{(k)}$ indicates the same possibility of the estimated label and the real label y in the v_k-th view. Instead, where $p_{j,N+1}^{(k)}$ denotes the probability that the predicted label from incorrect perspective is the same as $N+1$ label.

Specifically, there are the following steps.

(1) Input. Object images $\{x_k\}_{k=1}^{M}$ from M viewpoints and its labels $y \in \{1, 2, ..., N\}$. In order to increase the stability of SCNN, an incorrect category label $N+1$ is introduced.
(2) Training. Training viewpoint variables $v_k \in \{1, 2, ..., M\}$ with SCNN to output a category likelihood matrix $P(\hat{y} = y \mid x_k, v_k)$ where $k \in \{1, 2, ..., M\}$. During SCNN, the labels are given, whereas the $\{v_k\}$ are unknown. In other words, SCNN regards the $\{v_k\}$ as latent variables to update.
(3) Determination. In the light of the $P(\hat{y} = y \mid x_k, v_k)$ to determine the v_k.
(4) Optimization. According to the v_k to update the weights of SCNN by back propagation (BP).
(5) Repeat. Repeating (2), (3) and (4) steps to get more accuracy.

During the test, the process of test is similar to the training phase, except that object images from $M'(1 \leq M' \leq M)$ views.

4 Experiments

4.1 Dataset

The Modelnet10 dataset is introduced by Wu et al. [26] for multi-view images classification, which consists of 4899 (3991 for training and 908 for test) target objects. The resolution of the images is 224 × 224 for RGB channel. We resize the images to 32 × 32 pixels and set predefined viewpoints M of [9] to 20.

4.2 Experimental Parameter

In our experiments, we set batch size as 200 and learning rate as 0.1. The learning rate is updated by stochastic gradient descent (SGD) with momentum of 0.9. We set L2 loss weight to 0.000001 and dropout to 0.1. All experiments of classification are trained for 100 epochs.

4.3 Results

To verify the advantages of Dropout (after each max-pooling), we compare the number of training epochs to achieve some representative accuracy and their respective best precision between SCNN and SCNN-a.

Table 1 shows the results on Modelnet10 dataset. SCNN-a without the Dropout (after each max-pooling) takes 44 epochs to reach the classification result of 93.17%, whereas SCNN only needs 35 epochs to more than the precision of 93.17%. SCNN with Dropout (after each max-pooling) technology achieves 93.40% accuracy with 35 epochs, whereas SCNN-a never achieves the accuracy throughout the training period. SCNN with the Dropout reaches the maximum test accuracy of 93.50%, which is 0.33% higher than BSGCN-a to reach the best classification precision of 93.17%. It implies SCNN that each max-pooling layer followed by Dropout technology can get the more robust features of multi-view images, improve the generalization capability of model, and get more classification result.

Table 1. Comparison on epochs to max accuracy and max accuracy on $Modelnet10$

Methods	Epochs to 93.17%	Epochs to 93.40%	$ModelNet10$ (Max Accuracy)
SCNN (ours)	-	35	93.50%
SCNN-a (ours)	44	Not reach	93.17%

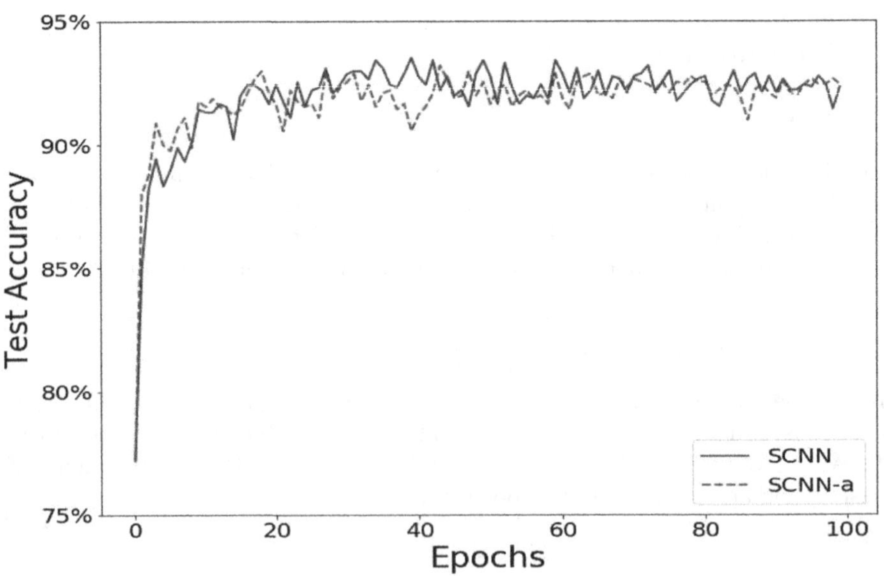

Fig. 3. A comparison of SCNN-a and SCNN.

Figure 3 shows the comparison of test accuracy between SCNN and SCNN-a on Modelnet10 dataset. The overall trend of SCNN is significantly higher than SCNN-a. The accuracy of SCNN is 0.19% (average, 40−100 epochs), 0.11% (average, 80–100 epochs) and 0.13% (average, 0–100 epochs) higher than SCNN-a, respectively. It implies that SCNN by Dropout (after each max-pooling) trick can improve accuracy.

Table 2. The comparison of our methods and voxel-based methods.

Methods	*ModelNet10*
3D-GAN [25]	91.0%
Xu and Todorovic [27]	88.00%
binVoxNetPlus [15]	92.32%
VSL [14]	91.0%
SCNN (ours)	93.50%
SCNN-a (ours)	93.17%

Table 2 shows the results comparison of our methods and voxel-based multi-view methods on Modelnet10 dataset. Compared to voxel-based multi-view methods [14,15,25,27], our methods of SCNN and SCNN-a achieve 93.50% and 93.50% accuracy respectively, which are at least 0.85% higher than [14,15,25,27]. Moreover, the input data of [14,15,25,27] is high dimensional. For example, the [25] with $64 \times 64 \times 64$ resolution generates high computation whereas SCNN with 32×32 pixels requires low computing resource.

Table 3. The comparison of our methods and 3D point cloud-based methods.

Methods	*ModelNet10*
PointNet [6]	77.6%
G3DNET [4]	93.1%
SCNN (ours)	93.50%
SCNN-a (ours)	93.17%

Table 3 shows the accuracy comparison of our methods and 3D point cloud-based multi-view methods [4,6] on Modelnet10 dataset. Compared to PointNet [6], SCNN achieves higher classification, with 20% relative improvement. SCNN is only 0.40% higher than G3DNET [4] of 93.1%. However, the framework of [4] with deep graph CNN includes multiple graph convolutional layers, which leads to high computational and memory resources. Moreover, SCNN has only two convolutional layers, saving valuable time resources.

Table 4. The comparison of our methods and graph CNN-based methods.

Methods	$ModelNet10$
Dominguez et al. [5]	74.3%
ECC [19]	90.0%
SCNN (ours)	93.50%
SCNN-a (ours)	93.17%

Table 4 shows the accuracy comparison of our methods and graph CNN-based multi-view methods [5,19] on Modelnet10 dataset. SCNN achieves higher result than graph CNN-based [5], with 26% relative improvement. ECC [19] is 3.5% lower than SCNN with classical convolution. Compared to SCNN without graph convolution, the methods of [5,19] require more calculation cost.

Table 5. The comparison of our methods and 2D image-based methods.

Methods	$ModelNet10$
Zanuttigh and Minto [29]	91.5%
VIPGAN [7]	94.05%
SCNN (ours)	93.50%
SCNN-a (ours)	93.17%

Table 5 shows the accuracy comparison of our methods and 2D image-based multi-view methods [7,29] on Modelnet10 dataset. The method of [29] is lower than SCNN-a and SCNN. VIPGAN [7] by VGG19 and RNN model achieves the state-of-the-art result of 94.05% for multi-view images classification. SCNN by 32×32 resolution includes 2 convolutional layers with 32/64 filters and 2 fully connected layers with 1280/220 neurons, whereas VGG19 [20] with 224×224 pixels consists of 16 convolutional layers (such as convolution with 512 filters) and 3 fully connected layers with 4096/4096/10 neurons. Compared to VIPGAN [7], SCNN achieves similar accuracy with less time and space complexity.

5 Conclusions

We propose two new shallow convolutional neural networks (SCNN-a and SCNN) by 2 convolutional layers for multi-view images classification. We compare the results of SCNN-a and SCNN, which indicate that SCNN with Dropout (after each max-pooling) trick can learn more robust features and get more result. The comparative experiments of our methods and classical methods prove that SCNN can achieve competitive precision with two convolutional layers. In the future work, we will extend our SCNN-a and SCNN to these tasks of [11–13,17, 18,24,28,30,31].

Acknowledgment. This research was funded by the Scientific and Technological Projects of Guangdong Province grant number (2017A050501039), the Guangdong Province General Colleges and Universities Featured Innovation grant number (2015GXJK080), the Qingyuan Science and Technology Plan Project grant number (170809111721-249, 170802171710591), and the Scientific and Technological Projects of Guangdong Province (2019A070701013).

References

1. Arsalan Soltani, A., Huang, H., Wu, J., Kulkarni, T.D., Tenenbaum, J.B.: Synthesizing 3D shapes via modeling multi-view depth maps and silhouettes with deep generative networks. In: Proceedings of the IEEE Conference on Computer Vision and Pattern Recognition, pp. 1511–1519 (2017)
2. Arvind, V., Costa, A., Badgeley, M., Cho, S., Oermann, E.: Wide and deep volumetric residual networks for volumetric image classification. arXiv preprint arXiv:1710.01217 (2017)
3. Cao, Z., Simon, T., Wei, S.E., Sheikh, Y.: Realtime multi-person 2D pose estimation using part affinity fields. In: Proceedings of the IEEE Conference on Computer Vision and Pattern Recognition, pp. 7291–7299 (2017)
4. Dominguez, M., Dhamdhere, R., Petkar, A., Jain, S., Sah, S., Ptucha, R.: General-purpose deep point cloud feature extractor. In: 2018 IEEE Winter Conference on Applications of Computer Vision (WACV), pp. 1972–1981. IEEE (2018)
5. Dominguez, M., Such, F.P., Sah, S., Ptucha, R.: Towards 3D convolutional neural networks with meshes. In: 2017 IEEE International Conference on Image Processing (ICIP), pp. 3929–3933. IEEE (2017)
6. Garcia-Garcia, A., Gomez-Donoso, F., Garcia-Rodriguez, J., Orts-Escolano, S., Cazorla, M., Azorin-Lopez, J.: Pointnet: a 3D convolutional neural network for real-time object class recognition. In: 2016 International Joint Conference on Neural Networks (IJCNN), pp. 1578–1584. IEEE (2016)
7. Han, Z., Shang, M., Liu, Y.S., Zwicker, M.: View inter-prediction GAN: unsupervised representation learning for 3D shapes by learning global shape memories to support local view predictions. arXiv preprint arXiv:1811.02744 (2018)
8. Hinton, G.E., Srivastava, N., Krizhevsky, A., Sutskever, I., Salakhutdinov, R.R.: Improving neural networks by preventing co-adaptation of feature detectors. arXiv preprint arXiv:1207.0580 (2012)
9. Kanezaki, A., Matsushita, Y., Nishida, Y.: RotationNet: joint object categorization and pose estimation using multiviews from unsupervised viewpoints. In: Proceedings of the IEEE Conference on Computer Vision and Pattern Recognition, pp. 5010–5019 (2018)
10. Krizhevsky, A., Sutskever, I., Hinton, G.E.: ImageNet classification with deep convolutional neural networks. In: Advances in Neural Information Processing Systems, pp. 1097–1105 (2012)
11. Lei, F.Y., Cai, J.: EIWCS: characterizing edges importance to weaken community structure. In: Applied Mechanics and Materials, vol. 556, pp. 6054–6057. Trans Tech Publ (2014)
12. Lei, F., Cai, J., Dai, Q., Zhao, H.: Deep learning based proactive caching for effective WSN-enabled vision applications. Complexity 2019, 12 p. (2019)

13. Lei, F.Y., Dai, Q.Y., Cai, J., Zhao, H.M., Liu, X., Liu, Y.: A Proactive Caching Strategy Based on Deep Learning in EPC of 5G. In: Ren, J., Hussain, A., Zheng, J., Liu, C.-L., Luo, B., Zhao, H., Zhao, X. (eds.) BICS 2018. LNCS (LNAI), vol. 10989, pp. 738–747. Springer, Cham (2018). https://doi.org/10.1007/978-3-030-00563-4_72
14. Liu, S., Giles, L., Ororbia, A.: Learning a hierarchical latent-variable model of 3D shapes. In: 2018 International Conference on 3D Vision (3DV), pp. 542–551. IEEE (2018)
15. Ma, C., Guo, Y., Lei, Y., An, W.: Binary volumetric convolutional neural networks for 3-D object recognition. IEEE Trans. Instrum. Meas. **99**, 1–11 (2018)
16. Qi, C.R., Su, H., Mo, K., Guibas, L.J.: PointNet: deep learning on point sets for 3D classification and segmentation. In: Proceedings of the IEEE Conference on Computer Vision and Pattern Recognition, pp. 652–660 (2017)
17. Ren, J., Wang, D., Jiang, J.: Effective recognition of MCCS in mammograms using an improved neural classifier. Eng. Appl. Artif. Intell. **24**(4), 638–645 (2011)
18. Ren, J., Xu, M., Orwell, J., Jones, G.A.: Multi-camera video surveillance for real-time analysis and reconstruction of soccer games. Mach. Vis. Appl. **21**(6), 855–863 (2010)
19. Simonovsky, M., Komodakis, N.: Dynamic edge-conditioned filters in convolutional neural networks on graphs. In: Proceedings of the IEEE Conference on Computer Vision and Pattern Recognition, pp. 3693–3702 (2017)
20. Simonyan, K., Zisserman, A.: Very deep convolutional networks for large-scale image recognition. arXiv preprint arXiv:1409.1556 (2014)
21. Solli, M., Bergstrom, S.: Image retrieval and processing systems and methods, US Patent App. 10/180,950, 15 Jan 2019
22. Su, H., Maji, S., Kalogerakis, E., Learned-Miller, E.: Multi-view convolutional neural networks for 3D shape recognition. In: Proceedings of the IEEE international conference on computer vision. pp. 945–953 (2015)
23. Su, H., Maji, S., Kalogerakis, E., Learned-Miller, E.: Multi-view convolutional neural networks for 3D shape recognition. In: Proceedings of the IEEE International Conference on Computer Vision, pp. 945–953 (2015)
24. Wang, Z., Ren, J., Zhang, D., Sun, M., Jiang, J.: A deep-learning based feature hybrid framework for spatiotemporal saliency detection inside videos. Neurocomputing **287**, 68–83 (2018)
25. Wu, J., Zhang, C., Xue, T., Freeman, B., Tenenbaum, J.: Learning a probabilistic latent space of object shapes via 3D generative-adversarial modeling. In: Advances In Neural Information Processing Systems, pp. 82–90 (2016)
26. Wu, Z., Song, S., Khosla, A., Yu, F., Zhang, L., Tang, X., Xiao, J.: 3D ShapeNets: a deep representation for volumetric shapes. In: Proceedings of the IEEE Conference on Computer Vision and Pattern Recognition, pp. 1912–1920 (2015)
27. Xu, X., Todorovic, S.: Beam search for learning a deep convolutional neural network of 3D shapes. In: 2016 23rd International Conference on Pattern Recognition (ICPR), pp. 3506–3511. IEEE (2016)
28. Yan, Y., et al.: Unsupervised image saliency detection with gestalt-laws guided optimization and visual attention based refinement. Pattern Recogn. **79**, 65–78 (2018)

29. Zanuttigh, P., Minto, L.: Deep learning for 3D shape classification from multiple depth maps. In: 2017 IEEE International Conference on Image Processing (ICIP), pp. 3615–3619. IEEE (2017)
30. Zhang, A., Sun, G., Ren, J., Li, X., Wang, Z., Jia, X.: A dynamic neighborhood learning-based gravitational search algorithm. IEEE Trans. Cybern. **48**(1), 436–447 (2016)
31. Zheng, J., Liu, Y., Ren, J., Zhu, T., Yan, Y., Yang, H.: Fusion of block and keypoints based approaches for effective copy-move image forgery detection. Multidimension. Syst. Sig. Process. **27**(4), 989–1005 (2016)

Low-Rank Laplacian Similarity Learning

Si-Bao Chen[1,2(✉)], Rui-Rui Wang[1], Bin Luo[1], and Jian Zhang[2]

[1] Key Lab of Intelligent Computing and Signal Processing of Ministry of Education, School of Computer Science and Technology, Anhui University, Hefei 230601, China
sbchen@ahu.edu.cn

[2] Peking University Shenzhen Institute, Shenzhen 518057, China

Abstract. Graph Laplacian methods are shown to be effective to reveal low-dimensional manifold which concealed in high-dimensional data features. However, the quality of constructed graph affects the final performance of graph Laplacian similarity. In this paper, we propose a low-rank Laplacian similarity learning method with local reconstruction restriction and selection operator type minimization. A low-rank constraint is added to the graph Laplacian matrix. An iterative algorithm is proposed to optimize the low-rank Laplacian similarity learning method. The proposed method is applied to clustering, classification and semi-supervised classification. Extensive experiments demonstrate the effectiveness of the proposed method.

Keywords: Similarity learning · Manifold learning · Low-rank · Laplacian eigenmaps

1 Introduction

Manifold learning method is the basic method in pattern recognition. There are many classical dimensionality methods, and divided into linear manifold learning algorithm and nonlinear manifold learning algorithm. Linear methods are traditional methods such as principal component analysis (PCA) [5] and linear discriminant analysis (LDA) [18]. Nonlinear manifold learning algorithms include Laplacian eigenmaps (LE) [2] and locally linear embedding (LLE) [11], etc. Most of these manifold learning algorithms have some similar parts, for example, they all need to construct an adjacency and calculate the similarity matrix between data points, and then compute eigenvalues and eigenvectors. In this paper, we mainly focus on the similarity learning in LE.

Similarity and distance are inseparable in the similarity learning algorithm. Distance-metric learning is very important to similarity learning, different measures of distance can lead to completely different results. Euclidean distance is the most classic distance measurement method, and it represents the real

This work was supported in part by NSFC Key Projects of International (Regional) Cooperation and Exchanges under Grant 61860206004 and in part by Shenzhen Science & Research Project under Grant JCYJ20170817155854115.

J. Ren et al. (Eds.): BICS 2019, LNAI 11691, pp. 34–44, 2020.
https://doi.org/10.1007/978-3-030-39431-8_4

distance between two points. Sparse representation [3] can better retain valid information and discard redundant information, such as [21] and [14]. Sparse representation can extract effective features better. Feature extraction can be applied to many places, for example [19] and [10].

As an important part of machine learning, pattern recognition and data mining, cluster learning plays an increasingly important role. Cluster analysis is based on similarity, with more similarities between things in one category than things that are not in the same category. Typical clustering algorithms include k-means clustering, spectral clustering, etc. And normalized cut (Ncut) [15] and ratio cut (Rcut) [9] are two commonly graph-based clustering algorithms. These graph-based methods first need to generate a graph and then invoke the optimize procedures on the data graph. But a disadvantage of the graph-based approach is that the resulting graph also needs to use the k-means algorithm to get the final clustering indicators. Non-negative matrix factorization (NMF) [6] is a matrix decomposition method that decomposes a large matrix into two small matrices so that the two small matrices can be restored to a large matrix after multiplication.

In these research directions especially for spectral clustering, similarity between samples is very important for clustering, different similarity learning methods may produce completely different clustering results. We proposed a new method that added rank constraints to our algorithm to ensure that the similarity matrix has k connected components. So, our similarity matrix can directly used for the clustering work and we can get cluster results directly without requiring any post-processing to extract the clustering indicators. Recently, some similarity learning methods have been proposed, such as [13] proposed two methods called constrained Laplacian rank based on the L1-norm (CLR-L1) and constrained Laplacian rank based on the L2-norm (CLR-L2), these two methods all learn a new data similarity matrix S that is a block diagonal matrix and has exactly c connected components, where the c is the number of clusters, and [4] proposed a method named LE sparse similarity learning (LESS) to learn similarity without constructing adjacency graph for neighborhood, and this method proposed two algorithms for mix-signed and nonnegative data.

Semi-supervised learning is an important issue in the field of pattern recognition and machine learning. It is a learning method that combines supervised learning with unsupervised learning [20]. It mainly considers how to train and classify with a small number of labeled samples and a large number of unlabeled samples. We test semi-supervised classification on our method, found that our method has good performance in semi-supervised classification compared with other methods.

2 Methodology

In this section, we first introduce a most important manifold learning algorithms LE, and then simply illustrate our similarity learning algorithms based on Low-Rank Laplacian.

We briefly introduce the notations used in this article. The matrices are written as uppercase, such as M, the elements of the matrix M are represented as M_{ij}, The trace of the matrix M is expressed as $Tr(M)$, and the transpose of the matrix M is expressed as M^T. The identity matrix is represented as I.

2.1 LE

Laplacian Eigenmaps establish relationships between data from a local perspective. It can reflect the intrinsic manifold structure of the data.

Given n data point $X_1, X_2, \ldots, X_n \in R^d$, where d is the dimension of the feature. Their low dimensional representation by LE is $Y_1, Y_2, \ldots, Y_n \in R^p (p < d)$. If the two data points i and j are very similar, after dimensionality reduction data points i and j should be as close as possible in the target subspace. Next is the detailed steps of the classic LE.

(1) Construct the adjacency graph with n nodes, using the k-NN algorithm to connect the nearest k points of each point. Nodes i and j are connected if X_i is among k nearest neighbors of X_j or X_j is among k nearest neighbors of X_i.

(2) Calculation weight, if nodes i and j are connected, we can simply set a similarity weight $S_{ij} = 1$ on it, otherwise zero. Or define the similarity weight S_{ij} by heat kernel

$$S_{ij} = exp\{-\frac{d_{ij}^2}{2r}\} \tag{1}$$

where $d_{ij} = \|X_i - X_j\|$, $r > 0$ is a suitable constant.

(3) Calculate the eigenvectors and eigenvalues of the Laplacian matrix L by solving the generalized eigenvector problem

$$Lv = \lambda Dv \tag{2}$$

where D is a diagonal matrix and its elements $D_{ii} = \sum_j S_{ij}$, and the Laplacian matrix is $L = D - S$. $p+1$ smallest eigenvalues 0 expressed as $0 = \lambda_0 \leq \lambda_1 \leq \ldots \lambda_p$, the corresponding feature vector is $v_0, v_1, \ldots, v_p$. Omitting the eigenvector corresponding to the 0 eigenvalue, point i can be mapped into $X_i \rightarrow Y_i = (v_1(i), v_2(i), \ldots, v_p(i))$. The feature vector corresponding to the smallest p nonzero eigenvalues is used as the result of the dimension reduction.

2.2 Low-Rank Laplacian Similarity Learning

For graph-based methods, it is particularly important to retain the local structure of data. How to learn the low-dimensional manifold structure from the high-dimensional manifold data has also become the main research problem of researchers in recent years.

Given a data matrix $X = \{X_1, X_2, \ldots, X_n\} \in R^{d \times n}$, where n is the number of data points and d is the dimension of feature. We think closer sample points are more similar and the corresponding reconstruction similarity are bigger, while distant sample points are less similar and the corresponding reconstruction similarity are smaller. So, if the distance between point i and point j is small, the similarity between them is high, and if the distance between point i and point j is large, the similarity between them is low. Therefore, the determination of probability W_{ij} can be seen as solving following problem:

$$\min_{W_i \in^{n\times 1}} \sum_{i,j}^{n} \|X_i - X_j\|_2^2 Wij$$
$$s.t.\ \forall i,\ W_i^T \mathbf{1} = 1,\ W_{ij} \geq 0. \tag{3}$$

In order to avoid some rows of W are all zeros, so we add a constraint that the sum of each row of W is one. The parameter $\alpha > 0$.

We think the similarity of our learning is similar to the initial similarity, so we add reconstruction restriction to learn new similarity

$$\min_{W} \sum_{i,j}^{n} \|X_i - X_j\|_2^2 W_{ij} + \alpha \|W - S\|_F^2$$
$$s.t.\ W_i^T \mathbf{1} = 1,\ W_{ij} \geq 0,\ i = 1, 2, \ldots, n. \tag{4}$$

where S is the initial similarity matrix that defined with heat kernel.

Then we adopt LASSO type minimization of $\|W\|_1$ to obtain the sparsity of W.

$$\min_{W} \sum_{i,j}^{n} \|X_i - X_j\|_2^2 W_{ij} + \alpha \|W - S\|_F^2 + \beta \|W\|_1$$
$$s.t.\ W_i^T \mathbf{1} = 1,\ W_{ij} \geq 0,\ i = 1, 2, \ldots, n. \tag{5}$$

where the parameter $\beta > 0$.

Since the similarity matrix W does not has exact c connected components (c is the number of classes), if we want to get the final result, we also need subsequent processing through other discretization methods such as k-means. In LE algorithm, Laplacian matrix of W is denote $L_W = D_W - (W^T + W)$, where $D_W \in R^{n\times n}$ is a degree matrix, and i-th diagonal element is $\sum_j (W_{ij} + W_{ji})/2$.

Then we add rank constraint $rank(L_W) = n - c$ to the Laplacian matrix. Then, our problem becomes

$$\min_{W} \sum_{i,j}^{n} \|X_i - X_j\|_2^2 W_{ij} + \alpha \|W - S\|_F^2 + \beta \|W\|_1$$
$$s.t.\ W_i^T \mathbf{1} = 1,\ W_{ij} = W_{ji} \geq 0,\ rank(L_W) = n - c,\ i = 1, 2, \ldots, n. \tag{6}$$

According to Theorem 1 [16], we know Laplacian matrix has a important property, so we can learn a similarity matrix that is block diagonal with proper permutation.

Theorem 1. *If Laplacian matrix L_W is nonnegative, the number of eigenvalues of the Laplacian matrix L_W is 0, which is equal to the number of connected components in the graph with the similarity matrix W.*

It assigns adaptive neighbours to each sample, then the similarity matrix W will be changed until it contains exact c connected component. Different from traditional graph-based clustering methods, the learned W can be directly used for clustering according to Tarjan's strongly connected components algorithm [17] without performing k-means or other discretization procedures.

3 Optimization Algorithm

In this section, we explain our optimization process. and our similarity learning algorithm can be used for both classification, clustering and semi-supervised classification work.

Through Theorem 1, we know that if we want to get c connected components of Laplacian matrix L_W, the sum of the c smallest eigenvalue of L_W should be zero. We denote $\sigma_i(L_W)$ is the i-th smallest eigenvalue of L_W, and because L_W is positive semi-definite, $\sigma_i(L_W) \geq 0$. Than we add rank constraint $rank(L_W) = n - c$ to L_W, we should be ensured $\sum_{i=1}^{c} \sigma_i(L_W) = 0$. According to Ky Fan's Theorem [7], we know

$$\sum_{i=1}^{c} \sigma_i(L_W) = \min_{F \in R^{n \times c}, F^T F = I} Tr(F^T L_W F). \tag{7}$$

Therefore, the problem (6) can be seen as the following problem

$$\min_{W,F} \sum_{i,j}^{n} \|X_i - X_j\|_2^2 W_{ij} + \alpha \|W - S\|_F^2 + \beta \|W\|_1 + 2\lambda Tr(F^T L_W F)$$
$$s.t.\ W_i^T \mathbf{1} = 1,\ W_{ij} \geq 0, F \in R^{n \times c}, F^T F = I,\ i = 1, 2, \ldots, n. \tag{8}$$

When W is fixed, the Eq. (8) turns into

$$\min_{F \in R^{n \times c}, F^T F = I} Tr(F^T L_W F). \tag{9}$$

The optimal solution of F is calculation by LE algorithm, it's value is the c eigenvectors of L_W corresponding to the c smallest eigenvalues.

When F is fixed, the Eq. (8) turns into

$$\min_{W} \sum_{i,j}^{n} \|X_i - X_j\|_2^2 W_{ij} + \alpha (W_{ij} - S_{ij})^2 + \beta W_{ij} + \lambda \sum_{i,j} \|f_i - f_j\|_2^2 W_{ij}$$
$$s.t.\ W_i^T \mathbf{1} = 1,\ W_{ij} \geq 0,\ i = 1, 2, \ldots, n. \tag{10}$$

We denote $U_{ij} = \|X_i - X_j\|_2^2$, and $V_{ij} = \|f_i - f_j\|_2^2$, so for each i, we can deal with following problem

$$\min_{W_i} \sum_{j=1}^{n} (\alpha_i W_{ij}^2 + U_{ij} W_{ij} - 2\alpha_i S_{ij} Wij + \beta_i + \lambda V_{ij})$$
$$s.t.\ \forall i,\ W_i^T \mathbf{1} = 1,\ W_{ij} \geq 0. \tag{11}$$

Algorithm 1. Algorithm of Low-Rank Laplacian Similarity Learning

Input: A n-by-p data matrix X which contains n p-dimensional training samples.

Output: An n-by-n similarity matrix W, and an n-by-c predicted label matrix F for all data points.

1: Compute initial similarity matrix S, with its elements being heat kernels $S_{ij} = exp\{-d_{ij}^2/2r\}$.
2: **repeat**
3: For each i, update each row of W as in Eq.(17).
4: Update F as in Eq.(9), where F is formed by the k eigenvectors of $L_W = D_W - (W^T + W)/2$ corresponding to the k smallest eigenvalues.
5: **until** converge

Then the above problem can be written as follow

$$\min_{W_i} \|W_i + \frac{U_{ij} + \lambda V_{ij} - 2\alpha_i S_{ij} + \beta_i}{2\alpha_i}\|_2^2$$
$$s.t.\ \forall i,\ W_i^T \mathbf{1} = 1,\ W_{ij} \geq 0. \tag{12}$$

We set $Q_{ij} = U_{ij} + \lambda V_{ij} - 2\alpha S_{ij} + \beta$, then the above formula can be simplified into

$$\min_{W_i} \|W_i + \frac{Q_{ij}}{2\alpha_i}\|_2^2$$
$$s.t.\ \forall i,\ W_i^T \mathbf{1} = 1,\ W_{ij} \geq 0. \tag{13}$$

The Lagrangian function of upper formula become

$$L_i(W) = \|W_i + \frac{Q_i}{2\alpha_i}\|_2^2 - \delta_i (W_i^T \mathbf{1} - 1) - \eta_i^T W_i, \tag{14}$$

where δ and η are Lagrangian multipliers and they all ≥ 0.

According to the [13], assume the number of neighbors k, the parameter α can be get by the following formula

$$\alpha_i = \frac{k}{2} Q_{i,k+1} - \frac{1}{2} \sum_{j=1}^{k} Q_{ij}. \tag{15}$$

Table 1. Clustering result in terms of accuracy on four benchmark datasets.

Data set	ORL	COIL-20	COIL-100	PIE-pose27
K-means	0.6475	0.5931	0.5153	0.3617
Rcut [9]	0.3025	0.5986	0.6304	0.1765
Ncut [15]	0.3675	0.7944	0.6535	0.3088
NMF [6]	0.6300	0.5979	0.5332	0.2686
LE [4]	0.4425	0.4465	0.4107	0.2125
LESS [4]	0.5950	0.5521	0.4625	0.8687
CLR-L1 [13]	0.6575	0.8535	0.8122	0.8746
CLR-L2 [13]	0.6325	0.8736	0.8035	0.9345
OUR	**0.6900**	**1.0000**	**0.8314**	**0.9580**

and the parameter β can be get by the following formula

$$\beta_i = U_{ij} + \lambda V_{ij} - 2\alpha_i S_{ij} - Q_{ij}. \tag{16}$$

and the iterative function of W is

$$W_{ij} = \frac{Q_{i,k+1} - Q_{ij}}{kQ_{i,k+1} - \sum_{e=1}^{k} Q_{ie}}, \tag{17}$$

if $j > k$, we set $W_{ij} = 0$.

4 Experiments

In this section, we will test our method compared with other related graph based methods on several benchmark data sets. We simply adopt gabor feature of each data set. In the following, we first introduce the data sets, then we test our algorithm from three aspects: classification, semi-supervised classification and clustering.

4.1 Datasets

ORL data set [1] is a face data set contain 400 images in 40 class, we extract gabor features with 2560 dimension from each images. AR data set [12] contain 3120 images in 120 class, we extract gabor features with 3200 dimension from each images. Yale data set [4] contain 166 images in 15 class, we extract gabor features with 2560 dimension from each images. COIL-20 data set [4] contain 1440 images in 20 class, we extract gabor features with 640 dimension from each images. COIL-100 data set [13] contain 7200 images in 100 class, we extract gabor features with 640 dimension from each images. PIE-pose27 [8] data set contain 2856 images in 68 class, we extract gabor features with 640 dimension from each images.

Table 2. Clustering result in terms of NMI on four benchmark datasets.

Data set	ORL	COIL-20	COIL-100	PIE-pose27
K-means	0.8043	0.7462	0.7530	0.6361
Rcut [9]	0.4702	0.8894	0.8435	0.2633
Ncut [15]	0.5466	0.6887	0.8473	0.4883
NMF [6]	0.7896	0.7340	0.7581	0.5033
LE [4]	0.6357	0.6118	0.6495	0.4074
LESS [4]	0.7420	0.6613	0.7641	0.9602
CLR-L1 [13]	0.8004	0.9450	0.9401	0.9577
CLR-L2 [13]	0.7816	0.9450	0.9407	0.9817
OUR	**0.8575**	**1.0000**	**0.9808**	**0.9890**

4.2 Clustering

For clustering, we test our method on four data sets of ORL, COIL-20, COIL-100, and PIE-pose27, and we test our methods with other seven clustering methods of K-means, Ratio Cut (Rcut) [9], Normalized Cut (Ncut) [15], NMF [6], CLR-L1 [13] and CLR-L2 [13], LE [4] and LESS [4] methods.

Because our similarity learning algorithm adds a rank constraint to the Laplacian matrix, the graph we learned will with c connected components, and the similarity matrix W will be a block diagonal matrix, so we can directly cluster with the similarity matrix.

In our experiment, there is still a parameter λ that is not determined. We can first initialize λ to a random value, then change according to the number of connected components of the similarity matrix. If the number of connected components of similarity matrix is greater than class number c, we can update λ to $\lambda/2$, If the number of connected components of similarity matrix is smaller than class number c, we can update λ to 2λ.

Table 3. Semi-supervised classification result in terms of accuracy on four benchmark datasets.

Data set	ORL	COIL-20	PIE-pose27	Yale
CLR-L1 [13]	0.8890	0.8470	0.8091	0.7203
CLR-L2 [13]	0.8655	0.8502	0.9687	0.7538
LE [4]	0.8546	0.9903	0.9718	0.6624
LESS [4]	0.8982	1.0000	**0.9941**	0.6792
OUR	**0.9044**	**1.0000**	0.9885	**0.7538**

We adopt two evaluation metric, accuracy and normalized mutual information (NMI) as our clustering indicator. As shown in Table 2, we can see that we proposed method outperform other methods in almost all experiments.

4.3 Semi-supervised Classification

For semi-supervised classification, we test our method on four data sets of ORL, COIL-20, Yale and PIE-pose27, and we compare our methods with other four methods of CLR-L1 [13], CLR-L2 [13], LE [4] and LESS [4] methods. For semi-supervised classification, we adopt accuracy to test the effectiveness of our algorithm. We select the front 20% data as labeled data, and the parameter λ update is the same as the previous update method.

Table 4. Classification result in terms of accuracy on four benchmark datasets.

Data set	ORL	COIL-20	AR	Yale
CLR-L1 [13]	0.8568	0.9204	0.6978	0.7437
CLR-L2 [13]	0.8745	0.9460	0.6757	0.7155
LE [4]	0.8750	0.9220	0.7596	0.6810
LESS [4]	0.8900	0.9840	0.7927	0.6930
OUR	**0.9311**	**1.0000**	**0.8864**	**0.7664**

As shown in Table 3, We compared the experimental results of our method and other methods on four different data sets. We can see that on the PIE dataset, the LESS method is better than our method, but on the other three data sets, our method experimental results are higher than the LESS methods. We can see that we proposed method outperform other methods in almost all experiments.

4.4 Classification

For classification, we compare our methods with four methods of CLR-L1 [13], CLR-L2 [13], LE [4] and LESS [4] methods, And the parameter λ update is the same as the previous update method. For classification, we use accuracy as an evaluation metric. We use ten-fold cross-validation method and then computer the classification accuracy by the k nearest neighbor classifier.

As shown in Table 4, our classification accuracy is higher than other methods. Particularly, on the COIL-20 data set, the accuracy of our algorithm reaches a maximum of 1.

5 Conclusions

In this paper, we proposed a low-rank Laplacian similarity learning method to learn a new manifold data similarity matrix with local reconstruction restriction, minimize the selection operator type and added a rank constraint to the Laplacian matrix. So our similarity matrix has with exactly c connected components, and this similarity matrix can directly useful for the clustering work. We obtained indicator matrix F by Laplacian mapping can be use for the classification work. Our experimental results show that our method has good performance in clustering, classification and semi-supervised classification.

References

1. Addlesee, M.D., Jones, A., Livesey, F., Samaria, F.: The ORL active floor [sensor system]. IEEE Pers. Commun. **4**(5), 35–41 (1997)
2. Belkin, M., Niyogi, P.: Laplacian eigenmaps for dimensionality reduction and data. Representation **15**, 1373–1396 (2003)
3. Cao, F., et al.: Sparse representation-based augmented multinomial logistic extreme learning machine with weighted composite features for spectral-spatial classification of hyperspectral images. IEEE Trans. Geosci. Rem. Sens. **56**(11), 6263–6279 (2018)
4. Chen, S., Ding, C.H.Q., Luo, B.: Similarity learning of manifold data. IEEE Trans. Cybern. **45**(9), 1744–1756 (2015)
5. Debruyne, M., Verdonck, T.: Robust kernel principal component analysis and classification. Adv. Data Anal. Classif. **4**(2–3), 151–167 (2010)
6. Ding, C.H.Q., He, X.: On the equivalence of nonnegative matrix factorization and spectral clustering. In: Proceedings of the 2005 SIAM International Conference on Data Mining, pp. 606–610 (2005)
7. Fan, K.: On a theorem of Weyl concerning eigenvalues of linear transformations. Proc. Natl. Acad. Sci. USA **36**(1), 31–35 (1950)
8. Gross, R., Matthews, I.A., Baker, S.: Eigen light-fields and face recognition across pose. In: 5th IEEE International Conference on Automatic Face and Gesture Recognition, pp. 3–9 (2002)
9. Hagen, L.W., Kahng, A.B.: New spectral methods for ratio cut partitioning and clustering. IEEE Trans. CAD Integr. Circ. Syst. **11**(9), 1074–1085 (1992)
10. Han, J., Zhang, D., Hu, X., Guo, L., Ren, J., Wu, F.: Background prior-based salient object detection via deep reconstruction residual. IEEE Trans. Circuits Syst. Video Techn. **25**(8), 1309–1321 (2015)
11. Hsieh, P., Yang, M., Gu, Y., Liang, Y.: Classification-oriented locally linear embedding. IJPRAI **24**(5), 737–762 (2010)
12. Martnez, A., Benavente, R.: The AR face database. CVC Technical report 24 (1998)
13. Nie, F., Wang, X., Jordan, M.I., Huang, H.: The constrained Laplacian rank algorithm for graph-based clustering. In: Proceedings of the Thirtieth AAAI Conference on Artificial Intelligence, pp. 1969–1976 (2016)
14. Qiao, T., et al.: Joint bilateral filtering and spectral similarity-based sparse representation: a generic framework for effective feature extraction and data classification in hyperspectral imaging. Pattern Recogn. **77**, 316–328 (2018)

15. Shi, J., Malik, J.: Normalized cuts and image segmentation. IEEE Trans. Pattern Anal. Mach. Intell. **22**(8), 888–905 (2000)
16. Spielman, D.A.: Spectral graph theory and its applications. In: 48th Annual IEEE Symposium on Foundations of Computer Science, pp. 29–38 (2007)
17. Tarjan, R.E.: Depth-first search and linear graph algorithms. SIAM J. Comput. **1**(2), 146–160 (1972)
18. Wang, X., Tang, X.: Dual-space linear discriminant analysis for face recognition. In: 2004 IEEE Computer Society Conference on Computer Vision and Pattern Recognition, pp. 564–569 (2004)
19. Wang, Z., Ren, J., Zhang, D., Sun, M., Jiang, J.: A deep-learning based feature hybrid framework for spatiotemporal saliency detection inside videos. Neurocomputing **287**, 68–83 (2018)
20. Yan, Y., et al.: Unsupervised image saliency detection with gestalt-laws guided optimization and visual attention based refinement. Pattern Recogn. **79**, 65–78 (2018)
21. Zhao, C., Li, X., Ren, J., Marshall, S.: Improved sparse representation using adaptive spatial support for effective target detection in hyperspectral imagery. Int. J. Rem. Sens. **34**(24), 8669–8684 (2013)

Long Short-Term Attention

Guoqiang Zhong[1(✉)], Xin Lin[1], Kang Chen[1], Qingyang Li[1], and Kaizhu Huang[2]

[1] Department of Computer Science and Technology, Ocean University of China, Qingdao 266100, China
gqzhong@ouc.edu.cn, 2410767409@qq.com, chenkoucer@qq.com, 1194094543@qq.com

[2] Department of Electrical and Electronic Engineering, Xian Jiaotong-Liverpool University, SIP, Suzhou 215123, China
Kaizhu.Huang@xjtlu.edu.cn

Abstract. Attention is an important cognition process of humans, which helps humans concentrate on critical information during their perception and learning. However, although many machine learning models can remember information of data, they have no the attention mechanism. For example, the long short-term memory (LSTM) network is able to remember sequential information, but it cannot pay special attention to part of the sequences. In this paper, we present a novel model called long short-term attention (LSTA), which seamlessly integrates the attention mechanism into the inner cell of LSTM. More than processing long short term dependencies, LSTA can focus on important information of the sequences with the attention mechanism. Extensive experiments demonstrate that LSTA outperforms LSTM and related models on the sequence learning tasks.

Keywords: Machine learning · Sequence learning · Attention mechanism · Long short-term memory · Long short-term attention

1 Introduction

With the attention mechanism, human can naturally focus on vital information and ignore irrelevant information during one's perception and cognition [1,2]. Based on this fact, many brain-inspired learning models have been deeply studied and widely applied in recent years [3–10]. However, although many machine learning models can learn effective representations of data and memorize the data information, they cannot pay attention to important part of the data. For instance, long short-term memory (LSTM) [11] is a widely used model for sequence learning. However, it lacks the attention mechanism. To address this problem, some work tries to apply the attention mechanism to LSTM. Nevertheless, most of these models only add the attention mechanisms outside the LSTM cells and have not thoroughly solved the issue that LSTM have no the attention mechanism itself [2,12,13].

J. Ren et al. (Eds.): BICS 2019, LNAI 11691, pp. 45–54, 2020.
https://doi.org/10.1007/978-3-030-39431-8_5

In this paper, we propose a novel model called long short term attention (LSTA), which seamlessly integrates the attention mechanism into the inner cell of LSTM. In this case, LSTA can simultaneously remember historical information and notice crucial details in the sequences. In the experiments for sequence learning, we demonstrate the advantage of LSTA over LSTM.

The rest of this paper is organized as follows. In Sect. 2, we introduce some previous work related to LSTA, including LSTM and some models using the attention mechanism. In Sect. 3, we present LSTA in detail. In Sect. 4, we report the experimental results on two sequence learning tasks, i.e. image classification and sentiment analysis. Section 5 concludes this paper.

2 Related Work

In this section, we review some previous work related to LSTA, including LSTM and several models using the attention mechanism.

2.1 LSTM

LSTM is a powerful learning model for sequential data and has been widely applied in many areas, such as speech recognition and handwritten character recognition [14,15]. The cell of LSTM includes an input gate, a forget gate and an output gate. These gate and the state of the cell can be updated as follows:

$$\boldsymbol{f}_t = \sigma(\boldsymbol{W}_f[\boldsymbol{h}_{t-1}, \boldsymbol{x}_t] + \boldsymbol{b}_f), \tag{1}$$

$$\boldsymbol{i}_t = \sigma(\boldsymbol{W}_i[\boldsymbol{h}_{t-1}, \boldsymbol{x}_t] + \boldsymbol{b}_i), \tag{2}$$

$$\tilde{\boldsymbol{C}}_t = \tanh(\boldsymbol{W}_{\tilde{c}}[\boldsymbol{h}_{t-1}, \boldsymbol{x}_t] + \boldsymbol{b}_{\tilde{c}}), \tag{3}$$

$$\boldsymbol{C}_t = \boldsymbol{f}_t * \boldsymbol{C}_{t-1} + \boldsymbol{i}_t * \tilde{\boldsymbol{C}}_t, \tag{4}$$

$$\boldsymbol{o}_t = \sigma(\boldsymbol{W}_o[\boldsymbol{h}_{t-1}, \boldsymbol{x}_t] + \boldsymbol{b}_o), \tag{5}$$

$$\boldsymbol{h}_t = \boldsymbol{o}_t * \tanh(\boldsymbol{C}_t). \tag{6}$$

Here, $\boldsymbol{W}_f, \boldsymbol{W}_i, \boldsymbol{W}_{\tilde{c}}, \boldsymbol{W}_o$ are the weight parameters and $\boldsymbol{b}_f, \boldsymbol{b}_i, \boldsymbol{b}_{\tilde{c}}, \boldsymbol{b}_o$ are biases. The forget gate $\boldsymbol{f}_t$ primarily controls the cell state by forgetting the previous moment information. In a similar way, the input gate $\boldsymbol{i}_t$ and output gate $\boldsymbol{o}_t$ control the information that will be input to the LSTM cell and output at the current moment, respectively. These three gates are crucial parts of the LSTM cell, which is used to update the current state of the LSTM cell $\boldsymbol{C}_t$ and obtain new cell output $\boldsymbol{h}_t$.

In order to optimize the performance of LSTM, many extensions of LSTM have been proposed recently [16–19]. In [20], the spatiotemporal LSTM (ST-LSTM) units are designed for memorizing both spatial and temporal information. [21] introduces a convolutional LSTM (ConvLSTM), which extends the fully connected LSTM to have convolutional architectures in both the input-to-gate and gate-to-gate transitions. In addition, [17] introduces a tensorized LSTM model, which represent the hidden states with tensors.

As discussed above, LSTM and most of its extensions mainly focus on processing the sequential data, but cannot pay attention to the important information in the sequences. In this paper, we present a model that can integrate the attention mechanism into the inner-cell of LSTM.

2.2 Models Using the Attention Mechanism

The primary function of the attention mechanism is selection and allocation [1,8]. It leads to quick processing of information, with an efficient information choice and concentration of the computing power on the crucial tasks [1]. [22] introduces the attention mechanism in the human cognitive system, with which human pays attention to the noteworthy information and ignores irrespective information [2,22,23]. In the cognitive computation area, the attention mechanism has been widely applied, such as the work to resolve the human visual neural computational problem [24] and that to model the retrieval mechanism of associations from the associative memory [25].

In particular, a large amount of attention based deep learning models have been proposed in recent years. For example, [26] presents the structured attention networks, which incorporate graphical models to generalize simple attention. Alternatively, [27] introduces a self-attention mechanism model, which is applied to replace the common recurrent and convolutional models. It relies entirely on the attention mechanism to compute representations of its input and output. Moreover, in [5], the selective attention for identification model (SAIM) is applied to visual search applications. The SAIM simulates the human ability to complete translation invariant recognition of multiple scenes. Additionally, in [28], a recurrent attention mechanism network is proposed. It is an end-to-end memory learning model used on several language modeling tasks.

As mentioned above, many attention based methods have been proposed to address visual or language processing problems. However, rare work has integrated the attention mechanism into the cell of LSTM to improve its performance in sequence learning.

3 Long Short-Term Attention

In this section, we introduce the proposed long short-term attention (LSTA) model in detail, which seamlessly integrates the attention mechanism into the

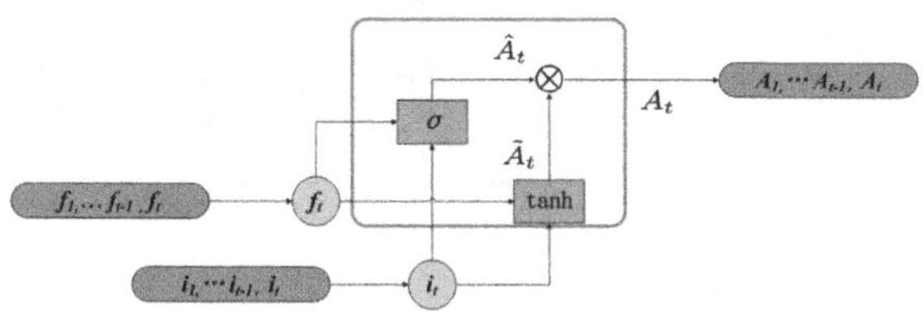

Fig. 1. An illustration of the attention gate.

cell of LSTM. For clarity, we first introduce the added attention gate in Sec. 3.1, and then the architecture and learning of LSTA in Sec. 3.2.

3.1 The Attention Gate

Figure 1 shows the structure of the attention gate of LSTA, which accepts the inputs from the input gate and the forget gate. Equation (7) is the update formula of the attention gate:

$$\boldsymbol{A}_t = \psi(\hat{\boldsymbol{A}}_t[\boldsymbol{f}_t, \boldsymbol{i}_t], \tilde{\boldsymbol{A}}_t[\boldsymbol{f}_t, \boldsymbol{i}_t]) = \hat{\boldsymbol{A}}_t \bigotimes \tilde{\boldsymbol{A}}_t, \tag{7}$$

where $\hat{\boldsymbol{A}}_t$ and $\tilde{\boldsymbol{A}}_t$ are defined as follows:

$$\hat{\boldsymbol{A}}_t = \boldsymbol{\sigma}(\boldsymbol{W}_{\hat{a}}[\boldsymbol{f}_t, \boldsymbol{i}_t] + \boldsymbol{b}_{\hat{a}}), \tag{8}$$

$$\tilde{\boldsymbol{A}}_t = \mathbf{tanh}(\boldsymbol{W}_{\tilde{a}}[\boldsymbol{f}_t, \boldsymbol{i}_t] + \boldsymbol{b}_{\tilde{a}}). \tag{9}$$

Here, $\boldsymbol{W}_{\tilde{a}}$ and $\boldsymbol{W}_{\hat{a}}$ are weight parameters, while $\boldsymbol{b}_{\tilde{a}}$ and $\boldsymbol{b}_{\hat{a}}$ are biases. The sigmoid function $\boldsymbol{\sigma}$ is employed to compute $\hat{\boldsymbol{A}}_t$, which indicates the ratios of the attention elements as shown in Eq. (7). Similarly, the **tanh** function is used to get the candidate attention values $\tilde{\boldsymbol{A}}_t$, which can be positive or negative.

In Eq. (7), $\bigotimes$ represents the element-wise multiplication. We multiply the elements between $\tilde{\boldsymbol{A}}_t$ and $\hat{\boldsymbol{A}}_t$ to obtain the output of the attention gate $\boldsymbol{A}_t$. The attention gate determines the attention distribution on the information at the current cell. In the following, we introduce how it can be seamlessly integrated into the cell of LSTM.

3.2 LSTA

In order to endow the attention mechanism to LSTM, we propose the LSTA model which integrates the attention gate introduced above inside the LSTM

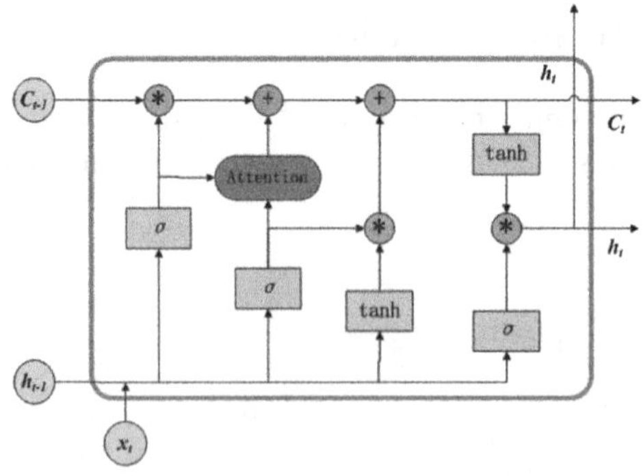

Fig. 2. The LSTA cell. The module with red color is the attention gate. (Color figure online)

cell. Figure 2 is a diagram of the LSTA cell. Particularly, LSTA can pay attention to important information in the sequences during its learning process.

LSTA inherits the three gates of LSTM. For the update of its cell state, we can compute it as

$$\begin{aligned}\hat{C}_t &= C_t + A_t \\ &= f_t * C_{t-1} + i_t * \tilde{C}_t + A_t \\ &= f_t * C_{t-1} + i_t * \tilde{C}_t + \tilde{A}_t \bigotimes \hat{A}_t.\end{aligned} \tag{10}$$

Here, A_t is the output of the attention gate and C_t is the original LSTM cell state. In this case, we integrate the attention mechanism into LSTM unit, such that the new model, LSTA, can not only memorize the sequential information, but also pay attention to important information in the sequences.

Accordingly, the output gate of LSTA can be updated as

$$h_t = o_t * \tanh(\hat{C}_t). \tag{11}$$

Note that, in LSTA, the attention mechanise is applied inside the LSTM cell, unlike previous attention based LSTM models, in which attention is added after the whole sequence has been handled by all the LSTM cells. Therefore, LSTA is quite different from LSTM and most of its attention based variants. LSTA enables the sequence learning to focus on important parts of the input data and automatically ignore irrelevant parts, so as to improve its performance.

4 Experiments

To evaluate the proposed model LSTA, we have conducted extensive experiments on two sequence learning tasks, image classification and semantic analysis. In the following, we report the experimental settings and results.

4.1 Experiments on the Image Classification Task

In this section, we used the MNIST and Fashion-MNIST data sets to test the performance of LSTA. MNIST is a handwritten digit data set. It contains seventy thousands of 28×28 gray scale images, which belong to 10 classes. For all the images, 60,000 are used for training and the other 10,000 for test [29]. Alternatively, Fashion-MNIST is an image data set, while its image format and number are both the same as the MNIST data set [30]. In our experiments, we considered the rows of an image as sequential data to perform image classification.

For testing the performance of LSTA, we compared it with some relevant models. As LSTA integrates the attention mechanism into the LSTM cell, the most closely related model to LSTA is LSTM. Hence, we set LSTM as our baseline. Furthermore, we also compared LSTA with gated recurrent unit (GRU) [31], bidirectional LSTM (Bi-LSTM) [32] and nested LSTM (NLSTM) [33] in our experiments. Note that, although there are many attention based variants of

LSTM, they are quite different from LSTA. We can also apply the attention mechanism outside the LSTA cell as same as them. Hence, we have not compared with them in our work.

Table 1 shows the image classification results obtained by LSTA and the compared models on the MNIST and Fashion-MNIST data sets. As we can see, LSTA outperforms all the compared models consistently. This demonstrate the advantage of LSTA over LSTM and its variants and the importance of the attention mechanism during sequence learning.

Table 1. Accuracy obtained by LSTA and related models on the MNIST and Fashion-MNIST data sets.

Data set	LSTM	GRU	Bi-LSTM	NLSTM	LSTA
MNIST	97.47%	97.79%	97.81%	97.75%	**97.85%**
Fashion-MNIST	87.46%	88.16%	88.18%	88.32%	**88.60%**

To further analyze the advantage of LSTA over LSTM, we draw the learning curves of LSTM and LSTA obtained on the Fashion-MNIST data set in Fig. 3. Note that, we used the same loss function for LSTM and LSTA in our experiments. Figure 3(a) shows the accuracy curves against the training steps, while Fig. 3(b) shows the loss curves against the training steps. As can be seen, due to the attention mechanism, LSTA consistently performs better, and converges faster than LSTM.

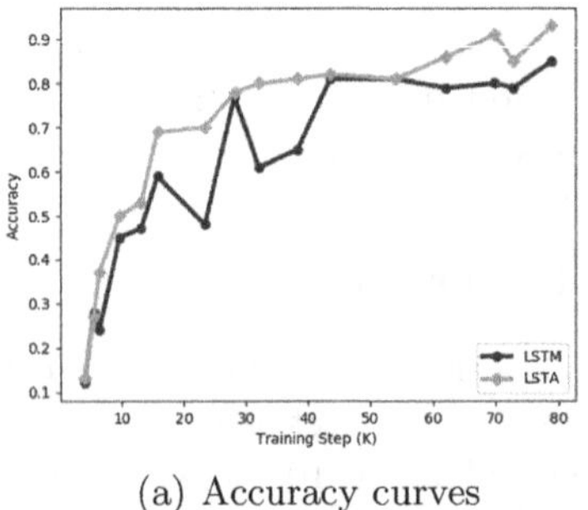

(a) Accuracy curves

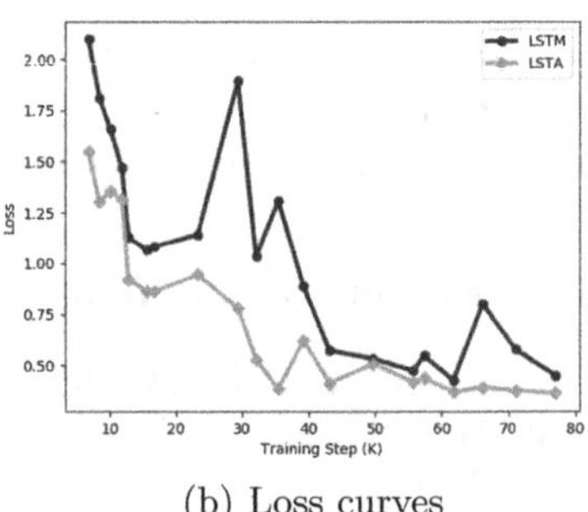

(b) Loss curves

Fig. 3. The accuracy and loss curves of LSTM and LSTA on the Fashion-MNIST data set. (a) shows the accuracy curves; and (b) shows the loss curves.

4.2 Experiments on the Sentiment Analysis Task

Sentiment analysis is an interesting and important learning task [34–36]. In order to evaluate the performance of LSTA, we conducted experiments on both the classical sentiment analysis and aspect based sentiment analysis.

Classical Sentiment Analysis. In this experiment, we used the internet movie review database (IMDB) [34] to test LSTA on classical sentiment analysis. IMDB is a crawler data set about the internet movie reviews. Based on the emotion of the reviews, it divides all the film reviews into the positive and negative categories.

In our work, we compared LSTA with LSTM and hybrid deep belief network (HDBN) [37], which is an effective deep network for sentiment analysis. The error rate and the running time of LSTA and the compared models are depicted in Fig. 4(a) and (b), respectively. As we can see, among the compared model, LSTA obtained the best classification accuracy and used the least running time.

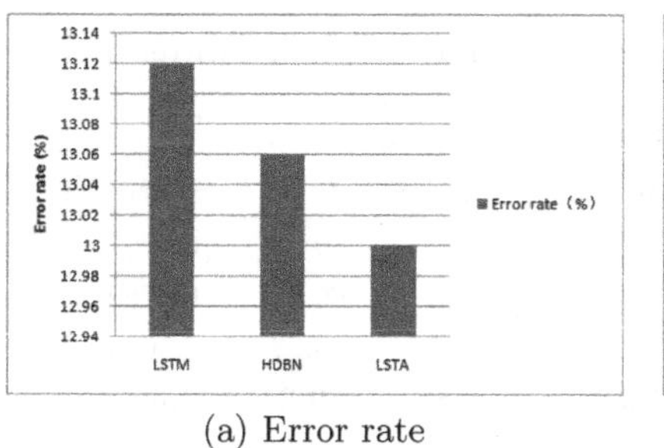

(a) Error rate

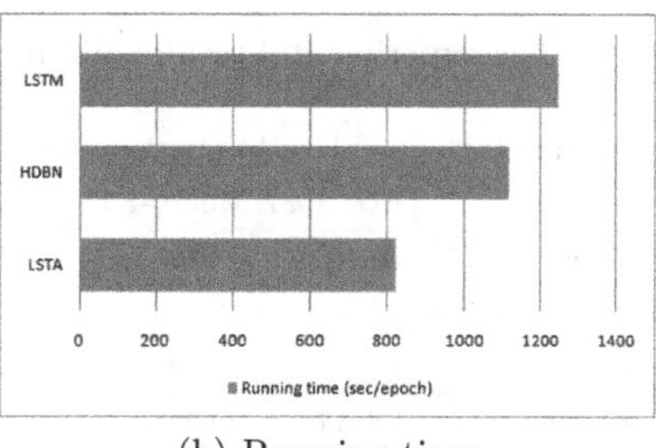

(b) Running time

Fig. 4. The error rate and the running time of LSTM, HDBN and LSTA on the IMDB data set. (a) shows the error rate obtained by the three models; (b) depicts their running time.

Aspect Based Sentiment Analysis. Aspect based sentiment analysis is one of the important tasks of semantic analysis [38]. In order to verify the effect of LSTA on aspect based sentiment analysis, we conducted experiments on two data sets. One was the SemEval-2014 Task 4 (SemEval14) data set [35], which contains two domains (Restaurant and Laptop). The other was the Twitter data set collected by Dong et al. [36]. In these two data sets, the aspect terms of each review are labeled by three sentiment polarities, which are positive, neutral and negative, respectively. For example, about an aspect term *fajitas*, when it is in a sentence *"I loved their fajitas, but the service is horrible."*, its polarity is positive, but for aspect term *service*, its polarity is negative. Concretely, the statistics of the two data sets are provided in Table 2.

Table 2. The statistics of the SemEval14 and Twitter data sets.

Data set	Positive		Neutral		Negative	
	Train	Test	Train	Test	Train	Test
SemEval14 (Restaurant)	2164	728	637	196	807	196
SemEval14 (Laptop)	994	341	464	169	870	128
Twitter	1561	173	3127	346	1560	173

In this experiment, we used Accuracy and Macro-averaged F-measure (Macro-F1) as the metrics to evaluate the effect of LSTA and the compared models [36,39]. The experimental results obtained by LSTA and the compared methods are shown in Table 3. In this table, "Cabasc" is a content attention model for aspect based sentiment analysis [38]. "ATAE-LSTM" is an attention-based LSTM with aspect embedding, which can focus on the parts of a sentence when several aspects are taken as input [40].

From Table 3, we can see that LSTA performs best among the compared models. That is, LSTA outperforms both LSTM and previous attention models, including that apply the attention mechanism outside the cell of LSTM.

Table 3. The experimental results obtained on the SemEval14 and Twitter data sets.

Method	SemEval14 (Restaurant)		SemEval14 (Laptop)		Twitter	
	Acc. (%)	Macro-F1	Acc. (%)	Macro-F1	Acc. (%)	Macro-F1
Cabasc	78.12	0.6743	70.84	0.6552	69.51	0.6707
ATAE-LSTM	77.86	0.6718	69.75	0.6425	69.65	0.6762
LSTM	77.41	0.6686	69.74	0.6394	68.93	0.6699
LSTA	**78.57**	**0.6801**	**71.16**	**0.6559**	**69.94**	**0.6911**

5 Conclusion

In this paper, we present a novel LSTA model to alleviate the problem that LSTM lacks the attention mechanism. The key idea behind this model is to seamlessly integrate the attention mechanism into the cell of LSTM. Experiments demonstrate that LSTA performs better than LSTM, many variants of LSTM and related attention models. Hence, LSTA can be seen as a substitute of LSTM in the sequence learning tasks.

Acknowledgment. This work was supported by the National Key R&D Program of China under Grant No. 2016YFC1401004, the National Natural Science Foundation of China (NSFC) under Grant No. 41706010, and No. 61876155, the Science and Technology Program of Qingdao under Grant No. 17-3-3-20-nsh, the CERNET Innovation Project under Grant No. NGII20170416, and the Fundamental Research Funds for the Central Universities of China.

References

1. Posner, M.I.: Cognitive Neuroscience of Attention. Guilford Press (2011)
2. Xu, K., et al.: Show, attend and tell: neural image caption generation with visual attention. In: ICML, pp. 2048–2057 (2015)
3. Luo, B., Hussain, A., Mahmud, M., Tang, J.: Advances in brain-inspired cognitive systems. Cogn. Comput. **8**(5), 795–796 (2016)
4. Taylor, J.G.: Cognitive computation. Cogn. Comput. **1**(1), 4–16 (2009)

5. Heinke, D., Backhaus, A.: Modelling visual search with the selective attention for identification model (VS-SAIM): a novel explanation for visual search asymmetries. Cogn. Comput. **3**(1), 185–205 (2011)
6. Aboudib, A., Gripon, V., Coppin, G.: A biologically inspired framework for visual information processing and an application on modeling bottom-up visual attention. Cogn. Comput. **8**(6), 1007–1026 (2016)
7. Gao, F., Zhang, Y., Wang, J., Sun, J., Yang, E., Hussain, A.: Visual attention model based vehicle target detection in synthetic aperture radar images: a novel approach. Cogn. Comput. **7**(4), 434–444 (2015)
8. Wischnewski, M., Belardinelli, A., Schneider, W.X., Steil, J.J.: Where to look next? Combining static and dynamic proto-objects in a TVA-based model of visual attention. Cogn. Comput. **2**(4), 326–343 (2010)
9. Katsuki, F., Constantinidis, C.: Bottom-up and top-down attention: different processes and overlapping neural systems. Neurocomputing **20**(5), 509–521 (2014)
10. Wang, Z., Ren, J., Zhang, D., Sun, M., Jiang, J.: A deep-learning based feature hybrid framework for spatiotemporal saliency detection inside videos. Neurocomputing **287**, 68–83 (2018)
11. Hochreiter, S., Schmidhuber, J.: Long short-term memory. Neural Comput. **9**(8), 1735–1780 (1997)
12. Luong, T., Pham, H., Manning, C.D.: Effective approaches to attention-based neural machine translation. In: EMNLP, pp. 1412–1421 (2015)
13. Lin, Z., et al.: A structured self-attentive sentence embedding. In: ICLR (2017)
14. Greff, K., Srivastava, R.K., Koutník, J., Steunebrink, B.R., Schmidhuber, J.: LSTM: a search space odyssey. IEEE Trans. Neural Netw. Learn. Syst. **28**(10), 2222–2232 (2017)
15. Wöllmer, M., Eyben, F., Graves, A., Schuller, B.W., Rigoll, G.: Bidirectional LSTM networks for context-sensitive keyword detection in a cognitive virtual agent framework. Cogn. Comput. **2**(3), 180–190 (2010)
16. Graves, A., Mohamed, A.-R., Hinton, G.: Speech recognition with deep recurrent neural networks. In: ICASSP, pp. 6645–6649 (2013)
17. He, Z., Gao, S., Xiao, L., Liu, D., He, H., Barber, D.: Wider and deeper, cheaper and faster: tensorized LSTMs for sequence learning. In: NIPS, pp. 1–11 (2017)
18. Wang, P., Song, Q., Han, H., Cheng, J.: Sequentially supervised long short-term memory for gesture recognition. Cogn. Comput. **8**(5), 982–991 (2016)
19. Neil, D., Pfeiffer, M., Liu, S.-C.: Phased LSTM: accelerating recurrent network training for long or event-based sequences. In: NIPS, pp. 3882–3890 (2016)
20. Wang, Y., Long, M., Wang, J., Gao, Z., Philip, S.Y.: PredRNN: recurrent Neural networks for predictive learning using spatiotemporal LSTMs. In: NIPS, pp. 879–888 (2017)
21. Xingjian, S., Chen, Z., Wang, H., Yeung, D.-Y., Wong, W.-K., Woo, W.-C.: Convolutional LSTM network: a machine learning approach for precipitation nowcasting. In: NIPS, pp. 802–810 (2015)
22. Corbetta, M., Shulman, G.L.: Control of goal-directed and stimulus-driven attention in the brain. Nat. Rev. Neurosci. **3**(3), 201–215 (2002)
23. Yan, Y., et al.: Unsupervised image saliency detection with gestalt-laws guided optimization and visual attention based refinement. Pattern Recogn. **79**, 65–78 (2018)
24. Cutsuridis, V.: A cognitive model of saliency, attention, and picture scanning. Cogn. Comput. **1**(4), 292–299 (2009)
25. Wichert, A.: The role of attention in the context of associative memory. Cogn. Comput. **3**(1), 311–320 (2011)

26. Kim, Y., Denton, C., Hoang, L., Rush, A.M.: Structured attention networks. In: ICLR (2017)
27. Vaswani, A., et al.: Attention is all you need. In: NIPS, pp. 6000–6010 (2017)
28. Sukhbaatar, S., Weston, J., Fergus, R., et al.: End-to-end memory networks. In: NIPS, pp. 2440–2448 (2015)
29. LeCun, Y., Cortes, C., Burges, C.J.: MNIST Handwritten Digit Database. AT&T Labs, February 2010
30. Xiao, H., Rasul, K., Vollgraf, R.: Fashion-MNIST: a novel image dataset for benchmarking machine learning algorithms. CoRR, abs/1708.07747 (2017)
31. Chung, J., Gülçehre, Ç., Cho, K., Bengio, Y.: Empirical evaluation of gated recurrent neural networks on sequence modeling. CoRR, abs/1412.3555 (2014)
32. Graves, A., Schmidhuber, J.: Framewise phoneme classification with bidirectional LSTM and other neural network architectures. Neural Netw. **18**(5–6), 602–610 (2005)
33. Moniz, J.R.A., Krueger, D.: Nested LSTMs. In: ACML, pp. 530–544 (2017)
34. Maas, A.L., Daly, R.E., Pham, P.T., Huang, D., Ng, A.Y., Potts, C.: Learning word vectors for sentiment analysis. In: ACL-HLT, pp. 142–150, June 2011
35. Pontiki, M., Galanis, D., Pavlopoulos, J., Papageorgiou, H., Androutsopoulos, I., Manandhar, S.: SemEval-2014 task 4: aspect based sentiment analysis. In: SemEval@COLING, pp. 27–35 (2014)
36. Dong, L., Wei, F., Tan, C., Tang, D., Zhou, M., Xu, K.: Adaptive recursive neural network for target-dependent Twitter sentiment classification. In: ACL, pp. 49–54 (2014)
37. Yan, Y., Yin, X.-C., Li, S., Yang, M., Hao, H.-W.: Learning document semantic representation with hybrid deep belief network. Comput. Intell. Neurosci. **2015** 650527:1–650527:9 (2015)
38. Liu, Q., Zhang, H., Zeng, Y., Huang, Z., Wu, Z.: Content attention model for aspect based sentiment analysis. In: WWW, pp. 1023–1032 (2018)
39. Tang, D., Qin, B., Liu, T.: Aspect level sentiment classification with deep memory network. In: EMNLP, pp. 214–224 (2016)
40. Wang, Y., Huang, M., Zhu, X., Zhao, L.: Attention-based LSTM for aspect-level sentiment classification. In: EMNLP, pp. 606–615 (2016)

EEG-Based Emotion Estimate Using Shallow Fully Convolutional Neural Network with Boost Training Strategy

Yuehan Yao[1], Chunmei Qing[1(✉)], Xiangmin Xu[1], and Yang Wang[2]

[1] School of Electronic and Information Engineering, South China University of Technology, Guangzhou 510000, China
qchm@scut.edu.cn
[2] School of Science, Hong Kong University of Science and Technology, Hong Kong, China

Abstract. Emotion recognition using Electroencephalogram (EEG) has drawn the attention of many scholars. However, there are few studies looking into regressive approach. Actually, human affective states are continuous rather than discrete. This paper focuses on how to estimate continuous affective status from EEG recordings. A Shallow Fully Convolutional Network (SFCN) with Boost Training Strategy is proposed to estimate affective status, including Valence, Arousal, Dominance, and Liking. SFCN is presented to extract the emotional relative features automatically from preprocessed EEG instead of using hand-crafted features. With Global Average Pooling (GAP) layer, SFCN can solve the effect of unreliability of label introduced by segmented-augmentation method. Moreover, Boost Training Strategy is designed to train model with low memory cost and further improves the performance of SFCN. Experiments on DEAP dataset demonstrate the effectiveness of proposed approaches. Results show that Mean Square Error (MSE) for Valence, Arousal, Dominance, Liking are 3.9181, 3.6009, 3.4441 and 4.806, respectively.

Keywords: Emotion Estimate · Shallow Fully Convolutional Neural Network · Global Average Pooling · Boost Training Strategy

1 Introduction

In human-computer interaction, affective computing helps to make interaction more adaptive to human emotion. For example, audio player can adaptively pick music to coordinate feelings of users. As part of affective computing, emotion recognition based on EEG has drawn the attention of many scholars from psychology to engineering. Modeling emotion recognition using EEG recordings remains a challenge.

Usually, emotion recognition is performed as classifier [1, 2, 19]. In these studies, human emotions are represented by a set of discretized categorizations (for example, anger, fear, joy, sad, surprise). These methods follow a similar paradigm: handcrafted features in EEG were extracted in the time or frequency domain, classifiers such as Naive Bayes and Support Vector Machine (SVM) were implemented [1, 2, 20, 21]. However, human affective states are continuous rather than discrete [3]. Soleymani et al.

J. Ren et al. (Eds.): BICS 2019, LNAI 11691, pp. 55–64, 2020.
https://doi.org/10.1007/978-3-030-39431-8_6

[4] studies in regression-based emotion recognition using power spectrum density feature extracted from EEG. Al-Fahad et al. [5] modeled 4-D affective space (Valence, Arousal, Dominance, Liking) using Support Vector Regression (SVR). In our work, we focus on how to estimate continuous affective space from EEG recordings.

Recently, inspired by the success of deep learning in computer vision and natural language processing [6], deep learning based methods such as Convolutional Neural Network (CNN) have been designed for EEG-based emotion recognition [7, 8]. However, these methods follow the same paradigm as above, using handcrafted features. The handcrafted features with a limited dimension will be a bottleneck to represent the emotion of subjects. In theory, CNN can provide promising performance because it is able to extract feature automatically. There are a few studies have looked into automatic EEG feature extraction. In particular, EEGNet [9] was designed to classify Event Related potential (ERP) signals. DeepConvNet and Shallow Convolutional Network (SCN) [10] were proposed to classify Motor Imagery (MI) EEG signals. More concretely, spatial and temporal features were extracted and fed into fully connected layers.

However, training deep network with EEG dataset is of great challenge. For example, in the publicly available dataset named DEAP [1], which was used in the work, the amount of data is too small to train deep network directly while the size of each sample is too large leading to dimensional disaster. Usually, to increase the number of training samples, EEG in a trial is divided into several fragments and assign the same self-reported final affective state to all EEG fragments. For simplicity, the method is called segmented-augmentation method in the following sections. According to [11], the fluctuation of affective state should be induced in a trial [11]. In segmented-augmentation method, there is a discrepancy between assigned label and real affective status for every EEG fragment due to the fluctuation of affective status. The discrepancy brings noise samples during training model.

In order to estimate continuous affective space from raw EEG recordings directly, a new EEG-based emotion estimation method is proposed in this paper. The main contributions of our work are summarized as follows:

- Shallow Fully Convolutional Network (SFCN) is proposed to extract features relative to emotion from raw EEG recordings directly. Also, SFCN alleviate the effect of unreliability of label introduced by segmented-augmentation method. With global average pooling layer, SFCN has less trainable parameters and allows different size input in time.
- Boost Training Strategy is employed to combine benefits of training model with short and long EEG fragments. Moreover, BTS costs less memory both in train and test stage to get similar amount of train data than segmented-augmentation method.
- Extensive experiments are implemented on DEAP dataset. Experimental results verify the effectiveness of the proposed methods.

The rest of the paper is organized as follows. Section 2 depicts the details of Shallow Fully Convolutional Network and proposed training technique. Section 3 describes EEG dataset used in the paper and the experimental results. Some conclusions are drawn in Sect. 4.

2 Methodology

The framework of the whole EEG-based emotion estimation method is illustrated in Fig. 1. Brief description is given below. Preprocess EEG data according to DEAP [1] as described in Sect. 3.1. Split dataset into 60%, 20% and 20% as training data, validation data and test data. Divide EEG data in a trial into several fragments and assign the self-reported final affective state to all segmented EEG fragments in a trial. Train Shallow Fully Convolutional Network (SFCN, described in Sect. 2.1) with segmented training data, early stopping on the loss of segmented validation data. Specially, Boost Training Strategy (BTS, described in Sect. 2.2) is applied. Predict segmented test data score using trained models. Finally, predicted score of a trial is the average of serval fragments' predicted scores. Repeat above steps to avoid the contingency of the experimental results. Performance analysis (Mean Square Error, MSE) on test data using self-reported and predicted score.

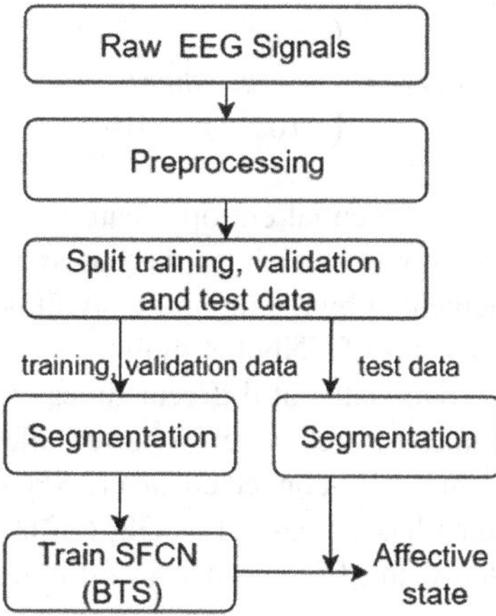

Fig. 1. Diagram of proposed method

2.1 Shallow Fully Convolutional Network (SFCN)

To extract directly features relative to human emotions from EEG recordings, the paper develops the base model named Shallow Convolutional Network (SCN) refer to the paper [10]. In segmented-augmentation method mentioned in Sect. 1, there is a difference between assigned label and real affective status for every EEG fragment. Thus, training SCN with the long EEG fragments is more accurate than using the short EEG fragments. However, due to the fully connected layer of SCN, training SCN with the long EEG fragments often causes dimensional disaster and overfitting.

To address the problem, Shallow Fully Convolutional Network (SFCN) is proposed to training model with longer EEG fragments. The architecture of Shallow Fully

Convolutional Network (SFCN) is shown in Fig. 2. Brief description is given below. The shape of input data is 1 × 32 (channels) × 512 (time samples). SFCN consists of serval parts: Feature Extractor, Feature Transformer and Local Prediction and Global Average Pooling (GAP) layer [13].

Feature Extractor consists of two convolution layers. The first convolution layer uses 40 filters with shape of (1, 13) to extract temporal features for every channel. The second convolution layer with kernel sizes of (32, 1) is used to combine temporal features of all electrodes. After the two convolutions, a batch normalization layer [14] follows to accelerate network training.

Feature Transformer is composed with a squaring activation function, a temporal mean pooling layer and a logarithmic activation function. Squaring and logarithmic activation function are defined as $f(\boldsymbol{x}) = x^2$ and $f(\boldsymbol{x}) = \log(\boldsymbol{x})$ respectively. Temporal mean pooling layer is utilized to smooth features and reduce the size of features over time. For numerical stability, the output of temporal mean pooling layer is truncated between $10e^{-8}$ and $10e^3$. Formally,

$$f(\boldsymbol{x}) = \begin{cases} 10e^{-8},\ x < 10e^{-8} \\ x,\ others \\ 10e^3,\ x > 10e^3 \end{cases} \tag{1}$$

These steps aim to extract differential entropy features [15] from EEG data. After logarithmic activation layer, dropout layer is applied to avoid overfitting [16].

Local Prediction is implemented by a temporal convolution layer with kernel sizes of (1, 3). Due to the weight sharing of CNN (as shown in Fig. 3), Local Prediction can be interpreted to predict affective status at different times. And the GAP layer aggregates emotions at different times to predict self-reported affective status.

Comparing with SCN using fully-connected layer, SFCN reduces 2640 trainable parameters when the input data has a shape of (1, 32, 512). On the other hand, SFCN allows to be trained and tested with EEG fragments of different size without increasing trainable parameters.

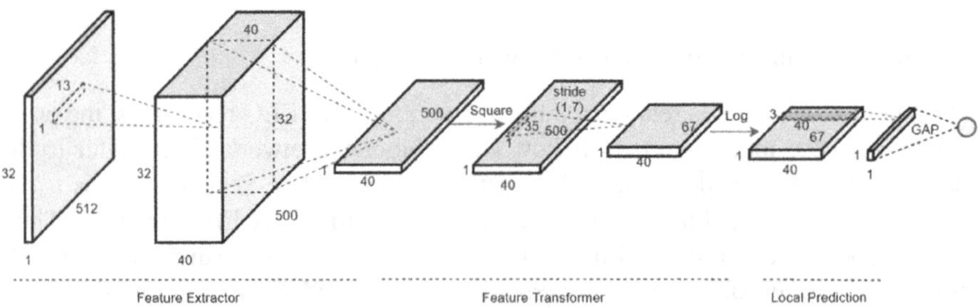

Fig. 2. Shallow Fully Convolutional Network architecture.

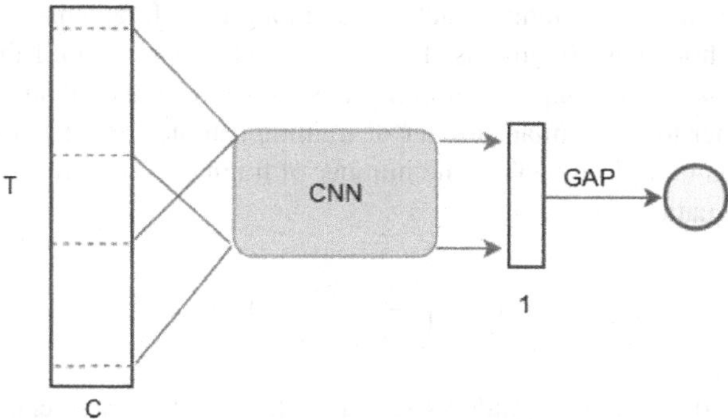

Fig. 3. Weight sharing of CNN. T is the number of time samples. C is the number of channels.

The objective function used in the model is Mean Square Error defined as:

$$L = \frac{1}{N}\sum\nolimits_{x \in S} \|y - f(\boldsymbol{x})\|^2 \tag{2}$$

Where S is the training set, N is the size of training set, x is the input of network and y is the label, f(x) is the output of the model.

2.2 Boost Training Strategy

To increase the number of training samples, EEG in a trial is divided into several fragments and all EEG fragments are assigned the same self-reported affective state. For simplicity, the paper names it segmented-augmentation method.

In order to investigate the influence of windows size on regression task, following the research [17], the preprocessed EEG in a trial is divided into different window sizes. The block diagram of window segmentation process is illustrated in Fig. 4. The set of window size is $\{4\text{s}, 8\text{s}, 16\text{s}\}$ and overlapping sample is implemented to make the similar amount of training data. Specially, the bigger windows size of EEG fragment is, the smaller step of EEG fragment is.

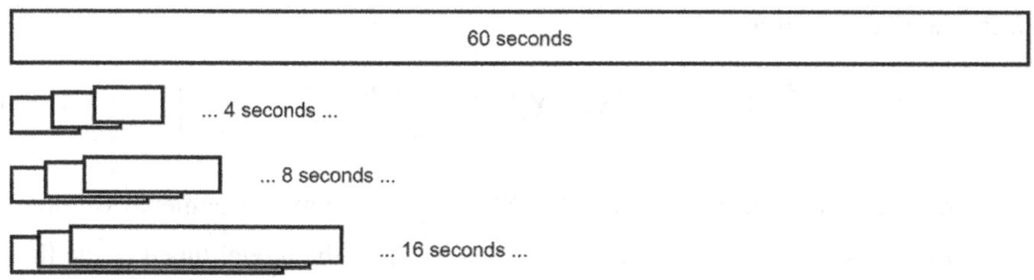

Fig. 4. Diagram of window segmentation process

As mentioned above, training model with the long EEG fragments is more accurate than using the short EEG fragments. However, as is illustrated in Table 1, the long EEG fragments with overlapping sampling cost more resources than the short EEG fragments in order to get similar number of training samples. For EEG data in a trial, the total length is 60 s. In the table, the number of fragments in a trial is calculated by the following equation.

$$\mathrm{N} = \left\lfloor \frac{60 - \mathrm{ws}}{step} \right\rfloor + 1 \tag{3}$$

Where ws and *step* is the windows size and step of EEG fragments in a trial.

Besides, we introduce Memory Expansion Rate (MER) metric to measure relative expansion of memory for a trial. For segmented-augmentation method, MER is defined as below:

$$\mathrm{MER} = \frac{\mathrm{N} \times \mathrm{ws}}{60} \tag{4}$$

Where N × ws is the total seconds of EEG in a trial after segmentation. The 60 represents the seconds of EEG in a trial before segmentation. The bigger MER means more memory consumption due to overlapping. Specially, if a 4 s windows size and 4 s step are used, the MER is 1.00.

Boost Training Strategy is proposed to combine benefits of training model with short and long EEG fragments by using various window sizes input, as illustrated in Fig. 5. In the first stage, the preprocessed EEG signals are segmented into non-overlapping and 4 s fragments which are fed into SFCN. Concretely, all fragments of a trial are organized as below:

$$\mathrm{D}_4^{(i)} = \left\{X_4^{(1)}, X_4^{(2)}, X_4^{(3)}, \ldots, X_4^{(j)}, \ldots, X_4^{(15)}\right\} \tag{5}$$

Where $X_4^{(j)}$ is the jth 4 s fragment of ith trial. Then, early stopping strategy is applied on validation data to find the best model. In the second stage, the above segmented EEG signals are grouped according to adjacent pairs, merged into 8 s fragments and fed into SFCN initialized by best model in previous stage. All fragments of a trial are organized as below:

$$\mathrm{D}_8^{(i)} = \left\{\left[X_4^{(1)}, X_4^{(2)}\right], \left[X_4^{(3)}, X_4^{(4)}\right], \ldots, \left[X_4^{(2j)}, X_4^{(2j+1)}\right], \ldots\right\} \tag{6}$$

Where $[.,.]$ denotes merging and $\left[X_4^{(2j)}, X_4^{(2j+1)}\right]$ is the jth 8 s fragment of ith trial. The third stage is the same as the previous stage. Finally, the model tuned at the third stage is used to predict 3 non-overlapping EEG fragments with the window size of 16 s. Predicted score of a trial is the average of the three fragments' predicted scores.

Table 1. The MER and N with different configurations. In the table, "BTS" represents the model using Boost Training Strategy.

Configurations	N (train)	MER (train)	N (test)	MER (test)
ws = 4 s, step = 2.33 s	25	1.67	25	1.67
ws = 8 s, step = 2.17 s	24	3.2	24	3.2
ws = 16 s, step = 1.75 s	26	6.93	26	6.93
BTS	25	**2.73**	**3**	**0.8**

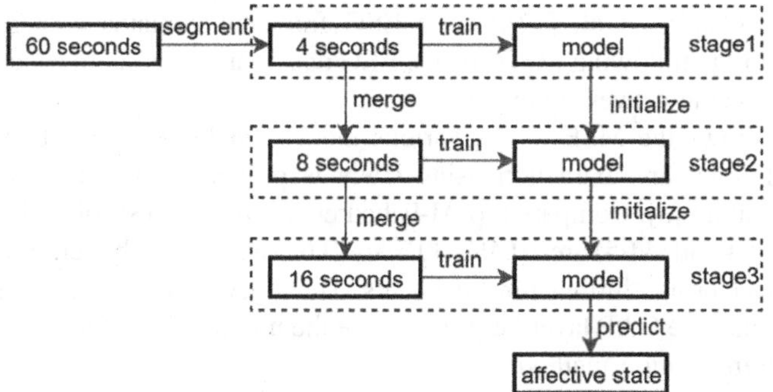

Fig. 5. Diagram of Boost Training Strategy

As is illustrated in Table 1, Boost Training Strategy costs less memory both in training and testing stage to get similar amount of train data than segmented-augmentation method. There are 25 fragments for a trial in total. The numbers of fragments are 15, 7 and 3 at corresponding stage. Also fitting model with BTS gets better performance as illustrated in Sect. 3.4.

3 Experiments and Results

3.1 Database and Preprocessing

DEAP dataset [1] is used in the study. In the study, 32 participants were asked to watch 40 videos to elicit their emotions. During watching video, EEG and physiological signals were recorded. At the end of each video, participants reported their levels of affective status using Self-assessment manikins (SAM) [12]. The data was recorded by BioSemi Active II system at 512 Hz. First, the EEG signals were downsampled to 128 Hz, and the electrooculogram (EOG) artifacts were removed. Then a 4.0–45.0 Hz bandpass frequency filter was applied.

In our tasks, we remove the first 3 s EEG fragment and only use the EEG data with shape of 32 × 7680 (channel number × sampling number) in a trial. The all data is a matrix of 32 × 40 × 32 × 7680 (participant number × video number × channel number × sampling number) with 1280 × 4 labels.

3.2 Training Details

We fit all models using Adam [18] as optimizer with a learning rate of 0.001. We run about 30 training epochs and perform early stopping strategy if no improvement in validation data in the past 5 epochs. All models are implemented through PyTorch and are deployed on a GeForce GTX1080TI GPU. All experiments are conducted 20 times and averaged results are reported.

3.3 Performance of Shallow Fully Convolutional Network

According to Candra et al. [17], a 4 s EEG fragment contains enough emotional information. In the following experiments, EEG data in a trial is segmented into several 4 s fragments without overlapping.

Figure 6 shows the MSE of the various models on DEAP dataset. As expected, automatic EEG feature extraction using CNN is proven to be stronger than using handcrafted feature [5]. Compared to Al-Fahad et al. [5], the MSE of SCN on test data (4.22, 3.71, 3.54 and, 4.95) are 10.4%, 39.7%, 49.6% and 33.1% better. Besides, SFCN with GAP layer brings further improvements. The ablation study based on SCN [10] demonstrates that the GAP layer helps to reduce the unreliability of label introduced by segmented-augmentation method.

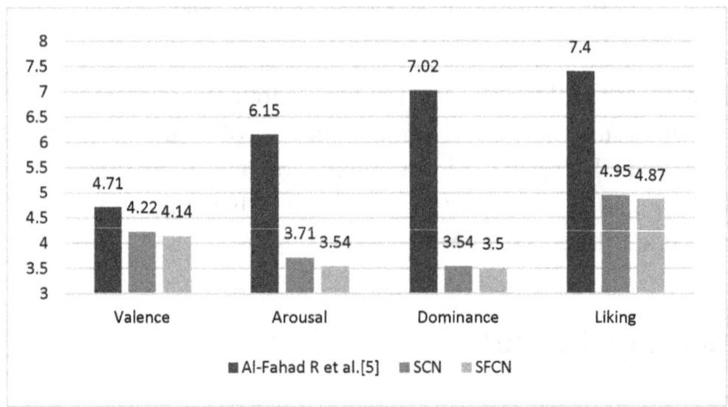

Fig. 6. Model comparison on DEAP dataset. The windows size of input EEG data is 4 s

3.4 Performance of Boost Training Strategy

Table 2 show the MSE of SFCN with different configurations. In the table, "ws" represents the windows size of input EEG data. "BTS" represents the model using Boost Training Strategy. By comparing the models, some conclusions are drawn. First, under the same window size of 4 s, using smaller step improves the performance slightly benefiting from increasing the size of train data. Second, the ablation study on using different window size shows that increasing the window size effectively improve the performance by reducing the effect of unreliability of label introduced by segmented-augmentation method. Third, Boost Training Strategy can improve stably

Table 2. MSE of SFCN with different configurations.

Configurations	Valence	Arousal	Dominance	Liking
ws = 4 s, step = 4 s	4.1359	3.6815	3.4964	4.8653
ws = 4 s, step = 2.33 s	4.0772	3.6545	3.4937	4.8379
ws = 8 s, step = 2.17 s	4.0545	3.6608	3.4549	4.8161
ws = 16 s, step = 1.75 s	3.9691	3.6447	3.4901	4.8476
BTS	**3.9181**	**3.6009**	**3.4441**	**4.806**

the performance of SFCN for continuous affective status including Valence, Arousal, Dominance, Liking with the smaller MER both in training and testing stage.

4 Conclusions

This paper focuses on how to estimate continuous affective space preprocessed raw EEG recordings directly. Using the handcrafted features to train model will be a bottleneck to represent the emotion of subjects. Shallow Fully Convolutional Network (SFCN) is proposed to extract the emotional relative features automatically from preprocessed EEG data. Compared with conventional method, the model can reduce a lot of feature engineering jobs and get better capability. With Global Average Pooling (GAP) layer, SFCN solves the effect of unreliability of label introduced by segmented-augmentation method. Moreover, Boost Training Strategy is designed to help training model with low memory cost and further improves the performance of SFCN. Extensive experiments verify the effectiveness of the proposed methods. Our future work is to conduct experiments on other databases to verify the effectiveness of the proposed method.

Acknowledgments. This work is supported by the National Natural Science Foundation of China (Grant No. U180120050, 61702192, and U1636218).

References

1. Koelstra, S., et al.: DEAP: a database for emotion analysis; using physiological signals. IEEE Trans. Affect. Comput. **3**(1), 18–31 (2012)
2. Kumar, N., Khaund, K., Hazarika, S.M.: Bispectral analysis of EEG for emotion recognition. Procedia Comput. Sci. **84**, 31–35 (2016)
3. Lan, Z., et al.: Using support vector regression to estimate valence level from EEG. In: IEEE International Conference on Systems, Man, & Cybernetics (2017)
4. Soleymani, M., et al.: Continuous emotion detection in response to music videos. In: 2011 IEEE International Conference on Automatic Face & Gesture Recognition and Workshops (FG 2011) (2011)
5. Al-Fahad, R., Yeasin, M.: Robust modeling of continuous 4-D affective space from EEG recording. In: 2016 15th IEEE International Conference on Machine Learning and Applications (ICMLA) (2016)

6. Bahdanau, D., Cho, K., Bengio, Y.: Neural machine translation by jointly learning to align and translate. In: Proceedings of the 3rd International Conference on Learning Representations (2015)
7. Tripathi, S., Acharya, S., Sharma, R.D., Mittal, S., Bhattacharya, S.: Using deep and convolutional neural networks for accurate emotion classification on DEAP dataset. In: Twenty-Ninth IAAI Conference (2017)
8. Qiao, R., et al.: A novel deep-learning based framework for multi-subject emotion recognition. In: International Conference on Information (2017)
9. Vernon, L., Amelia, S., Nicholas, W., et al.: EEGNet: a compact convolutional neural network for EEG-based brain–computer interfaces. J. Neural Eng. (2018)
10. Schirrmeister, R.T., Gemein, L., Eggensperger, K., et al.: Deep learning with convolutional neural networks for decoding and visualization of EEG pathology. Hum. Brain Mapp. **38**(11), 5391–5420 (2017)
11. Gunes, H., Schuller, B.: Categorical and dimensional affect analysis in continuous input: current trends and future directions. Image Vis. Comput. **31**(2), 120–136 (2013)
12. Morris, J.D.: SAM: the self-assessment manikin; an efficient cross-cultural measurement of emotional response. J. Adv. Res. **35**(8), 63–68 (1995)
13. Lin, M., Chen, Q., Yan, S.: Network in network. Comput. Sci. (2013)
14. Ioffe, S., Szegedy, C.: Batch normalization: accelerating deep network training by reducing internal covariate shift. In: International Conference on Machine Learning. JMLR.org (2015)
15. Shi, L.C., Jiao, Y.Y., Lu, B.L.: Differential entropy feature for EEG-based vigilance estimation. In: Proceedings of the Annual International Conference of the IEEE Engineering in Medicine and Biology Society, pp. 6627–6630 (2013)
16. Krizhevsky, A., Sutskever, I., Hinton, G.E.: ImageNet classification with deep convolutional neural networks. In: International Conference on Neural Information Processing Systems (2012)
17. Candra, H., et al.: Investigation of window size in classification of EEG-emotion signal with wavelet entropy and support vector machine. In: 2015 37th Annual International Conference of the IEEE on Engineering in Medicine and Biology Society (EMBC), pp. 7250–7253 (2015)
18. Kingma, D.P., Ba, J.: Adam: a method for stochastic optimization. In: Proceedings of 3rd International Conference on Learning Representations (2015)
19. Padfield, N., Zabalza, J., Zhao, H., Masero, V., Ren, J.: EEG-based brain-computer interfaces using motor-imagery: techniques and challenges. Sensors **19**(6), 1423 (2019)
20. Ren, J.: ANN vs. SVM: which one performs better in classification of MCCs in mammogram imaging. Knowl.-Based Syst. **26**, 144–153 (2012)
21. Zabalza, J., Clemente, C., Di Caterina, G., Ren, J., Soraghan, J.J., Marshall, S.: Robust PCA micro-doppler classification using SVM on embedded systems. IEEE Trans. Aerosp. Electron. Syst. **50**(3), 2304–2310 (2014)

Emotion Recognition Using Eye Gaze Based on Shallow CNN with Identity Mapping

Shan Jin[1], Chunmei Qing[1(✉)], Xiangmin Xu[1], and Yang Wang[2]

[1] School of Electronic and Information Engineering, South China University of Technology, Guangzhou 510000, China
qchm@scut.edu.cn

[2] School of Science, Hong Kong University of Science and Technology, Hong Kong, China

Abstract. Machine recognition of human emotions has attracted more and more attention for its wide application in recent years. As a spontaneous signal of human behavior, eye gaze is utilized for emotion recognition. Compared with electroencephalogram (EEG) signals, eye gaze data is more available, and it can be used in many practical applications, such as virtual reality (VR). In this paper, a new method of human emotion recognition based on eye gaze is proposed. Firstly, a new set of eye gaze features is proposed which consists of eye gaze sequences, extracted statistical feature sequences and spectral feature sequences. Then, the eye gaze feature set is input into the convolutional layer to extract high-level features. Finally, these high-level features and the eye gaze feature set are combined to complete the mapping of features to human emotions. Experiments on MAHNOB-HCI dataset demonstrate the effectiveness of this method.

Keywords: Eye gaze · Emotion recognition · Shallow CNN with identity mapping · Arousal · Valence

1 Introduction

Emotion is a kind of subjective experience and plays an important role in natural communication [1]. Dimensional space theory is proposed to explain the mechanism of emotion production [2, 3]. Various emotions can be represented by different spatial positions, the similarity and difference between different emotions are reflected by the distance in the dimensional space. The most commonly used dimensions include valence and arousal [4].

In the existing studies, emotion recognition based on eye gaze mainly consists of two aspects. One aspect is to identify the emotion of the participant from the data of eye gaze [5–7], the other aspect is to identify the emotion of the object which participant watched from eye gaze [8–11].

In human emotion recognition based on eye gaze, along the arousal dimension, the emotions are divided into calm, medium aroused and excited by Soleymani et al. [7] Emotions are also divided into unpleasant, neutral valence and pleasant along the valence dimension. The author extracts statistical and spectral features related to pupil diameter, fixation distance and so on. The libSVM [12] classifier based on RBF [13]

J. Ren et al. (Eds.): BICS 2019, LNAI 11691, pp. 65–75, 2020.
https://doi.org/10.1007/978-3-030-39431-8_7

kernel is used to perform single-mode human emotion recognition based on eye gaze features. The accuracies of emotion recognition based on eye gaze are 63.5% (arousal) and 68.8% (valence). Lu et al. collect data by themselves in [6]. They divide emotions into positive, neutral and negative. The linear kernel support vector machine is used for recognizing the participants' emotions. Although there are some achievements in the existing research, there are still some opportunities and difficulties in the study of human emotion recognition based on eye gaze data. First, using only manual features may miss some deep features hidden in the original data. Second, the statistical and spectral features cannot reflect the continuity of features in time. Third, because of the limited eye gaze data, deep learning has not been widely used. Although the neural network is used for human emotion recognition based on eye gaze data in [10], its recognition performance is not good enough.

In this paper, a novel way for feature extraction and an emotion recognition model based on eye gaze are proposed. The contribution points are summarized below:

(1) The temporally statistical features and the temporally spectral features are extracted, which can express the details of eye gaze and the trend of features change.
(2) A new shallow CNN with identity mapping is proposed for emotion recognition, where the convolutional layer in the proposed model is used for extracting high-level features. The high-level features are then concatenated with the raw feature set by identity mapping. The rest of the network is designed to map the concatenated features to human emotions.
(3) High accuracy of emotion recognition is obtained, which is 11.7%, 10.5% improved respectively in valence and arousal compared with state-of-the-art algorithms.

In this paper, the second section introduces the process of feature extraction of eye gaze. The method of emotion recognition we proposed are given in section three. The fourth section shows the experimental results and discussions. Section five is the conclusion.

2 Eye Gaze Feature Set

The Database MAHNOB-HCI [7] is used in this paper. It is collected in a rigorous laboratory environment, and contains the eye gaze data from 30 participants when they watched 20 videos separately. These video are from the online resources, including the weather forecast, popular video clips and so on. After each trial, their self-report of emotion, arousal and valence are recorded. Due to the partial information missing of some participants, only the data of 27 participants are used. The eye gaze data obtained from the dataset can be expressed as follows:

$$X_{data} = \left[X_{pdl}, X_{pdr}, X_{dl}, X_{dr}, X_{fpx}, X_{fpy}, X_{mfpx}, X_{mfpy}, X_{ft}\right] \quad (1)$$

X_{data} are the eye gaze data that used in this paper. X_{pdl} and X_{pdr} are pupil diameter sequences of left and right. X_{dl} and X_{dr} are distance sequences from the eye tracker to the eye (left and right). X_{fpx} and X_{fpy} are the abscissa and ordinate sequences of the fixation points collected by eye tracker. X_{mfpx} and X_{mfpx} are mapping sequences of abscissa and ordinate fixation points. X_{ft} is the fixation time sequence.

In this study, the missing values caused by collection problems are filled with the average values before and after the missing values. The pupil diameter lost due to blinking is filled by linear interpolation.

The change of pupil diameter is mainly caused by light. It takes the elimination of light reflection to get the change of pupil diameter caused by emotion. Principal component analysis (PCA) is used to estimate this common light reflection pattern for each video [5]. It is assumed that pupil diameter is mainly affected by illumination and emotion, among which illumination is the main factor.

In the pupil diameter sequences, for n samples based on the same video, the shortest sample length is used as the window of each sample. Each sample of the n samples is truncated to obtain n equal-length pupil diameter sequences. The right singular matrix of SVD [14] is used to extract the first principal component from these n equal-length pupil diameter sequences, which is approximately the pupil response caused by light. The calculation formula of singular value decomposition is as follows:

Assuming that matrix A is an n by m matrix. It can be expressed as:

$$A_{n*m} = U_{n*n} \sum\nolimits_{n*m} V_{m*m}^{T} \tag{2}$$

A is a matrix consisting of n equal-length pupil diameter sequences. U is a n * n matrix (the vectors of U is left singular vectors), Σ is a n * m matrix (the diagonal elements are singular values, in addition to the diagonal, the rest of the elements are 0), V is a m * m matrix (the vectors of V is right singular vectors).

Matrix A left multiplies transpose A^T. A square matrix (m * m) is obtained. It is used to find the eigenvalue and eigenvector, v_i is the right singular vector:

$$\left(A^{T}A\right)v_i = \lambda_i v_i \tag{3}$$

The singular value σ_i can be calculated according to the eigenvalues λ:

$$\sigma_i = \sqrt{\lambda_i} \tag{4}$$

The sequences of pupil diameter caused by emotion can be obtained as follows:

$$A'_{n*m} = A_{n*m} - \sigma_i \tag{5}$$

After the light reflection in the pupil diameter is removed, relevant features such as pupil diameter, fixation distance, blinking and closing eyes, and fixation coordinate can be obtained by referring to the method in [7], with a total of 51 dimensions.

It is worth noting that each dimension of 51-dimensional feature is a feature sequence. Each frame of each feature sequence is extracted from all the data before the corresponding frame in the eye gaze sequences, so the features are continuous. These features can be called as temporal feature sequences. Assuming the length of the eye gaze sequence (frame number of X_{data} captured by the instrument when participants watch videos) is n frames, the length of each dimension feature sequence in the 51-dimensional features is n frames. The i_{th} data frame in each feature sequence is extracted from 1 to i data frames in the X_{data}. But the features of each frame during the blink are extracted from the first frame to the end frame of the blink.

These 51-dimensional features can be represented as follows:

$$X_{temporal} = \left[X_{pd}, X_{fd}, X_{bce}, X_{fc}\right] \tag{6}$$

$X_{temporal}$ are the 51-dimensional features. X_{pd} are 12-dimensional features associated with pupil diameter. X_{fd} are 6-dimensional features associated with fixation distance. X_{bce} are 6-dimensional features associated with blinking and closing eyes. X_{fc} are 27-dimensional features associated with fixation coordinate.

In $X_{temporal}$, features associated with blinking or closing eyes is calculated by the unobtainable fragments. Emotions triggered by video content stimuli may cause participants to close eyes, and the depth at which participants close eyes can also be used to identify participants' emotions. The frequency with which participants approach or stay away from the screen can also be used to identify emotions triggered by video. Statistical features, such as standard deviation, kurtosis and skewness, are also related to participants' emotions. In order to represent the different oscillations of human eye fixation mode, the power spectral densities of different bands are extracted [7].

Specific features are shown in Table 1. As far as we know, these feature sequences in bold are the new feature sequences.

In Table 1, the scan path length is equal to the first-order difference of x-coordinate (or y-coordinate). The displacement is the Euclidean distance of gaze points between two adjacent frames.

The formula for calculating displacement is as follows:

$$\mathrm{D} = \sqrt{(x_{t+1} - x_t)^2 + (y_{t+1} - y_t)^2} \tag{7}$$

D is the displacement, x and y are abscissa and ordinate of the fixation point respectively, and t is the frame time.

The field of view is divided into four rectangles with equal area by a cross. In each rectangular zone, the standard deviation of x-coordinate (or y-coordinate) can be obtained, from which the average and standard deviation of coordinates in four zones (both x and y) can also be obtained.

$X_{temporal}$ is combined with X_{data} to form a 60-dimensional feature sequences. The 60-dimensional feature sequences can be expressed as follows:

$$X_{combine} = \left[X_{data}, X_{temporal}\right] \tag{8}$$

$X_{combine}$ are the 60-dimensional feature sequences.

Table 1. Feature details extracted from X_{data}.

Eye gaze data	Extracted features
Pupil diameter (both left and right) (12)	Average, standard deviation (SD), spectral power: [0, 0.2] Hz, [0.2, 0.4] Hz, [0.4, 0.6] Hz, [0.6, 1] Hz
Gaze distance (6)	Approach time ratio, avoidance time ratio, approach rate, avoidance rate, average of approach time, **average of avoidance time**
Eye blinking (6)	**Amount of blinking, SD of blinking amount,** blinking rate, length of the longest blink, length of the current blink, time spent with eyes close
Gaze coordinates (27)	SD (both x and y), skewness (both x and y), Kurtosis (both x and y), average fixation time, **scan path length** (both x and y), **displacement**, **SD of displacement**, **average of displacement**, number of fixation zones (normalized by the video length), spectral power (both x and y): [0, 0.2] Hz, [0.2, 0.4] Hz, [0.4, 0.6] Hz, [0.6, 0.8] Hz, [0.8, 1] Hz, **average of standard deviation of coordinates in four zones** (both x and y), **standard deviation of standard deviation of coordinates in four zones** (both x and y)

3 Methodology

3.1 Sample Construction

Inspired by [7], along the arousal dimension, emotions are divided into calm, medium aroused, and excited. Emotions are also divided into unpleasant, neutral valence and pleasant along the valence dimension. The mapping between emotions and categories are given in Table 2.

Table 2. The mapping of valence and arousal

Arousal class	Emotion
Calm	Sadness, disgust, neutral
Medium arousal	Joy and happiness, amusement
Excited/Activated	Surprise, fear, anger, anxiety
Valence class	Emotion
Unpleasant	Fear, anger, disgust, sadness, anxiety
Neutral valence	Surprise, neutral
Pleasant	Joy and happiness, amusement

In order to reduce the differences between participants, the min-max standardization is carried out among the same participants. The 60-dimensional feature sequences $X_{combine}$ are truncated with a window length of 800 frames (nearly 13 s) and overlap of

100 frames. Samples after truncation are represented by $x_{combine}$. Each sample size is 800 * 60 after truncation, and the label of each sample is consistent with the label of the original sample. Truncation mode is shown in Fig. 1 (see Fig. 1).

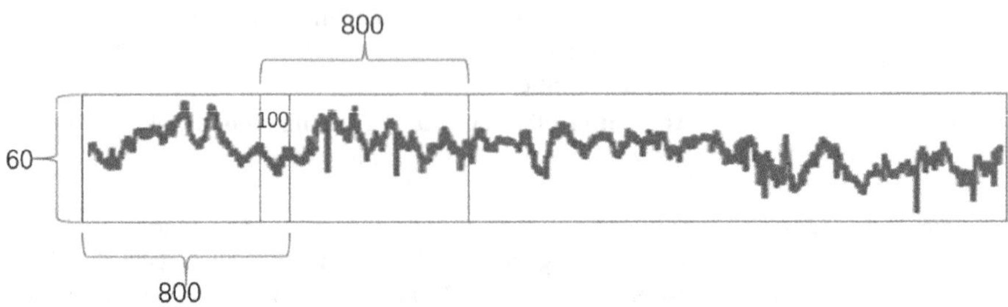

Fig. 1. Truncation mode.

3.2 Shallow CNN with Identity Mapping

In order to extract discriminative features, a shallow CNN with identity mapping (SCNN-IM) is proposed as an emotion classification model. In SCNN-IM, $x_{combine}$, as the lowest input of the network, pass through the convolutional layer to get the deep features. By adjusting the size of convolution kernels [15], SCNN-IM can automatically extract abstract features, which can be called high-level features. These high-level feature sequences can be expressed as $x_{high-level}$. $x_{high-level}$ are concatenated with $x_{combine}$ and used as input of the full connection layer. As mentioned earlier, $x_{combine}$ are transformed into 2-dimensional image format and used as input of SCNN-IM network. The details of the network are shown in Fig. 2 (see Fig. 2).

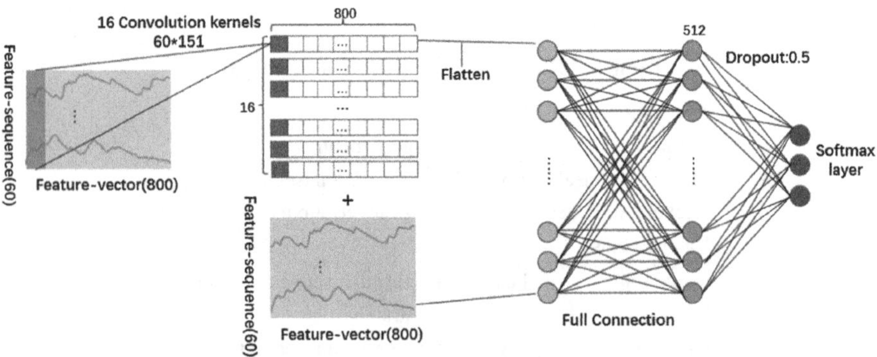

Fig. 2. The structure and settings of SCNN-IM.

In SCNN-IM, consider $x^i_{combine}$ as the i_{th} sample and y_i is the prediction result. The convolutional layer extract high-level features from $x^i_{combine}$. This process can be represented by the following formulas:

$$\mathrm{C}\left(x^i_{combine}\right) \rightarrow x^i_{high-level} \tag{9}$$

$$\mathrm{C}(\cdot) = ReLU\left(BN\left(W\left(x^i_{combine}\right)\right)\right) \tag{10}$$

$\mathrm{C}(\cdot)$ is considered to be operations to extract high-level features. W is the weight in convolution calculation. $x^i_{high-level}$ are the high-level feature sequences of the i_{th} sample.

The high-level feature sequences $x^i_{high-level}$ are then concatenated with $x^i_{combine}$ by identity mapping to get a new feature set. It can be represented as follows:

$$\mathrm{M}\left(x^i_{high-level}, x^i_{combine}\right) \rightarrow x^i_{set} \tag{11}$$

$$\mathrm{M}(\cdot) = \left[x^i_{high-level}, x^i_{combine}\right] \tag{12}$$

The new feature set x^i_{set} passes through two fully connected layers to get the prediction result y_i. This process can be represented by the following formulas:

$$\mathrm{F}\left(x^i_{set}\right) \rightarrow y_i \tag{13}$$

$$\mathrm{F}(\cdot) = Softmax\left(FC\left(ReLU\left(BN\left(FC\left(x^i_{set}\right)\right)\right)\right)\right) \tag{14}$$

In detail, the convolution layer does the convolution operation by 16 convolution kernels and the size is 60×151. The convolution operation is followed by an activation function ReLU [16]. At the output end of the first fully connected layer, the activation function ReLU and a dropout with the probability of 0.5 are followed. The activation function used after the final fully connected layer is SoftMax. Batch normalization [15] is used in the convolutional layer and the first fully connected layer to improve the network convergence speed.

The batch normalization used is as follows:

$$x'^{(k)} = \frac{x^{(k)} - E\left[x^{(k)}\right]}{\sqrt{Var\left[x^{(k)}\right]}} \tag{15}$$

In experiments, the epoch is 60 and the batch-size is 64. The Categorical Cross Entropy is chosen as the loss function. The loss function used is as follows:

$$\mathrm{Loss(x, class)} = -\log\left(\frac{\exp(x[class])}{\sum_j \exp(x[j])}\right) \tag{16}$$

Adam is chosen as the optimizer. The learning rate is 0.0001. The model is built through Pytorch. The choice of initialization methods in convolutional layer and full connection layer is critical to model performance. The initialization mentioned in [18] is used for the proposed network.

3.3 Validation and Classification Strategy

As mentioned in [7], the method of leave-one-participant-out is used as cross validation in this study. It can check whether a new participant's felt emotion can be estimated based on others. In detail, there are 27 people's data in total, and for each of them, the accuracy of the model is the result predicted by the model trained from the data of the remaining 26 people.

The feature sequences extracted by each person in each video are considered as a complete sample. Each complete sample is divided into several parts. The length of the complete sample is different, so the number of truncations of each complete sample is different. So that each complete sample is extended to several subsamples. These subsamples are obtained from the same complete sample, so they have the same emotion label. In the proposed network, the input units are subsamples. This will lead to a phenomenon that in the testing stage, subsamples from the same complete sample are used as network input, and different classification results will be obtained in the output end, such as [0, 0, 1, 0, 0, 0, 1, 2, 0]. These results are confusing, and the predictive label of the complete sample cannot be obtained intuitively from them. So, in the subsamples from the same complete sample, the category with the largest number is chosen as the prediction result of the complete sample.

4 Experimental Results

The effectiveness of the proposed method will be demonstrated in this section. This method is compared with the baseline, and the performance with different features, models and classification strategies are also compared.

4.1 Comparison with Baseline

In Table 3 includes the average accuracy as well as the best accuracy for proposed system. The best accuracy is in bold.

Table 3. The average accuracy rate with leave-one-participant-out cross validation.

Method	Arousal	Valence
MAHNOB-HCI [7]	63.5%	68.8%
Ours	**75.2%**	**79.3%**

The results in Table 3 show that the accuracy of the proposed method is better than the baseline in the MAHNOB-HCI dataset. The accuracy of the proposed method increases 11.7% on arousal, and 10.5% on valence, respectively. This is because the convolutional layer can extract high-level features which are difficult to be excavated manually, and the temporal feature sequences can also reflect the change trend of features.

4.2 Comparison of Using and Not Using Classification Strategy

Table 4 shows the effect of classification strategy. The accuracy is the average accuracy of 27 participants.

Table 4. The effect of classification strategy.

Method	Without classification strategy		With classification strategy	
Accuracy	Arousal	Valence	Arousal	Valence
	64.40%	68.44%	**75.26%**	**79.38%**

It can be seen from Table 4 that classification strategy has positive improvement on accuracy. Compared with the experimental results without using the classification strategy, there is 10.86% improved in arousal by using classification strategy, and there is 10.94% improved in valence. The classification strategy not only improves the accuracy, but can also intuitively reflect the predictive label of the complete sample. At the same time, the use of classification strategy can directly reflect the label of complete samples.

4.3 Comparison of Features

In order to demonstrate the effectiveness of the method of using $x_{combine}$ as network input, the methods of using x_{data} as network input and $x_{temporal}$ as network input are also tested respectively. The results are given in Table 5. The accuracy is the average accuracy of 27 participants.

Table 5. Comparison of feature selection.

Feature	Arousal	Valence
x_{data} (9)	66.67%	70.61%
$x_{temporal}$ (51)	74.02%	78.13%
$x_{combine}$ (60)	**75.26%**	**79.38%**

The results in Table 5 show that the recognition accuracy based on combined features gets the best performance in both arousal and valence. The performance of using only temporal feature sequences is better than that of using only eye gaze data, which indicates that temporal feature sequences contain more useful information than the eye gaze data. With the eye gaze data as the input of the proposed network, the accuracy is better than the baseline in terms of arousal and valence. This also reflects that the proposed method is superior than manually feature extraction method.

4.4 Comparison of Networks

In addition, the effects of SCNN-IM, SCNN (SCNN-IM without identity mapping) and SNN (SCNN-IM without convolutional layer) are also compared. The results are shown in Table 6. The accuracy is the average accuracy of 27 participants.

Table 6. Comparison between SCNN-IM, CNN and DNN.

Method	Arousal	Valence
SCNN	70.85%	77.49%
SNN	73.84%	79.11%
Ours (SCNN-IM)	**75.26%**	**79.38%**

It is easy to see that the proposed network performs better in arousal and valence than other networks. This shows that the use of convolution layer and identity mapping can not only preserve important information in manual features, but also extract high-level features contained in manual features.

5 Conclusion

A new human emotion recognition framework which mainly includes temporal feature sequence extraction, classification strategy and SCNN-IM is proposed in this paper. The network can find the mapping pattern of features to emotions from the eye gaze data, temporal feature sequences and high-level features. Experiments on MAHNOB-HCI dataset demonstrate the effectiveness of this framework, and high accuracy of emotion recognition is obtained. In arousal, the accuracy rate increases by 11.7%. In valence, the accuracy rate increases by 10.5%. The accuracies of different feature sequences as network input are also compared. The results show that the temporal feature sequences are effective for emotion recognition. At the same time, the classification strategy greatly improves the accuracy. It can also extract image features of gaze point area on video and fuse with eye gaze features to further improve the accuracy of emotion recognition.

Acknowledgments. This work is supported by the National Natural Science Foundation of China (Grant No. U180120050, 61702192, and U1636218).

References

1. Shu, L.: A review of emotion recognition using physiological signals. Sensors **18**(7), 2074 (2018)
2. Russell, J.A.: A circumplex model of affect. J. Pers. Soc. Psychol. **39**(6), 1161–1178 (1980)
3. Lane, R.D.: Is alexithymia the emotional equivalent of blindsight? Biol. Psychiatry **42**(9), 834–844 (1997)
4. Xie, J.: Research progress of mood measurement methods. Psychol. Sci. **2**, 488–493 (2011)
5. Zheng, W.: Multimodal emotion recognition using EEG and eye tracking data. In: 36th Annual International Conference of the IEEE Engineering in Medicine and Biology Society, pp. 5040–5043 (2014)
6. Lu, Y.: Combining eye movements and EEG to enhance emotion recognition. In: International Joint Conference on Artificial Intelligence, pp. 1170–1176 (2015)
7. Soleymani, M.: A multimodal database for affect recognition and implicit tagging. IEEE Trans. Affect. Comput. **3**(1), 42–55 (2012)
8. O'Dwyer, J.: Continuous affect prediction using eye gaze. In: IEEE International Conference on Bioinformatics and Biomedicine, pp. 2001–2007 (2017)
9. O'Dwyer, J.: Continuous affect prediction using eye gaze. In: 28th Irish Signals and Systems Conference, pp. 1–6 (2017)
10. Aracena, C.: Neural networks for emotion recognition based on eye tracking data. In: IEEE International Conference on Systems, Man, and Cybernetics, pp. 2632–2637 (2015)
11. Pantic, M.: Multimodal emotion recognition in response to videos. IEEE Trans. Affect. Comput. **3**(1), 211–223 (2012)
12. Chang, C.-C.: LIBSVM: a library for support vector machines. ACM Trans. Intell. Syst. Technol. **2**(3), 27 (2011)
13. Quinlan, J.R.: C4.5: Programs for Machine Learning. Morgan Kaufmann Publishers Inc., San Francisco (1992)
14. Golub, G.H.: Singular value decomposition and least squares solutions. Numer. Math. **14**(5), 403–420 (1970)
15. Lecun, Y.: Backpropagation applied to handwritten zip code recognition. Neural Comput. **1**(4), 541–551 (1989)
16. Nair, V.: Rectified linear units improve restricted Boltzmann machines. In: International Conference on Machine Learning, pp. 807–814 (2010)
17. Ioffe, S.: Batch normalization: accelerating deep network training by reducing internal covariate shift. In: International Conference on International Conference on Machine Learning, pp. 448–456 (2015)
18. He, K.: Delving deep into rectifiers: surpassing human-level performance on imagenet classification. In: IEEE International Conference on Computer Vision, pp. 1026–1034 (2015)

Height Prediction for Growth Hormone Deficiency Treatment Planning Using Deep Learning

Muhammad Ilyas[1], Jawad Ahmad[1](✉), Alistair Lawson[1], Jan Sher Khan[2], Ahsen Tahir[3], Ahsan Adeel[4], Hadi Larijani[5], Abdelfateh Kerrouche[1], M. Guftar Shaikh[6], William Buchanan[1], and Amir Hussain[1]

[1] Edinburgh Napier University, Edinburgh, UK
jawad.saj@gmail.com
[2] University of Gaziantep, Gaziantep, Turkey
[3] University of Engineering and Technology, Lahore, Pakistan
[4] University of Wolverhampton, Wolverhampton, UK
[5] Glasgow Caledonian University, Glasgow, UK
[6] Royal Hospital for Sick Children (RHSC), Edinburgh, UK

Abstract. Prospective studies using longitudinal patient data can be used to help to predict responsiveness to Growth Hormone (GH) therapy and assess any suspected risks. In this paper, a novel Clinical Decision Support System (CDSS) is developed to predict growth (in terms of height) in children with Growth Hormone Deficiency (GHD) just before the start of GH therapy. A Deep Feed-Forward Neural Network (DFFNN) model is proposed, developed and evaluated for height prediction with seven input parameters. The essential input parameters to the DFFNN are gender, mother's height, father's height, current weight, chronological age, bone age, and GHD. The proposed model is trained using the Levenberg Marquardt (LM) learning algorithm. Experimental results are evaluated and compared for different learning rates. Measures of the quality of the fit of the model such as Root Mean Square (RMSE), Normalized Root Mean Square (N-RMSE), and Mean Absolute Percentage Error (MAPE) show that the proposed deep learning model is robust in terms of accuracy and can effectively predict growth (in terms of height) in children.

Keywords: Growth Hormone Deficiency · Deep learning · Levenberg Marquardt (LM) learning · Root Mean Square · Normalized Root Mean Square · Height prediction

1 Introduction

Medical records of groups or individuals can be compared and analysed for a number of purposes (for example, if a child is Growth Hormone deficient or not, or risk of other conditions/disease). These records could be alike as well as

J. Ren et al. (Eds.): BICS 2019, LNAI 11691, pp. 76–85, 2020.
https://doi.org/10.1007/978-3-030-39431-8_8

different in many ways, with certain characteristics being common. The information extracted from such records could be used for a number of purposes or a particular outcome (such as observation of a particular ailment like GHD, diabetes, cancer, cardiovascular risk etc). The analysis or use of medical records in retrospective cohort studies [12] could be utilised for a risk ratio or odds ratio to have an assessment of relative risk. However, on the other hand, prospective cohort studies [12] are conducted or coordinated by starting at the current state or point, and following the progress/response of the conditions. Artificial Intelligence (AI), pattern recognition and machine learning [18] have undergone substantial development over the past few decades. A large amount of literature is available both for theoretical investigations and for practical applications [18]. A model based on a "supervised" machine learning algorithm [9] can be used to create a function which generates an output prediction given input data. The exact form of this function is determined during the training phase on the basis of a given set of input/output pairs included in the part of dataset which is used for training the model (i.e. the "training set"). The ability of a model to predict the output given an unseen input pattern is known as "generalization" and essentially represents the core aim of such tools.

Different techniques and models which are able to predict height, ranging from standard regression techniques [15] to the more sophisticated "artificial intelligence" techniques, including the popular neural networks and support vector machines, or more recent techniques such as artificial immune systems and eco state network [13] are critically reviewed. A recent literature review has revealed that to measure the effectiveness of GH treatment, in terms of height growth, the most frequently used methods are Multiple Linear Regression (MLR) [16] based. The MLR models assume near dependencies between input and output variables whereas sometimes there are also non-linear relationship(s) between them.

To analyse and address this problem and possibly to overcome these limitations of both linear and non-linear dependencies, there are many proposed solutions by applying machine learning techniques such as Artificial Neural Networks (ANN) [1]. There are different types of ANNs inspired by and resembling to neuronal connections in the brain. These, basically complex computational systems, can be used as prediction models in domains such as Growth Hormone Deficiency (GHD). For our research we have selected deep feed-forward neural network is selected as a model for height prediction. Such methods do not require feature calculations, and a deep neural network [7,17] can predict the desired output. A typical neural model consist of [16]:

- Input layer (explanatory data).
- Hidden (1 or more) layers (data processing).
- Output layer (delivering the prediction results).

There are several basic computational units within each of these neuron layers. These neurons or nodes (in each layer) have weighted connections to each of the nodes in the next layer. The hidden layer(s) and output layer neurons transform the calculated weighted sum of all their inputs by activation (sigmoid) functions [10]. The calculated results of each layer are passed to the next layer until the output is aligned to the final solution of the model [2,3,11].

During the training process the output weights of coefficients of all neurons are adjusted to produce an optimum results as close as possible to the expected outcome. For this adjustment of weights there are number of algorithms available [7]. Test dataset are used to evaluate the trained model for accuracy of prediction results. The accuracy of a model is measured as the difference between real and predicted values of the output attribute [16]. In recent years, since 2006, neural networks, deep structured learning, hierarchical learning or more commonly called deep learning are the terms used to represent the most recent enhancements in the use and improvement of machine learning algorithms [4,14]. The influence of techniques developed from deep learning research have proved to be remarkable . The significant contributions and impacts of such techniques in a wide range of applications especially in signal and information processing work is immense. There is wide scope of contribution of deep learning within the traditional information processing work, including key aspects of artificial intelligence and machine learning [9,10].

2 Related Knowledge

2.1 Deep Feed-Forward Neural Network

A feed-forward neural network sometimes called as a feed-forward or multilayer perception, A feed-forward neural network (also known as multilayer perception), is a network model in there is no feedback between layers and information only moves from the input layer towards the output layer. In neural network notation, the leftmost layer is known as the input layer and the rightmost layer is known as the output layer. Neurons in the input layer and the output layer are called input and output neurons, respectively. A neuron is a computational function that mimics the function of a biological neuron. The middle layers in a feed-forward neural network are called the hidden layers and neurons in the middle layers are known as hidden neurons. If neural network consists of only a single hidden layer the network is called a shallow network. In contrast to shallow networks, deep neural network consists of several hidden layers. Figure 1 shows the input, hidden and output layers of a typical feed-forward neural network. The connections in Fig. 1 are called as weights of the networks. Mathematically the output of the network is computed through a function:

$$\bar{O}_i = f(\sum_{j=1}^{n} X_j W_{ij} + B_i), \tag{1}$$

where O is the output, X is the input to the network, W is the connection weight and B is constant term.

2.2 Data Acquisition

The dataset we acquired from KIGS data pediatric growth disorders [18]. The acquired KIGS dataset was in fact the data provided to KIGS by Royal Hospital for Children (RHC), Glasgow (UK). Under the close supervision of clinical domain expert, the datasets about Growth Hormone Deficient patients were acquired and consolidated by utilising KIGS data as well as the data collected through utilisation of electronic data capture (EDC) devices in daily clinical practice. Some of the records were even manually extracted from previous registers of patients' records. As per General Data Protection Regulation (GDPR) requirements in place, the data was anonymised and stored securely.

2.3 Data Preprocessing

The dataset for training the proposed model is obtained from the Royal Hospital for Children, Glasgow, UK. A dataset comprises of a number of instances/records, in other words called data points expressed as inputs of the values of independent attributes/variables. Along with independent variables, one dependent variable is also defined as output of predicted values. The values of independent variables in each instance/record require close observation for any data anomaly. Therefore, the term data preprocessing involves various sub-processes to handle any missing, inconsistent, incomplete or inappropriate value of any attribute in order to develop an efficient and accurate prognostic model [6].

2.4 Data Normalisation

Data normalisation or standardisation [5] is a process to transform data of an attribute to have a common range for example 0 to 1. In data preprocessing step for machine learning algorithms, data normalization is one of the key step. In contrast to different scale, normalization of data is done so that dataset numeric values uses a common scale without loss of any important information. In some scenarios, various machine learning algorithms does not model data accurately without normalisation step.

2.5 Collinearity

One of the common problems is collinearity [5] among independent variables i.e. it becomes almost impossible to get unique estimates by a good predictor model if two or more independent attributes have close correlation among their data values. It could cause false consideration of not significant variable by a model even if it is critically significant independent variable. Therefore, the collinearity issue must be addresses prior to finalising a dataset for an input to any prediction model.

2.6 Missing Values

Another very challenging well known issue is missing values for any attribute in a dataset. The efforts should be made to collect as much information as possible and should have complete values for all attributes to avoid missing data issues. However, it is not always possible to acquire completely perfect datasets. Therefore, certain statistical test should be performed on the datasets to make sure the dataset is absolutely complete and appropriate for an input to a prognostic model. To handle missing data, the use of likelihood-based [15] approach is widely reported as useful technique which could handle data clustering and classification. This technique could also handle function approximation from missing or incomplete values in more appropriate way [5].

2.7 Feature Selection

To improve performance and accuracy of a prediction model, only significant features of a dataset should be selected carefully as an input. As too many features selected in a prediction or classification model could increase complexity hence result over-fitting and also causing lack of generalisation, leading to misleading results.

3 The Proposed Deep Learning Prediction Model

The proposed deep feed-forward neural network architecture is shown in Fig. 1. The input layer consist of seven essential inputs i.e., gender information, mother height, father height, current weight, chronological age, bone age, and growth hormone deficiency information. The network has three hidden layers: hidden layer 1, hidden layer 2, hidden layer 2, consisting 8, 6, and 4 neurons, respectively. The proposed model is trained with Levenberg-Marquardt (LM) training algorithm. LM algorithm is an iterative method which is used to solve the curve fitting problems. In non-linear problems, LM algorithm determines the minimum of a function. LM algorithm is the linear combination of both Gauss-Newton and gradient descent methods. Mathematically Levenberg-Marquardt training algorithm can be derived from Newton's Method. Let's say we have a performance matrix $F(z)$ and we need to optimize it using Newton method as follows [8]:

$$z_{n+1} = z_n - B_n^{-1} W_n \tag{2}$$

where $B_n \equiv \bigtriangledown^2 F(z)|_{z=z_n}$ and $W_n \equiv \bigtriangledown F(z)|_{z=z_n}$. Lets say that $F(x)$ sum up square functions i.e.,

$$F(z) = \sum_{n=1}^{N} U_n^2(z) = U^T(z)U(z) \tag{3}$$

Now the ith element of the gradient can be calculated as:

$$[\bigtriangledown F(z)]_i = \frac{\partial F(z)}{\partial z_i} = 2\sum_{n=1}^{N} U_n(z)\frac{\partial U(n)}{\partial z_i} \tag{4}$$

Equation 4 can also be written in matrix form as:

$$\nabla F(z) = 2J^T(z)U(z) \tag{5}$$

where $J(z)$ is the Jacobian matrix and can be computed as:

$$\mathsf{J(z)} = \begin{pmatrix} \frac{\partial U_1(z)}{\partial z_1} & \frac{\partial U_1(z)}{\partial z_2} & \cdots & \frac{\partial U_1(z)}{\partial z_N} \\ \frac{\partial U_2(z)}{\partial z_1} & \frac{\partial U_2(z)}{\partial z_2} & \cdots & \frac{\partial U_2(z)}{\partial z_N} \\ \frac{\partial U_N(z)}{\partial z_1} & \frac{\partial U_N(z)}{\partial z_2} & \cdots & \frac{\partial U_N(z)}{\partial z_N} \end{pmatrix} \tag{6}$$

Now the i and j elements of Hessian matrix can be calculated as:

$$[\nabla^2 F(z)]_{i,j} = \frac{\partial^2 F(z)}{\partial z_i \partial z_j}$$

$$= 2\sum_{n=1}^{N}\{\frac{\partial U_n(z)}{\partial z_i}\frac{\partial U_n(z)}{\partial z_j} + U_n(z)\frac{\partial^2 U_n(z)}{\partial z_i \partial z_j}\} \tag{7}$$

$$\nabla^2 F(z) = 2J^T(z)J(z) + 2S(z) \tag{8}$$

where
$S(z) = \sum_{n=1}^{N} U_n(z) \nabla^2 U_n(z)$
We assume that $S(x)$ is very small, therefore Eq. (8) can be rewrite as:

$$\nabla^2 F(z) = 2J^T(z)J(z) \tag{9}$$

Now Eq. (2) can be rearrange as:

$$z_{n+1} = z_n - B_n^{-1} W_n$$

$$Z_{n+1} = z_n - [2J^T(z_n)J(z_n)]^{-1} 2J^T(z_n)U(z_n)$$

2 will be cancel out and we will have

$$z_{n+1} = z_n - [J^T(z_n)J(z_n)]^{-1} J^T(z_n)U(z_n) \tag{10}$$

Now a small approximation μI is added to the matrix $H = J^T J$ i.e., $G = H + \mu I$, in order to solve the invertibility problem related with H. Due to this addition G will generate the same eigenvectors as of H and therefore, H can be inverted now [8]. Now the Levenberg-Marquardt training algorithm can be computed as:

$$z_{n+1} = z_n - [J^T(z_n)J(z_n) + \mu I]^{-1} J^T(z_n)U(z_n) \tag{11}$$

$$\nabla z_n = -[J^T(z_n)J(z_n) + \mu I]^{-1} J^T(z_n)U(z_n) \tag{12}$$

$$z_{n+1} = z_n - \frac{1}{\mu_n}(J^T(z_n)U(z_n))$$

$$z_{n+1} = z_n - (\frac{1}{2\mu_n})(\nabla F(z)) \tag{13}$$

The proposed deep feed-forward neural network predicts the height with respect to different parameters available in the dataset. The proposed network was trained with using 2589 data samples from the dataset. In training, different number of neurons, hidden layers and epochs were tried. The best ANN structure was 1 hidden layer with 10 neurons.

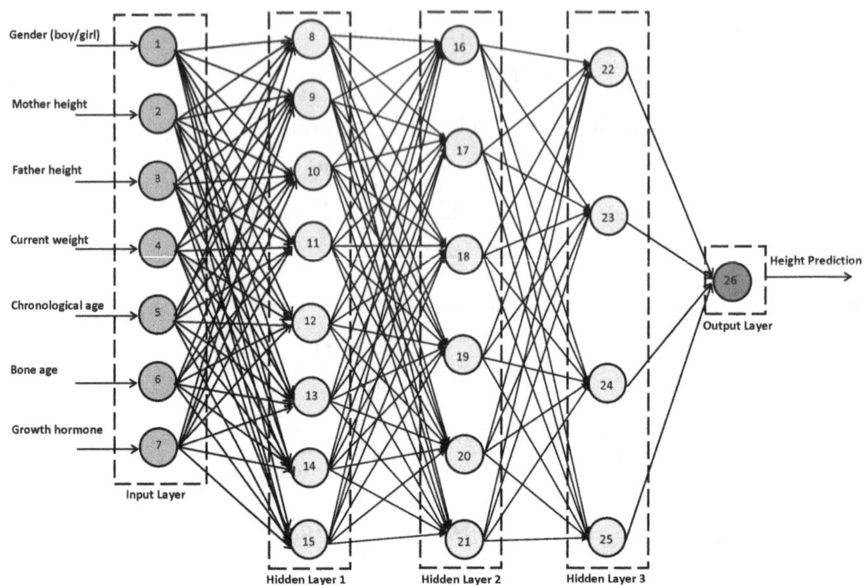

Fig. 1. The proposed deep feed-forward neural network architecture: 7 inputs.

4 Experimental Results

In order to find the accuracy of the proposed height prediction model, Root Mean Square (RMSE), Normalized Root Mean Square (NRMSE), Mean Absolute Percentage Error (MAPE) and R are computed. The accuracy of a prediction model can be calculated via Root Mean Square Error (RMSE). In RMSE, the difference between actual and predicted output is calculated using equation [11]:

$$RMSE = \sqrt{\frac{1}{n}\sum_{i=1}^{n}(O_j - O_i')^2}, \tag{14}$$

where n indicates the total number of samples, O and O' is the actual height and predicted height, respectively. Other parameters, such as NRMSE, MAPE and R is calculated using equations:

$$N\ RMSE = \sqrt{\frac{1}{n}\sum_{i=1}^{n}\left(\frac{O_i - O_i'}{O_i}\right)^2} \tag{15}$$

$$MAPE = \frac{1}{n}\sum_{i=1}^{n}\left|\frac{O_i - O_i'}{O_i}\right| \times 100\% \tag{16}$$

Table 1. Error values for 7-8-6-4-1 deep feed-forward neural network: $\eta = 0.1$.

Error	DFFNN train	DFFNN test
RMSE	14.2930	16.2961
N-RMSE	0.1530	0.1912
MAPE	8.7344%	10.5487%
R	0.9880	0.9840

Table 2. Error values for 7-8-6-4-1 deep feed-forward neural network: $\eta = 0.05$.

Error	DFFNN train	DFFNN test
RMSE	13.1405	15.6356
N-RMSE	0.1193	0.1407
MAPE	7.3535%	8.7290%
R	0.9899	0.9857

Table 3. Error values for 7-8-6-4-1 deep feed-forward neural network: $\eta = 0.01$.

Error	DFFNN train	DFFNN test
RMSE	9.0307	11.4221
N-RMSE	0.0730	0.1013
MAPE	4.8040%	6.7409%
R	0.9954	0.9921

$$R = 1 - \left(\frac{\sum_{i=1}^{n} (O_i - O_i')}{\sum_{i=1}^{n} O_i} \right)^2 \qquad (17)$$

The above-mentioned parameters are calculated for both seen and unseen datasets and these values are reported in Tables 1, 2 and 3 with different learning rate. From these tables, one can notice that that the proposed algorithm can predict the height with least errors. Moreover, one can also notice that for unseen dataset the deep feed-forward neural network has more error as compared to seen pattern. Moreover, it is evident from tables that when the learning rate decreases, the accuracy of prediction increases.

5 Conclusion

A new deep learning approach has been exploited for accurate prediction of height. The proposed model uses 7 inputs neuron, three hidden layers with 8-6-4 neurons, and one output neuron. The proposed height prediction model was trained via the LM algorithm after pre-processing steps such as normalisation and elimination of data points for which data is missing in any column. Prediction results are verified via RMSE, NRMSE, MAPE, and R with different learning rate. All experimental results proves that the proposed model is highly accurate when a slow learning rate i.e., $\eta = 0.01$ is selected. When the value of η is selected as 0.01, RMSE, NRMSE, MAPE, and R for unseen data is 11.4221, 0.1013, 6.7409%, and 0.9921 which was comparably less than for fast learning rate such as $\eta = 0.1$ and $\eta = 0.05$. The proposed prediction model could be used to give families/clinicians a more accurate estimation of final adult height compared to current prediction methods. In future, the dataset will be trained using a new technique known as Random Neural Network (RNN). Additionally, the proposed scheme will be integrated with light-weight encryption schemes for privacy protection.

Conflict of Interest. There is no conflict of interest.

References

1. Adeel, A., Larijani, H., Ahmadinia, A.: Random neural network based novel decision making framework for optimized and autonomous power control in LTE uplink system. Phys. Commun. **19**, 106–117 (2016)
2. Ahmad, J., Larijani, H., Emmanuel, R., Mannion, M., Javed, A.: An intelligent real-time occupancy monitoring system using single overhead camera. In: Arai, K., Kapoor, S., Bhatia, R. (eds.) IntelliSys 2018. AISC, vol. 869, pp. 957–969. Springer, Cham (2019). https://doi.org/10.1007/978-3-030-01057-7_71
3. Ahmad, J., Larijani, H., Emmanuel, R., Mannion, M., Javed, A., Phillipson, M.: Energy demand prediction through novel random neural network predictor for large non-domestic buildings. In: 2017 Annual IEEE International Systems Conference (SysCon), pp. 1–6. IEEE (2017)
4. Deng, L., Yu, D., et al.: Deep learning: methods and applications. Found. Trends® Sign. Process. **7**(3–4), 197–387 (2014)
5. Devos, O., Downey, G., Duponchel, L.: Simultaneous data pre-processing and SVM classification model selection based on a parallel genetic algorithm applied to spectroscopic data of olive oils. Food Chem. **148**, 124–130 (2014)
6. Farooq, K., et al.: A novel cardiovascular decision support framework for effective clinical risk assessment. In: 2014 IEEE Symposium on Computational Intelligence in Healthcare and e-health (CICARE), pp. 117–124. IEEE (2014)
7. Feng, W., Huang, W., Ren, J.: Class imbalance ensemble learning based on the margin theory. Appl. Sci. **8**(5), 815 (2018)
8. Hagan, M.T., Demuth, H.B., Beale, M.H., De Jesús, O.: Neural network design, vol. 20. PWS Publishing Co., Boston (1996)
9. Han, J., Pei, J., Kamber, M.: Data mining: concepts and techniques. Elsevier (2011)
10. Ieracitano, C., et al.: Statistical analysis driven optimized deep learning system for intrusion detection. In: Ren, J., et al. (eds.) BICS 2018. LNCS (LNAI), vol. 10989, pp. 759–769. Springer, Cham (2018). https://doi.org/10.1007/978-3-030-00563-4_74
11. Larijani, H., Ahmad, J., Mtetwa, N., et al.: A novel random neural network based approach for intrusion detection systems. In: 2018 10th Computer Science and Electronic Engineering (CEEC), pp. 50–55. IEEE (2018)

12. Lindgren, H.: Integrating clinical decision support system development into a development process of clinical practice – experiences from dementia care. In: Peleg, M., Lavrač, N., Combi, C. (eds.) AIME 2011. LNCS (LNAI), vol. 6747, pp. 129–138. Springer, Heidelberg (2011). https://doi.org/10.1007/978-3-642-22218-4_17
13. Lukoševičius, M.: A practical guide to applying echo state networks. In: Montavon, G., Orr, G.B., Müller, K.-R. (eds.) Neural Networks: Tricks of the Trade. LNCS, vol. 7700, pp. 659–686. Springer, Heidelberg (2012). https://doi.org/10.1007/978-3-642-35289-8_36
14. Najafabadi, M.N., Villanustre, F., Khoshgoftaar, T.M., Seliya, N., Wald, R., Muharemagic, E.: Deep learning applications and challenges in big data analytics. J. Big Data **2**(1), 1 (2015)
15. Quinlan, J.R.: C4.5: Programs for Machine Learning. Morgan Kaufmann Publishers Inc., San Francisco (1993)
16. Smyczyńska, U., Smyczyńska, J., Hilczer, M., Stawerska, R., Tadeusiewicz, R., Lewiński, A.: Pre-treatment growth and IGF-I deficiency as main predictors of response to growth hormone therapy in neural models. Endocr. Connect. **7**(1), 239–249 (2018)
17. Wang, Z., Ren, J., Zhang, D., Sun, M., Jiang, J.: A deep-learning based feature hybrid framework for spatiotemporal saliency detection inside videos. Neurocomputing **287**, 68–83 (2018)
18. Witten, I.H., Frank, E., Hall, M.A., Pal, C.J.: Data Mining: Practical Machine Learning Tools and Techniques. Morgan Kaufmann (2016)

Salient Object Detection Based on Deep Multi-level Cascade Network

Dengdi Sun[1], Hang Wu[1], Zhuanlian Ding[2(✉)], Sheng Li[1], and Bin Luo[1]

[1] School of Computer Science and Technology, Anhui University, Hefei 230601, People's Republic of China

[2] School of Internet, Anhui University, Hefei 230039, People's Republic of China

dingzhuanlian@163.com

Abstract. Fully convolutional neural networks (FCNs) have played an important role in current saliency detection task, since the multi-layer structure describe the depth features of an image in different scales. To reasonably and effectively aggregate and utilize the hierarchical features, we propose a novel multi-level convolution feature cascade model with an end-to-end way in this paper. Our model consists of two modules: one is the multi-level depth feature extraction module via our improved FCNs; the other module aim at combining the characteristics of multiple resolutions with coarse semantics and fine details via **C**ascade, **U**psampling and **D**econvolution operations, named as CUD module. Finally, the output of CUD module is used to predict the saliency map through further learning. The proposed model can efficiently and flexibly aggregate multi-layer convolution features and provides accurate saliency maps. The extensive experiments show that our method achieves satisfactory results compared with some current representative methods.

Keywords: Fully convolutional networks · Saliency detection · Multi-level feature maps

1 Introduction

The task of image saliency detection is to identify the most informative and important part of an image, which has received widely attention in computer vision [1–4], and a wealth of approaches have been invented in recent years. Some early research methods [5–10] used low-level visual features (such as color, texture, and contrast) and heuristic priors to detect significance targets. These methods contribute to the simulation and approximation of human visual saliency by reducing computation while maintaining image structure. However, such low-level features and priors are difficult to capture high-level semantic knowledge about objects and their surroundings. Therefore, these low-level feature-based methods are often incompetent in the real complex scenario.

In recent years, deep convolutional neural networks (CNNs), especially fully convolutional neural networks (FCNs) have achieved better results than traditional methods [11–14]. Features extracted using FCNs contain more advanced

J. Ren et al. (Eds.): BICS 2019, LNAI 11691, pp. 86–95, 2020.
https://doi.org/10.1007/978-3-030-39431-8_9

semantic information and are more robust for various objects in images. However, there are still two areas that need to be addressed. First, most of the previous FCNs-based methods [12,15–17] stack the max-pooling layer and the single-scale convolution layer sequentially, in order to generate deep features. Due to the limited receptive fields, the features lack rich context information, resulting in the salient objects with different scales and shapes cannot achieve the desired effect. Second, many current methods generate the final saliency map relied on the advanced features obtained by deep learning. These methods fail to take into account the low-level salient features. Later, some studies [12,18–20] try to make use of multi-level convolution features to make saliency prediction. These methods have produced good results, but the multi-scale features corresponding to convolution layers are not being fully utilized.

In order to solve this problem, this paper proposes a deep multi-level neural network. The framework makes effectively use of the multilevel features of FCNs for saliency detection. The main work is to propose a multi-level feature aggregation network which uses multi-level convolution features as saliency features for saliency objects detection. Make the most of different levels of deep features to achieve precise object boundary inference and semantic enhancement. The resulting framework can be trained through end-to-end gradient learning, which uses single-resolution ground truth without additional annotation. This model achieves satisfactory performance on currently common saliency detection datasets.

2 Related Work

Recently, deep learning based methods have achieved remarkable performance in many recognition tasks. A great deal of research has been done to develop a variety of deep architectures that describe salient features in different levels. Lee et al. [17] proposed to use the low-level distance graph and high-level symbol feature coding of deep CNNs for highlighting salient object detection. Liu et al. [11] proposed a deep level saliency network, which integrates context information and learns enough global structure to gradually refine the details of saliency map. In addition, Long et al. [21] proved the effectiveness of FCNs in image segmentation task for the first time. After that, Li et al. [22] designed a pixel-level fully convolutional stream and a segment-wise spatial pooling stream to produce pixel-level saliency predictions. Hou et al. [18] propose to add short connections between multiple side output layers to combine features of different levels. Wang et al. [15] developed deep recurrent FCNs, taking rough prediction as a saliency prior and gradually refining the generated prediction. In contrast to the above methods relied on limited level features, we propose a new multi-level feature aggregation method based on FCNs with end-to-end pattern. The results show that our method can refine the hierarchical feature maps and ensure the accuracy of saliency detection, achieving satisfactory results.

3 The Proposed Method

In this section, we first describe the overall architecture of our proposed model in Sect. 3.1. Then the detailed formula of multi-level feature cascade module named as CUD in Sect. 3.2 is given. Section 3.3 introduces the training details of our proposed network architecture.

3.1 Overview of Network Architecture

In this section, we outline the proposed network structure, which is composed of two parts: multi-level feature extraction and multi-scale cascade with coarse semantics and fine details (CUD). The overall architecture is shown in Fig. 1. The first component is based on the FCN architecture derived from pre-trained VGG-16 net [23]. This model is able to generate multi-level feature maps to capture hierarchical information from different scales. To better adapt to saliency detection tasks, we modified the VGG-16 network as follows. First, we removed all the fully connection layers from VGG-16 network because our task focused on pixel-level prediction. Second, in VGG-16 model, there are five max-pooling layers with kernel size of 2×2 and stride of 2. In order to balance the semantic context and fine image details, we remove the last max-pooling layer, and follow the rest part by the combination of dropout and convolution layers twice, to prevent the over-fitting and improve the generalization ability of extracting robust features simultaneously. In this way, the output feature mapping will be reduced to 1/16 of input image. Using this module, we extracted the side outputs from conv1_2 (64 feature maps), conv1_pool (64 feature maps), conv2_pool (128 feature maps), conv3_pool (256 feature maps), conv4_pool (512 feature maps) and conv7 (128 feature maps) as six hierarchical features.

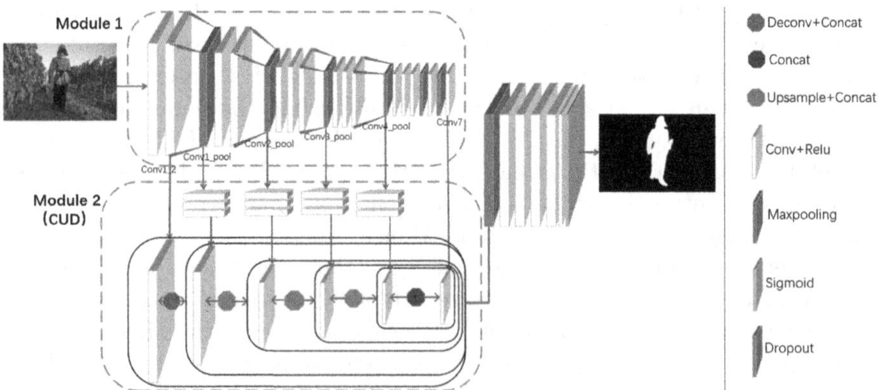

Fig. 1. The architecture of our multi-level feature-based visual saliency model. Our model takes a RGB image ($384 \times 400 \times 3$) as input, The final saliency map is formed by convolving the multilevel feature map with end-to-end way. (Color figure online)

Moreover, aiming at the inconsistency of multilevel convolution feature resolution, a multi-scale feature combination module (CUD) is proposed, which is the second component in our network architecture. Through the CUD module, the extracted multi-scale feature maps are merged together to form a tensor, which is fed integrally to a dropout layer with keeping probability of 0.7. After that, to further improve the prediction and generalization ability for salient objects, four convolution layers with the Relu activation function are connected behind. The kernel of the four layers is 3×3, and the number of channels is 512, 256, 128 and 64 respectively. Eventually, and a single channel convolution layer with sigmoid activation function and kernel size of 3×3 is added to learn the weights for different levels and produce the final saliency map.

3.2 CUD Module

It has been widely acknowledged that the features of different levels, which abstract scenes in different scales, are remarkably complementary. Specifically, the deeper features typically carry more global contextual information and are more likely to locate the salient object correctly, while the shallower features supply more spatial details. To exploit sufficiently the complementarity in multiple layers, we put forward a kind of context awareness-based multi-scale feature combination module (CUD) via cascade, upsampling and deconvolution operations. In particular, we first send the middle four side outputs (second to fifth level) into three convolution layers with 3×3 kernel respectively to capture the more detailed features. The number of channels for three layers is 256, 256 and 128, and the stride is set as 1 to ensure the size of feature maps stays the same. So, the above results were combined with outputs of conv1_2 and the last conv7 layers from module 1, to establish the multi-scale features $F = \{f_i, i = 1..., 6\}$(represents the feature map from level 6 to level 1). Using it, five cascade feature maps $H = \{H_i, i = 1..., 5\}$ can be generated as follows.

$$H_1 = \text{cat}\,(f_1, f_2)\,, \tag{1}$$

$$H_{i+1} = \text{cat}\,(\text{up}\,(H_i)\,, f_{i+2})\,, \quad i = 1, 2, 3 \tag{2}$$

$$H_5 = \text{cat}\,(\text{deconv}\,(H_4)\,, f_6)\,, \tag{3}$$

where, cat(·), up(·) and deconv(·) denote the cascade, upsampling and deconvolution operation respectively.

It's worth noting that using deconvolution operator can effectively preserve the semantic information in feature cascades, but also result in a very large number of parameters. So it's unfeasible to completely cascade all features only using a deconvolution operator. In contrast, upsampling operators have a small amount of parameters, but also causes loss of semantic information. Considering the above two factors, in this paper, we adopt the following combination strategy: (1) directly cascading the last two feature maps (level 5 and 6) together; (2) upsampling feature maps 4 through 2 level by level in reverse order; (3) attaching the first level to the previous series of features with deconvolution, as shown in Fig. 1.

3.3 Training

Given a set of training data $\boldsymbol{X} = \{X_i\}$, $i = 1, \cdots, n$ and corresponding ground truth $\boldsymbol{G} = \{G_i\}$, $i = 1, \cdots, n$, n is the number of training samples, so the saliency output from our deep network architecture can be expressed as:

$$S_i = f_S(X_i, \theta), \tag{4}$$

where $f_s(\cdot)$ denotes the mapping model built by the whole network from input image X_i to output saliency map S_i, while θ represents the set of all parameters used in the network. To minimize the pixel-level difference between predicted saliency score and ground truth, the minimum square error (MSE) should be included in the loss function. Since the range of ground truth values is often $[0, 1]$, so we have to normalize the predictions into the same interval through dividing by the maximum value. Furthermore, in most cases, the region of background takes up most of pixels in a picture, leading to the majority of ground truth values are close to zero. To highlight the salient objects, the pixels with high probability of ground-truth should be attached more attention. According these principles above, the overall loss function [24] is thus:

$$L(X_i) = \frac{1}{N}\sum_{i=1}^{N}\left\|\frac{\frac{f_S(X_i)}{\max(f_S(X_i))} - G_i}{\alpha - G_i}\right\|^2. \tag{5}$$

Here α is set to 1.15. In this paper, our model is based on Tensorflow-Keras environments, and the training utilize the Adam optimizer on DUT-ORMON [10] dataset. In the training process, the learning rate is 0.001, the batch size is set to 8, and the number of training epoch is 50. All the training and experiments are run in a Server with a 12G NVIDIA Titan X GPU.

4 Experiment

For the performance evaluation, we evaluate the proposed model on three public datasets including ECSSD [9], HKU-IS [25], DUT-OMRON [10], PASCAL-S [26] and SOD [9].

4.1 Evaluation Criteria

In terms of evaluation criteria, we first used the standard precision recall (PR) curve to evaluate the performance of our method. Precision is the ratio of real saliency pixels assigned to all the predicted salient pixels, and recall is defined as the ratio of the total saliency detected pixels to the ground-truth number. Here we calculate precision and recall by thresholding the predicted results from 0 to 255, and draw the PR-curve. We also evaluate our method using the overall performance measurement F-measure, which is computed as follows,

$$F_\beta = \frac{(1+\beta^2) \times \text{ Precision } \times \text{ Recall}}{\beta^2 \times \text{ Precision } + \text{Recall}}, \tag{6}$$

Table 1. The comparison results of F-measure and MAE on five datasets.

	DUT-MORON		ECSSD		HKU-IS		PASCAL-S		SOD	
Methods	F_β	MAE	F_β	MAE	F_β	MAE	F_β	MAE	F_β	MAE
OURS	**0.6866**	**0.0912**	**0.8674**	**0.0544**	**0.8583**	**0.0570**	**0.7566**	**0.0954**	**0.7659**	**0.1276**
DCL	0.6842	0.1573	0.8293	0.1495	0.8533	0.1359	0.7141	0.1807	0.7413	0.1938
DS	0.6028	0.1204	0.8255	0.1216	0.7851	0.0780	0.6590	0.1760	0.6981	0.1889
ELD	0.6109	0.0924	0.8102	0.0796	0.7694	0.0741	0.7180	0.1232	0.7116	0.1545
LEGS	0.5915	0.1334	0.7853	0.1180	0.7228	0.1193	-	-	0.6834	0.1955
MDF	0.6442	0.0916	0.8070	0.1049	0.8006	0.0957	0.7087	0.1458	0.7205	0.1639
BL	0.4988	0.2388	0.6841	0.2159	0.6597	0.2071	0.5742	0.2487	0.5798	0.2668
DRFI	0.5504	0.1378	0.7331	0.1642	0.7218	0.1445	0.6182	0.2065	0.6343	0.2238

here β^2 is set to 0.3. In addition to the PR-curve and the F-measure, we calculate MAE to measure the mean difference between the predicted saliency map and the ground truth. It is computed as:

$$\mathrm{MAE} = \frac{1}{W \times H} \sum_{x=1}^{W} \sum_{y=1}^{H} |S(x, y) - G(x, y)| \tag{7}$$

where S and G denote predicted saliency map and ground truth, respectively.

4.2 Comparison Results

We compare our model with other several algorithms (DCL [22], DS [27], ELD [17], LEGS [16], MDF [25], DRFI [8]) in five datasets. To be fair, all the results from compared methods are provided by the authors or running the available code or software.

Quantitative Evaluation. The comparison results are shown in Fig. 2 and Table 1. From Table 1, we can see the performance of different methods under the maximum F-measure and MAE value. The validity of the proposed model is proved by the fact that our method consistently outperforms other methods in all five datasets for different measurements. In addition, Fig. 2 shows the PR-curves for different methods in same datasets. We can see that our PR-curve is generally superior to other methods. Therefore, these results mean that our model can provide a more accurate saliency map, and is robust and reliable enough for the prediction region even on challenging datasets.

Qualitative Evaluation. Figure 2 shows a visual comparison of our method with other advanced saliency detection methods. It can be seen that our method will generate more accurate and robust saliency maps in all kinds of challenging situations, such as complex backgrounds, objects near the image boundary and multi-objects.

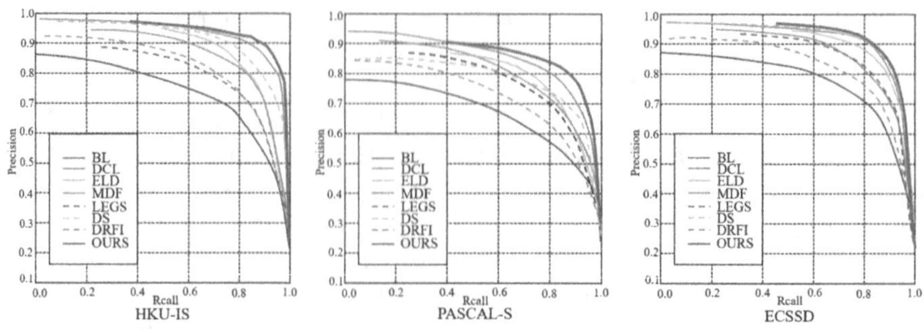

Fig. 2. The PR-curves of the proposed algorithm and other state-of-the-art methods.

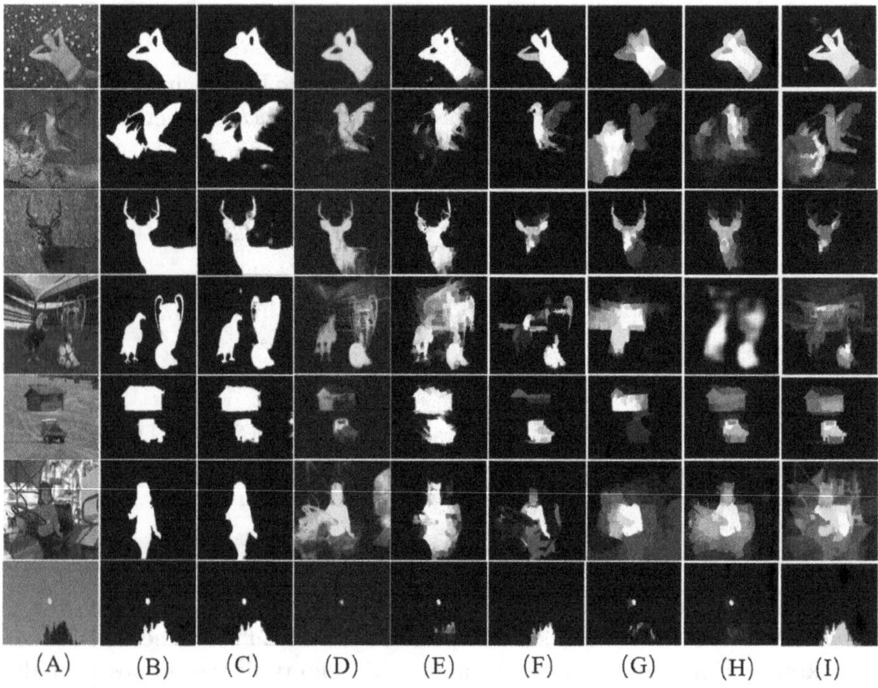

Fig. 3. Qualitative comparisons of the proposed method with the state-of-the-art algorithms. (a) Input images; (b) Ground truth; (c) Our method; (d) DCL; (e) ELD; (f) MDF; (g) DS; (h) DRFI.

4.3 Analysis for the CUD Module

We put forward in the multi-scale features cascade module (CUD) in Sect. 3.2, to combine the characteristics under different resolution level as a whole, via cascading, upsampling and deconvolution operators. In order to prove the effectiveness of combining strategy, we modify our CUD module using all upsampling cascade to replace the cascading-upsampling-deconvolution combination,

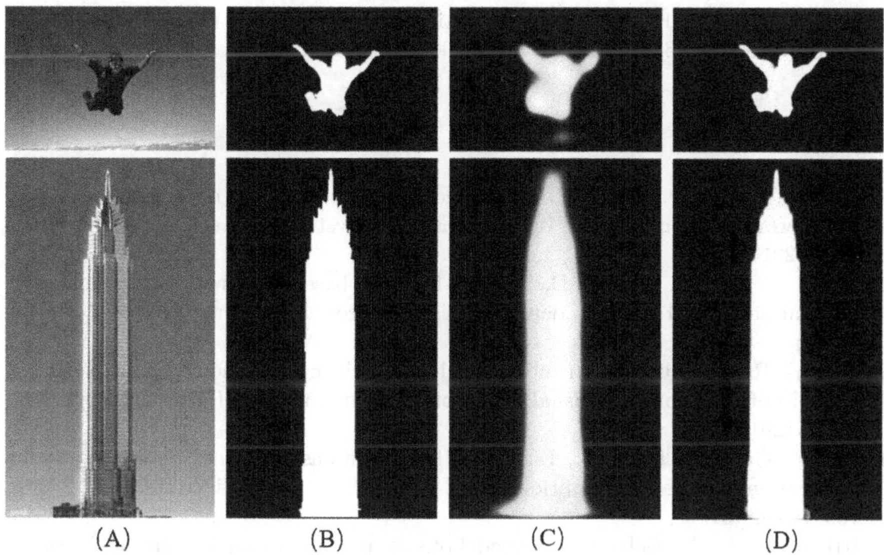

Fig. 4. Visual examples of our method and CUD module with all upsampling modules. From left to right: (a) input image, (b) ground truth, (c) saliency map of the method by CUD module with all upsampling module, (d) saliency map of the proposed method.

and compare it with our proposed method. Figure 4 shows a few representative visual comparison results as mentioned above. From this picture, the combination of deconvolution and upsampling can generate the most accurate and robust saliency map with the lowest computational cost, which fully prove the effectiveness of our CUD module to generate the cascaded multi-scale features. It's worth noting that it's unfeasible to employ all deconvolution operators to cascade the features, because of the huge number of parameters.

5 Conclusion

In this paper, an end-to-end deep network-based saliency detection is proposed. We improve the FCNs, and design a novel multi-scale feature cascade module, named as CUD module. Through our model, we can generate the final saliency map reflecting high-level semantic concepts and low-level spatial details simultaneously. So the predicted saliency could contain more robust spatial coherence and contour localization. Experimental results on five databases show the better performance of the proposed method. In the future, we will further optimize our architecture via DenseNet.

Acknowledgments. This work is supported by the Key Natural Science Project of Anhui Provincial Education Department (KJ2018A0023), the Guangdong Province Science and Technology Plan Projects (2017B010110011), the Anhui Key Research and Development Plan (1804a09020101), the National Basic Research Program (973

Program) of China (2015CB351705), the National Natural Science Foundation of China (61906002, 61402002, 61876002 and 61860206004).

References

1. Han, J., Zhang, D., Hu, X.: Background prior-based salient object detection via deep reconstruction residual. IEEE Trans. Circ. Syst. Video Technol. **25**(8), 1309–1321 (2014)
2. Wang, Z., Ren, J., Zhang, D.: A deep-learning based feature hybrid framework for spatiotemporal saliency detection inside videos. Neurocomputing **287**, 68–83 (2018)
3. Yan, Y., Ren, J., Sun, G.: Unsupervised image saliency detection with Gestalt-laws guided optimization and visual attention based refinement. Pattern Recogn. **79**, 65–78 (2018)
4. Ren, Z., Gao, S., Chia, L.T., Tsang, W.H.: Region-based saliency detection and its application in object recognition. IEEE Trans. Circ. Syst. Video Technol. **24**(5), 769–779 (2014)
5. Itti, L., Koch, C., Niebur, E.: A model of saliency-based visual attention for rapid scene analysis. IEEE Trans. Pattern Anal. Mach. Intell. **20**(11), 1254–1259 (1998)
6. Harel, J., Koch, C., Perona, P.: Graph-based visual saliency. In: Advances in Neural Information Processing Systems, pp. 545–552 (2007)
7. Perazzi, F., Krähenbühl, P., Pritch, Y., Hornung, A.: Saliency filters: contrast based filtering for salient region detection. In: IEEE Conference on Computer Vision and Pattern Recognition, pp. 733–740 (2012)
8. Jiang, H., Wang, J., Yuan, Z., Wu, Y., Zheng, N., Li, S.: Salient object detection: a discriminative regional feature integration approach. In: IEEE Conference on Computer Vision and Pattern Recognition, pp. 2083–2090 (2013)
9. Yan, Q., Xu, L., Shi, J., Jia, J.: Hierarchical saliency detection. In: IEEE Conference on Computer Vision and Pattern Recognition, pp. 1155–1162 (2013)
10. Yang, C., Zhang, L., Lu, H., Ruan, X., Yang, M.-H.: Saliency detection via graph-based manifold ranking. In: IEEE Conference on Computer Vision and Pattern Recognition, pp. 3166–3173 (2013)
11. Liu, N., Han, J.: DHSNet: deep hierarchical saliency network for salient object detection. In: IEEE Conference on Computer Vision and Pattern Recognition, pp. 678–686 (2016)
12. Zhang, P., Wang, D., Lu, H., Wang, H., Yin, B.: Learning uncertain convolutional features for accurate saliency detection. In: International Conference on Computer Vision, pp. 212–221 (2017)
13. Han, J., Zhang, D., Cheng, G.: Object detection in optical remote sensing images based on weakly supervised learning and high-level feature learning. IEEE Trans. Geosci. Remote Sens. **53**(6), 3325–3337 (2014)
14. Fang, L., Li, S., Duan, W.: Classification of hyperspectral images by exploiting spectral-spatial information of superpixel via multiple kernels. IEEE Trans. Geosci. Remote Sens. **53**(12), 6663–6674 (2015)
15. Wang, L., Wang, L., Lu, H., Zhang, P., Ruan, X.: Saliency detection with recurrent fully convolutional networks. In: Leibe, B., Matas, J., Sebe, N., Welling, M. (eds.) ECCV 2016. LNCS, vol. 9908, pp. 825–841. Springer, Cham (2016). https://doi.org/10.1007/978-3-319-46493-0_50

16. Wang, L., Lu, H., Ruan, X., Yang, M.-H.: Deep networks for saliency detection via local estimation and global search. In: IEEE Conference on Computer Vision and Pattern Recognition, pp. 3183–3192 (2015)
17. Lee, G., Tai, Y., Kim, J.: Deep saliency with encoded low level distance map and high level features. In: IEEE Conference on Computer Vision and Pattern Recognition, pp. 660–668 (2016)
18. Hou, Q., Cheng, M.-M., Hu, X., Borji, A., Tu, Z., Torr, P.: Deeply supervised salient object detection with short connections. In: IEEE Conference on Computer Vision and Pattern Recognition, pp. 3203–3212 (2017)
19. Li, G., Xie, Y., Lin, L., Yu, Y.: Instance-level salient object segmentation. In: IEEE Conference on Computer Vision and Pattern Recognition, pp. 2386–2395 (2017)
20. Zhang, L., Dai, J., Lu, H., He, Y., Wang, G.: A bi-directional message passing model for salient object detection. In: IEEE Conference on Computer Vision and Pattern Recognition, pp. 1741–1750 (2018)
21. Long, J., Shelhamer, E., Darrell, T.: Fully convolutional networks for semantic segmentation. In: IEEE Conference on Computer Vision and Pattern Recognition, pp. 3431–3440 (2015)
22. Li, G., Yu, Y.: Deep contrast learning for salient object detection. In IEEE Conference on Computer Vision and Pattern Recognition, pp. 478–487 (2016)
23. Simonyan, K., Zisserman, A.: Very deep convolutional networks for large-scale image recognition. arXiv preprint arXiv:1409.1556 (2014)
24. Serra, G., Cornia, M., Baraldi, L., Cucchiara, R.: A deep multi-level network for saliency prediction. In: International Conference on Pattern Recognition, pp. 3488–3493 (2016)
25. Zhao, R., Ouyang, W., Li, H., Wang, X.: Saliency detection by multi-context deep learning. In: IEEE Conference on Computer Vision and Pattern Recognition, pp. 1265–1274 (2015)
26. Li, Y., Hou, X., Koch, C., Rehg, J., Yuille, A.: The secrets of salient object segmentation. In: IEEE Conference on Computer Vision and Pattern Recognition, pp. 280–287 (2014)
27. Li, X., et al.: DeepSaliency: multi-task deep neural network model for salient object detection. IEEE Trans. Image Process. **25**(8), 3919–3930 (2016)

Real-Time Visual Tracking Base on SiamRPN with Generalized Intersection over Union

Zhihui Huang, Jin Zhan, Huimin Zhao(✉), Kaihan Lin, Penggen Zheng, and Jujian Lv

School of Computer Science, Guangdong Polytechnic Normal University, Guangzhou, China
zhihuihuangy@gmail.com,
{gszhanjin, zhaohuimin}@gpnu.edu.cn

Abstract. Deep learning-based tracking methods have great challenges to handle larger training data with aiming to be invariant to all sorts of appearance variations. In this paper, we incorporate a novel Generalized intersection over union (GIOU) as bounding box regression loss into Siamese framework based tracker, and propose a visual tracking method based on Siamese region proposal network (SiamRPN) with generalized intersection over union. We set out to bridge the gap between optimizing the commonly used bounding box regression loss and maximizing the Intersection over Union (IOU) metric value. Our target estimation component is trained to predict the overlap between the target object and an estimated bounding box. Moreover, it can relieve the case that non-overlapping bounding boxes in training phase. Experimental validations have shown that our tracker performs substantially improvement on the tracking benchmarks OTB100 and is effective to deformation, occlusion and other challenges in object tracking.

Keywords: Visual tracking · Generalized intersection over union · Deep learning · SiamRPN

1 Introduction

Visual object tracking is a basic problem in the field of computer vision and is widely applied in many high-level computer vision tasks such as automatic driving, intelligent monitoring system, human-computer interaction and robotics. However, because video contains rich and complex changes in both internal and external scenes, such as occlusion of the target, changes in attitude scale, motion blurring, illumination changes, background clutter and so on, it is a challenging problem to achieve efficient algorithms with robustness, accuracy and real-time.

Deep learning is a new branch of machine learning. Deep learning architecture can achieve complex function approximation by learning non-linear network structure and representing input data. In view of its powerful feature appearance performance, researchers began to introduce in-depth learning into visual tracking. Although deep learning-based trackers have high efficiency and great development advantages, different depth structure models have different advantages and disadvantages. For example,

J. Ren et al. (Eds.): BICS 2019, LNAI 11691, pp. 96–105, 2020.
https://doi.org/10.1007/978-3-030-39431-8_10

the tracking accuracy of CNN-based methods is increasing, but speed has always been a bottleneck, while the twin network (Siamese) breaks through the lag of depth vision tracking algorithm in speed, but its tracking accuracy becomes another shortboard.

There are two difficulties in the application of in-depth learning to tracking field. Firstly, the priori knowledge acquired from the first frame of video is far from meeting the requirement of label data volume in depth model training. Moreover, the data volume of positive and negative samples is imbalanced, and the rich appearance changes of the target cannot be captured. Secondly, the multi-layer structure of deep network leads to the increase of computational complexity, and many computations will reduce the real-time performance of the actual tracking process.

We summarize the contributions of the work as follows. Firstly, we adopt Siamese based framework to achieve real-time tracking, which can effectively learn temporal variation of target appearance by incorporating region proposal network (RPN). Aiming towards improving tracking accuracy, we introduce a new metric to optimize prediction candidate box in detection frame according to the ground truth. Secondly, to overcome the weaknesses of IOU by extending the concept to non-overlapping cases, we present an analytical solution that is replacing defaults ℓ_1-smooth loss with $\mathcal{L}_{Giou}$ loss during training phrase. Moreover, in order to meet the requirement of label data volume in depth model training, we apply GIOU based tracker which performs well in test phase. Furthermore, we successfully train a SiamRPN based tracker with $\mathcal{L}_{Giou}$ loss on several public visual tracking benchmarks datasets.

2 Related Work

In order to solve the complex scene changes in video tracking, many theoretical methods have been introduced into tracking problems, such as classifier [1–3], sparse representation [4–6], saliency detection [7–9], feature selection [12–15] and deep learning [16–27], etc. Target tracking applications have also developed from single target tracking to multi-view tracking [10] and three-dimensional tracking applications [11]. Deep learning has a powerful feature learning ability, which can extract the depth features of tracking objects, and brings a new research direction for solving various challenges in visual tracking. At present, there are three kinds of deep learning frameworks cited by tracking algorithms, namely Stacked Autoencoders (SAE), Convolutional Neural Networks (CNN) and Twin Networks (Siamese).

The problem of insufficient training samples should be solved firstly when deep learning is applied to target tracking. In 2013, Wang et al. [16] proposed a DLT tracking method for the first time, unsupervised off-line depth pre-training was performed on large-scale natural image data sets. Stacked Denoising Autoencoders (SDAE) was used to learn the general feature representation of targets, and then the pre-training model was fine-tuned online. The idea of transfer learning reduces the requirement of training samples and improves the performance of tracking algorithms. However, due to the low resolution of off-line training dataset, it is difficult to extract enough apparent features. SO-DLT [17] continues the strategy of non-tracking data pre-training and online fine-tuning, proposes using CNN network model instead of

DLT stack noise reduction coding model. The method solves the sensitivity of model updating and determines the location and size of the target boundary box in the current frame through multi-scale frame search strategy. Zhou et al. [18] proposed a tracking algorithm that combines deep learning technology with online AdaBoost framework, inherits the SDAE network structure of DLT, and is used to learn the appearance features of multi-layer images. Moreover, good experimental results are obtained.

Because of its network structure, CNN can learn more invariance in scaling, rotation, translation and other non-linear changes. This powerful feature extraction ability is in line with the requirements of target tracking. Nam et al. [19] proposed a multi-domain learning framework based on CNN. The model consists of a shared layer and a specific domain multi-branch layer. In order to avoid the occurrence of tracking drift, the hard negative sample mining method is used to obtain negative samples which are effective for classifier training. MDNet is relatively simple, and the computational complexity of the required model is lower than that of image recognition. In reference [20], a VITAL tracking method is proposed. High-quality positive samples are generated by embedding the Generation Countermeasure Network (GAN) in CNN structure. In addition, for the imbalance of positive and negative samples, a high-order cost-sensitive loss function is used to reduce the impact of simple negative samples on the training of classification model. Compared with the hard-negative sample mining method of MDNet, VITAL uses higher-order cost loss function to obtain useful negative samples, which not only improves target tracking accuracy, but also speeds up the training to the optimal state.

Siamese network is a measure of data similarity and is used to learn or match new objects. It is suitable for the situation that there are many kinds of data and the sample size of each kind is small. In 2016, Tao et al. [21] introduced Siamese network for pretraining a general matching function suitable for online tracking at the first time and gained high attention. In recent years, a series of related literatures [22–27] appeared. The algorithm is relatively simple to implement and reduces the time consumption of tracking process to a great extent. However, it has poor discrimination ability for similar interference items, and is prone to location errors, so it has great room for improvement.

The successful application of RPN network in FasterRCNN [27] tracking-by-detection algorithm has attracted wide attention. Instructively, RPN first integrate in Siamese architecture by SiamRPN [25]. Specifically, the experimental results show that it not only achieves real-time effect in speed, but also improve the accuracy significantly.

3 The Proposed Method

In the following we describe the proposed method in detail, which consists of SiameseRPN in tracking and Generalized Intersection over Union [28] (GIOU) algorithm. We build method upon the SiamRPN algorithm, which consists in traditional VGG module. Here we use modified AlexNet, where the groups from conv2 and conv4 are removed. As shown in Fig. 1, the framework of GIOU based SiameseRPN can be mainly divided into two modules. One is Siamese Network, which realizes feature extraction. Another module is Region Proposal Network (PRN) with aiming to generate proposals for target location. This paper mainly discusses RPN network.

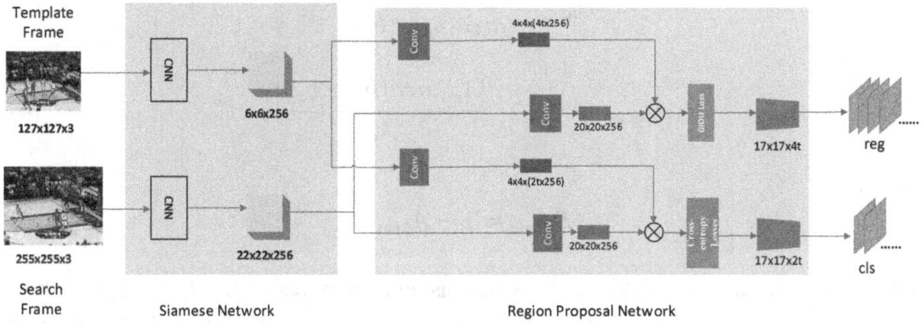

Fig. 1. The framework of the proposed method.

Region Proposal Network Module. In order to make RPN suitable for tracking task, this module contain two components, one realizes foreground-background classification, and the other completes proposal regression. During the training phrase, the sample will be labeled as positive or negative by classified branch. Afterwards, achieving accurate positioning in regression. Meantime, the output of the network contains t units, where t denotes the number of anchors adopted. It is means that the training channels need to be changed to $2t$ and $4t$ respectively to meet the requirements of classification and regression process. First of all, the output of template branch $z(x)$ and search branch $p(x)$ should be divided into $2t$ and $4t$ respectively, we denote $z(x)_{cls}$ and $p(x)_{cls}$ as input in classification. Similarly, $z(x)_{reg}$ and $p(x)_{reg}$ are used in regression. As shown in Fig. 1, $\otimes$ denotes the convolution operation in classification and regression. The cross-correlation in two branches can place, respectively, as flowing:

$$A_{cls} = z(x)_{cls} \otimes p(x)_{cls} \quad (1)$$

$$A_{reg} = z(x)_{reg} \otimes p(x)_{reg} \quad (2)$$

Loss. More importantly, the main goal of RPN is, accurately, estimate the target location with a bounding box of variable aspect ratio. In the end, the cross-entropy losses function in SiamRPN are employed during training the classification network here. Instead, we refer to connect the two regression branches by GIOU loss. IOU, is the most commonly used metric for comparing the similarity between two arbitrary shapes. It can be shown that there is not a strong correlation between minimizing the commonly used losses, e.g. l_n-norms, which are infeasible to optimize in the case of non-overlapping bounding boxes, and it cannot reflect how far the two shapes are from each other. Therefor, it will easily result in tracking drifting that the target is absent. In contrast to IOU loss, GIOU does not only focus on overlapping area. The empty space between target bounding box and prediction bounding box is also noticed and reduced in training phrase. GIOU inference process is as follows:

$$A_{iou} = \frac{area(b_p \cap b_g)}{area(b_p \cup b_g)} \tag{3}$$

$$A_{Giou} = A_{iou} - \frac{|A_c \backslash area(b_p \cup b_g)|}{|A_c|} \tag{4}$$

$$\mathcal{L}_{Giou} = 1 - A_{Giou} \tag{5}$$

where b_p denotes as (d_x, d_y, d_w, d_h), as well as let b_g denotes as (t_x, t_y, t_w, t_h), both of them are considered as the central coordinates and shapes of prediction bounding box and ground truth bounding box. Let A_c denotes the area of smallest enclosing convex object. Similar to IOU, GIOU as a distance, as function in Eq. 5. When minimizing the GIOU loss between arbitrary proposal box and ground truth box, the range of GIOU is defined as:

$$-1 \leq GIOU(b_p, b_g) \leq 1 \tag{6}$$

The largest value of GIOU occurs only when two objects overlay perfectly, like prediction bounding box is consistent with ground truth box. However, GIOU value asymptotically converges to -1 when the ratio between occupying regions of two shapes, or the area of the enclosing shape A_c are tends to be zero. As the condition in Fig. 2.

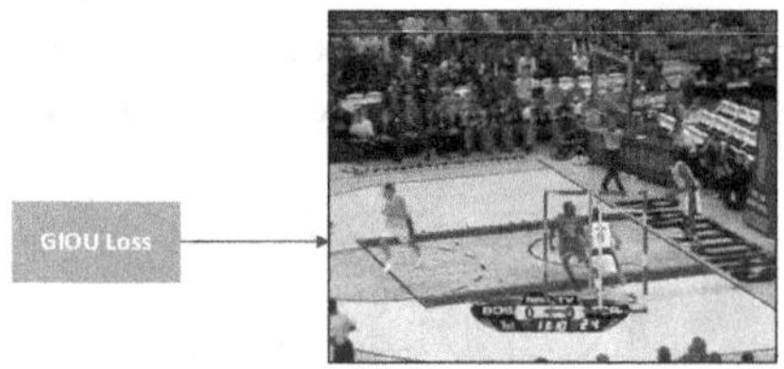

GIOU Loss Visualization

Fig. 2. The example of non-overlapping bounding box in tracking, including ground truth (red), prediction bounding box (blue) and the smallest convex shape (green) (Color figure online).

4 Experiments

4.1 Implementation Details

In this section, we conduct our experiments on several public visual tracking benchmarks datasets, *i.e.* OTB-50 [29], OTB-100 [30], VOT 2013 [31] and at all. For all of these tasks, the network architectures are based on SiamRPN. In experiments, we follow the idea that combines training and inference phase, and apply no module updating. The experimental equipment plays an essential role in the research of Deep Learning. There are totally 60 epochs performed and the learning rate set as 10^{-2}. To put that into context, all experiments were trained on 8G RAM and Nvidia GTX 1080 GPU. To train a model costs around 40 h on the only GPU.

Network Training. For the evaluation of OTB-50 and OTB-100 dataset, we adopt some annotated videos from VOT-2013, 2014 and 2016 datasets to train the introduced Siamese based network. Our training data consist of videos of objects, whose bounding box location is provided to us. It is also worthy to note that, the videos occur in the test dataset are all removed from the training datasets for fair comparison. In addition, to quickly validate the effectiveness of our proposed hard positive transformation network, we only implement this experiment on 10 videos from OTB dataset: *Dancer, FleetFace, Gym, Liquor, Crossing, Tiger1, Toy, Sylvester, Trans, Panda.* From every two frames in a video, we generate multiple pairs. The sample pairs are fed into temple branch and search branch respectively. Afterwards, temple patches are resized to 127×127, but unify search patches size to 255×255. Meanwhile, positive samples are defined as the anchors which have IOU > 0.6, while negative samples are considered as the anchors which have IOU not more than 0.3.

4.2 Evaluation on Tracking Benchmarks

We evaluate our algorithm introduced $\mathcal{L}_{Giou}$ in 10 videos from OTB dataset, and compare to the baseline loss ℓ_1-*smooth*. The final performances on the test set of the selective dataset have been reported in Table 1, where the optimal trackers are highlighted with red. The results in Table 1 show that training SiamRPN using GIOU based loss can slightly improve the performance on the benchmark. Overlapping rate per frame on video *Panda* and *Tiger1* is illustrated in Fig. 3, respectively. As shown in Fig. 3, overlap rate of our method (blue) performs better than ℓ_1-smooth (orange) at the most frames totally. Specially, our method keeps a high value even the default loss traps in the case of non-overlap bounding boxes.

Table 1. Average center location error (lower is better) between ℓ_1-*smooth* loss and $\mathcal{L}_{Giou}$ loss

Sequence	Dancer	FleetFace	Gym	Liquor	Crossing	Tiger1	Toy	Sylvester	Trans	Panda
ℓ_1-*smooth*	17.2	**149.7**	**16.0**	**37.5**	8.7	2402.6	777.3	**25.0**	43.4	15.3
Ours	**16.1**	426.5	18.6	40.7	**6.7**	**218.1**	**586.6**	26.0	**40.3**	**14.7**

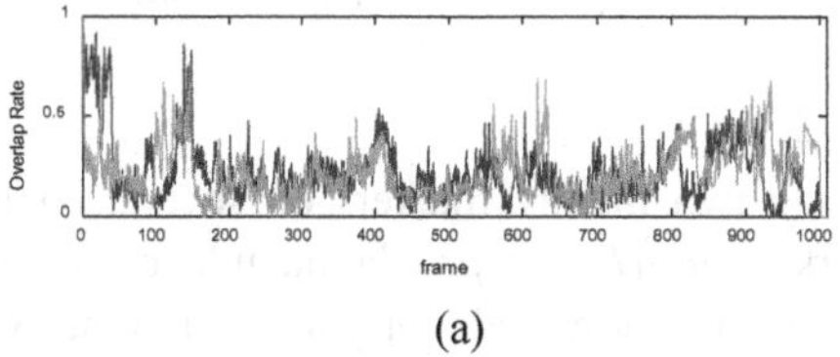

(a)

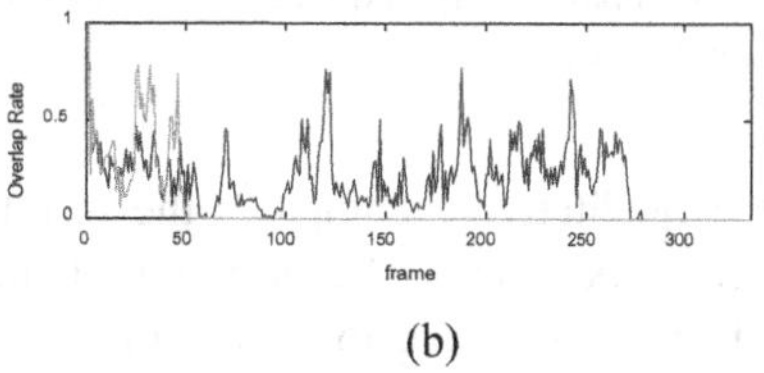

(b)

Fig. 3. Overlap rate evaluation, higher is better. (a) *Panda* (b) *Tiger1*, and $\mathcal{L}_{Giou}$ (blue) and ℓ_1-smooth (orange) (Color figure online).

It is essential to compare the proposed method with the ℓ_1-*norm* based line loss, which calculated depended on IOU. The evaluation is based on two metrics: pression and success plot (Fig. 4). The success plot shows the ratios of successful frames improved by using $\mathcal{L}_{Giou}$ as regression loss are over ℓ_1-smooth. Obviously, in order to predict the overlap between the target object and an estimated bounding box more robust, it is crucial to improve loss function of concerning bounding box as same as expanding dataset in training.

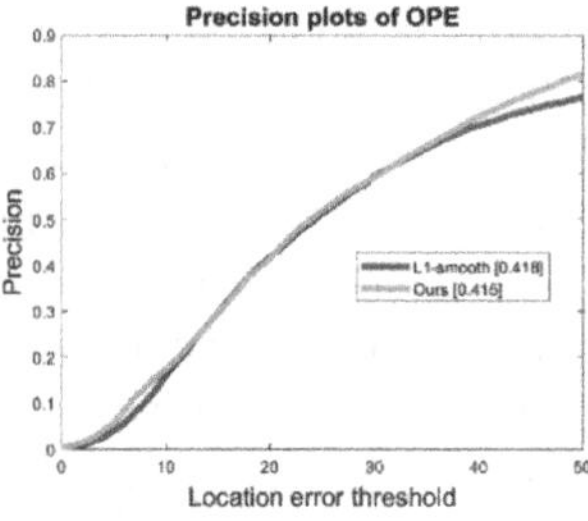

Fig. 4. Precision and success plots on the OTB-2015 dataset using one-pass evaluation.

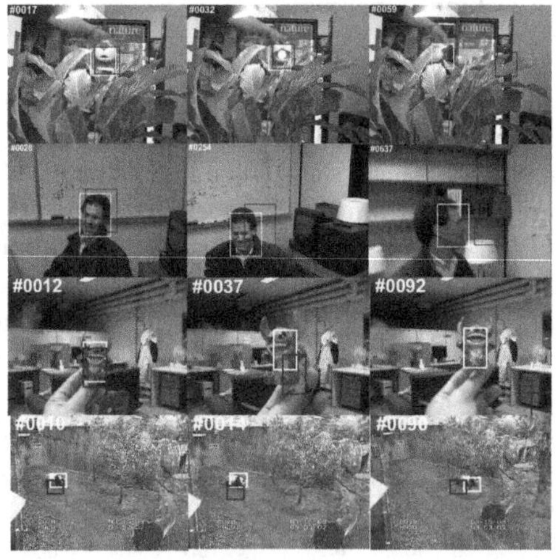

Fig. 5. Qualitative evaluation of our proposed tracker (green) and default SiameseRPN (blue) on three challenging sequence (from top to down: *Tiger1*, *FleetFace, Toy* and *Panda*) (Color figure online).

It qualitatively compares the results of the two mainly trackers on several challenging sequences. According to benchmark, *tigeral* and *panda* include common challenges of occlusion, deformation, in-plane rotation and out-plane rotation. As shown in Fig. 5, the tracker replacing L1 smooth loss with $\mathcal{L}_{Giou}$ loss performs well on fast motion (FM, *toy*), occlusion(OCC, *tiger1*), scale variation(SV, *panda*)and motion blur(MB, *fleetface*), while the tacker trained by ℓ_1-smooth loss occurs drifting in test process.

5 Conclusion

In this paper, we have replaced ℓ_1-*normal* loss with a new GIOU as bounding box regression loss. Instead of a metric loss calculated based on IOU, $\mathcal{L}_{Giou}$ loss can overcome the problem of optimizing in the case of non-overlapping bounding boxes. we adopt SiamRPN based framework to achieve real-time tracking by effectively learning temporal variation of target appearance with region proposal network. There is an opportunity to exploit loss function in module training excepting extend dataset. Moreover, in experiments, our method can achieve slightly improvement in OTB 2015.

Future work will include improved feature extraction and learning [32, 33], where fusion of multiple features [34, 35], especially the motion features [36] can be focused. In addition, deep learning model will be explored [37], along with feature detection and tracking [38, 39].

Acknowledgement. This study was partly supported by National Natural Science Foundation of China (61772144, 61672008), Innovation Team Project (Natural Science) of the Education Department of Guangdong Province (2017KCXTD021), Foreign Science and Technology Cooperation Plan Project of Guangzhou Science Technology and Innovation Commission (201807010059), Guangdong Provincial Application oriented Technical Research and Development Special Fund Project (2016B010127006), the Scientific and Technological Projects of Guangdong Province (2017A050501039), Innovation Research Project (Natural Science) of Education Department of Guangdong Province (2016KTSCX077), Foundation for Youth Innovation Talents in Higher Education of Guangdong Province (2018KQNCX139).

References

1. Grabner, H., Leistner, C., Bischof, H.: Semi-supervised on-line boosting for robust tracking. In: Forsyth, D., Torr, P., Zisserman, A. (eds.) Computer Vision – ECCV 2008. ECCV 2008. LNCS, vol. 5302, pp. 234–247. Springer, Heidelberg (2008). https://doi.org/10.1007/978-3-540-88682-2_19
2. Babenko, B., Yang, M.-H., Belongie, S.: Visual tracking with online multiple instance learning. In: Proceedings of the IEEE Conference on Computer Vision and Pattern Recognition (CVPR), pp. 983–990 (2009)
3. Kalal, Z., Mikolajczyk, K., Matas, J.: Tracking-learning-detection. IEEE Trans. Pattern Anal. Mach. Intell. (PAMI) **34**(7), 1409–1422 (2012)
4. Mei, X., Ling, H.: Robust visual tracking using l_1 minimization. In: Proceedings of the IEEE International Conference on Computer Vision (ICCV), pp. 1436–1443 (2009)
5. Wang, D., Lu, H., Yang, M.-H.: Online object tracking with sparse prototypes. IEEE Trans. Image Process. (TIP) **22**(1), 314–325 (2013)
6. Zhang, T., Liu, S., Xu, C., et al.: Structural sparse tracking. In: Proceedings of the IEEE Conference on Computer Vision and Pattern Recognition (CVPR), pp. 150–158 (2015)

7. Yan, Y., Ren, J., Sun, G., et al.: Unsupervised image saliency detection with Gestalt-laws guided optimization and visual attention based refinement. Pattern Recogn. **79**, 65–78 (2018)
8. Wang, Z., Ren, J., Zhang, D., et al.: A deep-learning based feature hybrid framework for spatiotemporal saliency detection inside videos. Neurocomputing **287**, 68–83 (2018)
9. Yan, Y., Ren, J., Zhao, H., et al.: Cognitive fusion of thermal and visible imagery for effective detection and tracking of pedestrians in videos. Cognitive Computation **10**(1), 94–104 (2018)
10. Ren, J., Xu, M., Orwell, J., et al.: Multi-camera video surveillance for real-time analysis and reconstruction of soccer games. Mach. Vis. Appl. **21**(6), 855–863 (2010)
11. Ren, J., Orwell, J., Jones, G.A., et al.: A general framework for 3D soccer ball estimation and tracking. In: 2004 International Conference on Image Processing, 2004. ICIP 2004, vol. 3, pp. 1935–1938 (2004)
12. Han, J., Zhang, D., Cheng, G., et al.: Object detection in optical remote sensing images based on weakly supervised learning and high-level feature learning. IEEE Trans. Geosci. Remote Sens. **53**(6), 3325–3337 (2014)
13. Zabalza, J., Ren, J., Zheng, J., et al.: Novel segmented stacked autoencoder for effective dimensionality reduction and feature extraction in hyperspectral imaging. Neurocomputing **185**, 1–10 (2016)
14. Tschannerl, J., Ren, J., Yuen, P., et al.: MIMR-DGSA: unsupervised hyperspectral band selection based on information theory and a modified discrete gravitational search algorithm. Inf. Fusion **51**, 189–200 (2019)
15. Zhang, A., Sun, G., Ren, J., et al.: A dynamic neighborhood learning-based gravitational search algorithm. IEEE Trans. Cybern. **48**(1), 436–447 (2016)
16. Wang, N., Yeung, D.Y.: Learning a deep compact image representation for visual tracking. In: Advances in Neural Information Processing Systems, pp. 809–817 (2013)
17. Wang, N., Li, S., Gupta, A., et al.: Transferring rich feature hierarchies for robust visual tracking. Comput. Sci. (2015)
18. Zhou, X., Xie, L., Zhang, P., et al.: An ensemble of deep neural networks for object tracking. In: Proceedings of the IEEE International Conference on Image Processing (ICIP), pp. 843–847, France (2014)
19. Nam, H., Han, B.: Learning multi-domain convolutional neural networks for visual tracking. arXiv: 1510.07945 (2016)
20. Song, Y., Ma, C., Wu, X., et al.: VITAL: visual tracking via adversarial learning. In: Proceedings of 2018 IEEE/CVF Conference on Computer Vision and Pattern Recognition, pp. 8990–8999, USA (2018)
21. Tao, R., Gavves, E., Smeulders, A.W.: Siamese instance search for tracking. In: Proceedings of IEEE Conference on Computer Vision and Pattern Recognition (CVPR), pp. 850–865, USA (2016)
22. Bertinetto, L., Valmadre, J., Henriques, J.F., Vedaldi, A., Torr, P.H.S.: Fully-convolutional siamese networks for object tracking. In: Hua, G., Jégou, H. (eds.) ECCV 2016. LNCS, vol. 9914, pp. 850–865. Springer, Cham (2016). https://doi.org/10.1007/978-3-319-48881-3_56
23. Guo, Q., Feng, W., Zhou, C., et al.: Learning dynamic siamese network for visual object tracking. In: Proceedings of IEEE International Conference on Computer Vision (ICCV), pp. 1763–1771, Italy (2017)
24. He, A., Luo, C., Tian, X., et al: A twofold siamese network for real-time object tracking. In: Proceedings of 2018 IEEE/CVF Conference on Computer Vision and Pattern Recognition, pp. 4834–4843, USA (2018)
25. Li, B., Yan, J., Wu, W., et al.: High performance visual tracking with siamese region proposal network. In: Proceedings of 2018 IEEE/CVF Conference on Computer Vision and Pattern Recognition, pp. 8971–8980, USA (2018)

26. Zhang, Y., Wang, L., Qi, J., et al.: Structured siamese network for real-time visual tracking. In: Proceedings of European Conference on Computer Vision (ECCV), pp. 351–366, Germany (2018)
27. Wang, X., Shrivastava, A., Gupta, A.: A-Fast-RCNN: hard positive generation via adversary for object detection r-CNN. Comput. Sci. 1440–1448 (2015)
28. Rezatofighi, H., Tsoi, N., Gwak, J.Y., et al.: Generalized intersection over union: a metric and a loss for bounding box regression. arXiv preprint https://arxiv.org/abs/1902.09630 (2019)
29. Wu, Y., Lim, J., Yang, M.-H.: Online object tracking: a benchmark. In: IEEE Conference on Computer Vision and Pattern Recognition (CVPR) (2013)
30. Wu, Y., Lim, J., Yang, M.-H.: Object tracking benchmark. IEEE Trans. Pattern Anal. Mach. Intell. **37**(9), 1834–1848 (2015)
31. Kristan, M., Pflugfelder, R., Leonardis, A., et al.: The visual object tracking VOT2013 challenge results. In: IEEE International Conference on Computer Vision Workshops, pp. 98–111 (2014)
32. Feng, W., Huang, W., Ren, J.: Class imbalance ensemble learning based on margin theory. Appl. Sci. **8**(5), 815 (2018)
33. Sun, G., Ma, P., et al.: A stability constrained adaptive alpha for gravitational search algorithm. Knowl.-Based Syst. **139**, 200–213 (2018)
34. Ren, J.: Fusion of intensity and inter-component chromatic difference for effective and robust colour edge detection. IET Image Process. **4**(4), 294–301 (2010)
35. Feng, Y., et al.: Object-based 2D-to-3D video conversion for effective stereoscopic content generation in 3D-TV applications. IEEE Trans. Broadcast. **57**(2), 500–509 (2011)
36. Ren, J., et al.: High-accuracy sub-pixel motion estimation from noisy images in Fourier domain. IEEE Trans. Image Process. **19**(5), 1379–1384 (2009)
37. Han, J., et al.: Background prior-based salient object detection via deep reconstruction residual. IEEE Trans. Circ. Syst. Video Technol. **25**(8), 1309–1321 (2014)
38. Ren, J., Vlachos, T.: Efficient detection of temporally impulsive dirt impairments in archived films. Sign. Process. **87**(3), 541–551 (2007)
39. Ren, J., et al.: Multi-camera video surveillance for real-time analysis and reconstruction of soccer games. Mach. Vis. Appl. **21**(6), 855–863 (2010)

Face Detection and Segmentation with Generalized Intersection over Union Based on Mask R-CNN

Kaihan Lin, Huimin Zhao, Jujian Lv(✉), Jin Zhan, Xiaoyong Liu, Rongjun Chen, Canyao Li, and Zhihui Huang

School of Computer Science, Guangdong Polytechnic Normal University, Guangzhou, China
{zhaohuimin, jujianlv}@gpnu.edu.cn

Abstract. As a research hotspot of computer vision and information security, face detection has been widely developed in the past few decades. However, most of the existing detection methods only realize the location of the bounding box, which leads to background noise in the face features as well as limited accuracy of detection. To overcome these drawbacks, a face detection and segmentation method with Generalized Intersection over Union (GIoU) based on Mask R-CNN is proposed in this paper, which is called G-Mask. In this method, ResNet-101 is used to extract features, RPN is used to generate RoIs, and RoIAlign faithfully retains the exact spatial locations to generate binary mask through Fully Convolution Network. In particular, to achieve better performance in multi-scale face detection tasks, we utilize GIoU as the bounding box loss function. Furthermore, a new face dataset with segmentation annotation information is constructed in this paper to train the model. The experimental results of the well-known benchmark FDDB and AFW show that the proposed G-Mask method achieves promising face detection performance compared with Faster R-CNN and the original Mask R-CNN method, and also can realize the instance-level face information segmentation while detecting.

Keywords: Face detection · Instance segmentation · Generalized Intersection over Union · Mask R-CNN

1 Introduction

Face detection is an important research direction in computer vision and information security, as well as a key branch of object detection, which has important research significance and application value. Face detection includes two processes of face localization and face recognition, which using image processing technology, machine learning and other methods to locate interested objects from images or videos. In recent years, with the importance of information security highlighted, face detection has been widely studied and developed in the field of pattern recognition.

In the field of object detection, region-based CNN detection methods is currently the mainstream scheme, such as R-CNN [1], Fast R-CNN [2], Faster R-CNN [3], as well as Mask R-CNN [4]. These methods are efficient and robust, as well as rapid

J. Ren et al. (Eds.): BICS 2019, LNAI 11691, pp. 106–116, 2020.
https://doi.org/10.1007/978-3-030-39431-8_11

detection speeds. Unlike the general object detection method, which has made great progress in the past few years, the method of face detection is lagged behind somewhat. The existing face detection methods mainly implements face detection and the location of the face bounding box, which may have some drawbacks such as the extracted face features has background noise, spatial quantization is rough, and can not be accurately positioned. Therefore, it is not conducive to further image processing, which leads to some efficient and practical application of image processing technologies (e.g. face image super-resolution reconstruction [5], face alignment of images [6, 28], etc.) difficult to apply on video images, so it is urgent to need a face detection and segmentation method for video images [7, 29].

Mask R-CNN [4] is an improved algorithm proposed by He et al. based on Faster R-CNN, which adds attention to instance segmentation. Benefiting from the state-of-the-art performance of Mask R-CNN, impressive results had been achieved in various object detection benchmarks, such as the COCO detection challenges and Cityscapes benchmarks. For face detection, most methods are still based on Faster RCNN or AdaBoost, which have limitations in accuracy and no instance segmentation for faces. In addition, since face detection is different from other detection tasks, the face may be smaller than other objects, and the situation is complex and diverse, the original algorithm is limited in the task of multi-scale face detection. In order to address the above problems, this paper proposes an improved Mask R-CNN with Generalized Intersection over Union (GIoU), which introduces Generalized Intersection over Union [23] as loss function for bounding box regression to improve detection accuracy of multi-scale face detection. The main contributions of this paper are as follows:

(1) A new dataset was created, which annotated 5115 images randomly selected from the FDDB [8] and ChokePoint datasets [9].
(2) An improved Mask R-CNN for face detection (G-Mask) was proposed, which introduces GIoU as loss function for bounding box regression, aims to improve the face detection accuracy.
(3) The results using our method are presented in the several mainstream benchmarks, including the FDDB and AFW [10].

2 Related Work

In recent years, researchers have done a lot of work on face detection, and some work has been applied to our daily lives. The existing face detection methods can be simply classified as traditional methods and the deep learning methods.

Traditional Methods: The well-known Viola-Jones [11] is the first real-time and effective face detection methods, which marks that face detection has entered the practical application stage. However, it also has several drawbacks, such as its relatively larger feature size and low recognition rate for complex situations.

To address these concerns, many scholars have done a lot of research and proposed more complicated features, such as HOG [12], SIFT [13], SUFT [14], LBP [15], etc. One of significant advances was Deformable Part Model (DPM), which proposed by Felzenszwalb et al. [16]. DPM carries out performance extension on the basis of HOG and SVM, fully utilized the advantages of them and making important breakthroughs in face detection, pedestrian detection and other tasks. However, the traditional machine learning methods still has two main defects. Firstly, the region selection strategy based on sliding window is not targeted, with high time complexity and window redundancy. Secondly, the characteristics of manual design are not robust to various challenges.

Deep Learning Methods: Since AlexNet used deep convolutional neural network in ImageNet challenge, and the accuracy of image classification has been greatly improved, researchers have attempted to apply deep learning to face detection, and achieved promising application effect. For example, Zhan et al. [17] utilized deep convolutional neural network to extract features and extract more valuable features from face and non-face images that have not been filtered by Adaboost, thus improving the detection accuracy. Ranjan et al. [18] proposed a deformation part model based on normalized features extracted by deep convolutional neural network. In recent years, with the rapid development of region-based CNN series object detection algorithm, the application of R-CNN series methods in the field of face detection is gradually emerging. Jiang et al. [19] trained Faster R-CNN model in WIDER dataset and implemented face detection in FDDB and IJB-A dataset. Wu et al. [20] proposed a DSFD algorithm based on Faster R-CNN for the problem of low accuracy of small-scale face detection. Sun et al. [21] improved the Faster R-CNN model, achieved better detection results through feature concatenation, hard negative mining, multi-scale training and other strategies. Face detection based on the deep learning mainly adopts convolutional neural network for feature extraction, which has better implementation effect in precision and multi-target detection task, and be able to spend acceptable time for accuracy significantly promoted. Therefore, face detection methods based on deep learning has become the mainstream of face detection research direction. In this paper, we propose a improved Mask R-CNN scheme, which is more suitable for face detection by improving the loss function.

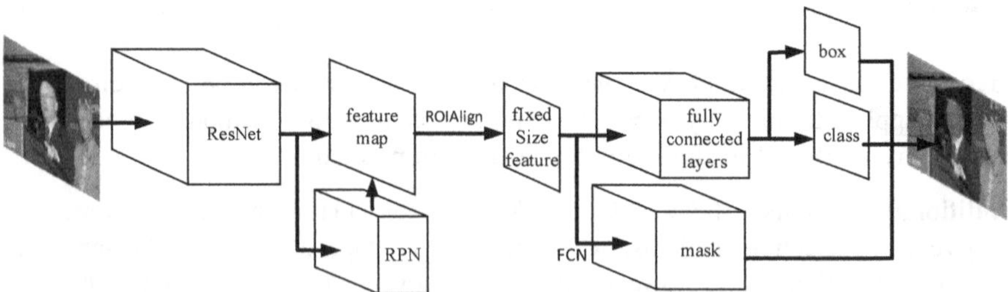

Fig. 1. Network architecture of the G-Mask

3 Our Approach

3.1 Network Architecture

Our model is similar to Mask R-CNN and mainly composed of two branches, one for object detection and the other for segmentation. The architecture of proposed network is illustrated in Fig. 1. Firstly, the ResNet-101 backbone is used to extract the face features of the whole image, so as to obtain the corresponding feature map. Then Region Proposal Network (RPN) is used to rapidly generate Regions of Interest (RoI) on the feature map, and the feature map output of the fixed size is obtained by the Region of Interest Align (RoIAlign). Finally, the bounding box is located and classified in the detection branch, and the corresponding face mask is drawn on the image in the segmentation branch through the Fully Convolution Network (FCN) [22].

3.2 Region Proposal Network

The RPN network rapidly generates RoIs by sliding windows on the feature map through anchors of different scales and different aspect ratios. Details are shown in Fig. 2(a). The background image in the figure represents the feature map extracted by the convolutional neural network, and the dotted line indicates that the anchor is the standard anchor. Assume that the standard anchor size is 16 pixels, and the three anchors contained therein respectively represent three anchors with aspect ratios of 1:1, 1:2, and 2:1. The dot-dash line and the solid line respectively represent anchors of 8 and 32 pixel. Similarly, each of them has three aspect ratios anchors. RPN uses the above three scales and three aspect ratios of nine scale anchors to slide in the feature map to generate RoIs. In this paper, the anchor of RPN used 5 scales and 3 aspect ratios.

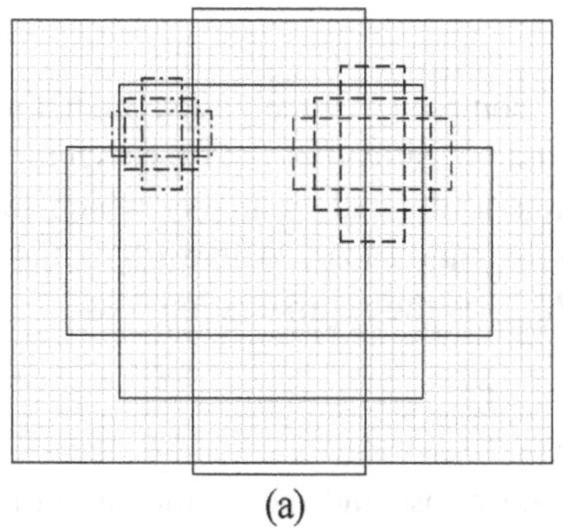
(a)

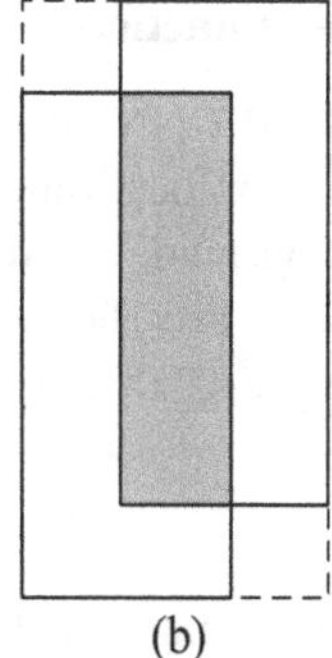
(b)

Fig. 2. (a) Illustration of RPN network. (b) Illustration of GIoU metric. The solid lines indicates the prediction box and ground truth box, the dotted line indicates the smallest enclosing box, and the shaded portion indicates the intersection of the prediction box and the ground truth box.

3.3 Region of Interest Align

The RoIAlign layer implements pooling of the RoIs generated by RPN, thereby pooling feature maps of different size into a fixed size feature map. In the Faster R-CNN model, RoIPool has two quantization operations, which produce quantization bias, resulting in misalignments of the extracted features.

When it comes to small object detection and instance segmentation tasks, RoIPool does not meet the requirements of instance-level mask. In response to the above problem, RoIAlign cancels the quantization process on the generated RoI feature map, and uses the bilinear interpolation to preserve the floating-number coordinates, thereby aligning the extracted features with the input image. The function of the bilinear interpolation is defined as follows:

Interpolate on the X-axis:

$$f(R_1) \approx \frac{x_2 - x}{x_2 - x_1} f(Q_{11}) + \frac{x - x_1}{x_2 - x_1} f(Q_{21}) \quad where \quad R_1 = (x, y_1), \tag{1}$$

$$f(R_2) \approx \frac{x_2 - x}{x_2 - x_1} f(Q_{12}) + \frac{x - x_1}{x_2 - x_1} f(Q_{22}) \quad where \quad R_2 = (x, y_2), \tag{2}$$

interpolate on the Y-axis:

$$f(P) = f(x, y) \approx \frac{y_2 - y}{y_2 - y_1} f(R_1) + \frac{y - y_1}{y_2 - y_1} f(R_2), \tag{3}$$

where $f(x, y)$ is the pixel value of the point P to be solved, $f(Q_{11})$, $f(Q_{12})$, $f(Q_{21})$, $f(Q_{22})$, are the pixel values of the four known points $Q_{11} = (x_1, y_1)$, $Q_{12} = (x_1, y_2)$, $Q_{21} = (x_2, y_1)$ and $Q_{22} = (x_2, y_2)$, and $f(R_1)$, $f(R_2)$ are the pixel value obtained by interpolating in the X-axis direction.

3.4 Loss Function

The Mask R-CNN model in this paper has completed three tasks, including face bounding box localization, face and background classification, and face segmentation from background. Therefore, the loss function is defined as in (4) which includes classification loss, bounding box loss and segmentation loss. Where L^*_{cls} is the classification loss, L^*_{box} is the bounding box loss, L^*_{mask} is the segmentation loss.

$$L = L^*_{cls} + L^*_{box} + L^*_{mask}. \tag{4}$$

In more detail, for this paper, the classification loss and the segmentation loss are following the Mask R-CNN, and the bounding box loss we introduce GIoU as the loss function. Generalized Intersection over Union (GIoU) [23] is a metric and a loss for bounding box regression proposed by Hamid Rezatofifighi et al. Its application in the state-of-the art object detection frameworks and has achieved the promising performance in many popular object benchmarks, so we attempts to improve the loss function by introducing this method. Figure 2(b) shows the details of GIoU.

For classification loss, the definition is as in (5)

$$L^*_{cls} = L(\{p_i\}) = \frac{1}{N_{cls}} \sum_i L_{cls}(p_i, p^*_i), \tag{5}$$

where i is the index of anchor and N_{cls} is the mini-batch size, p_i and p^*_i is the predicted probability and the ground-truth label of anchor i The ground-truth label $p^*_i = 1$ only when the anchor is positive, and $p^*_i = 0$ when the anchor is negative. The L^*_{cls} is the log loss between two classes which is defined as in (6)

$$L_{cls}(p_i, p_i*) = -\log[p_i * p_i + (1 - p_i*)(1 - p_i)]. \tag{6}$$

For bounding box loss, we adopt the GIoU as loss function. Assume the coordinates of predicted and ground-truth bounding box is $B_p = (x^p_1, y^p_1, x^p_2, y^p_2)$ and $B_g = (x^g_1, y^g_1, x^g_2, y^g_2)$. and ensure that $x_2 > x_1$, $y_2 > y_1$ in B_p and B_g, and the smallest enclosing box B_c can be found through

$$\begin{aligned} x^c_1 &= \min(x^p_1, x^g_1), \quad x^c_2 = \max(x^p_2, x^g_2), \\ y^c_1 &= \min(y^p_1, y^g_1), \quad y^c_2 = \max(y^p_2, y^g_2). \end{aligned} \tag{7}$$

In addition, the area of B_c can be computed as

$$A_c = (x^c_2 - x^c_1) \times (y^c_2 - y^c_1). \tag{8}$$

The IoU between B_p and B_g is defined as

$$IoU = \frac{A_I}{A_p + A_g - A_I}, \tag{9}$$

where A_p, A_g is the area of B_p and B_g, and A_I is the area where they intersect. Therefore, GIoU can be calculated by the definition of (10)

$$GIoU = IoU - \frac{A_c - (A_p + A_g - A_I)}{A_c}. \tag{10}$$

The loss of bounding box is defined as in (11)

$$L^*_{box} = 1 - GIoU. \tag{11}$$

For segmentation loss, the k-th mask contributes to the loss only when the region is related to the ground truth class k, and the loss function is defined as in (12)

$$L^*_{mask} = -\frac{1}{m^2} \sum_{1 \le i,j \le m} [y_{ij} \log \hat{y}^k_{ij} + (1 - y_{ij}) \log(1 - \hat{y}^k_{ij})], \tag{12}$$

where y_{ij} is the label value of a cell (i,j) for the region of size $m \times m$, and $\hat{y}^k_{ij}$ is the predicted value of the k-th class of this cell.

4 Experiments

4.1 Experimental Setup

Unlike object detection and generic face detection, there are no off-the-shelf face datasets with masks annotation that can be employed to train the model. The first step of our work is to create a new dataset. Different from other generic face datasets, a satisfactory face annotation of mask must contain both an object's category label and its accurate mask. Since annotating samples of face datasets with mask is a labor-intensive task, limited by time and labor, we annotated 5115 samples. In order to enhance the reliability of the samples, we randomly selected them from FDDB and ChokePoint datasets and annotated them with masks. After the annotation work, we trained the G-Mask model on our dataset.

We implemented G-Mask with Keras framework in Ubuntu 16.04 system and used the ResNet-101 network as the backbone network architecture. In the training phase, the epoch is set to 50, the steps of per epoch is 3000, the learning rate is 0.001, and the weight decay rate is 0.0001. The training and testing process is carried out on the same server, which is an Xeon E5 CPU of 128 GB memory and NVIDIA GeForce GTX 1080Ti GPU.

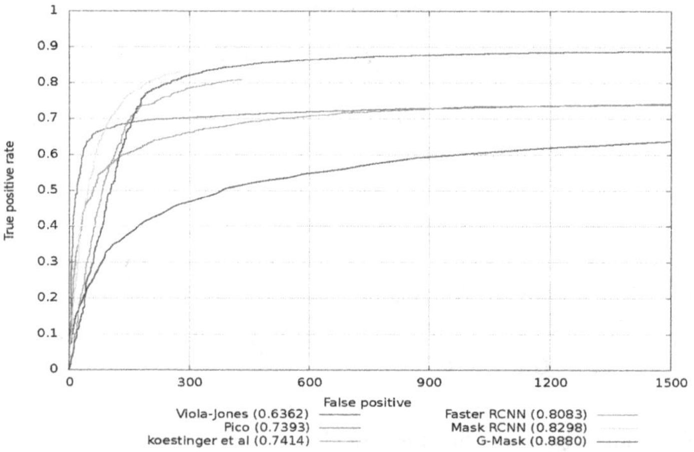

Fig. 3. Comparisons of face detection with other methods on FDDB benchmark.

4.2 Experimental Results

In this paper, our model not only completes the bounding box localization of face target, but also separates face information from background by binary mask. Therefore, the method can obtain more detailed face information through the above. In order to verify the G-Mask model, we compared the Faster R-CNN [19], Pico [24], Viola-Jones [25], and koestinger [26] methods on the FDDB benchmark. For effective comparison, the training data of the G-Mask, Mask R-CNN, and Faster R-CNN models are the same, which is the dataset constructed in this paper. We compared the true positive rate of 1500 false positives. The performance curve is shown in Fig. 3. It shows that G-Mask performs better than Faster R-CNN in more than 160 false positives, and was similar to Mask R-CNN in 280 false positives. In addition, our method achieved 88.80% true positive rate when there were 1500 false positives, which exceeds all comparison methods. Limited to the scale of the dataset and the difference in the format of the label, we did not achieve the state-of-the-art results, but our method can achieve better results on the same dataset than the compared method.

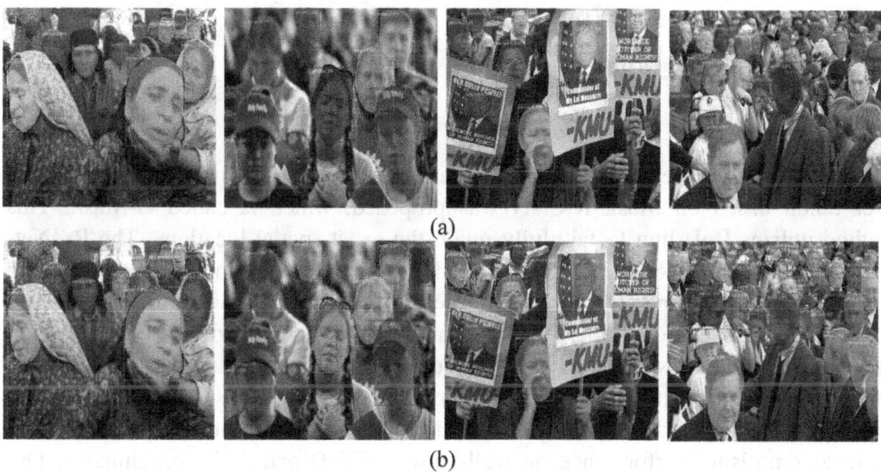

Fig. 4. Some different detection results of Mask R-CNN and G-Mask. (a) Mask R-CNN model, (b) G-Mask model.

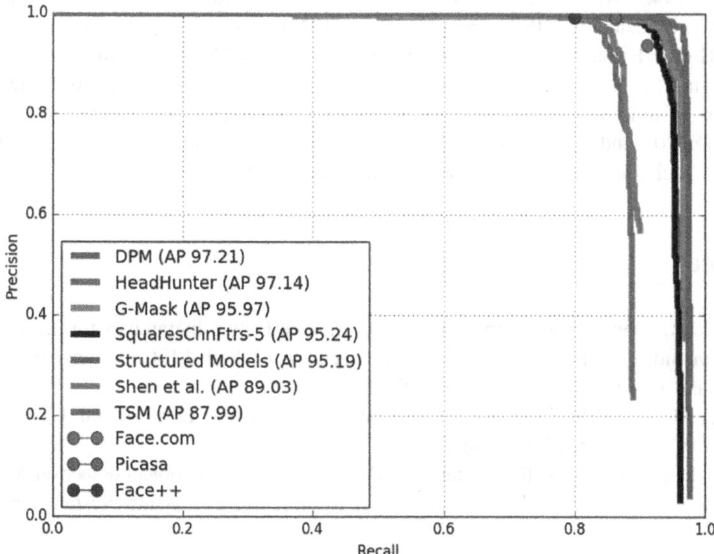

Fig. 5. Comparisons of face detection with other methods on AFW benchmark. Data of other models and code for evaluation are derived from [27].

Figure 4 shows the comparison of some detection results between the Mask R-CNN and the G-Mask model, and it is obvious that the G-Mask model performs better in multi-scale face tasks, which demonstrates the validity of the model.

In addition, in order to verify the validity of the model in different benchmark, we tested our model on the AFW benchmark and the performance curve are shown in Fig. 5. Due to the different label formats of our dataset and AFW benchmark, as well as the moderately sized training dataset, we did not get the best result, but still got 95.97 AP in this comparison, which demonstrates the generality of G-Mask in different benchmark.

5 Conclusion

In this work, a face detection and segmentation method with generalized intersection over union based on Mask R-CNN was proposed, which is called G-Mask. This method utilizes RoIAlign to faithfully retain the exact spatial locations. The ResNet-101 network and the RPN network are used to generate RoIs, and the corresponding face binary mask is generated through the Fully Convolution Network to segment face image from the background image. In particular, we introduce GIoU as a loss function based on the initial Mask R-CNN model to deal with multi-scale face tasks. In addition, a new face dataset with segmentation annotation information is constructed in this paper to train the model. The experimental results show that our proposed method achieves promising performance on well-known FDDB and AFW benchmarks. Our future work will extend the existing dataset to further improve the performance of our model. Secondly, optimize the model structure to improve detection accuracy.

Acknowledgement. This work was partly supported by National Natural Science Foundation of China (61772144, 61672008), Innovation Team Project (Natural Science) of the Education Department of Guangdong Province (2017KCXTD021), Foundation for Youth Innovation Talents in Higher Education of Guangdong Province (2018KQNCX139), Innovation Research Project (Natural Science) of Education Department of Guangdong Province (2016KTSCX077), Project for Distinctive Innovation of Ordinary Universities of Guangdong Province (2018KTSCX120), and Foreign Science and Technology Cooperation Plan Project of Guangzhou Science Technology and Innovation Commission (201807010059).

References

1. Girshick, R., Donahue, J., Darrell, T., Malik, J.: Rich feature hierarchies for accurate object detection and semantic segmentation. In: Proceedings of the IEEE Conference on Computer Vision and Pattern Recognition, pp. 580–587 (2014)
2. Girshick, R.: Fast R-CNN. In: Proceedings of the IEEE International Conference on Computer Vision, pp. 1440–1448 (2015)
3. Ren, S., He, K., Girshick, R.,. Faster R-CNN: towards real-time object detection with region proposal networks. In: Advances in Neural Information Processing Systems, pp. 91–99 (2015)

4. He, K., Gkioxari, G., Dollár, P., Girshick, R.: Mask R-CNN. In: Proceedings of the IEEE International Conference on Computer Vision, pp. 2961–2969 (2017)
5. Yang, J., Wright, J., Huang, T.S., Ma, Y.: Image super-resolution via sparse representation. IEEE Trans. Image Process. **19**(11), 2861–2873 (2010)
6. Zhang, K., Zhang, Z., Li, Z., et al.: Joint face detection and alignment using multitask cascaded convolutional networks. IEEE Signal Process. Lett. **23**(10), 1499–1503 (2016)
7. Wang, Z., Ren, J., et al.: A deep-learning based feature hybrid framework for spatiotemporal saliency detection inside videos. Neurocomputing **287**, 68–83 (2018)
8. Jain, V., Learned-Miller, E.: FDDB: a benchmark for facedetection in unconstrained settings. Technical report UM-CS-2010-009, University of Massachusetts, Amherst (2010)
9. Wong, Y., Chen, S., Mau, S., et al.: Patch-based probabilistic image quality assessment for face selection and improved video-based face recognition. In: Proceedings of the IEEE Conference on Computer Vision and Pattern Recognition, pp. 74–81 (2011)
10. Ramanan, D., Zhu, X.: Face detection, pose estimation, and landmark localization in the wild. In: Proceedings of the IEEE Conference on Computer Vision and Pattern Recognition, pp. 2879–2886 (2012)
11. Viola, P., Jones, M.J.: Robust real-time face detection. Int. J. Comput. Vision **57**(2), 137–154 (2004)
12. Dalal, N., Triggs, B.: Histograms of oriented gradients for human detection. In: Proceedings of the IEEE Conference on Computer Vision and Pattern Recognition, pp. 886–893 (2005)
13. Lowe, D.G.: Distinctive image features from scale-invariant keypoints. Int. J. Comput. Vis. **60**(2), 91–110 (2004)
14. Bay, H., Ess, A., Tuytelaars, T., Van Gool, L.: Speeded-up robust features (SURF). Comput. Vis. Image Underst. **110**(3), 346–359 (2008)
15. Ahonen, T., Hadid, A., Pietikainen, M.: Face description with local binary patterns: application to face recognition. IEEE Trans. Pattern Anal. Mach. Intell. **12**, 2037–2041 (2006)
16. Felzenszwalb, P.F., Girshick, R.B., McAllester, D., Ramanan, D.: Object detection with discriminatively trained part-based models. IEEE Trans. Pattern Anal. Mach. Intell. **32**(9), 1627–1645 (2009)
17. Zhan, S., Tao, Q.Q., Li, X.H.: Face detection using representation learning. Neurocomputing **187**, 19–26 (2016)
18. Ranjan, R., Patel, V.M., Chellappa, R.: A deep pyramid deformable part model for face detection. In: IEEE International Conference on Biometrics Theory, Applications and Systems, pp. 1–8 (2015)
19. Jiang, H., Learned-Miller, E.: Face detection with the faster R-CNN. In: IEEE International Conference on Automatic Face and Gesture Recognition, pp. 650–657 (2017)
20. Wu, W., Yin, Y., Wang, X., Xu, D.: Face detection with different scales based on faster R-CNN. IEEE Trans. Cybern. **99**, 1–12 (2018)
21. Sun, X., Wu, P., Hoi, S.C.: Face detection using deep learning: an improved faster RCNN approach. Neurocomputing **299**, 42–50 (2018)
22. Long, J., Shelhamer, E., Darrell, T.: Fully convolutional networks for semantic segmentation. In: Proceedings of the IEEE Conference on Computer Vision and Pattern Recognition, pp. 3431–3440 (2015)
23. Rezatofighi, H., Tsoi, N., Gwak, J., Sadeghian, A., Reid, I., Savarese, S.: Generalized intersection over union: a metric and a loss for bounding box regression. In: Proceedings of the IEEE Conference on Computer Vision and Pattern Recognition, pp. 658–666 (2019)
24. Markuš, N., Frljak, M., Pandzic, I.S., et al.: A method for object detection based on pixel intensity comparisons organized in decision trees. arXiv preprint arXiv:1305.4537, 8 (2013)

25. Jensen, O.H.: Implementing the Viola-Jones face detection algorithm. Master's thesis, Technical University of Denmark, DTU, DK-2800 Kgs. Lyngby, Denmark (2008)
26. Koestinger, M., Wohlhart, P., Roth, P.M., Bischof, H.: Robust face detection by simple means. In: Computer Vision in Applications Workshop (2012)
27. Mathias, M., Benenson, R., Pedersoli, M., Van Gool, L.: Face detection without bells and whistles. In: Fleet, D., Pajdla, T., Schiele, B., Tuytelaars, T. (eds.) ECCV 2014. LNCS, vol. 8692, pp. 720–735. Springer, Cham (2014). https://doi.org/10.1007/978-3-319-10593-2_47
28. Ren, J., Vlachos, T., Zhang, Y., Zheng, J., Jiang, J.: Gradient-based subspace phase correlation for fast and effective image alignment. J. Vis. Commun. Image Represent. **25**(7), 1558–1565 (2014)
29. Zabalza, J., et al.: Novel segmented stacked autoencoder for effective dimensionality reduction and feature extraction in hyperspectral imaging. Neurocomputing **185**, 1–10 (2016)

Semi-supervised Batch Mode Active Learning for Multi-class Classification

Jujian Lv[1(✉)], Huimin Zhao[1], Rongjun Chen[1], Jin Zhan[1], Jianhong Li[2], Kaihan Lin[1], and Canyao Li[1]

[1] School of Computer Science, Guangdong Polytechnic Normal University, Guangzhou, China
{jujianlv, zhaohuimin}@gpnu.edu.cn
[2] Laboratory of Language Engineering Computing, Guangdong University of Foreign Studies, Guangzhou, China

Abstract. Most of classification tasks typically require a large number of labelled samples to learn an accurate classifier, while labelled samples are usually limited in practice, and obtaining a lot of labelled samples is a time consuming and laborious work. Active learning is a paradigm to reduce the expensive human action by selecting the most valuable unlabeled samples iteratively. Existing works on active learning evaluate an unlabeled sample by one or two criteria, such as uncertainty, diversity, representativeness and so on. In this paper, three criteria, i.e., uncertainty based on a semi-supervised classifier, diversity based on the distance between samples and representativeness based on the distribution of data, are combined to design a batch mode sample selection strategy for multi-class active learning. By minimizing the expected error with respect to the optimal classifier, we can select the most valuable unlabeled samples for labeling. Experimental results on three public image datasets have demonstrated the effectiveness of our proposed method.

Keywords: Active learning · Semi-supervised learning · Multi-class classification

1 Introduction

In many machine learning applications, such as face recognition [1, 2], handwriting recognition [3, 4], image classification [5, 6] and object recognition [7] etc., unlabeled samples are usually easy to obtain, while labelling training data is expensive and time-consuming due to the involvement of human experts. Thus, it is desired to find ways to relieve the tedious work of labelling the training data. One of the important ways is active learning, which makes the most use of the scarce human labelling resources to maximize the classification performance by selecting the most valuable data from a candidate set for labelling.

The key problem of active learning is how to select the most valuable data, maximizing the performance of the model learned. During the past years, many active selection criteria have been proposed, such as uncertainty, diversity, density and representativeness etc. [8]. Although a lot of active learning algorithms have been

J. Ren et al. (Eds.): BICS 2019, LNAI 11691, pp. 117–127, 2020.
https://doi.org/10.1007/978-3-030-39431-8_12

proposed, most of them only deploy one criteria for query selection, which could significantly limit the performance of active learning. As an example, uncertainty sampling [9–12] queries those points whose predicted labels are most uncertain using the current trained model, which usually do not exploit the structure information of unlabeled data, leading to serious sample bias and consequently undesirable performance for active learning. Representative sampling [13–16] can exploit the distribution of unlabeled data, cannot make use of the label information even when labeled data are available. Although several active learning algorithms [17–20] have been proposed trying to consider different criteria simultaneously, they are still far from satisfactory and have several aspects to be improved.

In addition, most of the exiting research in active learning [8, 11, 19] is based on binary classification classifiers. To address the multi-class classification problem, many of them are direct extensions of binary active learning methods to the multi-class scenario by decomposing a multi-class problem as several independent binary classification subproblems, that may degrade the performance of active learning. Furthermore, the estimation of uncertainty in many active learning algorithms is based on supervised classifier, which often suffers from learning with a small number of labeled data in the early stage, leading fail to learn an accurate classification. Moreover, most existing active learning methods have focused on selecting a single most informative example in each data sampling iteration. This active learning framework must retrain the classifier on each iteration. Such a greedy incremental approach is inefficient and can only obtain suboptimal solution.

To overcome the above shortcomings, we proposed a semi-supervised batch mode active learning algorithm to handle multi-class classification problems in this paper. In the proposed algorithm, three criteria, i.e., uncertainty based on a semi-supervised classifier, diversity based on the distance between samples and representativeness based on the distribution of data, are combined to design a batch mode sample selection strategy for multi-class active learning. The information entropy is calculated based on the predicted value of semi-supervised classifier, which is used to estimate the uncertain information of samples. In addition, the diversity information value of the sample is calculated by the distance between samples. These two types of information are applied to the optimal experimental design framework as weighting factors to guide the model to select more valuable samples. An iterative optimization algorithm is proposed to solve the optimization problem. We have demonstrated our method on several benchmark image data set. All experimental results indicate that our proposed algorithm outperforms other state-of-the-art active learning algorithms.

The rest of this paper is organized as follows. In Sect. 2, we give a brief introduction to several typical related works. In Sect. 3, we give the objective function of our proposed method, and describe an efficient iterative algorithm to optimize the objective function in detail, and then describe the experiments to demonstrate the efficiency of our method in Sect. 4. Lastly, we conclude this paper in Sect. 5.

2 Related Work

The generic problem of active learning is the following. Given unlabeled data $\boldsymbol{X} = [\boldsymbol{x}_1, \cdots, \boldsymbol{x}_n] \in \mathbb{R}^{d \times n}$, find a subset $\mathbf{Z} = \{\mathbf{z}_1, \cdots, \mathbf{z}_m\} \subset \mathbf{X}$ which contains the most informative points, such that the potential performance the classifier can be maximized if they are labeled and used as training points. Such a problem can be formulated as the Transductive Experimental Design (TED) problem [14] to solve:

$$\begin{aligned} &\min \sum_{i=1}^{n} \|\mathbf{x}_i - \mathbf{Z}\mathbf{a}_i\|_2^2 + \lambda \|\mathbf{a}_i\|_2^2 \\ &s.t.\, \mathbf{Z} \subset \mathbf{X}, |\mathbf{Z}| = m \end{aligned} \tag{1}$$

where $\mathbf{a}_i \in \mathbb{R}^m$, λ is the regularization parameter controlling the amount of shrinkage. According to the above expressions, it can be intuitively seen that the best subset selected by the transductive experimental design can more accurately reconstruct all the data in the test set, and these points in the best subset are often referred to as the most representative data points. By introducing $\|\cdot\|_{2,0}$ norms, the above optimization problems are equivalent to:

$$\begin{aligned} &\min \sum_{i=1}^{n} \|\mathbf{x}_i - \mathbf{X}\mathbf{a}_i\|_2^2 + \lambda \|\mathbf{A}\|_{2,0} \\ &s.t.\, \mathbf{A} = [\mathbf{a}_1, \mathbf{a}_2 \cdots, \mathbf{a}_n] \in \mathbb{R}^{n \times n}, \|\mathbf{A}\|_{2,0} = m \end{aligned} \tag{2}$$

The first term in Eq. (2) is the loss of the representation, and the second term in Eq. (2) is the $\ell_{2,0}$-norm regularization on $\mathbf{A}$. The loss used in Eq. (4) is a squared loss, which is very sensitive to data outliers, and solving this problem is NP-hard because of the $\ell_{2,0}$-norm. To solve these two deficiencies, Nie [16] proposed an improved active learning method based on Robust Representation and Structured Sparsity (RRSS) with objective function:

$$\min_{\mathbf{A}} \sum_{i=1}^{n} \|\mathbf{x}_i - \mathbf{X}\mathbf{a}_i\|_2 + \lambda \|\mathbf{A}\|_{2,1} \tag{3}$$

which relax the objective to an efficient convex formulation by employing a structured sparsity-inducing norm. Above objective function can be written into a matrix format as follow:

$$\min_{\mathbf{A}} \|(\mathbf{X} - \mathbf{X}\mathbf{A})^T\|_{2,1} + \lambda \|\mathbf{A}\|_{2,1} \tag{4}$$

where the $\ell_{2,1}$-norm is applied to the loss function that is beneficial to reduce the effects of data outliers and improve the robustness of active learning. The most representative m data points corresponding to the top m rows of the ordered optimal $\mathbf{A}$ should be selected. The ordered optimal **A** is obtained by sorting the rows of optimal **A** in Eq. (4) by the row-sum values of the absolute **A** in the decreasing order.

According to [14, 16], TED and RRSS tend to select examples representative of all the unlabeled data which can reflect the structure distribution of the data set. Although these methods can exploit the distribution of unlabeled data and support batch selection, they cannot make use of the beneficial label information even when labeled data are available. In the next section, we will present our Semi-supervised Batch Mode Multi-class (SBMM) active learning which can effectively utilize the available label information to select the most valuable examples that are both representative and informative.

3 Semi-supervised Batch Mode Multi-class Active Learning

3.1 Objective Function

In this section, we give the proposed SBMM active learning algorithm. According to [14, 16], TED and RRSS are unsupervised active learning methods, which only consider the distribution information of the unlabeled data, but do not consider the label information even when labeled data are available. Therefore, our research focuses on how to make better use of the distribution information and label information of the data to guide the active sample selecting, when labeled data are available.

Suppose there are some labeled data points, we can learn a classifier from the data.

However, it is not appropriate to use supervised learning to train a classifier if fewer labeled samples are available, especially in the early stage of the active learning. On the one hand, when there are few labeled data points, the training of the model is prone to over-fitting, which easily leads to poor generalization ability of the classifier. On the other hand, it is a great waste of sample resources if we only use the few labeled samples but ignore the enormous number of unlabeled samples.

In order to make better use of labeled and unlabeled samples, we use graph-based semi-supervised classifier to predict the uncertainty of unlabeled data. This is because the semi-supervised classifier can achieve more accurate prediction results than the supervised classifier when the labeled samples are insufficient. In the graph-based semi-supervised learning, the harmonic function can extend the predictive values from the discrete form to the continuous form [21, 22]. It satisfies the following requirements: for the labeled samples, the harmonic function ensures that the output of the labeled sample is consistent with the real value as:

$$f(\boldsymbol{x}_i) = y_i, i = 1, \ldots, l \tag{5}$$

for unlabeled data, the weight average characteristics must be satisfied as:

$$f(\boldsymbol{x}_j) = \frac{\sum_{k=1}^{l+u} w_{jk} f(\boldsymbol{x}_k)}{\sum_{k=1}^{l+u} w_{jk}}, j = l+1, \ldots, l+u \tag{6}$$

Based on the harmonic function, by relaxing the predictive value to the real number domain, the following objective functions can be obtained:

$$\min_{f(x)\in R} \infty \sum_{i=1}^{l} (y_i - f(\mathbf{x}_i))^2 + \sum_{i,j=1}^{l+u} w_{ij}(f(\mathbf{x}_i) - f(\mathbf{x}_j))^2 \tag{7}$$

Defining the Laplace matrix as $\mathbf{L} = \mathbf{D} - \mathbf{W}$, $\mathbf{f} = [f(\mathbf{x}_1), \ldots, f(\mathbf{x}_{l+u})]^T$, where weight matrix $\mathbf{W}$ defined as follows:

$$\mathbf{W}_{ij} = \begin{cases} \exp\left(\frac{-\|x_i - x_j\|_2^2}{\sigma^2}\right) & if\, x_j \in N_k(x_i)\, or\, x_i \in N_k(x_j) \\ 0 & \text{otherwise} \end{cases} \tag{8}$$

Then the regularization term in the above formula can be rewritten as: $\sum_{i,j=1}^{l+u} w_{ij}(f(\mathbf{x}_i) - f(\mathbf{x}_j))^2 = \mathbf{f}^T\mathbf{L}\mathbf{f}$. Divide the Laplacian matrix into four sub-matrices

$$\mathbf{L} = \begin{bmatrix} \mathbf{L}_{ll} & \mathbf{L}_{lu} \\ \mathbf{L}_{ul} & \mathbf{L}_{uu} \end{bmatrix} \tag{9}$$

and $\mathbf{f}$ into $(\mathbf{f}_l, \mathbf{f}_u)$. Setting $\mathbf{y}_l = (y_1, \ldots y_l)^T$, then the predicted value of the data can be derived by Lagrange multiplier and some matrix operations as follow:

$$\begin{aligned} \mathbf{f}_l &= \mathbf{y}_l \\ \mathbf{f}_u &= -\mathbf{L}_{uu}^{-1}\mathbf{L}_{ul}\mathbf{y}_l \end{aligned} \tag{10}$$

For the multi-class classification problem,

$$\begin{aligned} \mathbf{F}_l &= \mathbf{Y}_l \\ \mathbf{F}_u &= -\mathbf{L}_{uu}^{-1}\mathbf{L}_{ul}\mathbf{Y}_l \end{aligned} \tag{11}$$

where $\boldsymbol{Y}_l, \boldsymbol{F}_l \in \mathbb{R}^{l\times c}$ and $\boldsymbol{F}_u \in \mathbb{R}^{u\times c}$. It can be verified that $\sum_{j=1}^{c} \mathbf{F}_{ij} = 1$. In this paper, we adopt the information entropy $h_{\mathrm{H}}(\mathbf{x}_i)$ ψ to evaluate the uncertainty of $\mathbf{x}_i$, which can be estimated by

$$h_{\mathrm{H}}(\mathbf{x}_i) = -\sum_{j=1}^{c} p(y_j|\mathbf{x}_i) \log p(y_j|\mathbf{x}_i) \tag{12}$$

where $p(y_j|\mathbf{x}_i) = \mathbf{F}_{ij}$ is regarded as the probability that $\mathbf{x}_i$ belongs to the j-th class, $\log p(\cdot)$ is the natural logarithm operator. A larger $h_{\mathrm{H}}(\mathbf{x}_i)$ indicates that the corresponding uncertainty of $\mathbf{x}_i$ is greater.

To make the selected unlabeled samples as diverse as possible and far away from the labeled samples simultaneously, we define the uncertainty $u_u(i)$ and diversity confidence value of the unlabeled data point $\mathbf{x}_i$ at the same scale as:

$$u_u(i) = \gamma - (\gamma - 1)\frac{h_{\mathrm{H}}(\mathbf{x}_i)}{\log_2(c)} \in [1, \gamma] \tag{13}$$

$$u_d(i) = \gamma - (\gamma - 1)\frac{\min_{j \in \mathbf{L}} d_{ji}}{\max_{k \in \mathbf{U}} d_{ji} \min_{j \in \mathbf{L}} d_{jk}} \in [1, \gamma] \tag{14}$$

where γ is a suitable constant. The combination of uncertainty and diversity can be given by:

$$u(i) = \sqrt{u_u(i) \times u_d(i)} \in [1, \gamma] \tag{15}$$

Then, by incorporating the combination of uncertainty and diversity (15) as the weighted coefficients of **A** into (4), we can get the following form of objective function as:

$$\min_{\mathbf{A}} \|(\mathbf{X} - \mathbf{XA})^T\|_{2,1} + \lambda\|\mathbf{UA}\|_{2,1} \tag{16}$$

where $\mathbf{U} = diag(u(1), u(2), \cdots, u(n))$ is a diagonal matrix. It is easy to see that the smaller the value of $u_u(i)$ and $u_d(i)$ is, the value of $u(i)$ is smaller, then the weight of corresponding row of matrix A is smaller, thus the probability of the corresponding unlabeled data point $\mathbf{x}_i$ will be selected is larger. In other words, the proposed algorithm is more inclined to select those unlabeled samples, which are great uncertainty and diversity, and can represent the structural distribution of data at the same time.

3.2 Efficient Optimization

Because the value of **U** is a fixed at each sample selection step, the objective function (16) is still a convex function. To solve this convex optimization problem, we define the following function:

$$f(\mathbf{A}) = \|(\mathbf{X} - \mathbf{XA})^T\|_{2,1} + \lambda\|\mathbf{UA}\|_{2,1} \tag{17}$$

Taking the derivative of Eq. (17) with regard to **A**, and setting the derivative to zero, we have

$$\frac{\partial f(\mathbf{A})}{\partial \mathbf{A}} = \mathbf{X}^T\mathbf{XAE} - \mathbf{X}^T\mathbf{XE} + \lambda\mathbf{FA} = 0 \tag{18}$$

where $\mathbf{E} = diag(e_i, \ldots, e_n)$ and $\mathbf{F} = diag(f_i, \ldots, f_n)$ are diagonal matrices, their diagonal elements are $e_i = 1/2\|\mathbf{x}_i - \mathbf{X}\mathbf{a}_i\|_2$ and $f_i = u(i)/2\|\mathbf{a}^i\|_2$ respectively. Then for each *i*, the following equations are established:

$$e_i\mathbf{X}^T\mathbf{X}\mathbf{a}_i - e_i\mathbf{X}^T\mathbf{x}_i + \lambda\mathbf{F}\mathbf{a}_i = 0 \tag{19}$$

and then $\mathbf{a}^i$ ψ can be calculated by

$$\mathbf{a}_i = e_i(e_i\mathbf{X}\mathbf{X}^T + \lambda\mathbf{F}\mathbf{a}_i)^{-1}\mathbf{X}\mathbf{x}_i \tag{20}$$

where the matrices **E** and **F** are unknown variables and their values depend on the matrix **A**. Since the objective function of our method have the similar form with RRSS

Algorithm 1 The optimization algorithm of SBMM active learning

input: dataset $\mathbf{D} = [\mathbf{L}, \mathbf{X}]$, the label of the labeled data $\mathbf{Y}_L$, the number of nearest neighbors k, the parameters λ, σ and γ.
output: matrix $\mathbf{A}$.

Construct a nearest neighbor graph with weight matrix **W** as in Eq.(8), calculate the graph Laplacian $\mathbf{L} = \mathbf{D} - \mathbf{W}$
Calculate predicted values $\mathbf{F}_u$ of unlabeled samples as in Eq.(11)
Calculate the information entropy $h_H(\mathbf{x}_i)$ of each unlabeled sample **W** as in Eq.(12)
Calculate $u_u(i)$ and $u_d(i)$ of each unlabeled sample $\mathbf{x}_i$ as in Eq.(13) and Eq.(14)
Calculate $u(i)$ of each unlabeled sample $\mathbf{x}_i$ as in Eq.(15), get $\mathbf{U} = diag(u(1), u(2), \cdots, u(n))$
while not converge do
    Calculate $e_i = 1/2\|\mathbf{x}_i - \mathbf{X}\mathbf{a}_i\|_2$, get $\mathbf{E} = diag(e_i, \ldots, e_n)$
    Calculate $f_i = u(i)/2\|\mathbf{a}^i\|_2$, get $\mathbf{F} = diag(f_i, \ldots, f_n)$
    update a_i as in Eq.(20)
end

active learning algorithm, we simple employ the iterative algorithms proposed by Nie [16] to solve the optimization problem, which can effective converge to the global solution to the problem (16). The detailed proof can be found in [16], which is omitted here. The detailed algorithm is described in Algorithm 1.

After obtaining the optimal **A** in Eq. (16), we can sort the rows of **A** by the row-sum values of the absolute **A** in the decreasing order. Therefore, the active learning task can be performed by selecting the *m* samples corresponding to the top *m* rows of **A**.

4 Experimental Results

In this section, we carry out classification experiments on three real-world data sets to compare different active learning algorithms quantitatively. Table 1 summarizes the detailed information of the datasets used in the experiment.

Table 1. Characteristics of data sets.

Name	Size	# of class	Application
Yale	165	15	Face recognition [23]
USPS	2000	10	Handwritten digits recognition [15]
Coil20	1440	20	Object classification [24]

4.1 Experiment Setup

To demonstrate the effectiveness of our proposed algorithm, we evaluate and compare five active learning methods:

- Active learning algorithm based on K-means Clustering (K-means): select the data points that are most close to K centroids.
- Transductive Experimental Design (TED) [14]: select the most representative data points that are most accurately reconstruct all the data.
- Question method (QUIRE) [20]: select the most both representative and uncertain data points.
- Active learning method based on robust representation and structured sparsity (RRSS) [16]: select the most representative data points through robust representation and structured sparsity.
- semi-supervised batch mode multi-class active learning algorithm (SBMM) proposed in this paper.

In our experiments, 50% data points of each dataset are randomly selected as candidate samples and the other 50% data points as the testing data. we use the points selected by each active learning algorithm from the candidate samples as the training data to train a classifier, and the unselected points are used as the testing data. The classification accuracy of the associated classifier is used to measure the performance of each active learning algorithm. The Support Vector Machine (SVM) classifier is used as the base classifier. We repeat every test case for 50 times and report the average classification performances.

4.2 Experimental Results

In face recognition experiments, each algorithm selects $5, 10\ldots, 45$ sample from the candidate samples as the training dataset to train a classifier. The experimental results are shown in Fig. 1(a). For handwritten digits recognition, we randomly select 2000 images, 200 for each digit from the USPS database as experimental data set. In this experiment, each algorithm selects $100, 200\ldots, 900$ sample from the candidate samples as the training dataset to train a classifier. The experimental results are shown in Fig. 1(b). In object classification experiment, each algorithm selects 50, 100..., 450 sample from the candidate samples as the training dataset to train a classifier. The experimental results are shown in Fig. 1(c).

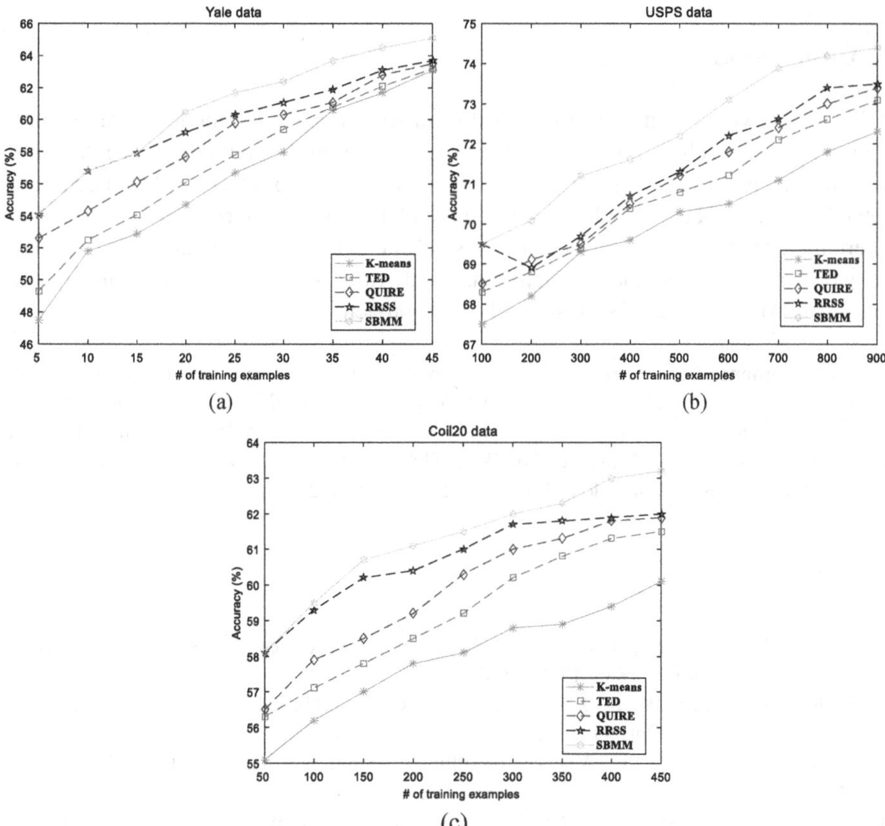

Fig. 1. A comparison of different active learning algorithms on Yale data set, USPS dataset and Coil 20 data set.

As can be seen, our SBMM algorithm significantly outperforms the other active learning algorithms in most cases. The performance difference gets larger as the number of training samples increases. The RRSS algorithm outperforms TED in most cases. Through the comparison and analysis, it can be found that the performance of the QUIRE algorithm is significantly better than the TED algorithm and the K-means algorithm. This shows that taking into account the uncertain and distribution information simultaneously can help the algorithm to select more valuable samples for improving the performance of the classifier. The label-independent algorithm RRSS which ignores the label information of samples, shows better performance than the label-dependent algorithm QUIRE, especially at the early stage of the experiment. This could be explained by the scarce labeled data at the early stage, and the class boundary is not accurate enough which cause the deviation of sample selection. That is to say, the selection of classifier is critical for the label-dependent algorithm. In conclusion, selecting reasonable evaluation criteria and fusion method is the guarantee of accurate sample selection.

5 Conclusion

In this paper, we have introduced a novel semi-supervised batch mode active learning method for multi-class image classification. Unlike most previous active learning methods which consider only single criteria or two criteria to select unlabeled data, our method design a robust sample selection model based on multi-criterion by integrating uncertainty, diversity and representativeness of the data. Experimental results on three real-world applications (face recognition, handwritten digits recognition, and image classification) show the effectiveness of our approach.

Acknowledgement. This work was partly supported by Foundation for Youth Innovation Talents in Higher Education of Guangdong Province (2018KQNCX139), National Natural Science Foundation of China (61772144, 61672008), Innovation Team Project of the Education Department of Guangdong Province (2017KCXTD021), Project for Distinctive Innovation of Ordinary Universities of Guangdong Province (2018KTSCX120).

References

1. Abate, A.F., Nappi, M., Riccio, D., et al.: 2D and 3D face recognition: a survey. Pattern Recognit. Lett. **28**(14), 1885–1906 (2007)
2. Fu, L., Chen, D., Lin, K., et al.: An improved SRC method based on virtual samples for face recognition. J. Mod. Opt. **99**, 1–12 (2018)
3. Ramteke, A.S., Rane, M.E.: A survey on offline recognition of handwritten. Int. J. Parasitol. **42**(5), 501–509 (2012)
4. Voigtlaender, P., Doetsch, P., Ney, H.: Handwriting recognition with large multidimensional long short-term memory recurrent neural networks. In: Proceedings of the International Conference on Frontiers in Handwriting Recognition (2017)
5. Wei, Y., Zhou, Y., Li, H.: Spectral-spatial response for hyperspectral image classification. Remote Sens. **9**(3), 203 (2017)
6. Liu, L., Wang, P., Shen, C., et al.: Compositional model based fisher vector coding for image classification. IEEE Trans. Pattern Anal. Mach. Intell. **39**(12), 2335–2348 (2016)
7. Khurana, P., Sharma, A., Singh, S.N., et al.: A survey on object recognition and segmentation techniques. In: Proceedings of the International Conference on Computing for Sustainable Global Development (2016)
8. Settles, B.: Active learning literature survey, Computer Sciences Technical Report 1648, University of Wisconsin, Madison, 26 January 2010
9. Lewis, D., Catlett, J.: Heterogeneous uncertainty sampling for supervised learning. In: Proceedings of the International Conference on Machine Learning, pp. 148–156 (1994)

10. Tong, S., Koller, D.: Support vector machine active learning with applications to text classification. In: Proceedings of the International Conference on Machine Learning, pp. 999–1006 (2000)
11. Tong, S., Chang, E.: Support vector machine active learning for image retrieval. In: Proceedings of the ACM International Conference on Multimedia, pp. 107–118 (2001)
12. Lindenbaum, M., Markovitch, S., Rusakov, D.: Selective sampling for nearest neighbor classifiers. Mach. Learn. **54**(2), 125–152 (2004)
13. Nguyen, H.T., Smeulders, A.: Active learning using pre-clustering. In: Proceedings of the International Conference on Machine Learning, pp. 79–86 (2004)
14. Yu, K., Bi, J., Tresp, V.: Active learning via transductive experimental design. In: Proceedings of the International Conference on Machine Learning, pp. 1081–1088 (2006)
15. Zhang, L., Chen, C., Bu, J.: Active learning based on locally linear reconstruction. IEEE Trans. Pattern Anal. Mach. Intell. **33**(10), 2026–2038 (2011)
16. Nie, F., Wang, H., Huang, H., et al.: Early active learning via robust representation and structured sparsity. In: Proceedings of the International Joint Conference on Artificial Intelligence, pp. 1572–1578 (2013)
17. Zhu, X., Lafferty, J., Ghahramani, Z.: Combining active learning and semi-supervised learning using Gaussian fields and harmonic functions. In: Proceedings of the International Conference on Machine Learning Workshop on the Continuum from Labeled to Unlabeled Data, pp. 58–65 (2003)
18. Xu, Z., Akella, R., Zhang, Y.: Incorporating diversity and density in active learning for relevance feedback. In: Amati, G., Carpineto, C., Romano, G. (eds.) ECIR 2007. LNCS, vol. 4425, pp. 246–257. Springer, Heidelberg (2007). https://doi.org/10.1007/978-3-540-71496-5_24
19. Zhang, Yu., Yeung, D.-Y.: Discriminative experimental design. In: Gunopulos, D., Hofmann, T., Malerba, D., Vazirgiannis, M. (eds.) ECML PKDD 2011. LNCS (LNAI), vol. 6913, pp. 585–596. Springer, Heidelberg (2011). https://doi.org/10.1007/978-3-642-23808-6_38
20. Huang, S.J., Jin, R., Zhou, Z.H.: Active learning by querying informative and representative examples. IEEE Trans. Pattern Anal. Mach. Intell. **36**(10), 1936–1949 (2014)
21. Zhu, X.: Semi-supervised learning literature survey. Technical report, University of Wisconsin-Madison (2008)
22. Zhu, X., Ghahramani, Z., Lafferty, J.D.: Semi-supervised learning using Gaussian fields and harmonic functions. In: Proceedings of the International Conference on Machine Learning (ICML), pp. 912–919 (2003)
23. Georghiades, A.S., Belhumeur, P.N., Kriegman, D.J.: From few to many: illumination cone models for face recognition under variable lighting and pose. IEEE Trans. Pattern Anal. Mach. Intell. **23**(6), 643–660 (2002)
24. Nene, S.A., Nayar, S.K., Murase, H.: Columbia object image library (COIL-20), Technical report CUCS-005-96. Columbia University (1996)

Dimensionality Reduction with Extreme Learning Machine Based on Manifold Preserving

Canyao Li, Jujian Lv[(✉)], Huimin Zhao, Rongjun Chen, Jin Zhan, and Kaihan Lin

School of Computer Science, Guangdong Polytechnic Normal University, Guangzhou 510665, China
{jujianlv, zhaohuimin}@gpnu.edu.cn

Abstract. As a nonlinear dimensionality reduction technique, manifold learning method is used to solve the computational complexity of high-dimensional data, which has been widely used in the visualization and feature extraction. However, most of existing methods are sensitive to noise and usually cannot get the accurate projection function, which limit its practical application. To overcome these problems, we propose a nonlinear dimensionality reduction method with Extreme Learning Machine based on Manifold Preserving called MP-ELM. MP-ELM takes both manifold structure and distance information into account, which can heighten dimensionality reduction effect and enhance noise immunity. The results of the visualization experiment on artificial data, clustering and face recognition experiment on several real-word database show that our method significantly outperforms the compared dimensionality reduction methods.

Keywords: Dimensionality reduction · Extreme Learning Machine · Manifold learning

1 Introduction

With the advent of the era of big data, big data has brought great opportunities for academia and industry, but also has brought many challenges. One representative of them is solving the computational complexity of high-dimensional data. To avoid being trapped into the "dimensional disaster", an effective method is to reduce the dimensionality of high-dimensional data. As an important method of data preprocessing, dimensionality reduction technology has been extensively applied in many areas of machine learning [1], pattern recognition [2] and computer vision [3].

The dimensionality reduction algorithms use some mapping methods to map the data points in original high dimensional space to a low dimensional space. The essence of dimensionality reduction algorithm is to learn a mapping function $f : x \rightarrow y$, where x is the expression of the original data point, and the y is the expression of the low dimensional vector after the data points are mapped. According to whether f is linear or nonlinear, the existing dimensionality reduction methods can be divided into linear dimensionality reduction and nonlinear dimensionality reduction. The linear dimensionality reduction method assumes that the high-dimensional observation data lie in a

J. Ren et al. (Eds.): BICS 2019, LNAI 11691, pp. 128–138, 2020.
https://doi.org/10.1007/978-3-030-39431-8_13

low dimensional linear subspace. High-dimensional data can be mapped to a low-dimensional subspace by linear projection. Representative linear dimensionality reduction methods include Principal Component Analysis (PCA) [4], Linear Discriminant Analysis (LDA) [5], Independent Component Analysis (ICA) [6], Locality Preserving Projections (LPP) [7], Neighborhood Preserving Embedding (NPE) [8], Sparsity Preserving Projections (SPP) [9] and so on. Although linear dimensionality reduction method has an explicit projection function that is beneficial to solve out-of-sample problem, the linear assumption makes it may fail to discover the essential data structures that are nonlinear. In order to explicitly discover the nonlinear structure concealed in the data, many nonlinear dimensionality reduction algorithms have been proposed in the past decade years, such as Kernel Principal Component Analysis (KPCA) [10, 25], Kernel Linear Discriminant Analysis (KLDA) [11], Kernel Independent Component Analysis (KICA) [12], Locally Linear Embedding (LLE) [13], Hessian Locally Linear Embedding (HLLE) [14], Isometric Mapping (ISOMAP) [15], Maximum Variance Unfolding (MVU) [16]. However, most of existing nonlinear dimensionality reduction methods are sensitive to noise and usually cannot get the accurate projection function, which limit its practical application.

In this paper, motivated by the recent development and the extension in dimensionality reduction of Extreme Learning Machine (ELM) [17–19, 23, 24], we propose a nonlinear dimensionality reduction method with Extreme Learning Machine based on Manifold Preserving (MP-ELM). Specifically, the proposed algorithm takes both manifold structure and distance information into account, which can heighten dimensionality reduction effect and enhance noise immunity. Moreover, our method has explicit projection function, which is beneficial to solve out-of-sample problem.

The rest of the paper is organized as follows. Section 2 reviews the related work ELMs. The proposed MP-ELM algorithm is introduced in Sect. 3. Experimental results are given in Sect. 4. Finally, we provide some concluding remarks and future work in Sect. 5.

2 ELMs

ELM algorithm is essentially a single hidden layer feed forward neural networks (SLFNs) [20], its structure as shown in Fig. 1. Unlike traditional SLFNs that all the parameters of hidden neurons need to be tuned, ELM assigns all the parameters of the hidden nodes randomly without any iterative tuning, which are independent with each other. Hence ELM has fast learning speed and universal approximation capability. The training process of ELM mainly consists of two stages.

The first stage is to construct the network structure: a fixed number n_h of hidden neurons are randomly generated, which map the data from the input space into a. n_h-dimensional feature space. Thehidden node output for the input data point $x \in R^{d_0}$ is $h(x) = [h_1(x), h_2(x), \cdots h_{n_h}(x)]$, where $h_1(x)$ is the output of the i-th hidden node which is defined as follows:

$$h_i(x) = g(a_i, b_i, x), a_i \in R^{d_0}, b_i \in R \tag{1}$$

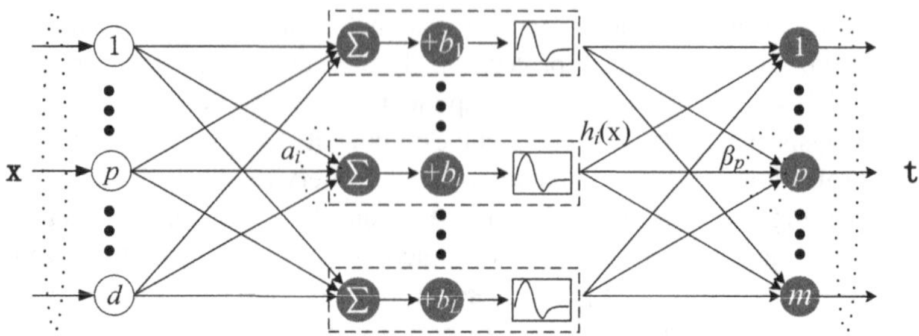

Fig. 1. ELM network structure

where $g(a_i, b_i, x)$ can be any nonlinear piecewise continuous functions, such as the Gaussian function (2) and Sigmoid function (3):

$$g(a_i, b_i, x) = exp(-b_i\|x - a_i\|) \tag{2}$$

$$g(a_i, b_i, x) = 1/\left(1 + exp\left(-a_i^T x + b_i\right)\right) \tag{3}$$

where a_i, b_i are the parameters of the mapping function which can be randomly generated, and the $\|\cdot\|$ denotes the Euclidean norm. For the whole data set X, the output of the hidden nodes is given by

$$H(X) = \begin{bmatrix} h(x_1) \\ \vdots \\ h(x_n) \end{bmatrix} = \begin{bmatrix} g(a_1, b_1, x_1) & \cdots & g(a_{n_h}, b_{n_h}, x_1) \\ \vdots & \ddots & \vdots \\ g(a_1, b_1, x_n) & \cdots & g(a_{n_h}, b_{n_h}, x_n) \end{bmatrix} \tag{4}$$

The network output of ELM is

$$Y = H(X)\beta \tag{5}$$

where $\beta = \left[\beta_{1,} \beta_{1,} \cdots, \beta_{n_h}\right]^T$ is the output weight matrix between the hidden nodes and the output nodes.

The second stage is to solve the output weights by minimizing the sum of the squared losses of the prediction errors, which leads to the following formulation:

$$\begin{gathered} min\frac{1}{2}\|\beta\|^2 + \frac{C}{2}\sum\nolimits_{i=1}^{n} \|e_i\|^2 \\ s.t. e_i^T = h(x_i)\beta - y_i^T \end{gathered} \tag{6}$$

where the first term in the objective function is a regularization term against over-fitting, the second term is the sum of error, and $e_i \in R^{n_1}$ is the error vector with respect to the i-th training pattern, and C is a penalty coefficient on the training errors.

Huang extend the ELM to unsupervised scenarios, propose an unsupervised ELM (US-ELM) base on the manifold regularization for clustering and dimensionality reduction as:

$$\begin{aligned} \min_{\beta}\|\beta\|^2 + \lambda tr\left(\beta^T H(X)^T LH(X)\beta\right) \\ s.t.(H(X)\beta^T H(X)\beta = I \end{aligned} \tag{7}$$

where $\boldsymbol{L}$ is the graph laplacian built from whole dataset. The second term is the manifold regularization, whose purpose is to make the output of the network preserve the manifold structure from the original data. When the dimension of network output is smaller than the dimension of input data, US-ELM is a nonlinear dimensionality reduction method.

3 Dimension Reduction of ELM Based on Manifold Preserving

In the US-ELM algorithm [19], the construction of Laplacian matrix L is very important, which directly affects the final result of dimension reduction. The US-ELM algorithm uses Gaussian distance to construct Laplacian matrix L, that is to say, it directly uses Gaussian distance to describe the manifold structure of data. However, with the increase of original data dimension, the classification performance of the distance measure between classes will be decreased. In this section, a new manifold distance measurement method is proposed, which combines Euclidean distance with geodesic distance, and is used to construct the Laplacian matrix L. That is, in the neighborhood of a sample, the ratio of geodesic distance to Euclidean distance is defined as the structural weight, the ratio of geodesic distance to median geodesic distance is defined as the distance weight, and the product of the structural weight and distance weight is used as the manifold structure distance weight, so that the information of manifold structure and distance can be combined organically [21]. On this basis, it is preferable to preserve the manifold structure of the original data into the new projection space.

The manifold neighbor weight of the sample x_i between the sample x_{ij} (x_{ij} is the jth neighbor of x_i) is defined as follows:

$$w_{ij}^S = E(x_i, x_{ij})/G(x_i, x_{ij}) \tag{8}$$

$$w_{ij}^D = exp[-G(x_i, x_{ij})/g_m] \tag{9}$$

$$w_{ij} = w_{ij}^S * w_{ij}^D \tag{10}$$

where $E(x_i, x_{ij})$ and $G(x_i, x_{ij})$ are Euclidean distances and geodesic distances between sample x_i and sample x_{ij} in its neighborhood respectively, g_m is the median of all geodesic distances in its neighborhood. In this paper, we use the classical Dijkstra algorithm to calculate geodesic distance, which is used in Isomap algorithm generally. By calculating formula (8), (9) and (10), the new manifold preserving neighbor weight matrix w_{ij} can be obtained. Then by repeating the above steps, the global manifold preserving neighbor weight matrix $W(W$ is an $n * n$ matrix) can be obtained.

For the distance weight w_{ij}^D, the g_m is fixed in its neighborhood. If a neighbor x_{ij} from the geodesic distance of the sample point x_i is farther, the $-G(x_i, x_{ij})/g_m$ is smaller, then the w_{ij}^D corresponding to the neighbor x_{ij} is smaller. This setting conforms to the theory that the neighbor is farther, the contribution to x_i reconstruction is smaller. The influence of noise on the weight can be reduced partly, by dividing the median g_m. The ratio of Euclidean distance $E(x_i, x_{ij})$ to geodetic distance $G(x_i, x_{ij})$ is used to measure the local neighborhood linearity of sample x_i. The more x deviates from the linear plane, the smaller the contribution of x_i is. The more the neighbor point x_{ij} deviates from the linear plane, the smaller the contribution of the neighbor point x_{ij} to reconstruct x_i is, then the structural weight w_{ij}^S of the nearest neighbor is smaller. Therefore, it can further emphasize the importance of the structure to the weight and improves the noise resistance.

We construct Laplacian Matrix

$$L_{MP} = D - W \tag{11}$$

where D is a diagonal matrix with its diagonal elements $D_{ii} = \sum_{j=1}^{N} w_{ij}$, W is the global manifold preserving neighbor weight matrix. Then, the objective function of the proposed MP-ELM algorithm is

$$\begin{gathered}\min_{\beta} \|\beta\|^2 + \lambda tr\left(\beta^T H(X)^T L_{MP} H(X)\beta\right) \\ s.t.(H(X)\beta^T H(X)\beta = I\end{gathered} \tag{12}$$

In order to obtain the optimal solution of output weight matrix β, Lagrange multiplier method is used to transform the objective function (12) as follow:

$$L(\beta) = tr\left(\beta^T \beta\right) + \frac{\lambda}{2} tr\left(\beta^T H(X)^T L_{MP} H(X)\beta\right) \varphi tr\left(\beta^T H(X)^T H(X)\beta - I\right) \tag{13}$$

Let $\frac{\partial L}{\partial \beta} = 0$, we can get

$$\left(I + \frac{\lambda}{2} H(X)^T L_{MP} H(X)\right)\beta = \varphi H(X)^T H(X)\beta \tag{14}$$

By calculating the generalized eigenvalue of (14), the minimum m eigenvalues and corresponding eigenvectors can be obtained to form the optimal output weight matrix β^*. When $n_h > n, H(X)^T H(X)$ has a higher dimension, which would consume more memory if we calculate the generalized eigenvalue of the formula (14) directly. For convenient application, let $\beta = H(X)^T \alpha$, and the both sides of the formula (14) is multiplied simultaneously $\left(H(X)H(X)^T\right)^{-1} H(X)$.

Then, we can get

$$\left(I + \frac{\lambda}{2} L_{MP} H(X) H(X)^T\right)\alpha = \varphi H(X) H(X)^T \alpha \tag{15}$$

Obviously, the formula (14) has the same eigenvalue as the formula (15). The solution matrix β^* and eigenvector matrix α^* have the following relationship

$$\beta^* = H(X)^T \alpha^* \tag{16}$$

Therefore, we can construct a matrix α^* from the corresponding eigenvectors of the minimum m eigenvalues by calculating the generalized eigenvalue of the formula (15). Then the solution matrix of the formula (14) can be obtained as $\beta^* = H(X)^T \alpha^*$. To sum up, MP-ELMalgorithm is summarized as follows.

Algorithms 1. MP-ELM algorithm

Input:the training data matrix $X \in R^{N \times n_i}$, parameter $\lambda \in \{10^{-4}, 10^{-3}, \cdots, 10^4\}$.

Output:the sample matrix $Y \in R^{N \times n_o} (n_o < n_i)$ after dimensionality reduction.

Step 1:Calculate the k-nearest neighbor graph.

Step 2:Calculate the global manifold neighbor matrix W by repeating the form the formula (8)-(10).

Step 3:Construct the Laplacian Matrix L_{MP} by the formula(11).

Step 4:Initialize ELM network. n_h is the number of hidden layer nodes. The input weight $a \in R^{n \times n_h}$ and the bias $b \in R^{nh}$ are randomly initialized, then the hidden layer output matrix $H(X) \in R^{n \times n_h}$ calculated according to the formula (4).

Step 5:When $n > n_h$, the output weight matrix β is calculated by the formula (14); otherwise, the output weight matrix $\beta = H(X)^T \alpha$ is calculated by the formula (15).

Step 6:Calculate the dimensionality reduction matrix:$Y = H(X)\beta$.

4 Experiments and Analysis

In order to verify the effectiveness of dimensionality reduction of MP-ELM algorithm, three experiments are carried out as follows: (1) The visualization experimentsof an artificialdata:reduce the original data dimension from 3 to 2; (2) The clustering experiment of real data: the original data are embedded from high-dimensional space to low-dimensional space for clustering. (3) The face recognition experiment: extract the low-dimensional features from the original high-dimensional face data for face recognition. All alorithms were implemented using MATLAB 2015b on a 3.4 GHz machine with 8 GB of memory.

4.1 Artificial Data Visualization Experiments

In this section, we use the classical manifold dataset Scurve as the visualization experiment data. 1000 data points were uniformly sampled from the three-dimensional

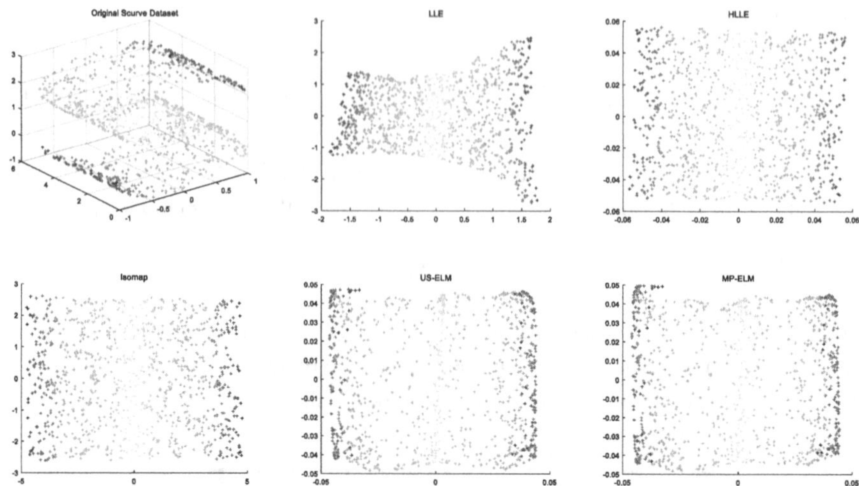

Fig. 2. Visualization experiment of the original Scurve data

Scurve as the test dataset of visualization experiments. Two experiments were conducted in order to evaluate the performance of the proposed MP-ELM algorithm: (1) the original data without noise; (2) the test data with Gaussian white noise. We compare it with that of relating algorithms, i.e. LLE, HLLE, Isomap, US-ELM. In the visualization experiments, the tradeoff parameters λ of US-ELM and MP-ELM were selected from the exponential sequence $\{10^{-4}, 10^{-3}, \cdots, 10^{4}\}$ based on the performances of visualization experiments.

Figure 2 shows the results of visualization experiment on the original Scurve data. We can observe that MP-ELM outperformed LLE significantly, and also outperformed

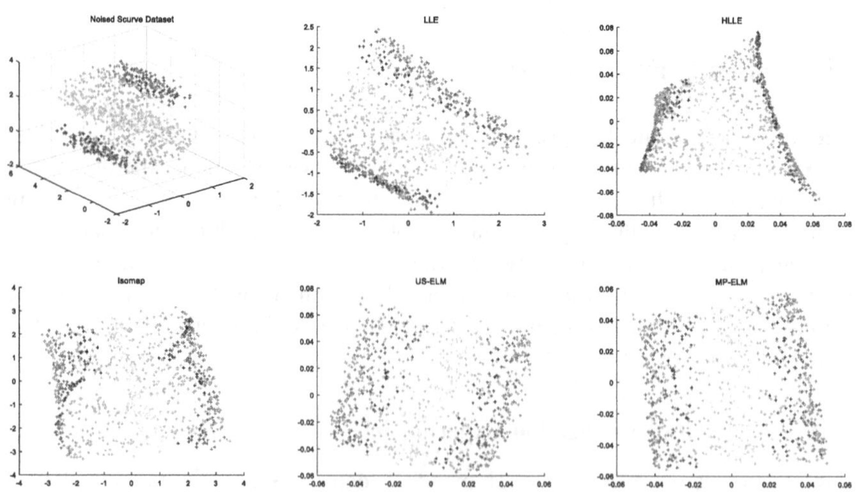

Fig. 3. Visualization experiment of the original Scurve data with Gaussian white noise

HLLE, Isomap and US-ELM. From the results of noised Scurve data in Fig. 3, we can observe that MP-ELM algorithms also achieved the best performance. Compared with the results of noise-free data in Fig. 2, the performance of Isomap and US-ELM have certain degradation, but the performance of LLE and HLLE algorithms were degraded greatly. Compared with other algorithms, the degradation degree of our algorithm is the smallest, which shows that our algorithm has excellent anti-noise ability.

4.2 Clustering Experiment on the IRIS Data Set

In this section, we test the feasibility of the proposed MP-ELM algorithm on the real-world IRIS data set and the clustering experiment results are shown in Table 1. The criterion for measuring clustering quality is the widely used Clustering Accuracy (ACC) [22] which as defined as

$$ACC = \frac{1}{n}\sum\nolimits_{i=1}^{n} \delta(y_i, map(c_i)) \quad (17)$$

where n is the number of training patterns, y_i and c_i are the true category label and the predicted cluster label of pattern x_i, respectively, $\delta(y_i, c)$ is a function that equals to 1 if $y = c$ or equals to 0 otherwise, $map(\cdot)$ is an optimal permutation function that maps each cluster label to a category label by the Hungarian algorithm. Three related algorithms, i.e., Isomap, LLE and US-ELM, are used for comparison. The tradeoff parameters λ of US-ELM and MP-ELMwere selected from the exponential sequence $\{10^{-4}, 10^{-3}, \cdots, 10^{4}\}$ based on the clustering performance.

In order to reduce the influence of randomness of the experiment, which caused by the random weights of US-ELM and MP-ELM methods and the random initial center selection of K-means, US-ELM and MP-ELM were run 10 times respectively, and then K-means clustering was performed 10 times on the dimension reduced data set each time. The average clustering accuracy of 100 times was taken as the final accuracy for US-ELM and MP-ELM methods, while the average of 10 times on K-means clustering accuracy for other dimension reduction methods. The average of clustering accuracy (variance, dimension) is given in the Table 1. In this table, the dimension number is the dimension corresponding to the optimal clustering result of each data set. The parameters corresponding to the optimal clustering results of US-ELM and the MP-ELM are listed in the table respectively. By comparing all the methods in Table 1, we can observe that MP-ELM outperformed US-ELM, and outperformed LLE and Isomap significantly.

Table 1. The average of clustering accuracy (%) on IRIS data set.

Data	Isomap	LLE	US-ELM (λ)	MP-ELM (λ)
IRIS	88.65	82.33	91.06	94.67
	(3.24, 3)	(6.82, 3)	(9.78, 3)	(8.92, 3)
			(0.1)	(1)

4.3 Face Data Recognition Experiment

Face recognition experiments on ORL face image and Yale face database are were conducted in this section. ORL Face Database is collected and organized by AT&T Laboratory of Cambridge University. There are 40 persons in total, each with 10 different 112 * 92 pixels face images. The images show the changes of different time, light, facial expression and facial ornaments. Yale Face database contains 15 persons, each with 11 different 243 * 320 pixels 165 gray-scale pictures. The images include different facial expressions or configurations: mid-light, glasses, happy, left-light, glasses-free, normal, right-light, sadness, sleepiness, surprise and blinking. Each face image database is divided into two groups as training set and testing set. 70%–80% of the images are selected as training set and the other images as testing set. Three related algorithms, i.e., Isomap, LLE and US-ELM, are used for comparison. The tradeoff parameters λ of US-ELM and MP-ELMwere selected from the exponential sequence $\left\{10^{-4}, 10^{-3}, \cdots, 10^{4}\right\}$ based on the performances of face recognition experiments.

Table 2. The maximum face recognition rates on ORL and Yale data sets.

Data type	Algorithm	Maximum recognition rate (%)	Neighbor value (k)	Dimensional reduction (d)
ORL	Isomap	90.46	14	85
	LLE	85.5	15	90
	US-ELM	92.67	12	95
	MP-ELM	94.33	12	95
Yale	Isomap	86.67	16	88
	LLE	80	18	88
	US-ELM	93	10	90
	MP-ELM	95.67	10	90

The best recognition rate and corresponding parameters of each algorithm are listed in Table 2. It can be clearly seen from Table 2 that our algorithm achieves the highest recognition accuracy (ORL 94.33 and Yale 95.67). The results of our algorithm are 8.83–15.67% points higher than the worst results (LLE, ORL 85.5 and Yale 80). MP-ELM algorithm is at least 1.66 percentage points higher than the second best result (US-ELM, ORL 92.67).

5 Conclusion

In this paper, we have proposed a nonlinear dimensionality reduction method with Extreme Learning Machine based on Manifold Preserving called MP-ELM, to extend the traditional ELMs for dimensionality reduction tasks. Compared to existing non-linear dimensionality reduction algorithms, the proposed MP-ELM can preserve manifold structure of data in the process of dimensionality reduction and get the accurate projection function. Experimental results demonstrate that MP-ELM gives favorable performance and noise immunity compared to the other related algorithms. In the future, we will extend our method to supervised and semi-supervised scenarios.

Acknowledgement. This work was partly supported by National Natural Science Foundation of China (61772144, 61672008), Innovation Team Project of the Education Department of Guangdong Province (2017KCXTD021), Foundation for Youth Innova-tion Talents in Higher Education of Guangdong Province (2018KQNCX139), Project for Distinctive Innovation of Ordinary Universities of Guangdong Province (2018KTSCX120).

References

1. Rosten, E., Drummond, T.: Machine learning for high-speed corner detection. In: Leonardis, A., Bischof, H., Pinz, A. (eds.) ECCV 2006. LNCS, vol. 3951, pp. 430–443. Springer, Heidelberg (2006). https://doi.org/10.1007/11744023_34
2. Qin, H., Tang, S.: A solution to dimensionality curse of BP network in pattern recognition based on RS theory. In: International Joint Conference on Computational Sciences and Optimization, Sanya (2009)
3. Wright, J., Ma, Y., Mairal, J., Sapiro, G., Huang, T.S., Yan, S.: Sparse representation for computer vision and pattern recognition. Proc. IEEE **98**(6), 1031–1044 (2010)
4. Huasheng, H., Aqing, Y.: Face recognition based on PCA. Electron. Sci. Technol. **28**(8), 98–101 (2015)
5. Altman, E.I., Marco, G., Varetto, F.: Corporate distress diagnosis: comparisons using linear discriminant analysis and neural networks (the Italian experience). J. Bank. Financ. **18**(3), 505–529 (1994)
6. Lacerda, G., Spirtes, P.L., Ramsey, J., et al.: Discovering Cyclic Causal Models by Independent Components Analysis. Grace: Uncertainty in Artificial Intelligence (2012)
7. He, X.F., Niyogi, P.: Locality preserving projections. Adv. Neural. Inf. Process. Syst. **16**(3), 153–160 (2004)
8. He, X.F., Cai, D., Yan, S., Zhang, H.J.: Neighborhood preserving embedding. In: Proceedings of the International Conference on Computer Vision, Bejing, China, pp. 1–6. IEEE (2005)
9. Qiao, L.S., Chen, S.C., Tan, X.Y.: Sparsity preserving projections with application to face recognition. Pattern Recognit. **43**(1), 331–341 (2010)
10. Alzate, C., Suykens, J.A.K.: Multiway spectral clustering with out-of-sample extensions through weighted kernel PCA. IEEE Trans. Pattern Anal. Mach. Intell. **32**(2), 335–347 (2010)
11. Mika, S., Ratsch, G., Weston, J., et al.: Fisher discriminant analysis with kernels. In: Proceedings of the Neural Networks for Signal Processing, pp. 41–48. IEEE Press(1999)
12. Jordan, M.L., Bach, F.R.: Kernel independent component analysis. J. Mach. Learn. Res. **3** (1), 1–48 (2002)
13. Roweis, S.T., Saul, K.L., Tan, X.Y.: Nonlinear dimensionality reduction by locally linear embedding. Science **290**(22), 2323–2326 (2010)
14. Donoho, D.L., Grimes, C.: Hessian eigenmaps: locally linear embedding techniques for high dimensional data. Proc. Natl. Acad. Sci. U. S. A. **100**(10), 5591–5596 (2003)
15. Balasubramanian, M., Schwartz, E.L.: The isomap algorithm and topological stability. Science **295**(5552), 7 (2002)

16. Weinberger, K.Q., Saul, L.K.: Unsupervised learning of image manifolds by semidefinite programming. In: IEEE Conference on Computer Vision and Pattern Recognition, vol. 2, pp. 988–995 (2004)
17. Huang, G.B., Ding, X., Zhou, H., Roweis, S.T., Saul, K.L., Tan, X.Y.: Optimization method based extreme learning machine for classification. Neurocomputing **74**, 155–163 (2010)
18. Peng, Y., Wang, S.H., Long, X.Z., Lu, B.L.: Discriminative graph regularized extreme learning machine and its application to face recognition. Neurocomputing **149**, 340–353 (2015)
19. Huang, G., Song, S., Jatinder, N.D., Cheng, W.: Semi-supervised and unsupervised extreme learning machines. IEEE Trans. Cybern. **44**(12), 2405–2417 (2014)
20. Kasun, L.L.C., Yang, Y., Huang, G.B., Zhnag, Z.Y.: Dimension reduction with extreme learning machine. IEEE Trans. Image Process. **25**(8), 3906–3918 (2016)
21. Liu, F.Y., Xia, K.W., Niu, W.J.: Improved reconstruction weight-based locally linear embedding algorithm. J. Image Graph. **23**(1), 0052–0060 (2018)
22. Wei-Wei, W., Xiao-Ping, L., Xiang-Chu, F., Si-Qi, W.: A survey on sparse subspace clustering. Acta Autom. Sin. **41**(8), 1373–1384 (2015)
23. Cao, F., Yang, Z., Ren, J., Chen, W., Han, G., Shen, Y.: Local block multilayer sparse extreme learning machine for effective feature extraction and classification of hyperspectral images. IEEE Trans. Geosci. Remote Sens. **57**, 5580–5594 (2019)
24. Cao, F., et al.: Sparse representation-based augmented multinomial logistic extreme learning machine with weighted composite features for spectral-spatial classification of hyperspectral images. IEEE Trans. Geosci. Remote Sens. **56**(11), 6263–6279 (2018)
25. Zabalza, J., et al.: Novel folded-PCA for improved feature extraction and data reduction with hyperspectral imaging and SAR in remote sensing. ISPRS J. Photogramm. Remote Sens. **93**, 112–122 (2014)

Quantifying the Effect of Cognitive Bias on Security Decision-Making for Authentication Methods

Tahani Albalawi(✉), Kambiz Ghazinour(✉), and Austin Melton(✉)

Department of Computer Science, Kent State University, Kent, USA
{talbalal,kghazino,amelton}@kent.edu

Abstract. The main challenge that can impact the effectiveness of authentication mechanisms is human error (unintentional threats). Irrational judgment associated with human error is often linked to a unique attribute called cognitive bias (CB). CB is a tendency to think irrationally in certain situations and make irrational judgment. The appearance of CB in human decisions is considered one of the implications of system usability. In the security filed, usability is recognized as one of the main issues that affect an individual's security decisions. Clearly, security decision-making is a result of three overlapping factors: security, usability and CB. In this paper, we quantify security decision making by providing a holistic view on how these factors affect the security decision. For this purpose, an experiment was conducted involving 54 participants who performed multiple security tasks related to authentication. An eye-tracking machine was used to record cognitive measurements that were used for decision analysis. Multi Criteria Decision Analysis (MCDA) approach was then used to evaluate the participants' decisions. The result showed that participants security decisions are varied depends on the authentication method. For instance, picture type was the authentication method least influenced by CB. Low system usability is one of the major causes of CB in decisions. This was not the case for the picture password method. The different levels of usability associated with the picture method resulted in low impact of CB on participants' security decision. This finding point to investigating how picture-based authentication methods are capable of handling the issue of the CB.

Keywords: Security · Usability · Human error · Decision · Authentication · MCDM · Cognitive bias

1 Introduction

Generally, the term *error* in the security domain refers to the situation when there is a violation of security requirements in the user's decision. However, people sometimes make an irrational judgment even without violating security requirements. In this case, the term *human error* is used. For instance, even though security requirements of generating passwords impose rules to maintain security, people continue to choose weak passwords (e.g. Abc123*). Weak passwords are not only easy to be detected by computers, but they can also by guessed by humans.

J. Ren et al. (Eds.): BICS 2019, LNAI 11691, pp. 139–154, 2020.
https://doi.org/10.1007/978-3-030-39431-8_14

The classical view of human error is characterized by a negative evaluation of erroneous behavior that must be avoided [1]. In the literature, many attempts were reported to identify and classify human causes of error [2–4]. Although there is no one strict definition of human error, most attempts to define it have agreed that it involves some degree of deviation. The irrational judgment (or human error) is often linked to a unique attribute of human behavior called a cognitive bias (CB). CBs are tendencies to think irrationally in certain situations and make an irrational judgment. The recognition of CB dates back to the early 1970s when psychologists Kahneman and Tversky demonstrated that there is a gap between how humans should make a decision and how they actually make a decision. They used the term *cognitive bias* to describe any human error that results from irrational judgment [5].

Kahneman and Tversky indicated some aspects that might be responsible for the manifestation of CB. For example, taking shortcuts in information-processing, emotional and moral motivations and cognitive limitations related to processing capacity and memory cognitive load (CL). Most of these aspects include the element of usability as an influencing element. For instance, information-processing shortcuts are a result of processing complicated information. To make a decision, people have to process information and when this involves a large amount of information or complicated data people usually use simple rules called heuristics. These heuristics are usually based on people's experiences. Using simple rules will result in fast decision making but not necessary a perfect decision or judgment. Similarly, the CL aspect is affected by usability. The CL reflects the level of mental effort used to process the information. High level CL indicates that there is difficulty in processing the information considered one of the implications of usability.

On the other hand, in the security filed, usability is known as of the key issues that affect an individual's security decision. The mismatch between security and usability goals contributes to making inappropriate security-related decisions. Security goals include confidentiality, integrity, and availability, all of which provide protection of data and resources. Meanwhile, usability goals concentrate on user preferences, such as effectiveness, efficiency, and satisfaction.

Clearly, we can see that the security decision-making is a result of three overlapping factors: security, usability and CB. In this paper, we present an attempt to quantify security decision making by using TOPSIS technique to offer a holistic view on how much these factors affect the security decision. This will assist individuals in their security decision process, promoting more effective security and encouraging security designers to consider the human factor in the early stages of the design cycle for more robust security policies. For this purpose, an experiment was conducted involving 54 participants who performed multiple security tasks. The security tasks were related to authentication. The goal was to explore which of the authentication methods was more capable of handling CB in a user's security decision making. To our knowledge, this is the first study that compares different authentication methods for CB (unintentional threats). An eye-tracking machine was used to record cognitive measurements that were used for decision analysis. Since the process of security decision is a result of prioritizing different factors (security and usability) to reach a certain decision, the proposed model was based on Multi Criteria Decision Analysis (MCDA) approach [6].

In this approach, different formal methods are used to analyze decisions that involve different or contradicting factors.

This paper is organized as follows; Section Two present the concept of CB and how it arises; Section Three presents authentication approaches and security evaluation. Section Four presents the approach of MCDA and some aggregation techniques used for the purpose of evaluation. Section Five present methodology of the experiment, the design, results and discussion. Finally, Section Six is the conclusion

2 What Is Cognitive Bias and How It Arises

CB has been proposed to understand the failures in human decision-making and judgment. Kahneman and Tversky discovery of CBs contradicted with the widely-believed assumption stating that human decision-making is a rational process based on logical and rational analysis. They demonstrated that human decision-making sometimes deviates from rationality due to many limitations related to the nature of the human approach to processing information. They called this phenomenon "Cognitive Bias" and defined it as "a pattern of deviation in judgment that occurs in particular situations, leading to perceptual distortion, inaccurate judgment, illogical interpretation, or what is broadly called irrationality" [5]. Extensive research in human psychology and cognitive biases outlined that human reasoning is best described as a list of biases and heuristics that refer to discrepancies between what decisions people should make and how they actually form those decisions [7]. It is difficult to distinguish which steps in the cognitive process can cause bias and there is no single explanation for this behavior. However, there are various processes that can contribute to the occurrence of bias in human decision-making. These are as follows:

(a) Information-processing shortcuts (heuristics) [8]: For System 1 reasoning, in order to manage and process a large amount of information simultaneously as well as effectively, a set of simple and efficient rules are performed to make certain decisions. In psychology, these rules are called heuristics, which are considered as mental shortcuts commonly focusing on one part of a complex problem while ignoring the other parts. The goal of heuristics is to simplify cognitive processes, speed up the response and make a decision quickly, especially when the decision is required in a short amount of time. Although individuals utilize heuristics to facilitate their decision-making process, the outcome of the decision might not lead to correct or optimal decision-making, but rather one that is just adequate and saves effort, or worse, leading to irrational decision-making.

(b) Cognitive limitation related to processing capacity and memory [9]: Human memory is part of the cognitive faculties that process information. Working memory (WM) is the main part of memory responsible for processing information, including the reasoning process. However, it is the most vulnerable type of memory as it is easily exposed to overload. Overload happens when the WM processes too much or too complex information (or both) at the same time. This leads to maximizing overload mental effort. This vulnerability is known as the *Cognitive Load Theory* (CLT). The resulting decision might deviate from rationality and can lead to cognitive biases in the decision-making.

(c) Emotional and moral motivations [10]: Recent research has shown that human emotions stimulate biases in the individual's decision-making [23]. They influence ability to process information in the correct way. Since feelings and emotional responses are linked to System 1 thinking in a fundamental way, it is not uncommon that System 1 limitations could influence an individual's decision-making leading to bias.

3 Authentication Types and Security Evaluation

Authentication approaches can be classified into three types according to the distinct characteristics they use [11]: (a) what the individual knows: knowledge-based authentication (KBA) e.g. passwords, PINs and pass codes, (b) what the individual has: smart cards, key fobs, USB tokens etc. and (c) what the individual is: biometric characteristics e.g. fingerprints and eyeprint. Since CB is related to knowledge processes, knowledge-based authentication is the most suitable approach to use in this study. KBA can be classified into two major categories. First, alphanumeric passwords, which are widely used. One of the main security challenges is how to create a complex alphanumeric password that improves system security without causing usability problems. Second, graphical password techniques that have been developed to enhance the security of alphanumeric authentication. Graphical passwords have emerged as potential alternatives to alphanumeric passwords. This is supported by evidence as psychologists have shown that images can be more memorable than words or sentences.

Existing graphical password techniques can be further categorized into [12]: (a) recall-based: the individual is asked to recall and reproduce a drawing with the mouse or stylus on a blank canvas or on a grid, (b) recognition-based: the individual should recognize all of the preselected pass-images from a portfolio of images during authentication and (c) cued-recall: cued-recall systems usually provide a background image and require the user to remember and target specific locations on the image. The image acts as a memory cue to reduce the memory load on users.

In the literature, various security studies were conducted to evaluate the 'guessability' of passwords for different authentication methods. Evaluation was based on the degree of intentional threat, e.g. dictionary attack, pattern recognition attack etc. Three authentication methods were selected in our experiments: alphanumeric, grid pattern (recognition-based) and picture password (cued-recall). The question of which is safer of these methods remains. Some researchers argue that alphanumeric passwords are the safest because, for instance, if you have a five-character password (i.e. 90 different character possibilities using a US English keyboard), then, this will require 90×90 $90 \times 90 \times 90 = 5{,}904{,}900{,}000$ attempts to guess the correct password. For grid pattern based passwords, since the user has to start with one of the nine points, the neighboring point has to be chosen next. Thus, $9 \times 8 \times 7 \times 6 \times 5 = 15{,}120$ permutations are required to find the correct pattern. Which is a fraction of the number of attempts a text password requires. For a picture password, all possible combinations must be exhausted on the picture. That is about 2^{30} passwords to try (i.e. over billion attempts), which is four times the number of attempts required for a 5-character password.

From the previous account, the security ranking of password guessability for the selected authentication methods that were used in this study is as follows, ranked from the most to the least effective: (picture password > text password > grid pattern password). However, the focus of this paper is on unintentional threat that results from CB. We would like to evaluate these authentication methods based on their capability of handling CB in users' security decision making. The evaluation model is derived from Multi Criteria Decision Analysis (MCDA) approach. The next Section introduces this approach.

4 Multiple-Criteria Decision Making (MCDM)

MCDM is a prescriptive decision tool to structure the decision-making processes and to assist in finding the optimal choice between conflicting goals, e.g. security and usability goals. In this analysis, different possibilities are reviewed and compared. The most distinguished character of the MCDM techniques is the ability to combine the performance of decision alternatives across several types of criteria, e.g. contradicting, qualitative or quantitative, to reach a compromise solution. While comparing different type of measurements for the set of criteria is a fundamental step in the MCDM process, the normalization of different measurements is performed in the initial steps of any MCDM technique. The MCDM structures complex decisions into clear and insightful results or outcomes that can be easily justified. It considers diverse and possibly conflicting criteria. The importance of the different criteria is considered and alternatives are reviewed when all materials are put together and analyzed, and finally advice can be generated. The MCDM process consists of four working principle steps. The next section introduces these steps.

4.1 MCDM Steps

First step, selection of criteria: deals with the formalizing and grouping the different criteria. In the decision-making context, the criterion considers some sort of standard for judgment. It makes one particular choice or course of action judged more desirable than another. The set of criteria represents a list of factors that matter for the final decision. Second step is the selection of alternatives: the alternatives represent the different types of possible solutions for the decision problem. Third step is weighing selection: when there is a multiple number of standards (criteria), the choice or course of action will not be simple, especially when such standards are in conflict to a substantial extent. Each standard (criterion) has a level of effect on the final decision. Therefore, the set of standard criteria has to be weighted to reflect the level of importance of each criterion. The forth step is the aggregation methods to represent importance: this step will separate the best alternative from the available options. This could be a set of mathematical models. Once the scores have been standardized and the weights have been ascribed, a ranking of alternatives can be generated by using aggregation methods. Methods used for MCDM include: Analytic hierarchy process

(AHP), ELECTRE (Outranking), Multi-attribute utility theory (MAUT) and Technique for Order of Prioritisation by Similarity to Ideal Solution (TOPSIS). In this paper, the last model (TOPSIS) was used to evaluate the security decision in our experiment. The following section explain this method.

4.2 TOPSIS Technique

TOPSIS technique is built based on the distance principle. It is assumed that there is an ideal and a non-ideal solution for each decision for a problem. The basic rule of TOPSIS is that it calculates the distance between the alternatives, the ideal and non-ideal solution, and the best alternative choice for the decision is the one that has the "shortest distance" from the positive ideal solution and the "farthest distance" from the negative ideal solution. The final output for the TOPSIS technique is a sorted list of alternatives based on their closeness to the ideal solution. The following are the steps of the TOPSIS technique [13]:

First: normalization of the decision matrix. This is done to transform various attribute dimensions into non-dimensional attributes, allowing for comparisons across different criteria.

Second: constructing the weighted matrix. Each criterion in the MCDA is associated with a weight that determines the importance of that criterion among the other criteria. The different weights directly influence the MCDA procedure. Thus, these weights must be employed in any MCDA technique. Each column of the normalized decision matrix is multiplied by its associated weight, $\boldsymbol{w_j}$.

$$v_{ij} = n_{ij}\, w_j \tag{1}$$

Third: determination of the ideal solution and the negative ideal solution. This is done by distinguishing between the best and worst attribute lists using Eqs. (2) and (3), respectively:

$$\{v_1^+, v_2^+, \ldots v_n^+\} = \{(\max v_{ij} \mid \in k)(\min v_{ij} \mid \in k'|)\}\ i = 1, 2, \ldots m \tag{2}$$

$$\{v_1^-, v_2^-, \ldots v_n^-\} = \{(\max v_{ij} \mid \in k)(\min v_{ij} \mid \in k'|)\}\ i = 1, 2, \ldots m \tag{3}$$

Where $\boldsymbol{k}$ is the index set of the best criteria and $\boldsymbol{k'}$ is the index set of the worst criteria.

Forth: calculation of the distance between the alternative and ideal solutions. This is accomplished by using the following Euclidean distance equation:

$$s_i^+ = \left\{\sum\nolimits_{j=1}^{n} x\left(v_{ij} - v_j^+\right)^2\right\} \mathrm{j} = 1, 2, \ldots \mathrm{n}; \quad \mathrm{i} = 1, 2, \ldots, \mathrm{m} \tag{4}$$

Similarly, the distance is calculated between the alternatives and the negative ideal solution.

Fifth: calculation of the relative closeness to the ideal solution. This is done by using the following equation:

$$Ci = \frac{s_i^-}{s_i^+ + s_i^-} = i = 1, 2, \ldots m; \quad 0 \leq Ci \leq 1 \tag{5}$$

$\boldsymbol{C_i} = 1$, if and only if the alternative solution has the best condition; and $\boldsymbol{C_i} = 0$, if and only if the alternative solution has the worst condition. The higher values of $\boldsymbol{C_i}$ mean that the rank is better. Thus, the final step in TOPSIS method means with ranking the alternatives according to $\boldsymbol{C_i}$.

5 Evaluation Methodology

5.1 Experiment Overview

An experiment was conducted to quantify the effect of CB on security decision-making. A number of 54 participants (28 male, 24 females and 2 other) were invited to register for a game based website using one of the authentication methods in order to play a game. All actions were recorded using an eye tracker to capture measurements related to cognitive processes and to observe the participants' behavior. At the end of the experiment, participants were asked to fill a short survey that included questions used to measure security and usability criteria.

Participants were divided into groups for three sections. The security task in each section was to register on the website with a username and a password. The registration method in each section involved one of the following authentication mechanisms: (a) alphanumeric based password; (b) grid pattern based and (c) picture password. Further, within each section participants were assigned randomly to one of the following conditions: (a) Low: representing low cognitive load which implies fewer password complexity rules (more usable) and (b) High: representing high cognitive load which implies more passwords complexity rules (less usable). The level of cognitive load here indicates the level of difficulty. It is clear that a higher level of CL is often related to increased difficulty in processing the information. The difficulty of the authentication problem is linked to password requirements and rules. Thus, the level of the condition (low, high) is manipulated by altering the requirements of the authentication model. For instance, participants in the TextL model had no constrains in choosing the password. While, participants in the TextH model had high requirement, e.g. a minimum of 10 characters' length and at least one lower case character, one capital letter, one number and one special character. Thus, in the end, the total number of groups was six, each represented an authentication model as follow: Group 1 (TextL model): participants used an alphanumeric based password with a low condition, Group 2 (TextH model): participants used an alphanumeric based password with a high condition. Similarly Group 3, Group 4, Group 5, and Group 6 for (Grid model) and (PicH model).

Since using more password complexity rules implies lower password vulnerability and more secure passwords, the security evaluation for authentication models in this study can be ranked as follows: PicH > PicL > TextH > TextL > GridH > GridL.

5.2 Observations

The CBs in the participants' decision were accounted for in the analysis when two or more participants had security behavior. In other words, when two participants chose the same password or similar passwords that followed the same pattern, this considers as bias. For instance, "Adam123*" and "Sam135*" are considered as similar passwords that follow one pattern (first letter is capital followed by a number and a special character in the end). Previous research has shown that there are preferred patterns used by many people when choosing alphanumeric passwords [14]. This bias increases password guessability. Table 1 shows the list of observations and the number of CB patterns in each group. The frequency represents the total number of all CBs that participants exhibited in their security decisions. For instance, in the Text authentication group with high cognitive load (TextH), the total number of CB types was 5 as follows: 7 participants used the uppercase letter in the beginning of the selected password, 6 participants used the concept of simple passphrases in their passwords, 4 participants included their first name in the password, 3 participants used an arranged number and 8 participants placed the symbol requirement at the end of the password. Thus, the frequency of CB in this group was 28. Note that it is possible for a participant to have more than one CB in his/her decision, e.g. a participant could include a capital letter in the beginning and add a symbol at the end of the chosen password.

5.3 Using MCDA to Quantify Security Decision-Making in the Authentication

First Step: Selection of Criteria

Selecting the set of criteria in the authentication problem was somewhat complex due to human and other errors. One of the main issues to address when selecting the criteria was finding appropriate measurement standards for human error in the security evaluation. Since CB in security decision is mainly connected to security and usability, the evaluation standards were required to involve factors related to these aspects. Doing so in the quantification process provides an idea about which authentication method is most capable of providing the desired balance between the contradictory factors of security and usability.

A number of existing studies proposed evaluation that involved several criteria to assess security and usability in a system [12, 15, 16]. However, these evaluation studies suffered from several issues such as: (a) inability to deal with human error: most of the security and usability evaluations were focused primarily on malicious intent of threat (not from legitimate users), neglecting the threats that result from human error which have non-malicious intent; (b) the use of limited criteria measurements: careful attention should be given to the selection of a suitable number of criteria. A limited number of criteria can affect the overall evaluation. Because each criterion in the MCDM reflects the importance of each part of the evaluated system, the inclusiveness of the list of criteria is important to mitigate the vulnerability caused by neglecting the evaluation of each part of the system; and (c) the focus of these evaluations tended to lean more towards either security or usability.

Table 1. Cognitive Bias observation list

Group	Type of CB	Frequency
TextL	– Simple passphrases (3) – Include first name (4) – Include arranged number, e.g. 123 or 987 (2)	9
TextH	– Capital letter in the beginning (7) – Simple passphrases (6) – Include or derive first name (4) – Include arranged number (3) – Symbol at the end (8)	28
GridL	– Start from the upper left (5) – Start from the upper middle (2) – Stay at the border (6)	13
GridH	– Start from the upper left (4) – Start from the bottom left (2) – Start from the upper right (2) – Spiral pattern (2) – Cross pattern (3) – Letter shape (Z, U, S) (3) – Stay at the border (2)	16
PicL	– Building border (2) – Long building, circle shape (3) – Inner building, cross shape (2)	7
PicH	– The pattern includes square, triangle and circle shapes (3) – Include only circles (4)	7

In 2010, Kainda et al. [17] managed to address the problem of criteria selection by developing a security threat model that included a balance between security and usability to evaluate the system based on non-malicious threat. Thus, the selection of authentication criteria was derived from the highlighted study. The MCDM process for the authentication problem defined two sets of criteria: usability and security. The following section presents each set with its measurement.

(a) Usability criteria

- *Effectiveness:* This refers to the ability of the individual to achieve the intended goals. The goal here is the registration task, where participants were asked to create a password in order to login to the website. The task completion rate was measured using the following equation:

$$\frac{number\ of\ tasks\ completed\ successfully}{total\ number\ of\ tasks\ undertaken} \times 100 \quad (6)$$

Where a successful attempt occurred when the number of errors equaled 0 when creating a password. In other words, this refers to a successful attempt when performing the task for the first time.

- Efficiency: The goal (the registration task) needed to be achieved within an acceptable amount of time and with minimal effort. This was measured in terms of task time as follows:

$$Efficiency = \frac{\sum_{j=1}^{R}\sum_{i=0}^{N}\frac{n_{ij}}{t_{ij}}}{NR} \quad (7)$$

Where
N = the total number of tasks
R = the number of users
n_{ij} = the result of task i by user j; if the user successfully completed the task, then n_{ij} = 1, if not, then n_{ij} = 0
t_{ij} = The time spent by user j to complete task i, if the task was not successfully completed, then time was measured until the user quit the task.

- *Satisfaction:* This refers to user satisfaction about the registration method. This was measured through standardized satisfaction questionnaires, such as post-task questionnaires. In this study, SEQ (Single Ease Question) type was used in the experiment survey. In the survey, the participants were asked to rate (on a 7-point scale) their satisfaction about the registration method.
- *Accuracy*: This refers to the success rate of performing the registration task. This can be calculated as:

$$Accuracy = \frac{1}{number\ of\ all\ attempt} \times 100 \quad (8)$$

- Memorability: This criterion was measured simply by calculating the duration time of the attempt to recall the password in the second phase of the experiment.
- *Knowledge/skill:* This refers to the learnability aspect, i.e. how easy it is to learn to use a system. It can be measured by using post-task questionnaires. In this study, SEQ type was used where participants were asked how easy it was for them to learn the method of authentication. The participants rated their response on a 7-point scale.

(b) Security criteria

- *Attention:* This is the ability to focus and to maintain interest in a given task or idea while avoiding distractions [18]. Since attention is considered a cognitive process, it can be tracked and measured by using an eye-tracking tool. When the visual gaze was constant on a single location, the occurrence of distraction in that moment was non-existent. Thus, the eye tracker recorded this location as an AOI (Area of Interest), calling this situation as a fixation point.

- *Vigilance:* This is the process of paying close and continuous attention. The expectation for security systems is for individuals to proactively assess the state of the security before using a system or software. However, the reality is different, as an individual can be easily distracted. Similar to the attention criterion, vigilance is also considered a cognitive process. Its measurement depends on both attention and task duration, as shown in the equation:

$$\text{Vigilance} = \frac{\textit{number of fixation points}}{\textit{task duration}} \tag{9}$$

- *Motivation:* This refers to which concept that motivated an individual to make a security decision. In other words, whether the choice of the password by the participant was made to be more usable, e.g. easy to remember, or because it is more secure. This criterion was measured by a focused question that required selecting one choice from two provided answers. Participants were asked why they chose their selection (password or pattern), where the provided choices were (a) more secure or (b) more usable (coded as 1 and 0, respectively, for data analysis, where the higher the value, the more secure the choice). The obvious expectation of individuals for password selection was for security reasons, usability reasons, or both. However, this experiment desired to more precisely identify the main dormant motivation for the participants. Even if the participants' choice was "both", the security and usability remained uneven as a motivation. Normally, one must dominate the other. For this reason, the choice of "both" was intentionally omitted in this portion of questions.
- *Social context:* This refers to the social aspects of human beings that influences their actions, such as sharing a password among family members, or sharing a software digital certificate in a joint project. This criterion was also measured by using a scenario-based question in the survey. Participants were asked the following question: "If you want to retrieve an extremely important email and you do not have internet connection would you" and the choices to answer this question were: (a) call your (close friend/relative/someone you trust) and give (her/him) your email and password to retrieve the information for you, or (b) wait until you have internet connection. The options were encoded as 0 and 1, respectively. The lower the value, the more secure the chosen act or behavior.
- *Conditioning:* This refers to the tendency of the individual to repeat the security task due to a reliance on a previous or an expected outcome. For example, when choosing a password, many users tended to not read the password requirements or instructions, which sometimes led to errors when performing the security task "choosing a password". This would inevitably end with the participant repeating the process of the task. In this experiment, the conditioning criterion was measured by counting how many repetitive errors resulted from ignoring the authentication rules and requirements.

Second Step the Selection of Alternatives
The alternatives of the authentication problem included three types of authentication techniques (alphanumeric, grid and picture). Each had two models. The models were different, depending on the amount of CL associated with each authentication type. Therefore, each group in our experiment represented an alternative as follows: TextL, TextH, GridL, GridH, PicL and PicH.

Third Step: Selection of Weights. The importance of different criteria in MCDA are represented with different weights. Different weights will directly influence the choice of the best alternative from the others. Thus, different weight methods were evaluated from the literature. The importance of each criterion can be evaluated from the point of view of the decision maker. Weight methods included subjective weighting, i.e. direct assignment of weights to each criterion; pairwise comparison using a rating scale; or swing weighting, which assigns weights to attributes based on a rank-order.

Subjective weighting and pairwise comparisons require the involvement of the decision maker from the beginning before making the decision, while the swing weighting method offers more flexibility since it can be used to extract implicit weights and assign them a rank-order. Therefore, because the intention of this study was to measure the participants' decision-making after the decision had been made, the swing weighting method was used using the following formula:

$$w(xi) = \frac{n - rank(xi) + 1}{n + 1} \tag{10}$$

Where:

n = number of criteria
xi = criterion value
$rank(xi)$: the rank of the criterion xi
$w(xi)$: the weight of the criterion xi

Table 2. Weighted normalized decision matrix

	Attention	Vigilance	Condition-ing	Motiva-tion	Social context	Memora-bility	Skill/ knowledge	Effective-ness	Efficiency	Satisfac-tion	Accuracy
TextL	0.0313	0.0268	0.0000	0.0295	0.0350	0.0402	0.0363	0.0107	0.0067	0.0363	0.0312
TextH	0.0322	0.0287	0.0130	0.0290	0.0353	0.1073	0.0359	0.0054	0.0041	0.0341	0.0270
GridL	0.0325	0.0271	0.0069	0.0296	0.0342	0.0685	0.0355	0.0064	0.0028	0.0359	0.0297
GridH	0.0338	0.0300	0.0000	0.0292	0.0342	0.0700	0.0349	0.0071	0.0032	0.0353	0.0272
PicL	0.0275	0.0259	0.0069	0.0302	0.0342	0.0209	0.0355	0.0053	0.0036	0.0359	0.0271
PicH	0.0337	0.0284	0.0135	0.0289	0.0341	0.0954	0.0360	0.0085	0.0029	0.0362	0.0275

Forth Step: Aggregation Methods to Represent Importance
In this paper, the TOPSIS method was used to find the relative closeness of each alternative authentication model with an ideal solution and to finalize the rank of each alternative model. The first step was the normalization of the decision matrix. The vector method was used for normalization. Second, each column in the normalized decision matrix was multiplied by the associated weights, w_j, of the authentication

criteria by using Eq. 1. Table 2 shows the weighted normalized decision matrix. The third step was determination of the ideal solution and the negative ideal solution. TOPSIS distinguishes two types of attribute lists: (a) best list (s_i^+), which includes attributes that have a positive impact and need to be maximized to achieve the best solution; and (b) worst list (s_i^-), which includes attributes that have a negative impact and need to be minimized. The best list related to the authentication problem includes the following criteria: Attention, Vigilance, Skill/Knowledge, Effectiveness, Efficiency, Satisfaction, and Accuracy. The worst list includes the following criteria: Conditioning, Motivation, Social Context, and Memorability.

The fourth step was to calculate the distance between the alternative, id{\displaystyle i}Ieal, and negative solutions using Euclidean distances in Formula 4. Table 3 shows s_i^+, s_i^- and *Ci*. The fifth step involved calculating the relative closeness to the ideal solution. Using Formula 5, the relative closeness to the ideal solution was calculated as shown in Table 4, where the higher values of *Ci* means that the rank is better.

Table 3. The ideal solutions and the negative ideal solutions

Model	s_i^+	s_i^-	*Ci*
TextL	0.0672	0.0254	0.2741
TextH	0.0140	0.0866	0.8612
GridL	0.0280	0.0486	0.6346
GridH	0.0379	0.0516	0.5769
PicL	0.0873	0.0071	0.0747
PicH	0.0190	0.0749	0.7976

Table 4. TOPSIS Rank for model

Model	*Ci* Rank
TextL	5
TextH	1
GridL	3
GridH	4
PicL	6
PicH	2

5.4 Results and Analysis

By using the TOPSIS technique, the participants' security decision was quantified based on their preferences. The authentication models were ranked based on their relative closeness to the ideal solution. The security and usability factors were both considered in the evaluation. Figure 1 shows the authentication model ranks based on TOPSIS, security-only evaluation and rank of the authentication models based on the number of CBs that appeared in their security decision.

The models least affected by participants' CBs were the picture password methods. Both models that used picture passwords (PicL, PicH) had an equal number of CBs. In addition, picture passwords achieved the highest rank in the security evaluation (first and second ranks). In terms of TOPSIS evaluation, the PicL model using picture passwords was the model that best handled the security and usability factors followed by TextL model based on text passwords. Hence, the security rank of the PicL model was higher than that of the TextL and the CBs were lower in the PicL method. Low usability systems represent a major cause of CB in security decisions. Figure 1 shows this is not the case in the picture password type of method. The different levels of system usability (in term of CL level) associated with the picture method resulted in the same number of CBs and low CB impact on participants' security decisions compared to other authentication types. This finding points to investigating how the picture method is capable of handling the issue of human error.

The design of the picture method followed nudge strategies. Participants' passwords were generated without requiring the participant to fully understand their security choices. Nudge is considered as an influential behavioral intervention tailored to the password choice. It is used to guide individuals to make better choices without awareness of the consequences [19]. "An intervention can only be considered a nudge if individuals are able easily to resist its influence [20]". Nudges are of use in relation to authentication because the goal is to promote best practice in password creation. Nevertheless, this may not be an issue for authentication if the motivation is to promote optimal decisions at the moment of password creation. Some researches argue that when people create their passwords they tend to do this without due thought by engaging their basic cognitive level rather than using sophisticated thought processes. Sunstein [21] explains that nudges can have an impact when associated with educational efforts to encourage the individual and motivate them into thinking at an advanced and more engaged level. This can allow individuals to create better passwords. Jeske et al. [22] experimented with nudging users to select the most secure network from a set. The authors concluded that nudging was effective, however personal differences among users had an impact on their security decisions.

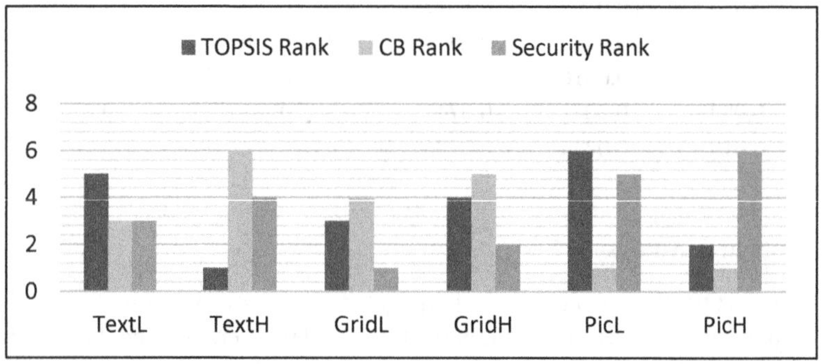

Fig. 1. TOPSIS, CB and Security ranks of the authentication models

6 Conclusion

The main challenges that impact the performance and effectiveness of authentication mechanisms is human error (i.e. unintentional threats). People sometimes make irrational judgment even without violating security requirements. The irrational judgment (human error) is often linked to a unique attribute of human behavior called cognitive bias (CB). The usability of the system is the main factor that contributes to CB in decisions. Security decision-making is a result of three overlapping factors: security, usability and CB. This paper uses the MCDM approach to quantify the effect of cognitive biases on security decision-making in authentication methods. For the purpose of evaluation, an experiment was conducted involving 54 participants who performed multiple security tasks related to authentication. Three different types of KBA authentication approach were used (text, grid and picture). The goal was to explore which of the authentications' methods was more capable of handling CB in user's security decision making. The result showed that the picture method was the authentication method least influenced by CB. Low system usability is one of the major causes of CB in decisions. This was not the case for the picture password method. The different levels of usability associated with the picture method resulted in low impact of CB on participants' security decision. This finding point to investigating how picture-based authentication methods are capable of handling the issue of the CB.

References

1. Edwards, W.: Conservatism in human information processing (excerpted). In: Kahneman, D., Slovic, P., Tversky, A. (eds.) Judgment Under Uncertainty: Heuristics and Biases. Cambridge University Press, New York (1982). ISBN 978-0521284141. Original work published 1968
2. Senders, J.W., Moray, N.P.: Human Error: Cause, Prediction, and Reduction, p. 25. Lawrence Erlbaum Associates, Mahwah (1991)
3. Health and Safety Executive. http://www.hse.gov.uk/humanfactors/topics/humanfail.htm
4. Reason, J.: Human Error. Cambridge University Press, Cambridge [England] (1990)
5. Kahneman, D., Tversky, A.: Subjective probability: a judgment of representativeness. Cogn. Psychol. **3**(3), 430–454 (1972)
6. Belton, V., Stewart, T.: Multiple Criteria Decision Analysis: An Integrated Approach. Springer, Boston (2002). https://doi.org/10.1007/978-1-4615-1495-4
7. Birnbaum, M.H., Mellers, B.A.: Bayesian inference: combining base rates with opinions of sources who vary in credibility. J. Pers. Soc. Psychol. **45**(4), 792 (1983)
8. Kahneman, D., Slovic, P., Tversky, A.: Judgment Under Uncertainty: Heuristics and Biases, 1st edn. Cambridge University Press, Cambridge (1982)
9. Simon, H.A.: A behavioral model of rational choice. Q. J. Economics. **69**(1), 99–118 (1955). https://doi.org/10.2307/1884852
10. Staggers, N.; Norcio, A.F.: Mental models: concepts for human-computer interaction research (1993)
11. Erlich, Z., Zviran, M.: Authentication practices from passwords to biometrics. In: Encyclopedia of Information Science and Technology, 3rd edn, pp. 4248–4257. IGI Global (2015)
12. Gao, H., et al.: Usability and security of the recall-based graphical password schemes. In: 2013 IEEE 10th International Conference on. High Performance Computing and Communications & 2013 IEEE International Conference on Embedded and Ubiquitous Computing (HPCC_EUC). IEEE (2013)
13. Shanian, A., Savadogo, O.: TOPSIS multiple-criteria decision support analysis for material selection of metallic bipolar plates for polymer electrolyte fuel cell. J. Power Sources **159**, 1095–1104 (2006)
14. Uellenbeck, S., et al.: Quantifying the security of graphical passwords: the case of android unlock patterns. In: Proceedings of the 2013 ACM SIGSAC Conference on Computer & Communications Security. ACM (2013)

15. Florêncio, D., Herley, C.: A large-scale study of web password habits. In: Proceedings of the 16th International Conference on World Wide Web, Banff, Alberta, Canada, pp. 657–666. ACM Press (2007)
16. Wiedenbeck, S., et al.: Authentication using graphical passwords: effects of tolerance and image choice. In: Proceedings of the 2005 Symposium on Usable Privacy and Security. ACM (2005)
17. Kainda, R., Flechais, I., Roscoe, A.W.: Security and usability: analysis and evaluation. In: 2010 International Conference on Availability, Reliability, and Security, ARES 2010. IEEE (2010)
18. Anderson, J.R.: Cognitive Psychology and Its Implications, 6th edn, p. 519. Worth Publishers, New York City (2004)
19. Oliver, A.: Is nudge an effective public health strategy to tackle obesity? Yes. Br. Med. J. **342**, d2168 (2011)
20. Thaler, R.H., Sunstein, C.R.: Nudge: Improving Decisions About Health, Wealth, and Happiness. Yale University Press, New Haven (2008)
21. Sunstein, C.R.: Nudges do not undermine human agency. J. Consum. Policy **38**(3), 207–210 (2015)
22. Jeske, D., Coventry, L., Briggs, P., van Moorsel, A.: Nudging whom how: it proficiency, impulse control and secure behaviour. In: Personalizing Behavior Change Technologies CHI Workshop, Toronto, 27 April 2014. ACM (2014)
23. Kahneman, D.: Thinking, Fast and Slow. Farrar, Straus and Giroux, New York (2011)

Pixel-Wise Segmentation of SAR Imagery Using Encoder-Decoder Network and Fully-Connected CRF

Fei Gao[1], Yishan He[1(✉)], Jun Wang[1], Fei Ma[1(✉)], Erfu Yang[2], and Amir Hussain[3]

[1] Beihang University, Beijing 100191, China
hys1009hys@126.com, mafeimf@buaa.edu.cn
[2] University of Strathclyde, Glasgow G1 1XJ, UK
[3] Cognitive Big Data and Cyber-Informatics (CogBID) Laboratory, Edinburgh Napier University, Edinburgh EH10 5DT, UK

Abstract. Synthetic Aperture Radar (SAR) image segmentation is an important step in SAR image interpretation. Common Patch-based methods treat all the pixels within the patch as a single category and do not take the label consistency between neighbor patches into consideration, which makes the segmentation results less accurate. In this paper, we use an encoder-decoder network to conduct pixel-wise segmentation. Then, in order to make full use of the contextual information between patches, we use fully-connected conditional random field to optimize the combined probability map output from encoder-decoder network. The testing results on our SAR data set shows that our method can effectively maintain contextual information of pixels and achieve better segmentation results.

Keywords: SAR image segmentation · Encoder-decoder network · Fully-connected CRF

1 Introduction

Synthetic Aperture Radar (SAR) is an advanced instrument for earth observation and is widely used in various areas of the country's economy and defense construction [1, 2, 16]. SAR image segmentation plays an important role in SAR image interpretation [3] and it is a prerequisite for many further applications. For example, in the task of assessing crop coverage, different types of crops need to be segmented first [4] and areas with oil slick need to be first segmented when detecting slick on the sea surface [5].

The segmentation of SAR image means categorizing SAR image pixel by pixel, meanwhile maintaining the spatial structure of different regions. Patch-based methods are commonly used in recent research. These methods mainly compose of three steps: (1) divide the whole SAR image into patches; (2) extract the feature of each patch for classification; (3) combine the classification results of patches into segmentation results. For example, Geng [6] proposed a deep convolutional autoencoders (DCAE) to extract and optimize patch features. DCAE consists of a feature extractor, an average

J. Ren et al. (Eds.): BICS 2019, LNAI 11691, pp. 155–165, 2020.
https://doi.org/10.1007/978-3-030-39431-8_15

pooling layer, and sparse autocoders. The feature extractor extracts gray-level cooccurrence matrix (GLCM) and Gabor features from images patches. The pooling layer conducts scale transformation. And the sparse autocoders are used for feature optimization. In [7], the author uses the pretrained Alexnet to extract patch features. K-means clustering is then applied for visual word encoding. Finally, a Naive Bayesian classifier is adopted to classify the coded patches. In [8], a hierarchically adversarial network is introduced to extract features of superpixels. Duan [9] integrates dual-tree complex wavelet transform into convolutional neural network as a hidden layer to improve the feature extraction ability of the network. Inspired by biological vision system, Gao [10] presents a hierarchical method for river detection, where biologically visual saliency modeling is used to extract superpixels' features. However, a common drawback exists in these patch-based methods. Although the patch is relatively small, it may still contain different categories of pixels. The accuracy of segmentation results will be reduced if treating the whole patch as a single category.

One way to overcome the above disadvantage is to adopt pixel-wise segmentation methods. In the field of optical image segmentation, pixel-based methods are mainstream. In these methods, the original image is fed as input of specially designed convolutional neural network. The feature extraction process is automatically accomplished through hidden layers. And the pixel-wise segmentation result is obtained from the output of the network. For example, Long [11] proposes a fully convolutional network (FCN) for semantic segmentation of optical images. By replacing the fully-connected layer with convolution layer, the input image size of FCN can be arbitrary. The pixel-wise segmentation results are acquired directly from the output of FCN. In [12], the author proposes a U-shaped convolutional neural network, called Unet. Unet first downsamples the input image to small feature maps and then upsamples them to pixel-wise segmentation results. It achieves good performance in biomedical image segmentation. Segnet [13] is a fully convolution network with encoder-decoder structure. It is initially used to deal with the semantic segmentation tasks of driverless vehicles or intelligent robots. The structure of its encoder and decoder is symmetrical. To make the segmentation result more accurate, the spatial information saved by the downsampling layer of encoder is then utilized in the upsampling layers of the decoder. In this way, more accurate segmentation result can be achieved by Segnet and it runs faster as well. The pixel-based method in optical image segmentation includes mainly two benefits. The first is that it is an end-to-end model that makes full use of the strong feature extraction ability of convolutional neural network. The second is that it can directly output pixel-level segmentation results, which makes the segmentation result more accurate. However, for high-resolution SAR images, the computational cost is unacceptable if we directly take the whole SAR image as an input. In order to address this problem, we can first divide the SAR images into patches and get the pixel-level segmentation results of patches through the network. Final segmentation results can be obtained by combining them together. But in this way, the spatial relationships between patches is neglected, which makes the segmentation results of neighbor patches not consistent enough.

Conditional random field (CRF) is a discriminative model based on undirected graph. It can naturally combine the feature information of image patches and contextual information between patches to model the posterior probability of labels. The traditional CRF model used in SAR image segmentation is based on patches. For example, in order to effectively integrate contextual prior into segmentation process, Chu [14] combines CRF with Bayesian network to optimize the over-segmented SAR images. However, patch-based CRF is not suitable for the pixel-wise segmentation in this paper. In [15], a pixel-wise CRF called fully-connected CRF with gaussian edge potentials is proposed. In addition to taking pixel-wise features into consideration, this model can integrate the spatial relationship among all pixels to optimize the segmentation result. Besides, an optimization algorithm is also proposed to make inference of pixel-wise CRF feasible.

For the above reasons, in this paper, we first divide the original SAR image into patches so as to reduce the computational complexity. Then we choose Segnet to conduct pixel-level segmentation on the patches. In order to further utilize the contextual information between patches and improve the neighborhood label consistency, we use fully-connected CRF to optimize the whole combined segmentation map.

The segmentation results of our approach show that we can obtain more accurate segmentation results within patches by using Segnet and achieve better neighborhood label consistency among different patches by adopting fully-connected CRF.

2 Proposed Method

The flow diagram of our segmentation method is shown in Fig. 1. In our approach, the original SAR image is first cropped into small image patches. Then these patches are fed into the encoder-decoder network, i.e. Segnet, to obtain patch-wise probability maps, which show the probability that each pixel belongs to different categories within the patches. The combined probability map, together with the grayscale and position features of the original SAR image pixels, are fed into fully-connected CRF for optimization. Final segmentation results can be obtained after several iteration steps using fully-connected CRF.

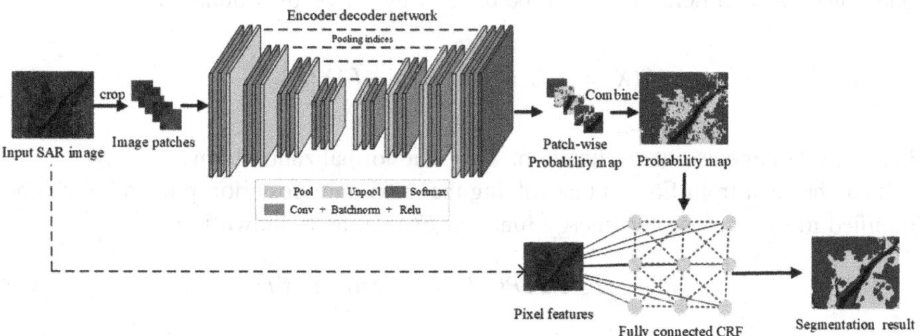

Fig. 1. The flow diagram of our method

2.1 Encoder-Decoder Network for Pixel-Wise Segmentation

For pixel-wise segmentation network, we use Segnet proposed in [13], which achieves pixel-wise segmentation through end-to-end training. The network can be divided into two parts: encoder and decoder. The specific structure of these two parts is shown in Fig. 2. The encoder structure includes the first 13 convolution layers in VGG16. Five pooling layers is adopted to reduce the size of the feature maps. The structure of the decoder is symmetrical to the encoder, which consists of five upsampling layers and 13 convolution layers. The upsampling layer utilizes the position information stored during pooling. In this way, the spatial relationship can be maintained when upsamping the feature maps to the original size. Besides, the number of the training parameters are greatly reduced. The feature maps are sparse after upsampling, so trainable convolution layers are adopted to generate dense feature maps. The output of the decoder is fed into the softmax classifier to obtain the category probability of each pixel.

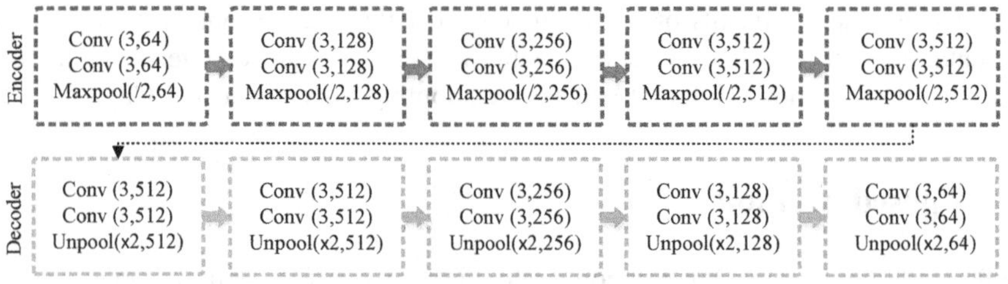

Fig. 2. The structure of encoder and decoder used in Segnet, the first item in bracket means kernel size, the second item in bracket means output dimension.

2.2 Fully-Connected CRF for Posteriori Probability Optimization

Random field **I** is a set of random variables $\{I_1, I_2, \cdots, I_N\}$, which represents a high resolution the SAR image. I_i represents the feature vector of pixel i. Random field **X** is a set of random variables $\{X_1, X_2, \cdots, X_N\}$, X_i representing the label of pixel i. Conditional random field $(\mathbf{I}, \mathbf{X})$ can be defined by Gibbs distribution as:

$$P(X = x|I) = \frac{1}{Z(I)}\exp(-E(X|I)) \tag{1}$$

where $E(X|I)$ denotes energy function, $Z(I)$ is a normalization term.

It can be seen from Eq. (1) that solving the maximum posteriori probability can be simplified to minimizing the energy function $E(X|I)$, as is shown in (2).

$$x^* = \arg\max_x P(x|I) = \arg\min_x E(x|I) \tag{2}$$

The energy function is composed of unary term ψ_u and pairwise term ψ_p:

$$E(x) = \sum\nolimits_i \psi_u(x) + \sum\nolimits_{i \neq j} \psi_p(x_i, x_j) \tag{3}$$

For fully-connected CRF, the output probability map by Segnet can be used for unary term ψ_u. And the pairwise term ψ_p considers the relationship between each pixel and all other pixels, which can be describe by (4).

$$\psi_p(x_i, x_j) = \mu(x_i, x_j) \underbrace{\sum\nolimits_{m=1}^{K} \omega^{(m)} k^{(m)}(\mathbf{f}_i, \mathbf{f}_j)}_{k(\mathbf{f}_i, \mathbf{f}_j)} \tag{4}$$

where μ denotes label compatibility function, $\omega^{(m)}$ is the weight coefficient and $k(\mathbf{f}_i, \mathbf{f}_j)$ indicates two-kernel potentials, which is shown in (5).

$$k(\mathbf{f}_i, \mathbf{f}_j) = \omega^{(1)} \exp\left(-\frac{|p_i - p_j|^2}{2\theta_\alpha^2} - \frac{|g_i - g_j|^2}{2\theta_\beta^2} \right) + \omega^{(m)} \exp\left(-\frac{|p_i - p_j|^2}{2\theta_\gamma^2} \right) \tag{5}$$

where p_i and p_j denotes the position of pixel i and pixel j, g_i and g_j denotes the grayscale value of the pixels in SAR image. θ_α and θ_β control the degree of nearness and similarity, θ_γ controls the degree of smoothness. These parameters are not trainable in our experiment.

According to mean field approximation theory, the problem of estimating the maximum posteriori probability can be transformed into minimizing the K-L divergence of a distribution function $Q(x)$ and the probability function $P(x)$ by iteration. The iteration process is as follows:

$$Q_i(x_i = l) = \frac{1}{Z_i} \exp\left\{ -\psi_u(x_i) - \sum_{l' \in L} \mu(l, l') \sum_{m=1}^{K} \omega^{(m)} \sum_{j \neq i} k^{(m)}(\mathbf{f}_i, \mathbf{f}_j) Q_j(l') \right\} \tag{6}$$

3 Experiment

3.1 Experiment Data

The SAR data set for experiment includes 36 airborne SAR images, which were acquired in Fangchenggang, Guangxi, China. These images cover an area of about 30 km × 30 km in total. The size of each image is 1419 × 1122 and the resolution is 2 m. For training and testing, we labeled all the images manually according to Google Map, categorizing the area into four classes: urban, farmland, river and background.

For the purpose of comparison, 7 of all 36 SAR images were selected as training set and the rest 29 SAR images belong to test set in all experiments. Several SAR images and corresponding ground truth in the training set are shown in Fig. 3 It can be seen that although the distribution of different regions in high resolution images is not uniform, each category of regions is relatively concentrated. It reflects the neighborhood consistency of SAR images.

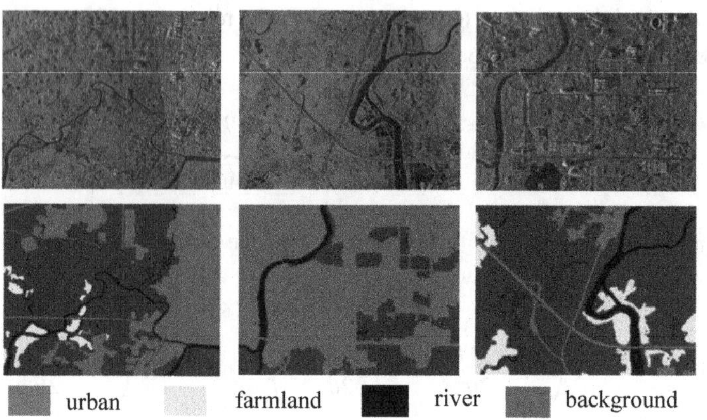

Fig. 3. Several SAR images and corresponding ground truth from our dataset

3.2 Evaluation Metrics

In our experiment, we choose four pixel-wise metrics, including overall accuracy (OA), overall precision (OP), f1-score and kappa coefficient to quantitatively evaluate the performance of segmentation methods. These metrics are calculated according to (7)–(10). Our experiment platform is configured with 32 G memory, Intel (R) Xeon (R) CPU L5639 @ 2.13 GHz * 1, and one Tesla K20c GPU.

$$OA = \sum_{i=1}^{c} x_{ii}/N \tag{7}$$

where x_{ii} denotes the diagonal elements of the confusion matrix, N stands for the total number of pixels of SAR image and c represents the number of the categories.

$$OP = (\sum_{i=1}^{c} \alpha_i x_{ii})/N \tag{8}$$

where $\alpha_i = \sum_{j=1}^{c} x_{ji} / \sum_{j=1}^{c} x_{ij}$, x_{ij} is the element in the i_{th} row and j_{th} column of the confusion matrix.

$$\text{f1-score} = \frac{2 \cdot \text{precision} \times \text{recall}}{\text{precision} + \text{recall}} \tag{9}$$

$$\kappa = \frac{p_0 - p_e}{1 - p_e} \tag{10}$$

where $p_0 = OA$, $p_e = \sum_{i=1}^{c} \gamma_i / N$, $\gamma_i = \sum_{j=1}^{c} x_{ji} \times \sum_{j=1}^{c} x_{ij}$.

3.3 Experiment Settings

We conduct three experiments for comparison, finetune Alexnet [7], deep convolutional autoencoder (DCAE) [6], and Segnet without fully-connected CRF.

In the Alexnet model, the convolution and pooling layers of Alexnet pretrained on Imagenet dataset are used as feature extractor, which outputs 256-dimensional features. These features are then fed into a fully-connected network with a hidden layer for classification. During training, the parameters of convolution and pooling layers are fixed and the parameters of the full connection layer are updated by backward propagation algorithm. The loss function used in this model is mean square error function; learning rate is set to 1e−4; batch size is set to 330; the number of epochs is 40; the weight decay coefficient is 0.0005. As suggested in [7], the patches are cropped with the size of 21*21 and the step of 10.

In DCAE model, GLCM and Gabor features are first extracted using convolutional kernels. Average pooling is then employed for scale transformation and Principal Component Analysis (PCA) is used to reduce the computational cost. Two cascaded autoencoders are then utilized to optimize these features. The training of the autoencoders is conduct through greedy layer-wise strategy. Finally, a fully-connected layer with the softmax activation function is used to classify the optimized features. Mean square error function is used as loss function; the learning rate is set to 1e−4; batch size is set to 330; the number of epochs is set to 40; the weight decay coefficient is 1e-8 and the patch size is 32*32 with a step of 16.

The Segnet model is introduced in Sect. 2. For hyperparameters, we adopt mean square error function as the loss function; the learning rate is set to 0.01; batch size is set to 300; the training epochs is set to 50; the weight decay coefficient is 1e−8 and patch size is 32*32.

3.4 Experiment Result

In this part, we will quantitatively compare our method with the aforementioned methods, i.e. Segnet, DCAE and Alexnet. Table 1 lists the segmentation results of these methods on test set. As is shown in Table 1, the segmentation results of Segnet combined with fully-connected CRF is better than other methods in OA, OP, f1-score and kappa, reaching 86.36, 86.54, 85.69, 0.7187 respectively. And the segmentation result of Segnet is better than DCAE and Alexnet. The results suggest that Segnet is capable of making more accurate prediction within patches. Fully-connected CRF makes further improvement thanks to its ability of utilizing contextual information.

In order to further compare the segmentation performance of different methods in different categories, Table 2 gives the f1-score in different categories achieved by each method. We can see from the table that fully-connected CRF greatly improves the segmentation result in different categories, especially in farmland and urban areas.

Table 1. The overall performance metrics for each method

Metrics	Segnet-full CRF	Segnet	DCAE	Alexnet
OA	**86.36**	81.86	81.09	78.32
OP	**86.54**	83.02	82.66	78.09
f1-score	**85.69**	81.98	80.99	76.56
κ	**0.7187**	0.6233	0.6076	0.5289

Figures 4 and 5 visually illustrate the segmentation results of the methods on two SAR images in the test set. It is shown in Fig. 4 that the segmentation result of Segnet is better than other patch-based methods. After further optimization by fully-connected CRF, the label consistency of farmland and river areas is strengthened and the edges between different categories of areas are preserved. It proves that the contextual information between patches is effectively utilized by fully-connected CRF.

Table 2. f1-score in different categories

Category	Segnet-full CRF	Segnet	DCAE	Alexnet
Urban	**66.62**	56.69	61.63	45.79
Farmland	**80.71**	61.45	43.25	25.12
River	**79.84**	75.00	76.20	70.15
Background	**90.50**	87.80	86.98	80.69

The segmentation results shown in Fig. 5 clearly indicate that the label consistency of farmland area is enhanced and the edges of river and farmland become smoother after optimization by fully-connected CRF. In addition, many misclassified pixels in the river and background area are corrected after optimization. It verifies that fully-connected CRF model is capable of jointly utilizing the gray feature of pixels and the contextual information so that better segmentation can be achieved.

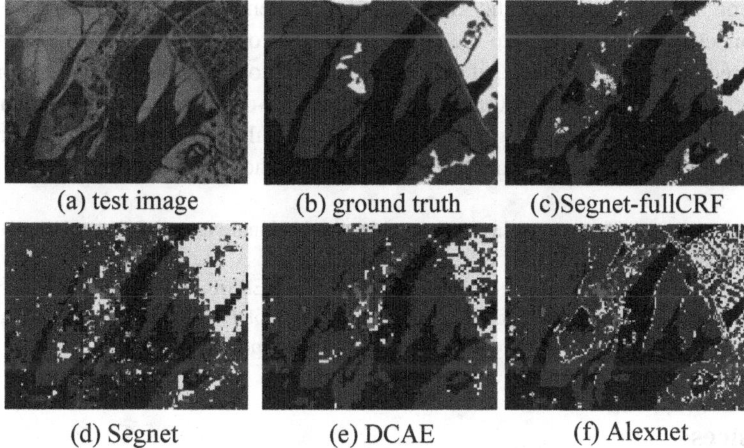

Fig. 4. The segmentation results of each model (a) Input SAR image (b) Ground truth. (c) Segnet-full CRF (OA = 86.36) (d) Segnet (OA = 81.86) (e) DCAE (OA = 81.09) (f) Alexnet (OA = 78.32)

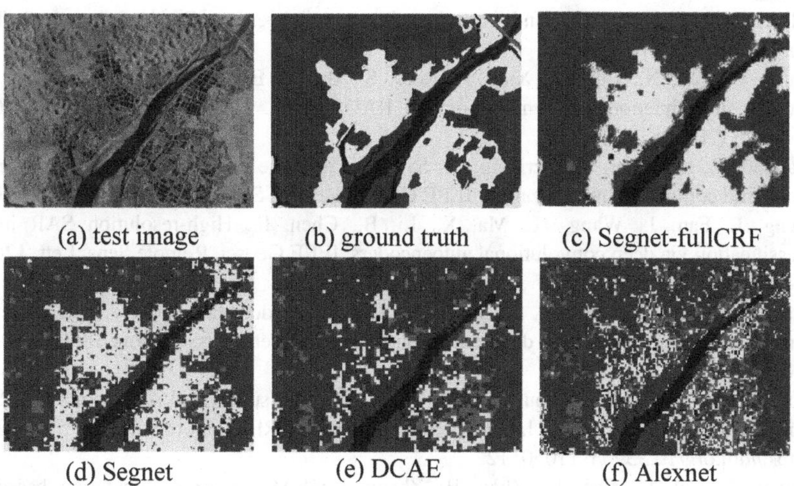

Fig. 5. The segmentation results of each model (a) Input SAR image. (b) Ground truth. (c) Segnet-full CRF. (d) Segnet. (e) DCAE. (f) Alexnet

4 Conclusion

In this paper, we combine the encoder-decoder network used in optical image segmentation with fully-connected CRF for high resolution SAR image segmentation. To improve the segmentation accuracy within the patch, we use Segnet to obtain pixel-wise segmentation result of the patches. In order to make full use of contextual information and strengthen neighborhood label consistency between patches, we adopt fully-connected CRF to optimize the probability maps output by Segnet. This method is compared with several other patch-based segmentation methods in our experiment. The experiment result demonstrates that the encoder-decoder network has superior performance in SAR image segmentation, and that fully-connected CRF effectively utilizes contextual information and greatly optimizes the segmentation results.

Acknowledgements. This research was funded by the National Natural Science Foundation of China, grant nos. 61771027, 61071139, 61671035. Professor A. Hussain was supported by the UK Engineering and Physical Sciences Research Council (EPSRC) grant no. EP/M026981/1. The SAR images used in the experiments are the courtesy of Beijing Institute of Radio Measurement, the authors would like to thank them for their support in this work.

References

1. Gao, F., Huang, T., Wang, J., Sun, J., Hussain, A., Yang, E.: Dual-branch deep convolution neural network for polarimetric SAR image classification. Appl. Sci. **7**(5), 447–460 (2017)
2. Fei, G., Zhenyu, Y., Jun, W., Jinping, S., Erfu, Y., Huiyu, Z.: A novel active semisupervised convolutional neural network algorithm for SAR image recognition. Comput. Intell. Neurosci. **14**(7), 1–8 (2017)
3. Oliver, C., Quegan, S.: Understanding Synthetic Aperture Radar Images. SciTech Publishing, Chennai (2004)
4. Shao, Y., Fan, X., Liu, H., Xiao, J., Ross, S., Brisco, B., et al.: Rice monitoring and production estimation using multitemporal RADARSAT. Remote Sens. Environ. **76**(3), 310–325 (2001)
5. Galland, F., Réfrégier, P., Germain, O.: Synthetic aperture radar oil spill segmentation by stochastic complexity minimization. IEEE Geosci. Remote Sens. Lett. **1**(4), 295–299 (2004)
6. Geng, J., Fan, J., Wang, H., Ma, X., Li, B., Chen, F.: High-resolution SAR image classification via deep convolutional autoencoders. IEEE Geosci. Remote Sens. Lett. **12**(11), 1–5 (2015)
7. Tian, T., Chang, L., Jinkang, X., Jiayi, M.: Urban area detection in very high resolution remote sensing images using deep convolutional neural networks. Sensors **18**(3), 904–910 (2018)
8. Ma, F., Gao, F., Sun, J., Zhou, H., Hussain, A.: Weakly supervised segmentation of SAR imagery using superpixel and hierarchically adversarial CRF. Remote Sens. **11**, 512 (2019). https://doi.org/10.3390/rs11050512
9. Duan, Y., Liu, F., Jiao, L., Zhao, P., Zhang, L.: SAR Image segmentation based on convolutional-wavelet neural network and Markov random field. Pattern Recogn. **64**, 255–267 (2017). https://doi.org/10.1016/j.patcog.2016.11.015
10. Gao, F., Ma, F., Wang, J., Sun, J., Zhou, H.: Visual saliency modeling for river detection in high-resolution SAR imagery. IEEE Access **6**, 1000–1014 (2017)
11. Long, J., Shelhamer, E., Darrell, T.: Fully convolutional networks for semantic segmentation. IEEE Trans. Pattern Anal. Mach. Intell. **39**(4), 640–651 (2014)
12. Ronneberger, O., Fischer, P., Brox, T.: U-Net: convolutional networks for biomedical image segmentation. In: Navab, N., Hornegger, J., Wells, W.M., Frangi, A.F. (eds.) MICCAI 2015. LNCS, vol. 9351, pp. 234–241. Springer, Cham (2015). https://doi.org/10.1007/978-3-319-24574-4_28

13. Badrinarayanan, V., Kendall, A., Cipolla, R.: Segnet: a deep convolutional encoder-decoder architecture for image segmentation (2015)
14. Chu, H., Xinlong, L., Di, F., Bo, S., Bin, L., Mingsheng, L.: Hierarchical terrain classification based on multilayer Bayesian network and conditional random field. Remote Sens. **9**(1), 96–108 (2017)
15. Krähenbühl, P., Koltun, V.: Efficient inference in fully-connected CRFs with Gaussian edge potentials. Paper Presented at the Advances in Neural Information Processing Systems (2011)
16. Zabalza, J., et al.: Novel folded-PCA for improved feature extraction and data reduction with hyperspectral imaging and SAR in remote sensing. ISPRS J. Photogramm. Remote Sens. **93**, 112–122 (2014)

Biologically Inspired Systems

Gabor Based Lipreading with a New Audiovisual Mandarin Corpus

Yan Xu, Yuexuan Li, and Andrew Abel(✉)

Research Institute of Big Data Analytics (RIBDA), Xi'an Jiaotong-Liverpool University, Suzhou 215123, China
{Yan.Xu,Andrew.Abel}@xjtlu.edu.cn, Yuexuan.Li15@student.xjtlu.edu.cn

Abstract. Human speech processing is a multimodal and cognitive activity, with visual information playing a role. Many lipreading systems use English speech data, however, Chinese is the most spoken language in the world and is of increasing interest, as well as the development of lightweight feature extraction to improve learning time. This paper presents an improved character-level Gabor-based lip reading system, using visual information for feature extraction and speech classification. We evaluate this system with a new Audiovisual Mandarin Chinese (AVMC) database composed of 4704 characters spoken by 10 volunteers. The Gabor-based lipreading system has been trained on this dataset, and utilizes the Dlib Region-of-Interest(ROI) method and Gabor filtering to extract lip features, which provides a fast and lightweight approach without any mouth modelling. A character-level Convolutional Neural Network (CNN) is used to recognize Pinyin, with 64.96% accuracy, and a Character Error Rate (CER) of 57.71%.

Keywords: Audiovisual · Speech recognition · Chinese · Gabor transform

1 Introduction

Human speech is multimodal, with audio and visual information used both in the perception and production of speech. This relationship has been heavily investigated in the literature, with a detailed summary in Abel and Hussain [2]. Lipreading is an approach that interprets lip movement [13], inspired by human cognitive abilities. This can be used in speech recognition, identity recognition, human-computer intelligent interfaces and multimedia systems. Many proposed lipreading systems have very high recognition rates, for instance, the LipNet [4] and 'Watch, Listen, Attend, and Spell' (WLAS) [12] systems. However, most of them use an English corpus such as Grid. Chinese is spoken by around one fifth of the world's population, but written Chinese does not indicate its pronunciation from its character. However, "Pinyin" can be used to mark the pronunciation of Chinese Mandarin [6]. Lipreading is a difficult task to apply to Pinyin, with difficult to identify ambiguities, like similar lip shapes (e.g. 'p' and 'b'), liquids and

J. Ren et al. (Eds.): BICS 2019, LNAI 11691, pp. 169–179, 2020.
https://doi.org/10.1007/978-3-030-39431-8_16

nasals (e.g. 'n' and 'l', are similar to 'ni' and 'li'), blade-alveolars and retroflexes (e.g. 'ci' and 'chi'), and front and back nasal sounds (e.g. 'nin' and 'ning').

In this paper proposes an improved Chinese lipreading system to recognize Pinyin and tone in Chinese speech. To evaluate this, we introduce a new AVMC database, composed of 4704 Pinyin words spoken by 10 volunteers in a clean visual and acoustic environment. For feature extraction, an improved fast and lightweight architecture based on Gabor transforms was developed. A CNN was used to test these lip features, with a character-level performance of 64.96%.

2 Related Work

Traditionally, lipreading has two key components: feature extraction and recognition. Recently, some end-to-end lipreading systems have been developed, such as LipNet [4], and Long Short-Term Memory (LSTM) systems [17]. Chung et al. [12] proposed a character-level architecture called WLAS, with a 3% Word Error Rate(WER), Weng [18] achieved 82.0% word recognition rate for the LRW corpus, and Petridis et al. [11] obtained a 94.7% recognition rate for OuluVS2. These end-to-end approaches use an image directly to self-learn features, and are difficult to explain. We are more interested in extracting lip features, as they can be used for more than just model results. Classic methods are arguably more lightweight and explainable [3]. These include Active Appearance Models (AAM), Discrete Cosine Transform (DCT), and Gabor Wavelet Transform (GWT). DCT is good at concentrating energy into lower order coefficients, but is sensitive to illumination changes, and is difficult to form an intuitive understanding of [1].

Gabor features are insensitive to variance in illumination, rotation, and scale. They can focus on facial features such as eyes, mouth and nose, with optimal localization properties in both spatial and frequency domains [5]. We propose GWT to extract lip features, which is a fast and lightweight approach without any mouth modelling. Compared to deep learning models, GWT reduces speech recognition training time, and is more suitable for small datasets. Sujatha and Santhanam [14] used GWT to correct mouth openness after using a height-width model when extracting 2D lip features, with word recognition of 66.83%. We extract seven lip features, which includes six 2D features and one 3D feature. Hursig et al. used Gabor features to detect the overall lip region [10], while we obtain detailed features. Dakin and Watt proposed that horizontal Gabor feature performance is good for facial feature recognition by using Gabor filters of different orientations [7], and was implemented by the authors [1]. Here, we present an improved visual feature extraction system.

3 A New Audiovisual Mandarin Speech Corpus

Many English-language audiovisual speech corpora have been published, including LRS [12], AVLetter, AV-TIMIT, CUAVE, Grid,OuluVS and XM2VTSDB [20]. However, Chinese lipreading research suffers from a shortage of published and available corpora. Zhang et al. in 2009 collected a large-scale Chinese corpus by recording CCTV news broadcasts, which includes 20495 natural Chinese sentences [19]. However, there is a complex visual background and a noisy speech environment. This paper introduces a new audiovisual Chinese corpus recorded in a clean environment. Chinese is a tonal language, consisting of individual characters, each of which have an initial, a final, and a tone associated with them. To perform accurate initial speech recognition and further analysis, we require a labelled video corpus of distinct Chinese characters, recorded in a clean environment, and we therefore created the AVMC dataset.

Data Acquisition: 162 Chinese characters were collected from the general specification table published by the Chinese ministry of education. These characters are chosen with a reasonable distribution of initials, finals and tones. 10 native Mandarin Chinese volunteers were used (see Fig. 1). The data acquisition procedure for each volunteer was: (1) sign participant information and consent form; (2) read caption list; (3) practice recording for 1–2 min; (4) record for all captions and repeat 3 times. During recording, volunteers were asked to pause between each word, and if they made mistakes, paused and repeated. Mistakes not identified during recording were identified later in the editing process. This produced 30 videos, each being a volunteer reciting all 162 characters in a quiet environment, with a plain blue screen as background. To ensure they were looking directly at the screen, a teleprompter was used. As some Chinese characters have the same pronunciation, there are in total 158 types of pronunciations including both correct and wrong utterances. The video was recorded at a resolution of 1920 × 1080, at 50 fps, and the audio was recorded at 48 kHz.

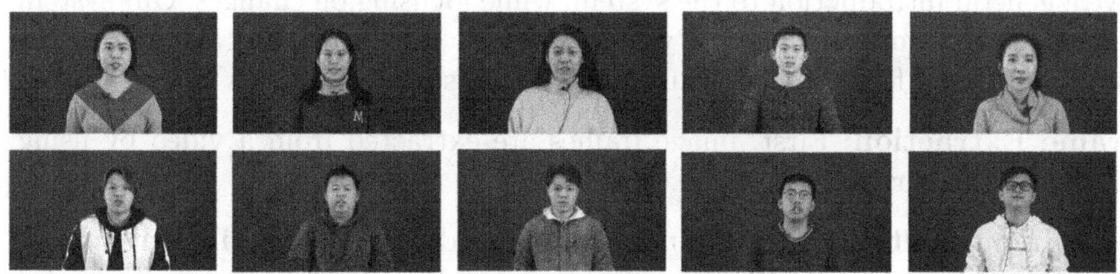

Fig. 1. Example frames of all speakers in AVMC

Data Pre-processing: The 30 raw videos were edited using Adobe Premiere Pro to remove silent pauses, breaks, coughs, off-camera noise, and maintain a consistent order of characters. The processed videos are stored in mp4 format.

Data Labeling: The pauses were manually identified, and video captioning software (Arctime) was used to label initial, final, tone and Pinyin. The occasional vocalized mistakes were not corrected but labelled with actual pronunciations. In a character level representation, the classes for initials, finals, and tones are given shown as follows:

- initials: 0, b, c, d, f, g, h, j, k, l, m, n, p, q, r, s, t, w, x, y, z
- finals 0, a, e, g, i, n, o, r, u and v
- tones 1, 2, 3, 4

For lipreading, the model uses a distinct Pinyin character representation, as shown in Fig. 2. Here, the Pinyin for zhong with the first tone would be represented as having the characters ‘1’, ‘z’, ‘h’, ‘o’, ‘n’, ‘g’. However, Pinyin such as ‘ban’ with second tone would be shorter and could be represented as ‘2’, ‘b’, ‘a’, ‘n’, ‘0’, ‘0’. Here, 0 means there is no character in this location.

	0	a	b	c	d	e	f	g	h	i	j	k	l	m	n	o	p	q	r	s	t	u	v	w	x	y	z	1	2	3	4
1	0	0	0	0	0	0	0	0	0	0	0	0	0	0	0	0	0	0	0	0	0	0	0	0	0	0	0	1	0	0	0
z	0	0	0	0	0	0	0	0	0	0	0	0	0	0	0	0	0	0	0	0	0	0	0	0	0	0	1	0	0	0	0
h	0	0	0	0	0	0	0	0	1	0	0	0	0	0	0	0	0	0	0	0	0	0	0	0	0	0	0	0	0	0	0
o	0	0	0	0	0	0	0	0	0	0	0	0	0	0	0	1	0	0	0	0	0	0	0	0	0	0	0	0	0	0	0
n	0	0	0	0	0	0	0	0	0	0	0	0	0	0	1	0	0	0	0	0	0	0	0	0	0	0	0	0	0	0	0
g	0	0	0	0	0	0	0	1	0	0	0	0	0	0	0	0	0	0	0	0	0	0	0	0	0	0	0	0	0	0	0

Fig. 2. Character level representation of Pinyin for “zhong” with the first tone

4 Improved Gabor-Based Lip Feature Extraction System

Previous research identified that horizontal Gabor features could be used to identify facial features [7]. This resulted in an initial lightweight Gabor-based lip feature extraction system in previous work by the authors [1]. Here, we present an improved visual feature extraction system. Due to space limitations, we will give a general introduction to the system, while focusing on changes. Our system is now quicker, implemented in Python, more accurate, and can calculate height as an additional feature. The feature extraction system is shown in Fig. 3.

Frame Extraction: First, image frames are extracted from a video by using the Python **cap.read()** function.

ROI Identification: Lip regions are extracted using the **Dlib** method, an improvement on the Viola-Jones method used in [1]. We also identify the centre point to select the correct region after Gabor filtering. To demonstrate this, the image in Fig. 4 is labelled with 68 points, with the ROI located using points 6, 10, and 13. The x and y centre co-ordinates are calculated as follows:

$$X = (point(48).x - point(6).x) + \frac{point(54).x - point(48).x}{2} \tag{1}$$

$$Y = (point(51).x - point(13).x) + (shape.part(62).y - shape.part(51).y) + \frac{point(66).x - point(62).x}{2} \tag{2}$$

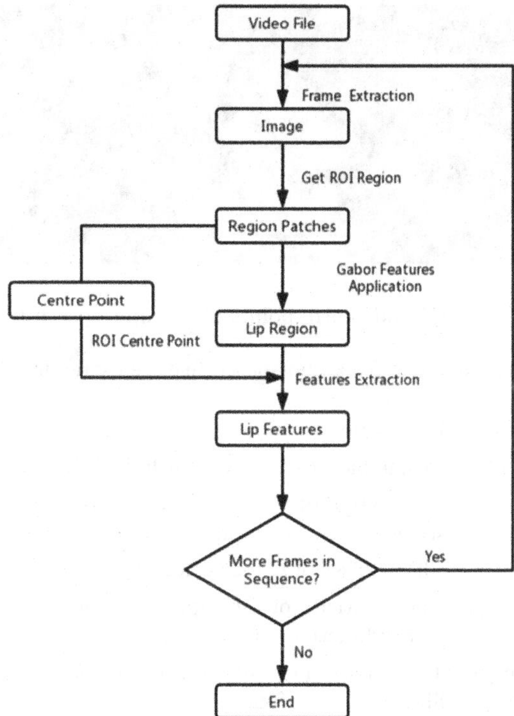

Fig. 3. Key steps of lip feature extraction

Gabor Features: Lip region was identified by using GWT. In OpenCV Python, this can be done using **cv2.getGaborKernel(**$ksize$, σ, θ, λ, γ, ψ, $ktype$**)**. This requires a number of parameters, and after experimentation, optimal parameters for this dataset are listed in Table 1.

The parameters chosen in Table 1 are heavily dependent on factors such as image size, distance from the camera, and speaker pose. The parameters were suitable for the majority of videos, although some occasional small adjustments $\pm$ 1 were made to optimise results. It should be noted that no changes were needed within video sequences. Example results are shown in Fig. 5. Here, Fig. 5(a) shows an original frame, and (b) and (c) show an extracted open and closed mouth respectively. The effect of the GWT is shown in Fig. 5(d) and (e) showing an open mouth and a closed mouth. It can be seen that the dark area of the open mouth is obvious, but the closed mouth is very faint. Finally, Fig. 5(f) shows precise feature extraction, as will be discussed next.

Feature Extraction: The Python function **skimage.filters.threshold_yen** determines whether each pixel in transformed image should belong to the target or background region, calculated automatically depending on the individual image. This produces a corresponding binary image. This method returned a

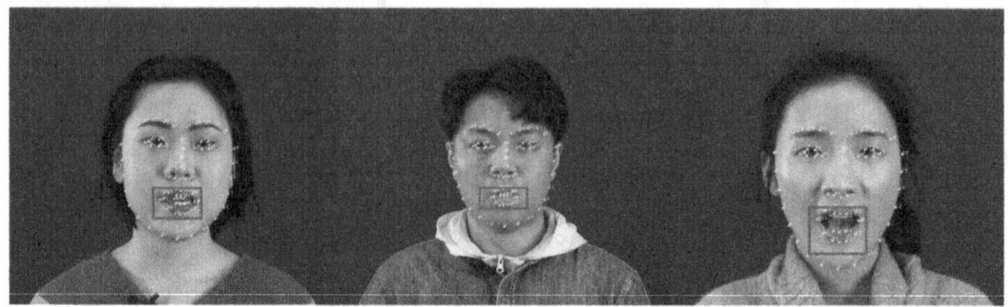

Fig. 4. The ROI and centre points of example speech frames

Table 1. Suitable parameters for Gabor-based feature extraction of AVMC data

Parameter	Description	Value
Wavelength (λ)	Cosine factor of the Gabor filter kernel	16
Orientation (θ)	Orientation of the normal to the parallel stripes of a Gabor function	90
Phase offset (ϕ)	Phase offset of Gabor cosine factor	0
Aspect ratio (γ)	The ellipticity of the support of the Gabor function	0.5
St. deviation (σ)	The standard deviation of the Gabor filter Gaussian function	4
ktype	The type and range of values that each pixel in the Gabor kernel can hold	CV_32F
Ksize	The size of the Gabor kernel	12

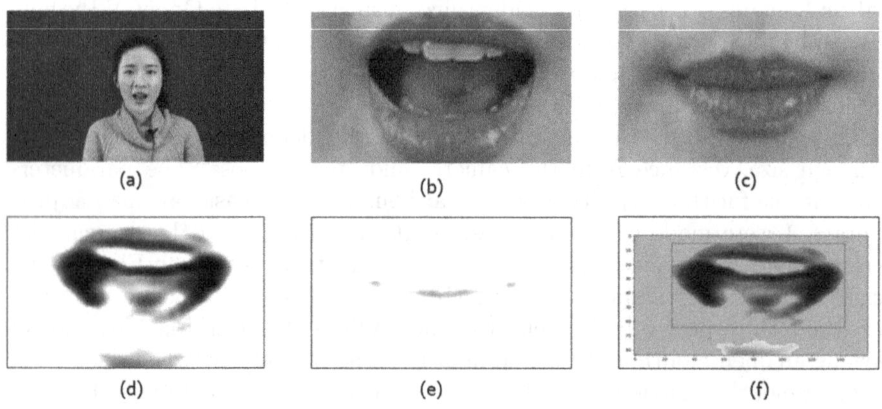

Fig. 5. Example of the feature extraction process from one frame

higher threshold value which more accentuated lip features in comparison to the **skimage.filters.threshold_otsu** function.

The Python **regionprops** function is then used to label all connected pixels and to find the mouth region according to the distance between ROI centre point and the centre point of the labelled regions. The **Regionprops** function identifies region properties in an image, and the result of GWT is a number of regions, with the closest region to the ROI centre point being chosen as the lip region R, with several parameters then obtained. Figure 5(f) shows a final result. Seven properties of the blue region represent the lip features. These are:

- Width: The width of R.
- Height: The height of R. Width and height temporal changes provide intuitive and effective lip information.
- Centre (X,Y): Centre point of R. Tracks lip position.
- Mass: Sum of each pixel value within R. Provides 3D mouth depth information, including tongue and teeth changes.
- Area: Number of pixels within R. A clear measurement of mouth openness.
- Orientation: the mouth angle in degrees, mapping pose of speaker.

Table 2. Configuration of Pinyin recognition network for visual speech recognition

Input Layer: (None, 35, 7)					
Conv1D filter: 64 kernel: 3 strides: 1 padding: same activation: linear bias: true	**Conv1D** filter: 128 kernel: 8 strides: 1 padding: same activation: linear bias: true	**Conv1D** filter: 256 kernel: 13 strides: 1 padding: same activation: linear bias: true	**Conv1D** filter: 256 kernel: 18 strides: 1 padding: same activation: linear bias: true	**Conv1D** filter: 256 kernel: 25 strides: 1 padding: same activation: linear bias: true	**Conv1D** filter: 960 kernel: 35 strides: 1 padding: valid activation: linear bias: true
MaxPooling1D strides: 2 pool:2 padding: valid	**MaxPooling1D** strides: 2 pool:2 padding: valid	**MaxPooling1D** strides: 2 pool:2 padding: valid	**MaxPooling1D** strides: 2 pool:2 padding: valid	**MaxPooling1D** strides: 2 pool:2 padding: valid	
Concatenate					
Add					
Batch Normalization					
Conv1D filter: 256 kernel: 6 stride: 1 padding: valid activation: linear bias: true					
MaxPooling1D strides: 2 pool: 2 padding: valid					
Dropout rate: 0.25					
TimeDistributed(Dense) units: 31 activation: softmax bias: true					
Output Layer: (None, 6, 31)					

Table 3. Precision, recall, and f1-score for all Pinyin characters

	precision	recall	f1-score
0	0.743	0.949	0.833
a	0.597	0.573	0.583
b	0.535	0.618	0.573
c	0.559	0.284	0.374
d	0.187	0.186	0.182
e	0.624	0.183	0.281
f	0.067	0.040	0.050
g	0.494	0.099	0.164
h	0.551	0.250	0.343
i	0.541	0.714	0.615
j	0.331	0.311	0.317
k	0.393	0.200	0.257
l	0.316	0.459	0.368
m	0.470	0.435	0.444
n	0.450	0.243	0.313
o	0.511	0.147	0.227
total	0.449	0.372	0.377

	precision	recall	f1-score
p	0.462	0.250	0.321
q	0.294	0.375	0.328
r	0.579	0.500	0.532
s	0.324	0.486	0.387
t	0.606	0.375	0.457
u	0.550	0.482	0.507
v	0.800	0.200	0.314
w	0.212	0.300	0.247
x	0.343	0.361	0.349
y	0.238	0.391	0.295
z	0.258	0.267	0.261
1	0.431	0.453	0.440
2	0.438	0.192	0.255
3	0.491	0.685	0.569
4	0.512	0.524	0.516

4.1 Lipreading with Inception-ResNet, Results and Discussion

To test our improved feature extraction system with our new corpus, we perform visual speech recognition in an Inception-ResNet network [16]. This combines the Inception CNN module with residual connections. The Inception module has an efficient utilization of the computing resources inside the network, which increases network depth and width while keeping the computational cost low. Residual connections have been shown to contribute to faster training of the Inception network [15]. Based on initial trials, the proposed architecture of this network is shown in Table 2. This model is character based, meaning that rather than estimating the Pinyin, given a sequence of visual vectors, it attempts to identify each character.

After 5 runs, the overall character level validation accuracy of this system is 64.96% with an Interquartile Range (IQR) of 0.003, and the CER is 57.72% with an IQR of 0.005. This is in line with other visual systems that consider only single words without sentence level context. The detailed results are shown in Table 3. However, some analysis of the table is required. Firstly, a single model was trained for all characters, and this meant there were more cases of 0 (i.e. no character present), which is a result of having more smaller Pinyin words (i.e. '1yi' has 3 more '0' characters than '1zhong'). Despite the data being evenly distributed at Pinyin level, at character level, this results in a skew to '0', affecting the results. It should also be noted that when the character results are combined into a single Pinyin character, the overall word accuracy is only 11.76%. However, this is not an unexpected result.

Table 3 shows that according to both accuracy scores and f1-scores of 26 letters, the most accurate characters are 'a', 't', and 'r'. Furthermore, 'v' is distinctive, with highest precision but low recall, which may due to the lower distribution rate. It should also be pointed out that the results can be grouped into initials, finals, shared initials and finals, and tones. Excluding zeros, the respective mean f1-score for the 16 dedicated initials is 0.327, for the 6 dedicated finals it is 0.421, for the 3 shared initials and finals, it is 0.335, and for tones it is 0.445. This suggests that performance is better for finals than initials, with the shared initials and finals likely causing confusion. In addition, the overall validation accuracy is likely to be much higher for finals than for initials, which is unsurprising, given that more information is present in the visualisation of a final. Also, conventional deep learning algorithms are likely to not perform well in this test, due to a lack of training data. So above all, an overall character level validation accuracy of 64.96% is along the lines of what is expected.

The results support that recognition is being performed accurately in many cases, considering that visual information alone will only ever generate incomplete information, and that tone is overwhelmingly a function of the vocal cord, and is not visualised. To generate accurate Pinyin matching, then separate models should be trained for initials, finals, and tones, since we are dealing with three distinct word components. We can also improve the very low word accuracy scores by training these separate models, and also improving the formulation of Pinyin, post character generation. There is always likely to be skew in the data, this is a feature of character-level Pinyin generation, and the structure of Pinyin makes direct comparison to English language lip-reading challenging.

Much research has found that it is possible to train deep learning models at the character level, as it allows the model to learn internal word structures. However, to the best knowledge of the authors, this approach has not been used widely for Chinese, with research limited to been text based work, such as by Huang and Wang [9]. Due to the new approaches, we have used in this paper, and the new form of analysis, there is no direct comparison between our results and other results in the literature, as other research tends to consider the Pinyin at a word level, rather than considering it separately at a character level, which as our research has shown, is an important factor. Overall, we can conclude that firstly, the improved feature extraction method improved on that proposed by Abel et al. [1], using a more advanced ROI detection method (Dlib rather than Viola-Jones). Qualitative comparisons identified that our features were more reliable and accurate, with additional features (i.e. height measurements). In addition, using Gabor features rather than CNN features is more suitable for a smaller corpus, and also reduced the training time considerably. Our new AVMC corpus is available on request, and fills a role of clean Chinese speech data, focusing on individual characters, that other corpora do not currently meet. Finally, the initial experiments presented in this paper suggested that results were along the lines of what was expected, and that using a different approach to what is used for non-tonal languages will improve results.

5 Conclusions

This paper introduced a new audiovisual speech corpus, AVMC, which is recorded in a good quality studio environment, and contains 10 speakers reading distinct Chinese characters from a teleprompter. This dataset is fully labelled, and is freely available on request. To demonstrate its effectiveness, we performed initial visual speech recognition with an improved lightweight Gabor-based feature extraction system, with character based recognition results of 64.96% for recognition rate and 57.72% CER when trained with a deep neural network. Future work will be to improve the feature extraction process by making it more robust and easier to configure, as well as improving our database by adding more speakers and more utterances to make it more suitable for deep learning use, and considering training with individual models for different speech components. In addition, for the recognition model, it could be improved to a different Inception-ResNet network by adding 1*1 convolution to reduce the computational cost [15]. Furthermore, after getting lip Gabor images, the stacked denoising autoencoders need to be used to reduce noisy and hypothesis ROI regions [8].

Acknowledgments. This work was supported by XJTLU Grant RDF 16-01-35, and partially funded by the Research Institute of Big Data Analytics.

References

1. Abel, A., Gao, C., Smith, L., Watt, R., Hussain, A.: Fast lip feature extraction using psychologically motivated Gabor features. In: 2018 IEEE Symposium Series on Computational Intelligence (SSCI), pp. 1033–1040. IEEE (2018)
2. Abel, A., Hussain, A.: Novel two-stage audiovisual speech filtering in noisy environments. Cogn. Comput. **6**(2), 200–217 (2014)
3. Abel, A., Hussain, A.: Cognitively Inspired Audiovisual Speech Filtering. SCC, vol. 5. Springer, Cham (2015). https://doi.org/10.1007/978-3-319-13509-0
4. Assael, Y.M., Shillingford, B., Whiteson, S., De Freitas, N.: LipNet: end-to-end sentence-level lipreading (2016)
5. Bhadu, A., Tokas, R., Kumar, D.V.: Facial expression recognition using DCT, Gabor and Wavelet feature extraction techniques. Int. J. Eng. Innovative Technol. **2**(1), 92–95 (2012)
6. Cao, J.: Chinese pronunciation: the complete guide for beginner. https://www.digmandarin.com/chinese-pronunciation-guide.html
7. Dakin, S.C., Watt, R.J.: Biological "bar codes" in human faces. J. Vis. **9**(4), 2.1–10 (2009)
8. Han, J., Zhang, D., Hu, X., Guo, L., Ren, J., Wu, F.: Background prior-based salient object detection via deep reconstruction residual. IEEE Trans. Circ. Syst. Video Technol. **25**(8), 1309–1321 (2014)
9. Huang, W.: Character-level convolutional network for text classification applied to Chinese corpus (2016)
10. Hursig, R.E., Zhang, J.X., Kam, C.: Lip localization algorithm using Gabor filters (2011)
11. Petridis, S., Wang, Y., Li, Z., Pantic, M.: End-to-end multi-view lipreading. In: British Machine Vision Conference, London, September 2017
12. Chung, J.S., Senior, A., Vinyals, O., Zisserman, A.: Lip reading sentences in the wild. In: The IEEE Conference on Computer Vision and Pattern Recognition (CVPR), July 2017
13. Sterpu, G., Harte, N.: Towards lipreading sentences with active appearance models. arXiv preprint arXiv:1805.11688 (2018)

14. Sujatha, B., Santhanam, T.: A novel approach integrating geometric and gabor wavelet approaches to improvise visual lip-reading. Int. J. Soft Comput. **5**, 13–18 (2010)
15. Szegedy, C., Ioffe, S., Vanhoucke, V., Alemi, A.A.: Inception-v4, inception-ResNet and the impact of residual connections on learning. In: Thirty-First AAAI Conference on Artificial Intelligence (2017)
16. Szegedy, C., et al.: Going deeper with convolutions. In: Proceedings of the IEEE Conference on Computer Vision and Pattern Recognition, pp. 1–9 (2015)
17. Wand, M., Koutník, J., Schmidhuber, J.: Lipreading with long short-term memory. In: 2016 IEEE International Conference on Acoustics, Speech and Signal Processing (ICASSP), pp. 6115–6119. IEEE (2016)
18. Weng, X.: On the importance of video action recognition for visual lipreading. arXiv preprint arXiv:1903.09616 (2019)
19. Zhang, X., Gong, H., Dai, X., Yang, F., Liu, N., Liu, M.: Understanding pictograph with facial features: end-to-end sentence-level lip reading of Chinese (2019)
20. Zhou, Z., Zhao, G., Hong, X., Pietikäinen, M.: A review of recent advances in visual speech decoding. Image Vis. Comput. **32**(9), 590–605 (2014)

Graph Embedded Multiple Kernel Extreme Learning Machine for Music Emotion Classification

Xixian Zhang[1], Zhijing Yang[1(✉)], Jinchang Ren[2], Meilin Wang[1], and Wing-Kuen Ling[1]

[1] School of Information Engineering, Guangdong University of Technology, Guangzhou 510006, China
yzhj@gdut.edu.cn
[2] Department of Electronic and Electrical Engineering, University of Strathclyde, Glasgow G1 1XW, UK

Abstract. Music emotion classification is one of the most importance parts of music information retrieval (MIR) because of its potential commercial value and cultural value. However, music emotion classification is still a tough challenge, due to the low representation of music features. In this paper, a novel Extreme Learning Machine (ELM), combining graph regularization term and multiple kernel, is proposed to enhance the accuracy of music emotion classification. We use nonnegative matrix factorization (NMF) to find the optimal weights of combining multiple kernels. Furthermore, the graph regularization term is added to increase the relevance between predictions from the same class. The proposed Graph embedded Multiple Kernel Extreme Learning Machine (GMK-ELM) is tested on three music emotion datasets. Experiment results show that the proposed GMK-ELM outperforms several well-known ELM methods.

Keywords: Music emotion classification · Extreme Learning Machine (ELM) · Graph embedded · Multiple kernel learning

1 Introduction

As an important domain of music information retrieval (MIR), music emotion recognition (MER) aims to explore affective information from music signal automatically with the help of signal processing technology, computer science, psychology, etc. The typical MER tasks adopt signal processing technology to extract music feature which reflect the relationship between music and emotions from raw audio signal frame by frame. Katayose [1] took into account melody, rhythm, etc. as the music emotion factors for piano song emotion classification. Inspired by Katayose, Feng and Zhuang proposed a music emotion detecting model [2] to predict the four basic emotion types (happiness, sadness, indignation, panic) of music emotion in 2003, and achieved many breakthrough results. However, the small size of testing data makes this model unpersuasive.

Choosing correct music feature plays a vital role in music emotion classification (MEC). Some researchers try to discover music feature with related physics knowledge for improving performance. They employ spectrum feature, such as shapes, center,

J. Ren et al. (Eds.): BICS 2019, LNAI 11691, pp. 180–191, 2020.
https://doi.org/10.1007/978-3-030-39431-8_17

slope, skewness of each spectrum sub-bands. Ren [3] proposed a type of modulation spectrum features for music emotion classification. The modulation spectrum feature can capture more information of harmonic component and nonharmonic component. Then SVM classifier is used to divide testing data into four classes. Experiments showed that modulation spectrum features can improve performance of classification.

Unlike the aforementioned works, some researchers try to improve performance of automatic music classification (AMC) by exploring more information with classifier. Scardapane utilizes Extreme Learning Machine (ELM) for music classification [4]. In Scardapane's work, ELM achieves slightly better performance than feedforward neural network architecture but spends much less computation cost. Because the weights of input layer in ELM are generated at random, implying that there is no need to tune parameter of input layer. The function of input layer in ELM is to map low dimensional feature into high dimensional space with nonlinear transform.

Recently, ELM and its extension version are widely applied in different fields, especially in hyperspectral image (HSI) classification [19, 20]. Kernel extension of ELM called spectral and spatial K-ELM (SSK-ELM) [7] explores the spectral and spatial information to improve kernel ELM for hyperspectral images classification. In the same time, multi-kernel methods [21] are also popular and effective in many fields. Hence, it's reasonable to combine multi-kernel methods and ELM model. Multi-kernel versions of ELM (MK-ELM) [5, 6] integrate kernels with different types into one kernel, which obtains more nonlinear representation. Previously works have shown that multi-kernel ELM make good use of kernel information. However, MK-ELM doesn't take local consistency of data into consideration, and ignores the class imbalance problem [22]. Aiming at solving weak data consistency of MK-ELM, we try to add the graph regularization term into the object function of MK-ELM.

In this paper, we propose a novel MK-ELM called Graph embedded Multiple Kernel Extreme Learning Machine (GMK-ELM), inspired by Gu [8] and Iosifidis [9]. Furthermore, GMK-ELM is employed to recognize music emotion on three music datasets.

The remainder of this paper is summarized as follows. In Sect. 2, we introduce the basic concept of MK-ELM and Graph Embedded kernel ELM (GEK-ELM). Details of GMK-ELM and procedure of extracting music feature are given in Sect. 3. Section 4 shows the experiment results of music emotion classification. Finally, we will make a summary of our work in Sect. 5.

2 Review of Related Works

2.1 Kernel ELM

Extreme Learning Machine (ELM) [10] is a single layer network proposed by Huang. There are two characteristics in ELM. One is random input weights of input layer, and another is analytic expression of output weight. Details of ELM and its variants will be presented in this section.

Suppose we have N training samples with d dimension, denoted as $\mathrm{X} = [x_1, x_2, \ldots, x_N] \in R^{N \times d}$. The output with m category is denoted as $\mathrm{Y} = [y_1, y_2, \ldots, y_N] \in R^{N \times m}$, $y_i \in R^{1 \times m}$, $i = 1, 2, \ldots, N$. Input weights and biases in input layer are given respectively as $\mathrm{W} = [w_1, w_2, \ldots, w_L] \in R^{d \times L}$ and $\mathrm{B} = [b_1, b_2, \ldots, b_N] \in R^{N \times L}$, where L is the number of hidden layer node. Nonlinear projection takes place in input layer according to following equation:

$$H = g(XW + B) \tag{1}$$

Hidden matrix $H \in R^{N \times L}$ is the output of input layer, and $g(\cdot)$ is the activation function. The output of ELM classifier can be formulated as following equation:

$$H\beta = Y \tag{2}$$

The output weight of ELM is $\beta \in R^{L \times m}$. We need to find the optimal β to make H approximate Y as much as possible. In order to guarantee well generalization capability of ELM, regulation term should be taken into account. Combine the above two points, optimization problem of β can be formulated as following problem:

$$min_{\beta} \frac{1}{2} \|\beta\|_2^2 + \frac{C}{2} \sum_{i=1}^{N} \|\varepsilon_i\|_2^2$$

$$\text{s.t. } \mathrm{h}(x_i)\beta = y_i - \varepsilon_i,\ i = 1, 2, \ldots, N \tag{3}$$

In above problem, ε_i denotes the error of $\mathrm{h}(x_i)$ form hidden matrix of the ith sample, and C is the constant. We can use Lagrange multiplier method to solve the above convex problem. The analytic expression of optimal output weight β^* is given as following equation:

$$\beta^* = H^T \left(\frac{I}{C} + HH^T \right)^{-1} Y \tag{4}$$

Suppose we have $\mathrm{K} = HH^T \in R^{N \times N}$, $\mathrm{K}(x_i, x_j) = \mathrm{h}(x_i)h(x_j)^T = \Phi(x_i)\Phi(x_j)^T$, where $\Phi(\cdot)$ represents the unknown transform in hidden layer. Obviously, HH^T has the same form as the kernel matrix. Thus, we can rewrite Eq. (4) into kernel version ELM (K-ELM).

$$\beta_{KELM} = H^T \left(\frac{I}{C} + \Omega_{KELM} \right)^{-1} Y^* \tag{5}$$

$$Y_{KELM} = H^* \beta_{KELM} = H^* H^T \left(\frac{I}{C} + HH^T \right)^{-1} Y^* = \Omega_{test} \left(\frac{I}{C} + \Omega_{train} \right)^{-1} Y^* \tag{6}$$

where β_{KELM} is the RBF kernel, Y_{KELM} is the output of K-ELM,Y^* is the label of training data, $\Omega_{test} = \mathrm{K}(x_i^*, x_j)$ is the kernel matrix of testing data, $\Omega_{train} = \mathrm{K}(x_i, x_j)$ is the kernel matrix of training data.

Instead of using a single kernel ELM, [5] defines multiple kernels ELM (MK-ELM) for EEG classification. Difference kernels are combined according to the following equation:

$$\tilde{K}\left(x_i, x_j\right) = \sum\nolimits_{q=1}^{Q} \lambda_q \mathrm{K}_q(x_i, x_j) \tag{7}$$

where $\tilde{K}\left(x_i, x_j\right)$ is the mixed kernel of Q pre-defined kernels, and λ_q is the weight of corresponding kernel.

$$\beta_{MK} = H^T\left(\frac{I}{C} + \tilde{K}\left(x_i, x_j\right)\right)^{-1} Y^* \tag{8}$$

$$Y_{MK} = H^* \beta_{MK} \tag{9}$$

where β_{MK} is the output weight of MK-ELM, and Y_{MK} is the output of MK-ELM.

2.2 Multiple Kernel Learning via NMF

The weight factors λ_q in Eq. (7) determined the performance of mixed kernel [11]. To compares the typical multiple kernel learning (MKL) methods with NMF method, it's found that NMF-MKL achieve well performance of most case in Gu's works. The details of NMF-MKL are given as follows.

Given a kernel set K_Q with Q basic kernels $\left\{K_q,\ q = 1, 2, \ldots, Q;\ K_q \in R^{N \times N}\right\}$. Then using vectorization function $vec(\cdot)$ to transform K_q into one dimensional vector $k_q \in R^{N^2 \times 1}$. Combine Q vector k_q into a two dimensional matrix P, where $P = [k_1, k_2, \ldots, k_q]$, $q = 1, 2, \ldots, Q$; $P \in R^{N^2 \times Q}$. The NMF algorithm [12] is used to find two low-dimensional nonnegative matrixes $V \in R^{N^2 \times l}$ and $D \in R^{Q \times l}$ to represent P. The Objective function is given as following equation:

$$O = \left\|P - VD^T\right\|_F^2 \tag{10}$$

Here, V and D are the optimal nonnegative vectors. $V \in R^{N^2 \times l}$ is made up of l selected kernels. Using the function $vec(\cdot)^{-1}$ to reshape V into $K^* \in R^{N \times N}$, which can be seen as the optimal kernel of NMF. $D \in R^{Q \times l}$ can be view as weight factors to combine kernel.

2.3 Graph Embedded ELM

Graph version ELM [9, 13] take graph regularize term into account in ELM objective function. Assume we have C classes and N samples. N_c denotes the size of class c, where $c = 1, 2, \ldots, C$. The graph can be defined as $G = \{X, W\}$, where X is the raw data, and W is the connecting matrix of corresponding vertices. In the case of Linear Discriminant Analysis (LDA) [14], the main idea is that finding a low-dimension subspace to represent feature where data can be separated easily. The LDA graph can be defined as follows:

$$W_{i,j} = \begin{cases} \frac{1}{N_c}, & if\ x_i\ and\ x_j\ belong\ to\ class\ c \\ 0, & otherwise \end{cases} \tag{11}$$

$$W^p_{i,j} = \begin{cases} \frac{1}{N} - \frac{1}{N_c}, & if\ x_i\ and\ x_j\ belong\ to\ class\ c \\ \frac{1}{N}, & otherwise \end{cases} \tag{12}$$

where W is the intrinsic graph, W^p is the penalty graph. Calculate the graph Laplacian matrix as the following equations:

$$D_{i,i} = \sum\nolimits_{j=1}^{N} W_{i,j} \tag{13}$$

$$D^p_{i,i} = \sum\nolimits_{j=1}^{N} W^p_{i,j} \tag{14}$$

$$\mathrm{L} = \mathrm{D} - \mathrm{W} \tag{15}$$

$$L^p = D^p - W^p \tag{16}$$

For graph embedded kernel ELM (GEK-ELM), we can formulate the output weight β_G as following equations:

$$\mathrm{A} = \left(\mu_1 I + \mu_2 (L^p)^{\dagger} L + \Omega\right)^{-1} Y^* \tag{17}$$

$$\beta_G = H^T A \tag{18}$$

where $\mathrm{A} \in R^{N \times C}$ is a matrix containing intrinsic information and penalty information. μ_1, μ_2 are constants. Operation symbol $\dagger$ denotes pseudo-inverse operator. Ω can be arbitrary kernel matrix. Y^* is the label of training data.

The output Y_G of GEK-ELM is as follow equation:

$$Y_G = H^* \beta_G = H^* H^T \left(\mu_1 I + \mu_2 (L^p)^{\dagger} L + \Omega_{train}\right)^{-1} Y^* = \Omega_{test} A \tag{19}$$

where $\Omega_{test} = \mathrm{K}\left(x_i^*, x_j\right)$ is the kernel matrix of testing data and training data. $\Omega_{train} = \mathrm{K}\left(x_i, x_j\right)$ is the kernel matrix of training data.

3 Proposed Method for MEC

3.1 Proposed ELM Models

The core idea of multiple kernel strategy is that combining various kernels by appropriate rule, which improve separableness as higher as possible. The mixed kernel generally contains higher dimension feature information and robustness than a single kernel. We propose a multiple kernel version ELM called Nonnegative Matrix Factorization Multiple Kernel Extreme Learning Machine (NMF-ELM) to capture more feature information. As mentioned In Sect. 2, we have Q kernels, and apply NMF algorithm to solve the optimal weights D and V, then adopt the $vec(\cdot)^{-1}$ function to reshape V into optimal kernel $\Omega_{NMF} \in R^{N \times N}$. The output weight and output of NMF-ELM are as follows.

$$\beta_{NMF} = H^T \left(\frac{I}{C} + \Omega_{NMF} \right)^{-1} Y^* \tag{20}$$

$$Y_{NMF} = H^* \beta_{NMF} = H^* H^T \left(\frac{I}{C} + HH^T \right)^{-1} Y^* = \Omega_{test}^{NMF} \left(\frac{I}{C} + \Omega_{train}^{NMF} \right)^{-1} Y^* \tag{21}$$

After mapping feature into high nonlinear space, the distance information of data may loss in different degree. Meanwhile, there may exist coincident information between two kernels after fusing. In order to solve this problem we add graph regulation regularize term into account in NMF-ELM, and propose a novel ELM call Graph embedding Multiple Kernel Extreme learning machine (GMK-ELM). The output weight and output of GMK-ELM are as follows.

$$A_{GMK} = (\mu_1 I + \mu_2 (L^p)^{\dagger} L + \Omega_{NMF})^{-1} Y^* \tag{22}$$

$$\beta_{GMK} = H^T A_{GMK} \tag{23}$$

$$Y_{GMK} = H^* \beta_{GMK} = H^* H^T (\mu_1 I + \mu_2 (L^p)^{\dagger} L + \Omega_{train}^{NMF})^{-1} Y^* = \Omega_{test}^{NMF} A_{GMK} \tag{24}$$

The flowchart of our proposed method is given in Fig. 1.

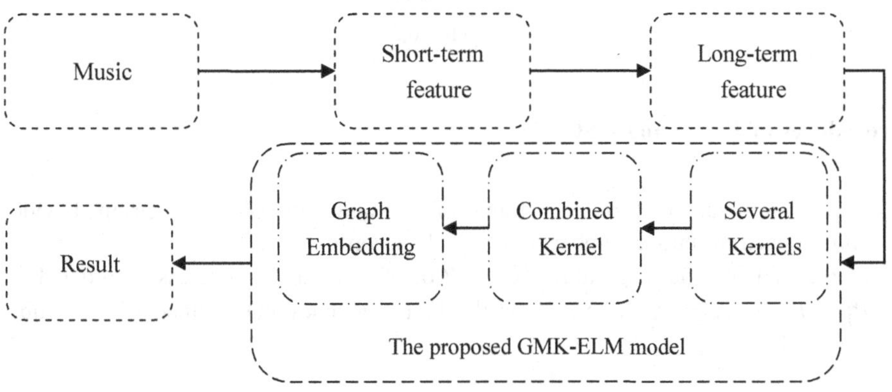

Fig. 1. Flowchart of Proposed Method

3.2 Extracting Music Feature

We adopt the modulation feature called Modulation Octave-Based Spectral Contrast (MOSC) mentioned in [3]. Different from the short-term frame-based feature as Octave-Based-Spectral Contrast (OSC) [16], MOSC is the long-term feature captured form texture windows which consist of several frames. Rhythm information and speech syllabic rates exist in corresponding modulation frequency sub-band [15]. And the procedures of extracting OSC and MOSC are as follows:

Table 1. Frequency ranges of OSC sub-band

Filter number	Frequency range
1	[0,100]
2	(100,200]
3	(200,400]
4	(400,800]
5	(800,1600]
6	(1600,3200]
7	(3200,6400]
8	(6400,11025]

Table 2. Frequency ranges of modulation sub-band

Filter number	Frequency range
1	[0,0.33)
2	[0.33,0.66)
3	[0.66,1.32)
4	[1.32,2.64)
5	[2.64,5.28)
6	[5.28,10.56)
7	[10.56,21.03]

Procedures of Extracting OSC:

Step 1: Applying FFT on each frame of raw audio to acquire spectrum. Divide above spectrum into a number of subbands according to Table 1.
Step 2: To sort the magnitude spectra P of ath sub-band in decreasing order. Let $P_1^a \geq P_2^a \geq \ldots \geq P_{N_a}^a$, where N_a is the FFT frequency bins numbers in a^{th} sub-band, where $a \in [1, 8]$.

Step 3: Calculating spectral peak (SP), spectral valley (SV), spectral contrast (SC) of ath sub-band as following equations:

$$SP(a) = log\left(\frac{1}{\eta N_a}\sum\nolimits_{i=1}^{\eta N_a} P_i^a\right) \tag{25}$$

$$SV(a) = log\left(\frac{1}{\eta N_a}\sum\nolimits_{i=1}^{\eta N_a} P_{N_a-i+1}^a\right) \tag{26}$$

$$SC(a) = SP(a) - SV(a) \tag{27}$$

Step 4: To combine $SP(a)$ and $SC(a)$ into one vector to represent $OSC(a)$ in a^{th} sub-band. To calculate mean and standard deviation of each frame, we set $\eta = 0.2$ according to [3]. The dimension of short-term feature OSC is 16 of each frame.

Procedures of Extracting MOSC:

Step 1: Determinate the size of texture window. To capture the OSC spectrum from above procedures by defined texture window with 50% overlap. Here, the size of window is 256 frames, $W_{text} \in R^{16\times 256}$, and the modulation frequency bins is correspond to 128.
Step 2: Apply FFT on Each OSC spectrum to obtain modulation feature spectrogram $M_t(m, d)$ of each texture window. And compute the averaged texture window $\overline{M_t}(m, d) = \frac{1}{T}\sum_{t=1}^{T} |M_t(m, d)|$; $1 \le m \le L$, $1 \le d \le D$. Here, T is the number of texture window, $L = 128$ is the modulation frequency bins. $D = 16$ is dimension of OSC spectrum.
Step 3: To take logarithm on each value of averaged texture window. Computing modulation spectral peak (MSP), modulation spectral valley (MSV), modulation spectral contrast (MSC) of each modulation sub-band shown in Table 2, according to following equations:

$$MSP(b, d) = \max\left(\overline{M_t}(m, d)\right);\ \phi_{b,l} \le m \le \phi_{b,h},\ 1 \le b \le B,\ 1 \le d \le D \tag{28}$$

$$MSV(b, d) = \min\left(\overline{M_t}(m, d)\right);\ \phi_{b,l} \le m \le \phi_{b,h},\ 1 \le b \le B,\ 1 \le d \le D \tag{29}$$

$$MSC(b, d) = MSP(b, d) - MSV(b, d);\ 1 \le b \le B,\ 1 \le d \le D \tag{30}$$

where B is the number of modulation sub-band, which is 7 here. $\phi_{b,l}$ and $\phi_{b,h}$ respectively denote the lowest modulation frequency and highest modulation frequency of the bth modulation sub-band.
Step 4: Calculating mean and standard deviation of each row and column from MSC matrix and MSV matrix. Then we obtain four row statistics and four column statistics, and combine above statistics into a vector with the length of (4D + 4B). Finally, this is the MOSC feature we need.

4 Experiments for MEC

4.1 Experimental Setup

In this section, five ELM models (original ELM, K-ELM, GEK-ELM, NMF-ELM, GMK-ELM) are tested on three music emotion datasets (Sound-track dataset [17], MIREX-like, Song's dataset [18]). The details of all dataset are given in Table 3. For all the dataset, In order to reduce redundancy of feature, we use Gradient Boosting Decision Tree (GBDT) to calculate the importance of each dimension, and drop out the bottom 10 dimension. The number of hidden node of ELM is set to 50. The mixed kernel ELM is consisted of 5 gaussian kernels with $\sigma = [1, 2, 4, 8, 16]$.

We evaluate five ELM models on each dataset for 10 times randomly, and adopt mean of accuracy, standard deviation of accuracy, mean of macro-F1 and their corresponding standard deviation as classification criteria.

Table 3. Information of music emotion datasets

Dataset	Class	Sample	Training proportion
Sound-track	6	180	50%
MIREX-like	5	903	50%
Song's dataset	4	2904	50%

4.2 Experimental Results and Discussions

As can be seen in Table 4, two single kernel ELM (K-ELM, GEK-ELM) could not perform well on the small size dataset. The multiple kernel ELM (NMF-ELM, GMK-ELM) achieve good performance of Sound-track dataset, especially the GMK-ELM, which achieve the best performance of accuracy and macro-F1.

As can be seen in Table 5, single kernel ELM perform better than original ELM. Though the multiple kernel ELM get slightly improvement of marcro-F1 on MIREX-like dataset, the GMK-ELM still achieve the best performance.

As shown in Table 6, GMK-ELM achieves the best performance in all criteria, and NMF-ELM get the second best performance. The differences among K-ELM, GEK-ELM and ELM are not obvious.

Table 4. Performance of fives ELM on Sound-track dataset (Best result is marked in bold type)

Classifier	Accuracy	Standard deviation	Macro-F1	Macro-F1-std.
ELM	0.3444	0.0399	0.3571	**0.0299**
K-ELM	0.3278	**0.0386**	0.3373	0.0435
GEK-ELM	0.3311	0.0456	0.3351	0.0478
NMF-ELM	0.3656	0.0411	0.3783	0.0309
GMK-ELM	**0.3700**	0.0426	**0.3807**	0.0354

Table 5. Performance of fives ELM on MIREX-like dataset (Best result is marked in bold type)

Classifier	Accuracy	Standard deviation	Macro-F1	Macro-F1-std.
ELM	0.3688	0.0217	0.3541	0.0242
K-ELM	0.3797	**0.0217**	0.3760	**0.0225**
GEK-ELM	0.3790	0.0250	0.3774	0.0242
NMF-ELM	0.3834	0.0243	0.3763	0.0272
GMK-ELM	**0.3854**	0.0273	**0.3777**	0.0291

Table 6. Performance of fives ELM on Song's dataset (Best result is marked in bold type)

Classifier	Accuracy	Standard deviation	Macro-F1	Macro-F1-std.
ELM	0.5233	0.0144	0.5256	0.0156
K-ELM	0.5328	0.0123	0.5351	0.0130
GEK-ELM	0.5298	0.0126	0.5319	0.0134
NMF-ELM	0.5405	0.0105	0.5428	0.0126
GMK-ELM	**0.5411**	**0.0101**	**0.5429**	**0.0117**

Based on above results, we can summarize that the proposed NMF-ELM and GMK-ELM obtains the better result than single kernel ELM and original ELM on music emotion classification. The strategy of multiple plays an important role in enlarge the feature space. The larger feature space provides more information for classification. Furthermore, the graph embedding strategy preserves distance information of data, and reduces superfluous information. Hence, GMK-ELM obtains the best result of all ELM classifiers.

5 Conclusion

This paper proposes two novel multiple kernel ELM (NMF-ELM and GMK-ELM), which is applied on music emotion classification to improve the performance of the original ELM. For NMF-ELM, nonnegative matrix factorization algorithm is used to optimize the combining weight of multiple kernels. The robustness of NMF-ELM thereby is enhanced effectively. Furthermore, we find out that the graph regularization term is an important part to make the similar samples closer. As a result, we combine NMF-ELM and Graph Embedded ELM to propose the GMK-ELM. The Experiment results show that the two proposed ELMs can improve the accuracy and marco-F1 in music emotion classification tasks.

In the future, we will lay emphasis on finding self-adaption graph matrix for GMK-ELM. It is more reasonable that the weight of graph matrix should be learned from specific case rather than determined previously. Meanwhile, learning a self-adaption graph matrix needs huge computation. Therefore, reducing computation of ELM not allow to ignore.

Acknowledgement. This work is supported in part by the National Nature Science Foundation of China (nos. U1701266, 61471132), the Innovation Team Project of Guangdong Education Department (no. 2017KCXTD011), Natural Science Foundation of Guangdong Province China (no. 2018A030313751), and Science and Technology Program of Guangzhou, China (nos. 201803010065, 201802020010).

References

1. Katayose, H., Imai, M., Inokuchi, S.: Sentiment extraction in music. In: 9th International Conference on Pattern Recognition, pp. 1083–1087. IEEE (1988)
2. Feng, Y., Zhuang, Y., Pan, Y.: Popular music retrieval by detecting mood. In: Proceedings of the 26th Annual International ACM SIGIR Conference on Research and Development in Information Retrieval, pp. 375–376. ACM (2003)
3. Ren, J., Wu, M., Jang, J.S.R.: Automatic music mood classification based on timbre and modulation features. IEEE Trans. Affect. Comput. **6**(3), 236–246 (2015)
4. Scardapane, S., Comminiello, D., Scarpiniti, M., Uncini, A.: Music classification using extreme learning machines. In: 8th International Symposium on Image and Signal Processing and Analysis (ISPA), pp. 377–381. IEEE (2013)
5. Zhang, Y., et al.: Multi-kernel extreme learning machine for EEG classification in brain-computer interfaces. Expert Syst. Appl. **96**, 302–310 (2018)
6. Ergul, U., Bilgin, G.: MCK-ELM: multiple composite kernel extreme learning machine for hyperspectral images. Neural Comput. Appl. 1–11 (2019)
7. Yang, Z., Cao, F., Zabalza, J., Chen, W., Cao, J.: Spectral and spatial kernel extreme learning machine for hyperspectral image classification. In: Ren, J., et al. (eds.) BICS 2018. LNCS (LNAI), vol. 10989, pp. 394–401. Springer, Cham (2018). https://doi.org/10.1007/978-3-030-00563-4_38
8. Gu, Y., Wang, Q., Wang, H., You, D., Zhang, Y.: Multiple kernel learning via low-rank nonnegative matrix factorization for classification of hyperspectral imagery. IEEE J. Sel. Top. Appl. Earth Obs. Remote Sens. **8**(6), 2739–2751 (2015)
9. Iosifidis, A., Tefas, A., Pitas, I.: Graph embedded extreme learning machine. IEEE Trans. Cybern. **46**(1), 311–324 (2016)
10. Huang, G., Zhou, H., Ding, X., Zhang, R.: Extreme learning machine for regression and multiclass classification. IEEE Trans. Syst. Man Cybern. **42**(2), 513–529 (2012)
11. Gu, Y., Chanussot, J., Jia, X., Benediktsson, J.A.: Multiple kernel learning for hyperspectral image classification: a review. IEEE Trans. Geosci. Remote Sens. **55**(11), 6547–6565 (2017)
12. Lee, D., Seung, H.S.: Learning the parts of objects by non-negative matrix factorization. Nature **401**(6755), 788 (1999)
13. Peng, Y., Wang, S., Long, X., Lu, B.L.: Discriminative graph regularized extreme learning machine and its application to face recognition. Neurocomputing **149**, 340–353 (2015)
14. Zhu, M., Martinez, A.M.: Subclass discriminant analysis. IEEE Trans. Pattern Anal. Mach. Intell. **28**(8), 1274–1286 (2006)
15. Sukittanon, S., Atlas, L.E., Pitton, J.W.: Modulation-scale analysis for content identification. IEEE Trans. Signal Process. **52**(10), 3023–3035 (2004)
16. Lee, C.H., Shih, J.L., Yu, K.M., Lin, H.S.: Automatic music genre classification based on modulation spectral analysis of spectral and cepstral features. IEEE Trans. Multimedia **11**(4), 670–682 (2009)
17. Eerola, T., Vuoskoski, J.K.: A comparison of the discrete and dimensional models of emotion in music. Psychol. Music **39**(1), 18–49 (2011)

18. Song, Y., Dixon, S., Pearce, M.: Evaluation of musical features for emotion classification. In: 13th International Society for Music Information Retrieval Conference, ISMIR, pp. 523–528 (2012)
19. Cao, F., Yang, Z., Ren, J., Ling, W.K., Zhao, H., Sun, M., et al.: Sparse representation-based augmented multinomial logistic extreme learning machine with weighted composite features for spectral-spatial classification of hyperspectral images. IEEE Trans. Geosci. Remote Sens. **56**(11), 6263–6279 (2018)
20. Cao, F., Yang, Z., Ren, J., Ling, W.K.: Extreme sparse multinomial logistic regression: a fast and robust framework for hyperspectral image classification. Remote Sens. **9**(12), 1255 (2017)
21. Fang, L., Li, S., Duan, W., Ren, J., Benediktsson, J.A.: Classification of hyperspectral images by exploiting spectral–spatial information of superpixel via multiple kernels. IEEE Trans. Geosci. Remote Sens. **53**(12), 6663–6674 (2015)
22. Feng, W., Huang, W., Ren, J.: Class imbalance ensemble learning based on the margin theory. Appl. Sci. **8**(5), 815 (2018)

Short-Term Electricity Demand Forecasting Based on Multiple LSTMs

Binbin Yong[1,2], Zebang Shen[1], Yongqiang Wei[1], Jun Shen[3,4], and Qingguo Zhou[1(✉)]

[1] School of Information Science and Engineering, Lanzhou University, Lanzhou, Gansu, China
{yongbb,shenzb12,weiyq18,zhouqg}@lzu.edu.cn
[2] School of Physical Science and Technology, Lanzhou University, Lanzhou, Gansu, China
[3] School of Computing and Information Technology, University of Wollongong, Wollongong, NSW, Australia
jshen@uow.edu.au
[4] Department of EE and CS, Research Lab of Electronics, Massachusetts Institute of Technology, Cambridge, MA 02139, USA

Abstract. In recent years, the problem of unbalanced demand and supply in electricity power industry has seriously affected the development of smart grid, especially in the capacity planning, power dispatching and electric power system control. Electricity demand forecasting, as a key solution to the problem, has been widely studied. However, electricity demand is influenced by many factors and nonlinear dependencies, which makes it difficult to forecast accurately. On the other hand, deep neural network technologies are developing rapidly and have been tried in time series forecasting problems. Hence, this paper proposes a novel deep learning model, which is based on the multiple Long Short-Term Memory (LSTM) neural networks to solve the problem of short-term electricity demand forecasting. Compared with autoregressive integrated moving average model (ARIMA) and back propagation neural network (BPNN), our model demonstrates competitive forecast accuracy, which proves that our model is promising for electricity demand forecasting.

Keywords: Electricity demand forecasting · Deep neural network · LSTM · Short-term

1 Introduction

Nowadays, the smart power grid has been gradually replacing the traditional power grid. One of the most important advantages of the smart power grid is that it can control the generated energy precisely and automatically, which is based on the electricity demand prediction. By forecasting the electricity demand accurately, power resources can be dispatched more intelligently by the smart grid [1]. Unfortunately, error estimation of electricity demand is still one of the

J. Ren et al. (Eds.): BICS 2019, LNAI 11691, pp. 192–200, 2020.
https://doi.org/10.1007/978-3-030-39431-8_18

most common reasons of the power grid collapse [2]. Therefore, it is useful to study more efficient methods for electricity demand forecasting, which is still a complex issue [3]. Generally, the electricity demand forecasting is divided into three categories: short-term, mid-term and long-term forecasting, based on the forecasting period. The duration of short-term forecasting ranges from minutes to a week, while the mid-term forecasting ranges from one week to one year. And duration for long-term forecasting can be more than one year. All these three types forecasting are essential tools for smart control in the smart grid. Because great economic value and social value are implied in this problem, the electricity demand forecasting has became a widely researched field recently, and many approaches are proposed for this issue. For example, Alfares et al. [4] reviewed many models for electricity demand forecasting, which are divided into two series: time series (univariate) forecasting models and causal models. The time series models, by which the electricity demand is modeled as a function fitted by past observations, mainly include the dynamic linear [5] or nonlinear [6] models, Kalman filtering models [7–9]. On the other hand, the causal models include the autoregressive moving average (ARMA) [10,11], optimization model [12], nonparametric regression model [13], structural model [14] and curve-fitting models [15].

In recent years, machine learning methods have been widely used in electricity demand forecasting. Park et al. [16] presented an artificial neural network (ANN) based approach for electricity demand forecasting. Hsu et al. [17] built an export system using fuzzy set theory in 1992. Chen et al. [18] used the support vector machine (SVM) model to solve the electricity demand forecasting problem. Peng et al. [19] raised an improved ANN approach which utilized past electricity demand and temperature as inputs to forecast the demand. Peng et al. proposed an forecasting idea which is slightly similar to RNNs. Afterwards, Vermaak et al. [20] used the RNN model to forecast the electricity demand. Yong et al. [2] used an Monte Carlo based neural network to solve the problem. [21] and [22] are forecasting models based on optimized neural network, which both achieved good forecasting accuracy, compared to benchmark algorithms.

In order to further improve the forecasting accuracy, we pay attention to the field of deep learning. Since Hinton et al. [23] firstly proposed to use deep neural network to convert high-dimensional data to low-dimensional data, deep learning have dramatically became the state-of-the-art method in speech recognition, visual object recognition, object detection and many other domains, such as drug discovery and genomics [24]. Conventional machine learning method can not process raw data well, and many prior knowledge is needed when solving time series problem. Deep learning methods can process raw data well with the help of multi-levels representations extracted by many non-linear layers. For time series task, Long Short-Term Memory (LSTM) [25] is a widely used deep neural network, which is in fact a special kind of recurrent neural networks (RNNs) [3] network that shares parameters in the time axis. Based on the above, in this paper, we proposed a multi-LSTMs model to forecast the short-term electricity demand.

The rest of this paper is organized as follows. Section 2 introduces the proposed short-term electricity demand forecasting method. Section 3 presents the experimental results for short-term electricity demand forecasting. In Sect. 4, we conclude the paper.

2 Short-Term Electricity Demand Forecasting Method

The proposed forecasting method is shown in Fig. 1. Figure 1(a) shows the preprocessing methods for electricity demand data, which include normalization and

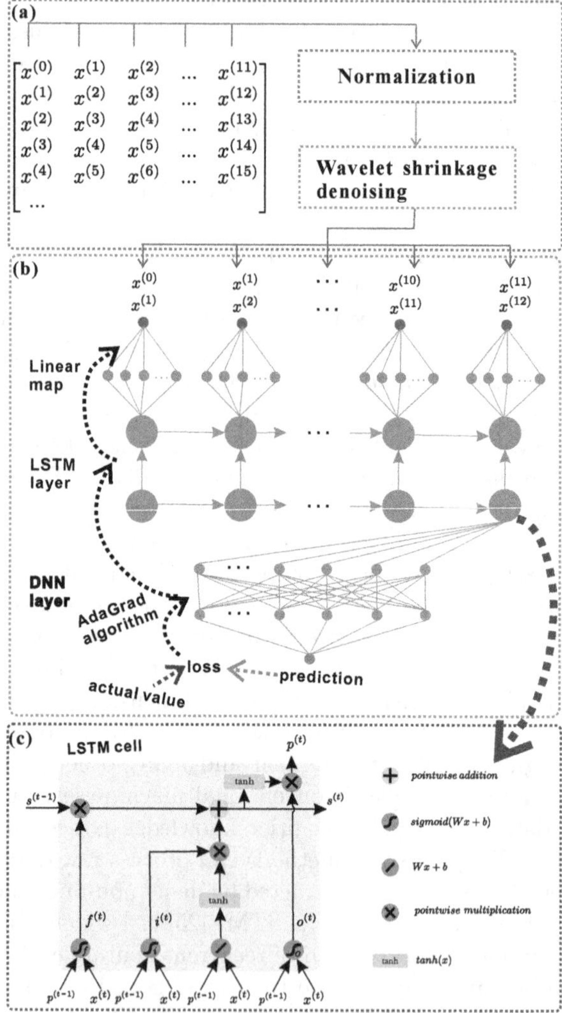

Fig. 1. The structure and training process of proposed forecasting method

denoising methods. The raw data is normalized between 0 and 1, and wavelet shrinkage denoising technique is adopted. In our design, 12 continuous electricity load data is used to forecast the next electricity load data. Therefore, our forecasting model is designed to have 12 input nodes and 1 output node.

2.1 Multi-LSTMs Model

Figure 1(b) shows the structure of the multi-LSTMs forecasting model, and each node in the LSTM layer is a LSTM cell as shown in Fig. 1(c). At the beginning of the model, we add linear map layer for each input to map the input $\boldsymbol{x}^{(i)}$ to 10 dimensions.

After the linear map layer, two LSTM layers are stacked sequentially by the sequential model, as shown in Fig. 1(b). That is, data flow through two LSTM layers in turn. 12×2 LSTM cells are adopted in the network in total. For each LSTM layer, the size of output is $[batch\_size, 12, 10]$, and the number of hidden units is fixed as 10. According to our experiment, stacking two LSTM layers can bring a better performance than a single LSTM layer, which can be seen in the next section. We only focus on the forecasting value, and the output of the last LSTM cell is used as the final forecasting value.

At the end of the forecasting model, two fully connected (FC) layers are added to the model and each FC layer has 10 hidden neurons with nonlinear activation function ReLU [26]. In order to produce a 1 dimension forecasting result, we add a linear regression layer at last to denote the final prediction result.

3 Experimental Results

The electricity load data used in this paper is public and can be accessed online. It is collected from Queensland, Australia and has an interval of 30 min. That is to say, 48 continuous electricity load values are collected everyday, and 336 continuous electricity load values are collected each week. In our experiments, the time series data of the first 8 days is used as the training data, and the data of the last day is used as the test data. When training the forecasting model, all weights of the multi-LSTMs model are initialized randomly in truncated normal distribution with standard deviation of 0.1 and biases 0. Training data with small batches of size 20 are used for training the deep learning model.

In order to measure the performance of the proposed forecasting model, root mean square error (RMSE), mean absolute error (MAE) and mean absolute percentage error (MAPE) are adopted as performance metrics, which are defined as Eq. (1–3):

Table 1. Experimental results: short-term electricity demand forecasting for Queensland in summer and autumn

Day	Error	Summer			Autumn		
		BPNN	ARIMA	Proposed	BPNN	ARIMA	Proposed
Mon.	RMSE	136.270	70.534	**58.674**	151.131	78.953	**72.117**
	MAPE	1.65%	0.83%	**0.70%**	2.25%	0.92%	**0.90%**
	MAE	110.054	54.475	**46.755**	117.687	49.851	**44.207**
Tue.	RMSE	172.867	72.689	**69.917**	148.016	66.859	**61.936**
	MAPE	1.91%	0.79%	**0.77%**	1.89%	0.89%	**0.86%**
	MAE	129.780	53.350	**53.317**	111.938	53.350	**51.031**
Wed.	RMSE	173.446	86.262	**66.789**	159.127	69.243	**66.364**
	MAPE	2.01%	0.94%	**0.82%**	2.12%	0.89%	**0.85%**
	MAE	135.253	64.436	**54.692**	123.765	51.519	**49.259**
Thu.	RMSE	179.221	74.205	**66.474**	178.823	71.413	**70.292**
	MAPE	2.01%	0.83%	**0.77%**	2.43%	0.94%	**0.90%**
	MAE	138.493	58.841	**51.224**	142.212	54.283	**50.682**
Fri.	RMSE	148.055	71.281	**62.447**	133.942	72.163	**70.973**
	MAPE	1.89%	0.87%	**0.76%**	1.89%	0.94%	**0.86%**
	MAE	118.143	56.820	**48.649**	105.057	54.048	**50.021**
Sat.	RMSE	141.079	64.618	**57.827**	137.088	72.607	**61.761**
	MAPE	1.96%	0.86%	**0.77%**	1.91%	0.95%	**0.88%**
	MAE	110.943	49.834	**44.973**	103.374	51.711	**47.772**
Sun.	RMSE	135.515	53.234	**48.967**	142.317	81.766	**63.323**
	MAPE	2.13%	0.74%	**0.72%**	1.97%	1.03%	**0.91%**
	MAE	114.940	40.969	**39.243**	106.234	56.026	**49.118**

$$\mathrm{RMSE} = \sqrt{\frac{1}{n}\sum_{t=1}^{n}(y^{(t)} - p^{(t)})^2} \tag{1}$$

$$\mathrm{MSE} = \frac{1}{n}\sum_{t=1}^{n}(y^{(t)} - p^{(t)})^2 \tag{2}$$

$$\mathrm{MAPE} = \sum_{t=1}^{n}\frac{1}{n}\left|\frac{y^{(t)} - p^{(t)}}{y^{(t)}}\right| \times 100\% \tag{3}$$

in which $y^{(t)}$ denotes the observation value at time t, while $p^{(t)}$ means the prediction value at time t.

Table 1 shows the forecasting errors for different days in a week for Queensland in summer and autumn, and forecasting errors of ARIMA and BPNN models are compared. The ARIMA model is configured with autoregressive order parameter 8, moving average parameter 3 and difference term parameter 1.

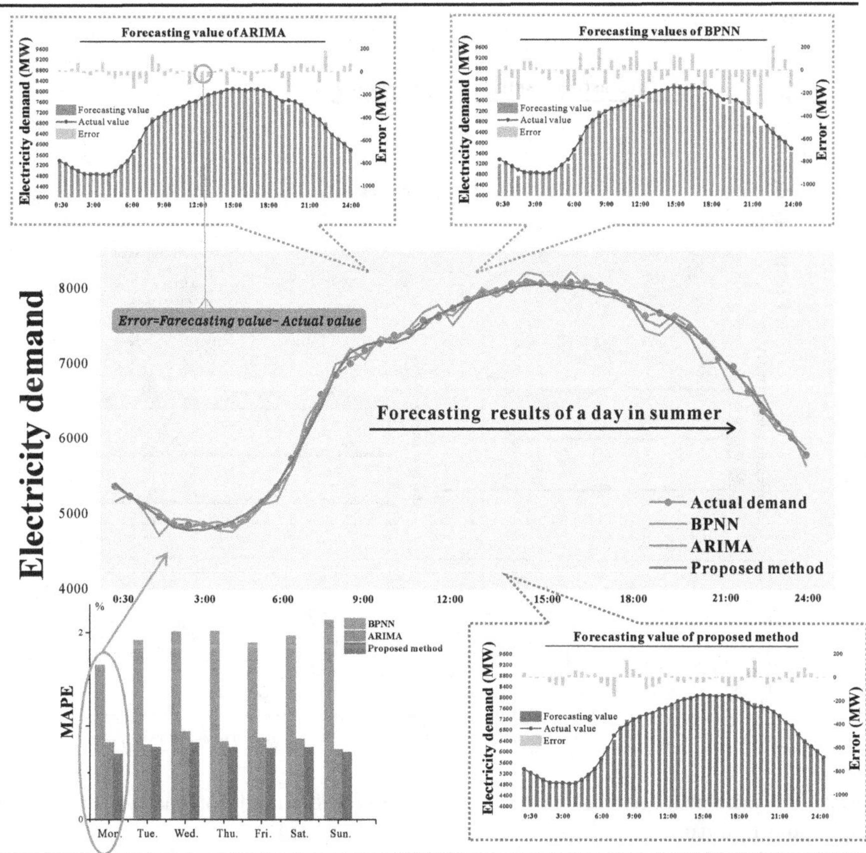

Fig. 2. Experimental results: short-term electricity demand forecasting curves for Queensland in summer

The BPNN is designed with 12 input nodes, 50 hidden nodes and one output node, which is determined by many experiments and performs best. According to results in Table 1, we can find that proposed method achieves highest forecasting accuracy for each day. Especially for the MAPE metric, the performance of the proposed method is remarkable.

Figure 2 shows more intuitive comparisons of forecasting model for summer days by forecasting electricity demand of Monday. After a lot of training, BPNN still has high prediction errors. The ARIMA model and proposed method both perform well, and the proposed method give smaller forecasting deviation between the actual electricity demand. Figure 2 also shows the comparison of MAPE metrics between three models, and the proposed model achieves minimum prediction error. Figure 3 shows the detailed forecasting results of autumn model.

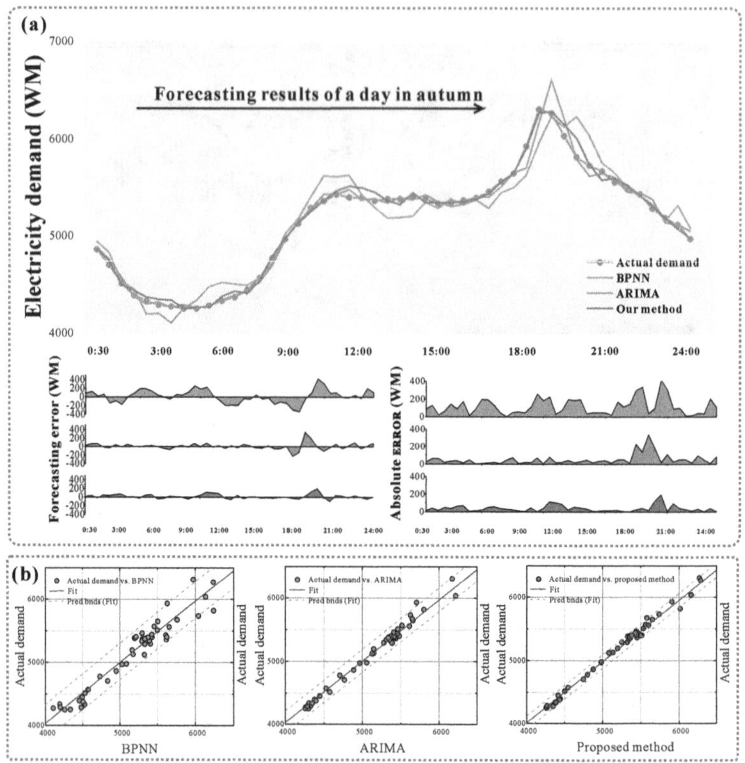

Fig. 3. Experimental results: short-term electricity demand forecasting curves for Queensland in autumn

Figure 3(a) gives another forecasting results in autumn of these three models. Obviously, the forecasting result of proposed method is closest to the real electricity demand. Figure 3(b) show the comparison of forecasting deviations, from which we can easily see that our model is more accurate with smaller deviations.

4 Conclusion

In this paper, a deep learning based multiple LSTMs model is proposed for short-term electricity demand forecasting. Real electricity demand data for Queensland in summer and autumn is preprocessed and used for model training and testing. Meanwhile, ARIMA and BPNN forecasting models are designed for comparisons. Results show that proposed model has competitive performances compared to traditional forecasting models.

Acknowledgment. This work was supported by National Natural Science Foundation of China under Grant No. 61402210 and 60973137, State Grid Corporation Science and Technology Project under Grant No. SGGSKY00FJJS1700302, Program for

New Century Excellent Talents in University under Grant No. NCET-12-0250, Major National Project of High Resolution Earth Observation System under Grant No. 30-Y20A34-9010-15/17, Strategic Priority Research Program of the Chinese Academy of Sciences with Grant No. XDA03030100, Google Research Awards and Google Faculty Award.

References

1. Chen, J.-F., Lo, S.-K., Do, Q.H.: Forecasting monthly electricity demands: an application of neural networks trained by heuristic algorithms. Information **8**(1), 31 (2017)
2. Yong, B., et al.: Neural network model with Monte Carlo algorithm for electricity demand forecasting in Queensland. In: The Australasian Computer Science Week Multiconference, pp. 1–7 (2017)
3. Mansouri, V., Akbari, M.E.: Efficient short-term electricity load forecasting using recurrent neural networks. J. Artif. Intell. Electr. Eng. **3**(9), 46–54 (2014)
4. Alfares, H.K., Nazeeruddin, M.: Electric load forecasting: literature survey and classification of methods. Int. J. Syst. Sci. **33**(1), 23–34 (2002)
5. Douglas, A.P., et al.: The impacts of temperature forecast uncertainty on Bayesian load forecasting. IEEE Trans. Power Syst. **13**(4), 1507–1513 (1998)
6. Sadownik, R., Barbosa, E.P.: Short-term forecasting of industrial electricity consumption in Brazil. J. Forecast. **18**(3), 215–224 (1999)
7. Infield, D.G., Hill, D.C.: Optimal smoothing for trend removal in short term electricity demand forecasting. IEEE Trans. Power Syst. **13**(3), 1115–1120 (1998)
8. Park, J.H., Park, Y.M., Lee, K.Y.: Composite modeling for adaptive short-term load forecasting. IEEE Trans. Power Syst. **6**(2), 450–457 (1991)
9. Sargunaraj, S., Gupta, D.P.S., Devi, S.: Short-term load forecasting for demand side management. IEE Proc.-Gener. Transm. Distrib. **144**(1), 68–74 (1997)
10. Wang, H., Schulz, N.N.: Using AMR data for load estimation for distribution system analysis. Electr. Power Syst. Res. **76**(5), 336–342 (2006)
11. Magnano, L., Boland, J.W.: Generation of synthetic sequences of electricity demand: application in South Australia. Energy **32**(11), 2230–2243 (2007)
12. Yu, Z.: A temperature match based optimization method for daily load prediction considering DLC effect. IEEE Trans. Power Syst. **11**(2), 728–733 (1996)
13. Charytoniuk, W., Chen, M.S., Olinda, P.V.: Nonparametric regression based short-term load forecasting. IEEE Trans. Power Syst. **13**(3), 725–730 (1998)
14. Harvey, A., Koopman, S.J.: Forecasting hourly electricity demand using time-varying splines. J. Am. Stat. Assoc. **88**(424), 1228–1236 (1993)
15. Taylor, J.W., Majithia, S.: Using combined forecasts with changing weights for electricity demand profiling. J. Oper. Res. Soc. **51**(1), 72–82 (2000)
16. Park, D.C., et al.: Electric load forecasting using an artificial neural network. IEEE Trans. Power Syst. **6**(2), 442–449 (1991)
17. Hsu, Y.Y., Ho, K.L.: Fuzzy expert systems: an application to short-term load forecasting. IEE Proc. C Gener. Transm. Distrib. **139**(6), 471–477 (1992)
18. Chen, B.J., Chang, M.W., Lin, C.J.: Load forecasting using support vector machines: a study on EUNITE competition 2001. IEEE Trans. Power Syst. **19**(4), 1821–1830 (2004)
19. Peng, T.M., Hubele, N.F., Karady, G.G.: Advancement in the application of neural networks for short-term load forecasting. IEEE Trans. Power Syst. **7**(1), 250–257 (1992)

20. Vermaak, J., Botha, E.C.: Recurrent neural networks for short-term load forecasting. IEEE Trans. Power Syst. **13**(1), 126–132 (1998)
21. Hu, R., et al.: A short-term power load forecasting model based on the generalized regression neural network with decreasing step fruit fly optimization algorithm. Neurocomputing **221**, 24–31 (2016)
22. Rana, M., Koprinska, I.: Forecasting electricity load with advanced wavelet neural networks. Neurocomputing **182**, 118–132 (2016)
23. Hinton, G.E., Salakhutdinov, R.R.: Reducing the dimensionality of data with neural networks. Science **313**(5786), 504–507 (2006)
24. Lecun, Y., Bengio, Y., Hinton, G.: Deep learning. Nature **521**(7553), 436–444 (2015)
25. Hochreiter, S., Schmidhuber, J.: Long short-term memory. Neural Comput. **9**(8), 1735 (1997)
26. Glorot, X., Bordes, A., Bengio, Y.: Deep sparse rectifier neural networks. J. Mach. Learn. Res. **15**, 315–323 (2011)

Adaptive Video Summarization via Robust Representation and Structured Sparsity

Manjin Sheng[1], Jiayu Shi[1], Dengdi Sun[1(✉)], Zhuanlian Ding[2], and Bin Luo[1]

[1] School of Computer Science and Technology, Anhui University, Hefei 230601, China
sundengdi@163.com

[2] School of Internet, Anhui University, Hefei 230039, China

Abstract. To improve faster browsing and more efficient content indexing of huge video collections, video summarization has emerged as an important area of research for the multimedia community. One of the mechanisms to generate video summaries is to extract keyframes which represent the most important content of the video. However, there are still some problems like image imperfection and noise interference, which seriously affect the performance of keyframe selection. Aiming at above problems, in this paper, we propose a linear reconstruction framework to summarize the videos. The first model in our framework seeks the most informative keyframes (base vectors) using the structure sparsity of the ℓ_{21} norm regularization, to represent all the frames as the linear combination of them in a video. Furthermore, we also propose another more robust model via ℓ_{21} norm based loss function to suppress the outlier, and form the joint sparsity with ℓ_{21} norm regularization. For the optimization, we design two efficient algorithms for two proposed models respectively. Finally the extensive experiments on real world video datesets are presented to show the effectiveness of the proposed framework.

Keywords: Video summarization · Keyframe extraction · Robust representation · Structured sparsity

1 Introduction

With the rapid development in video acquisition, storage and distribution technologies, the volume of video data in the daily life are growing explosively, which makes it very difficult to browse, manage and retrieve the huge amount of video content quickly and efficiently. To address this challenge, video summarization is an available and promising strategy, which provides a condensed version of a full length video through searching the most important content in video streams, and therefore has been widely applied in video indexing, event detection and interactive browsing systems [1].

J. Ren et al. (Eds.): BICS 2019, LNAI 11691, pp. 201–210, 2020.
https://doi.org/10.1007/978-3-030-39431-8_19

Generally, most videos contain significant redundancy and only a small fraction of the frames are informative, so one of the important video summarization technique is to automatically select a subset of the most representative frames from a video to describe its content [2], known as keyframe extraction. The existing keyframe extraction algorithms can be roughly divided into three categories: segmentation-, clustering- and sequential-based approaches. The segmentation-based algorithms [3] segment a video into a series of shots at first, and then select a small number of keyframes from each shot. However, the shots duplication, overlap and segmentation error can seriously affect the extraction of keyframes. The clustering-based approach [4] groups the similar frames of a video into some clusters, and then chooses typically one frame that is closest to cluster centroid as a keyframe. In fact, a number of video data are not fit the clustering model, and the quality of selected keyframes heavily depends on the effect of clustering. The sequential-based method [5] measures the difference between the frames, and then compares with a predefined threshold to confirm the keyframes. Nevertheless, this approach trend to find the significant changes in video sequences, and hence may not be enough to represent the most informative visual content.

In this paper, we present a linear reconstruction framework to solve frame-extraction problem, and the key idea is to express all the frame feature vectors with the linear combination of a small number of base vectors. The proposed framework consists of two components: a convex reconstruction loss function and a regularizer for keyframe selection. Under this framework, we first employ the structured sparse regularization based on ℓ_{21} norm to select the representative keyframes. Moreover, the robust reconstruction loss function is further utilized to suppress the influence of noise and outlier frames. For optimization, we design two efficient algorithms to iteratively solve the two models respectively to obtain the convergence solution. Experiments on real world video database have shown that the proposed algorithms achieve better performance compared to existing state-of-the-art algorithms, and are able to select the accurate and robust keyframes automatically.

2 Reconstruction Framework for Video Summarization

Assuming that a video contains n frames f_i, $i \in [1....n]$, we extract a d-dimensional column feature vector x_i for each frame image f_i, to form a feature matrix $X = [x_1, x_2, \cdots, x_n] \in \mathbb{R}^{d\times n}$. The task of keyframe-based video summarization is to select the m $(m \ll n)$ most informative frame images to represent the entire video. Such a problem can be formulated as the linear combination of the basis in the original feature space X,

$$\min_{B,S} \sum_{i=1}^{n} \|x_i - Bs_i\|_2^2, \quad s.t. \quad B \subset X, \ \ Card(B) = m, \tag{1}$$

where, $Card(\cdot)$ denote the column number of matrix, $B = [b_1, b_2, \cdots, b_m] \in \mathbb{R}^{d\times m}$ is the basis matrix consisted of m column vectors. In video summarization, the m columns are usually treated as m keyframes and should therefore be a subset of X. $S = [s_1, s_2, \cdots, s_n] \in \mathbb{R}^{m \times n}$ is the coefficient matrix, and s_i indicates the coefficient vector of x_i linear combination by m basis $b_1, b_2, \cdots, b_m$. Equation (1) is similar to Transductive Experimental Design (TED) [6] problem, whose key idea is to select the samples that can best represent the whole data using a linear representation. However, Eq. (1) is nonconvex and difficult to optimize because of the product of two unknown matrices B and S. To address the drawback, we replace the basis matrix B as original feature matrix X directly and minimize the residual of linear reconstruct: $\min_W \sum_{i=1}^{n} \Theta(x_i - Xw_i)$ with the new coefficient matrix $W = [w_1, w_2, \cdots, w_n] \in \mathbb{R}^{n \times n}$, where $\Theta(\cdot)$ is a convex function of residual. In other words, we minimize the reconstruction error of each data point as a linear combination of all the data. Thus, our reconstruction framework can be generally written into a matrix format:

$$\min_{E,W} \Theta(E) + \gamma \Psi(W), \quad s.t. \;\; X = XW + E, \tag{2}$$

where $E \in \mathbb{R}^{d \times n}$ denotes the residual of linear reconstruct, and $\Theta(E)$ is the loss function of reconstruction, which can be with different forms depending on the data characteristic and task requirement. $\Psi(W)$ stands for the regularizer on W, which define the mechanism for keyframe selection, and γ is the coefficient controlling the importance of the regularizer.

3 Methodology

Under the reconstruction framework of Eq. (2), we formulate the keyframe extraction problem using the structured sparsity-inducing norms and propose two novel models with efficient optimization algorithms.

3.1 Linear Reconstruction with Structured Sparsity

We first consider the reconstruct error as a least square loss function, that is $\Theta(E) = \sum_{i=1}^{n} \|x_i - Xw_i\|_2^2$. To choose $m \ll n$ representatives, we enforce that there are only m nonzero elements in w_i. Thus, if $w_{ij} = 0$, the corresponding column vector x_j does not participate in the linear combination of x_i, which means the frame f_j is not a valid representation of frame f_i. On the contrary, the frame images corresponded with nonzero elements in w_i should be selected to represent f_i. Therefore, the previous problem is converted into the framework of sparse linear reconstruction. Furthermore, to select a common subset of representative frames from all vectors, we introduce the structure sparsity constrain via ℓ_{21} norm as the regularizer in Eq. (2) as:

$$\min_{W} \sum_{i=1}^{n} \|x_i - Xw_i\|_2^2 + \gamma \|W\|_{21}, \tag{3}$$

where $\|W\|_{21} = \sum_{j=1}^{n} \sqrt{\sum_{i=1}^{n} (w_{ji})^2}$, and when W is row-sparse enough, the objective function achieve the global minimum. In other words, the indices of the nonzero rows of W correspond to the indices of the columns of X which are chosen as the data representatives. Furthermore, we want the selection of representatives to be invariant with respect to a global translation of the data [7]. We thus enforce the affine constraint $\mathbf{1}^{\mathrm{T}}W = \mathbf{1}$. As a result, we have the following **Model I** in matrix format:

$$\min_{W} \|X - XW\|_F^2 + \gamma\|W\|_{21}, \quad s.t. \; \mathbf{1}^{\mathrm{T}}W = \mathbf{1}^{\mathrm{T}} \tag{4}$$

where $\mathbf{1}$ denote all-ones vector. Using Model I, each frame in a video can be represented adaptively as an affine combination of $k \ll n$ keyframes.

Solution:
To optimize Eq. (4), we add a relaxation constraint $W = C$, and convert it to the Augmented Lagrange Multiplier (ALM) [8] function as following:

$$\begin{aligned} \mathcal{L}_1 = \|X - XW\|_F^2 + \gamma \|C\|_{2,1} + \frac{\mu}{2}\left(\|W - C\|_F^2 + \left\|\mathbf{1}^{\mathrm{T}}W - \mathbf{1}^{\mathrm{T}}\right\|_2^2\right) \\ + \operatorname{Tr}\left[\Lambda_1^{\mathrm{T}}(W - C)\right] + \operatorname{Tr}\left[\Lambda_2^{\mathrm{T}}\left(\mathbf{1}^{\mathrm{T}}W - \mathbf{1}^{\mathrm{T}}\right)\right], \end{aligned} \tag{5}$$

where Λ_1 and Λ_2 are Lagrange multipliers and $\mu > 0$ is a penalty parameter. The above problem can be solved by alternative iteration. Calculating the partial derivatives of Eq. (5) with respect to each variable and parameter respectively, we can first get the solution of W as follows,

$$W = \left(2X^{\mathrm{T}}X + \mu\left(I + \mathbf{1}\mathbf{1}^{\mathrm{T}}\right)\right)^{-1}\left(2X^{\mathrm{T}}X + \mu\left(P + \mathbf{1}Q\right)\right) \tag{6}$$

where $P = C - \frac{\Lambda_1}{\mu}$, $Q = \mathbf{1}^{\mathrm{T}} + \frac{\Lambda_2}{\mu}$. Similarity, C is solved via the following operator [9]:

$$c_i = \begin{cases} \frac{\|r_i\| - \frac{\gamma}{\mu}}{\|r_i\|} r_i & if \; \frac{\gamma}{\mu} < \|r_i\| \\ 0 & otherwise \end{cases} \tag{7}$$

where $R = W + \frac{\Lambda_1}{\mu}$. Finally, the solutions to Λ_1, Λ_2 Eqs. (8) and (9) are obtained.

$$\Lambda_1 = \Lambda_1 + \mu(W - C) \tag{8}$$

$$\Lambda_2 = \Lambda_2 + \mu(\mathbf{1}^{\mathrm{T}}W - \mathbf{1}^{\mathrm{T}}) \tag{9}$$

The complete algorithm is outlined in Algorithm 1. Also, we conduct the keyframe selection from a single shot to briefly show the performance of Model I. From Fig. 1, in this single shot with transitional segments, our model select the 4-th frame as the keyframe in this shot, which is most representative and successfully avoids the unclear transition between the head and the tail.

3.2 Robust Linear Reconstruction with Structured Sparsity

In Model I, $\Theta(E) = \sum_{i=1}^{n} \|x_i - Xw_i\|_2^2$. However, the least square loss function used in linear reconstruction is sensitive to data outliers, thus the Model I is not

Algorithm 1. Linear Reconstruction with Structured Sparsity

Input: feature matrix $X \in \mathbb{R}^{d \times n}$, parameter γ.

1: **Initialize:** $W = C = \mathbf{0}, \Lambda_1 = 0, \Lambda_2 = 0, \mu = 10^{-6}, max_\mu = 10^{10}, \rho = 1.1, \varepsilon = 10^{-8}$.

2: **while** not converge **do**

  2.1: fix the others and update W by Eq.(6);

  2.2: fix the others and update C by Eq.(7);

  2.3: update the multipliers Λ_1 and Λ_2 by Eq.(8) and Eq.(9);

  2.4: update the parameter μ by $\mu = \min(\rho\mu, max_\mu)$;

  2.5: check the convergence conditions $max|W - C| < \varepsilon$ and $max|\mathbf{1}^{\mathrm{T}}W - \mathbf{1}^{\mathrm{T}}| < \varepsilon$.

3: **end while**

Output: coefficient matrix $W \in \mathbb{R}^{n \times n}$.

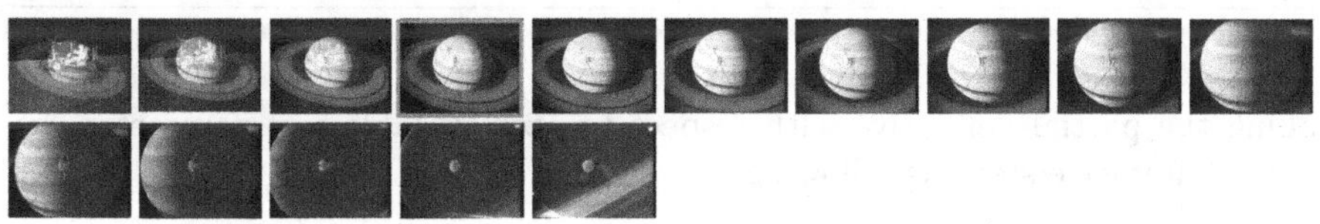

Fig. 1. Extract the keyframe from one shot by model I.

suitable for the real-world video summarization task with large noisy frames. To this end, we further consider the robust reconstruction loss function via ℓ_{21} norm to select the keyframes insensitive to the effect of noises and outliers, that is $\Theta(E) = \sum_{i=1}^{n} \|x_i - Xw_i\|_2$ [10], Therefore we propose to solve the following problem:

$$\min_{W} \sum_{i=1}^{n} \|x_i - Xw_i\|_2 + \gamma \|W\|_{21}, \tag{10}$$

In the same way, we also enforce the affine constraint $\mathbf{1}^{\mathrm{T}}W = \mathbf{1}$ to form the **Model II** in matrix format:

$$\min_{W} \left\|(X - XW)^{\mathrm{T}}\right\|_{21} + \gamma \|W\|_{21}, \quad s.t. \;\; \mathbf{1}^{\mathrm{T}}W = \mathbf{1}^{\mathrm{T}} \tag{11}$$

In Model II, by using ℓ_{21} norm in loss function, the ℓ_1 norm is imposed among data points and the ℓ_2 norm is used for features.

Solution:

To optimize Eq. (4), considering the non-smooth ℓ_{21} norm in both components, we add the relaxation constraint $W = C$ and $X - XW = E$, and convert Model II into the following ALM objective:

$$\begin{aligned} \mathcal{L}_2 = & \left\|E^{\mathrm{T}}\right\|_{21} + \gamma \|C\|_{2,1} + \frac{\mu}{2}\left[\|W - C\|_F^2 + \left\|\mathbf{1}^{\mathrm{T}}W - \mathbf{1}^{\mathrm{T}}\right\|_2^2 + \|X - XW - E\|_F^2\right] \\ & + \mathrm{Tr}\left[\Lambda_1^{\mathrm{T}}(W - C)\right] + \mathrm{Tr}\left[\Lambda_2^{\mathrm{T}}\left(\mathbf{1}^{\mathrm{T}}W - \mathbf{1}^{\mathrm{T}}\right)\right] + \mathrm{Tr}\left[\Lambda_3^{\mathrm{T}}(X - XW - E)\right], \end{aligned} \tag{12}$$

Algorithm 2. Robust Linear Reconstruction with Structured Sparsity

Input: feature matrix $X \in \mathbb{R}^{d \times n}$, parameter γ.

1: **Initialize:** $W = C = \mathbf{0}$, $\Lambda_1, \Lambda_2, \Lambda_3 = 0$, $\mu = 10^{-6}, max_\mu = 10^{10}, \rho = 1.1, \varepsilon = 10^{-8}$.

2: **while** not converge **do**

2.1: fix the others and update W by Eq.(13);

2.2: fix the others and update C by Eq.(7);

2.3: fix the others and update E by Eq.(14);

2.4: update the multipliers Λ_1, Λ_2 and Λ_3 by Eq.(8), Eq.(9) and Eq.(15);

2.5: update the parameter μ by $\mu = \min(\rho\mu, max_\mu)$;

2.6: check if $max|W - C| < \varepsilon$, $max|\mathbf{1}^{\mathrm{T}}W - \mathbf{1}^{\mathrm{T}}| < \varepsilon$ and $max|X - XW - E| < \varepsilon$.

3: **end while**

Output: coefficient matrix $W \in \mathbb{R}^{n \times n}$.

Taking the partial derivative with respect to each variable and parameter, we have the iterative steps as following:

$$W = \left(2X^{\mathrm{T}}X + \mu\left(I + \mathbf{1}\mathbf{1}^{\mathrm{T}}\right)\right)^{-1}\left(2U^{\mathrm{T}}X + \mu\left(P + \mathbf{1}Q\right)\right) \tag{13}$$

where $U = X - E + \frac{\Lambda_3}{\mu}$. Then, C is solved by Eq. (7), and E is updated via the same operator:

$$e_i = \begin{cases} \frac{\|v_i\| - \frac{1}{\mu}}{\|v_i\|} v_i & if \ \frac{1}{\mu} < \|v_i\| \\ 0 & otherwise \end{cases} \tag{14}$$

where $V = X - XW + \frac{\Lambda_3}{\mu}$. At last, Lagrange multiplier Λ_3 are updated as:

$$\Lambda_3 = \Lambda_3 + \mu(X - XW - E) \tag{15}$$

The detailed algorithm is described in Algorithm 2.

Here, we show the performance of Model II using the same example in Model I. Within this shot, we replace three frames with noisy images. As shown in Fig. 2, Model II selects the same keyframe (red box) as Model One. The outlier and noise frame are well avoided, and the frame with better visual representativeness is selected.

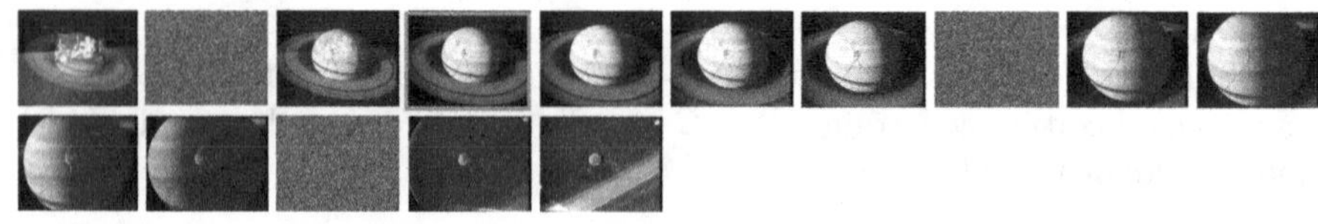

Fig. 2. Extract the keyframe from one shot by model II. (Color figure online)

4 Implementation

To capture high-level semantics information, we use the pretrained convolution neural network to extract deep features. In particular, the network is a modified VGG-16 model, in which the fc_8 layer is replaced with two fully-connected layers followed by a mean pooling layer to fuse feature maps of multi-frames. The unit size of the two fully connected layers to 1,000 and 300 respectively, which means our deep feature is a 300-dimensional vector. Considering the temporal association between frames, we uniformly cut out continuous 5 frames $f_i, \cdots, f_{i+4}$ using a temporal sliding window manner, where the window is shifted by 1 frame, then feed integrally the 5 frames into the modified VGG network. So the output is treated as the feature of the i-th frame f_i.

After obtaining the reconstructed coefficient matrix W, each row of the matrix is frame-to-video contribution information, so we can calculate the row-sum values $w^j = \sum_{i=1}^{n} |w_{ji}|$ of the absolute W to quantify the representativeness of the frame to the reconstruction process. The larger the value, the more significant the frame is. Thus we sort the row-sum values in the decreasing order, and the keyframe extraction task can be performed by further selecting the m frames corresponding to the top m row-sum values of W to obtain a video storyboard.

Within two models, γ controls the sparsity of regularizer, so influent the quality of obtaining representatives. In this paper, we run our proposed algorithm with $\gamma = \alpha\gamma_0$, where $\alpha > 1$ and γ_0 is analytically computed from the data. Actually, depending on the amount of activities in a video, we could obtain an appropriate number of representatives for that video.

5 Experiments

5.1 Database and Experiment Setup

We validate our methods by Open Video Project. This dataset collects a series of real-world videos in common video set [11], including various subjects such as Documentary, Educational, Lecture and so on, and comes with a storyboard and content description. As a standard, the groundtruth keyframes are obtained by curve simplification algorithm and some manual intervention from the open video storyboard. Here, we compared our two models with the groundtruth, time difference method (TD) [12], K-means clustering algorithm, and robust principal component analysis key frame extraction (RPCA-KFE) [13].

5.2 Comparison Results

To evaluate the performance of our algorithms, we extract the same number (m) of key frames as the storyboard by various methods independently, and compare them with the groundtruth. If the content of a result keyframe f_i is same to groundtruth, we record $score_i = 1$. In the same way, $score_i = 0.5$ for similar keyframe, and $score_i = 0$ for different keyframe. We selected 20 videos from

Table 1. Average accuracy of keyframe extraction.

Category	TD		K-Means		RPCA		Model 1		Model 2	
	Org	+Noise	Org	+Noise	Org	+Noise	Org	+Noise	Org	+Noise
Documentary	43.5%	22.3%	61.4%	49.4%	67.7%	55.2%	**74.9%**	64.3%	71.3%	**67.5%**
Historical	39.7%	21.4%	67.1%	53.2%	68.4%	54.6%	**76.3%**	66.3%	75.3%	**71.3%**
Lecture	42.8%	26.3%	66.8%	51.0%	70.5%	60.2%	**73.7%**	60.1%	69.1%	**66.8%**
Average	42.0%	23.3%	65.1%	51.2%	68.9%	56.7%	**74.6%**	63.6%	71.9%	**68.5%**

the three categories: Documentary, Historical and Lecture, and carried out the comparison experiments with and without noise respectively. The average frame accuracy is calculated as $\frac{\sum_{i=1}^{m} score_i}{m}$, and is shown in Table 1.

By analyzing the results in Table 1, we can see that the traditional TD algorithm has the worst effect, and our model have the best performance among all the methods. Especially after adding noise, the accuracy of TD algorithm and K-means algorithm is greatly decreased, while our robust model II still achieve satisfactory results.

5.3 Case Study for Story Integrity

In order to further evaluate our experimental results, we randomly selected a video here to demonstrate the results in terms of story integrity and anti-noise ability (see next subsection). In this section, we choose the video named "New Indian", a part of the Indian documentary, whose duration is 28 s and the frame rate is 29.7 fps. The experimental results are shown below.

From Fig. 3 we can see that as the simplest traditional method, TD method only selects 10 key frames, which does not completely summarize the whole story, and only 4 frames are correct. K-means find 7 right frames with 3 similar frames (yellow box) and 4 wrong frames (blue box). The RPCA method has the 8 frames as same as the standard storyboard, and 2 frames are similar. Both of our two models have more than 10 correct frames. Specifically, Model I correctly selects 11 frames, and there are 2 frames with similar contents, meanwhile Model II select 10 right frames and 2 similar frames. Comparison results show that our methods can generate better story integrity, and fully represent the entire content except a small amount of frame redundancy and loss.

5.4 Case Study on Corrupted Video

In order to verify the anti-noise ability of the proposed methods, we randomly select some frames from each video and manually corrupt them with plenty of pepper and salt noise. As shown in Fig. 4, we find that corrupted frames have a significant impact on TD and K-means algorithms. Especially, TD algorithm has not almost any anti-noise ability. Due to noise interference, the TD and K-means algorithms easily lead to the storyboard to be broken and scattered, and automatically select a lot of error and noise images. The RPCA method based

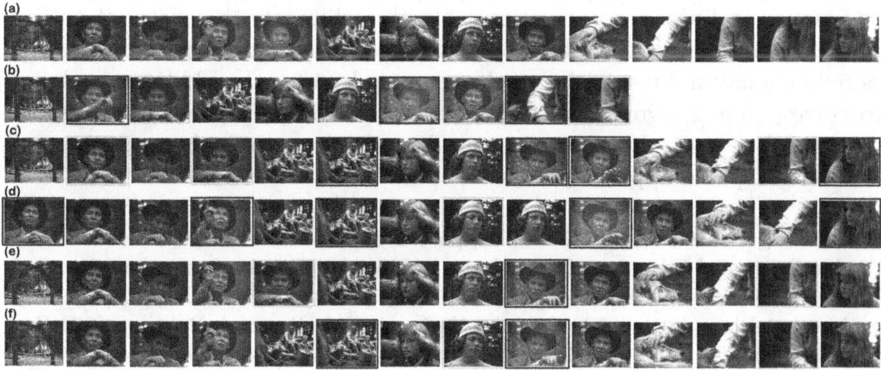

Fig. 3. Extraction results by (a) Open Video Storyboard (b) TD (c) K-Means (d) RPCA (e) Model I (f) Model II (Color figure online)

Fig. 4. Extraction results by (a) TD (b) K-means (c) RPCA (d) Model I (e) Model II

on low-rank sparse decomposition of matrix and has certain noise immunity, but it also inevitably selects a part of corrupted frames. On the contrary, neither of our two models has extracted the noise pictures. However, comparing the keyframe sequences before and after adding noise (Figs. 3 and 4), we can apparently observe that the contents of some key frames of Model I are affected by noise; the key frame redundancy increases while the accuracy decreases. Moreover, The key frames extracted by Model 2 not only contain no noise, but also preserve the content invariant because of the robust linear reconstruction in Model II. Therefore, we conclude that Model 2 has the best anti-noise ability.

6 Conclusion

In this paper, we propose two video keyframe extraction algorithms based on the linear reconstruction framework. At first, the ℓ_{21} norm based structured sparse regularization is utilized to select the most representative frames with large coefficients. Then, we introduce the robust sparse representation based loss function in linear reconstruction to further eliminate the effects of outlier. As a result, the keyframes selected by our models are most representative and less redundancy, and insensitive to the corrupted frames. In addition, we design two corresponding algorithms for two models, and apply them to real video summarization tasks. In all experimental results, our methods outperform all the other compared approaches.

Acknowledgments. This work was supported by the Key Natural Science Project of Anhui Provincial Education Department (KJ2018A0023), the Guangdong Province Science and Technology Plan Projects (2017B010110011), the Anhui Key Research and Development Plan (1804a09020101), the National Basic Research Program (973 Program) of China (2015CB351705), the National Natural Science Foundation of China (61906002, 61402002, 61876002 and 61860206004) and 2018 College Students Innovation and Entrepreneurship Training Program (201810357352).

References

1. Elkhattabi, Z., Tabii, Y., Benkaddour, A.: Video summarization: techniques and applications. Int. J. Comput. Electr. Autom. Control Inf. Eng. **9**(4), 928–933 (2015)
2. Khosla, A., Hamid, R., Lin, C.J., Sundaresan, N.: Large-scale video summarization using web-image priors. In: IEEE Conference on Computer Vision and Pattern Recognition, pp. 2698–2705 (2013)
3. Ren, J., Jiang, J., Feng, Y.: Activity-driven content adaptation for effective video summarization. J. Vis. Commun. Image Represent. **21**(8), 930–938 (2010)
4. Ren, J., Jiang, J.: Hierarchical modeling and adaptive clustering for real-time summarization of rush videos. IEEE Trans. Multimed. **11**(5), 906–917 (2009)
5. Ejaz, N., Tariq, T., Balik, S.: Adaptive key frame extraction for video summarization using an aggregating mechanism. J. Vis. Commun. Image Represent. **23**, 1031–1040 (2012)
6. Yu, K., Bi, J., Tresp, V.: Active learning via transductive experimental design. In: International Conference on Machine Learning, pp. 1081–1088. ACM (2006)
7. Elhamifar, E., Sapiro, G., Vidal, R.: See all by looking at a few: sparse modeling for finding representative objects. In: IEEE Conference on Computer Vision and Pattern Recognition, pp. 1600–1607. IEEE (2012)
8. Lin, Z., Chen, M., Ma, Y.: The augmented lagrange multiplier method for exact recovery of corrupted low-rank matrices. arXiv preprint arXiv:1009.5055 (2010)
9. Liu, G., Lin, Z., Yu, Y.: Robust subspace segmentation by low-rank representation. In: International Conference on Machine Learning, pp. 663–670 (2010)
10. Nie, F., Wang, H., Huang, H., Ding, C.: Early active learning via robust representation and structured sparsity. In: International Joint Conference on Artificial Intelligence, pp. 1572–1578 (2013)
11. http://www.open-video.org/
12. Dang, C., Radha, H.: RPCA-KFE: key frame extraction for video using robust principal component analysis. IEEE Trans. Image Process. **24**(11), 3742–3753 (2015)
13. Kim, G., Sigal, L., Xing, E.: Joint summarization of large-scale collections of web images and videos for storyline reconstruction. In: IEEE Conference on Computer Vision and Pattern Recognition, pp. 4225–4232. IEEE (2014)

Eye Fixation Assisted Detection of Video Salient Objects

Xinyu Yan, Zheng Wang(✉), and Meijun Sun

College of Intelligence and Computing, Tianjin University, Tianjin, China
{xinyuyan,wzheng,sunmeijun}@tju.edu.cn

Abstract. With the increasing maturity of image saliency detection, more and more people are focusing their research on video saliency detection. Currently, video saliency detection can be divided into two forms, eye fixation detection and salient objects detection. In this article, we focus on exploring the relationship between them. Firstly, we propose a network called fixation assisted video salient object detection network (FAVSODNet), which uses the eye gaze information in videos to assist in detecting video salient objects. A fixation assisted module (FAM) is designed to connect FP task and SOD task deeply. Under the guidance of the eye fixation information, multiple salient objects in complex scene can be detected more correctly. Moreover, when the scene suddenly changes or a new person appears, it can better to detect the correct salient objects with the aid of fixation maps. In addition, we adopt an extended multi-scale feature extraction module (EMFEM) to extract rich object features. Thus, the neural network can aware the objects with variable scales in videos more comprehensively. Finally, the experimental results show that our method advances the state-of-art in video salient object detection.

Keywords: Video salient object detection · Eye fixation prediction · Deep learning

1 Introduction

The human visual system (HVS) aims to localize the most important objects or regions immediately within the range of human visual, which helps people to process information quickly in complex scenes. To make it easier and faster for computers to process video data, more and more people have begun to study video saliency detection to simulate human visual attention mechanisms in the past few decades. It is often used as a pre-processing step for many computer vision tasks such as video captioning [23], scene classification [21], object detection [11,26], and video compression [12,13], etc.

Video saliency models can be generally classified into two categories: salient object detection (SOD) and eye fixation prediction (FP). The purpose of salient object detection is to locate and segment the most eye-catching objects. Eye fixation prediction focuses on locating lots of points that attract attention. At

J. Ren et al. (Eds.): BICS 2019, LNAI 11691, pp. 211–223, 2020.
https://doi.org/10.1007/978-3-030-39431-8_20

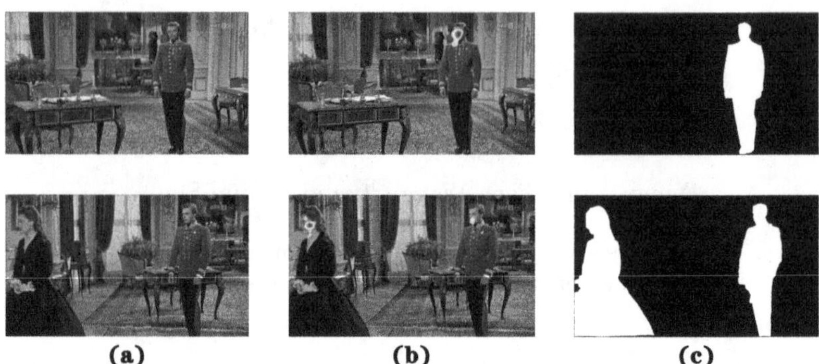

Fig. 1. Given two frames in a video like (a). We can find that there is a strong correlation between their eye fixation maps (b) and salient object maps (c)

present, although both tasks have been relatively mature, we have found that many video salient object models are not able to perform satisfactorily when handling complicated situations. For example, in a messy scene, there will usually be more than one salient object, and the current video salient object model cannot detect them all. Furthermore, when the lens switches, it is difficult to detect the salient objects correctly in a suddenly changing scene.

In this work, we utilize the prior of eye fixation obtained from an eye gaze prediction branch to detect salient objects in videos more accurately. Eye fixation points are collected by eye trackers when people watch videos. In a free viewing task, they show the combination of the influence of low-level features, high-level semantic features and temporal information between frames in videos, and intuitively shows the location of the most interesting regions. As shown in Fig. 1, the objects on which these points fall are the salient objects in each frame of the video. Our method is based on the strong correlation between the salient object and the eye fixation points, which is further confirmed by our experimental results.

The proposed fixation assisted video salient object detection network (FAV-SODNet) is a multi-branch neural network. It takes two consecutive frames as input and then extracts the features of the two frames and the temporal information between them. The FP branch predicts the eye fixation map of the current frame. Then we designed a Fixation Assisted Module (FAM) to connect the two tasks deeply, so that the result obtained by the FP branch provide a high-level guide for the SOD branch to detect the salient objects more accurately. In addition, in order to adapt to the variable size of the object in the video due to the movement of the lens and the case of multiple objects of different scales in a complex scene, we design an extended multi-scale feature extraction module (EMFEM), using stacked expansion convolution to obtain different sizes of receptive fields to extract more abundant multi-scale features of object.

Our contributions are summarized as three folds.

- We design a two-branch neural network called fixation assisted video salient object detection network (FAVSODNet), which takes two consecutive frames as input. First, we predict the eye fixation of the video. Then, we detect the salient object by combining the prior of eye gaze map.
- We propose a Fixation Assisted Module (FAM), which establishes a link between the FP branch and the SOD branch. In this way, the eye fixation map guides the SOD branch to extract salient objects more accurately.
- A multi-scale feature module (EMFEM) is put forward to capture rich multi-scale features to locate salient objects of different scales in videos.

2 Related Work

2.1 Video Salient Object Detection (VSOD)

Early methods of video saliency object detection [6,8,9,18,19,22,25,40] are based on shallow, hand-crafted features, such as color, edge, location and so on, and rely on optical flow to extract motion information. A majority of them utilize heuristic saliency priors, such as background prior [34] and center prior [7]. However, these methods have limited ability to express features, resulting in low accuracy. Furthermore, the calculation of optical flow causes serious time-consuming.

Later, with the success of deep neural network, various video salient object detection models based on deep learning have emerged. [32] introduced a video saliency network consists of two FCN modules, which extracts temporal and spatial saliency information respectively and achieves a speed of 2 fps. [17] presented a flow guided recurrent neural encoder (FGRNE), exploiting both motion information in terms of optical flow and sequential feature evolution encoding in terms of LSTM networks. [28] proposed a PDB-ConvLSTM based on recurrent network architecture, which utilized ConvLSTM structure to effectively fuse the temporal and spatial features of five consecutive frames and predict the salient map of the current frame.

However, these methods can not cope with some complex situations well. When there are many salient objects or lens switching, these methods can not really reflect the correct judgment of human visual mechanism.

2.2 Video Fixation Prediction (VFP)

Traditional video saliency prediction methods mostly consist of two steps: feature extraction and feature fusion. For videos, both spatial and temporal features have a significant impact on the final prediction. They explored the way of integrating spatial and temporal saliency features through different computational mechanisms, such as motion based features [14,39], temporal difference [15,27] and compressed domain methods [10,36]. Similarly, these hand-crafted features have great limitations, which makes the accuracy of the models not high enough.

Later, deep learning based models [1,2,5,16] began to emerge. For instance, [1] studied two different two-stream convolutional networks for dynamic saliency prediction. [2] proposed a spatiotemporal attentional model that learns where to look in a video directly from human fixation data. [16] used an object-to-motion convolutional neural network (OM-CNN) to learn spatio-temporal features for predicting the intra-frame saliency via exploring the information of both objectness and object motion.

2.3 The Combination of VSOD and VFP

Although FP and SOD are two tasks of saliency detection, there is a strong correlation between them, which has been analyzed in [3]. [33] build a neural network called Attentive Saliency Network (ASNet) that learned to detect salient objects from fixation maps in images. In this paper, we will concentrate on video-based saliency, using the relationship between the two to detect salient objects more accurately.

3 Our Approach

In this section, we first describe the overall architecture of our proposed method in Sect. 3.1. Then we introduce the extended multi-scale feature extraction module (EMFEM) in detail in Sect. 3.2. Section 3.3 provides implementation of the fixation assisted module (FAM). Finally, the implementation details are introduced in Sect. 3.4.

3.1 Overview of Network Architecture

At a high level, our goal is to feed frame pairs in videos into the network and continuously output pixel-wise maps of salient objects. Figure 2 shows the archi-

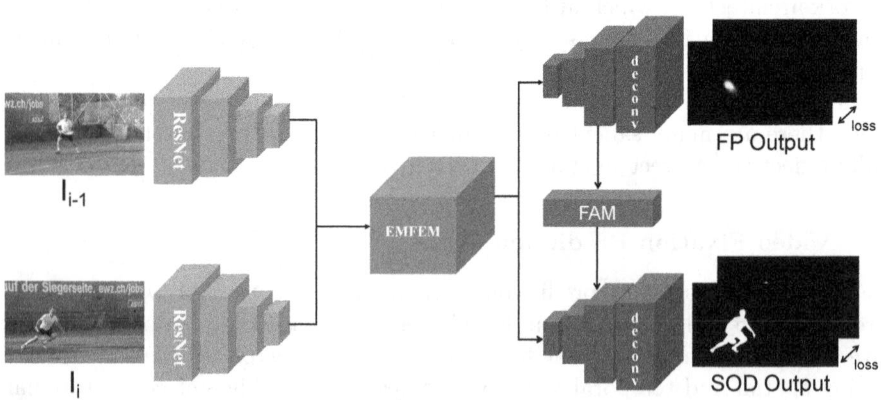

Fig. 2. The overall architecture of the proposed fixation assisted video salient object detection network. We utilize the EMFEM (Sect. 3.2) to obtain rich multi-scale features and design a fixation assisted module (Sect. 3.3) to provide an high-level prior for the detection of salient objects.

tecture of proposed fixation assisted video salient object detection network (FAV-SODNet).

At first, we input pair frames I_{i-1}, I_i, with a typical resolution of $224 * 224 * 3$, into the first four blocks of ResNet50 to extract features. The low-level blocks will extract shallow appearance features, while the deep-level blocks will extract semantic features. And every time a block passes, the resolution of the output feature map will be reduced by half. Subsequently, the features extracted from ResNet50 are fed into an extended multi-scale feature extraction module (EMFEM) to obtain rich multi-scale features. These features are then fed into two different branches: FP branch and SOD branch. In order to get salient maps of the same size as the original images, we used deconvolution blocks to restore the resolution of the feature maps in both branches. At the end of FP branch, we use a $3 * 3$ kernel with sigmoid activation function to get a rough binary fixation map FP_i. SOD branch and FP branch are not completely independent. We design a fixation assisted module (FAM), which feeds the features extracted from FP branch into SOD branch to provide an high-level prior for the detection of salient objects. Finally, in the SOD branch, we input multi-scale features from EMFEM and eye fixation assistant features from FAM into the deconvolution block, and obtain the binary salient object map SOD_i with the same resolution as the original input.

3.2 Extended Multi-scale Feature Extraction Module

It is particularly important to extract multi-scale features to detect salient objects in videos, as the distance between the object and the shot is constantly changing. Previous CNN models consist of stacked convolution layers and downsampling layers. Although the downsampling operation can expand the receptive field, it will cause the loss of the resolution of the feature maps. In order to adapt to the prediction task of pixel-wise in this paper, we design an extended multi-scale feature extraction module (EMFEM), which contains a stack of dilated convolutional layers to embed multi-scale knowledge of objects.

Table 1. Details of extended multi-scale feature extraction module (EMFEM)

Layer	Filter	Dilation rate	Output
stage1_relu1	3 * 3, 64	1/3/6/12/18	64 * 112 * 112
stage2_relu8	3 * 3, 64	1/3/6/12/18	64 * 56 * 56
stage3_relu12	3 * 3, 512	1/3/6/12/18	512 * 28 * 28
stage4_relu18	3 * 3, 1024	1/3/6/12/18	1024 * 14 * 14

We will input the feature maps at four levels extracted from each block in ResNet50, which are represented as $\mathrm{F} = \{f_i, \mathrm{i} = 1, 2, 3, 4\}$ into EMFEM. Table 1 describes the details of the proposed EMFEM. For feature map f_i, we extract features of different scales by using five dilated convolutions with different dilated rates. Dilated convolution [38] is a specially designed convolution with holes, which can increase the receptive field without losing the resolution. We set the dilation rates to $\{1, 3, 6, 12, 18\}$. Finally, we concatenate the feature maps from different dilated convolution layers and get the multi-scale features $\mathrm{F}' = \{f_i', \mathrm{i} = 1, 2, 3, 4\}$.

3.3 Fixation Assisted Module

The multi-scale features $\mathrm{F}' = \{f_i', \mathrm{i} = 1, 2, 3, 4\}$ obtained from EMFEM are fed into two decoders composed of deconvolution. Firstly, for FP branch, we directly feed f_4' into the decoder, and through four deconvolution blocks, we restore the resolution of the feature map layer by layer. The features obtained by each deconvolution block are named $\mathrm{FPF} = \{fpf_i, \mathrm{i} = 1, 2, 3, 4\}$. Finally, we add a $3 * 3$ kernel with sigmoid activation function after fpf_4 to get a rough binary fixation map FP_i.

Next, in FAM, we connect the feature $\mathrm{FPF} = \{fpf_i, \mathrm{i} = 1, 2, 3, 4\}$ obtained from each deconvolution block of FP branch with $\mathrm{F}' = \{f_i', \mathrm{i} = 1, 2, 3, 4\}$ obtained from EMFEM, and get $\mathrm{FAF} = \{faf_i, \mathrm{i} = 1, 2, 3, 4\}$. Finally, in SOD branch, we first feed faf4 into the first deconvolution block, and then connect the result with faf_3 and feed it into the next deconvolution block. Repeat this until the last convolution block, and after the last deconvolution block, we add a $3 * 3$ kernel with sigmoid activation function to get a binary salient object map SOD_i.

3.4 Implementation Details

Overall Loss. For both the FP branch and the SOD branch, we propose a fused loss function that accounts for multiple evaluation metrics to produce the saliency map more accurately. For the FP branch, the loss function is defined as follows:

$$Loss(S_{FP}) = L_{cross_entropy}(S_{FP}) + L_{MAE}(S_{FP}) \tag{1}$$

For the SOD branch, the loss function is defined as follows:

$$Loss(S_{SOD}) = L_{cross_entropy}(S_{SOD}) + L_{MAE}(S_{SOD}) \tag{2}$$

where $L_{cross-entropy}$ and L_{MAE} denote cross entropy loss and MAE loss respectively. $L_{cross-entropy}$ is defined as:

$$L_{corss-entropy} = -\sum_{x,y} I_{x,y} log(P_{x,y}) + (1 - l_{x,y}) log(1 - p_{x,y}) \tag{3}$$

where $l_{x,y}$ is the label of pixel (x,y) and $P_{x,y}$ is the probability of pixel (x,y). L_{MAE} is used in saliency detection widely which is defined as:

$$L_{MAE} = \sum_{x,y} |l_{x,y} - p_{x,y}| \tag{4}$$

Training Settings. Since there are few video datasets that offer annotations for both FP and SOD tasks, we train our network for two steps. First, we train the FP branch using two video fixation dataset: Hollywood-2 [29] and UCF Sports [29]. Initial learning rate of Adam algorithm is 10^{-5}. Then, we train the SOD branch only using two video salient object dataset: Densely Annotated Video Segmentation (DAVIS) [24] and Freiburg-Berkeley Motion Segmentation (FBMS) [4]. Initial learning rate is also set as 10^{-5}. We augment the training set by mirror reflection and image cropping to relieve the over-fitting problem. We use the Keras framework to implement the model. The parameters of the first 4 convolutional layers are initialized by ResNet50 pretrained on ImageNet. A NVIDIA GTX 1080 Ti GPU is used for experience. It takes about 30 h to accomplish the training process of our model.

4 Experimental Results

4.1 Experimental Setup

Dataset. We evaluate our approach on three public benchmark datasets: DAVIS, FBMS, and the Video Salient Object Detection (ViSal) [31]. DAVIS dataset is one of the most challenging video segmentation benchmarks, which consists of 50 high-quality video sequences and fully-annotated pixel-level segmentation ground-truth for each frame. We use its training set to train our model, which contains 30 videos. We test our models on its test set, which consists of 20 videos. The FBMS dataset contains 59 natural video sequences, where the training set includes 29 video sequences and the test set has 30 video sequences. We train our models on its training set and report the performance on the test set. ViSal includes 17 challenging video clips. It is a dataset specially designed for video salient object. We evaluate our models on the whole ViSal dataset.

Evaluation Criteria. In our experiments, we choose three widely used metrics, namely precision-recall (PR) curve, F-measure and mean absolute error (MAE) score, to evaluate the performance of our method as well as other state-of-the-art models for traditional video saliency detection. Specifically, the precision value is defined as the ratio of ground truth salient pixels in the detected salient region. And the recall value corresponds to the percentage of the predicted salient pixels and all ground truth area. The curves are averaged over each video sequence. The F-measure denotes the weighted harmonic mean of precision and recall for an overall evaluation. It can be computed as:

$$F_{\beta} = \frac{(1+\beta^2) \times Precision \times Recall}{\beta^2 \times Precision + Recall} \tag{5}$$

We set $B^2 = 0.3$ to weight precision more than recall as suggest in [37]. The maximum F-measure from all precision-recall pairs is shown as a good summary of the methods detection performance. Different from PR curve and F-measure,

MAE measures a more balanced comparison between the predicted saliency map and ground truth. It is defined as:

$$MAE = \frac{1}{W \times H} \sum_{x=1}^{W} \sum_{y=1}^{H} |S(x,y) - G(x,y)| \tag{6}$$

where W and H are predicted the width and height of video frame, S and G are predicted saliency map and ground truth respectively.

4.2 Performance Comparison with State-of-the-art

We make an comparison of the accuracy of video salient object detection between our and other 6 famous saliency approaches: FCNs [32], SAG [35], SGSP [20], GAFL [31], SFLR [6] and MST [30].

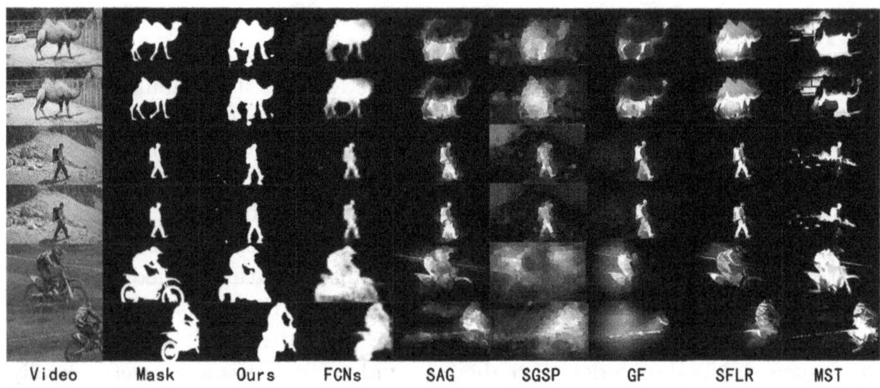

Fig. 3. Qualitative comparison against other 6 saliency methods with groundtruths on three example videos.

Quantitative Evaluation. The proposed model is compared with 6 state-of-the-art saliency detection algorithms on three datasets. Figure 4 and Table 2 show the comparison results. The PR curves on the test sets of DAVIS and ViSal datasets are plotted in Fig. 4. It can be observed that the PR curves of the proposed algorithm perform better than other methods on above three datasets. The performance of different methods under the metrics of maximum F-measure and MAE are illustrated in Table 2. Overall, our method achieves the best results among three datasets using all the evaluation metrics which means our model is more robust than other competitors.

Qualitative Evaluation. Figure 3 presents some saliency maps generated by our model as well as other 6 state-of-the-art algorithms on three example videos. It can be seen that our method can accurately detect video salient objects.

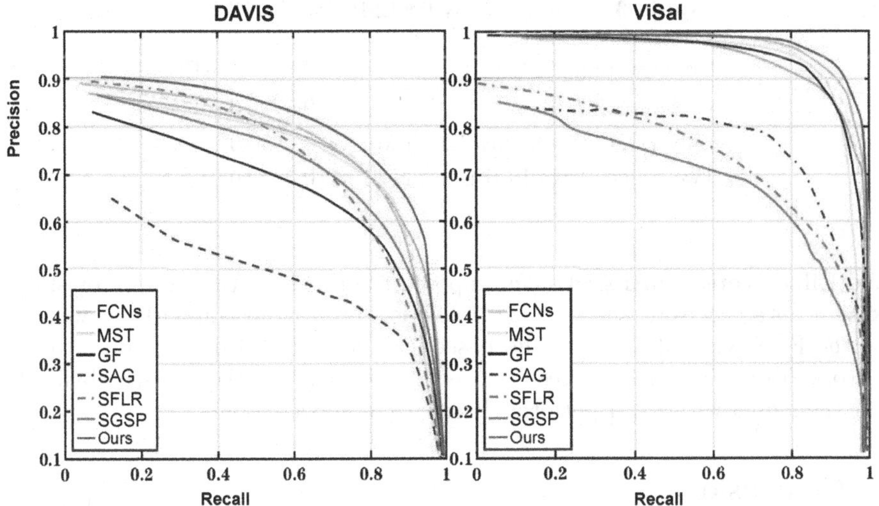

Fig. 4. PR curve.

Table 2. Quantitative comparison results against 6 saliency methods.

Methods	Year	DAVIS		FBMS		ViSal	
		MAE↓	F^{max} ↑	MAE↓	F^{max} ↑	MAE↓	F^{max} ↑
FCNs [32]	TIP'18	0.053	0.729	0.100	0.735	0.041	0.877
SAG [35]	CVPR'15	0.105	0.479	0.142	0.581	0.096	0.734
SGSP [20]	TCSVT'17	0.128	0.677	0.171	0.571	0.172	0.648
GAFL [31]	TIP'15	0.091	0.578	0.150	0.551	0.099	0.726
SFLR [6]	TIP'17	0.056	0.727	0.117	0.660	0.062	0.779
MST [30]	CVPR'16	0.165	0.429	0.177	0.500	0.095	0.673
OURS		**0.049**	**0.732**	**0.091**	**0.801**	**0.039**	**0.880**

4.3 Analysis of the Proposed Approach

The proposed model is composed of two modules, including the extended multi-scale feature extraction module (EMFEM) and the fixation assisted module (FAM). We design a series of experiments to investigate the contribution of each module.

The Effectiveness of EMFEM. The EMFEM is proposed to capture more multi-scale context information to detect salient objects in video. To demonstrate the effectiveness of the EMFEM, we remove the EMFEM in our model. The maximum F-measure and MAE of above models are shown in Table 3. It can be observed that our EMFEM brings the best performance since the dilated convolutional layers capture multi-scale features without loss of resolution.

Table 3. Ablation study for EMFEM and FAM

Model setting	F^{max}	MAE
Without EMFEM	0.672	0.053
Only SOD branch with EMFEM	0.683	0.058
Two branch with EMFEM and FAM	0.732	0.049

The Effectiveness of FAM. We proposed the FAM to utilize the prior of eye fixation obtained from an eye gaze prediction branch. In comparison, we first use the FCN without FAM as the baseline. Then add the FAM model to the network. Table 3 reports the results over DAVIS dataset. We can see obviously that the model with FAM performs better than above model.

5 Conclusions

In this paper, a network called fixation assisted video salient object detection network (FAVSODNet) is proposed to detect video salient objects with the assist of eye fixation information. In order to obtain rich multi-scale features, we design an extended multi-scale feature extraction module (EMFEM), which adapts to the changing size of objects in videos by using dilated convolution. Moreover, a fixation assisted module (FAM) is introduced to provide an advanced guidance for eye fixation in video salient object detection. Experiment results demostrate that our proposed method advances the state-of-art in video salient object detection under different evaluation metrics.

Acknowledgment. The authors wish to acknowledge the support for the research work from the National Natural Science Foundation, China under grant Nos. 61572351, 61876125 and 61772360.

References

1. Bak, Ç., Erdem, A., Erdem, E.: Two-stream convolutional networks for dynamic saliency prediction, July 2016
2. Bazzani, L., Larochelle, H., Torresani, L.: Recurrent mixture density network for spatiotemporal visual attention, March 2016
3. Borji, A., Sihite, D.N., Itti, L.: Salient object detection: a benchmark. In: Fitzgibbon, A., Lazebnik, S., Perona, P., Sato, Y., Schmid, C. (eds.) ECCV 2012. LNCS, vol. 7573, pp. 414–429. Springer, Heidelberg (2012). https://doi.org/10.1007/978-3-642-33709-3_30
4. Brox, T., Malik, J.: Object segmentation by long term analysis of point trajectories. In: Daniilidis, K., Maragos, P., Paragios, N. (eds.) ECCV 2010. LNCS, vol. 6315, pp. 282–295. Springer, Heidelberg (2010). https://doi.org/10.1007/978-3-642-15555-0_21. http://dl.acm.org/citation.cfm?id=1888150.1888173
5. Chaabouni, S., Benois-Pineau, J., Hadar, O., Ben Amar, C.: Deep learning for saliency prediction in natural video, April 2016

6. Chen, C., Li, S., Wang, Y., Qin, H., Hao, A.: Video saliency detection via spatial-temporal fusion and low-rank coherency diffusion. IEEE Trans. Image Process. **26**(7), 3156–3170 (2017). https://doi.org/10.1109/TIP.2017.2670143
7. Cheng, M., Zhang, G., Mitra, N.J., Huang, X., Hu, S.: Global contrast based salient region detection. In: CVPR 2011, pp. 409–416 (2011). https://doi.org/10.1109/CVPR.2011.5995344
8. Guo, C., Ma, Q., Zhang, L.: Spatio-temporal saliency detection using phase spectrum of quaternion Fourier transform. In: 2008 IEEE Conference on Computer Vision and Pattern Recognition, pp. 1–8, June 2008. https://doi.org/10.1109/CVPR.2008.4587715
9. Fang, Y., Wang, Z., Lin, W.: Video saliency incorporating spatiotemporal cues and uncertainty weighting. In: 2013 IEEE International Conference on Multimedia and Expo (ICME), pp. 1–6, July 2013. https://doi.org/10.1109/ICME.2013.6607572
10. Fang, Y., Lin, W., Chen, Z., Tsai, C.M., Lin, C.W.: A video saliency detection model in compressed domain. IEEE Trans. Circuits Syst. Video Technol. **24**(1), 27–38 (2014). https://doi.org/10.1109/TCSVT.2013.2273613
11. Girshick, R.: Fast R-CNN, April 2015. https://doi.org/10.1109/ICCV.2015.169
12. Guo, C., Zhang, L.: A novel multiresolution spatiotemporal saliency detection model and its applications in image and video compression. IEEE Trans. Image Process. **19**(1), 185–198 (2010). https://doi.org/10.1109/TIP.2009.2030969
13. Hadizadeh, H., Baji, I.V.: Saliency-aware video compression. IEEE Trans. Image Process. **23**(1), 19–33 (2014). https://doi.org/10.1109/TIP.2013.2282897
14. Harel, J., Koch, C., Perona, P.: Graph-based visual saliency. In: Proceedings of the 19th International Conference on Neural Information Processing Systems, NIPS 2006, pp. 545–552. MIT Press, Cambridge (2006). http://dl.acm.org/citation.cfm?id=2976456.2976525
15. Itti, L., Dhavale, N., Pighin, F.: Realistic avatar eye and head animation using a neurobiological model of visual attention. In: Proceedings of SPIE - The International Society for Optical Engineering, vol. 5200, January 2004. https://doi.org/10.1117/12.512618
16. Jiang, L., Xu, M., Wang, Z.: Predicting video saliency with object-to-motion CNN and two-layer convolutional LSTM, September 2017
17. Le, T., Sugimoto, A.: Video salient object detection using spatiotemporal deep features. IEEE Trans. Image Process. **27**(10), 5002–5015 (2018). https://doi.org/10.1109/TIP.2018.2849860
18. Le, T.-N., Sugimoto, A.: Contrast based hierarchical spatial-temporal saliency for video. In: Bräunl, T., McCane, B., Rivera, M., Yu, X. (eds.) PSIVT 2015. LNCS, vol. 9431, pp. 734–748. Springer, Cham (2016). https://doi.org/10.1007/978-3-319-29451-3_58
19. Liu, T., Yuan, Z., Sun, J., Wang, J., Zheng, N., Tang, X., Shum, H.: Learning to detect a salient object. IEEE Trans. Pattern Anal. Mach. Intell. **33**(2), 353–367 (2011). https://doi.org/10.1109/TPAMI.2010.70
20. Liu, Z., Li, J., Ye, L., Sun, G., Shen, L.: Saliency detection for unconstrained videos using superpixel-level graph and spatiotemporal propagation. IEEE Trans. Circuits Syst. Video Technol. **27**(12), 2527–2542 (2017). https://doi.org/10.1109/TCSVT.2016.2595324
21. Lu, X., Zheng, X., Yuan, Y.: Remote sensing scene classification by unsupervised representation learning. IEEE Trans. Geosci. Remote Sens. **55**(9), 5148–5157 (2017). https://doi.org/10.1109/TGRS.2017.2702596

22. Mahadevan, V., Vasconcelos, N.: Spatiotemporal saliency in dynamic scenes. IEEE Trans. Pattern Anal. Mach. Intell. **32**(1), 171–177 (2010). https://doi.org/10.1109/TPAMI.2009.112
23. Pan, Y., Yao, T., Li, H., Mei, T.: Video captioning with transferred semantic attributes. In: 2017 IEEE Conference on Computer Vision and Pattern Recognition (CVPR). pp. 984–992, July 2017. https://doi.org/10.1109/CVPR.2017.111
24. Perazzi, F., Pont-Tuset, J., McWilliams, B., Gool, L.V., Gross, M., Sorkine-Hornung, A.: A benchmark dataset and evaluation methodology for video object segmentation. In: 2016 IEEE Conference on Computer Vision and Pattern Recognition (CVPR), pp. 724–732, June 2016. https://doi.org/10.1109/CVPR.2016.85
25. Rahtu, E., Kannala, J., Salo, M., Heikkilä, J.: Segmenting salient objects from images and videos. In: Daniilidis, K., Maragos, P., Paragios, N. (eds.) ECCV 2010. LNCS, vol. 6315, pp. 366–379. Springer, Heidelberg (2010). https://doi.org/10.1007/978-3-642-15555-0_27
26. Ren, S., He, K., Girshick, R., Sun, J.: Faster R-CNN: towards real-time object detection with region proposal networks. IEEE Trans. Pattern Anal. Mach. Intell. **39**, 1137–1149 (2015). https://doi.org/10.1109/TPAMI.2016.2577031
27. Ren, Z., Gao, S., Chia, L., Rajan, D.: Regularized feature reconstruction for spatio-temporal saliency detection. IEEE Trans. Image Process. **22**(8), 3120–3132 (2013). https://doi.org/10.1109/TIP.2013.2259837
28. Song, H., Wang, W., Zhao, S., Shen, J., Lam, K.M.: Pyramid dilated deeper ConvLSTM for video salient object detection. In: Proceedings of the 15th European Conference, Munich, Germany, 8–14 September 2018, Part XI, pp. 744–760, September 2018
29. Stefan, M., Cristian, S.: Actions in the eye: dynamic gaze datasets and learnt saliency models for visual recognition. IEEE Trans. Pattern Anal. Mach. Intell. **37**(7), 1408–1424 (2015)
30. Tu, W., He, S., Yang, Q., Chien, S.: Real-time salient object detection with a minimum spanning tree. In: 2016 IEEE Conference on Computer Vision and Pattern Recognition (CVPR), pp. 2334–2342, June 2016. https://doi.org/10.1109/CVPR.2016.256
31. Wang, W., Shen, J., Shao, L.: Consistent video saliency using local gradient flow optimization and global refinement. IEEE Trans. Image Process. **24**(11), 4185–4196 (2015). https://doi.org/10.1109/TIP.2015.2460013
32. Wang, W., Shen, J., Shao, L.: Video salient object detection via fully convolutional networks. IEEE Trans. Image Process. **27**(1), 38–49 (2018). https://doi.org/10.1109/TIP.2017.2754941
33. Wang, W., Shen, J., Xingping, D., Borji, A.: Salient object detection driven by fixation prediction, May 2018. https://doi.org/10.1109/CVPR.2018.00184
34. Wei, Y., Wen, F., Zhu, W., Sun, J.: Geodesic saliency using background priors. In: Fitzgibbon, A., Lazebnik, S., Perona, P., Sato, Y., Schmid, C. (eds.) ECCV 2012. LNCS, vol. 7574, pp. 29–42. Springer, Heidelberg (2012). https://doi.org/10.1007/978-3-642-33712-3_3
35. Wang, W., Shen, J., Porikli, F.: Saliency-aware geodesic video object segmentation. In: 2015 IEEE Conference on Computer Vision and Pattern Recognition (CVPR), pp. 3395–3402, June 2015. https://doi.org/10.1109/CVPR.2015.7298961
36. Xu, M., Jiang, L., Sun, X., Ye, Z., Wang, Z.: Learning to detect video saliency with HEVC features. IEEE Trans. Image Process. **26**(1), 369–385 (2017). https://doi.org/10.1109/TIP.2016.2628583

37. Yang, C., Zhang, L., Lu, H., Ruan, X., Yang, M.H.: Saliency detection via graph-based manifold ranking. In: Proceedings of the IEEE Conference on Computer Vision and Pattern Recognition, pp. 3166–3173 (2013)
38. Yu, F., Koltun, V.: Multi-scale context aggregation by dilated convolutions, November 2016
39. Zhong, S., Liu, Y., Ren, F., Zhang, J., Ren, T.: Video saliency detection via dynamic consistent spatio-temporal attention modelling. In: Proceedings of the Twenty-Seventh AAAI Conference on Artificial Intelligence, AAAI 2013, pp. 1063–1069. AAAI Press (2013). http://dl.acm.org/citation.cfm?id=2891460.2891608
40. Zhou, F., Kang, S.B., Cohen, M.F.: Time-mapping using space-time saliency. In: 2014 IEEE Conference on Computer Vision and Pattern Recognition, pp. 3358–3365, June 2014. https://doi.org/10.1109/CVPR.2014.429

Layered RGBD Scene Flow Estimation with Global Non-rigid Local Rigid Assumption

Xiuxiu Li[1,2(✉)], Yanjuan Liu[1,2], Haiyan Jin[1,2(✉)], Lei Cai[1,2], and Jiangbin Zheng[3]

[1] Xi'an University of Technology, Xi'an, China
{lixiuxiu, jinhaiyan}@xaut.edu.cn, liuyanjuan@stu.xaut.edu.cn, caileid@gmail.com

[2] Shaanxi Key Laboratory for Network Computing and Security Technology, Xi'an, China

[3] Northwestern Polytechnical University, Xi'an, Shaanxi, China
zhengjb@nwpu.edu.cn

Abstract. RGBD scene flow has attracted increasing attention in the computer vision community with the popularity of depth sensor. To accurately estimate three-dimensional motion of object, a layered scene flow estimation with global non-rigid, local rigid motion assumption is presented in this paper. Firstly, depth image is inpainted based on RGB image due to original depth image contains noises. Secondly, depth image is layered according to K-means clustering algorithm, which can quickly and simply layer the depth image. Thirdly, scene flow is estimated based on the assumption we proposed. Finally, experiments are implemented on RGBD tracking dataset and deformable 3D reconstruction dataset, and the analysis of quantitative indicators, RMS (Root Mean Square error) and AAE (Average Angular Error). The results show that the proposed method can distinguish moving regions from the static background better, and more accurately estimate the motion information of the scene by comparing with the global rigid, local non-rigid assumption.

Keywords: Scene flow · RGBD image · Local rigid · Global non-rigid

1 Introduction

3D scene Flow estimation is a significant problem in computer vision, which describes a 3D motion field formed by the motion of space scene. With the development of computer science and artificial intelligence, the related technologies of scene flow estimation have been rapidly developed, and scene flow is used widely in virtual reality, intelligent robot, cultural relic protection, 3DTV and so on.

Some research efforts have been dedicated to the estimation of the scene flow. There are three types of methods to estimate the scene flow according to the equipment used, which include monocular vision-based methods [7], stereo vision-based methods [1–3] and RGBD based methods [4–6]. In the estimation of scene flow, some methods estimate the dense scene flow directly [1, 9, 10], while others estimate the scene flow based on the assumption of rigid motion in local area [8, 11, 12].

J. Ren et al. (Eds.): BICS 2019, LNAI 11691, pp. 224–232, 2020.
https://doi.org/10.1007/978-3-030-39431-8_21

In monocular vision-based methods, Xiao et al. [7] proposed an energy function on the scene flow constructed with a brightness constancy assumption, a gradient constancy assumption, a short time object velocity constancy assumption, and two smooth operators. In stereo vision-based methods, Vedula et al. [1] firstly presented a framework for the computation of the dense, non-rigid scene flow from stereoscopic vision. Wedel et al. [11] presented a decoupling of the disparity estimation from the velocity estimation to estimate dense scene flow. Huguet and Devernay [2] estimated the 3-D displacement field of scene points in the original scene flow estimation method. In RGBD-based methods, Hadfield and Bowden [5] presented a novel formulation for scene flow estimation, which used a particle filter to estimate the surface in each frame. This method requires a complex resampling process. Gottfried et al. [6] presented a multi-modal flow algorithm, which is robust against typical (technology dependent) range estimation artifacts.

The result of estimating scene flow directly is high dimensional, thus other widely used methods are based on the assumption of 3D local rigid motion, which can reduce the solution space. In [4], Scene flow is estimated by Lucas Kanade framework with the assumption of 3D local rigidity of the scene, so the scene flow is the rigid translation flow of surface patches. In [10, 12], Scene flow is estimated by the assumption of local rigid motion and the flexible motion of each point are combined to obtain more detailed motion. Rene Schuster et al. [13] proposed using dense interpolation of sparse matches between two stereo image pairs to estimating scene flow. In fact the initial sparse matches can be regarded as the local rigid motions. Sun et al. [8] proposed a layered RGBD scene flow method, in which the depth information from RGBD data is used to solve the depth ordering problem directly.

In [8], the layered RGBD scene flow is a promising method as spatial smoothness is separated from the modeling of discontinuities and occlusions, which can model occlusion boundaries by obtaining the relative depth order. Depth image is layered based on the depth information. In order to estimate the motion of the scene, the assumption that pixels belonging to the same layer do rigid motion is proposed by [8]. In practical applications, this assumption is used to estimate that the motion of the scene is inaccurate because pixels of the same layer may have different motions. In this paper, we propose an assumption of global non-rigid, local rigid motion, which can accurately estimate the motion of each layer by dividing the each layer into different blocks.

The rest of this paper is organized as follows: Sect. 2, describes the processing of depth image, which involves painting and layering depth image. Section 3 describes how scene flow is estimated, Sect. 4, provides the detailed experimental evaluation of proposed method compared with others. Finally, Sect. 5 provides some concluding remarks.

2 Depth Image Processing

Depth image layering is a key part of the layered scene flow. Before layering, the depth image need to be inpainted for handling such situations which involves occlusions, lack of point correspondences, sensor imperfection etc. Corresponding preprocessing steps mainly includes image inpainting, and layering.

For depth image inpainting, the algorithm based on combining RGB image information are applied [16]. In this algorithm, holes in depth image and small noises are all regarded as noises, but holes have larger connected areas and the depth value is 0, while small noises has smaller connected areas. Holes are inpainted according to domain similarity and color consistency from the depth image and its aligned color image. Small noises are removed according to local bilateral filter.

Based on inpainted depth image, the layering of depth images is implemented. In layering stage, K-means clustering algorithm is used to segment and labeled the depth image, by which scene can be quickly and simply layered based on the depth information.

3 Scene Flow Estimation

In this section, an objective function of scene flow is presented as in [8, 14, 15]. Given a RGBD image sequence are $\{I_t, Z_t\}$, where $1 \leq t \leq T$, the objective function is represented as:

$$E(\vec{u}, g, R, \tau) = \sum_{t=1}^{T-1} \left\{ \sum_{k=1}^{K} \{\lambda_{data} E_{data}(\vec{u}_{tk}, g_{tk}) + \lambda_{spa} E_{spa}(\vec{u}_{tk})\} \right\} + \sum_{t=1}^{T} \sum_{k=1}^{K-1} \lambda_{sup} E_{sup}(g_{tk}) \tag{1}$$

Where $\vec{u}_{tk} = \{u_{tk}, v_{tk}, w_{tk}\}$ is the scene flow of each layer, which includes the 2D motion $\{u_{tk}, v_{tk}\}$ and depth variation w_{tk} of the layer k. E_{data} reflects RGBD data consistency between the tth frame and the $t + 1^{th}$ frame with the motion $\vec{u}$; E_{spa} reflects motion correlation in different directions within the same layer; E_{sup} is a spatial coherence layer support term. λ_{data}, λ_{spa} and λ_{sup} represent the corresponding weight of E_{data}, E_{spa}, E_{sup} respectively. $-1.5 \leq g_{tk} \leq 1.5$ is the support function, which represents the probability size that the pixel belongs to layer k in frame t.

The assumption of global non-rigid, local rigid motion is proposed to describe the behavior of the scene. Layered information of depth image can be obtained according to the K-means clustering. Each layer is divided into a number of sufficiently small blocks due to the pixels' direction of motion in each layer may different. The size of block is 3×3. The method in this paper proposed that pixels in the block share the common 3D rotation R_{tk} and translation τ_{tk} relative to the camera.

For RGB and depth image sequence, the calculation model of the initial scene flow is as follows: A point $\alpha_1 = (x_1, y_1)$ at the tth frame corresponds to the point. $\alpha_2 = (x_2, y_2)$ at the $t + 1^{th}$ frame. The optical flow is $(u_1, v_1) = (x_2 - x_1, y_2 - y_1)$. The depth value of point α_1 is z_1 and the point α_2's is z_2. The depth change data is $z = z_2 - z_1$, According to the mapping between 3D and 2D as Eq. (3), the 3D transformation of the corresponding pixel can be calculated as Eq. (2).

$$u = X_2 - X_1,\ v = Y_2 - Y_1,\ z = z_2 - z_1 \tag{2}$$

Where $\alpha_{12} = (X_1, Y_1, Z_1)$ is the 3D space coordinate of the point α_1 and $\alpha_{22} = (X_2, Y_2, Z_2)$ is the 3D space coordinate of the point α_2.

$$\begin{cases} X_1 = z_1 \bullet (x_1 - c_x)/f_x,\ Y_1 = z_1 \bullet (y_1 - c_y)/f_y \\ X_2 = z_2 \bullet (x_2 - c_x)/f_x,\ Y_2 = z_2 \bullet (y_2 - c_y)/f_y \end{cases} \tag{3}$$

Where $(f_x, f_y)^T$ and $(c_x, c_y)^T$ respectively represent the camera focal length and distortion co-efficient. When the image scene motion includes rotation R_{tk} and translation τ_{tk}, the 3D space coordinate of the spatial point α_{22} can be calculated from the spatial point:

$$\alpha_{22} = R_{t,k}\alpha_{12}^T + \tau_{t,k} \tag{4}$$

The image coordinates corresponding to the spatial point α_{22} is:

$$(f_x \frac{X_2}{z_2} + c_x,\ f_y \frac{Y_2}{z_2} + c_y) \tag{5}$$

The corresponding scene flow is:

$$u_{t,k}^R(\alpha_{22}) = f_x \frac{X_2}{z_2} + c_x - x_1 \tag{6}$$

$$v_{t,k}^R(\alpha_{22}) = f_y \frac{Y_2}{z_2} + c_y - y_1 \tag{7}$$

$$w_{t,k}^R(\alpha_{22}) = z_2 - z_1 \tag{8}$$

The semi-parametric model for the horizontal motion, vertical motion and depth change can be obtained as followed Eqs. (9), (10) and (11).

$$\begin{aligned} E_{spa\_u}(u_{tk}, R_{tk}, \tau_{tk}) = \sum_x \sum_{x' \in N_x} \lambda_b \rho_b((u_{tk}(x) - u_{tk}^R(x)) - (u_{tk}(x') - u_{tk}^R(x'))) \\ + \sum_{x' \in N_x} \rho_u(u_{tk}(x) - u_{tk}^R(x')) \end{aligned} \tag{9}$$

$$\begin{aligned} E_{spa\_v}(v_{tk}, R_{tk}, \tau_{tk}) = \sum_x \sum_{x' \in N_x} \lambda_b \rho_b((v_{tk}(x) - v_{tk}^R(x)) - (v_{tk}(x') - v_{tk}^R(x'))) \\ + \sum_{x' \in N_x} \rho_v(v_{tk}(x) - v_{tk}^R(x')) \end{aligned} \tag{10}$$

$$E_{spa\_w}(w_{tk}, R_{tk}, \tau_{tk}) = \sum_{x} \sum_{x' \in N_x} \lambda_b \rho_b((w_{tk}(x) - w_{tk}^R(x)) - (w_{tk}(x') - w_{tk}^R(x'))) + \sum_{x' \in N_x} \rho_w(w_{tk}(x) - w_{tk}^R(x')) \quad (11)$$

Where ρ_u, ρ_v, ρ_w and ρ_b are robust penalty function.

The coordinate descent method is used to minimize the RGBD scene flow energy function in Eq. (1). Firstly, estimate the initial scene flow according to the inter-frame optical flow and segmentation of the depth image. Secondly, obtain the optimized scene flow by image warping while keeping the layering result fixed. Thirdly, calculate the optimized layered support function with coordinate descent method while keeping the scene flow fixed. Finally, get the final scene flow by looping computing the second and third operations.

4 Experiments

In this section, scene flow estimation with global non-rigid, local rigid assumption is implemented on the dataset RGBD tracking and deformable 3D reconstruction.

RGBD Tracking Dataset. RGBD tracking dataset contains multiple independent moving targets and large areas of occlusion. In this section, Bear_back sequence is used to test the method in this paper, and the results are shown in Fig. 1. In Fig. 1, the motion of the scene is produced by the opposite movement of hands, where the body also has some motion. The first row is the image sequence in the dataset, the second row is Sun's estimation results, and the third row is the estimation result of this paper. The depth image is divided respectively into five layers by the Sun's method and the method in this paper, but the calculation result of occlusion is more accurate in the method of this paper. By comparing the scene flow of the region in the red box, it can be found that the results of the proposed method are closer to the motion region of the real image.

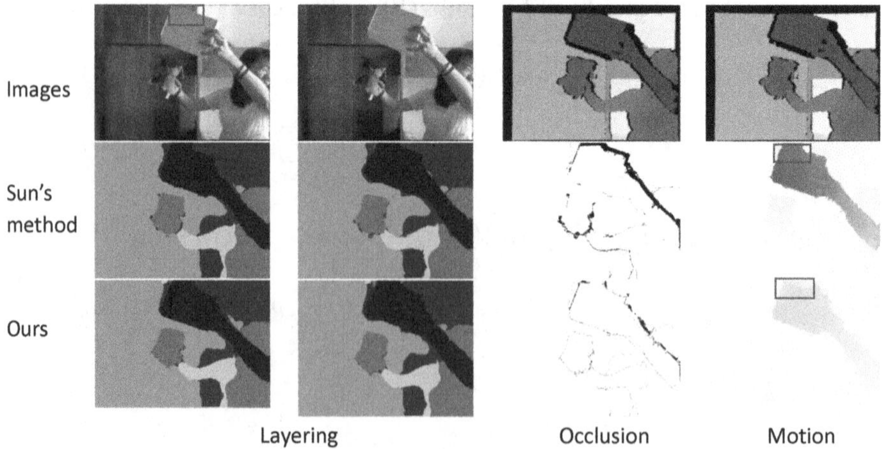

Fig. 1. Bear_back sequence test results (Color figure online)

Deformable 3D Reconstruction Dataset [17]. Deformable 3D reconstruction dataset contains Hat and Alex sequence, which is a set of non-rigid data. In Hat sequence, the motion of scene is produced by wearing the hat and some movement of the arm. In Alex sequence, the motion of scene is produced by waving arm and some movement of clothes. In this section, Hat and Alex sequence are used to test the proposed method, and the corresponding result are shown respectively in Fig. 2(a) and Fig. 2(b). In Fig. 2 (a) and Fig. 2(b), the first row is test image sequence, which contains respectively RGB image and depth image of the tth frame and the $t + 1^{th}$ frame. The second and the third row is respectively the result of Sun's method and the proposed method in this paper. The depth image is divided respectively into two layers, which can accurately identify the foreground and background information by the K-means clustering algorithm.

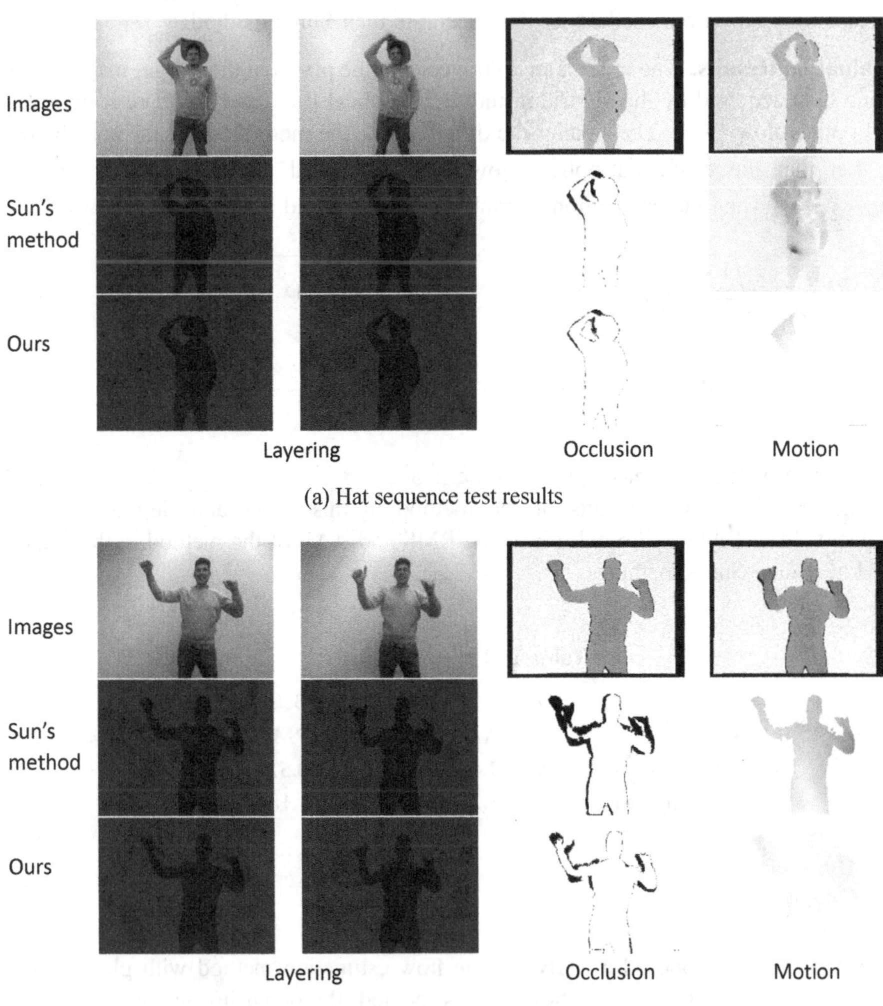

Fig. 2. Deformable 3D reconstruction dataset test results

Occlusion calculation is an important part of the layered scene flow, therefore, the occlusion images are also considered in this section.

By comparing the scene flow estimation result, it can be found that in Fig. 2(a) the result of Sun's method estimate the motion region is the whole body, and the scene flow is estimated even in the scene without the object. The result of Sun's method has errors may due to the pixels in same layer share a common motion, which result in pixels without moving are also estimated scene flow. However, our method can estimate the motion region of the object such as arm, head, and the hat because the every layer is divided into different blocks. Scene flow is estimated by estimating the motion of each block in the every layer. In Fig. 2(b), the motion intensity of the whole body is considered to be the same in Sun's method, however the motion of arm is more obvious than other parts of whole body in the proposed method. Otherwise the result of occlusion based on our method is more accurate than Sun's method.

Evaluation Results. The criteria are to traverse all the pixels in the image, map the 3D scene flow acquired by the algorithm into a 2D optical flow, and compare it with the real optical flow value. The smaller the difference is, the more accurate the calculation is. Let that the estimated optical flow is $(u, v)^T$, and the true optical flow is $(u_{GT}, v_{GT})^T$, Then the calculation formula of the RMS and AAE are as follows:

$$RMS = \sqrt{\frac{1}{N}\sum\nolimits_{(x,y)}((u_{GT}(x, y) - u(x, y)^2) + (v_{GT}(x, y) - v(x, y))^2)} \tag{12}$$

$$AAE = \frac{1}{N}\arccos\left(\frac{1 + u_{GT} \times u + v_{GT} \times v}{\sqrt{u_{GT}^2 + v_{GT}^2 + 1} \cdot \sqrt{u^2 + v^2 + 1}}\right) \tag{13}$$

Where N is the number of pixels in the image.

The error estimation results of the method in this paper and Sun are shown respectively in Table 1. From Table 1, the RMS and AAE of the method in this paper are lower than Sun's method.

Table 1. Error comparison

	Hat		Alex		Bear_back	
Method	RMS	AAE	RMS	AAE	RMS	AAE
Our method	**0.97**	**2.48**	**1.44**	**2.17**	**0.57**	**1.14**
Sun's method [8]	1.96	3.31	1.55	2.56	1.18	1.73

5 Conclusion

In this paper, we proposed a RGBD scene flow estimation method with global non-rigid, local rigid motion assumption. In this method, the depth image can be layered according to the K-means clustering algorithm firstly to process the occlusions, and scene flow is estimated with global non-rigid, local rigid motion assumption in each layer. In the estimation of scene flow, each layer is divided into a number of sufficiently small blocks based on the assumption that the pixels' motion in the same block is consistency and the pixels' motion in the different block is inconsistency. Experiments on different datasets show that the scene flow can be more accurately estimated by the method in this paper than [7]. However, the running time of the code is longer than [7] due to every layer is divided into different blocks. In future work, we will refer to the optimization of the model we proposed, using other fusion strategies [18, 19], improved motion estimation [20, 21] and optimization [22, 23]. Besides trained deep neural network methods can predict scene flow rapidly, so we will refer to the existing methods to study learning-based methods [24, 25].

Acknowledgment. This work has been supported by the National Natural Science Foundation of China under grant Nos. 6150238, 61501370 and 61703333. Thanks Deqing Sun et al. for providing the code.

References

1. Vedula, S., Baker, S., Rander, P., Collins, R., Kanade, T.: Three-dimensional scene flow. In: The 17th IEEE International Conference on Computer Vision, 1999, vol. 2, pp. 722–729. IEEE (1999)
2. Huguet, F., Devernay, F.: A variational method for scene flow estimation from stereo sequences. In: The 11th International Conference on Computer Vision, 2007, pp. 1–7. IEEE (2007)
3. Vogel, C., Schindler, K., Roth, S.: Piecewise rigid scene flow. In: 2013 IEEE International Conference on Computer Vision, 2013, pp. 1377–1384. IEEE (2013)
4. Quiroga, J., Devernay, F., Crowley, J.: Scene flow by tracking in intensity and depth data. In: 2012 IEEE Computer Society Conference on Computer Vision and Pattern Recognition Workshops (CVPRW), 2012, pp. 50–57. IEEE (2012)
5. Hadfield, S., Bowden, R.: Kinecting the dots: particle based scene flow from depth sensors. In: IEEE International Conference on Computer Vision, 2012, pp. 2290–2295. IEEE (2012)
6. Gottfried, J.-M., Fehr, J., Garbe, C.S.: Computing range flow from multi-modal *Kinect* Data. In: Bebis, G., et al. (eds.) ISVC 2011. LNCS, vol. 6938, pp. 758–767. Springer, Heidelberg (2011). https://doi.org/10.1007/978-3-642-24028-7_70
7. Xiao, D., Yang, Q., Yang, B., Wei, W.: Monocular scene flow estimation via variational method. Multimedia Tools Appl. **6**(8), 10575–10597 (2017)
8. Sun, D., Sudderth, E., Pfister, H.: Layered RGBD scene flow estimation. In: Proceedings of the IEEE Conference on Computer Vision and Pattern Recognition, pp. 548–556. IEEE (2015)
9. Hadfield, S., Bowden, R.: Scene particles: unregularized particle-based scene flow estimation. IEEE Trans. Pattern Anal. Mach. Intell. **36**(3), 564–576 (2014)
10. Xiang, X., Zhai, M., Zhang, R., Xu, W., El Saddik, A.: Scene flow estimation based on 3D local rigidity assumption and depth map driven anisotropic smoothness. IEEE Access **6**, 30012–30023 (2018)
11. Wedel, A., Rabe, C., Vaudrey, T., Brox, T., Franke, U., Cremers, D.: Efficient dense scene flow from sparse or dense stereo data. In: Forsyth, D., Torr, P., Zisserman, A. (eds.) ECCV 2008. LNCS, vol. 5302, pp. 739–751. Springer, Heidelberg (2008). https://doi.org/10.1007/978-3-540-88682-2_56

12. Schuster, R., Wasenmuller, O., Kuschk, G., Bailer, C., Stricker, D.: SceneFlowFields: dense interpolation of sparse scene flow correspondences. In: 2018 IEEE Winter Conference on Applications of Computer Vision (WACV), 2018, pp. 1056–1065. IEEE (2016)
13. Ren, Z., Sun, D., Kautz, J., Sudderth, E.: Cascaded scene flow prediction using semantic segmentation. In: 2017 International Conference on 3D Vision (3DV), 2017, pp. 225–233. IEEE (2017)
14. Sun, D., Sudderth, E., Black, M.: Layered image motion with explicit occlusions, temporal consistency, and depth ordering. In: Advances in Neural Information Processing Systems (NIPS), 2010, pp. 2226–2234 (2016)
15. Sun, D., Wulff, J., Sudderth, E., Pfister, H., Black, M.: A fully-connected layered model of foreground and background flow. In: Proceedings of the IEEE Conference on Computer Vision and Pattern Recognition, 2013, pp. 2451–2458. IEEE (2013)
16. Zhang, Y., Dai, J., Zhang, H., Yang, L.: Depth inpainting algorithm of RGB-D camera combined with color image. In: 2nd IEEE Advanced Information Management, Communicates, Electronic and Automation Control Conference (IMCEC), 2018, pp. 1391–1395. IEEE (2018)
17. Slavcheva, M., Baust, M., Cremers, D., Ilic, S.: KillingFusion: non-rigid 3D reconstruction without correspondences. In: 2017 IEEE Conference on Computer Vision and Pattern Recognition (CVPR), pp. 5474–5483 (2017)
18. Yan, Y., et al.: Cognitive fusion of thermal and visible imagery for effective detection and tracking of pedestrians in videos. Cogn. Comput. **10**(1), 94–104 (2018)
19. Ren, J.: Fusion of intensity and inter-component chromatic difference for effective and robust colour edge detection. IET Image Process. **4**(4), 294–301 (2010)
20. Feng, Y., et al.: Object-based 2D-to-3D video conversion for effective stereoscopic content generation in 3D-TV applications. IEEE Trans. Broadcast. **57**(2), 500–509 (2011)
21. Ren, J., et al.: High-accuracy sub-pixel motion estimation from noisy images in Fourier domain. IEEE Trans. Image Process. **19**(5), 1379–1384 (2009)
22. Feng, W., Huang, W., Ren, J.: Class imbalance ensemble learning based on margin theory. Appl. Sci. **8**(5), 815 (2018)
23. Sun, G., Ma, P., et al.: A stability constrained adaptive alpha for gravitational search algorithm. Knowl.-Based Syst. **139**, 200–213 (2018)
24. Wang, Z., et al.: A deep-learning based feature hybrid framework for spatiotemporal saliency detection inside videos. Neurocomputing **287**, 68–83 (2018)
25. Han, J., et al.: Background prior-based salient object detection via deep reconstruction residual. IEEE Trans. Circuits Syst. Video Technol. **25**(8), 1309–1321 (2014)

Fine-Grained Image Classification with Object-Part Model

Jinlong Hong[1], Kaizhu Huang[2(✉)], Hai-Ning Liang[1], Xinheng Wang[2], and Rui Zhang[3]

[1] Department of Computer Science and Software Engineering, Xi'an Jiaotong-Liverpool University, Suzhou, China
Jinlong.Hong15@studentxjtlu.edu.cn, HaiNing.Liang@xjtlu.edu.cn

[2] Department of Electrical and Electronic Engineering, Xi'an Jiaotong-Liverpool University, Suzhou, China
{Kaizhu.Huang,Xinheng.Wang}@xjtlu.edu.cn

[3] Department of Mathematical Sciences, Xi'an Jiaotong-Liverpool University, Suzhou, China
Rui.Zhang02@xjtlu.edu.cn

Abstract. Fine-grained image classification is used to identify dozens or hundreds of subcategory images which are classified in a same large category. This task is challenging due to the subtle inter-class visual differences. Most existing methods try to locate discriminative regions or parts of objects to develop an effective classifier. However, there are two main limitations: (1) part annotations or attribute descriptions are usually labor-intensive, and (2) it is less effective to find spatial relationship between the object and its parts. To alleviate these problems, we propose a novel object-part model that relies on an attention mechanism. The main improvements of our method are threefold: (1) an object-part spatial constraint which selects highly representative parts, able to keep parts both discriminative and integrative, (2) a novel heatmap generation method, able to represent comprehensively the discriminative parts by regions, and (3) a speed up of the part selection by filtering image patch candidates using a fine-tuned CNN. With these improvements, the proposed method achieves encouraging results compared to the state-of-the-art methods benchmarking on the Stanford Cars and Oxford-IIIT Pet datasets.

Keywords: Fine-grained image classification · Object-part model · Weakly supervised learning

1 Introduction

In the past few years, image classification has received increasingly attention as an essential task in computer vision. With the development of deep learning, the performance of coarse image classification on large scale datasets such as ImageNet 1K is improved unexpectedly. Yet, fine-grained image classification

J. Ren et al. (Eds.): BICS 2019, LNAI 11691, pp. 233–243, 2020.
https://doi.org/10.1007/978-3-030-39431-8_22

is still challenging currently. Fine-grained image classification is to recognize hundreds of subcategories which are classified in a large basic category. The differences between coarse image classification and fine-grained image classification are shown in Table 1. Developing better technologies on fine-grained image classification has several objectives such as reducing expensive expert resources and providing a better life for human beings.

Table 1. Differences between coarse and fine-grained image classification

Input				
Coarse image classification	Car	Car	Dog	Dog
Fine-grained image classification	Aston Martin Vantage 2012	Audi RS4 2008	Bulldog	Pit bull terrier

The technical challenges of fine-grained image recognition are mainly in two aspects: locating discriminative regions and selecting discriminative parts under certain criteria. Previous works have achieved good performance on localizing coarse object regions [5,17] but they rely on the heavily labor consuming annotations for object, parts or even pixels information. An unsupervised approach [13] of detecting salient objects is a bottom-up mechanism guided by the gestalt-laws of perception but a simpler method is implemented in this paper. For searching parts information, Zhang et al. [14] proposed an automatic selective deep filters method. However, they ignored the spatial relationship between object and its parts. The characteristic of selected parts should have strong relationship with the object and little redundant overlapping information among the part regions. In another approach to exploit part regions, a recurrent attention convolutional neural network was recurrently applied by training alternatively the classification network and the attention proposal network [1]. However, it can only find one part of the object and the other discriminative part regions are ignored.

To deal with the above challenges, this paper proposes an object-part framework with spatial constraints based on the object-part attention model (OPAM) [8]. The proposed framework contains the following two major components:

Object-Level Model. It is crucially important to develop a good model with high performance which can learn general features [15]. One possible way to do this is to augment the training dataset so as to boost the performance. Image patch candidates are created by selective search. Moreover, a fine-tuned pertained CNN works for filtering irrelevant background noise. Many existing works rely on object or part annotations [5], but they are heavily labor consumed. This problem is tried to be solved in a semi-supervised approach where the class activation map method is used to get the saliency value of all images at each pixel. The boundary of the class activation map is set for localizing the bounding box of the object.

Part-Level Model. Discriminative parts are critical for fine-grained image classification. For example, the prediction may be influenced by the brand of cars or body shape of cars in a great extent. The proposed method is to select the best n parts from image patches. The algorithm contains both object-level spatial constraints and part-level spatial constraints. For object-level spatial constraints, the relationship between object and its parts are closely combined. For part-level spatial constraints, the relationship among parts is balanced to be not only exclusive but also integrative.

Using the above mentioned methods, the proposed object-part model has achieved additional 0.9%, 0.5% performance lift on two benchmark data set, e.g., Stanford Cars, Oxford-IIIT Pet respectively against the baseline model. Various empirical analysis is also conducted to show the high competitiveness of the proposed framework against those state-of-the-art methods.

2 Proposed Object-Part Model

The proposed approach is to solve the fine-grained image classification task bases on an intuitive idea: identifying and distinguishing the objects and their discriminative parts within the subcategory. For instance, classifying an image of Jeep car, the first step is to localize the car and then distinguish the most distinct parts which differ from the other cars such as the seven-hole front grille and the rectangular design for the door. Therefore, the object-part model is proposed based on OPAM and it makes lots of improvements. The object-part model is also implemented with the semi-supervised method requiring no many annotations in both training and testing.

2.1 Object-Level Model

In the object-level model, the bounding boxes of objects are firstly obtained and then these bounding boxes are adopted to get finer features with the objects. There are two operations here: the patches filtering operations and the bounding box generation operation.

Patches Filtering. The performance of CNN model can be improved by data augmentation [3]. Therefore, selective search, a bottom up approach to union small similar regions in color, texture, shape, is designed to generate thousands of image patch candidates. However, such thousands of image patch candidates are not at the appropriate scales. Since irrelevant background patches are too many and some of patches are not representative at all for the object, a fine-tuned CNN is used for choosing only representative patches. The CNN model is pre-trained on the ImageNet 1K dataset and fine-tuned on the training data. The filtering algorithm is to check the label with top-1 prediction whose confidence is bigger than a threshold. The patches selected with the original image are additionally incorporated into the training set in order to train a better CNN which is called ClassNet.

Bounding Box Generation. The class activation map (CAM) [16] is selected to generate the object proposal, which is much easier to be implemented and trained on any CNN models than other optional methods. The CAM represents the saliency map for all of sub-categories where the saliency value on each pixel presents the discriminative degree for the object. To obtain the CAM, an average global pooling layer is added before the last fully connected layer of the CNN. The function of the average global pooling layer is to keep the spatial information from previous convolutional layers rather than using fully connected layers to filter it.

Concretely, given an image I, the saliency value of the image is the summative saliency value of the weighted sub-category c. The heatmap for image I is computed as follows:

$$M_c(x, y) = \sum_u w_u^c f_u(x, y) \tag{1}$$

where $M_c(x, y)$ represents the importance of activation at spatial location (x, y). w_u^c is the weight corresponding to subcategory c for neuron u, and $f_u(x, y)$ is the activation of neuron u in the last convolutional layer at spatial location (x, y). Then the boundary of the heatmap is set to be the bounding box of the object. The bounding box images from the segmentations of original images, are used to train the second CNN model named ObjectNet which contains features at the object level.

The overall sequence and structure of the object-level model can be visualized in Fig. 1. Using Car-196 dataset as an example, filtered patches, heatmaps and finer scale regions of cars can be obtained.

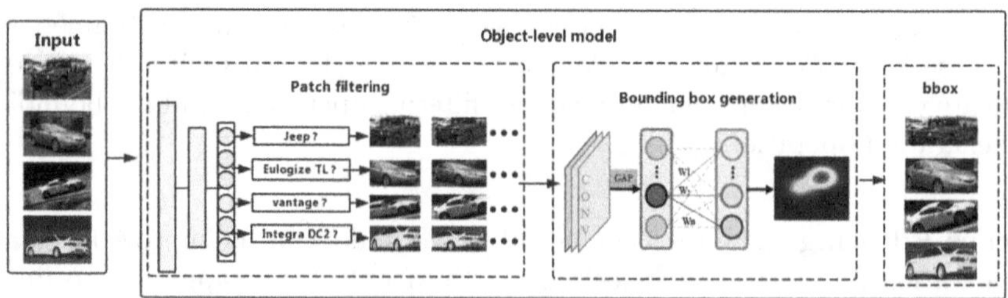

Fig. 1. The overall structure of object-level model

2.2 Part-Level Model

The discriminative parts of an object, e.g., the head, the body shape, the brand of a car in a vehicle, are crucial for identifying subtle inter-class differences on fine-grained image classification. The proposed part-level model is designed in three steps: object spatial constraint, part spatial constraint, and part alignment. It is also noted that all these steps in implemented in semi-supervised learning.

Object spatial constraints define the spatial relationship between object and its parts, while part spatial constraints define the spatial relationship among these parts. The idea is to combine the object level spatial constraints and the part level spatial constraints to meet the selection criteria. Therefore, for selecting n most discriminative parts from a given image I, the final scoring function P^* can be designed to fuse two spatial constraints equally as follows:

$$P^* = arg \max_P \Delta(P), \text{ where } \Delta(P) = \Delta_{box}(P)\Delta_{part}(P) \tag{2}$$

The purpose of object spatial constraints is to select highly parts, while the aim of part spatial constraints is to balance spatial relationships among part candidates and their discriminative degree. In addition, to speed up the following parts selection approach, the previously fine-tuned CNN is used to filter the part candidates with much background noise and the number of the part candidates can be reduced to approximate a quarter consequently. Two spatial constraints will be introduced in details.

Object Spatial Constraints. The spatial relationship between object and its parts is important because the selected parts should occupy the most discriminative regions of object and contain weak relationships with background. The measurement of Intersection-over-Union is utilized to keep the representative of the selected parts. The object spatial constraint is defined as follows:

$$\Delta_{box}(P) = \prod_{i=1}^{n} fb(p_i), \text{ where } \quad fb(p_i) = \begin{cases} 1, & IoU(p_i) > threshold \\ 0, & otherwise \end{cases} \tag{3}$$

Moreover, $IoU(p_i)$ represents the proportion of Intersection-over-Union over the part area and object area. The bounding box of object is calculated using the CAM. The product operation is to make sure every selected part has similar property as required above. Therefore, the combination of several part candidates cannot be selected as long as one of part candidates has the IoU value under a given threshold.

Part Spatial Constraints. The part spatial constraints are used to balance the parts relationship in two aspects. First, the parts should contain as much object discriminative information as possible, or namely has few overlap among parts. Second, the saliency value from heatmap is used to identify the most discriminative regions.

The part spatial constraint is defined as follows:

$$\Delta_{part}(P) = log(A_U - A_I - A_O) + norm(Mean(M_{A_U})) \tag{4}$$

Here, A_U is the union area of n parts, A_I is the intersection area of n parts, and A_O is the area outside the object region. The first term of the part spatial constraint is to avoid large overlapping among parts where subtraction of A_I is to reduce the overlapping, and subtraction of A_O is to generate the largest areas inside the object region. The second term of the spatial constraint is to find the most discriminative part regions of the object. In addition, $Mean(M_{A_U})$ is defined as follows:

$$Mean(M_{A_U}) = \frac{1}{|A_U|}\sum_{i,j} M_{ij} \tag{5}$$

where M_{ij} refers to the saliency value of pixel (i, j) in the union area of parts, and $|A_U|$ refers to the number of pixels that are located in the union area of n parts. Norm operation is to calculate the discriminative degree of parts and to keep the output in a certain range.

To obtain the saliency value, the intuitive idea is to use the CAM to find the boundary of objects. However, there are two problems with the CAM. First, the heatmap always has the hottest point to represent the most discriminative location of the object. Yet, there usually exists a discriminative region for the object rather than a discriminative point. Second, the heatmap is the sum of saliency values of all the weighted sub-categories. The point has subtle deviation due to the influence of minor sub-categories. Therefore, we are inspired to image patch candidates in the patches filtering section. Since the fine-tuned CNN model has already learned how to classify fine-grained images, the patches filtered by the fine-tuned CNN are representative for the objects. The heatmap can be created by calculating the overlapping regions of filtered image patches. The hottest region of the heatmap represents the most overlapping area for image patches on each image. In addition, the patches with highly overlapping areas should be removed to reduce the space complexity, but the overlapping patches should be kept in heatmap creation section.

The selected parts are used to train a CNN model named PartNet which can represent discriminative regions of the objects.

Part Alignment. Although part regions are selected for classification, the regions may be disordered semantically which may affect the final prediction performance. For example, the brand of BMW and Benz in vehicle recognition have totally different meaning for the categories but both represent a brand semantically.

Since intermediate layers of ClassNet can show certain clustering patterns, grouping neurons is used so as to represent different regions of the object. Specifically, we engage the similarity matrix S, where $S(i, j)$ is the cosine similarity of weights between two neurons u_i and u_j at an intermediate layer of the ClassNet, to partition the neurons into n groups. The clustering score of a part is the overall scores of neurons in one cluster. Then the parts will be sorted according to

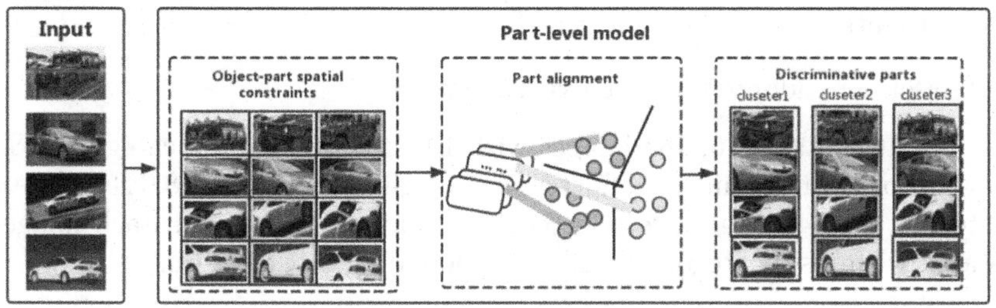

Fig. 2. Overall structure of part-level model. (Color figure online)

their scores. In this paper, the penultimate convolutional layer is set to represent the corresponding values of parts as suggested by the OPAM model.

The overall sequence of the part level model is shown in Fig. 2. In addition, the blue, yellow and green colors used in each stage represent the corresponding clusters the part-level model should group.

2.3 Final Prediction

As described above, three CNN models named ClassNet, ObjectNet, and PartNet are trained respectively to improve the performance of classification. Containing representations or features in multiple views, the proposed model can perform much better than merely using one model. The overall prediction result is the combination of three models' predictions:

$$\mathit{final\_score} = \alpha * CS + \beta * OS + \gamma * PS \tag{6}$$

where CS, OS, and PS denote the original score, object score, and part score given by the softmax values of ClassNet, ObjectNet and PartNet respectively. α, β, γ are selected by using the k-fold cross validation [4].

3 Experiments

The proposed object-part model is evaluated on two benchmark datasets for fine-grained image classification: Cars-196 dataset and Oxford-IIIT Pet dataset. Comparisons with the baseline OPAM and several other important models are also performed. Following the baseline OPAM, VGGNet-19 is adopted as the CNN models in our approach. The evaluation metric is given by $Accuracy = \frac{N_a}{N}$, where N means the number of testing images and N_a means the number of images which are correctly discriminated. The experiments are run three times and the average accuracy is reported.

3.1 Datasets

Two datasets are adopted for the experiments:

Cars-196: It contains 16, 185 images with 196 different car subcategories. The proportion of training images and testing images is 8,144 and 8,041. For each subcategory, 24–84 images are selected for training and testing. Each image is annotated with a subcategory label and a bounding box of object.

Oxford-IIIT Pet: It contains 7,349 images of 37 pet subcategories, and is a combination of 12 cat subcategories and 25 dog subcategories. It is divided as follows: 3,680 images for training and 3,669 images for test. For each subcategory, 93–100 images are selected for training and 88–100 images for testing.

3.2 Results

The experimental results on Cars-196 and Oxford-IIIT Pet dataset are reported in Tables 2 and 3 respectively. The columns represent the annotations, accuracy and model structure all approaches are used. For annotations, the selected columns indicate the annotations are used in selected stages. For features column, the candidates can be CNN models such as AlexNet, VGGNet, and ResNet-50. As clearly observed, the performance of the proposed model are comparable with the other state-of-the-art or popular models on Cars-196, while it attains the highest performance on Oxford-IIIT Pet.

Table 2. Comparison on Cars-196 dataset.

Method	Train annotation		Test annotation		Acc. (%)	Features
	Object	Parts	Object	Parts		
Ours					**93.06**	VGGNet
OPAM [8]					92.19	VGGNet
DFL-CNN [11]					93.10	ResNet-50
A^3M-SSL [2]					91.80	VGGNet
Bilinear-CNN [6]					91.30	VGGNet & VGG-M
PG Alignment [5]	✓				92.60	VGGNet
VGG-BGLm [17]	✓		✓		90.50	VGGNet
A^3M [2]		✓		✓	95.40	VGGNet

Specifically, in Table 2, the state-of-art performance on Cars-196 dataset is A^3M which is 2.34% higher than our proposed approach. However, the A^3M is a supervised model based on attribute description, where the attribute annotation is significantly more labor-intensive than part annotation. Its semi-supervised counterpart called A^3M-SSL has the performance 1.26% lower than the proposed model. On the other hand, as seen in Table 3, The proposed model achieves the

Table 3. Comparison on Oxford-IIIT Pet dataset.

Method	Train annotation		Test annotation		Acc. (%)	Features
	Object	Parts	Object	Parts		
Ours					**94.28**	VGGNet
OPAM [8]					93.81	VGGNet
NAC [10]					91.60	VGGNet
InterActive [12]	✓				93.45	VGGNet
AGAL [7]		✓		✓	92.60	VGGNet
MsML+ [9]	✓		✓		87.70	AlexNet

performance of 94.28% on Oxford-IIIT Pet, which is superior to all the other methods. Comparing with the baseline OPAM, 0.47% is improved by the object-part model in this paper.

The ablation analysis is also conducted to further examine the proposed object-part model. Concretely, the Cars-196 dataset is token as one illustrative example to examine the effectiveness of using $log(A_U - A_I - A_O)$, and the effectiveness of using $norm(Mean(M_{A_U}))$. The analysis is reported in Table 4. It is observed that the best accuracy can be achieved when the object-part constraints are both applied.

Table 4. Performance applying different constraints

Methods	Accuracy
$log(A_U - A_I - A_O)$	92.71%
$+norm(Mean(M_{A_U}))$	**93.06%**

4 Conclusion

In conclusion, this paper proposed an effective framework involving the object-part model for fine-grained image classification. The main novelties are: (1) generating more discriminative and integrative parts by new spatial constraints, (2) exploiting the patches created by the fine-tuned deep convolutional neural network to generate heat-map, (3) proposing spatial constraints to reduce significantly the time as required by creating parts. Encouraging results are achieved compared to the state-of-the-art methods benchmarking on the Stanford Cars and Oxford-IIIT Pet datasets.

Acknowledgement. The work was partially supported by the following: National Natural Science Foundation of China under no. 61876155, and 61876154; The Natural Science Foundation of the Jiangsu Higher Education Institutions of China under no. 17KJD520010; Suzhou Science and Technology Program under no. SYG201712,

SZS201613; Natural Science Foundation of Jiangsu Province BK20181189 and BK20181190; Key Program Special Fund in XJTLU under no. KSF-A-01, KSF-P-02, KSF-E-26, and KSF-A-10; XJTLU Research Development Fund RDF-16-02-49.

References

1. Fu, J., Zheng, H., Mei, T.: Look closer to see better: recurrent attention convolutional neural network for fine-grained image recognition. In: 2017 IEEE Conference on Computer Vision and Pattern Recognition (CVPR), pp. 4476–4484 (2017). https://doi.org/10.1109/CVPR.2017.476
2. Han, K., Guo, J., Zhang, C., Zhu, M.: Attribute-aware attention model for fine-grained representation learning. arXiv preprint (2019)
3. Huang, K., Hussain, A., Wang, Q., Zhang, R.: Deep Learning: Fundamentals, Theory and Applications. Springer, Cham (2019). https://doi.org/10.1007/978-3-030-06073-2. ISBN 978-3-030-06072-5
4. Kohavi, R.: A study of cross-validation and bootstrap for accuracy estimation and model selection. In: Proceedings of the 14th International Joint Conference on Artificial Intelligence, vol. 2, pp. 1137–1143. Morgan Kaufmann Publishers Inc. (1995)
5. Krause, J., Jin, H., Yang, J., Li, F.F.: Fine-grained recognition without part annotations. In: 2015 IEEE Conference on Computer Vision and Pattern Recognition (CVPR), pp. 5546–5555 (2015). https://doi.org/10.1109/CVPR.2015.7299194
6. Lin, T., RoyChowdhury, A., Maji, S.: Bilinear CNN models for fine-grained visual recognition. In: 2015 IEEE International Conference on Computer Vision (ICCV), pp. 1449–1457 (2015)
7. Liu, X., Wang, J., Wen, S., Ding, E., Lin, Y.: Localizing by describing: attribute-guided attention localization for fine-grained recognition. In: AAAI Conference on Artificial Intelligence (2017). https://www.aaai.org/ocs/index.php/AAAI/AAAI17/paper/view/14323
8. Peng, Y., He, X., Zhao, J.: Object-part attention model for fine-grained image classification. IEEE Trans. Image Process. **27**(3), 1487–1500 (2018)
9. Qian, Q., Jin, R., Zhu, S., Lin, Y.: Fine-grained visual categorization via multi-stage metric learning. In: 2015 IEEE Conference on Computer Vision and Pattern Recognition (CVPR), pp. 3716–3724 (2015)
10. Simon, M., Rodner, E.: Neural activation constellations: unsupervised part model discovery with convolutional networks. In: 2015 IEEE International Conference on Computer Vision (ICCV), pp. 1143–1151 (2015)
11. Wang, Y., Morariu, V.I., Davis, L.S.: Learning a discriminative filter bank within a CNN for fine-grained recognition. In: 2018 IEEE/CVF Conference on Computer Vision and Pattern Recognition, pp. 4148–4157 (2018)
12. Xie, L., Zheng, L., Wang, J., Yuille, A., Tian, Q.: Interactive: inter-layer activeness propagation. In: 2016 IEEE Conference on Computer Vision and Pattern Recognition (CVPR), pp. 270–279 (2016)
13. Yan, Y., et al.: Unsupervised image saliency detection with Gestalt-laws guided optimization and visual attention based refinement. Pattern Recogn. **79**, 65–78 (2018). https://doi.org/10.1016/j.patcog.2018.02.004
14. Zhang, X., Xiong, H., Zhou, W., Lin, W., Tian, Q.: Picking deep filter responses for fine-grained image recognition. In: 2016 IEEE Conference on Computer Vision and Pattern Recognition (CVPR), pp. 1134–1142 (2016). https://doi.org/10.1109/CVPR.2016.128

15. Zhong, G., Yan, S., Huang, K., Cai, Y., Dong, J.: Reducing and stretching deep convolutional activation features for accurate image classification. Cogn. Comput. **10**(1), 179–186 (2018). https://doi.org/10.1007/s12559-017-9515-z
16. Zhou, B., Khosla, A., Lapedriza, A., Oliva, A., Torralba, A.: Learning deep features for discriminative localization. In: 2016 IEEE Conference on Computer Vision and Pattern Recognition (CVPR), pp. 2921–2929 (2016). https://doi.org/10.1109/CVPR.2016.319
17. Zhou, F., Lin, Y.: Fine-grained image classification by exploring bipartite-graph labels. In: 2016 IEEE Conference on Computer Vision and Pattern Recognition (CVPR), pp. 1124–1133 (2016)

Action Recognition in Videos with Temporal Segments Fusions

Yuanye Fang, Rui Zhang, Qiu-Feng Wang, and Kaizhu Huang(✉)

Xi'an Jiaotong-Liverpool University,
No. 111 Ren'ai Road, Suzhou 215123, People's Republic of China
Yuanye.Fang15@student.xjtlu.edu.cn,
{rui.zhang02,qiufeng.wang,kaizhu.huang}@xjtlu.edu.cn

Abstract. Deep Convolutional Neural Networks (CNNs) have achieved great success in object recognition. However, they are difficult to capture the long-range temporal information, which plays an important role for action recognition in videos. To overcome this issue, a two-stream architecture including spatial and temporal segments based CNNs is widely used recently. However, the relationship among the segments is not sufficiently investigated. In this paper, we proposed to combine multiple segments by a fully connected layer in a deep CNN model for the whole action video. Moreover, the four streams (i.e., RGB, RGB differences, optical flow, and warped optical flow) are carefully integrated with a linear combination, and the weights are optimized on the validation datasets. We evaluate the recognition accuracy of the proposed method on two benchmark datasets of UCF101 and HMDB51. The extensive experimental results demonstrate encouraging results of our proposed method. Specifically, the proposed method improves the accuracy of action recognition in videos obviously (e.g., compared with the baseline, the accuracy is improved from 94.20% to 97.30% and from 69.40% to 77.99% on the dataset UCF101 and HMDB51, respectively). Furthermore, the proposed method can obtain the competitive accuracy to the state-of-the-art method of the 3D convolutional operation, but with much fewer parameters.

Keywords: Action recognition · Temporal segments models · Segments fusion · Convolutional Neural Networks

1 Introduction

Aiming to study and analyze the behaviors of objects through videos, action recognition has attracted much attention and achieved tremendous advance [13]. In the early research of action recognition, one big challenge is how to extract features to represent the visual characteristics [4]. Later, deep learning algorithm is widely considered to be a suited way to deal with this problem in an end-to-end fashion [7].

J. Ren et al. (Eds.): BICS 2019, LNAI 11691, pp. 244–253, 2020.
https://doi.org/10.1007/978-3-030-39431-8_23

The main goal of motion recognition is to determine the type of human behavior in videos, so it is also called human action recognition. Firstly, valuable information of visual characteristics needs to be extracted from videos or still images; then the suitable internal representation or feature vectors should be designed to represent the information; finally, the learning system (often a classifier) is constructed to classify the actions in videos or images.

Recently, Convolutional Neural Networks (CNNs) models [10] become one of the most popular deep learning models for classifying images of objects [8]. The common CNN models are powerful to extract and model the appearance of still images, however, they are not good at modeling temporal dynamics information which plays an important role for action recognition in videos. Depending on how to utilize the temporal information, we can divided the current video-based action recognition methods into three categories, i.e., Long-short term memory (LSTM) model based [3], two-stream based [13], and 3D-CNN based [15]. LSTM based models have achieved great success in the recognition of sequence problems, Donahue et al. [3] used a CNNs + LSTM model for action recognition where the CNNs were utilized to extract features and LSTM was used to integrate features over time. However, LSTM based models are difficult to apply parallel computation due to the dependency among the states in the sequence. To investigate the CNN models in the temporal information, Karpsathy et al. [8] studied multiple approaches for extending CNN models in time domain to take advantage of local spatiotemporal information on a large-scale video dataset Sports-1M. Furthermore, Simonyan et al. [13] proposed a two-stream based CNN model framework which contains two CNN models of spatial and temporal network. Instead of using two-stream based CNN models, Tran et al. [15] directly modelled both temporal and appearance information in the 3D convolution operations as a 3D CNN model. Recently, Carreira et al. [2] proposed I3D networks using two stream CNNs with inflated 3D convolutions on both single-frame still RGB images and multi-frame consecutive optical flow images, and the state-of-the-art result was achieved by this method on the Kinetics dataset [9], however, the 3D CNN based method involves a large number of parameters due to the 3D convolution.

To model the long-range temporal context, Wang et al. [18] proposed a temporal segment network which assembles an end-to-end temporal structure model on the entire video under the two-stream framework without 3D convolution and gets a competitive accuracy with higher efficiency. However, the work [18] did not utilize the segments information sufficiently. In this work, we proposed to consider the relationship among the multiple segments, which was modelled by a fully connected layer in the common CNN models, so this is very efficient and easily extends to different CNN models. In addition, we combine the four streams (i.e., RGB, RGB differences, optical flow, and warped optical flow) to improve the accuracy further. To evaluate the performance of the proposed method, we test on the two benchmark datasets of UCF101 [14] and HMDB51 [11], and the extensive experimental results show that the proposed method improves the accuracy of action recognition in videos obviously (e.g., the accuracy is improved from 94.20% to 97.30% and from 69.40% to 77.99% on the dataset UCF101 and HMDB51, respectively). Furthermore, the proposed method can obtain the competitive accuracy to the state-of-the-art method of the 3D convolutional operation, but with much fewer parameters.

2 Two-Stream Convolutional Neural Network

The proposed method is based on the framework of two-stream CNN models [13], which usually consists of two CNN models, i.e., a spatial stream CNN and a temporal stream CNN. The spatial stream CNN operates on single frame still RGB images to obtain appearance information, and the temporal stream CNN processes multi-frame consecutive optical flow images in a short snippet to obtain the motion information.

However, this original two-stream CNN model is difficult to access long temporal context, since only a single stack of consecutive frames in a short snippet was considered by the temporal CNN.

To overcome this issue, the temporal segment networks (TSN) model was proposed to extract long-range temporal information by splitting the whole video into multiple segments, which is especially useful to classify the complex motions with a relatively long period. The overall procedure of TSN [18] can be represented by

$$TSN(T_1, T_2, ..., T_k) = H(g(F(T_1; W), F(T_2; W), ..., F(T_k; W))), \tag{1}$$

where T_k represents the sequence of snippets; $F(T_k; W)$ is the function that produces class scores of all the classes by a CNN operating on the short snippet k with parameters W; g is the segment consensus function that is used to derive the video-level prediction by combining the class scores from multiple short snippets; H is the prediction function used to obtain the probability of each action class for the entire video.

3 Proposed Method

In the framework of two-stream CNN models, we use the temporal segment network (TSN) based method to capture long-range temporal information in the whole video [18]. To further utilize the relationship among the segments, we propose to fuse multiple temporal segments in the TSN models.

In addition, we combine four streams extracted from the whole video (i.e., RGB, RGB differences, optical flow, and warped optical flow) to improve the recognition accuracy further.

3.1 Temporal Segments Fusion

To capture the long-range temporal context, the video is divided into multiple segments in the TSN models, however, the relationship among the segments is

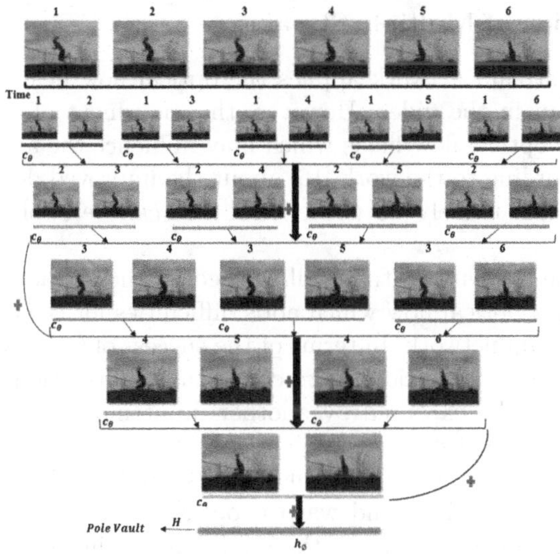

Fig. 1. An example of 2-frame fusion of $K = 6$ temporal segments

not considered in the work [18]. Our work is inspired by the temporal relational reasoning [12], which refers to the ability to link useful information of a sequential activity over time at short-term and long-term. To capture more information of the appearance's change between frames of some sequential activities, we integrate the relationship among the temporal segments into the TSN model, which can be defined as

$$net(T_1, T_2, ..., T_k) = H[h_\phi(\sum_{i=1}^{k-1}(c_\theta\langle T_i, T_{i+1}; W\rangle, c_\theta\langle T_i, T_{i+2}; W\rangle, ..., c_\theta\langle T_i, T_k; W\rangle))] \tag{2}$$

where h_ϕ is the function that combines the relationship between multiple segments T_k to get the result of the final classification; c_θ represents the relationship information between each pair of segments. Here both h_ϕ and c_θ are integrated into the common TSN by adding several fully connected layers with parameters ϕ and θ respectively.

To improve the efficiency of the TSN model, we utilize the sparse snippet sampling scheme for the predefined K segments of the whole video [18], where only one frame of the RGB stream is randomly sampled during each segment. For the total K segments, we can have K fusion methods, i.e., 2-frame, 3-frame, $\cdots$, K-frame. Figure 1 shows one example of 2-frame fusion of $K = 6$ segments.

In the TSN based models of the two-stream CNN framework, the predefined number of segments K in a video is important. The model will become a plain two-stream CNN if $K = 1$, which will be difficult to capture the long-range temporal context. With the increase of K, the temporal context information will be more considered. In the experiment, we will evaluate the recognition accuracy with the segments number varied from $K = 1$ to $K = 9$.

3.2 Combination of Multiple Streams

The popular two-stream network applies the optical flow fields to capture the motion information in the video. However, the movement of camera can also be encoded in the optical flow fields which may influence the action recognition performance. According to the work [16] about the improved dense trajectories, another input stream namely warped optical flow can be applied after remove camera motion.

In addition, the tremendous time will be used for the extraction of both optical flow and warped optical flow which adds difficulties for the on-time application of the two-stream network. In terms of the success of frame volumes [15] for obtaining the motion information, more contextual information about previous and next frames can be captured by another input modality, RGB difference with lower computation cost.

In summary, we will consider the four streams for the TSN model, i.e., RGB, RGB differences, optical flow, and warped optical flow. In this work, we will compare the multiple combination of these four steams in the experiments.

4 Experiments

4.1 Datasets and Experimental Setting

We evaluate the proposed method on two benchmark datasets of the action recognition, i.e., UCF101 [14] and HMDB51 [11]. UCF101 contains 13,320 video clips from 101 action classes, which is about 180 frames/video on average. And HMDB51 [11] includes 6,766 video clips from 51 action classes.

Followed by the baseline work [18], the data set is divided into three splits, and the average recognition accuracy over the three splits are reported to compare the performance with the existed methods. To save the computation cost, we also show the accuracy only in the split-1 of the dataset in some experiments. The model training details are followed by the work [18].

4.2 Evaluation of Segment Number

In evaluating the effects of the segment number K, we use the baseline two-stream CNN models with the two streams of RGB and optical flow as the input. To save the computation cost, we only show the recognition accuracy on the split-1 of the dataset UCF101, which is shown in Fig. 2.

It can be observed that a better performance can generally be achieved when the number of segments is increased. The network becomes a plain two-stream network if the number of segment equals to one. The results indicate that more information can be captured with more temporal segments for modeling long-range temporal structure. In addition, the performance saturated when the number of segments increases from 7 to 9. After consideration of the computational cost and the recognition performance, $K = 9$ is set in the spatial CNN and $K = 7$ in the temporal CNN in the following experiments.

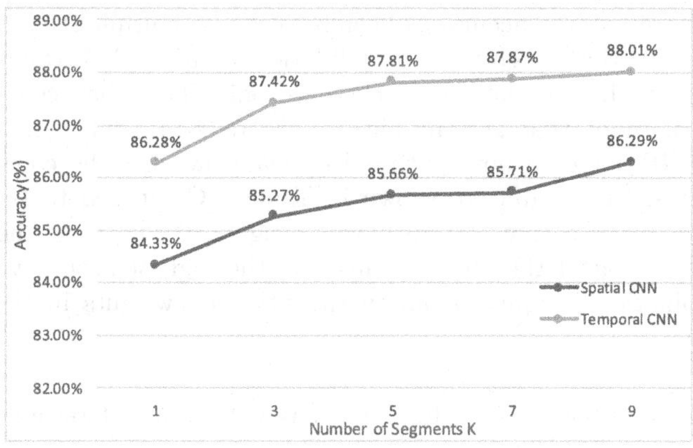

Fig. 2. Recognition accuracy with different K on UCF101 (split-1)

4.3 Evaluation of Combination of Multiple Streams

In the evaluation of combination of multiple streams, we first combine them with the predefined weights followed by the baseline work [18], and the recognition accuracy is shown in Table 1.

It can be found that the combination of streams of RGB and RGB differences boosts the recognition accuracy to 90.79%. The results indicate that the motion information can be captured by RGB difference although the accuracy is not as good as optical flow. The accuracies of optical flow and warped optical flow as well as their combination with RGB stream are very similar. The highest accuracy is achieved by combining RGB, optical flow and warped optical flow (93.83%) while it is slightly reduced by combining all streams.

Table 1. Accuracy of combining different streams with predefined weights on UCF101 (split 1).

Modality	Accuracy
RGB image	85.29%
RGB difference	88.03%
Optical flow	87.70%
Warped optical flow	87.79%
RGB image + RGB difference	90.79%
RGB image + Optical flow	93.55%
RGB image + Warped optical flow	93.63%
RGB image + RGB difference + Optical flow	93.73%
RGB image + Optical flow + Warped optical flow	93.83%
All streams	93.71%

To further analyze the accuracy of combination of multiple streams, we optimized the combination weights on the validation set instead of using predefined weights. To save the computational cost, we only show the accuracy of two combination methods that get the highest accuracy in Table 1, i.e., the combination of RGB + optical flow + warped optical flow, and the combination of all four streams, the results are shown in Table 2. Compared to the accuracy in Table 1, we can find that the optimized weights can improve the accuracy, and the combination of the four streams gets the highest accuracy. We hence use the combination of four streams with optimized weights in the following experiments.

Table 2. Accuracy of combining different streams with optimized weights on UCF101 (split 1)

Modality	Accuracy	Weights
RGB image + Optical flow + Warped optical flow	94.05%	5:3:2
RGB image + RGB difference + Optical flow + Warped optical flow	94.37%	8:3:5:7

4.4 Evaluation of Temporal Segments Fusion

In evaluating the effects of the temporal segments fusion, we consider all the fusion methods of 2-frame, 3-frame, $\cdots$, K-frame in the spatial CNN on the split-1 of the data set UCF101, and the results are shown in Table 3.

Table 3. Accuracy of temporal segments fusion in the spatial CNN on UCF101 (split-1).

Temporal segments fusion	Top1 accuracy	Top5 accuracy
2-frame	85.96%	96.28%
3-frame	85.22%	96.09%
4-frame	86.25%	96.27%
5-frame	**86.44%**	96.83%
6-frame	86.28%	96.64%
7-frame	86.16%	96.54%
8-frame	86.02%	97.01%
9-frame	86.20%	97.25%

We can see that the 5-frame fusion achieves the highest top 1 accuracy due to the appropriate number of parameters, and the accuracy is improved by about 0.5% compared to the one without considering the temporal segments fusion. The results show that the fusion of temporal segments can add the trajectories information in the spatial stream CNN, we hence use the 5-frame fusion in the following experiments.

4.5 Evaluation of Pre-training

The pre-training of CNN models is usually useful. We hence use the pre-training of the model on the two large data sets of Kinetics and ImageNet. Kinetics is a large-scale human action dataset released by Google DeepMind [9]. There are about 300,000 video clips from 400 classes contained in this dataset. The video clips were taken from YouTube videos and each of them lasts about 10 s. Kinetics is a much larger dataset than UCF101 and HMDB51. Moreover, we also consider the pre-training on the ImageNet, and the results are shown in Table 4. We can see that a considerable improvement can be achieved with Kinetics pre-training on the proposed method for all CNN models on both data sets.

Table 4. Accuracy with pre-training on UCF101 and HMDB51 (split-1).

Pre-training	Dataset	Spatial CNN	Temporal CNN	Two-stream CNN
ImageNet	UCF101	86.44%	88.01%	93.79%
ImageNet	HMDB51	54.38%	65.29%	70.78%
ImageNet + Kinetics	UCF101	90.62%	94.44%	96.89%
ImageNet + Kinetics	HMDB51	62.55%	74.38%	78.17%

4.6 Comparison with State-of-the-Art Methods

To further show the effectiveness of the proposed method, we compare the performance with several benchmark methods on all three splits of the datasets UCF101 and HDMB51. In this evaluation, the pre-training on both ImageNet and Kinetics was used, and the frame-5 temporal segments fusion was applied with the optimized weights. We set the number of segments as 9 and 7 in spatial CNN and temporal CNN, respectively.

Table 5 shows the accuracies of different methods, and the proposed method is based on the Temporal Segment Network [18]. We can see that the proposed method improves the accuracy obviously, which are improved from 94.20% to 97.30% on the dataset of UCF101 and from 69.40% to 77.99% on the dataset of HMDB51. Moreover, the proposed method outperforms the most methods except the two-stream I3D, which utilized a 3D CNN models with larger computational cost and more parameters. Additionally, IDT refers to improved trajectories while TDD means trajectory-pooled deep-convolutional descriptor.

Table 5. Average accuracy on three splits of UCF101 and HMDB51.

Model	#Params	UCF101	HMDB51
IDT [16]	-	86.40%	61.70%
Dynamic image networks + IDT [1]	-	89.10%	65.20%
TDD + IDT [17]	-	91.50%	65.90%
Two-stream fusion + IDT [6]	-	93.50%	69.20%
Temporal segment networks [18]	-	94.20%	69.40%
ST-ResNet + IDT [5]	-	94.60%	70.30%
Deep networks, Sports 1M pre-training [8]	-	65.20%	-
Two-Stream CNN [13]	12M	88.00%	89.40%
C3D ensemble + IDT, Sports 1M pre-training [15]	39M	90.10%	-
TSN (BN-inception), ImageNet + Kinetics pre-training [19]	-	97.00%	-
Two-stream I3D, ImageNet + Kinetics pre-training [2]	25M	97.90%	80.20%
Proposed method, ImageNet + Kinetics pre-training	10M	**97.30%**	**77.99%**

5 Conclusion

In this paper, we investigated the fusion of multiple temporal segments in the framework of temporal segment network for action recognition in videos. In addition, we combined the four streams of RGB, RGB differences, optical flow, and warped optical flow with the optimized weights. To improve the accuracy further, we use the pre-training of the model on both Kinetics and ImageNet. The experimental results on the datasets of UCF101 and HMDB51 show that the proposed method improves the recognition accuracy obviously, and it can achieve the competitive accuracy to the state-of-the art method with fewer parameters and lower computational cost. In the future, we will consider more temporal segments information to capture the long-range temporal context.

Acknowledgement. The work was partially supported by the following: National Natural Science Foundation of China under no. 61876155, and 61876154; The Natural Science Foundation of the Jiangsu Higher Education Institutions of China under no. 17KJD520010; Suzhou Science and Technology Program under no. SYG201712, SZS201613; Natural Science Foundation of Jiangsu Province BK20181189 and BK20181190; Key Program Special Fund in XJTLU under no. KSF-A-01, KSF-P-02, KSF-E-26, and KSF-A-10; XJTLU Research Development Fund RDF-16-02-49.

References

1. Bilen, H., Fernando, B., Gavves, E., Vedaldi, A., Gould, S.: Dynamic image networks for action recognition. In: Proceedings of the IEEE Conference on Computer Vision and Pattern Recognition, pp. 3034–3042 (2016)
2. Carreira, J., Zisserman, A.: Quo vadis, action recognition? A new model and the kinetics dataset. In: Proceedings of the IEEE Conference on Computer Vision and Pattern Recognition, pp. 6299–6308 (2017)

3. Donahue, J., et al.: Long-term recurrent convolutional networks for visual recognition and description. In: Proceedings of the IEEE Conference on Computer Vision and Pattern Recognition, pp. 2625–2634 (2015)
4. Duda, R.O., Hart, P.E., Stork, D.G.: Pattern Classification. Wiley, Hoboken (2001)
5. Feichtenhofer, C., Pinz, A., Wildes, R.: Spatiotemporal residual networks for video action recognition. In: Advances in Neural Information Processing Systems, pp. 3468–3476 (2016)
6. Feichtenhofer, C., Pinz, A., Zisserman, A.: Convolutional two-stream network fusion for video action recognition. In: Proceedings of the IEEE Conference on Computer Vision and Pattern Recognition, pp. 1933–1941 (2016)
7. Huang, K., Hussain, A., Wang, Q., Zhang, R.: Deep Learning: Fundamentals, Theory and Applications. Springer, Cham (2019). https://doi.org/10.1007/978-3-030-06073-2. ISBN 978-3-030-06072-5
8. Karpathy, A., Toderici, G., Shetty, S., Leung, T., Sukthankar, R., Fei-Fei, L.: Large-scale video classification with convolutional neural networks. In: Proceedings of the IEEE Conference on Computer Vision and Pattern Recognition, pp. 1725–1732 (2014)
9. Kay, W., et al.: The kinetics human action video dataset. arXiv preprint. arXiv:1705.06950 (2017)
10. Krizhevsky, A., Sutskever, I., Hinton, G.E.: ImageNet classification with deep convolutional neural networks. In: Advances in Neural Information Processing Systems, pp. 1097–1105 (2012)
11. Kuehne, H., Jhuang, H., Garrote, E., Poggio, T., Serre, T.: HMDB: a large video database for human motion recognition. In: 2011 International Conference on Computer Vision, pp. 2556–2563. IEEE (2011)
12. Santoro, A., et al.: A simple neural network module for relational reasoning. In: Advances in Neural Information Processing Systems, pp. 4967–4976 (2017)
13. Simonyan, K., Zisserman, A.: Two-stream convolutional networks for action recognition in videos. In: Advances in Neural Information Processing Systems, pp. 568–576 (2014)
14. Soomro, K., Zamir, A.R., Shah, M.: UCF101: a dataset of 101 human actions classes from videos in the wild. arXiv preprint. arXiv:1212.0402 (2012)
15. Tran, D., Bourdev, L., Fergus, R., Torresani, L., Paluri, M.: Learning spatiotemporal features with 3D convolutional networks. In: Proceedings of the IEEE International Conference on Computer Vision, pp. 4489–4497 (2015)
16. Wang, H., Schmid, C.: Action recognition with improved trajectories. In: Proceedings of the IEEE International Conference on Computer Vision, pp. 3551–3558 (2013)
17. Wang, L., Qiao, Y., Tang, X.: Action recognition with trajectory-pooled deep-convolutional descriptors. In: Proceedings of the IEEE Conference on Computer Vision and Pattern Recognition, pp. 4305–4314 (2015)
18. Wang, L., et al.: Temporal segment networks: towards good practices for deep action recognition. In: Leibe, B., Matas, J., Sebe, N., Welling, M. (eds.) ECCV 2016. LNCS, vol. 9912, pp. 20–36. Springer, Cham (2016). https://doi.org/10.1007/978-3-319-46484-8_2
19. Xiong, Y.: TSN Pre-trained Models on Kinetics Dataset (2017). http://yjxiong.me/others/kinetics_action/

Impervious Surface Extraction from Hyperspectral Images via Superpixels Based Sparse Representation with Morphological Attributes Profiles

Jun Rong[1,2], Genyun Sun[1,2(✉)], Aizhu Zhang[1,2], and Hui Huang[1,2]

[1] School of Geosciences, China University of Petroleum (East China), Qingdao 266580, China
genyunsun@163.com

[2] Laboratory for Marine Mineral Resources, Qingdao National Laboratory for Marine Science and Technology, Qingdao 266071, China

Abstract. Impervious surface is an important factor in monitoring urban development and environmental analysis. However, spectral differences and structural differences exist on impervious surfaces, which leads to accurate extraction of impervious surfaces is a difficult task. Therefore, this paper proposes a superpixel sparse representation based on morphological profiles and raw data to extract the impervious surface on hyperspectral imagery. Specifically, the segmentation map of the image is first generated by the mean shift segmentation. Then, the morphological attribute profiles of the hyperspectral image are extracted and stacked with raw data. Finally, the segmentation map is masked onto the stacked image and each resulting superpixel is classified via sparse representation. Experiments show that the method has good performance in impervious surface extraction and has advantages in the comparison method. This shows the effectiveness of the proposed method.

Keywords: Impervious surface · Hyperspectral · Sparse representation · Superpixel · Morphological attribute profiles

1 Introduction

Impervious surfaces refer to artificial objects that are impervious to water, including cement, asphalt pavements, houses, parking lots, etc. [1]. With the development of the city, the impact of impervious surface on the water cycle and heat transfer is increasing. Therefore, accurate extraction of impervious surfaces is of great significance for studying urban development and solving urban environmental problems. However, there are some problems in extracting the impervious surface, mainly because the spectral confusion, such as low albedow impervious surface is easily confused with water, vegetation, bare soil and shadows. And there is spatial heterogeneity due to intra-class structure differences [2].

Impervious surface extraction is mainly based on methods in the field of remote sensing [3, 4]. Based on multispectral imagery (MSI), there have been many research

J. Ren et al. (Eds.): BICS 2019, LNAI 11691, pp. 254–262, 2020.
https://doi.org/10.1007/978-3-030-39431-8_24

results [5, 6]. It mainly includes spectral mixture analysis [6], impervious surface index [7], multiple regression [8], classification [2] and regression tree (CART) algorithm [9]. However, due to the limited spectral bands in MSI, it does not adequately represent the spectral difference between the impervious surface and the pervious surface.

In recent years, with the development of imaging sensor, hyperspectral images (HSI) can be widely obtained globally. Due to the rich spectral information of HSI, the impervious surface extraction based on HSI has become a hot issue in the field of remote sensing [10, 11]. The extraction method includes sub-pixel-based methods [12], but with the increase of spatial resolution of HSI, pixel-level methods have attracted more attention [13], and in which SVM classifier-based methods have achieved good performance [14]. However, due to the high dimensionality of hyperspectral images, the SVM method is susceptible to dimensional curse, and pixel-based classifiers cannot solve the spatial heterogeneity of impervious surfaces, resulting in noise extraction results. Therefore, methods based on spectral-spatial information has been proposed and achieved good results [15].

Recently, sparse representation methods have been widely used in the fields of recognition [16], unmixing [17], and classification [18]. Chen et al. proposed a joint sparse representation (JSRC) method [18] and applied to HSI classification. JSRC construct a linear relationship between the samples in a window neighborhood and the dictionary atoms selected from the dictionary consisting of training samples, so that a sparse coefficient matrix is obtained to encode the label information of the samples. Liu et al. introduced sparse representation into impervious surface extraction based on the combination of multichannel gray level co-occurrence matrix and raw data [19]. Although this method considers the spectral-spatial characteristics, it cannot sufficiently solve the spatial heterogeneity of the impervious surface due to the adopted fixed window neighborhood. Therefore, a superpixel neighborhood which is adaptive to the structure of land covers has been widely used as spatial information [20, 27, 28]. Superpixels embody the structural diversity of land covers, thus they are more suitable for the representation of impervious surface.

In addition to the influence of the spatial neighborhood, the feature extraction method can further extract effective spectral-spatial features. Since the impervious surface is an artificial object, its characteristics such as texture and shape are quite different from those of natural objects. Therefore, methods for texture feature extraction, such as gabor features [21] and gray level co-occurrence matrix [19], are applied to the extraction of impervious surfaces. However, these features are highly demanding on the regularity of the texture, the spatial heterogeneity of the impervious surface cause difficulty to adapt to these features. In the literature [22], a kind of morphological attribute profiles (MAPs) is proposed, which includes four structural attribute profiles (APs): area, moment of inertia, length of bounding box and standard deviation. MAPs can well solve the spatial heterogeneity of the impervious surface, and it also has a good distinguishing for stripe objects such as roads.

Therefore, we proposed a impervious surface extraction method based on joint superpixel sparse representation for the stacked MAPs and raw image (JSMRSR).

Specifically, construct a superpixel map first by mean shift segmentation method. Then, attribute profiles are calculated on principal components (PCs) from principal component analysis (PCA) and stacked with raw image. Finally, the superpixel map is masked onto the stacked image to form superpixels, and then JSRC is applied to a superpixel level classification. Experiments on the HSI from Hyperion imaging sensor show that the proposed method has great advantages compared with the comparison methods, indicating the effectiveness of the proposed method.

2 Methodology

As Fig. 1 illustrated, the flowchart of the proposed method can be summarized into three steps: generation of superpixel map, acquisition of MAPs-Raw (MAPs stacked with raw data) map, and joint sparse representation of superpixels.

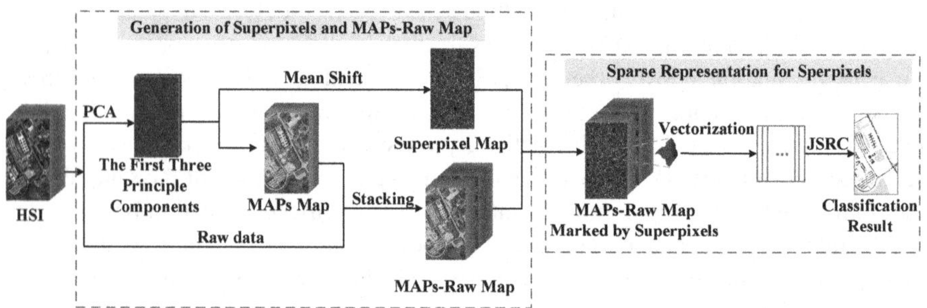

Fig. 1. Workflow of the proposed method.

2.1 Generation of Superpixel Map

A superpixel is a set of pixels that are adaptively divided according to the structure of land covers, therefore, it can adaptively represent impervious surface with different spatial shapes. There are many methods to segment superpixels [23, 24, 26], where mean shift segmentation method [23] is a very efficient way to generate superpixels. The main idea of the mean shift segmentation algorithm is to find the position where the largest probability density of the samples in the feature space is. Then the region is divided by classifying the samples on the drift path and the samples in a certain range into one class. In this paper, we use PCA to reduce the dimension of HSI, and then fed several PCs into mean shift algorithm to gain superpixel map.

2.2 Acquisition of MAPs-Raw Map

For the spatial heterogeneity of the impervious surface, MAPs can characterize impervious surfaces from four APs, including area, moment of inertia, length of bounding box and standard deviation. The calculation of AP is a series of thinning and thickening [22]. Assuming a grayscale image is f, then the AP is:

$$AP(f) = \{\phi_n(f), \cdots, \phi_1(f), \gamma_1(f), \cdots, \gamma_n(f)\} \tag{1}$$

where $\phi(f)$ and $\gamma(f)$ is thinning and thickening.

MAP are collections of AP on several grayscale images, that is:

$$MAP(F) = \{AP(f_1), AP(f_2), \cdots, AP(f_b)\} \tag{2}$$

where $F = \{f_1, f_2, ..., f_b\}$ is a set of gray images. When the four APs are separately extracted on F, the MAPs can be obtained by stacking these feature images.

In this paper, due to too many HSI bands, the PCA is first used for dimensionality reduction. The first few PCs were extracted for MAPs calculation. Taking into account the information loss caused by dimensionality reduction, the obtained MAPs are further superimposed with the original HSI to enhance the features.

2.3 Joint Sparse Representation for Superpixels

After obtaining the superpixel map and MAPs-Raw data, the superpixel map is then masked onto the MAPs-Raw data, so that the feature data can be divided into independent superpixels. Next, the superpixel is jointly sparse represented to sufficient extract spectral-spatial information.

Given a superpixel $\mathbf{X} = [\boldsymbol{x}_1, \boldsymbol{x}_2, ..., \boldsymbol{x}_T]$, where T is the number of pixels in a superpixel. $\mathbf{X}$ can be represented with JSRC with a dictionary $\boldsymbol{D} = [\boldsymbol{D}_1, \boldsymbol{D}_2] \in \boldsymbol{R}^{B \times N}$, where $\boldsymbol{D}_1$ is the collection impervious surface training samples, $\boldsymbol{D}_2$ is the training samples for pervious surface. N is the total number of training samples, and B is the bands dimension of HSI. In sparse representation, impervious surface includes different land covers can be attributed to same dictionary class, because the representation of samples can always finds the most linearly related dictionary atoms. Then, $\mathbf{X}$ can be represented as:

$$\mathbf{X} = [\boldsymbol{D}\boldsymbol{A}_1, \boldsymbol{D}\boldsymbol{A}_2] = \boldsymbol{D}\boldsymbol{A} \tag{3}$$

where $\boldsymbol{A} = [\boldsymbol{A}_1, \boldsymbol{A}_2] \in \boldsymbol{R}^{N \times T}$ is the sparse coefficients matrix of $\boldsymbol{X}$. By enforcing a row sparsity on $\boldsymbol{A}$, the position of nonzero rows in $\boldsymbol{A}$ corresponds to the position of selected dictionary atoms, which ensures that test samples are represented by a common dictionary atoms. The coefficients matrix $\boldsymbol{A}$ can be obtained by solving the optimization problem:

$$\hat{\boldsymbol{A}} = \underset{\boldsymbol{A}}{\operatorname{argmin}} \|\boldsymbol{X} - \boldsymbol{D}\boldsymbol{A}\| \ s.t. \ \|\boldsymbol{A}\|_{row,0} \leq K \tag{4}$$

where $\|\cdot\|_{row,0}$ represents the Frobenius norm of row sparsity, K is the sparsity of $\boldsymbol{A}$. The optimization problem of Eq. (4) is NP-hard problem, but the simultaneously orthogonal matching pursuit (SOMP) [25] algorithm can be used to find the approximate solution. After obtaining $\boldsymbol{A}$, the category of superpixel $\boldsymbol{X}$ can be obtained by:

$$class(\boldsymbol{X}) = \text{argmin}||\boldsymbol{X} - \boldsymbol{D}_c\hat{\boldsymbol{A}}_c||_F \quad c = 1, 2 \tag{5}$$

where $\hat{\boldsymbol{A}}_c$ denotes the coefficients of c-th class in $\hat{\boldsymbol{A}}$, and $||\cdot||_F$ is the Frobenius norm.

3 Results and Discussion

3.1 Dataset

In this article, we use the Earth Observing-1 (EO-1) Hyperion data for experiment. The data was taken at the south-central part of Maryland, USA on October 2, 2006, with a size of 200*190 pixels and a spatial resolution of 20 m. Hyperion dataset has 242 bands in the spectral range of 356–2577 nm. During the experiment, the low-quality bands in the following spectral range are removed, including 8–57 (427–925 nm), 79 (933 nm), 83–119 (973–1336 nm), 133–164 (1477–1790 nm), 183–184 (1982–1992 nm), and 188–220 (2032–2355 nm). This dataset has reference data and can be acquired in the 2006 National Land Cover Database (NLCD) products. According to the division of NLCD, there are the following categories in the experimental area, open water, open space (impervious surface account for less than 20% of total cover), low intensity (impervious surface account for 20% to 49% of total cover), medium intensity (impervious surface account for 50% to 79% of total cover) and high intensity (impervious surface account for 80% to 100% of total cover), deciduous forest, evergreen forest, cultivated crops and woody wetlands. High and medium intensity areas are considered impervious surface and others are considered to be permeable surface. The color image composited by first three PCs of Hyperion is showed in Fig. 2(a) and ground truth map is showed in Fig. 2(b).

3.2 Experiment Setup

In the experiment, the comparison methods include JSRC, JSRC for gabor features stacked with raw data (JGRSRC), JSRC for multichannel gray level co-occurrence matrix (GLCM) stacked with raw data (JCRSRC), JSRC for MAPs-Raw data (JMRSRC), and the proposed method (JSMRSR). The window scale of JSRC based method is set as 3×3 and sparsity level is 3. The number of PCs is 3. The 8 directions of gabor filter is $\{0, \pi/4, \pi/2, 3\pi/4, \pi, 5\pi/4, 3\pi/2, 7\pi/4\}$ of JGRSRC. The parameter of GLCM is the same with the literature [19]. The JSMRSR uses 3 attribute profiles, area, moment of inertia, and length of bounding box. The training samples are randomly selected 10% of each class from the labeled pixels, which tabled in Table 1. For the quantitate estimation, three commonly used quantitative metrics were adopted to estimate the accuracies of methods, including overall accuracy (OA), average accuracy (AA) and kappa coefficient (K).

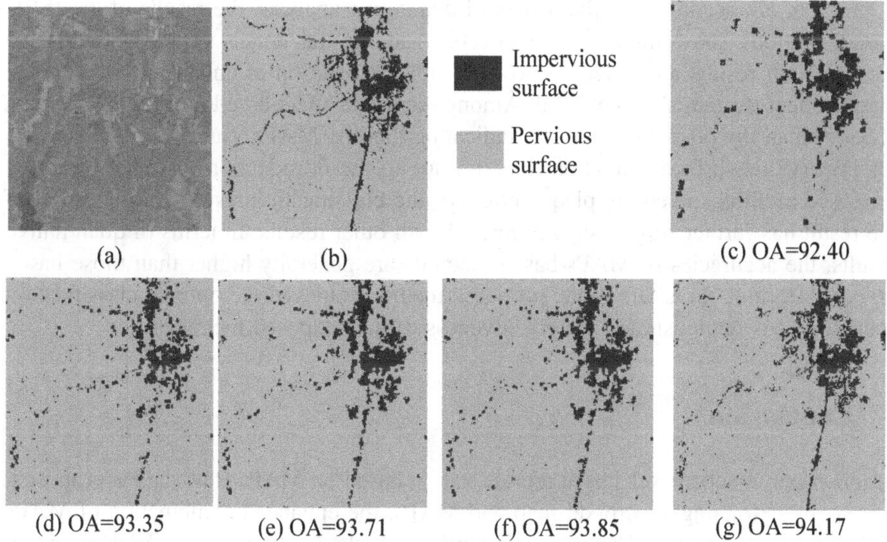

Fig. 2. Hyperion image: (a) composite color image; and (b) ground truth; Estimation map obtained by: (c) JSRC; (d) JGRSRC; (e) JCRSRC; (f) JMRSRC; (g) JSMRSR

Table 1. Reference classes in Hyperion

Class	Name	Train	Test
1	Impervious surface	366	3292
2	Pervious surface	3654	36902
Total		4020	40194

3.3 Analysis of Experimental Results

The classification maps of comparison methods are illustrated in Figs. 2(c)–(g), and the accuracies is tabled in Table 2, where IS denotes impervious surface and PS denotes pervious surface.

Table 2. Classification accuracies of comparision methods

Class	JSRC	JGRSRC	JCRSRC	JMRSRC	JSMRSR
IS	59.12	52.22	63.88	63.46	**66.28**
PS	95.81	**97.34**	96.65	96.78	96.73
OA	92.47	93.23	93.67	93.75	**93.96**
AA	77.46	74.78	80.27	80.12	**81.51**
K	54.68	54.77	61.26	61.46	**63.30**

First of all, according to the results of qualitative analysis, the results of the JSRC based methods show more plaque effects. And for the details of land covers, the classification results are rough. However, with the addition of enhanced features, the plaque effect is gradually alleviated. Among them, the effect based on MAPs-Raw data is better than the other two features, indicating that the MAPs feature is more suitable for impervious surface extraction. Finally, due to the introduction of superpixels, the proposed method solved the plaque effect of the classification result, and the noise of the result has further suppression compared with other results. In terms of quantitative results, the accuracies of MAPs-based methods are generally higher than those based on other features. In addition, the proposed method achieved the optimal classification accuracy. It is demonstrated the effectiveness of the proposed method.

4 Conclusion

In this paper, a superpixel sparse representation based on MAPs-Raw data is proposed. Firstly, by extracting superpixel map and MAPs, the enhanced combination of MAPs and raw data is obtained. Then superpixel map is masked onto the stacked data to obtain superpixels, and then JSRC is used for superpixel level classification. Experiments show that the MAPs feature is superior to Gabor and GLCM in describing the impervious surface on the Hyperion dataset. Moreover, spatial information based on superpixels is superior to window neighborhoods. The proposed method combined with the advantages of the both, and utilized the rich spectral features of HSI, which led to the solution of the spectral confusion and spatial heterogeneity of the impervious surface. In the future, we will apply new techniques applications for feature extraction [29–31] and band selection [32] as well as some application driven development [33, 34].

References

1. Weng, Q.: Remote sensing of impervious surfaces in the urban areas: requirements, methods, and trends. Remote Sens. Environ. **117**, 34–49 (2012)
2. Hsieh, P.F., Lee, L.C., Chen, N.Y.: Effect of spatial resolution on classification errors of pure and mixed pixels in remote sensing. IEEE Trans. Geosci. Remote **39**(12), 2657–2663 (2002)
3. Zhenfeng, S., Chong, L.: The integrated use of DMSP-OLS nighttime light and MODIS data for monitoring large-scale impervious surface dynamics: a case study in the Yangtze River Delta. Remote Sens. **6**(10), 9359–9378 (2014)
4. Ma, Q., He, C., Wu, J., et al.: Quantifying spatiotemporal patterns of urban impervious surfaces in China: an improved assessment using nighttime light data. Landscape Urban Plan. **130**, 36–49 (2014)
5. Song, X.P., Sexton, J.O., Huang, C., et al.: Characterizing the magnitude, timing and duration of urban growth from time series of Landsat-based estimates of impervious cover. Remote Sens. Environ. **175**, 1–13 (2016)
6. Li, L., Lu, D., Kuang, W.: Examining urban impervious surface distribution and its dynamic change in Hangzhou metropolis. ISPRS J. Photogramm. **109**(109), 1–16 (2016)

7. Zhiqiang, C., Jianfei, C.: Investigation on extracting the space information of urban land-use from high spectrum resolution image of ASTER by NDBI method. Geo-Information Sci. **24**(2), 213–221 (2006)
8. Chen, L., Zhang, Y., Chen, B.: Support vector regression with genetic algorithms for estimating impervious surface and vegetation distributions using ETM + data. In: Geoinformatics: Remotely Sensed Data & Information. International Society for Optics and Photonics (2007)
9. Li, Q., Rui, H., Zheng, D., et al.: Extracting impervious surface by CART method according to different brightness values from remote sensing imagery. In: International Conference on Geoinformatics. IEEE (2011)
10. Tan, K., Jin, X., Du, Q., et al.: Modified multiple endmember spectral mixture analysis for mapping impervious surfaces in urban environments. J. Appl. Remote Sens. **8**(1), 85–96 (2014)
11. Tang, F., Xu, H.Q.: Comparison of performances in retrieving impervious surface between hyperspectral (hyperion) and multispectral (TM/ETM+) images. Spectrosc. Spect. Anal. **34**(4), 1075–1080 (2014)
12. Phinn, S., Stanford, M., Scarth, P., et al.: Monitoring the composition of urban environments based on the vegetation-impervious surface-soil (VIS) model by subpixel analysis techniques. Int. J. Remote Sens. **23**(20), 4131–4153 (2002)
13. Sunde, M.G., He, H.S., Zhou, B., et al.: Imperviousness change analysis tool (I-CAT) for simulating pixel-level urban growth. Landscape Urban Plan. **124**, 104–108 (2014)
14. Cheng, X., Luo, J., Shen, Z., et al.: Estimation of impervious surface based on integrated analysis of classification and regression by using SVM. In: Geoscience and Remote Sensing Symposium (2011)
15. Luo, L., Mountrakis, G.: Converting local spectral and spatial information from a priori classifiers into contextual knowledge for impervious surface classification. ISPRS J. Photogramm. **66**(5), 579–587 (2011)
16. Wright, J., Ganesh, A., Zhou, Z., et al.: Demo: robust face recognition via sparse representation. In: IEEE International Conference on Automatic Face & Gesture Recognition (2009)
17. Iordache, M.D., Bioucasdias, J.M., Plaza, A.: Sparse unmixing of hyperspectral data. IEEE Trans. Geosci. Remote Sens. **49**(6), 2014–2039 (2011)
18. Yi, C., Nasrabadi, N.M., Tran, T.D.: Hyperspectral image classification using dictionary-based sparse representation. IEEE Trans. Geosci. Remote Sens. **49**, 3973–3985 (2011)
19. Liu, S., Gu, G.: Improving the impervious surface estimation from hyperspectral images using a spectral-spatial feature sparse representation and post-processing approach. Remote Sens. **9**, 456 (2017)
20. Hu, X., Weng, Q.: Impervious surface area extraction from IKONOS imagery using an object-based fuzzy method. Geocarto Int. **26**(1), 3–20 (2011)
21. Bhaskaran, S., Paramananda, S., Ramnarayan, M.: Per-pixel and object-oriented classification methods for mapping urban features using Ikonos satellite data. Appl. Geography **30**(4), 0–665 (2010)
22. Zhu, C., Li, J., et al.: Impervious surface extraction from multispectral images via morphological attribute profiles based on spectral analysis. IEEE J.-Stars **11**(12), 4775–4790 (2019)
23. Huang, X., Zhang, L.: An adaptive mean-shift analysis approach for object extraction and classification from urban hyperspectral imagery. IEEE Trans. Geosci. Remote Sens. **46**(12), 4173–4185 (2008)
24. Comaniciu, D., Meer, P.: Mean shift: a robust approach toward feature space analysis. IEEE Trans. Pattern. Anal. PAMI **24**, 603–619 (2002)

25. Tropp, J.A.: Algorithms for simultaneous sparse approximation. Part II: convex relaxation. Sig. Process. **86**, 572–588 (2006)
26. Zabalza, J., et al.: Novel segmented stacked autoencoder for effective dimensionality reduction and feature extraction in hyperspectral imaging. Neurocomputing **185**, 1–10 (2016)
27. Fang, L., Li, S., Duan, W., Ren, J., Benediktsson, J.A.: Classification of hyperspectral images by exploiting spectral–spatial information of superpixel via multiple kernels. IEEE Trans. Geosci. Remote Sens. **53**(12), 6663–6674 (2015)
28. Sun, H., Ren, J., Zhao, H., Yan, Y., Zabalza, J., Marshall, S.: Superpixel based feature specific sparse representation for spectral-spatial classification of hyperspectral images. Remote Sens. **11**(5), 536 (2019)
29. Ren, J., et al.: Effective feature extraction and data reduction in remote sensing using hyperspectral imaging. IEEE Sig. Process. Mag. **31**(4), 149–154 (2014)
30. Zabalza, J., et al.: Novel folded-PCA for improved feature extraction and data reduction with hyperspectral imaging and SAR in remote sensing. ISPRS J. Photogramm. Remote Sens. **93**, 112–122 (2014)
31. Zabalza, J., Ren, J., Zheng, J., et al.: Novel segmented stacked autoencoder for effective dimensionality reduction and feature extraction in hyperspectral imaging. Neurocomputing **185**, 1–10 (2016)
32. Tschannerl, J., et al.: Unsupervised hyperspectral band selection based on information theory and a modified discrete gravitational search algorithm. Inf. Fusion **51**, 189–200 (2019)
33. Tschannerl, J., Ren, J., Jack, F., et al.: Potential of UV and SWIR hyperspectral imaging for determination of levels of phenolic flavour compounds in peated barley malt. Food Chem. **270**, 105–112 (2019)
34. Qiao, T., et al.: Quantitative prediction of beef quality using visible and NIR spectroscopy with large data samples under industry conditions. J. Appl. Spectrosc. **82**(1), 137–144 (2015)

Dilated Convolutional Network for Road Extraction in Remote Sensing Images

Yuke Wang[1], Nailiang Kuang[3], Jiangbin Zheng[1(✉)], Pengyi Xie[1], Min Wang[2], and Chao Zhao[3]

[1] School of Software, Northwestern Polytechnical University, Xi'an, Shaanxi Province, China
wyk0704@163.com, zhengjb@nwpu.edu.cn
[2] North Electronics Research Institute Co., LTD., Xi'an, Shaanxi Province, China
[3] Xi'an Microelectronics Technology Institute, Xi'an, Shaanxi Province, China

Abstract. According to the characteristics of the road in the remote sensing images, we de-sign a dilated convolutional neural network (DCN) for road extraction. In order to minimize the problem of feature disappearance caused by down-sampling, we use dilated convolution of the traditional convolution in partial convolutional process instead. (dilated convolution has been used to partly replace traditional convolution) At the same time, DCN reduces the number of pooling layers. The ad-vantage is that the receptive field largely increases without increasing the number of parameters. As the road area is a small proportion in remote sensing images, the training set is pre-filtered according to the proportional distribution of positive and negative samples, which avoids the bad influences of the imbalance between positive and negative samples in training process. The experimental results show that DCN outperforms all the baselines in terms of precision, recall, and F1 scores.

Keywords: Dilated convolution · Road extraction · Sample imbalance

1 Introduction

As a major component of transportation, roads play an irreplaceable role in human activities. In modern society, roads are also important identification objects in maps and geographic information systems. With the widespread use of traffic geographic information systems, roads automatic extraction technology emerges and continues to evolve. In the past, people have done a lot of research on the automatic road ex-traction technology in remote sensing images. Most of these studies use the idea of "feature matching and road connection". These methods determine the roads by finding their general characteristics, such as gray features [1], edge features [2, 3], intersections [4], etc., and then following a connection algorithm to extract road locations [5, 6]. These methods play an active role in certain applications. But in the feature design and connection algorithm, there are many threshold parameters needing to be manually adjusted to achieve better results under certain types of images. Threshold problem limits the application of methods on large-scale data.

J. Ren et al. (Eds.): BICS 2019, LNAI 11691, pp. 263–272, 2020.
https://doi.org/10.1007/978-3-030-39431-8_25

With the development of deep learning technology in the field of computer vision, image classification, object recognition and semantic segmentation tasks have all achieved major breakthroughs. The road extraction task of remote sensing image is equivalent to a subset of the semantic segmentation task of the image. With the progress of deep semantic segmentation research [7–9], research on road extraction technology in remote sensing images has been also developed. Such as FCN [10], DeconvNet [11], SegNet [12], U-Net [13]. Most of the existing networks for segmentation will take a problem of multiple down-samples of feature maps. Because the road occupies a small proportion in the image, multiple down-sampling will cause feature loss. It will affect the results of road extraction. Recently, some advanced methods in other fields that may be used for reference have also been proposed. For example, significant detection [16, 17], object detection [18, 22], edge detection [19, 20], image forgery detection [21].

Section 2 introduces some related work. Section 3 describes the proposed Dilated Convolutional Neural Network (DCN). According to the characteristics of the road target, DCN is designed in this paper. In order to preserve the rich low-level details of the road, DCN adopts the skip connection from low-level features to high-level features. And the number of sampling in the encoding process is reduced to ensure the resolution of the intermediate feature maps. DCN uses the dilated convolution to partly replace the traditional convolution. Dilated convolution can obviously enhance the perceptive ability of the convolution kernel, without increasing the number of parameters. Hence, DCN is easy to train. As for the problem of sample imbalance, we pre-filter the training data. In Sect. 4, the effectiveness of DCN is compared with other methods by several objective and subjective experiments. Section 5 shows the conclusion. The contributions of this paper are summarized as follows.

1. We designed a lightweight network for remote sensing image road extraction, which is achieved by reducing the pooling layer and adding a hole convolution method. It maintains the integrity of the road structure.
2. We crop and screen the image while improving the cross entropy loss function, which ensures the balance of positive and negative samples in the training set. Our method has a good effect in the process of training the model.

2 Related Work

2.1 Deep Learning for Semantic Segmentation

Semantic segmentation algorithm is usually used to solve the pixel marking problem based on the convolutional neural network (CNN). Many state-of-the-art supervised learning algorithms for extracting the underlying feature hierarchy have been proposed. Long et al. [10] proposed a classification networks incorporating Alex, VGG and Google networks into fully CNN. In this method, some of the pooling layers were skipped: layer 3 (FCN-8s), layer 4 (FCN-16s), and layer 5 (FCN-32s). Ronneberger et al. [13] proposed U-Net, a CNN for image segmentation. It consists of an encoding path and a symmetric decoding path that enable localization. Badrinarayanan et al. [12]

proposed SegNet, which is a CNN for image segmentation. It also consists of an encoding path and a symmetric decoding path. SegNet is deeper than U-Net.

2.2 Dilated Convolution

Reference [14] points out that pooling and convolution operation will greatly reduce the resolution of feature maps, and dilated convolution can alleviate this problem. Compared with the ordinary convolution, the dilated convolution has a dilation rate parameter which is mainly used to indicate the size of the dilation. The kernel size of dilated convolution is the same as the ordinary convolution. In the convolutional neural network, the number of parameters is the same, while the difference is that the dilated convolution has a larger receptive field.

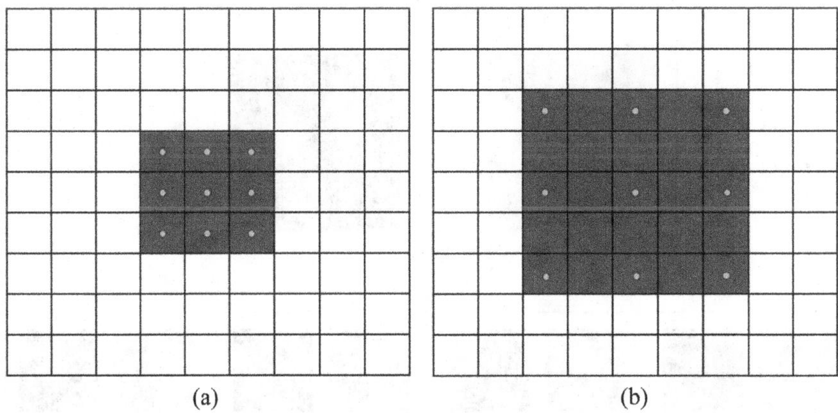

Fig. 1. (a) Ordinary convolution: 1-dilated convolution, (b) dilated convolution: 2-dilated convolution

Figure 1 shows an ordinary convolution and a dilated convolution with a dilation rate of 2. It can be seen that the dilated convolution increases the receptive field of the convolution kernel while keeping the number of parameters constant. At the same time, it can keep the size of the feature maps unchanged. The receptive field of a 3×3 convolution kernel with dilation rate of 2 is the same as the 5×5 convolution kernel, but the number of parameters is only 9, which is 36% of the number of parameters of the 5×5 convolution kernel.

3 Methodology

3.1 Dataset Processing

We enlarge the dataset (Massachusetts Roads, made publicly available by Mnih [15] on website: http://www.cs.toronto.edu/?vmnih/data/) by cropping the image. The original images are standardized and each image contains 1500×1500 pixels. For each image we crop it into 9 small images. Due to sample imbalance in the data, we calculate the proportion of positive samples in each image after cropping by Eq. (1). According to the calculation results, we decide whether to remove this picture.

$$\begin{cases} R = \frac{N_{pos}}{N_{total}} \\ R \geq T \end{cases} \tag{1}$$

where the N_{pos} represents the number of positive samples. N_{total} indicates the total number of samples. T is the threshold, which is determined manually.

Through a large number of experiments, we generally think that T takes 0.1 and the image that satisfies Eq. (1) can be retained.

Figure 2 shows an image crop into 9 images. Since two of the images do not satisfy Eq. (1), they are discarded.

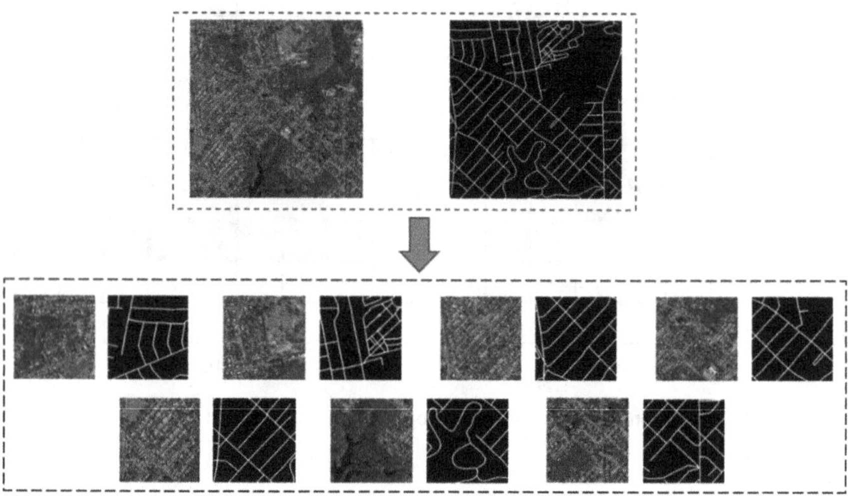

Fig. 2. Dataset amplification

3.2 DCN Architecture

The road is linear and has a special structure with a mesh distribution. The details are rich, but the semantic information is relatively simple. Such characteristics put forward higher requirements for the feature extraction ability of the segmentation network.

The classical semantic segmentation network processes complex and diverse images, requiring higher extraction of semantic information. Most of their encoding parts use pretrained models of classical classification networks (such as VGG16). In these network architectures, the input image is down-sampled multiple times, and the feature map in the middle of the network is compressed many times. For example, in the SegNet architecture, the smallest feature map is compressed 32 times, thus losing some of the details of the target. Although the network uses up-sampling to decode detailed information of the image, it is still not sufficient for road targets to effectively restore the details. At the same time, the simple characteristics of the semantic information of the road target also determine that the road extraction task does not have to adopt the pretraining model of the large-scale image classification network for feature extraction. This paper proposes a DCN architecture with lower depth, and its structure is shown in Fig. 3.

Firstly, DCN performs four ordinary convolution operations and two average pooling operations on the input image. At this time, the size of the feature map is 1/4 of the original image. Then, it performs 6 dilated convolution operations on the feature maps with dilation rate of 2. Subsequently, the feature maps are sent to the decoding network. After completing two up-samplings, the feature maps have the same size as the original image. Finally, the output is mapped to the probability of pixel classification using a single channel convolution layer. The size of convolution kernel is 1×1.

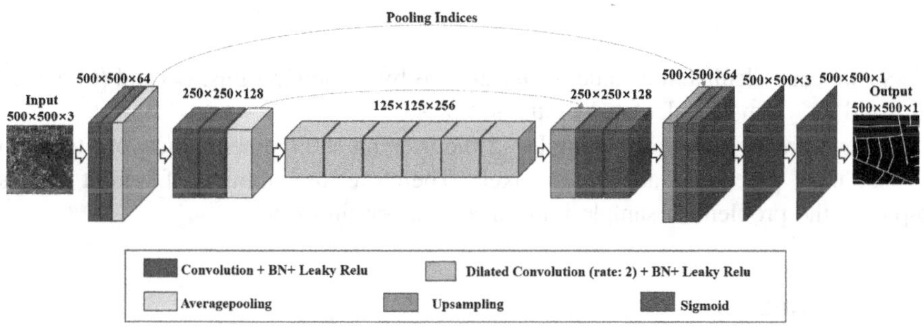

Fig. 3. DCN architecture

3.3 Loss Function

Cross-entropy [13] is widely used as a loss function for processing two-class problems in deep convolutional neural networks, which calculates the probability of being one specific class or not. Thus, our loss function is also based on the cross-entropy loss function L.

$$L = -\frac{1}{n}\sum\nolimits_{i=1}^{n} (y_i loga_i + (1 - y_i)log(1 - a_i)) \tag{2}$$

where y_i indicates the real category of the input x_i, in which $y_i = 1$ means that the i_{th} pixel belongs to the road. The a_i is the category of the pixel in output image, which is modeled by the following sigmoid function:

$$a_i = \frac{1}{1 + e^{-z_i}} \tag{3}$$

where z_i donates the input of the last convolution layer.

Since the input image has a sample imbalance problem, it is unreasonable to assign the same weight to the positive and negative samples. Therefore, we added weighting factors to Eq. (2).

$$L_{DCN} = -\frac{1}{n}\sum\nolimits_{i=1}^{n} (\omega_1 y_i log a_i + \omega_2 (1 - y_i) log(1 - a_i)) \tag{4}$$

where ω_1 and ω_2 are both positive numbers and they satisfy Eq. (5).

$$\omega_1 + \omega_2 = W \tag{5}$$

where W is usually chosen as 1 or 2.

In order to ensure the balance of positive and negative samples, we should make:

$$\frac{\omega_1 \times N_{pos}}{\omega_2 \times N_{neg}} = 1 \tag{6}$$

So we can calculate the values of ω_1 and ω_2 by combining Eqs. (5) and (6), where N_{pos} and N_{neg} can be calculated by the samples.

If there are more negative samples in the training set, the neural network tends to classify most pixels as background pixels. Therefore, the addition of weight factors improves the problem of sample imbalance to a certain extent.

4 Experiments

4.1 Performance Evaluations

Let TP denote the number of correctly classified road pixels. TN denotes the number of correctly classified non-road pixels. FP denotes the number of mistakenly classified road pixels. And FN denotes the number of mistakenly classified non-road pixels.

The metrics used are precision, recall, F1 score and IoU (intersection over union), as shown in the Eqs. (7)–(10). Precision is the percentage of road pixels that the classifier correctly classifies in all predicted pixels. The recall is the percentage of road pixels that are correctly classified in all actual road pixels. F1 score is a combination of precision and recall. IoU denotes the intersection of the predicted pixels and the ground-truth divided by the union.

$$Precision = \frac{TP}{TP + FP} \tag{7}$$

$$Recall = \frac{TP}{TP + FN} \tag{8}$$

$$F1score = \frac{2 \times Precision \times Recall}{Precision + Recall} \tag{9}$$

$$IoU = \frac{area(Predict) \cap area(GT)}{area(Predict) \cup area(GT)} \tag{10}$$

4.2 Experimental Results and Analysis

The dataset uses the remote sensing image road dataset, Massachusetts Roads. The dataset uses satellite remote sensing images covering more than 2,600 square kilometers in Massachusetts, USA. Each image is a 1500 × 1500 pixels RGB image with a ground resolution of about 1 m/pixel. The comparison methods selected in this paper are U-Net and SegNet. We also experimented with FCN on the data, but FCN is difficult to extract road details, so our comparative experiment ruled out FCN. The training set of the network uses a total of 3120 images and corresponding annotation maps of the cut images obtained according to the method mentioned in Sect. 3.1. The test set evaluated the DCN performance using 438 images and their annotations. The results obtained are shown in Table 1.

It can be seen that our approach significantly outperforms all other approaches. In particular, our DCN approach reaches the highest precision among three approaches. Meanwhile, our DCN approach significantly increases the precision rate. Then, F1-score is measured by precision and recall. As we can see, the F1-score of our approach is 0.7654, which is better than 0.661 of U-Net and 0.7042 of SegNet. The IoU of DCN is also higher than SegNet and U-Net.

Table 1. A comparison between our proposed method and others in terms of precision, recall, and F1 score

Model	Precision	Recall	F1-score	IoU
U-Net	0.5847	0.7601	0.6610	0.6567
SegNet	0.6358	0.7891	0.7042	0.7053
Our (DCN)	**0.7311**	**0.8030**	**0.7654**	**0.7294**

Besides, Fig. 4 shows the subjective results of roads extraction by three approaches, as well as ground truth. From Fig. 4(a) and (b), we can see that many background pixels are determined to be roads in the extraction results from SegNet and U-Net. But the results of DCN contain fewer pixels mistaken for roads. Figure 4(b)–(d) show that there are fractures in the roads from the results of the three methods. Among them, the results obtained from SegNet and U-Net have more road breaks. However, DCN is less, which benefits from its good information retention ability and detail extraction ability. In addition, many of the roads in the image are obscured by trees. As can be seen from Fig. 4(b) and (d), DCN even extracts a portion of the road that is obscured by trees.

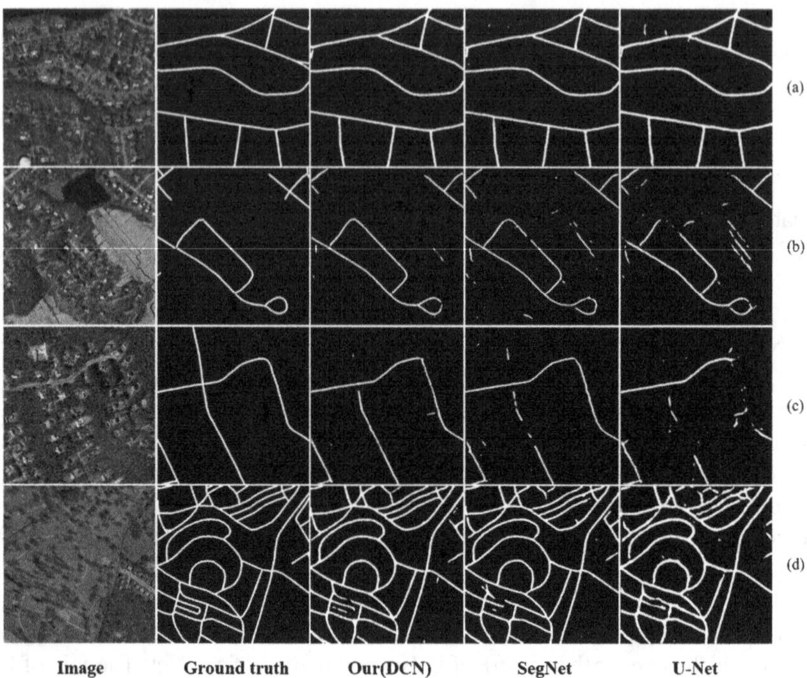

Fig. 4. Subjective results of road extraction by our DCN and other two approaches. (a) scene 1, (b) scene 2, (c) scene 3, (d) scene 4

Figure 5 shows the P-R (Precision-Recall) curve and ROC curve. Both of the two curves show that DCN performs better than SegNet and U-Net.

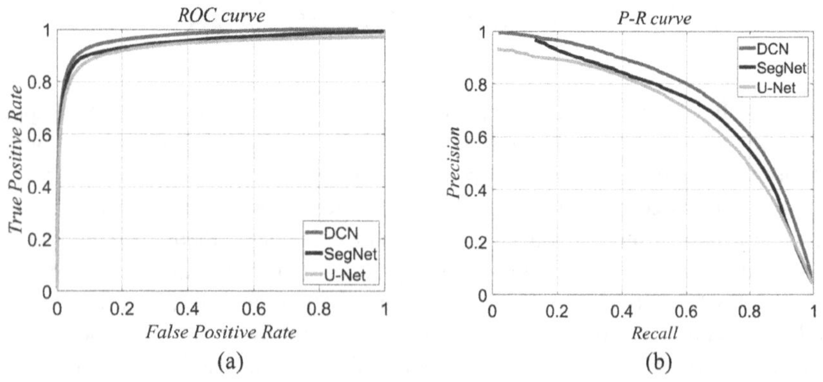

Fig. 5. ROC and P-R curve. (a) ROC curve of three models, (b) P-R curve of three models

5 Conclusions

In this paper, we proposed a novel convolutional neural network to extract road objects from aerial images. The network is similar to a traditional image segmentation network and includes an encoding network and a decoding network. In order to reduce the information loss caused by pooling, we reduced the number of pooling layers. At the same time, we use the dilated convolution layer to replace part of the ordinary convolution layer. The dilated convolution can improve the perceived ability of the network without increasing the number of parameters. It allows the network to extract detailed information better. At the same time, we screen the training samples and add the proportion factor of positive and negative samples in the loss function, which solves the problem of sample imbalance to some extent. The experiments were conducted on Massachusetts roads dataset and compared to the existing techniques. The results show that the DCN outperforms other models in precision, recall and F1-score. From the subjective experimental results, we can also intuitively see that the performance of DCN is better than the other contrastive models. In future work, we will investigate and compare other image segmentation techniques to get a better architecture for road extraction.

Acknowledgements. This work has been supported by HGJ, HJSW and Research & Development plan of Shaanxi Province (Program No. 2017ZDXM-GY-094, 2015KTZDGY04-01).

References

1. Steger, C.: An unbiased detector of curvilinear structures. IEEE Trans. Pattern Anal. Mach. Intell. **20**(2), 113–125 (1998)
2. Tupin, F., Maitre, H., Mangin, J.F., et al.: Detection of linear features in SAR image: application to road network extraction. IEEE Trans. Geosci. Remote Sens. **36**(2), 434–453 (1998)
3. Wenzhong, S., Changqing, Z.: The line segment match method for extracting road network from high-resolution satellite images. IEEE Trans. Geosci. Remote Sens. **40**(2), 511–514 (2002)
4. Jiuxiang, H., Razdan, A., Femiani, J.C., et al.: Road network extraction and intersection detection from aerial images by tracking road footprints. IEEE Trans. Geosci. Remote Sens. **45**(12), 4144–4157 (2007)
5. Christophe, E., Inglada, J.: Robust road extraction for high resolution satellite images. In: Proceedings of 2007 IEEE International Conference on Image Processing, vol. 5, pp. 437–440. IEEE, San Antonio (2007)
6. Poullis, C., You, S.: Delineation and geometric modeling of road networks. ISPRS J. Photogram. Remote Sens. **65**(2), 165–181 (2010)
7. Girshick, R., Donahue, J., Darrell, T., et al: Rich feature hierarchies for accurate object detection and semantic segmentation. In: Proceedings of 2014 IEEE Conference on Computer Vision and Pattern Recognition, pp. 580–587. IEEE, Columbus (2014)
8. Simonyan, K., Zisserman, A.: Very deep convolutional networks for large-scale image recognition. In: Proceedings of the 3rd International Conference on Learning Representations, San Diego (2015)

9. Szegedy, C., Liu, W., Jia, Y., et al: Going deeper with convolutions. In: Proceedings of 2015 IEEE Conference on Computer Vision and Pattern Recognition (CVPR), pp. 1–9. IEEE, Boston (2015)
10. Shelhamer, E., Long, J., Darrell, T.: Fully convolutional networks for semantic segmentation. IEEE Trans. Pattern Anal. Mach. Intell. **39**(4), 640–651 (2017)
11. Noh, H., Hong, S., Gan, B.: Learning deconvolution network for semantic segmentation. In: Proceedings of 2015 IEEE International Conference on Computer Vision (ICCV), pp. 1520–1528 IEEE, Santiago (2015)
12. Badrinarayanan, V., Kendall, A., Cipolla, R.: SegNet: a deep convolutional encoder-decoder architecture for image segmentation. IEEE Trans. Pattern Anal. Mach. Intell. **39**(12), 2481–2495 (2017)
13. Ronneberger, O., Fischer, P., Brox, T.: U-Net: convolutional networks for biomedical image segmentation. In: Navab, N., Hornegger, J., Wells, William M., Frangi, Alejandro F. (eds.) MICCAI 2015. LNCS, vol. 9351, pp. 234–241. Springer, Cham (2015). https://doi.org/10.1007/978-3-319-24574-4_28
14. Chen, L.-C., Papandreou, G., Schroff, F., Adam, H.: Rethinking atrous convolution for semantic image segmentation. https://arxiv.org/abs/1706.05587. Accessed Jun 2017
15. Mnih, V.: Machine learning for aerial image labeling. University of Toronto, Toronto (2013)
16. Han, J., Zhang, D., Hu, X., Guo, L., Ren, J., Wu, F.: Background prior-based salient object detection via deep reconstruction residual. IEEE Trans. Circ. Syst. Video Technol. **25**(8), 1309–1321 (2015)
17. Yan, Y., Ren, J., Sun, G., Zhao, H., Han, J., Zhan, J.: Unsupervised image saliency detection with Gestalt-laws guided optimization and visual attention based refinement. Pattern Recogn. **79**, 65–78 (2018)
18. Han, J., Zhang, D., Cheng, G., Guo, L., Ren, J.: Object detection in optical remote sensing images based on weakly supervised learning and high-level feature learning. IEEE Trans. Geosci. Remote Sens. **53**(6), 3325–3337 (2014)
19. Ren, J., Jiang, J., Wang, D., Ipson, S.S.: Fusion of intensity and inter-component chromatic difference for effective and robust colour edge detection. IET Image Proces. **4**(4), 294–301 (2010)
20. Sun, G., Zhang, A., Ren, J., Ma, J., Wang, P.: Gravitation-based edge detection in hyperspectral images. Remote Sens. **9**(6), 592 (2017)
21. Zheng, J., Liu, Y., Ren, J., Zhu, T., Yan, Y., Yang, H.: Fusion of block and keypoints based approaches for effective copy-move image forgery detection. Multidimension. Syst. Signal Process. **27**(4), 989–1005 (2016)
22. Han, J., Zhang, D., Hu, X., Guo, L., Ren, J., Wu, F.: Background prior-based salient object detection via deep reconstruction residual. IEEE Trans. Circ. Syst. Video Technol. **25**(8), 1309–1321 (2014)

MSA-Net: Multiscale Spatial Attention Network for the Classification of Breast Histology Images

Zhanbo Yang[1,2], Lingyan Ran[2], Yong Xia[1,2(✉)], and Yanning Zhang[2]

[1] Research & Development Institute of Northwestern Polytechnical University in Shenzhen, Shenzhen 518057, China
yxia@nwpu.edu.cn
[2] National Engineering Laboratory for Integrated Aero-Space-Ground-Ocean Big Data Application Technology, School of Computer Science and Engineering, Northwestern Polytechnical University, Xi'an 710072, China

Abstract. Breast histology images classification is a time- and labor-intensive task due to the complicated structural and textural information contained. Recent deep learning-based methods are less accurate due to the ignorance of the interfering multiscale contextual information in histology images. In this paper, we propose the multiscale spatial attention network (MSA-Net) to deal with these challenges. We first perform adaptive spatial transformation on histology microscopy images at multiple scales using a spatial attention (SA) module to make the model focus on discriminative content. Then we employ a classification network to categorize the transformed images and use the ensemble of the predictions obtained at multiple scales as the classification result. We evaluated our MSA-Net against four state-of-the-art methods on the BACH challenge dataset. Our results show that the proposed MSA-Net achieves a higher accuracy than the rest methods in the five-fold cross validation on training data, and reaches the 2nd place in the online verification.

Keywords: Breast cancer · Histology image classification · Multiscale · Spatial attention · Convolutional neural networks

1 Introduction

Breast cancer is one of the severe types of cancers in women, which accounts for 25.16% of all cancers with 1.68 million new cases worldwide in 2012 [13]. During the diagnosis of breast cancer, hematoxylin-eosin (H&E) stained histology images of tissue regions resulted from needle biopsy are evaluated to determine the type, including normal, benign, in situ carcinoma, and invasive carcinoma. Due to the complexity of histology images, detecting carcinoma by pathologists is time-consuming, labor-intensive, and subjective. The scientific community has been working on the development of automated detection and diagnosis tools

J. Ren et al. (Eds.): BICS 2019, LNAI 11691, pp. 273–282, 2020.
https://doi.org/10.1007/978-3-030-39431-8_26

over the past years. For instance, the Grand Challenge on BreAst Cancer Histology images (BACH) [2] organized in conjunction with the 15th International Conference on Image Analysis and Recognition (ICIAR 2018) aims at the classification and segmentation of H&E stained breast histology microscopy images.

Automated classification of H&E stained breast histology microscopy images is challenging in two aspects. First, microscopy images usually have an extremely high resolution, and hence contain rich structural information and details, which are hard to be characterized effectively at a single scale. Second, microscopy images from different categories may exhibit partly overlapped patterns, which interfere carcinoma detection, such as the hard mimics from benign lesion which have similar morphological appearance with carcinoma.

To address both issues, various deep learning-based methods have been designed as a result of the success of deep convolutional neural networks (DCNNs) in computer vision [1,3–6,10–12,15,16]. Araujo et al. [1] proposed a patches-based "DCNN + SVM" model to address the breast microscopy image classification problem. In this model, a DCNN is designed for feature extraction and a support vector machine (SVM) is used as a classifier. Chennamsetty et al. [3] constructed an ensemble of three DCNNs, each of which was pre-trained on different preprocessing regimes, and achieved the 1st place on the BACH challenge at the first stage. Besides, attention-based methods [8] were also proposed for this purpose. For instance, following the design trends of squeeze-and-excitation network (SE-Net) [8], Vu et al. [14] incorporated the self-attention mechanism into an encoder-decoder network. Despite the improved performance, these DCNN-based methods still suffer from less-discriminative power resulted mainly from the inadequate quantity of training data. We suggest exploring the multiscale and spatial attention aided contextual information, which have been commonly used by human histology image reader.

In this paper, we propose the multi-scale spatial attention deep convolutional neural network (MSA-Net) for the automated classification of H&E stained breast histology microscopy images. To exploit the multiscale information of images, we first convert each image to three scales, then perform adaptive spatial transformation on the microscopy patches cropped at each scale by the spatial attention (SA) module, which is followed by a classification network to categorize the transformed patches, and finally combine the results to generate the image label. We expect that can learn how to perform spatial transformation on the microscopy patches for precise classification. We evaluated the proposed algorithm on the BACH challenge dataset and achieved an accuracy of $94.50 \pm 1.27\%$ in the five-fold cross validation on training data and an accuracy of 94.00% in the online verification.

2 Method

Given a H&E stained breast histology microscopy image $X \in \mathbb{R}^{H \times W \times C}$, our goal is to predict the image label $Y \in \{0, 1, 2, 3\}$, which includes four classes: Normal (0), Benign (1), In situ carcinoma (2), and Invasive carcinoma (3). The

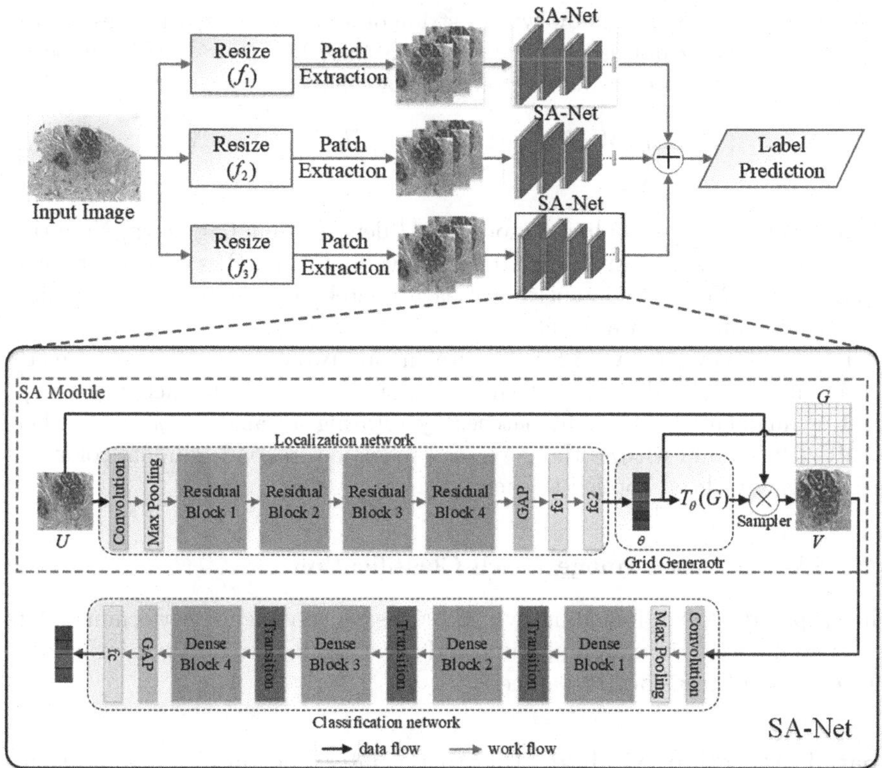

Fig. 1. Diagram of the proposed MSA-Net algorithm. For a histology microscopy image, we first extract microscopy patches at multiple scales, then classify these patches by SA-Net, and finally predict image label by ensemble of the classification results. The SA-Net includes two parts: the SA module consisting of localization network, grid generator and sampler, and the classification network. An input patch U is passed to localization network which regresses the transformation parameters θ, then the regular spatial grid G over V is transformed to the sampling grid $T_\theta(G)$, which is applied to U, and producing the warped output patch V, and lastly V is passed to classification network to get label prediction.

proposed MSA-Net algorithm consists of three steps: (1) multiscale image patch extraction, (2) SA-Net based image patch classification, and (3) multi-branch ensemble. The diagram that summarizes this algorithm is shown in Fig. 1. We now delve into the details of each step.

2.1 Multiscale Image Patch Extraction

For an breast histology microscopy image with size of $H \times W$, we first down-sample the images by factors f_1, f_2 and f_3 to get resized images at three scales, where the down-sampling factor $f \in [1, inf)$ with $f = 1$ being the original image.

Then we slide a $h \times w$ window with a stride of s on the resized images at each scale for extracting multiscale microscopy patches. In this way, the number of microscopy patches we extracted from an image is

$$N = \left(\left\lfloor \frac{W/f - w}{s} \right\rfloor + 1 \right) \times \left(\left\lfloor \frac{H/f - h}{s} \right\rfloor + 1 \right) \quad (1)$$

where f is the down-sampling factor, and $\lfloor\rfloor$ denotes rounding down. Note that the resized images were divided into partly overlapped patches to generate more training data. Next, the intensities of each microscopy patch are standardized to zero mean and unit variance.

To alleviate overfitting of SA-Net, we employ two data augmentation methods to increase the diversity of the training dataset. First, each microscopy patch is augmented into eight patches by rotating an angle of $k \cdot \pi/2$, where $k = \{0, 1, 2, 3\}$, and with/without vertical reflection. Second, random color perturbations have been applied to each patch.

2.2 SA-Net Based Image Patch Classification

The proposed SA-Net including two parts: the SA module for performing adaptive spatial transformation on inputs, and the classification network for predicting the label of transformed patches.

Spatial Attention Module. Due to the inter- and intra-confusing structural and textural information, we perform adaptive spatial transformation on microscopy patches by SA module before categorizing them. The SA module is split into three parts: (i) localization network, (ii) grid generator, and (iii) sampler, as shown in Fig. 1.

First, a localization network takes the extracted microscopy patch $U \in \mathbb{R}^{h \times w \times C}$, with h, w and C being the height, width and number of channels respectively, and outputs the transformation parameters θ. Due to their outstanding performance in non-linear transformation, we choose residual network [7] with 152 learnable layers named ResNet-152 as the backbone network for the localization network. ResNet-152 includes a convolutional layer with the kernel size of 7×7, a 3×3 max pooling layer, four residual blocks, which have 3, 8, 36, and 3 triple-layer residual groups, respectively, and an average pooling layer followed by the softmax operation. To adapt to our problem, we remove the classification layer and add two weight layers to predict the transformations: (i) fully-connected layer to reduce the length of feature vectors from 1024 to 128; (ii) fully-connected layer with 6-D output.

Then, the predicted transformation parameters are used to create a sampling grid by the grid generator, which is a set of points where the input map should be sampled to produce the transformed patch $V \in \mathbb{R}^{h \times w \times C}$. In detail, the output pixels are defined to lie on a regular grid $G = \{G_i\}$ of pixels $G_i = (x_i^O, y_i^O)$, where $i \in [0, 1, \ldots, hw - 1]$, forming an output patch V. The spatial transformation formula is

$$\begin{pmatrix} x_i^I \\ y_i^I \end{pmatrix} = \mathrm{T}_\theta(G_i) = A_\theta \begin{pmatrix} x_i^O \\ y_i^O \\ 1 \end{pmatrix} = \begin{bmatrix} \theta_{11} & \theta_{12} & \theta_{13} \\ \theta_{21} & \theta_{22} & \theta_{23} \end{bmatrix} \begin{pmatrix} x_i^O \\ y_i^O \\ 1 \end{pmatrix} \tag{2}$$

where (x_i^O, y_i^O) are the target coordinates of the regular grid in the output patch, (x_i^I, y_i^I) are the source coordinates in the input patch that define the sample points, and A_θ is a 6-DoF affine transformation matrix.

Lastly, a sampler takes the set of sampling points, along with the input patch U and produces the sampled output patch V. For doing that, bilinear interpolation sampling is applied in coordinates define the spatial location in U to generate the value at a particular pixel in V, where bilinear interpolation sampling is an extension of linear interpolation sampling for interpolation function of two variables on a rectilinear 2D grid.

Classification Network. For the transformed microscopy patches, we categorize them by classification network which using fine-tuned DenseNet-161 [9] model. Similar to ResNet models, DenseNet-161 consists of 161 learnable layers, including a convolutional layer with the kernel size of 7×7, a 3×3 max pooling layer, four dense blocks, three transition layers, and a global average pooling layer followed by the softmax operation. Those four dense blocks contain 6, 12, 36, and 24 dual-layer dense groups, respectively. To adapt the DenseNet-161 to our problem, we keep only four neurons in the layer before softmax.

2.3 Ensemble of the Classification Results

Through the SA-Net, a microscopy patch is spatially transformed and recognized as one of the four classes. The probabilities that a resized image belongs to a category are determined by the ratio of number of patches belongs to this category to the number of patches extracted from this image. Finally, the category of each histology microscopy image is recognized by the average prediction on three images resized from that image.

2.4 Training Procedure

Since each module of MSA-Net is differentiable, we train this deep learning model in an end-to-end fashion. To avoid the impact of the SA module in the initial training stage, the final layer of localization net is initialized to regress the identity transform of input patches. To train the SA-Net at each scale, we adopt the Adam optimizer to minimize the cross entropy loss, and set the batch size to 16, learning rate to 0.0001 with a decay of 10% every 10 training epochs, and the maximum epoch number to 30.

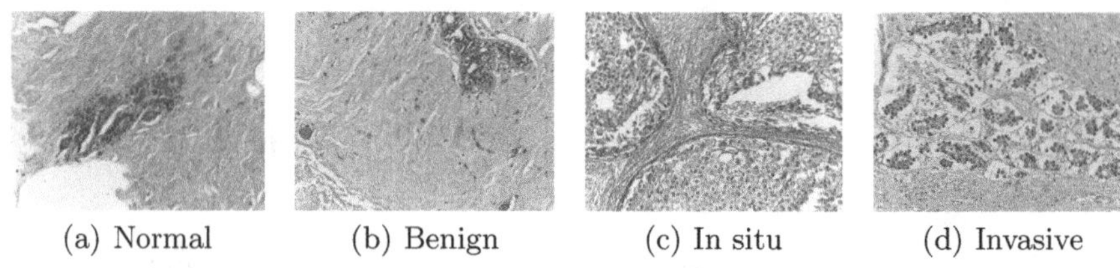

(a) Normal (b) Benign (c) In situ (d) Invasive

Fig. 2. Four H&E stained breast histology microscopy images from different categories.

3 Experiments and Results

3.1 BACH Dataset

The ICIAR 2018 grand challenge on BACH dataset [2] was used for this study. This dataset is composed of 400 H&E stained breast histology microscopy images with a size of 2048×1536 for training a classification model and 100 similar images with the same size for testing. Training images have four class labels including normal, benign, in situ carcinoma and invasive carcinoma (see Fig. 2). Each of four category contains 100 training images. The 100 testing images were officially presented for online verification, and their labels are not available.

3.2 Implementation Details

During offline training procedure, we evaluated the proposed MSA-Net algorithm using 400 training images with the five-fold cross validation.

In the training stage, microscopy patches of size 224×224 were extracted from 320 training images at three scales and were augmented to train SA-Net. We set the down-sampling factor f_1 as 2 which means the size of resized images is 1024×768 (Scale I), and f_2 as 4 which means the size of resized images is 512×384 (Scale II). The minimum size of image we down-sampled is 296×224 (Scale III), which corresponds to f_3 as 6.86. We set the stride to 133 at Scale I, 36 at Scale II, and 5 at Scale III for training patch extraction. In the testing stage, the patches were extracted from resized testing images with twice strides againest training data for computing acceleration.

3.3 Results

We show the accuracy, precision, recall, the area under the receiver operating characteristic (ROC) curve (AUC), and the ROC curve of the proposed algorithm in differentiating each category of images and the overall classification accuracy in Table 1 and Fig. 3. It shows that it is easy for the proposed algorithm to separate invasive carcinoma tissues from others, but difficult to separate normal tissues from others. Nevertheless, we achieved an average AUC of more than 98.26% in all categories and an overall accuracy of $94.50 \pm 1.27\%$, which

Table 1. Performance (mean ± standard deviation) of the proposed MSA-Net algorithm on BACH training images with five-fold cross validation.

Category	Accuracy (%)	Precision (%)	Recall (%)	series AUC (%)
Normal	96.50 ± 1.84	93.04 ± 3.91	93.00 ± 4.00	99.57 ± 0.24
Benign	97.00 ± 1.00	95.02 ± 2.90	93.00 ± 4.00	99.61 ± 0.26
In situ	97.25 ± 2.15	93.10 ± 7.45	97.00 ± 2.45	99.10 ± 0.79
Invasive	98.25 ± 1.87	98.05 ± 2.39	95.00 ± 4.75	98.26 ± 1.29
All	**94.50 ± 1.27**	94.80 ± 4.16	94.50 ± 3.80	99.14 ± 0.65

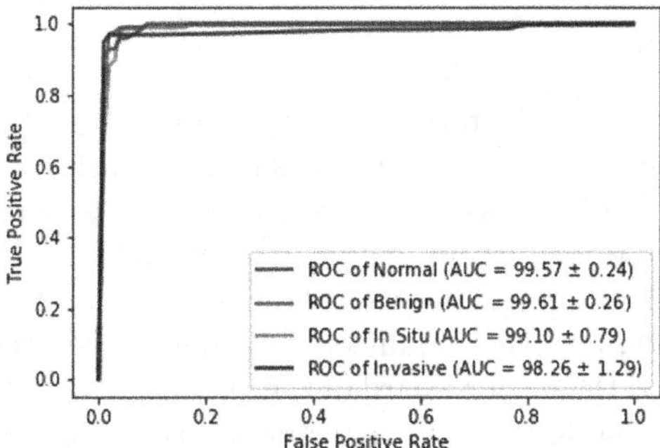

Fig. 3. The ROC curves. The True positive Rate and False Positive Rate are calculated through a one-vs.-rest strategy based on the classification results.

Table 2. Accuracy (%) of the proposed MSA-Net algorithm on BACH training dataset using five-fold cross valiation and four leading methods.

Method	Accuracy (%)
DCNN+SVM, 2017 [1]	77.80
Pre-trained VGG-16, 2018 [2]	83.00
Pre-trained Inception-Resnet-v2, 2018 [2]	87.00
Ensemble of three DCNNs, 2018 [2]	87.00
MSA-Net (proposed)	**94.50**

demonstrate the effectiveness of the proposed algorithm in the classification of breast histology microscopy images.

Next, we compare the proposed MSA-Net algorithm to four recent methods: (1) using a custom DCNN for feature extraction and a SVM for classification [1], (2) using a pre-trained VGG-16 together with a variety of data augmentation methods [2], (3) using a pre-trained Inception-Resnet-v2 together with a training process of two stages [2], and (4) using ensemble of three pre-trained DCNNs [2]. Table 2 shows the overall accuracy of those four methods, and the accuracy of

Table 3. The leader-board of the BACH challenge on testing dataset (ranked by accuracy on Task Part A).

Position	Participants	Accuracy (%)
1	hanwang.0501	95.00
2	young(ours)	**94.00**
3	bamboo	93.00
4	HeechanYang	93.00
5	YUN1503	92.00
6	heechan	92.00

our algorithm. It reveals that proposed algorithm is substantially more accurate than those four methods on this image classification task.

Moreover, besides 400 labeled training images, the organizers of BACH challenge also provided 100 microscopy images without labels for online testing. We submitted the classification results, which we obtained on those testing images, to the official website, and the organizers calculated the accuracy of our algorithm. We synthesized the leader-board of the challenge at first and second stages and displayed it in Table 3. It shows that our algorithm achieved an accuracy of 94.00% in the online validation and won the 2nd place on the leader-board.[1]

To further demonstrate the validity of the proposed MSA-Net, we also design the experiment on another histopathological dataset named Breast Cancer Histopathological Database (BreakHis), which is composed of 2,480 benign and 5,429 malignant microscopic images of breast tumor tissue with 700×460 pixels and 3 channels collected from 82 patients using different magnifying factors (40X, 100X, 200X, and 400X). To match the resolution of images in BACH dataset, we use microscopic images with 40X magnifying factor for experimentation, which contains 625 benign and 1370 malignant samples. We randomly select 20% of microscopic images for testing and other images for training. As shown in Table 4, we achieved an AUC of 99.99% in all categories and an overall accuracy of 99.75%, which further demonstrate the effectiveness of the proposed algorithm in the classification of breast microscopy images.

Table 4. Performance of the proposed MSA-Net algorithm on BreakHis dataset.

Category	Accuracy (%)	Precision (%)	Recall (%)	AUC (%)
Benign	99.75	100.00	99.20	99.99
Malignant	99.75	99.65	100.00	99.99
All	**99.75**	99.83	99.60	99.99

[1] Available at: https://iciar2018-challenge.grand-challenge.org/evaluation/results/.

Table 5. Accuracy of the proposed algorithm with different values of down-sampling factor f.

f	Size of resized image	Accuracy (%)
1	2048 × 1536	86.25
2	1024 × 768	92.50
4	512 × 384	93.75
6.86	296 × 224	91.25

4 Discussion

The down-sampling factor f represents the resolution of histology microscopy images input to the MSA-Net, hence plays an important role in classifying images. To determine the best value of f, we performed the proposed algorithm with different values of f and show their accuracy in Table 5. Due to the size of patches we input SA-Net are 224×224, the minimum size of image we down-sampled is 296×224, which corresponds f as 6.86. Table 5 shows that when f is 4, the proposed algorithm has best accuracy, however, when f is 1, the algorithm has worst accuracy. Hence we empirically set f to 2, 4 and 6.86 respectively in our experiments.

5 Conclusion

In this paper, we propose the MSA-Net algorithm to classify H&E stained breast microscopy images into four categories including normal, benign, in situ carcinoma, invasive carcinoma. Our results demonstrate the superior performance of the proposed algorithm with the 2nd place on the BACH challenge official leader-board and a five-fold cross validation accuracy of $94.50 \pm 1.27\%$ on BACH training images. In the future, the proposed MSA-Net algorithm serves great potential to the development of semi-supervision mechanism when identifying microscopy images using unlabeled samples.

Acknowledgement. This work was supported in part by the Science and Technology Innovation Committee of Shenzhen Municipality, China, under Grant JCYJ20180306171334997, in part by the National Natural Science Foundation of China under Grant 61771397 and 61902322, in part by the Fundamental Research Funds for the Central Universities under Grant 3102019G2019KY0001, in part by the Seed Foundation of Innovation and Creation for Graduate Students in Northwestern Polytechnical University under Grants ZZ2019029, and in part by the Project for Graduate Innovation team of Northwestern Polytechnical University.

References

1. Araújo, T., et al.: Classification of breast cancer histology images using convolutional neural networks. PlOS ONE **12**(6), 1–14 (2017)

2. Aresta, G., et al.: BACH: grand challenge on breast cancer histology images. arXiv preprint arXiv:1808.04277 (2018)
3. Chennamsetty, S.S., Safwan, M., Alex, V.: Classification of breast cancer histology image using ensemble of pre-trained neural networks. In: Campilho, A., Karray, F., ter Haar Romeny, B. (eds.) ICIAR 2018. LNCS, vol. 10882, pp. 804–811. Springer, Cham (2018). https://doi.org/10.1007/978-3-319-93000-8_91
4. Deng, J., Dong, W., Socher, R., Li, L.J., Li, K., Fei-Fei, L.: ImageNet: a large-scale hierarchical image database. In: Proceeding of the IEEE Conference on Computer Vision and Pattern Recognition (CVPR), pp. 248–255. IEEE (2009)
5. Han, J., Zhang, D., Cheng, G., Guo, L., Ren, J.: Object detection in optical remote sensing images based on weakly supervised learning and high-level feature learning. IEEE Trans. Geosci. Remote Sens. **53**(6), 3325–3337 (2014)
6. Han, J., Zhang, D., Hu, X., Guo, L., Ren, J., Wu, F.: Background prior-based salient object detection via deep reconstruction residual. IEEE Trans. Circ. Syst. Video Technol. **25**(8), 1309–1321 (2014)
7. He, K., Zhang, X., Ren, S., Sun, J.: Deep residual learning for image recognition. In: Proceeding of the IEEE Conference on Computer Vision and Pattern Recognition(CVPR), pp. 770–778 (2016)
8. Hu, J., Shen, L., Sun, G.: Squeeze-and-excitation networks. In: Proceedings of the IEEE Conference on Computer Vision and Pattern Recognition (CVPR), pp. 7132–7141 (2018)
9. Huang, G., Liu, Z., Van Der Maaten, L., Weinberger, K.Q.: Densely connected convolutional networks. In: Proceeding of the IEEE Conference on Computer Vision and Pattern Recognition (CVPR), pp. 2261–2269. IEEE (2017)
10. Ragab, D.A., Sharkas, M., Marshall, S., Ren, J.: Breast cancer detection using deep convolutional neural networks and support vector machines. PeerJ **7**, e6201 (2019)
11. Ren, J.: ANN vs. SVM: which one performs better in classification of MCCs in mammogram imaging. Knowl.-Based Syst. **26**, 144–153 (2012)
12. Ren, J., Wang, D., Jiang, J.: Effective recognition of MCCs in mammograms using an improved neural classifier. Eng. Appl. Artif. Intell. **24**(4), 638–645 (2011)
13. Stewart, B., Wild, C.P., et al.: World cancer report 2014. The International Agency for Research on Cancer (2014)
14. Vu, Q.D., To, M.N.N., Kim, E., Kwak, J.T.: Micro and macro breast histology image analysis by partial network re-use. In: Campilho, A., Karray, F., ter Haar Romeny, B. (eds.) ICIAR 2018. LNCS, vol. 10882, pp. 895–902. Springer, Cham (2018). https://doi.org/10.1007/978-3-319-93000-8_102
15. Wang, Z., Ren, J., Zhang, D., Sun, M., Jiang, J.: A deep-learning based feature hybrid framework for spatiotemporal saliency detection inside videos. Neurocomputing **287**, 68–83 (2018)
16. Yan, Y., et al.: Unsupervised image saliency detection with gestalt-laws guided optimization and visual attention based refinement. Pattern Recogn. **79**, 65–78 (2018)

VIP-STB Farm: Scale-up Village to County/Province Level to Support Science and Technology at Backyard (STB) Program

Yijun Yan[1], Sophia Zhao[1], Yuxi Fang[1], Yuren Liu[1], Zhongxin Chen[2], and Jinchang Ren[1(✉)]

[1] Department of Electronic and Electrical Engineering, University of Strathclyde, Glasgow, UK
Jinchang.Ren@strath.ac.uk
[2] Institute of Agricultural Resources and Regional Planning, Chinese Academy of Agricultural Sciences, Beijing, China

Abstract. In this paper, we introduce a new concept in VIP-STB, a funded project through Agri-Tech in China: Newton Network+ (ATCNN), in developing feasible solutions towards scaling-up STB from village level to upper level via some generic models and systems. There are three tasks in this project, i.e. normalized difference vegetation index (NDVI) estimation, wheat density estimation and household-based small farms (HBSF) engagement. In the first task, several machine learning models have been used to evaluate the performance of NDVI estimation. In the second task, integrated software via Python and Twilio is developed to improve communication services and engagement for HBSFs, and provides technical capabilities. In the third task, crop density/ population is predicted by conventional image processing techniques. The objectives and strategy for VIP-STB are described, experimental results on each task are presented, and more details on each model that has been implemented are also provided with future development guidance.

Keywords: Precision agriculture · Machine learning · Information fusion

1 Introduction

According to the national statistics announced in Dec 2017, ~25% of the population or ~314million people in China are working in the agriculture sector, where less than 20% is below 35-year old. Among them, over 43% have been educated up to primary school level, and only less than 8.5% have achieved the senior high-school level. Within these, ~96% are household-based small farms (HBSF). For the aging and poor-educated HBSFs, their poverty has been a persistent problem that affects the social and economic development of China.

To tackle this serious problem, the Chinese government has put strategic plans to innovate HBSF, where STB is one of the successful examples. In STB, skilled and well-educated researchers are assigned to villages to identify problems and provide solutions. By closely monitoring the environmental parameters and crop growing

J. Ren et al. (Eds.): BICS 2019, LNAI 11691, pp. 283–292, 2020.
https://doi.org/10.1007/978-3-030-39431-8_27

conditions with sensors and smartphones, the production yield has been improved by 90% whilst the environmental factors have been reduced by 30–40%.

Although STB shows a successful model for innovation of HBSF, several critical drawbacks have constrained its migration from village level to the county or province level as detailed below.

(1) Labour intensive: manual acquisition of data for monitoring growing conditions and estimation of yield is very labour intensive and costly thus economically inviable and non-scalable;
(2) Lack of automation: Empirical guidance was adopted followed by estimated plant density and yield which seems to be not statistical sound and effective as modern HPC and machine learning can offer smart decision-making with negligible extra cost;
(3) Inefficient communications in response to recommendations sent in texts;
(4) Environmental issues and limited sustainability due to uncontrolled waste of water and other resources as well as potential land degradation by over-applying fertiliser and chemicals.

Taking STBs in Laoling City and Yangxin County of Shandong Province for a case study, we aim to demonstrate feasible solutions to improve the balanced, quality-ensured and sustainable innovation of rural areas of China. Some effective techniques and systems are used in the project and three contributions are summarized as follows:

(1) Automatic NDVI estimation agricultural digital camera (ADC) from multispectral data acquired from Landsat satellite;
(2) Effective TTS interface is built up to ensure HBSFs understand the recommendations and act timely;
(3) Automation of the process to reduce the labour cost, where estimation from remote sensing data will be derived to replace the labour-intensive manual data acquisition from fields which are separately located and can be hard to access under severe weather conditions, where image processing techniques will be used to estimate crop population density based on readily available datasets;

The outline of this paper is as follows: Sect. 2 evaluates the performance of different regression methods for the ADC-NDVI estimation purpose. Section 3 describes the implementation of the test-to-speech (TTS) module. Automatic estimation of crop density is introduced in Sect. 4. Finally, some concluding remarks and future work are summarized in Sect. 5.

2 Estimation of ADC-NDVI from Remote Sensing Data

As one of the most important index, NDVI is usually used to detect vegetation growth status and coverage, etc. Generally, the NDVI value is calculated by TM data acquired from remote sense, and we name it as TM-NDVI in this paper. For more accurate statistics, agricultural digital camera (ADC) is used to determine the NDVI which is named as ADC-NDVI in the rest of the paper, where several students are needed to work for days to serve one particular STB site. However, manual acquisition of data is very labor intensive and costly, which is economically inviable and affect the scalability of STB to the upper level. To reduce the labour cost, the estimation from remote sensing data will be derived to replace the labour-intensive manual data acquisition from fields which are separately located and can be hard to access under severe weather conditions. In this section, we design two experiments to estimate the ADC-NDVI through TM data. As the TM-NDVI is calculated by NIR and red band which are TM3 and TM4, thus, TM3-4 is set as a baseline feature to compare. Five machine learning models (i.e. Ridge regression [1], Support vector regression (SVR) [2, 3], Cascade neural network [4], Random forest [5] and Gaussian kernel regression [6, 7]) are used in this work to evaluate the prediction performance in terms of RMSE and r^2. The reason for choosing these models is because they are all classic models and have good capabilities for many regression problems in the real world [8–10].

The TM data is acquired from Landsat, and SPAD, LAI and ADC-NDVI data is provided by a Chinese partner. There are 110 fields with one ADC-NDVI value and 6 TM bands data where TM1 is blue band ranging from 0.45–0.52 um, TM2 is green band ranging from 0.52–0.60 um, TM3 is red band ranging from 0.62–0.69 um, TM4 is near infrared ray (NIR) band ranging from 0.76–0.97 um, TM5 is middle-infrared band ranging from 1.55–1.75 um and TM6 is thermal infrared band ranging from 10.4–12.5 um. We use 50% data for training and 50% data for testing. The prediction performance is evaluated in terms of RMSE and r^2 followed by the standard deviation in the bracket which is used to show their stability.

In the first strategy, TM1-6 multispectral information is used to be training and testing features. From Table 1, it can be seen TM1-6 shows better overall performance than TM3-4, which means more spectral information from remote sense is helpful for the estimation of ADC-NDVI. The cascade neural network shows the best prediction performance on TM1-6 but it cost much computation source. This is because the initial weight of the hidden layer in the neural network is randomly selected, and some ill-suited initial value will cause the convergence time longer. Ridge regression has the lowest computation cost, and the second-best stability and prediction performance.

Table 1 Performance evaluation in terms of RMSE and r^2 in strategy 1

Regressors	TM3-4		TM1-6		
	RMSE	r^2	RMSE	r^2	Time (s)
Ridge	0.030 (±0.0017)	0.708 (±0.0465)	0.028 (±0.0024)	0.731 (±0.0704)	**0.0089**
SVR	0.106 (±0.0072)	0.698 (±0.0574)	0.101 (±0.0129)	0.720 (±0.0800)	3.7471
Random forest	0.035 (±0.0021)	0.596 (±0.0488)	0.036 (±0.0028)	0.579 (±0.0479)	0.1094
Cascade neural network	0.030 (±0.0027)	0.702 (±0.0632)	**0.025** (±0.0032)	**0.778** (±0.0636)	3.1944
Gaussian kernel	0.031 (±0.0022)	0.674 (±0.0615)	0.028 (±**0.0019**)	0.726 (±**0.0542**)	0.0371
Overall	0.046	0.676	0.044	**0.705**	

Table 2. Performance evaluation in terms of RMSE and r^2 in strategy 2

Regressors	TM3-4		TM3-4+LAI+SPAD		
	RMSE	r^2	RMSE	r^2	Time (s)
Ridge	0.030 (±0.0017)	0.708 (±0.0465)	0.028 (±0.0024)	0.742 (±0.0449)	**0.0228**
SVR	0.106 (±0.0072)	0.698 (±0.0574)	0.095 (±0.0129)	0.764 (±0.0576)	3.8931
Random forest	0.035 (±0.0021)	0.596 (±0.0488)	0.033 (±0.0028)	0.648 (±**0.0241**)	0.1859
Cascade neural network	0.030 (±0.0027)	0.702 (±0.0632)	**0.025** (±0.0032)	**0.793** (±0.0355)	2.4197
Gaussian kernel	0.031 (±0.0022)	0.674 (±0.0615)	0.028 (±**0.0019**)	0.737 (±0.0497)	0.1508
Overall	0.046	0.676	0.042	**0.735**	

This is because ridge regression is mainly used to solve the linear regression problem. Although ADC-NDVI and TM-NDVI are derived from different sources, it still has some linear connection between each other. In addition, Gaussian kernel regression and SVR have similar prediction performance, but the former has the best stability. Random forest has the worst performance. As a result, ridge regression and cascade neural network can be considered as the top two methods with either best usefulness or efficiency.

In the second strategy, TM3-4, SPAD and LAI are used to be training and testing features. SPAD and LAI are two important parameters of crops, which have been already given by the Chinese partner. Therefore, how are those parameters and spectral data related to ADC-NDVI will be investigated in our experiment. From Table 2, the random forest regression still performs the worst. For the other four techniques, their performance in strategy 2 is better than that in strategy 1. Gaussian kernel and ridge have just little gap between each other but are still not as good as cascade neural network and SVR. The prediction accuracy and stability of cascade neural network are better than SVR and the computation time is lower in strategy 2 than that in strategy 1. As a result, cascade neural network works the best in strategy 2. However, it relies on the feature selection, which affects its performance and computation cost much.

From the experimental results, some findings are summarized as follows:

(1) LAI and SPAD are more useful than TM 1,2,5,6 for ADC-NDVI estimation.
(2) ADC-NDVI can be potentially predicted through remote sensing data.
(3) Both cascade neural network and ridge are the best two model which either has best prediction performance or the most efficient.
(4) With better feature selection, the prediction performance of most regression model can be well improved.

For the future work, instead of using TM1-6, SWIR data (1000-1700 nm) can be also used for NDVI prediction. Then some novel band selection methods [11, 12] can be used to extract the most useful information and help to get more accurate prediction results. In addition, some novel deep learning methods such as segmented auto encoder [13] and deep neural network [14] can be also used to improve the prediction performance.

3 Text to Speech Module for HBSFs Engagement

This section will present a TTS module which can send a voice call message to farmers and remind them to finish the farming task(s). It is very important since each type of crop has different growth condition, irrigation and cultivation strategies. Wrong cultivation strategies or wrong irrigation time may affect the yield of the crops. Although smartphones are recommended as the best way to communicate with HBSFs to provide them crop conditions and suggested operations, these may not be fulfilled as 50% HBSFs failed to receive the text message or to respond accordingly. Also, it is found 57% HBSfs have no smartphones and only 31% using social media such as WeChat, due to the aging and poorly-educated background and limited income. This leads to a communication barrier where effective solutions are needed, simply because a large portion of them cannot read or understand the instructions in texts. Therefore, it is necessary to develop a TTS module to help those farmers make the right move.

Fig. 1. Concept of TTS module.

Figure 1 shows the concept of the TTS module. Twilio is an open PaaS (platform as a service) platform which focuses on communication services and provides technical capabilities. It is a well-known and leading cloud computing communication company in the world, which has more than 50 million registered develops and three billion market cap. Twilio packages the complex underlying communication function into API which allows software developers to programmatically make the function of phone calls, messaging and VoIP (voice on internet protocol) on any web, desktop and mobile applications. In another word, any function can be achieved by a few lines of code. Although the Twilio service is not free, the price is still very cheap. It uses pay-as-you-go model and the price of voice and message is $0.0218/min and $0.028/min, respectively. In addition, it has not only web platform, but also mobile Twilio Client which can be used to Android and iphone platform. It means the voice and messaging functions can be also added into any mobile app, which benefits the users a lot. In the future, we can also develop a special TTS app for HBSFs.

Fig. 2. Basic GUI for TTS

Due to too many advantages, we employ the Twilio's voice and messaging functions and build a basic interactive GUI (Fig. 2) in Python to call its functions. Once the farmer's phone number and command are input, the farmer's phone will receive a voice call. If the farmer doesn't hear the voice call clearly, he can also call back to the server and rehear it. The workflow of the TTS module involves the following steps:

(1) Input message
(2) Encode message to be used in a URL and create a XML file
(3) Return XML file to Twilio cloud server
(4) Transfer the XML file to a MP3 file
(5) Call from Twilio's number to target's number and play the MP3.

4 Automatic Estimation of Crop Density/Population from Images

In this section, a threshold-based segmentation method is introduced to calculate the crop density (d) in an image. With the growth of the crops, the density of crops, as a key factor of the final yield, is increasing as well. Therefore, the precise calculation of the crop density is very helpful for yield prediction. However, the existing challenge is most official agricultural data is acquired from the satellite and the resolution of those image data is very low, which leads to density calculation difficult.

Although we don't have the satellite data, we simulate the low-resolution condition by rescaling the image data acquired from some Chinese field (Fig. 3). Leaf detection in this work is performed by color discrimination. Unlike the traditional Red-Green-Blue (RGB) color space, the Hue-Saturation-Value (HSV) approach involves parametrization including not only true color (hue) but also color depth (saturation) and color darkness (value), as can be seen in Fig. 4. As a result, the HSV color space is much more suited for addressing real-world environments consisting of light reflections, shadows and darkened regions etc. Therefore, the real-time image processing workflow involves the following steps (Fig. 4): (i) transformation from RGB image to HSV image, (ii) binalization of HSV image, by means of applying the selected HSV color range thresholds, and (iii) posterior treatment of the binary image, including size filtering and morphologies, to avoid the detection of unrelated pixels. Finally, the crop density (D) is calculated by the ratio of foreground pixels (F_p) and whole pixels (W_p) in the segmented result.

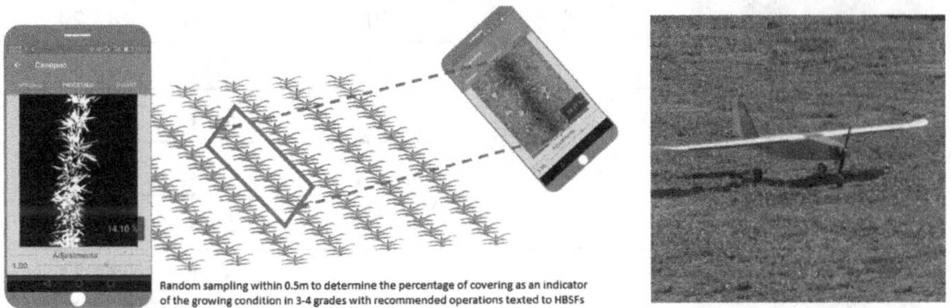

Fig. 3. Manual data acquisition for crop density estimation.

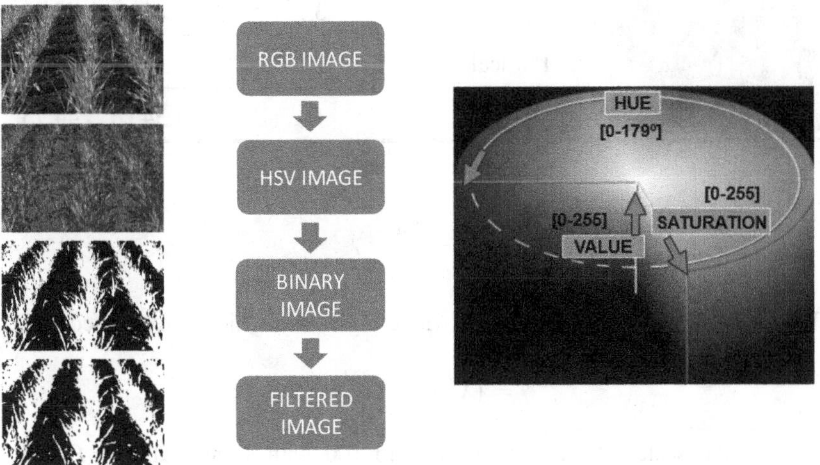

Fig. 4. Workflow of leaf area calculation method. (Color figure online)

Due to the color of crop leaf is mostly green include light and dark green. The selected color range thresholds of H, S and V is usually defined by $H \in [35^\circ, 99^\circ]$, $S \in [43, 255]$, $V \in [46, 255]$, respectively. With reducing the resolution of the image, the bit per pixel (bpp) is also getting lower and lower. In the experiment, we also notice that the density value will become larger when the resolution of the image decreases. To avoid too much variate, we introduce a penalty value γ so that the final density value (Eq. 1) can keep constant under different image scale.

Table 3. Visualization of low resolution image and density value under different scale.

Image	Legend	*X* (%)	Bpp	*D* (%)
	50% scale	Ground-truth 100	17.03	45.26
		50	14.94	45.29
		10	7.17	45.39
	8% scale	9	6.71	45.12
		8	6.21	45.40
		7	5.68	45.11
	5% scale	6	5.41	45.43
		5	4.81	45.08
		4	4.23	45.46
	1% scale	3	3.81	45.02
		2	3	45.60
		1	1.34	44.75

$$D = \frac{F_p}{W_p} - \gamma \tag{1}$$

The penalty value γ is estimated by ridge regression which is expressed in Eq. 2:

$$\gamma = \left(X^T X + \lambda \mathrm{I}\right)^{-1} X^T y \tag{2}$$

where X is the scale rate ranging from 1 to 100 with 1 interval, $\mathrm{y} = F_p * W_p^{-1} - groundtruth$, $\lambda = 0.001$.

From Table 3, we can see the density value under different scale is very close to the that of the ground-truth, and the MAE is 0.02. However, due to limited sample, the performance of this model needs to further validate on more samples in the future. To further improve the segmentation method, saliency detection [15], image segmentation [16] and deep learning method [17] can be employed to get better segmentation performance and also get more accurate density/population estimation.

5 Conclusion

In this paper, by introducing data fusion and AI-driven machine learning techniques, three solutions are derived towards three different challenges of Chinese agriculture. The performance still has many rooms to improve, but the STB programme for economic growth in precision agriculture is scaled up with such concepts, especially in promoting the largest and most vulnerable groups, i.e. HBSFs, and has a significant impact to improve the balanced, quality-ensured and sustainable innovation of rural areas of China. Our future work mainly focuses on the improvement of current three solutions which are summarised as follows:

(1) Fusion of multi-modal and multi-source data for accurate modeling and prediction including field measurements and remotely sensed.
(2) AI-driven method for more accurate estimation of crop population.
(3) Improvement of TTS module where a more interactive function will be included for more effective communication with HBSFs to fulfill the recommended operations.

References

1. Hoerl, A.E., Kannard, R.W., Baldwin, K.F.: Ridge regression: some simulations. Commun. Stat.-Theory Methods **4**, 105–123 (1975)
2. Smola, A.J., Schölkopf, B.: A tutorial on support vector regression. Stat. Comput. **14**, 199–222 (2004)
3. Chang, C.-C., Lin, C.-J.: LIBSVM a library for support vector machines. ACM Trans. Intell. Syst. Technol. (TIST) **2**, 27 (2011)
4. Warsito, B., Santoso, R., Yasin, H.: Cascade forward neural network for time series prediction. J. Phys.: Conf. Ser. **1025**, 012097 (2018)
5. Breiman, L.: Random forests. Mach. Learn. **45**, 5–32 (2001)
6. Huang, P.-S., Avron, H., Sainath, T.N., Sindhwani, V., Ramabhadran, B.: Kernel methods match deep neural networks on timit. In: 2014 IEEE International Conference on Acoustics, Speech and Signal Processing (ICASSP), pp. 205–209 (2014)
7. Rahimi, A., Recht, B.: Random features for large-scale kernel machines. In: Advances in Neural Information Processing Systems, pp. 1177–1184 (2008)
8. Tschannerl, J., Ren, J., Jack, F., Krause, J., Zhao, H., Huang, W., et al.: Potential of UV and SWIR hyperspectral imaging for determination of levels of phenolic flavour compounds in peated barley malt. Food Chem. **270**, 105–112 (2019)
9. Padfield, N., Zabalza, J., Zhao, H., Masero, V., Ren, J.: EEG-based brain-computer interfaces using motor-imagery: techniques and challenges. Sensors **19**, 1423 (2019)
10. Zhang, W., Goh, A.T.: Multivariate adaptive regression splines and neural network models for prediction of pile drivability. Geosci. Front. **7**, 45–52 (2016)
11. Tschannerl, J., Ren, J., Yuen, P., Sun, G., Zhao, H., Yang, Z., et al.: MIMR-DGSA: unsupervised hyperspectral band selection based on information theory and a modified discrete gravitational search algorithm. Inf. Fusion **51**, 189–200 (2019)
12. Wang, Q., Lin, J., Yuan, Y.: Salient band selection for hyperspectral image classification via manifold ranking. IEEE Trans. Neural Netw. Learn. Syst. **27**, 1279–1289 (2016)

13. Zabalza, J., Ren, J., Zheng, J., Zhao, H., Qing, C., Yang, Z., et al.: Novel segmented stacked autoencoder for effective dimensionality reduction and feature extraction in hyperspectral imaging. Neurocomputing **185**, 1–10 (2016)
14. Silver, D., Huang, A., Maddison, C.J., Guez, A., Sifre, L., Van Den Driessche, G., et al.: Mastering the game of go with deep neural networks and tree search. Nature **529**, 484 (2016)
15. Yan, Y., Ren, J., Sun, G., Zhao, H., Han, J., Li, X., et al.: Unsupervised image saliency detection with Gestalt-laws guided optimization and visual attention based refinement. Pattern Recogn. **79**, 65–78 (2018)
16. Xie, X., Xie, G., Xu, X., Cui, L., Ren, J.: Automatic image segmentation with superpixels and image-level labels. IEEE Access **7**, 10999–11009 (2019)
17. Xu, X., Li, G., Xie, G., Ren, J., Xie, X.: Weakly supervised deep semantic segmentation using CNN and ELM with semantic candidate regions. Complexity **2019**, 1–12 (2019). Paper ID 9180391

A User Profile Based Medical Recommendation System

Jun Cai, Xuebin Hong, Qingyun Dai, Huimin Zhao, Yan Liu(✉), Jianzhen Luo, and Zhijie Wu

Guangdong Polytechnic Normal University, GuangZhou 510665, China
liuyan_sysu@163.com

Abstract. With the rapidly development of Internet, online medical platform has become an essential part of medicines trade. In order to help users quickly find satisfying products in a large number of commodities, the recommendation system has been proposed. The traditional recommendation algorithm usually only takes the user-item rating into consideration, which leads low accurate of prediction. In this paper, we propose a user profile based recommendation method, which uses deep learning to analyze user behavior and construct user multi-dimensional attribute features. user profile can be constructed by analyzing information of drugs. By analyzing the historical information of user's action, including purchasing, browsing, and collecting, we can dynamically predict rating of user on drug by a trained neural network. The experimental verification on B2B medical platform shows that the accuracy of prediction is higher than other algorithms. The proposed system can not only improve user experience, but also increase the sales of the platform.

Keywords: Recommendation system · Online medical platform · User profiles · Deep learning

1 Introduction

With the rapid development of technology, people's lives are more tightly integrated with the Internet. The data on the Internet is growing at an unprecedented rate. Now, 5G will be commercialized, and the era of the Internet of Everything will come. According to IDC, global data will grow from 33ZB in 2018 to 175ZB in 2025, with 1ZB equivalent to 1 trillion GB. Big data has brought a lot of convenience to people, but it has also brought new challenges, such as information overload. One solution of information overload is searching engine. However, the problem is that users usually cannot define their key words of searching properly. The other solution is recommendation system, which is based on users' behavior and can help users quickly retrieving desired information. The recommendation system has been widely used by academia and industry.

J. Ren et al. (Eds.): BICS 2019, LNAI 11691, pp. 293–301, 2020.
https://doi.org/10.1007/978-3-030-39431-8_28

The core of recommendation system is recommendation algorithm, which is responsible for finding the user's potentially interested items through the information of user and item. The traditional recommendation algorithms can be classified into tree classes: collaborative filtering [1], content-based algorithms [2], and hybrid recommendation algorithms [3]. Various recommendation algorithms are proposed for different application scenarios and environments.

Providing users with high-quality personalized services must be based on understanding users. In recent years, user profile has been used to build multiple dimension tags of user. It depicts the user's background, interests, identity, psychology, needs, personality, etc., and adequately describes the user's information. In this paper, we propose a user profile based recommendation algorithm, which can reflect user's preferences and purchase intention dynamically.

In recent years, deep learning has achieved excellent results in computer vision [4], speech recognition [5], and natural language understanding [6]. Since deep learning can automatically learn features and the implicit relationship between features [7], the deep learning based recommendation algorithms can overcome the problem of data sparsity and cold start suffered by other existing recommendation algorithms. In this paper, we propose a dynamic user profile based recommendation algorithm. Firstly, user profile is constructed dynamically, then the rating of user-drug is predicated by a trained neural network. Experimental results show that the proposed algorithm performs much better than other recommendation algorithms.

The rest of the paper is structured as follows, Sect. 2 gives an overview of related works; Sect. 3 introduces our proposed framework. Section 4 simulates the performance of different recommendation algorithms; and Sect. 5 concludes the paper.

2 Related Works

User profile is an essential part of our recommendation. Skillen et al. built an extensible user profiles method from the user's profiles, which focuses on the user's dynamic and static information [8]. Pazzani et al. tried to classify users' topics using bayesian algorithm, which was derived from user-generated text information [9]. Fawcett et al. used user behavior, recording and clicking historical data to build a user profile, which reflects the real psychological needs of the user at that time [10]. Rosenthal et al. used text features and social features to create user profiles and conduct age classification research [11]. They began building users from multiple dimensions through data from various feature types. Obviously, Multidimensional data is a reliable source for constructing stereoscopic user profiles, which can significantly improve the quality of user profile.

User profile technology plays a vital role in many areas, such as advertising marketing and personalized recommendation services, mainly in the form of information association and target users. For the recommendation system, recommendation algorithms are responsible for finding the items interested by users with high probability. The collaborative filtering algorithm is the most used recommendation algorithm. Classification algorithm classifies and predicts whether a user purchases a specific type of item based on the data characteristics and historical behavior of the user and item. The famous classification algorithms are decision tree, support vector machine, and logistic regression. Breiman et al. proposed a random forest algorithm [12]. It is an integrated learning method, and the GBDT algorithm uses the bagging integration method, which has strong generalization ability. In recent years, deep learning based recommendation algorithms are proposed to overcome the limitations of traditional model and can achieve better performance [13]. Deep learning effectively captures non-linear and non-trivial user-drug relationships and supports the union of more complex abstractions into higher-level data representations [14–17].

3 Methods

In this section, we propose a user profiles based recommendation algorithm. Firstly, characteristics of users and drugs are extracted. Then deep neural network (DNN) is trained to make prediction.

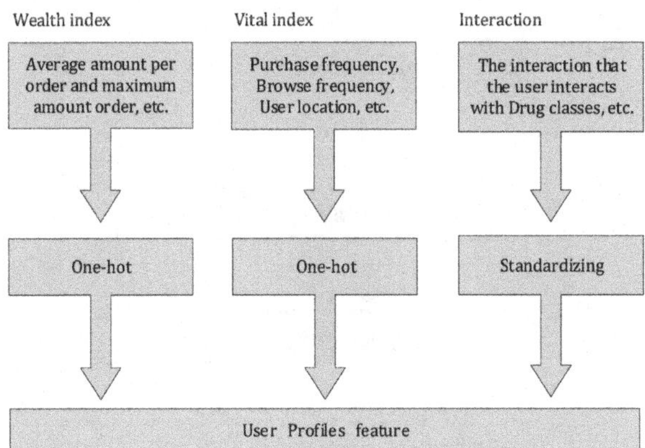

Fig. 1. User profiles

3.1 Feature Representation

The features of user profile and drug are shown in Figs. 1 and 2. The features of user profile are constructed by analyzing information from three dimensions, wealth index, activity index and interaction behavior. Wealth index is generated from sales; activity index describes the information of user activities, such as, frequency of browser and purchase; interacting behavior indicates the relationship between user and different types of drugs. By analyzing efficacy, factory and price of drugs, we can obtain features of drugs, as shown in Fig. 2.

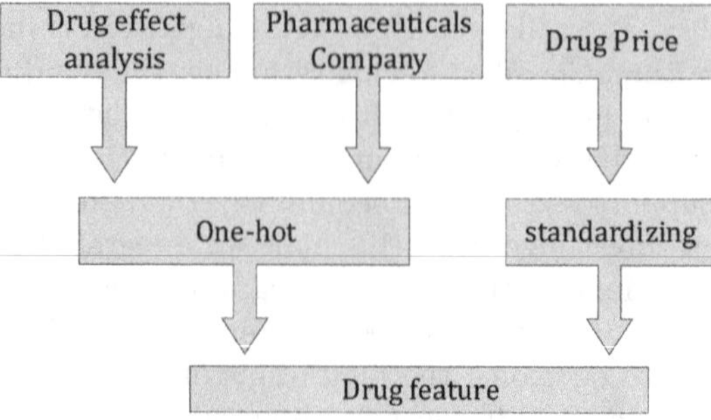

Fig. 2. Drug feature

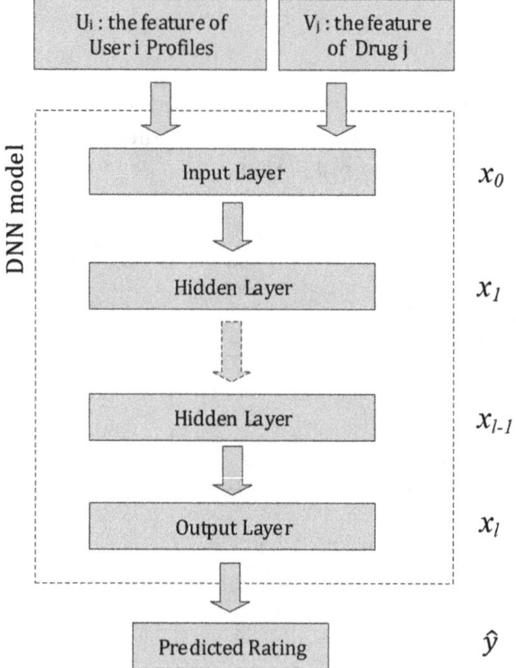

Fig. 3. DNN model

3.2 DNN Model

As a nonlinear model, a deep neural network has strong ability of fitting, it can learn the implicit relationship between features and improve the performance of recommendation algorithm. The input of our deep neural network is the combination of features of user and drug as shown in Fig. 3, the dimension of input data is 623 × 1. The input data x_0 is given by:

$$x_0 = [U_i, V_j] \tag{1}$$

where U_i is the feature vector of the user i, and V_j is the feature vector of the drug j. In our model, the DNN contains four hidden layers. The activation function uses the ReLU as activation function since it is more convenient and efficient comparing with other activation functions. The output of last hidden layer is given by Eq. 2.

$$x_l = ReLU(W_l * x_{l-1} + b_l) \tag{2}$$

where x_{l-1} is the output of $(l-1)^{th}$ layer, W_l is the weight of lth layer, and b_l is bias of the lth layer. The output of DNN model is given by following:

$$\widehat{y} = softmax(W_{out} * x_l + b_{out}) \tag{3}$$

where W_{out} is the weight of output layer, and b_{out} is bias of output layer. We will one-hot encode the user's score on the drug, and the corresponding neuron output and relevant scores are as follows:

$$\widehat{r}_{ui} = \arg\max_{\gamma}(\widehat{y}) \tag{4}$$

where $\widehat{y}$ is the predicted score value, and y is the output of the corresponding neuron. We use the cross-entropy loss function to measure the difference between actual rating and predicted rating, given by following:

$$loss = -\sum_{1}^{d}(yln(\widehat{y}) + (1-y)ln(1-\widehat{y})) \tag{5}$$

where $d = 5$ is the dimension of vector $\widehat{y}$ and vector y. In the adaptive learning rate optimizer, we use the Adam algorithm, which can converge faster than other optimizers.

4 Experiments

We investigate the performance of proposed algorithm on a server equipped with two GPUs (NVIDIA 1080TI), and one CPU (Intel(R) Xeon(R) e5-2670), 256G of memory. The dataset is collected from a B2B medical platform, include user purchase, browsing, collection, and other behavior data. It contains 1.83 million ratings, recording 103,799 users and 5,919 drugs. The statistics of the dataset are shown in Table 1.

There are many parameters to evaluate the performance of recommendation algorithm, such as coverage, accidental discovery, and prediction accuracy. In this paper, we adopt Mean Absolute Error (MAE), and Root Means Square Error (RMSE) to evaluate the performance. They can directly prove whether the model can capture the essential characteristics of the training data. The value of MAE reflects the change in the actual error value, and the cost of RMSE demonstrates the difference in the amount of its maximum error. The expressions of MAE and RMSE are given by following:

Table 1. Statistics of dataset

# of users	103799
# of items	5919
# of ratings	1830000
# of ratings per user	17.63
# of ratings per item	309.17
Rating sparsity	99.7%

$$MAE = \frac{1}{N}\sum_{i,j}|R_{ij} - \widehat{R}_{ij}| \tag{6}$$

$$RMSE = \sqrt{\frac{1}{N}\sum_{i,j}(R_{ij} - \widehat{R}_{ij})^2} \tag{7}$$

where N refers to the number of samples in the test set, R_{ij} is the user's true score value, and $\widehat{R}_{ij}$ is the predicted score value of the recommendation algorithm. The smaller these two values are, the better performance of the algorithm model can achieve.

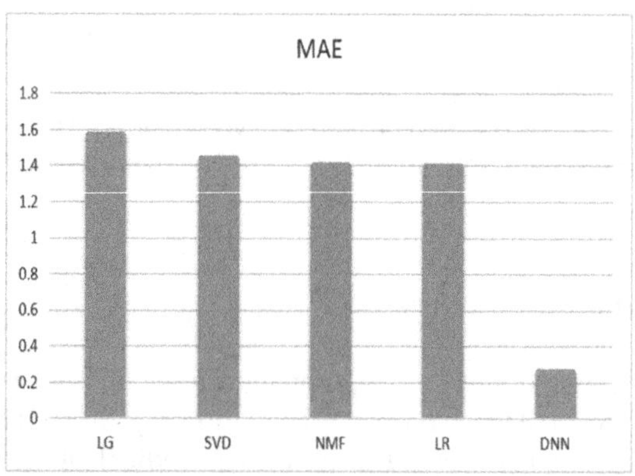

Fig. 4. MAE of different recommendation methods

In our simulations, we compare the proposed algorithm with other algorithms, including linear regression (LG), matrix decomposition singular value decomposition (SVD) [18], non-negative matrix factorization (NMF) [19], and logistic regression (LF). From Figs. 4 and 5, we can see that the proposed algorithm achieves best performance. We used a four-layer hidden network. The first layer is the input layer, which is 623 dimensions. The second layer to the fifth layer is hidden layers. The number of neurons of hidden layer is 1000, 500,

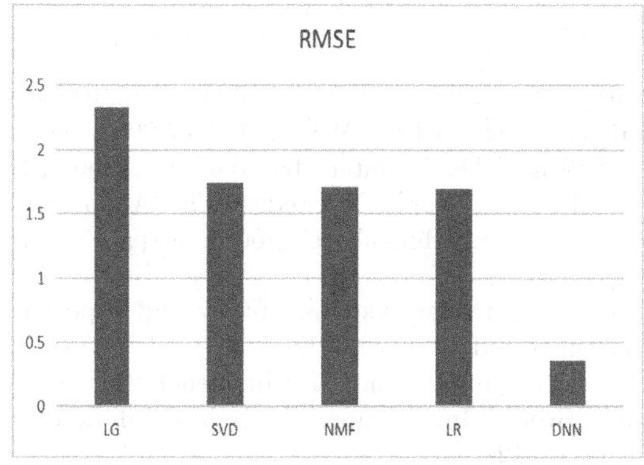

Fig. 5. RMSE of different recommendation methods

200, and 100. We chose ReLu as activation function. The output layer has five neurons, and softmax is used as the activation function.

5 Conclusion

In this paper, we have proposed a user profile based recommendation algorithm for online medical platform, and deep neural network is used to calculate prediction of user-drug rating according to user profile and features of drug. Our framework is simple and versatile. The experimental results show that the proposed model achieves a very high prediction performance, which proves that the application of the deep learning model is a successful attempt on the user's profiles. In the future work, we will use other deep learning techniques to improve the performance of the system on the user's profiles, such as convolutional neural networks, Recurrent Neural Network, etc.

Acknowledgments. This work was supported by the National Natural Science Foundation of China (No. 61571141, No. 61702120); Guangdong Natural Science Foundation (No. 2017A030310591); The Excellent Young Teachers in Universities in Guangdong (No. YQ2015105); Guangdong Provincial Application-oriented Technical Research and Development Special fund project (No. 2015B010131017, No. 2017B010125003); Science and Technology Program of Guangzhou (No. 201604016108); Guangdong Future Network Engineering Technology Research Center (No. 2016GCZX006); Science and Technology Project of Nan Shan (No. 2017CX004); The Project of Youth Innovation Talent of Universities in Guangdong (No. 2017KQNCX120); Guangdong science and technology development project (No. 2017A090905023); The Key projects of Guangdong science and Technology (No. 2017B030306015); The science and technology project in Guangzhou (No. 201803010081).

References

1. Sarwar, B.M., Karypis, G., Konstan, J.A., Riedl, J., et al.: Item-based collaborative filtering recommendation algorithms. WWW **1**, 285–295 (2001)
2. Pazzani, M.J., Billsus, D.: Content-based recommendation systems. In: Brusilovsky, P., Kobsa, A., Nejdl, W. (eds.) The Adaptive Web. LNCS, vol. 4321, pp. 325–341. Springer, Heidelberg (2007). https://doi.org/10.1007/978-3-540-72079-9_10
3. Burke, R.: Hybrid recommender systems: survey and experiments. User Model. User-Adap. Inter. **12**(4), 331–370 (2002)
4. Krizhevsky, A., Sutskever, I., Hinton, G.E.: Imagenet classification with deep convolutional neural networks. In: Advances in Neural Information Processing Systems, pp. 1097–1105 (2012)
5. Hinton, G., et al.: Deep neural networks for acoustic modeling in speech recognition: the shared views of four research groups. IEEE Sig. Process. Mag. **29**(6), 82–97 (2012)
6. Collobert, R., Weston, J., Bottou, L., Karlen, M., Kavukcuoglu, K., Kuksa, P.: Natural language processing (almost) from scratch. J. Mach. Learn. Res. **12**(Aug), 2493–2537 (2011)
7. Zhang, S., Yao, L., Sun, A., Tay, Y.: Deep learning based recommender system: a survey and new perspectives. ACM Comput. Surv. **52**(1), 5:1–5:38 (2019). https://doi.org/10.1145/3285029
8. Skillen, K.-L., Chen, L., Nugent, C.D., Donnelly, M.P., Burns, W., Solheim, I.: Ontological user profile modeling for context-aware application personalization. In: Bravo, J., López-de-Ipiña, D., Moya, F. (eds.) UCAmI 2012. LNCS, vol. 7656, pp. 261–268. Springer, Heidelberg (2012). https://doi.org/10.1007/978-3-642-35377-2_36
9. Pazzani, M., Billsus, D.: Learning and revising user profiles: the identification of interesting web sites. Mach. Learn. **27**(3), 313–331 (1997). https://doi.org/10.1023/A:1007369909943
10. Fawcett, T., Provost, F.J.: Combining data mining and machine learning for effective user profiling. In: KDD, pp. 8–13 (1996)
11. Rosenthal, S., McKeown, K.: Age prediction in blogs: a study of style, content, and online behavior in pre-and post-social media generations. In: Proceedings of the 49th Annual Meeting of the Association for Computational Linguistics: Human Language Technologies, vol. 1, pp. 763–772. Association for Computational Linguistics (2011)
12. Breiman, L.: Random forests. Mach. Learn. **45**(1), 5–32 (2001)
13. Sullivan, E., et al.: Reading news with a purpose: explaining user profiles for self-actualization, pp. 241–245, January 2019
14. Burbach, L., Lidynia, C., Brauner, P., Ziefle, M.: Data protectors, benefit maximizers, or facts enthusiasts: identifying user profiles for life-logging technologies. Comput. Hum. Behav. **99**, 9–21 (2019). http://www.sciencedirect.com/science/article/pii/S0747563219301797
15. Maleszka, B.: A method for knowledge integration of ontology-based user profiles in personalised document retrieval systems. Enterp. Inf. Syst. **13**(7–8), 1143–1163 (2019). https://doi.org/10.1080/17517575.2018.1560505
16. Ruas, P.H.B., et al.: Identification and characterisation of Facebook user profiles considering interaction aspects. Behav. Inf. Technol. **38**(8), 858–872 (2019). https://doi.org/10.1080/0144929X.2019.1566498

17. Wang, Z., Ren, J., Zhang, D., Sun, M., Jiang, J.: A deep-learning based feature hybrid framework for spatiotemporal saliency detection inside videos. Neurocomputing **287**, 68–83 (2018). http://www.sciencedirect.com/science/article/pii/S0925231218301097
18. Golub, G.H., Reinsch, C.: Singular value decomposition and least squares solutions. In: Bauer, F.L. (ed.) Linear Algebra. HDBKAUCO, vol. 2, pp. 134–151. Springer, Heidelberg (1971). https://doi.org/10.1007/978-3-662-39778-7_10
19. Lee, D.D., Seung, H.S.: Algorithms for non-negative matrix factorization. In: Advances in Neural Information Processing Systems, pp. 556–562 (2001)

Hyperspectral Image Classification via Hierarchical Features Adaptive Fusion Network

Zehui Sun, Qin Xu(✉), Fenglei Li, Yiming Mei, and Bin Luo

Key Laboratory of Intelligent Computing and Signal Processing of Ministry of Education, School of Computer Science and Technology, Anhui University, Hefei 230601, China
cvsunzehui@163.com, {xuqin,luobin}@ahu.edu.cn

Abstract. Recently, convolutional neural networks have attracted much attention due to its good performance in hyperspectral image classification. However, excessively increasing the depth of the network will lead to overfitting and vanishing gradient. Besides, previous networks rarely consider the related information among different convolution layers. In this paper we propose a hierarchical deep features adaptive fusion network (FAFNet) to address the above two problems. On the one hand, we use dense connectivity to overcome vanishing gradient and overfitting. On the other hand, we adaptively fuse different convolution layers by the learned weights which utilizing softmax to calculate. Experimental results on two well-known datasets demonstrate the excellent performance of the proposed method compared with other state-of-the-art methods.

Keywords: Hyperspectral image classification · Dense connectivity · Feature adaptive fusion · Convolutional neural networks

1 Introduction

Hyperspectral images [1,2] are composed of hundreds of spectral bands from the visible spectrum to infrared spectrum, which can provide plentiful spectral information. They have been widely used in many remote sensing applications, such as environmental management [3], object detection [4,5] and military [6]. Hyperspectral image classification which assigns each pixel vector to a certain set of classes in the scene is one of the most significant applications in remote sensing area.

Over the past few years, a lot of machine learning-based methods have been used in hyperspectral image classification, such as K-nearest neighbor (KNN) [7], random forest (RF) [8], and extreme learning machine (ELM) [9]. Among these methods, K-nearest neighbor has been widely used as the simplest method that employs Euclidean distance to measure the similarity between training data and testing data. The support vector machine (SVM) [10], which determines the

J. Ren et al. (Eds.): BICS 2019, LNAI 11691, pp. 302–310, 2020.
https://doi.org/10.1007/978-3-030-39431-8_29

boundary in a high-dimensional space using the kernel method, is considered as a breakthrough method for hyperspectral image classification since it can handle the well-knowed Hughes phenomenon and require a small size of training data. Sparse presentation, as an effective signal processing method, is also introduced in hyperspectral image classification [11,12]. The ASMLELM is proposed in [12] to alleviate the illposed problem of ELM and achieves good results. But the ability of representation of hand-crafted features may not be enough to distinguish subtle variation between the different classes.

Recently, deep learning methods have attracted more attention due to its excellent performances in hyperspectral image classification [26]. The main reason is that deep learning methods can extract the invariant and discriminant features from hyperspectral data automatically. The first attempt to use deep learning methods for hyperspectral image classification was proposed by Chen et al. [13], where the stacked auto encoders (SAEs)were built to extract deep features. After that, deep belief network (DBN) was also explored in [14] for hyperspectral image classification. But the above-mentioned methods transform the input data into a 1D vector, which would lose the significant spatial information. To solve the problem, the convolutional neural network based methods are developed. To simultaneously learn the spectral and spatial features, 3D CNN [15] was proposed to take the original hyperspectral image cube as an input. Zhang et al. [25] proposed a dual-channel CNN model, where a 1D CNN was used to automatically extract the hierarchical spectral features and a 2D CNN was applied to extract the hierarchical space-related features. Recently, Sheng et al. [17] proposed a multi-scale dynamic graph convolutional network for hyperspectral image classification. It can conduct the convolution on arbitrarily structured non-Euclidean data and is applicable to the irregular image regions represented by graph topological information.

The above-mentioned methods have two major problems unsolved. (1) Inordinately increasing the network depth will bring some negative effects such as overfitting and gradient vanishing, the discriminant features cannot be effectively extracted. (2) Considering that the network is composed of multiple different hierarchical layers, the strong related and complementary information among different hierarchical layers is not utilized sufficiently. To solve the problem, we propose a hierarchical features adaptive fusion network in this paper.

The three contributions of this paper are shown as follows. (1) We utilize a dense convolutional neural network embracing three dense blocks for HSI classification. The major advantage of this method includes the dense connection which enables the reuse of features, and reduces the dependency between layers. (2) Considering that different layers can extract different level features, we further employ a fusing mechanism to make full use of the different layers. (3) In addition, features of different layers should contribute unequally. Our method can smartly acquire the hierarchical layer weights to adaptively aggregate them by utilizing softmax fuction.

The rest of this paper can be summarized as follows. Section 2 introduces the proposed classification framework. The experiments and analysis are shown in Sect. 3. Section 4 concludes this paper.

2 Hierarchical Features Adaptive Fusion Network

2.1 Hierarchical Features Extract Module

Inspired by Densenet [16], dense blocks are designed to extract more discriminant features. Assume that a network has i convolution layers, X_i is the output of the i-th layer and $F_i(*)$ means the nonlinear transformation in the i-th convolution layer. Traditional CNN can be formulated as follows.

$$X_i = F_i(X_{i-1}), i \in N^+ \tag{1}$$

Densenet utilizes an extremely densely-connected structure, with the output of the zeroth to the $(i-1)$th layers acting as the input to the ith layer. The structure can be formulated as follows.

$$X_i = F_i([X_0, X_1, ..., X_{i-1}]), i \in N^+ \tag{2}$$

The hierarchical features extract module is shown in Fig. 1. First of all the principal component analysis (PCA) algorithm is performed to extract the most informative components of hyperspectral images. Then three dense blocks are adopted to extract the shallow, middle and high level features. d_1, d_2, d_3 represent the feature maps acquired three dense blocks respectively. To simultaneously learn the spectral and spatial features, we adopt 3D convolution as the basic unit

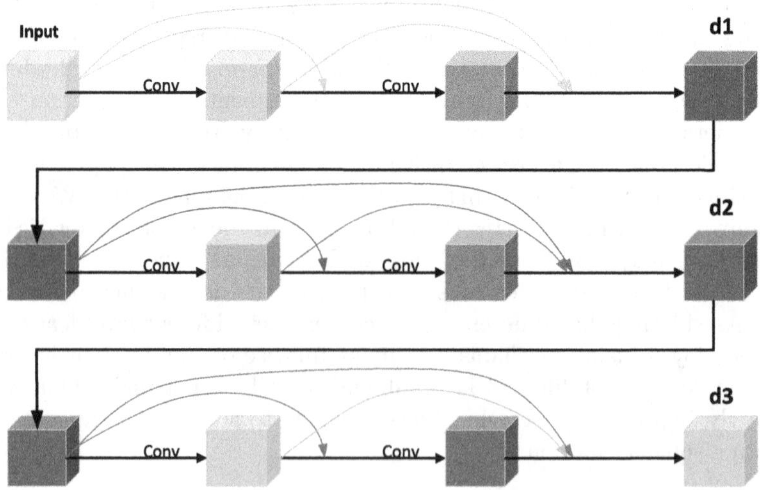

Fig. 1. d_1, d_2, d_3 represent the low, middle and high level features respectively.

in the proposed methods. To reduce the training time and prevent overfitting, we utilize the rectified linear unit (relu). We set paddingmode same to ensure that all the feature maps have the same scale in the network, so the feature maps can be contact conveniently.

2.2 Hierarchical Features Adaptive Fusion Module

Inspired by SKNet [18], we employ softmax to calculate hierarchical layers weights to adaptively exploit the strong correlated and complementary information among different convolution layers. The hierarchical features adaptive fusion module is shown in Fig. 2. As above-mentioned, d_1, d_2, d_3 are the features extracted from three dense blocks. f_1, f_2, f_3 represent fully connected layers, which includes dropout, fully connected and relu operations. $\oplus$ denote the operations of concatenation. W_n indicates the n-th layer weight, and $D_{contact}$ denotes the transformed feature of different layers, which would be sent to the softmax layer to calculate different layers weights.

$$\begin{aligned} D_1 &= f_1(d_1) \\ D_2 &= f_2(d_2) \\ D_3 &= f_3(d_3) \\ D_{contact} &= D_1 \oplus D_2 \oplus D_3 \\ W_n &= softmax(D_{contact}) \end{aligned} \tag{3}$$

$$Z = W_1 d_1 \oplus W_2 d_2 \oplus W_3 d_3 \tag{4}$$

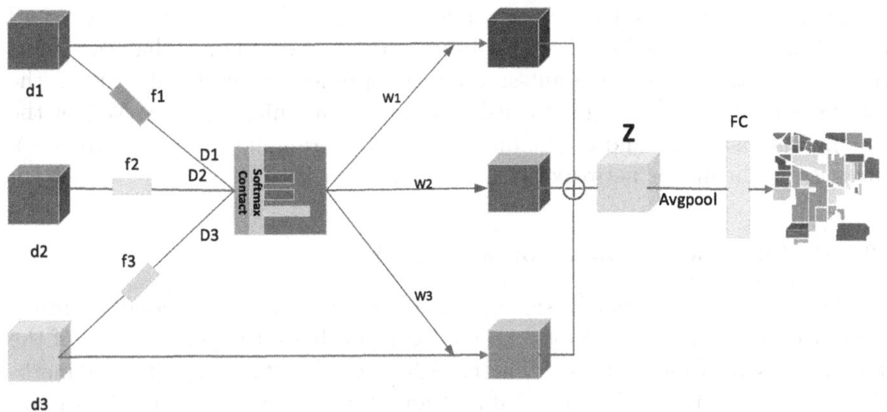

Fig. 2. d_1, d_2, d_3 represent features obtained by Hierarchical Features Extract module, they are sent to the softmax layer to calculate their weights, then they multipy the weights and contacted as the fusion feature Z.

After extracting the fusing feature Z, the average pooling is utilized to reduce the parameters and remove the noise. After processing by several fully connected layers, the fused feature is transformed into an output feature vector. Then, the feature vector is input to a softmax layer to calculate the conditional probabilities of each class. The cross entropy loss function is employed as the loss function.

3 Experimental Results and Discussion

In this section, we conduct several experiments to evaluate the performance of the proposed method on two well-known hyperspectral datasets: Indian Pines Dataset and Pavia University Dataset. The compared methods include: CNN [19], CNN-PPF [20], SS-CNN [21], DHNN [22], SVM [24], 3D-CNN [13], SSRN [23]. All the experiments are implemented in Tensorflow-gpu-1.80 with the gpu of NVIDIA GTX1070 and cpu of INTEL I7-7700K.

3.1 Datasets and Experiment Setup

(1) **Indian Pines Dataset:** The Indian Pines dataset was collected by Airborne Visible/Infrared Imaging Spectrometer (AVIRIS) sensor in the northwestern Indiana with a spatial resolution of 20 m. It contains 145 × 145 pixels and 220 spectral bands, from 0.4–2.5 µm, where 20 bands were discarded because of atmospheric affection. The number of samples is 10249.
(2) **Pavia University Dataset:** The Pavia University dataset was obtained by the Reflective Optics System Imaging Spectrometer (ROSIS) sensor in the University of Pavia with a spatial resolution of 1.3 m. It contains 600 × 340 pixels and generates 115 bands ranging from 0.43–0.86 µm, where 12 bands were discarded. The number of samples is 42776.

For the Indian Pines dataset, we randomly select 15% as the training set, and the testing set consisted of the remaining samples. Considering that the Pavia University dataset has abundant samples, we randomly select only 200 as the training set, and the testing set consisted of the remaining samples. We set the training batchsize 128 and a dynamic learning rate ranging from 2e−3 to 1e−4, which is significant for network optimization.

3.2 Performance Comparison and Analysis

According to the experimental setting described previously, the overall accuracy (OA), average accuracy (AA) were recorded to evaluate the performance of the different classification methods. The classification results using different methods on two datasets are shown in Tables 1 and 2, respectively. From Tables 1 and 2, for two datasets, we can obviously see that the proposed method can greatly improve the classification accuracy compared with other competitive methods. For the Indian Pines dataset, our method has 1.17 and 2.22% point improvement in OA and AA compared with other results. For the Pavia University dataset, our method has 0.93 and 0.75% point improvement in OA and AA compared with other results. The results demonstrate the proposed method excellent classification performance.

Table 1. Classification accuracy (%) for the Pavia University Dataset.

Class	CNN [19]	CNN-PPF [20]	SS-CNN [21]	DHNN [22]	Proposed
1	88.38	97.42	97.40	97.94	**99.71**
2	91.27	95.76	99.40	98.84	**99.91**
3	85.88	94.05	94.84	**99.01**	98.08
4	97.24	97.52	99.16	96.50	**99.65**
5	99.91	**100**	**100**	**100**	99.91
6	96.41	99.13	98.70	**99.69**	98.99
7	93.62	96.19	**100**	99.86	99.12
8	87.45	93.62	94.57	98.32	**98.69**
9	99.57	99.60	99.87	98.09	**100**
OA	92.27	96.48	98.22	98.61	**99.54**
AA	93.36	97.03	98.41	98.59	**99.34**

Table 2. Classification accuracy (%) for the Indian Pines Dataset.

Class	SVM [24]	CNN [19]	3D-CNN [13]	SSRN [23]	Proposed
1	68.04	65.87	89.13	97.53	**100**
2	83.55	81.04	98.33	98.45	**99.10**
3	73.82	79.07	98.05	97.70	**99.14**
4	71.98	82.70	98.23	89.46	**100**
5	94.29	69.25	97.56	99.16	**100**
6	97.32	88.29	98.93	99.80	**100**
7	88.21	67.86	83.57	**100**	**100**
8	98.16	96.26	99.41	**99.80**	97.84
9	52.00	67.00	65.00	94.64	**100**
10	79.49	68.82	97.22	96.75	**97.84**
11	86.83	86.55	98.12	98.13	**99.61**
12	83.41	73.41	93.09	**99.00**	98.80
13	97.41	94.54	99.80	**100**	99.43
14	96.14	96.24	99.43	**100**	**100**
15	67.31	85.39	90.18	96.58	**98.20**
16	92.47	92.90	89.73	93.12	**98.70**
OA	86.24	82.98	97.01	98.07	**99.24**
AA	83.15	80.95	96.98	97.07	**99.29**

To visualize the effectiveness of our method, we compare it with CNN, 3DCNN and our method. From Figs. 3 and 4, we can obviously see that our method acquires the best performance compared with other methods. Among all methods, our proposed method achieved a classification map that was the

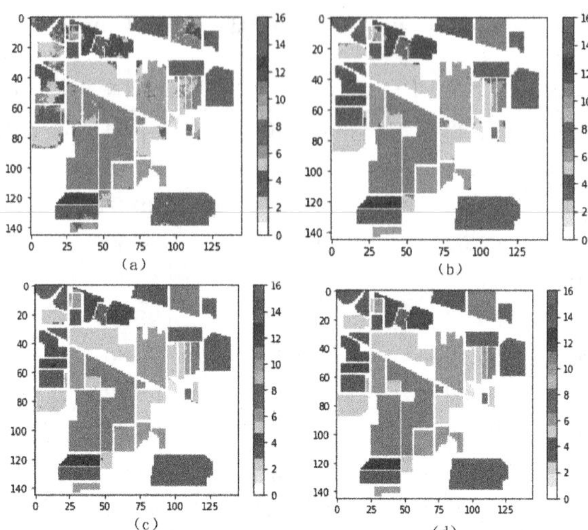

Fig. 3. The classification results in Indian Pines dataset. (a) CNN, (b) 3DCNN, (c) Proposed, (d) Groundtruth.

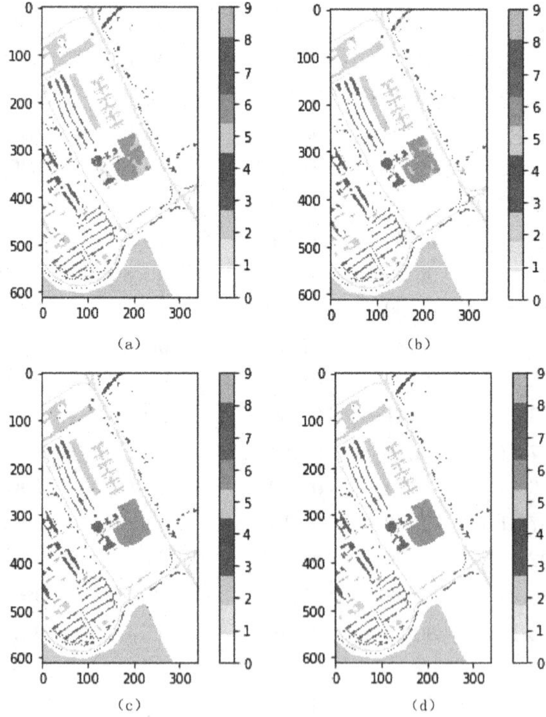

Fig. 4. The classifcation results in Pavia University dataset. (a) CNN, (b) 3DCNN, (c) Proposed, (d) Groundtruth.

closest to the groundtruth and the class boundaries were accurately defined and the background pixels were better classified. The major advantage of our method includes the dense connection which enables the reuse of features, and reduces the dependency between layers. We utilize dense connection to overcome vanishing gradient so that we can extract discriminative features. Besides, features from different layers should contribute unequally in feature fusing. Different from fusing hierarchical features directly, our method adaptively fuse different convolution layers by the learned weights to make full use of the discriminative features from different layers.

4 Conclusion

In this paper, we propose a novel hierarchical features adaptive fusion network for hyperspectral image classification. Compared with the previous methods, the proposed network can not only overcome the gradient vanishing and overfitting by using dense connectivity, but also make full use of the multiple-layer features with the learned adaptive weights. Experimental results demonstrate the superiority of the proposed method over several state-of-the-art methods. In the future work, we will explore new strategies to replace dense blocks and explore attention mechanism to further extract discriminant features.

Acknowledgments. The authors would like to thank the anonymous referees for their constructive comments which have helped improve the paper. This work was supported by National Natural Science Foundation of China (61502003, 71501002, 61472002, 61671018, 61860206004), by the Key Research Project of Humanities and Social Sciences in Colleges and Universities of Anhui Province under Grant SK2019A0013.

References

1. Ren, J., Zabalza, J., et al.: Effective feature extraction and data reduction with hyperspectral imaging in remote sensing. IEEE Sig. Process. Mag. **31**(4), 149–154 (2014)
2. Zabalza, J., Ren, J., et al.: Novel segmented stacked autoencoder for effective dimensionality reduction and feature extraction in hyperspectral imaging. Neurocomputing **185**, 1–10 (2016)
3. Bioucas-Dias, J.M., et al.: Hyperspectral remote sensing data analysis and future challenges. IEEE Geosci. Rem. Sens. Mag. **1**(2), 6–36 (2013)
4. Li, W., Wu, G., Du, Q.: Transferred deep learning for anomaly detection in hyperspectral imagery. IEEE Geosci. Rem. Sens. Lett. **14**(5), 597–601 (2017)
5. Zhang, Y., Du, B., Zhang, L.: A sparse representation-based binary hypothesis model for target detection in hyperspectral images. IEEE Trans. Geosci. Rem. Sens. **53**(3), 1346–1354 (2015)
6. Zhang, L., Tao, D., Huang, X., Du, B.: Hyperspectral remote sensing image subpixel target detection based on supervised metric learning. IEEE Trans. Geosci. Rem. Sens. **52**(8), 4955–4965 (2014)

7. Blanzieri, E., Melgani, F.: Nearest neighbor classification of remote sensing images with the maximal margin principle. IEEE Trans. Geosci. Rem. Sens. **46**(6), 1804–1811 (2008)
8. Ham, J., Chen, Y., et al.: Investigation of the random forest framework for classification of hyperspectral data. IEEE Trans. Geosci. Rem. Sens. **43**(3), 492–501 (2005)
9. Cao, F., et al.: Linear vs nonlinear extreme learning machine for spectral-spatial classification of hyperspectral image. Sensors **17**, 2603 (2017)
10. Melgani, F., Bruzzone, L.: Classification of hyperspectral remote sensing images with support vector machines. IEEE Trans. Geosci. Rem. Sens. **42**(8), 1778–1790 (2004)
11. Fang, L., et al.: Hyperspectral image classification via multiple-feature-based adaptive sparse representation. IEEE Trans. Instrum. Measur. **66**(7), 1646–1657 (2017)
12. Qiao, T., Yang, Z., et al.: Joint bilateral filtering and spectral similarity-based sparse representation: a generic framework for effective feature extraction and data classification in hyperspectral imaging. Pattern Recogn. **77**, 316–328 (2017)
13. Chen, Y., et al.: Deep learning-based classification of hyperspectral data. IEEE J. Sel. Top. Appl. Earth Observ. Rem. Sens. **7**(6), 2094–2107 (2014)
14. Chen, Y., et al.: Spectral spatial classification of hyperspectral data based on deep belief network. IEEE J. Sel. Top. Appl. Earth Observ. Rem. Sens. **8**(6), 1–12 (2015)
15. Chen, Y., et al.: Deep feature extraction and classification of hyperspectral images based on convolutional neural networks. IEEE Trans. Geosci. Rem. Sens. **54**(10), 6262–6251 (2016)
16. Huang, G., Liu, Z., et al.: Densely connected convolutional networks. In: Proceedings of the IEEE Conference on CVPR, pp. 2261–2269 (2017)
17. Sheng, W., et al.: Multi-scale Dynamic Graph Convolutional Network for Hyperspectral Image Classification. arXiv:1905.06133 (2019)
18. Li, X., et al.: Selective Kernel Networks. arXiv:1903.06586 (2019)
19. Hu, W., et al.: Deep convolutional neural networks for hyperspectral image classification. J. Sens. **2**, 1–12 (2015)
20. Li, W., Wu, G., et al.: Hyperspectral image classification using deep pixel-pair features. IEEE Trans. Geosci. Rem. Sens. **55**(2), 844–853 (2016)
21. Mei, S., et al.: Learning sensor-specific spatial-spectral features of hyperspectral images via convolutional neural networks. IEEE Trans. Geosci. Rem. Sens. **55**(8), 4520–4533 (2017)
22. Fang, L., Liu, Z., Song, W.: Deep hashing neural networks for hyperspectral image feature extraction. IEEE Geosci. Rem. Sens. Lett., 1–5 (2019)
23. Zhong, Z., Li, J., et al.: Spectral-spatial residual network for hyperspectral image classification: a 3-D deep learning framework. IEEE Trans. Geosci. Rem. Sens. **56**, 847–858 (2018)
24. Waske, B., et al.: Sensitivity of support vector machines to random feature selection in classification of hyperspectral data. IEEE Trans. Geosci. Rem. Sens. **48**(7), 2880–2889 (2010)
25. Zhang, H., Li, Y., Zhang, Y., Shen, Q.: Spectral-spatial classification of hyperspectral imagery using a dual-channel convolutional neural network. Rem. Sens. **8**, 438–447 (2017)
26. Wang, L., Peng, J., Sun, W.: Spatial-spectral squeeze-and-excitation residual network for hyperspectral image classification. Rem. Sens. **11**, 884 (2019)

Image Recognition, Detection, Tracking and Classification

Collaborative-Representation-Based Nearest Neighbor Classifier for Hyperspectral Image Classification Combined with Superpixel and Loopy Belief Propagation

Danning Lin[1], Zhijing Yang[1](✉), Meilin Wang[1], Yongqiang Cheng[2], and Qing Pan[1]

[1] School of Information Engineering, Guangdong University of Technology, Guangzhou 510006, China
yzhj@gdut.edu.cn

[2] School of Engineering and Computer Science, University of Hull, Hull HU6 7RX, UK

Abstract. The k nearest neighbor (KNN) is one of the most popular classifiers for hyperspectral images (HSI). However, in hyperspectral imagery classification, since the pixel spectral signatures are usually mixed due to the relatively low spatial resolution, traditional KNN on pixel-level cannot handle it. To improve the performance of classification, a new KNN method based on superpixel and the collaborative-representation (KNNSCR) has been proposed. This proposed method can effectively overcome the intra-class variations and inter-class interference. Furthermore, we combine KNNSCR with loopy belief propagation (LBP) to catch more detailed spatial information. The proposed method can greatly improve the accuracy of HSI classification. The experiments demonstrate that the proposed method obtain very good results by comparing with some well-known methods.

Keywords: Hyperspectral imagery classification · K nearest neighbor · Superpixel · Collaborative-representation · Loopy belief propagation

1 Introduction

Over the past several decades, hyperspectral imaging has experienced a tremendous interest in the remote sensing community due to its capability to achieve more detailed spectral measures [1, 29–31]. Thus, it has been widely used in various application of remote sensing field, such as precision agriculture [2–5], environment monitoring [6–8], national defense [9], and ocean exploration [10].

Since each pixel of HSI has many spectral features with limited label samples, it is very difficult to classify HSI with limited samples and high spectral resolution at each pixel. So HSI classification remains a challenging problem. In recent years, various supervised classification methods have been proposed, such as extreme learning machine [11], sparse representation [12], Bayesian theory [13], support vector machine [14–17] and random forest [18]. And in order to make classification performance well, some feature extraction and band selection methods have been searched [19–24].

J. Ren et al. (Eds.): BICS 2019, LNAI 11691, pp. 313–321, 2020.
https://doi.org/10.1007/978-3-030-39431-8_30

The KNN classifier is one of the most popular classifiers for HSI classification [25, 26]. It is a nonparametric classifier in which a test sample is simply assigned with a label occur most commonly in its KNNs. Several extensions of KNN have been investigated. In [27], a local mean-based nearest neighbor was developed by using class-specific mean vectors for similarity comparison, in [28], cosine-based nonparametric feature extraction combined with KNN was discussed. In [26], the Euclidean distance in a low-dimensional space was studied. Local manifold learning was combined with KNN in [25].

To overcome the drawback of the traditional KNN, a new KNN classifier based on superpixel and the collaborative-representation (KNNSCR) was proposed in this paper. First, we use an entropy rate superpixel (ERS) segmentation method to generate the superpixel map, from which the spatial-spectral feature is extracted. Then in each superpixel region, the test sample can be represented as linear combination of all the training samples. In the collaborative-representation (CR), we can know which training samples are more important to decide the class label of the test sample. So finally the KNNSCR can effectively classify all the pixels. Furthermore, we propose to combine the KNNSCR with LBP. LBP can catch more spatial information for HSI classification. It is based on the principle that if a sample belongs to a class, then the probability of its adjacent samples belonging to the same class is relatively large. With more spatial and spectral feature extracted in the HSI, the classification accuracy of HSI can be improved, to some extent.

The remaining of this paper is divided into the following sections: some related work is reviewed in Sect. 2. The proposed method is presented detailed in Sect. 3. Section 4 shows the experimental results and analysis. Finally, conclusion is given in Sect. 5.

2 Review of Related Work

2.1 Review of KNN

The nearest neighbor classifier attempts to find the training sample nearest to the testing sample according to a given distance measure and assigns the former's class label to the latter. Commonly, Euclidean distance is used to measure the similarity between a training sample x_i and a test sample y, i.e.,

$$d(x_i, y) = \|x_i - y\|_2^2 \tag{1}$$

The KNN classifier is a straightforward extension of the original nearest neighbor classifier. Instead of using only one sample closest to the testing point y, the KNN classifier chooses the k nearest samples from training data X, and majority voting is employed to decide the class label of y.

2.2 Review of CR

CR is based on the concept that the test sample can be represented as a linear combination of all the training samples X. Assume α is an n $\times$ 1 vector of weighting coefficients. The weight vector α for the linear combination is solved by an $\ell 2$-norm regularization, i.e.,

$$\alpha = \arg \min_{\alpha^*} \|y - X\alpha^*\|_2^2 + \lambda \|\Gamma_y \alpha^*\|_2^2 \quad (2)$$

where Γ_y is a biasing Tikhonov matrix, and λ is a global regularization parameter that balances the minimization between the residual part and the regularization term. Note that α^* is an estimate of α with size of n $\times$ 1. Specifically, the regularization term is designed in the form of

$$\Gamma_y = \begin{bmatrix} \left\|y - x_2^{(1)}\right\| & & 0 \\ & \ddots & \\ 0 & & \left\|y - x_2^{(n)}\right\| \end{bmatrix} \quad (3)$$

where $x^{(1)}$, $x^{(2)}$, …, $x^{(n)}$ are the columns of matrix X. Then, the weight vector α can be determined in a closed-form solution as

$$\alpha = (X^T X + \lambda^2 \Gamma_y^T \Gamma_y)^{-1} X^T y. \quad (4)$$

After obtaining $\alpha = \{\alpha_1, \alpha_2, \ldots, \alpha_n\}$, the k largest elements are found.

2.3 Review of LBP

LBP can extract the spatial information for classification. Its main principle is that if a node belongs to one class, the probability of its adjacent samples belonging to the same class is relatively large. It is an iterative algorithm and in the t-th iteration, the message sent from node i to the neighboring node of i node $j \in N(i)$ can be given by the following equation:

$$m_{ij}^t(y_j) = \frac{1}{Z} \sum_{y_i} \psi(y_i, y_j) \phi(y_i, x_i) \prod_{k \varepsilon N(i) \setminus \{j\}} m_{ki}^{t-1}(y_i) \quad (5)$$

where Z is a normalization constant, $\psi\left(y_i, y_j\right) = p\left(y_i, y_j\right)$ denotes that the interaction potential that penalizes the dissimilar pair of neighboring label, $\phi(y_i, x_i) = p(y_i|x_i)$ stands for the association potential of label y_i with respect to evidence x_i.

Assuming that $b_i^t(y_i)$ is the belief of node i at the iteration t, $b_i^t(y_i)$ can be presented by the following equation:

$$b_i^t(y_i = k) = q(y_i = k|x) = \phi(y_i = k) \prod_{j \in N(i)} m_{ji}^t(y_i = k) \quad (6)$$

Finally, we can estimate the final solution using maximize of the posterior marginal for I, which can be presented by following equation:

$$y_{\hat{i}} = \arg\max_{y_i} q(y_i|x) = \arg\max_{y_i} b_i^t(y_i) \tag{7}$$

3 The Proposed Approach

In hyperspectral imagery, pixel spectral signatures are usually mixed due to relatively low spatial resolution, and one pixel may be over two or more different classes of materials, leading to mixed spectra. The resulting phenomena of intra-class variation and inter-class similarity increase the difficulty of hyperspectral image classification. The traditional KNN method can't solve this problem. To tackle this problem, we propose the KNNSCR method in this paper. The algorithm includes the following four steps:

3.1 Superpixel Segmentation

PCA is first employed on the original hyperspectral image I to obtain the first three principal components $\mathrm{I} = \{I^1, I^2, I^3\}$, and the first three principal components are utilized as the ERS segmentation. By this way, the hyperspectral image can be segmented into N nonoverlapping 2-D superpixel regions.

3.2 Spatial-Spectral Feature Extraction

The domain transform recursive filtering (RF) is performed to each band of the hyperspectral image I to obtain the RF feature image as follows:

$$\mathrm{O} = \mathrm{RF}(\mathrm{I}) \tag{8}$$

where RF represents the domain transform RF operation. O is the resulting RF feature image.

3.3 Collaborative-Representation-Based KNN

For a superpixel map Y, it is composed of the N nonoverlapping superpixel regions, i.e., $\mathrm{Y} = \{Y_1, Y_2, \ldots, Y_N\}$. Y_n represents the nth region in the superpixel map. $Y_n = \{y_{n,1}, y_{n,2}, \ldots, y_{n,k_n}\}$, in which $y_{n,i}$ represents the ith test sample in the nth region. K_n is the total number of pixels in the nth superpixel.

In each superpixel region, a test sample can be represented by all the training sample like Eq. (2), and from the Eq. (4), we can know the most important training sample of each class, for the larger α is, the more important corresponding training sample is. And then the Euclidean distance among the test sample and the most important training sample of each class is considered as the Euclidean distance among the test sample and each class.

$$\mathrm{D}(y_{n,i},\mathrm{X}) = \{\mathrm{D}(y_{n,i},X_1),\mathrm{D}(y_{n,i},X_2),\ldots,\mathrm{D}(y_{n,i},X_C)\} \tag{9}$$

where $X_j(j = 1, 2, \ldots, C)$ denotes the jth class.

3.4 KNN Labeling

From the step C, the Euclidean distance among the superpixel Y_n and various class is

$$D(Y_n, X) = \{D(y_{n,1}, X); D(y_{n,2}, X); \ldots; D(y_{n,k_n}, X)\} \tag{10}$$

It is a $k_n \times j$ matrix.

The label of superpixel $\mathrm{Y_n}$ depends on the k pixels which are nearest to class j.

$$\mathrm{D}(Y_n, X_j) = \{\mathrm{D}(\hat{y}_{n,1}, X_j), \mathrm{D}(\hat{y}_{n,2}, X_j), \ldots, \mathrm{D}(\hat{y}_{n,k}, X_j)\}, \tag{11}$$

where $\hat{y}_{n,i}$ is the sorted test samples in superpixel Y_n according to the Euclidean distance among them and class j. Then, the resulting distance among superpixel Y_n and class j can be calculated by:

$$\widehat{D}(Y_n, X_j) = \frac{sum(D(Y_n, X_j))}{k} \tag{12}$$

Finally, the label of superpixel $\mathrm{Y_n}$ can be obtained by

$$\mathrm{Class}(Y_n) = argmin_{j=1,2,\ldots,C}\widehat{D}(Y_n, X^j) \tag{13}$$

4 Experiments and Analysis

4.1 Data Set

The scene was acquired over a mixed agricultural/forest area, provided along with a 16-class ground truth data, which is shown in Fig. 1. It contains 145 lines and 145 samples in each line, while the ground-truth map only comprises 10366 pixels. The original data set is composed of 220 spectral channels, from which 50 bands are removed for the sake of noise and water absorption phenomena. This scene is widely utilized for the validation of hyperspectral classification due to its unbalance of sample numbers and the high mixture. The number of training and testing samples of each class for the Indian Pines HSI data are shown in Table 1. There are about 1043 labeled samples used for training, about 10% of the total sample. In the testing process, we use rest labeled samples for testing.

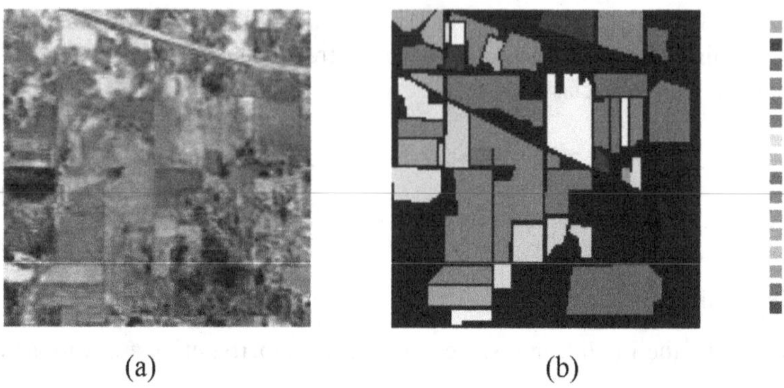

(a) (b)

Fig. 1. AVIRIS Indian Pines scene with 16 classes: (a) False color map. (b) Ground truth.

Table 1. The train samples and test samples of Indian Pines

Class	Train	Test	Class	Train	Test
C1	6	48	C9	2	18
C2	144	1290	C10	97	871
C3	84	750	C11	247	2221
C4	24	210	C12	62	552
C5	50	447	C13	22	190
C6	75	672	C14	130	1164
C7	3	23	C15	38	342
C8	49	440	C16	10	85

4.2 The Experiments and Result Analysis

In this section, an experiment is performed on the Indian Pines dataset to show the performance of the proposed method. In this experiment, the training samples account for 10% of the reference data. To evaluate the HSI classification accuracy, Table 2 shows the OA (overall accuracy), AA (average accuracy), k (kappa coefficient) and each class accuracy of KNN, KNNSCR, ELM-LBP and KNNSCR-LBP. The results demonstrate that our proposed method have a better performance. OA is the proportion of number of correctly predicted items in total of item to predict. AA is the average of each accuracy per class (sum of accuracy for each class predicted/number of class), kappa coefficient is a statistic which measures inter-rater agreement for qualitative (categorical) items.

From Table 2, compared with traditional KNN, KNNSCR improves the classification accuracy by 27.86% and 31.1% on OA and AA, respectively. The improvement is due to that the superpixel overcomes the intra-class variations and inter-class interference problem. Furthermore, LBP can catch more detailed spatial information from HSI, which can further improve the classification result. ELM-LBP, which combines ELM with LBP, achieves a good performance, but the performance of KNNSCR-LBP is better than it.

Table 2. Indian Pines: overall, average and individual class accuracy (in percent) and k statistic of different classification methods with 10% train samples. The best accuracy in each row is showed in bold.

Class	KNN	KNNSCR	ELM-LBP	KNNSCR-LBP
C1(Alfalfa)	89.47	**100**	81.67	97.56
C2(Corn-no till)	52.62	95.71	**97.60**	96.11
C3(Corn-min till)	64.11	94.71	**97.37**	95.45
C4(Corn)	48.29	91.56	95.86	**98.59**
C5(Grass/pasture)	80.88	93.17	94.09	**94.71**
C6(Grass/tree)	79.33	92.31	98.21	**98.63**
C7(Grass/pasture-mowed)	68.97	85.71	43.91	**100**
C8(Hay-windrowed)	92.07	98.85	99.98	**100**
C9(Oats)	71.43	**83.33**	3.33	**83.33**
C10(Soybeans-no till)	55.60	94.78	93.59	**96.69**
C11(Soybeans-min till)	65.73	96.74	**99.42**	97.74
C12(Soybeans-clean till)	45.47	95.21	97.41	**97.75**
C13(Wheat)	86.10	94.89	**98.16**	95.65
C14(Woods)	91.95	95.05	99.45	**100**
C15(Bldg-grass-tree-drivers)	44.30	97.90	98.63	**98.85**
C16(Stone-steel towers)	98.67	92.59	78.82	**95.24**
OA	67.49	95.35	97.29	**97.51**
AA	62.81	93.91	86.09	**96.64**
k	70.94	94.70	96.91	**97.16**

5 Conclusion

In this paper, we have proposed a new classification method which combines KNNSCR with LBP. In the KNNSCR, the spatial and spectral features is extracted, and then more detailed spatial information can be caught in the LBP. The experiment demonstrates that our proposed method obtains good performance compared with traditional method.

Acknowledgement. This work is supported in part by the National Nature Science Foundation of China (nos. U1701266, 61471132), the Innovation Team Project of Guangdong Education Department (no. 2017KCXTD011), Natural Science Foundation of Guangdong Province China (no. 2018A030313751), and Science and Technology Program of Guangzhou, China (nos. 201803010065, 201802020010).

References

1. Plaza, A., Benediktsson, J.A., Boardman, J.W., Brazile, J., Bruzzone, L., Camps-Valls, G.: Recent advances in techniques for hyperspectral image processing. Remote Sens. Environ. **113**(1), 110–122 (2009)

2. Lee, M.A., Huang, Y., Yao, H., et al.: Determining the effects of storage on cotton and soybean leaf samples for hyperspectral analysis. IEEE J. Sel. Topics Appl. Earth Observ. Remote Sens. **7**(6), 2562–2570 (2014)
3. Kanning, M., Siegmann, B., Jarmer, T.: Regionalization of uncovered agricultural soils based on organic carbon and soil texture estimations. Remote Sens. **8**(11), 927 (2016)
4. Chi, J., Crawford, M.M.: Spectral unmixing-based crop residue estimation using hyperspectral remote sensing data: a case study at purdue university. IEEE J. Sel. Topics Appl. Earth Observ. Remote Sens. **7**(6), 2531–2539 (2014)
5. Tschannerl, J., Ren, J., Jack, F., et al.: Potential of UV and SWIR hyperspectral imaging for determination of levels of phenolic flavour compounds in peated barley malt. Food Chem. **270**, 105–112 (2019)
6. Brook, A., Dor, E.B.: Quantitative detection of settled dust over green canopy using sparse unmixing of airborne hvperspectral data. IEEE J. Sel. Topics Appl. Earth Observ. Remote Sens. **9**(2), 884–897 (2016)
7. Clark, M.L., Roberts, D.A.: Species-level differences in hyperspectral metrics among tropical rainforest trees as determined by a tree-based classifier. Remote Sens. **4**(6), 1820–1855 (2012)
8. Ryan, J., Davis, C., Tufillaro, N., et al.: Application of the hyperspectral imager for the coastal ocean to phytoplankton ecology studies in Monterey Bay CA, USA. Remote Sens. **6** (2), 1007–1025 (2014)
9. Shimoni, M., Tolt, G., Perneel, C., et al.: Detection of vehicles in shadow areas using combined hyperspectral and lidar data. In: Proceedings of IEEE International Geoscience Remote Sensing Symposium, pp. 4427–4430 (2011)
10. Muller-Karger, F., Roffer, M., Walker, N., Oliver, M.: Satellite remote sensing in support of an integrated ocean observing system. IEEE Geosci. Remote Sens. Mag. **1**(4), 8–18 (2013)
11. Cao, F., Yang, Z., Ren, J.C., et al.: Local block multilayer sparse extreme learning machine for effective feature extraction and classification of hyperspectral images. IEEE Trans. Geosci. Remote Sens. **57**(8), 5580–5594 (2019)
12. Qiao, T., Yang, Z., Ren, J., et al.: Joint bilateral filtering and spectral similarity-based sparse representation: a generic framework for effective feature extraction and data classification in hyperspectral imaging. Pattern Recogn. **77**, 316–328 (2018)
13. Yang, H.: A back-propagation neural network for mineralogical mapping from aviris data. Int. J. Remote Sens. **20**(1), 97–110 (1999)
14. Chen, C.H., et al.: Statistical pattern recognition in remote sensing. Pattern Recognit. **41**, 2731–2741 (2008)
15. Melgani, F., Bruzzone, L.: Classification of hyperspectral remote sensing images with support vector machines. IEEE Trans. Geosci. Remote Sens. **42**(8), 1778–1790 (2004)
16. Fauvel, M., Benediktsson, J.A., Chanussot, J., Sveinsson, J.R.: Spectral and spatial classification of hyperspectral data using SVMS and morphological profiles. IEEE Trans. Geosci. Remote Sens. **46**(11), 3804–3814 (2008)
17. Heikkinen, V., Tokola, T., Parkkinen, J., Korpela, I., Jaaskelainen, T.: Simulated multispectral image for tree species classification using support vector machines. IEEE Trans. Geosci. Remote Sens. **48**(3), 1355–1364 (2010)
18. Mountrakis, G., Im, J., Ogole, C.: Support vector machines in remote sensing: a review. ISPRS J. Photogrammetry Remote Sens. **66**(3), 247–259 (2011)
19. Dalponte, M., Orka, H.O., Gobakken, T., Gianelle, D., Naesset, E.: Tree species classification in boreal forests with hyperspectral data. IEEE Trans. Geosci. Remote Sens. **51**(5), 2632–2645 (2013)
20. Sun, H., Ren, J., Zhao, H., et al.: Superpixel based feature specific sparse representation for spectral-spatial classification of hyperspectral images. Remote Sens. **11**(5), 536 (2019)

21. Zabalza, J., Ren, J., Zheng, J., et al.: Novel segmented stacked autoencoder for effective dimensionality reduction and feature extraction in hyperspectral imaging. Neurocomputing **185**, 1–10 (2016)
22. Tschannerl, J., et al.: Unsupervised hyperspectral band selection based on information theory and a modified discrete gravitational search algorithm. Inf. Fusion **51**, 189–200 (2019)
23. Ren, J., et al.: Effective feature extraction and data reduction in remote sensing using hyperspectral imaging. IEEE Sig. Process. Mag. **31**(4), 149–154 (2014)
24. Zabalza, J., et al.: Novel folded-PCA for improved feature extraction and data reduction with hyperspectral imaging and SAR in remote sensing. ISPRS J. Photogrammetry Remote Sens. **93**, 112–122 (2014)
25. Ma, L., Crawford, M.M., Tian, J.: Local manifold learning-based k-nearest-neighbor for hyperspectral image classification. IEEE Trans. Geosci. Remote Sens. **48**(11), 4099–4109 (2010)
26. Samaniego, L., Bardossy, A., Schulz, K.: Supervised classification of remotely sensed image using a modified k-NN technique. IEEE Trans. Geosci. Remote Sens. **46**(7), 2112–2125 (2008)
27. Mitani, Y., Hamamoto, Y.: A local mean-based nonparametric classifier. Pattern Recogn. Lett. **27**(10), 1151–1159 (2006)
28. Yang, J.M., Yu, P.T., Kuo, B.C.: A nonparametric feature extraction and its application to nearest neighbor classification for hyperspectral image data. IEEE Trans. Geosci. Remote Sens. **48**(3), 1279–1293 (2010)
29. Md Noor, S., Ren, J., Marshall, S., Michael, K.: Hyperspectral image enhancement and mixture deep-learning classification of corneal epithelium injuries. Sensors **17**(11), 2644 (2017)
30. Cao, F., Yang, Z., Ren, J., Ling, W.-K., Zhao, H., Sun, M., Benediktsson, J.A.: Sparse representation-based augmented multinomial logistic extreme learning machine with weighted composite features for spectral-spatial classification of hyperspectral images. IEEE Trans. Geosci. Remote Sens. **56**(11), 6263–6279 (2018)
31. Qiao, T., et al.: Quantitative prediction of beef quality using visible and NIR spectroscopy with large data samples under industry conditions. J. Appl. Spectroscopy **82**(1), 137–144 (2015)

A Character Superposition Method Based on Object Detection

Wenkai Xu[1], Jian Cen[1(✉)], Hushan Li[1], Jie Zhao[2], and Lianyue Hu[1]

[1] Guangdong Polytechnic Normal University, Guangzhou 510665, China
986412676@qq.com
[2] Guangzhou Shengneng Electronic Technology Co. LTD., Guangzhou 510100, China

Abstract. In this paper, the video data collected by the monitoring system in the urban underground integrated pipe gallery and the sensor data are independent of each other, which leads to the problem that the information value cannot be fully utilized. A character superposition method based on object detection is proposed. The method uses the sensor data as a character in the video, which solves the problem of information island between sensor data and video data. It is verified by experiments that the accuracy of object detection algorithm proposed by this paper is 13.94% higher than that of traditional target detection algorithm, and the false alarm rate is reduced by 14.29%. It solves the problem of accurate monitoring under the complex environment of urban underground integrated pipe gallery.

Keywords: Object detection · Character superposition · Wisdom pipe gallery

1 Introduction

Urban underground integrated pipe gallery is a new type of urban underground infrastructure, which can effectively reduce the excavation of road surface, release road space, and facilitate the renewal and maintenance of municipal pipelines. But because the pipeline is laid centrally in a unified confined narrow space, it is easy to cause the cascade disaster and safety risk before the pipeline. In order to ensure the long-term stable and safe operation of the urban underground integrated pipe gallery, the new generation of information technology such as Internet, Internet of things, big data and artificial intelligence is used to realize the real-time monitoring, danger alarm, intelligent decision-making and efficient management of the integrated pipe gallery.

During the first industrial revolution in Europe, urbanization led to the outbreak of urban population, and the original urban infrastructure could not adapt to the pace of urbanization [1]. In the intelligent project of urban underground integrated pipe gallery, video monitoring camera will be used to collect some real-time video data and record the video, so as to facilitate the subsequent query and return visit. But currently on the sensor display instrument is a digital instrument, the LED display, refresh rate often do not synchronized with the frequency of the camera, display data such as jitter and network interference, lead to cannot watch video, and after using character superposition technique can realize real-time synchronous display images and data, and can be

J. Ren et al. (Eds.): BICS 2019, LNAI 11691, pp. 322–330, 2020.
https://doi.org/10.1007/978-3-030-39431-8_31

observed through the real-time video review, provide efficient and can watch video resources for post-processing.

Video character superposition technology [2] originated in the 1980s. It is a technology that mixes digital characters or time signals into video signals, so as to display character data at a specific position on the screen. This technology is widely used and plays an important role in video monitoring system. At present, video character superposition technology [3] uses a special integrated circuit to display mixed character signals formed by video signal line, field synchronization signal and character generator at a predetermined time point by controlling the timing relationship. This method requires each camera to be equipped with a character superposition device, and the hardware cost increases with the increase of the number of cameras [19–22]. In addition, designing a set of video processing software using image processing technology can achieve the same function, thus greatly reducing the hardware cost.

2 Principle of Object Detection in Pipe Gallery

Pipe rack target detection principle is to use in the deep learning algorithms will monitor video sensor identification mark, and the real-time data in the database in the form of characters superimposed to the video data, heterogeneous data integration from the pipe rack, display the fusion method compared with the traditional manual inspection methods can save at least half of the time, greatly improving the efficiency of comprehensive pipe gallery management. Considering the obvious color difference between the target to be detected and the background in the pipe gallery environment, the color target area in video frame was firstly extracted by establishing a color model, and then the target area was further classified and identified by using the convolutional neural network. Compared with the traditional image recognition method, the recognition accuracy was higher. There are five stages: input stage, pre-processing stage, identification stage, marking stage and character superposition stage. The target detection schematic diagram to be adopted in this paper is shown in Fig. 1.

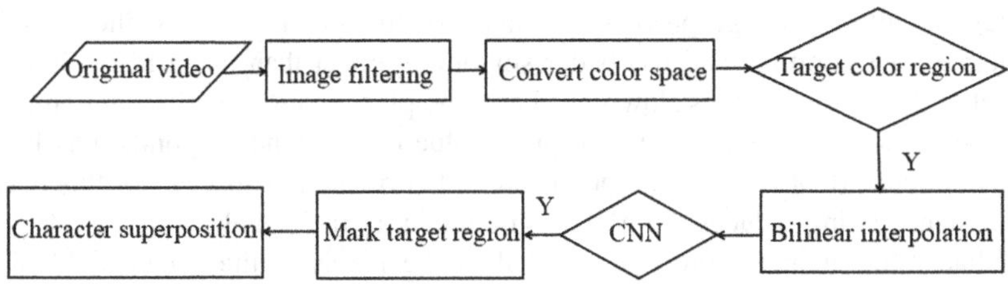

Fig. 1. Schematic diagram of target detection

2.1 Image Preprocessing

Image preprocessing refers to the extraction of image frames in video, and the image frames are processed through a series of processes to obtain the required image to be processed, and then the target detection in the next step is carried out.In this paper, HSV color space [4–6] is used, which is more consistent with human understanding of color than RGB color space. Screenshots of video in RGB space are shown in Fig. 2, and screenshots of video in HSV space are shown in Fig. 3.

Fig. 2. RGB color space

Fig. 3. HSV color space

In the experiment, Hikvision camera was used to read RGB color and then convert RGB color into HSV color. When RGB is converted to HSV in Open CV, the range of value of H channel is [0, 360], while OpenCV uses a byte (8 bits, which can represent 0 to 256) to store H channel, so the range of value of H should be compressed twice to be [0, 180]. The range of other two values are [0, 255].

2.2 Filtering Processing

The video data of the pipe gallery is acquired by using the Hikvision camera, and each frame image is smoothed and filtered:

1. Gaussian filtering image processing. Gaussian filter is a low-pass filter which is suitable for smoothing and has better smoothing effect than mean filter. Since the pixel of the image changes slowly in space, the pixel change of adjacent points will not be particularly obvious, but the pixel value of two random points may have a big difference (that is, the noise points are not correlated in space). For this reason, Gaussian filtering reduces the noise while retaining the signal.
2. Median filtering image processing. Median the pixels in the square field of the center pixel and replace the middle pixel. Mean filtering is very sensitive to large noise images (especially images with large outliers), and even a small number of large differences will lead to large fluctuations of the mean value. Therefore, the selection of median filtering can avoid the influence of these large noises.

Because of the above reasons, this paper selects Gaussian filter and median filter to preprocess the image to make the processed image smoother and reduce noise.

2.3 Color Space Conversion

The formula for converting color space RGB to HSV is as formula (1).

$$
\begin{aligned}
&V = max(R, G, B) \\
&S = \begin{cases} \frac{V - min(R,G,B)}{V}, & V \neq 0 \\ 0, & otherwise \end{cases} \\
&H = \begin{cases} 60(G - B)/(V - min(R, G, B)), & V = R \\ 120 + 60(B - R)/(V - min(R, G, B), & V = G \\ 240 + 60(R - B)/(V - min(R, G, B)), & V = B \end{cases}
\end{aligned}
\tag{1}
$$

In the above formula, R, G and B are red, green and blue channel components in RGB color space, and H, S and V are hue, saturation and value channel components in HSV color space.

2.4 Create Sliders and Threshold Treatments

The slider is created to get the threshold of the target color parameter. This experiment set up a total of eight adjustable parameters are respectively the Hue min, Sat min, Val min and Max Hue, Sat, Max, Max Val, Erode the size, Dilate the size. The return values of the 8 adjustable parameters set above are obtained so as to obtain the parameter interval of the object. Figure 4 shows the parameter adjustment slider.

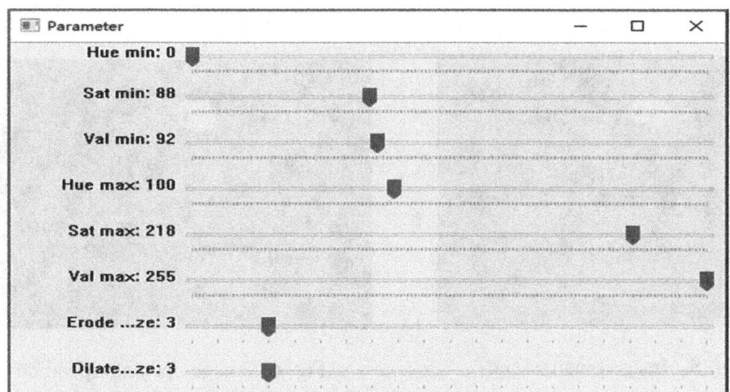

Fig. 4. Parameter adjustment slider

2.5 Image Morphological Processing

The threshold value is set to obtain the binary image of the image, but the obtained image still has some noise. In order to eliminate the noise, the image morphology processing is required next.

In this paper, the image is processed by the open operation in the form of corrosion followed by expansion and morphology. The open operation can remove the outliers outside the target, can obviously remove the noise in the binary image, and obtain the maximum connected target body.

Corrosion refers to the operation that the image is convolved with the kernel of specified size to obtain the local minimum value. Its formula is formula (2).

$$dst(x,y) = min\{src(x+x',y+y')\} \qquad (x',y') \in kernel \tag{2}$$

In the formula, DST represents the output, SRC represents the input, and kernel represents the expansion or corrosion of the nuclear matrix.

Expansion is the reverse of corrosion. The expansion operation calculates the maximum number of pixels in the core region. Its formula is formula (3).

$$dst(x,y) = max\{src(x+x',y+y')\} \tag{3}$$

Corrosion reduces the area, expansion expands the area, corrosion can eliminate the bulge, expansion can fill the cavity. Corrosion is used to eliminate speckle noise in the image and retain large areas in the image. Inflation is used to find connected areas in an image. In this paper, the method of corrosion before expansion can effectively remove the influence of noise and isolated small spots in the image. Figure 5 shows the binarization image, in which it is obvious that there are many small spots. Figure 6 shows the image after open operation. The expansion and corrosion cores used in this paper are both 3 × 3.

Fig. 5. Image binarization

Fig. 6. Image opening operation

2.6 Data Training

Convolutional neural network [7–13] is a kind of feedforward neural network, which is further designed on the basis of ordinary neural network. The special structure of convolutional neural network is used to process two-dimensional data such as image and speech. The network structure diagram of the convolutional neural network used in this paper is shown in Fig. 7.

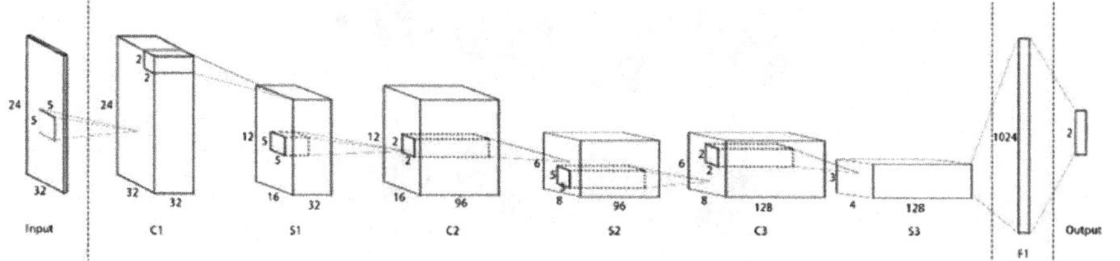

Fig. 7. Schematic diagram of network structure of convolutional neural network

Convolutional neural network generally includes Input layer, convolution layer (C1, C2, C3), pooling layer (S1, S2, S3), full connection layer (F1) and Output layer. The convolutional layer, pooling layer and full connection layer belong to the hidden layer in the neural network [14–19].

The parameter configuration table of the above convolutional neural network is shown in Table 1.

The data set used by CNN for training and testing is the same as the data set used by HOG+SVM method. The image size is 32 × 24 pixels. Adopt the method of random combination of CNN for training, where each randomly selected from a data set of 100 images of the classifier is trained a training set, a total of 5000 sets of data, equivalent to about 500000 images for training, in this way can be achieved using small data set for the purpose of the network, a large number of training. Some images in the data set are shown in Fig. 8.

The results of the comparison experiment in the convolutional neural network are shown in Table 2. The result is the classification effect of the classifier on the test set after half a million times of training in the way of random combination.

Table 1. Network parameter configuration table

Layer	Categories	Feature	Kernel	Step	Output dimension
Input	Input	3	\	\	3 × 32 × 24
C1	Convolution	32	5 × 5	1	32 × 32 × 24
S1	Pooling	32	\	2	32 × 16 × 12
C2	Convolution	96	5 × 5	1	96 × 16 × 12
S2	Pooling	96	\	2	96 × 8 × 6
C3	Convolution	128	5 × 5	1	128 × 8 × 6
S3	Pooling	128	\	2	128 × 4 × 3
F1	Fully connect	Number of neurons: 1024			
F2	Output	Number of neurons: 2			

Through the experiment, it is found that each time 100 pictures are randomly selected for training, and 2000 epochs of training can train the network to a better recognition effect, and the recognition rate of the training set can reach more than 96%.

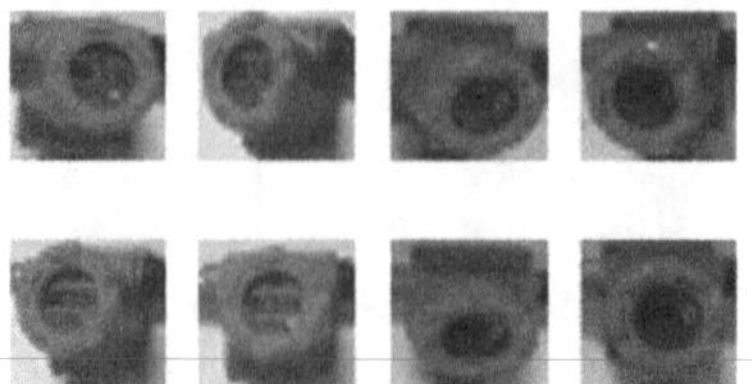

Fig. 8. Partial image of sensor dataset

Table 2. SVM and CNN classification experiment results

Method	Epochs	Training time	Accuracy
HOG+SVM	500000	30 min	65%
CNN	500000	230 min	96%

2.7 Character Superposition

The method of character superposition adopted in this paper uses python language to call OpenCV library to read video data. The target is detected through the target detection box, and then a request is sent to the database. Finally, the requested data is added to video in real time. The putText() function of the OpenCV library is used to write data to video. The results without character superposition are shown in Fig. 9, and the results with character superposition are shown in Fig. 10. Through character superposition, various sensor data of the current environment in the pipe gallery can be displayed in the form of Numbers. Compared with video without character superposition, it is easier to check for abnormalities and find out environmental changes that cannot be observed by the naked eye. Corresponding measures should be taken immediately.

Fig. 9. Result without character superposition

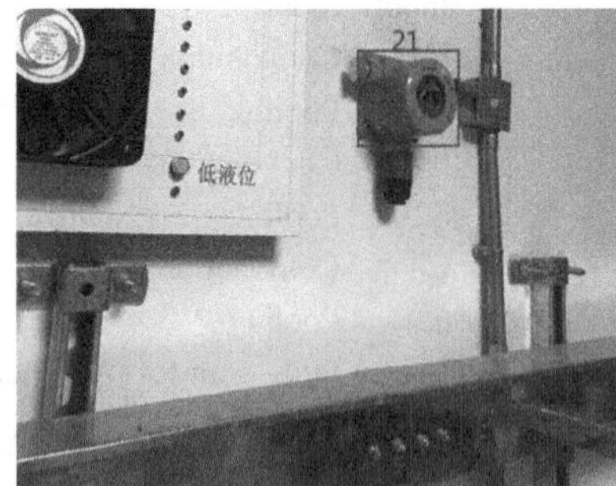

Fig. 10. Result with character superposition

3 The Analysis of Experimental Results

In this paper, the self-produced video data set is used to compare the algorithm in this paper with the traditional HOG+SVM algorithm. The accuracy, false alarm rate, sensitivity and omission rate are used for comparative analysis. Accuracy rate: refers to the proportion of frames with real target in all tested video that are detected. False alarm rate: refers to the proportion of frames that are detected as targets by non-targets in all tested video. The experimental statistical results are shown in Table 3.

Table 3. Experimental statistical results

Algorithm	Accuracy	False alarm rate
HOG+SVM	82.63%	17.72%
HSV+CNN	96.58%	3.48%

The analysis of experimental results:

It can be found from the experimental results of the two groups that the algorithm proposed in this paper has higher accuracy and lower false alarm rate than the traditional target detection algorithm.

4 Conclusion

The target detection algorithm for urban underground pipe gallery designed in this paper has better performance than the traditional target detection algorithm in classification recognition rate. It can detect the video with the presence of the target more accurately, and the detection of video can achieve the real-time effect basically.

Acknowledgment. This work was supported by the science and technology major project of education department of Guangdong province (2017KZDXM052), the Guangdong science and technology major project (2017B030305004).

References

1. Zhao, Q.: Current situation of construction of intelligent comprehensive pipe gallery at home and abroad. Urban Arch. (32), 79–81 (2018)
2. Wu, S.: Application of video superposition technology in intelligent engineering. Intell. Build. (02), 58–60 (2018)
3. Tian, J., Wang, W., Sun, Y.: A video superposition Chinese character recognition method without binarization. J. Chin. Acad. Sci. **35**(03), 402–408 (2008)
4. Zhou, J.: Underwater moving target extraction based on HSV color space. Comput. Knowl. Technol. **14**(21), 230–232 (2008)
5. Peng, M., Wang, J., Wen, X., Cong, X.: Detection of water surface image features based on HSV space. Chin. J. Image Graph. **23**(04), 526–533 (2008)

6. Tian, C., Xian, Y., Xia, J.: Method for detection and shadow removal of water targets based on HSV space. Chin. Foreign Ship Sci. Technol. (04), 34–38 (2017)
7. Hinton, G.E., Srivastava, N., Krizhevsky, A., et al.: Improving neural networks by preventing co-adaptation of feature detectors. arXiv preprint arXiv:1207.0580,2012
8. Zhou, F., Jin, L., Dong, J.: Research review of convolutional neural networks. Acta Computica Sinica 1–23 (2017)
9. Krizhevsky, A., Sutskever, I., Hinton, G.E.: ImageNet classification with deep convolutional neural networks. In: Proceedings of NIPS, pp. 1097–1105 (2012)
10. Szegedy, C.: Going deeper with convolutions. In: Proceedings of IEEE Computer Society Conference on Computer Vision and Pattern Recognition, pp. 1–9 (2015)
11. Lei, F., Dai, Q., Cai, J., Zhao, H., Liu, X., Liu, Y.: A proactive caching strategy based on deep learning in EPC of 5G. In: Ren, J., et al. (eds.) BICS 2018. LNCS, vol. 10989, pp. 738–747. Springer, Cham (2018). https://doi.org/10.1007/978-3-030-00563-4_72
12. Lei, F., Cai, J., Dai, Q., et al.: Deep learning based proactive caching for effective WSN-enabled vision applications. Complexity **2019**, 12 (2019)
13. Lei, F.Y., Cai, J.: EIWCS: characterizing edges importance to weaken community structure. In: Applied Mechanics and Materials, vol. 556 pp. 6054–6057. Trans Tech Publications (2014)
14. Yan, Y., et al.: Unsupervised image saliency detection with Gestalt-laws guided optimization and visual attention based refinement. Pattern Recogn. **79**, 65–78 (2018)
15. AlKhateeb, J.H., et al.: Knowledge-based baseline detection and optimal thresholding for words segmentation in efficient pre-processing of handwritten Arabic text. In: Fifth International Conference on Information Technology: New Generations (ITNG 2008). IEEE (2008)
16. Zheng, J., et al.: Fusion of block and keypoints based approaches for effective copy-move image forgery detection. Multidimens. Syst. Signal Process. **27**(4), 989–1005 (2016)
17. Ren, J., Vlachos, T.: Efficient detection of temporally impulsive dirt impairments in archived films. Sig. Process. **87**(3), 541–551 (2007)
18. Yan, Y., et al.: Cognitive fusion of thermal and visible imagery for effective detection and tracking of pedestrians in videos. Cogn. Comput. **10**(1), 94–104 (2018)
19. Wang, Z., et al.: A deep-learning based feature hybrid framework for spatiotemporal saliency detection inside videos. Neurocomputing **287**, 68–83 (2018)
20. Han, J., Zhang, D., Cheng, G., Guo, L., Ren, J.: Object detection in optical remote sensing images based on weakly supervised learning and high-level feature learning. IEEE Trans. Geosci. Remote Sens. **53**(6), 3325–3337 (2014)
21. Han, J., Zhang, D., Hu, X., Guo, L., Ren, J., Wu, F.: Background prior-based salient object detection via deep reconstruction residual. IEEE Trans. Circuits Syst. Video Technol. **25**(8), 1309–1321 (2014)
22. Ren, J., et al.: Multi-camera video surveillance for real-time analysis and reconstruction of soccer games. Mach. Vis. Appl. **21**(6), 855–863 (2010)

Blind Detection Based on Color SIFT

Tingge Zhu[1(✉)], Jiangbin Zheng[1], Mingchen Feng[1], Jinchang Ren[2], and Weihua Liu[3,4]

[1] Department of Computer Science and Engineering, School of Computers, Northwestern Polytechnical University, Xi'an, China
tgzhu@xupt.edu.cn, zhengjb0163@163.com, mingchen@mail.nwpu.edu.cn

[2] Department of Electronic and Electrical Engineering, University of Strathclyde, Glasgow, UK
jinchang.ren@strath.ac.uk

[3] School of Communication and Information Engineering, Xi'an University of Posts and Telecommunications, Xi'an, Shaanxi, China
liuweihua201@xupt.edu.cn

[4] Key Laboratory of Electronic Information Processing Technology for Crime Scene Investigation Application, Ministry of Public Security, Xi'an, China

Abstract. Blind detection algorithm based on keypoints has a small amount of computation and faster speed, however, its accuracy is lower, comparing with blind detection based on block. One factor is that keypoints are extracted in a grayscale image, which leads to loss of the color information of the image. In order to solve it, this paper proposes a novel blind detection algorithm based on key point image. Firstly, an image is changed from RGB space to HSV space, the color local binary patterns feature of each pixel is computed based on the HSV image. Then keypoints are extracted from the color local binary patterns image. which also carry color information. Then the nearest neighbors are used to find matching keypoints in all keypoints. Finally, wrong matching is filtered by the angle between matching points and morphology operations are used to come into being a forgery detection map to locate the tampered regions. Experimental results show that the proposed method based on color scale-invariant feature transform keypoint outperforms these methods based on traditional scale-invariant feature transform keypoint in the reliability of detection and the block-based method in efficiency.

Keywords: Color LBP · Color SIFT Keypoint · Blind detection

1 Introduction

With the development of image processing technology, anyone can easily edit image content without leaving any perceptible artifacts. If the editing of the image is malicious, it will cause a series of very bad social effects. Therefore, more and more researchers have begun to focus on image forgery detection, and many methods have been proposed [1]. Copy-move forgery is one of the most common image forgeries,

J. Ren et al. (Eds.): BICS 2019, LNAI 11691, pp. 331–341, 2020.
https://doi.org/10.1007/978-3-030-39431-8_32

wherein one or more region have been copied and pasted within the same image [2–4]. many blind methods, over the last decade, have been proposed for copy-move forgery. In general, they are divided into two major categories: block-based and keypoint-based methods.

Block-based approaches divide an image into overlapping or non-overlapping blocks and extract block feature. Similar blocks are searched among all blocks. Finally, tampered regions are located. Hayat et al. [5] proposed a blind detection method after DWT transform and an image is divided into many blocks. Then DCT is applied to the individual blocks, and they are compared based on correlation coefficients. In [6] an image is segmented based on color to achieve blur invariance, and search tampered regions by employing stationary wavelet transform (SWT) and singular value decomposition (SVD). Zhong et al. [7] extracted the feature of the overlapped circular blocks by the Discrete Radial Harmonic Fourier Moments (DRHFMs) and 2 Nearest Neighbors (2NN) is employed to search the similar feature vectors of blocks by test. These methods have a common drawback, which is heavy time-consumption. So many dimensionality reduction methods are used to speed up detection. For instance, principal component analysis (PCA) in [8], block clustering in [9], and so on. However, these methods based on block matching are still inferior to keypoint-based ones in term of time-consumption.

Many keypoint-based methods are proposed in recent years. These methods [10, 11] firstly detect keypoints, and then similar keypoints are searched in all keypoints. For keypoint-based approaches, a lower computation cost is usually acquired because of a sharp drop in the number of points, compared to the number of blocks proposed in the block-based method. In general, SIFT(Scale-invariant feature transform) and SURF (Speed up robust features) keypoints are employed. In [12–14, 24], these methods employ SIFT (SURF) keypoints to locate tampered regions based on different keypoint matching method. In [15] adaptive over-segmentation and keypoints matching are used to detect tampered regions. In these methods. Because of Few keypoints in smooth regions, so their detection accuracy is lower than block-based method's. In order to solve it, in [16, 17], a two-stage detection method is proposed. Yu et al. [16] use Harris corners and extract multi-support region order-based gradient histogram and hue histogram descriptors to detect tampered regions. Emam et al. [17] employ SIFT keypoints from the textured regions and Harris corner keypoints from non- textured regions to raise detection accuracy. Although these algorithms can locate the matched keypoints in detecting the duplicated regions, they all use the pure gray-based detectors to extract keypoints where the significant color information is ignored, which lead to lower accuracy.

In this paper, firstly, an image is pre-processed, which is change from RGB to HSV, and then we compute color LBP of every pixel to achieve color LBP image. We extract SITF points from HSV image by employing the SIFT detector. Then similar points are searched in all keypoints. Finally, wrong matching is filtered by the angle between matching points and morphology operations are used to come into being a forgery detection map to locate the tampered regions.

2 The Proposed Method

Most of the feature points are extracted in the grayscale image, and the color information of the image is lost. In order to solve this problem, an image is preprocessed before feature points are extracted. Firstly, an image is transformed from the RGB space to the HSV space, then color local binary pattern(LBP) is computed. So we get a color LBP image, and we extract feature points from the color LBP image, which also carry color information. Then similarity matching is performed on feature points. Wrong matching is filtered by the angle between matching points. Finally, morphology operations are used to come into being a forgery detection map to locate the tampered regions. The technical implementation of the proposed approach is presented in detail as follows (see Fig. 1).

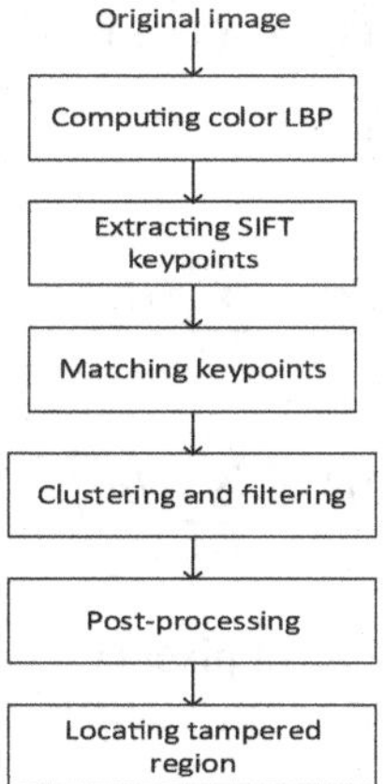

Fig. 1. The flow of the proposed method

2.1 Color LBP

In an image, the distribution of grayscale is similar between some regions, but the distribution of color is different. Mismatching may occur when we employ blind detection algorithms based on keypoints, such as SIFT features and surf features, which extracted in the grayscale image. According to [18] and [19], we compute the color LBP feature of an image with color and texture information. It not only retains the three channels of color image information but also extracts the LBP texture features, so that it achieves a balance between color information and computation, as well as a higher accuracy of feature extraction and matching.

Firstly, an image I is transformed from the RGB space to the HSV space, Let each channel of the normalized HSV image be $HC_i(i = 1, 2, 3)$. We compute $CoLBP(x, y)$ of every pixel (x, y) to get color LBP image. Here, $HC_i^j\ (i = 1, 2, 3; j = 1, 2 \ldots 8)$ represent the value of the ith channel of the jth point in the neighborhood of the pixel (x, y). $HC_i^0(i = 1, 2, 3)$ represent the value of three channels of the pixel (x, y). As shown in Fig. 2.

HC_1^1 HC_2^1 HC_3^1	HC_1^2 HC_2^2 HC_3^2	HC_1^3 HC_2^3 HC_3^3
HC_1^4 HC_2^4 HC_3^4	HC_1^0 HC_2^0 HC_3^0 (x, y)	HC_1^5 HC_2^5 HC_3^5
HC_1^6 HC_2^6 HC_3^6	HC_1^7 HC_2^7 HC_3^7	HC_1^8 HC_2^8 HC_3^8

(a) The neighborhood of the pixel (x, y)

2^7	2^6	2^5
2^4	(x, y)	2^3
2^2	2^1	2^0

(b) weight

Fig. 2. Color LBP

Let TH and $TH_j (j = 1, 2 \ldots 8)$ be

$$TH = \sum_{i=1}^{3} (HC_i^0)^2 \tag{1}$$

$$TH_j = \sum_{i=1}^{3} (HC_i^j)^2 \tag{2}$$

If the jth point in the neighborhood of pixel (x, y) satisfies the following conditions. Then we can get T_j of the jth point.

$$T_j = \begin{cases} 1 & if\ TH_j \geq TH \\ 0 & if\ TH_j < TH \end{cases} \tag{3}$$

According to the weight, we compute $CoLBP(x, y)$ of each pixel as follows to get color LBP image with color and texture information. As seen in Fig. 3.

$$CoLBP(x, y) = \sum_{j=1}^{8} T_j \times 2^{8-j} \tag{4}$$

(a) Original image

(b) Color LBP image of (a)

Fig. 3. Color LBP image

2.2 SIFT Keypoint Extraction and Matching

The traditional SIFT feature is extracted in the grayscale image, and the proposed algorithm is used to extract SIFT feature in the color LBP image with color and texture. Figure 4 shows the two extraction methods. We can see that the traditional SIFT feature extraction has few SIFT feature points in the smooth region, but the color LBP image can do.

(a) Color SIFT (b) Traditional SIFT

Fig. 4. Comparison of two feature extraction methods

$P = \{p_k, k = 1, 2 \ldots n\}$ is a set of all SIFT keypoints. Then the g2NN strategy [4] is used to find matching keypoints in all keypoints. Euclidean distance between two SIFT keypoints is calculated and form a distance vector set. Let *dis* be the distance set sorted in lexicographic sort and $dis = \left\{d_1, d_2, d_3 \ldots d_{n \times (n-1)}\right\}$, where n is the number of SIFT keypoints. Suppose d_i and d_{i+1} be two adjacent distance vectors in *dis*. Candidate matched feature points are these feature points which satisfy the following inequality.

$$\frac{d_i}{d_{i+1}} < Td, i = 1, 2, \ldots n \times (n-1) \tag{5}$$

Let k be the maximum value of i which satisfies the above formula. $Simd = \{d_1, d_2, \ldots d_k\}$ represents the set which that satisfies the above formula. Here, according to [12], Td is empirically set to 0.

2.3 Clustering and Filtering

Suppose p_a and p_b are the matching point pairs of any distance vector $d_i (i = 1, 2 \ldots k)$ in *Simd*, accordingly their coordinates are (x_a, y_a) and (x_b, y_b) respectively. Let the Angle between their line and the horizontal axis be θ_i (See Fig. 5). $S\theta = \{\theta_1, \theta_2, \ldots \theta_k\}$ is a set which represents all θ_i. $S\theta$ are sorted in descending order. Let $S\theta' = \{\theta'_1, \theta'_2, \ldots \theta'_k\}$ represent the sorted set. If θ'_i and θ'_{i+1} satisfy the following formula.

$$\theta'_i - \theta'_{i+1} < T\theta \tag{6}$$

The corresponding keypoints belong to the same class. So we can get $2t$ $(t < k)$ classes. $nt_i(i = 1, 2, \ldots 2t)$ is the number of the ith class. According to [16], if $nt_i < 3$, these keypoints belonging to the ith class are removed. Thereby, the false matching is removed. As shown in Fig. 6a and b $T\theta$ is an empirical value, which is set to 0.01.

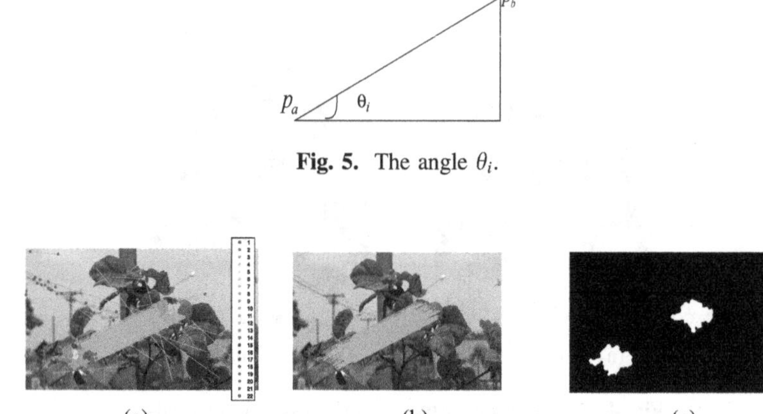

Fig. 5. The angle θ_i.

(a) (b) (c)

Fig. 6. A detection example

2.4 Post-processing

Although the match point pairs are found, they are very sparse. So as the final step, post-processing is needed to locate tampered regions. Morphology operations are used to come into being a forgery detection map to locate the tampered regions (see Fig. 6c).

3 Experimental Results and Discussions

In this section, we evaluate the performance of the proposed approach. Our algorithm was implemented on a computer (Intel 2.10 GHz processor, 16 GB RAM) using Matlab2016a. Details about the database, evaluation metrics, and performance of the proposed scheme under different circumstances can be found in the following subsection.

3.1 Databases

We use two databases to evaluate the performance of the proposed scheme. The first database is provided by Christlein et al. [4], which can be downloaded from [20]. The second database is the CoMoFoD_small_v2 database presented in [21]. It consists of 200 image sets with 512 × 512. The image region(s) are selected for duplication range from smooth to highly textured. The duplicated region can vary in size (e.g., small, medium, or large) and in quantity (e.g., one, or more). In summary, the total number of images with post-processed images is 10400.

3.2 Evaluation Metrics

As most of the literature, we use precision, recall and F_1 to quantitatively evaluate the performance. They are defined as follows:

$$Precision = \frac{T_p}{T_p + F_p} \times 100\% \quad (7)$$

$$Recall = \frac{T_p}{T_p + F_N} \times 100\% \quad (8)$$

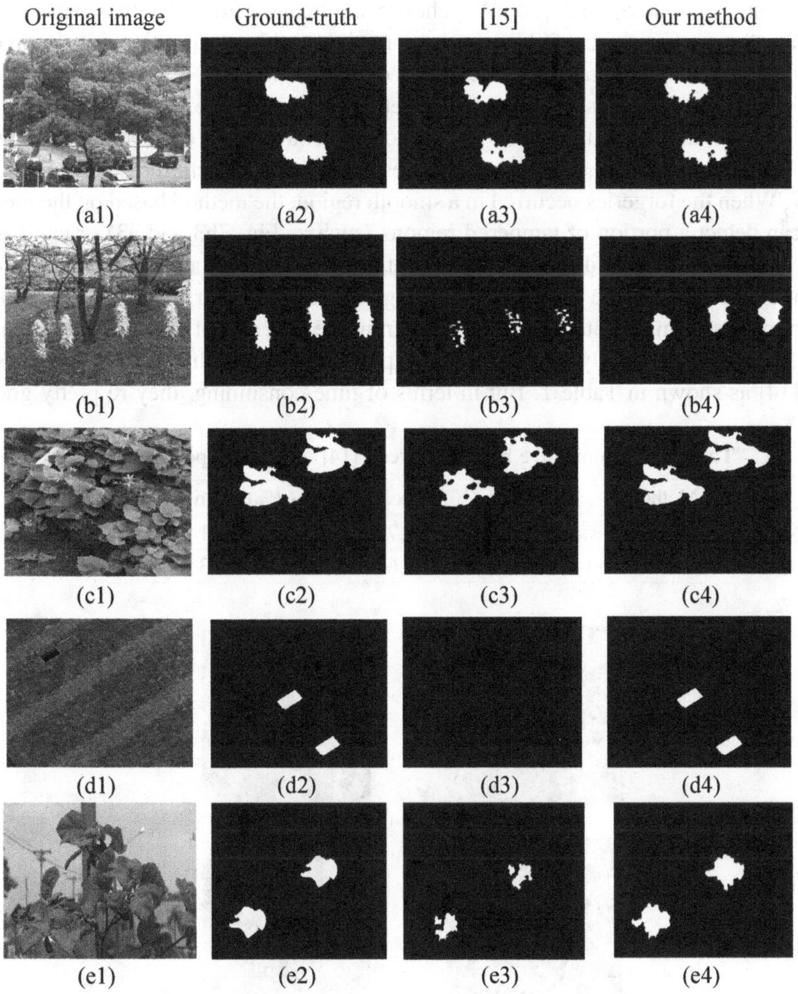

Fig. 7. Detection results of [14] scheme and the proposed scheme. From left to right, the four columns show the test images, ground truth, and detected results using [14] scheme, Zernike moments method and our proposed scheme, respectively.

$$F_1 = \frac{2 \times precision \times recall}{precision + recall} \quad (9)$$

Where T_p, F_p and F_N are the number of correctly identified pixels, the number of mistakenly detected pixels and the number of missed pixels, respectively. F_1 is a trade-off between precision and recall. The higher Precious, Recall and F_N, the more superior performance.

3.3 Experimental Results for Plain Tampered Operation and Discussions

In fact, most of the tampered image are visually indistinguishable, and the tampered regions are smooth or textured. We choose all images from the two databases to evaluate the performance of the proposed method, without applying any geometric distortions or image degradation operations on cloned regions.

Since original images in the first dataset have a large size, block-based methods don't work on the first database. So the proposed method is just compared with method [14]. We test our method without post-processing. Part of detection results is shown in Fig. 7. When the forgeries occurred in a smooth region, the method based on the method [14] can detect a portion of tampered regions (such as Fig. 7b3 and e3) or can't work (such as Fig. 7c3). It is due to that few feature points can be extracted from smooth regions, as shown in the second row of Fig. 8. However, our method can extracted feature points from smooth regions, as shown in the first row of Fig. 8. And compared with [14], they are evenly distributed. The proposed method has better detect results than [14] as shown in Table 1. But in terms of time-consuming, they're pretty good.

Table 1. Comparative results between [14] and the proposed method

Methods	Precision (%)	Recall (%)	F_1 (%)	Run time (s)
[14]	86.31	87.73	87.01	121
Our method	94.53	91.68	93.08	103

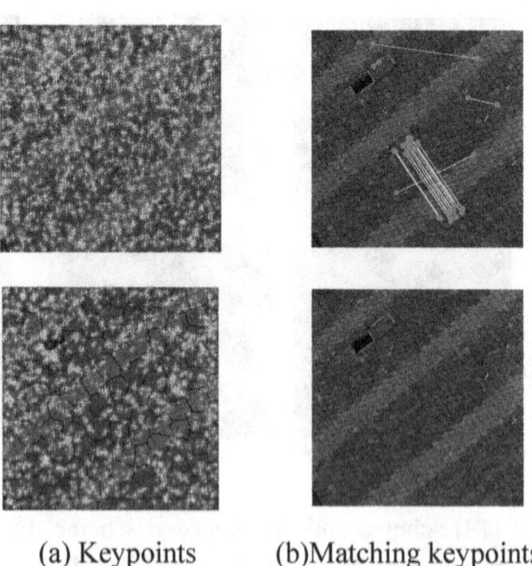

(a) Keypoints (b)Matching keypoints

Fig. 8. Keypoints and matching keypoints

3.4 Experimental Results for Post-processing Detection and Discussions

The two datasets provide tampered images with post-processing operation, such as blurring, rotation, scaling, noise and so on. our method can detection scaling, rotation, contrast adjustment, and combination attack. As seen Fig. 9. The proposed method can resist these attacks. We test dozens of these images. Their average precision, recall, and F_1 are 84.1, 82.7 and 83.39 respectively. In addition, keypoint extraction in the smooth region is not ideal. So our method doesn't resist the other attacks, such as noise, JPEG compression and so on.

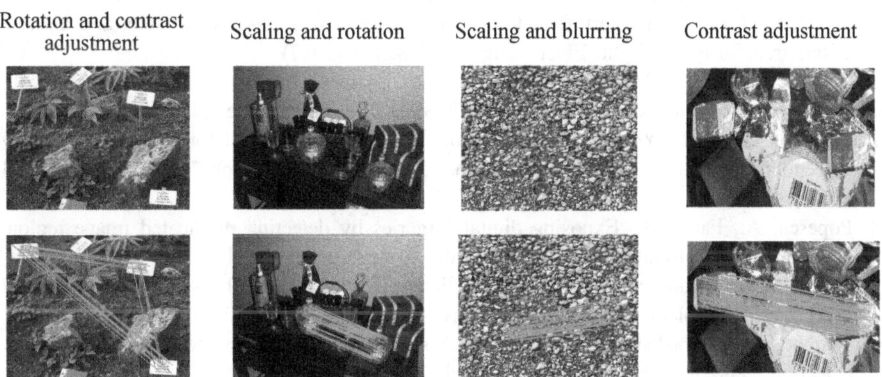

Fig. 9. Detection results with post-processing

4 Conclusion

This paper presents a novel image forgery detection approach based on color SIFT. An image is changed from RGB space to HSV space, and color LBP feature of every pixel is computed. In this way, we get a color LBP image. SIFT keypoints are extracted based on the color LBP image. Because SIFT feature can carry color information, so tampered regions are effectively located. But the proposed algorithm is less resistant to noise and JPEG compression attacks. In addition, most blind detection algorithms can't detect many tampering operations, in the same way, the proposed method can only detect the two combination attacks. Considering there are a few keypoins in smooth regions, in future work, we will study how to extract more keypoints in smooth regions to achieve the purpose of detecting various image tampering methods [23], or new approaches for feature extraction [24, 25], feature fusion [26] and feature tracking [27] as well as saliency based feature learning [28–30] and optimization [31].

Acknowledgment. The author would like to acknowledge the financial support of the following research grants: Grant No. 2018GABJC39 from Special project of science and technology foundation of the ministry of public security; and Grant No. 2018GY-135 from Key Research and Development Project of Shaanxi Science and Technology.

References

1. Dixit, R., Naskar, R.: Review, analysis and parameterization of techniques for copy-move forgery detection in digital images. IET Image Proc. **11**(9), 746–759 (2017)
2. Soni, B., Das, P.K., Thounaojam, D.M.: CMFD: a detailed review of block-based and key feature based techniques in image copy-move forgery detection. IET Image Proc. **12**(2), 167–178 (2018)
3. Manjunatha, S., Patil, M.: A survey on image forgery detection techniques. Digit. Image Process. **9**(5), 103–108 (2017)
4. Christlein, V., Riess, C., Jordan, J., et al.: An evaluation of popular copy-move forgery detection approaches. IEEE Trans. Inf. Forensics Secur. **7**(6), 1841–1854 (2012)
5. Hayat, K., Qazi, T.: Forgery detection in digital images via discrete wavelet and discrete cosine transforms. Comput. Electr. Eng. **62**, 448–458 (2017)
6. Dixit, R., Naskar, R., Mishra, S.: Blur-invariant copy-move forgery detection technique with improved detection accuracy utilizing SWT-SVD. IET Image Proc. **11**(5), 301–309 (2017)
7. Zhong, J., Gan, Y., Young, J., et al.: A new block-based method for copy-move forgery detection under image geometric transforms. Multimed. Tools Appl. **76**(13), 14887–14903 (2017)
8. Popescu, A., Farid, H.: Exposing digital forgeries by detecting duplicated image region. Department of Computer Science, Dartmouth College, USA (2004)
9. Sekeh, M.A., Maarof, M., Rohani, M.: Efficient image duplicated region detection model using sequential block clustering. Digit. Investig. **10**(1), 73–84 (2013)
10. Warbhe, A., Dharaskar, R., Thakare, V.: A survey on keypoint based copy-paste forgery detection techniques. Procedia Comput. Sci. **78**, 61–67 (2016)
11. Chauhan, D., Kasat, D., Jain, S., Thakare, V.: Survey on keypoint based copy-move forgery detection methods on image. Procedia Comput. Sci. **85**, 206–212 (2016)
12. Amerini, I., Ballan, L., Caldelli, R.: A SIFT-based forensic method for copy-move attack detection and transformation recovery. IEEE Trans. Inf. Forensics Secur. **6**(3), 1099–1110 (2011)
13. Amerini, I., Ballan, L., Caldelli, R., Bimbo, A., Tongo, L., Serra, G.: Copy-move forgery detection and localization by means of robust clustering with J-Linkage. Sig. Process. Image Commun. **28**(6), 659–669 (2013)
14. Manu, V.T., Mehtre, B.M.: Detection of copy-move forgery in images using segmentation and SURF. Advances in Signal Processing and Intelligent Recognition Systems. AISC, vol. 425, pp. 645–654. Springer, Cham (2016). https://doi.org/10.1007/978-3-319-28658-7_55
15. Pun, C., Yuan, X., Bi, X.: Image forgery detection using adaptive over segmentation and feature point matching. IEEE Trans. Inf. Forensics Secur. **10**(8), 1705–1716 (2015)
16. Yu, L., Han, Q., Niu, X.: Feature point-based copy-move forgery detection: covering the non-textured areas. Multimed. Tools Appl. **75**(2), 1159–1176 (2016)
17. Emam, M., Han, Q., Zhang, H.: Two-stage keypoint detection scheme for region duplication forgery detection in digital images. J. Forensic Sci. **63**(1), 101–111 (2018)
18. Porebski, A., Nicolas, V., Macaire, L.: Haralick feature extraction from LBP images for color texture classification. In: 2008 First Workshops on Image Processing Theory, Tools and Applications, Sousse, pp. 1–8 (2008). https://doi.org/10.1109/ipta.2008.4743780
19. Silva, E., Carvalho, T., Ferreira, A., Rocha, A.: Going deeper into copy-move forgery detection: exploring image telltales via multi-scale analysis and voting processes. J. Vis. Commun. Image Represent. **29**, 16–32 (2015)
20. http://www5.cs.fau.de/research/data/image-manipulation/

21. Tralic, D., Zupancic, I., Grgic, S.: CoMoFoD-new database for copy-move forgery detection. In: IEEE International Symposium, pp. 49–54 (2013)
22. Zhao, F., Fan, J., Liu, H., Lan, R., Chen, C.: Noise-robust multi-objective evolutionary clustering image segmentation motivated by intuitionistic fuzzy information. IEEE Trans. Fuzzy Syst. **27**(2), 387–401 (2019)
23. Zheng, J., et al.: Fusion of block and keypoints based approaches for effective copy-move image forgery detection. Multidimens. Syst. Signal Process. **27**(4), 989–1005 (2016)
24. Ren, J., Vlachos, T.: Efficient detection of temporally impulsive dirt impairments in archived films. Sig. Process. **87**(3), 541–551 (2007)
25. Zhou, Y., et al.: Hierarchical visual perception and two-dimensional compressive sensing for effective content-based color image retrieval. Cogn. Comput. **8**(5), 877–889 (2016)
26. Yan, Y., et al.: Cognitive fusion of thermal and visible imagery for effective detection and tracking of pedestrians in videos. Cogn. Comput. **10**(1), 94–104 (2018)
27. Ren, J., et al.: Multi-camera video surveillance for real-time analysis and reconstruction of soccer games. Mach. Vis. Appl. **21**(6), 855–863 (2010)
28. Wang, Z., et al.: A deep-learning based feature hybrid framework for spatiotemporal saliency detection inside videos. Neurocomputing **287**, 68–83 (2018)
29. Han, J., et al.: Object detection in optical remote sensing images based on weakly supervised learning and high-level feature learning. IEEE Trans. Geosci. Remote Sens. **53**(6), 3325–3337 (2014)
30. Yan, Y., et al.: Unsupervised image saliency detection with Gestalt-laws guided optimization and visual attention based refinement. Pattern Recogn. **79**, 65–78 (2018)
31. Sun, G., et al.: A stability constrained adaptive alpha for gravitational search algorithm. Knowl.-Based Syst. **139**, 200–213 (2018)

Evaluation of Deep Learning and Conventional Approaches for Image Steganalysis

Guoliang Xie[1], Jinchang Ren[1(✉)], Huimin Zhao[2], Sophia Zhao[1], and Stephen Marshall[1]

[1] Department of Electronic and Electrical Engineering, University of Strathclyde, Glasgow, UK
jinchang.ren@strath.ac.uk

[2] School of Computer Science, Guangdong Polytechnic Normal University, Guangzhou, People's Republic of China

Abstract. Steganography is the technique that's used to embed secret messages into digital media without changing their appearances. As a countermeasure to steganography, steganalysis detects the presence of hidden data in a digital content. For the last decade, the majority of image steganalysis approaches can be formed by two stages. The first stage is to extract effective features from the image content and the second is to train a classifier in machine learning by using the features from stage one. Ultimately the image steganalysis becomes a binary classification problem. Since Deep Learning related architecture unify these two stages and save researchers lots of time designing hand-crafted features, the design of a CNN-based steganalyzer has therefore received increasing attention over the past few years. In this paper, we will examine the development in image steganalysis, both in spatial domain and in JPEG domain, and discuss the future directions.

Keywords: Steganalysis · Deep-learning · Feature extractor

1 Introduction

Image steganography is the method for communicating secret messages under the cover images, which needs a cover source, a secret message and a secure steganographic scheme that hides the secret message under the cover source. Once a cover image is embedded with the secret message, it becomes a stego image. Usually the change of embedding is extremely subtle that people can't differentiate between a cover image and a stego image by their looks.

During the last decade, many adaptive steganographic algorithms have been proposed to hide secret messages inside carriers, which are much difficult to detect. Such algorithms can be found in spatial domain, for example, MiPOD [1], S-UNIWARD [2], HILL [3], WOW [4] and HUGO [5]. And in frequency domain or JPEG domain, J-UNIWARD [2] and UED-JC [6] are the recently developed adaptive steganographic algorithm. When designing such algorithm, the objective is to provide an approach that changes the cover image as litter as possible.

J. Ren et al. (Eds.): BICS 2019, LNAI 11691, pp. 342–352, 2020.
https://doi.org/10.1007/978-3-030-39431-8_33

Image steganalysis, on the other hand, is the method used for analyzing whether an image is a cover image or a stego one. Overall, image steganalysis can be divided into two different types, the first is called specific steganalysis and the second is called universal steganalysis. Specific steganalysis means a steganalysis method is designed for a designated steganographic method. While universal steganalysis means it works for any steganographic method in a specific domain. Since specific steganalysis is no-longer updated for the last decade, we will focus on universal steganalysis only in this paper, both in spatial and JPEG domain.

In this paper, we will divide the universal image steganalysis into conventional image steganalysis and deep-learning based image steganalysis. To avoid confusion, we defined conventional image steganalysis as: using hand-crafted feature extractors to produce features from images for training the classifiers in machine learning. In conventional image steganalysis, statistical features are usually used in training the classifiers while in deep-learning based methods, features are learned automatically by Neural Networks.

Figure 1 shows the comparison of the structures between conventional methods and deep-learning based methods, and the figure is extracted from Qian's work [25]. For a better comparison between conventional steganalysis and deep learning based steganalysis, we further divide the two-stage into three parts in Fig. 1. As Fig. 1 suggests, a conventional steganalysis technique is consist of pre-processing part, feature representation part and classification part. Researchers need to find out how to combine these three parts effectively to make a good steganalyzer. Although a deep-learning based technique is also composed of three parts, they are in fact inside the same architecture.

Starting from 2015 [25], researchers began to focus more on deep-learning based image steganalysis methods as effective conventional hand-crafted feature extractors becomes more and more difficult to design, and conventional methods tend to have large dimensionalities in their features, which makes the computation difficult. Deep-learning based methods, however, merge the pre-processing part (image processing layer), feature extraction part (convolutional layer) and classification part (fully connected layer) into a complete convolutional neural network. These networks have helped the researchers saving lots of time finding the effective feature extraction techniques as the networks themselves would do so automatically. Besides, deep-learning based methods are usually performed on GPUs (Graphics Processing Unit, GPU), which makes the computation much faster than the ones that uses CPUs [7].

2 Conventional Universal Image Steganalysis

2.1 Conventional Universal Image Steganalysis in Spatial Domain

Due to space limitation, our survey will start with SPAM feature [8], which was a powerful feature extractor in spatial domain. In this paper, the authors believed the secret messages can be regarded as addictive noise to the cover images, and they modeled the "local dependences" in cover image as a Markov chain. The empirical probability transition matrixes in Markov chain are used as features to train the SVMs.

Later, Fridrich et al. [9] proposed a model called Spatial Rich model (SRM), which used linear and nonlinear high-pass filters to acquire stego signal and resulting in a large feature vector compared to SPAM. Besides, they proposed to use ensemble classifiers [10] as the steganalyzer owing to its superior time performance compared to the SVMs, while its performance was competitive to the linear kernel SVMs. From then on, researchers mainly use ensemble classifiers proposed in [10] to verify their proposed methods, whose featural dimensionalities are relatively large, such as [11–14].

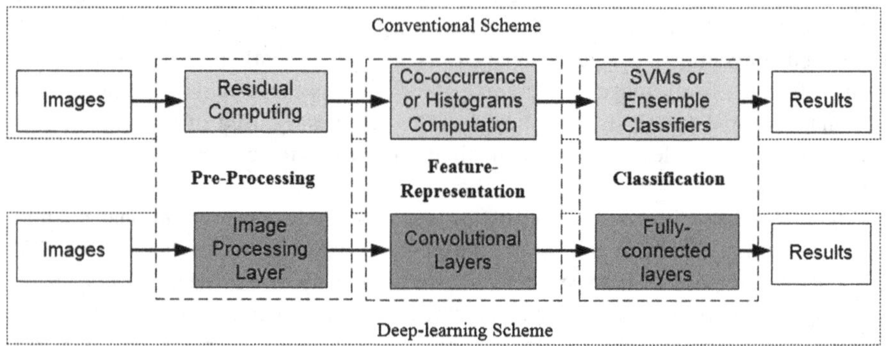

Fig. 1. Framework comparison between conventional methods (up) and deep-learning based methods (down).

Instead of using the co-occurrence matrix as in [9], Holub et al. projected residuals of the images onto a set of random vectors and this method is called PSRM (Projection Spatial Rich model) [12]. The method surpassed SRM in accuracy while reducing featural dimensionality. Besides, this method can be used in JPEG domain, just as SRM.

In paper [12, 13], the authors had found that by using the so called "Selection channel" in steganalysis, detection accuracy can be further improved, and Boroumand et al. [36] also proved it useful by using this technique in deep-learning based methods later. The "Selection channel" is in fact the probabilities of the elements in cover images that being modified. By far, the maxSRM proposed in [13] is the most effective conventional feature extractor for image steganalysis.

Later, Li et al. [14] also proposed an effective approach based on "Threshold LBP (Local Binary Pattern) Operation" in 2017. In this paper, although the authors still use co-occurrence matrix to characterize pixel relationship, they found that TLBP operation may be complementary to it in capturing local features. The results had proved that the TLBP is competitive to SRM, although it had not exceeded maxSRM in performance.

2.2 Conventional Universal Image Steganalysis in JPEG Domain

In frequency domain, the images are usually compressed and coded according to some predefined transformation rules, and when performing image steganalysis in frequency domain, the transformation rules have to be considered. In real world application, the

JPEG format is the most common image format, which adopts discrete cosine transform to compress the images.

Since the modern adaptive steganographic schemes, such as J-UNIWARD [2], Uniform Embedding Distortion (UED) [6], would not "introduce easily detected artifacts" in DCT coefficients, these techniques can be better detected using Machine Learning instead of designing the specific steganalysis scheme.

Starting from Chen's feature extractor in JPEG domain [15], whose scheme was classic and effective. They proposed to use both the "intrablock and interblock correlations" of the coefficients in JPEG images as features to train classifiers, where "interblock" means the JPEG coefficients in the same place in a 8×8 blocks and this correlation can be used. And we can capture the "intrablock correlation" by transition probability matrices of difference JPEG 2-D arrays using Markov processes.

"Calibration" is the technique that helps to improve the accuracy both in JPEG and spatial image steganalysis by "providing the steganalyst with a reference image". Although Calibration was first proposed in 2002 by Fridrich et al. [16], Kodovsky provides more detail in [17] to reveal the benefit of this technique and shows that it may have no benefit at all. By using the calibration technique, Liu's method [18] managed to surpass the CC-PEV (Cartesian calibration, CC) technique proposed in [17] in terms of accuracy.

As high-dimensional representation of images can provide better capability in capturing the complex features, Kodovský et al. proposed their first high-dimensional rich model in JPEG domain named CC-C300 [19]. Besides, they proposed their first ensemble classifier to deal with "the curse of dimensionality" reported in [19] as CC-C300 produces a 48600D feature for every jpeg image.

Kodovský et al. proposed their JPEG rich model (JRM) with 11255D and its cartesian-calibrated version abbreviated as CC-JRM with 22510D in paper [20], they also confirmed that "steganalysis can benefits from multiple-domain approaches" through the results tested by combining the Spatial Rich model (SRM) and CC-JRM.

To solve the dimensionality-cursed problem, Holub et al. provided a relatively low computational complexity scheme named DCTR (Discrete Cosine Transform Residual) [21], which can be implemented quickly while still being competitive to the high-dimensional ones. The DCTR feature set is constructed from "the first-order statistics of quantized noise residuals" using 64 kernels of DCT.

Holub et al. found that smaller kernels are better in capturing the artifacts introduced by the adaptive JPEG steganographic schemes, therefore they proposed their PHARM (PHase Aware of pRojection Model) scheme [22]. This method used a bunch of "small-support kernels" to obtain residuals, and project them randomly as in PSRM. Also, they further confirmed that by decompressing the JPEG images to spatial domain, adaptive steganographic schemes can be better detected. Later, Xia et al. [41] improves this method both in efficiency and effectiveness.

In paper [23], Song et al. proposed to use 2D Gabor filters to acquire residuals from the decompressed JPEG images, and then they extracted the histogram features and merged them as the so called GFR (Gabor Filter Residuals) feature set. Although this rich model sounds simple, they acquired relatively good performance in experiments.

To provide a JPEG-version's selection channel aware feature set, Denemark et al. utilized selection channel technique to improve the performance of DCTR, PHARM and GFR in [24]. They proved that a selection channel can help to increase the performance significantly, especially when applied to the low-embedding rate situations.

In paper [42], Feng et al. proposed to use "diverse base filters" to extract stego noise. The MD-CFR (Maximum Diversity Cascade Filter Residual) they proposed jointly with SCA-GFR (Selection Channel Aware, SCA) managed to be the most effective feature extractor for JPEG image steganalysis. In this scheme, they designed "various base filters" and then "cascaded" these base filters to get the needed "high order" filters, which are finally optimized through their "filter selection" method.

3 Deep-Learning Based Image Steganalysis

In a steganalysis-designed CNN (Convolutional Neural Networks, CNN), it is usually composed of the following parts: a pre-processing part, a convolution part and a classification part. The pre-processing part is a set of high-pass filters for capturing the stego-like high frequency signal. The convolution part is usually made of a convolution, an activation function, a pooling step and a normalization step. The classification part is usually equipped with a Sofamax function which normalize the output value between [0, 1].

3.1 CNNs for Spatial Image Steganalysis

Qian's work [25] is in literature the first to used CNN in image steganalysis successfully, inspired by Krizhevsky's CNN [26] in 2012. However, they achieved the performance well, which was just 3%–4% worse than EC with Rich Model. This paper sent a message that CNN could be very powerful in steganalysis if tuned and trained carefully.

Pibre [27] followed up, and showed the steganalysis results when steganographer uses the same embedding key for different images all the time. In their report, they showed that when well parameterized, the CNN can provide a result better than that of the combination of a Rich Model (RM) with an Ensemble Classifier (EC).

Xu [28] reported a CNN architecture that considers the advantages taken from conventional steganalysis. We refer this network as Xu-Net is this paper. Although Xu-Net used only one high-pass filter, the proposed CNN was competitive when compared with the SRM with ensemble classifiers on the BOSSbase [44]. The CNN they proposed did defeat the SRM + EC in detecting the S-UNIWARD and HILL algorithms.

In paper [29], Xu et al. improved the results by using ensemble scheme. They formed a group of CNNs and trained them independently on a "random subsample of the training dataset", and then their "intermediate feature representations" were extracted and pooled, which were then feed into next classification. Performance of the ensemble methods were evaluated on BOSSbase dataset.

Hoping to use transfer learning in image steganalysis, Qian et al. [30] proposed a transfer learning framework to help the training of CNN. In this work, they reported that the performance of a CNN on a low payload steganographic algorithm can be improved by transferring a pre-train CNN that detects this steganographic algorithm with a high payload to it.

Ye [31] proposed the first CNN architecture that outperformed the best conventional spatial steganalysis scheme, maxSRM, and we refer this work as Ye-Net. In this paper, they finally used 30 high-pass filters instead of one in previous works to extract the stego noise, and they proposed their own activation function in their CNN model. To further boost the performance, they used the selection-channel information from maxSRM.

Yedrouj etc. proposed an efficient Yedrouj-Net in [32], and claimed that their CNN provides better performance than Ye-Net even without the knowledge of the selection channel. That will raise a question: Is the selection channel really helping in deep learning technique? Since the networks themselves may learn the possible embedding positions when sufficiently trained.

Li et al. proposed a wide structure named ReST-Net in paper [33], and they proposed to use diverse activation modules (DAMs) in this CNN architecture. The different activation module will "activate the convolution outputs differently" and by using a parallel structure of CNN subnets, the ReST-Net can capture more "preprocessed information".

Zhang et al. proposed their Zhu-Net in [34]. They proposed to use smaller kernels in the preprocessing layer, and used "separable convolution" for extracting "spatial and channel correlation of residuals". Furthermore, "spatial pyramid pooling" is used to process the images with arbitrary size, which also helps to "aggregate local features".

Wu's work [35] also used one kernel in preprocessing layer, which's the same as in [25], but they proposed to use "residual learning" for preserving the stego noise. Experiments showed promising results when compared with maxSRMd2 + EC scheme.

Boroumand et al. proposed their SRNet in [36], and SRNet is the first net in literature that can be used both for spatial images and JPEG images. Besides, according to the paper, the network is also the first to use selection channel for JPEG domain steganalysis. The most important thing about this network is that they managed to free the designer from introducing the elements needed in training a CNN for image steganalysis, for example, the fixed kernels.

Note that Xu-Net, Ye-Net, Yedroudj-Net and Zhu-Net are using a fixed high-pass filter(s), some of these filters are updated during the CNN training process. However, SRNet randomly initialized these filters and they are updated during the training process. This scheme is proved to be one more step closer to automatic image steganalysis.

3.2 CNNs for JPEG Image Steganalysis

Xu proposed a convolutional neural network to detecting J-UNIWARD in paper [37]. In this report, different from the one in [36], where the authors disabled pooling in their front end, Xu confirmed that the pooling method is critical for performance. The 20-layer CNN proposed in the paper had been confirmed to outperform the best feature-based method, SCA-GFR. To better verify the performance, Xu used a dataset called "CLS-LOC" from ImageNet [46], which contains over 1.2 million images.

Chen proposed two CNNs for JPEG images called VNet and PNet in [38], they varied both in volume and in accuracy. Besides, these networks were the first to take JPEG phase-awareness into consideration. To further boost the performance, they proposed the "catalyst kernel" to capture the stego noise, which works much better than KV kernel proposed in Qian's work [25]. That's because the high frequency noise in spatial domain was changed when being transformed in JPEG domain, and the kernel that worked well in spatial domain was no longer effective. Still in this paper, the authors needed to rely on the insights taken from conventional steganalysis approaches.

Yang et al. [39] proposed a relatively deep CNN, which is composed of 32 layers. The network was designed so deep to "reuse the features by concatenating all features form the previous layers", and in this way, model parameters are greatly reduced. Besides, this is the first paper that combines CNN and SCA-GFR method by using the ensemble technique.

Zeng et al. proposed their "Hybrid Deep-Learning" framework [40], which was composed of two parts. The first part includes convolution, quantization and truncation as in classic method [14], while the second part is composed of "multiple deep sub-nets". That was the first work reported to use more than five million cover images in image steganalysis, which provides a benchmark for large-scale JPEG image steaganalysis.

Hu et al. proposed their scheme based on "visual attention and reinforce learning" [43], which sounds like a new way to solve steganalysis problem. In their scheme, they used "attention-focused regions" to mark the area of interest, and they replace the images that are wrongly classified with the "SoAFRs (the Summary of attention-focused regions)", which is "merged by continuous decision-making" through "reinforcement learning".

4 Results Comparisons

In this section, we would like to provide the direct comparisons between some classic methods, both in spatial domain and in JPEG domain. In spatial domain, we selected S-UNIWARD, WOW, HUGO and HILL as representative steganographic schemes, while in JPEG domain, we chose J-UNIWARD and UED-JC. We put the results for 0.1 bpp (bit per pixel) and 0.4 bpp in spatial schemes, and the results for 0.1 bpac (bit per AC coefficient) and 0.4 bpac in JPEG schemes since these payloads are the most frequently used.

For conventional methods, two databases BOSSbase [44] and BOWS-2 [45] are frequently used, they both contain 10,000 gray scale images. For deep-learning methods, besides the two datasets listed above, the CLS-LOC dataset [46] from "ImageNet" is used as well, in which 250,000 images were used.

In Table 1, the experimental results shown in the second column (SPAM + EC) to the fifth coloum (TLBP + EC) are tested by us on BOSSbase dataset only. The last two columns are extracted from paper [36], and the experiments were performed on BOSSbase and BOWS-2.

Table 1. Comparison of error-rate results from different steganalyzers in Spatial domain.

Feature extractor	SPAM [8] (686D)	SRM [9] (34671D)	maxSRM [13]	TLBP [14] (29040D)	SCA-YeNET [31]	SRNeT [36]
S-UNI/0.1 bpp	0.4561	0.4013	0.3682	0.4079	0.3220	0.3104
S-UNI/0.4 bpp	0.3270	0.2074	0.1990	0.1913	0.1281	0.1023
HUGO/0.1 bpp	0.4641	0.3666	0.3066	0.3768	–	–
HUGO/0.4 bpp	0.3065	0.1807	0.1654	0.2014	–	–
WOW/0.1 bpp	0.4740	0.4009	0.3015	0.3957	0.2442	0.2587
WOW/0.4 bpp	0.3785	0.2092	0.1634	0.2081	0.0959	0.0893
HILL/0.1 bpp	0.4765	0.4332	0.3796	0.4120	0.3380	0.3134
HILL/0.4 bpp	0.3848	0.2509	0.2251	0.2325	0.1708	0.1414

Table 2 shows the results from four conventional methods and three CNNs for JPEG images. The results for conventional methods were extracted from paper [24], while the results for CNNs were extracted from [36]. The leftmost column means the steganographic method is J-UNIWARD or UED-JC with quality factor 75 or 95, and the embedding rate is 0.1 bpac or 0.4 bpac.

As the results suggest, although maxSRM method was proposed in 2014, it is still a powerful tool in image steganalysis. Note that "selection channel" technique was not used in TLBP. Also, we can see from the result provided by SPAM that it can detect adaptive steganographic scheme to some extent, but fails in comparing with any rich models. For deep-learning methods, we showed only two state-of-art networks, and the SCA-YeNET means Ye-Net [31] with "selection channel".

In Table 2, we put only one of the selection channel aware version of the rich model in JPEG domain, SCA-GFR due to space constraints. Also, it can provide the best performance in these rich models. Besides, SRNeT is capable in detecting adaptive steganographic methods in both domains, so we put the results in this table.

Although CNN related methods had surpassed conventional methods in both domains, we still recommend researching in conventional and deep-learning methods simultaneously. The reason is easy, as Boroumand et al. suggested in [36], we are still far away from fully automatic steganalysis, thus we still need insights from conventional methods to help improve the detecting performance.

Table 2. Comparison of error-rate results from different steganalyzers in JPEG domain.

Feature extractor	DCTR [21] (8000D)	GFR [23] (17000D)	PHARM [22] (12600D)	SCA-GFR [24]	J-XuNeT [37]	SRNeT [36]
J-UNI/75/0.1 bpac	0.4400	0.4095	0.4284	0.3589	0.4310	0.3201
J-UNI/75/0.4 bpac	0.1553	0.1005	0.1259	0.0792	0.1207	0.0670
UED-JC/75/0.1 bpac	0.3593	0.3153	0.3376	0.2352	0.2144	0.1311
UED-JC/75/0.4 bpac	0.0593	0.0346	0.0418	0.0377	0.0287	0.0188
J-UNI/95/0.1 bpac	0.4826	0.4756	0.4835	0.4634	0.4812	0.4277
J-UNI/95/0.4 bpac	0.3081	0.2721	0.3079	0.2617	0.3232	0.1762
UED-JC/95/0.1 bpac	0.4598	0.4323	0.4490	0.3931	0.3848	0.3044
UED-JC/95/0.4 bpac	0.2180	0.1663	0.1947	0.1662	0.1292	0.0877

5 Conclusions

Throughout this paper, we can conclude that the research in conventional image steganalysis has slowed down, while deep-learning based image steganalysis is attracting more and more researchers. However, although many deep-learning based methods have shown remarkable performance when compared with conventional methods, most of these schemes still rely on classical conventional methods. The fully-automatic image steganalysis is still far from reaching, therefore we still need to research both on classic methods and CNN-related ones.

Papers such as Zeng's [40], revealed that GAN (Generative Adversarial Network) related work will be one of the interesting points in the future. However, since training a GAN equals training two CNNs simultaneously, how to accelerate the training speed and how to use the limited GPU resources effectively will become our problems. Furthermore, as training any of these networks usually takes an expensive graphic card or more, keep finding effective and efficient CNNs will always be the tasks.

Acknowledgement. This work was partly supported by National Natural Science Foundation of China (61772144, 61672008), Innovation Team Project (Natural Science) of the Education Department of Guangdong Province (2017KCXTD021), Foundation for Youth Innovation Talents in Higher Education of Guangdong Province (2018KQNCX139), Innovation Research Project (Natural Science) of Education Department of Guangdong Province (2016KTSCX077), Project for Distinctive Innovation of Ordinary Universities of Guangdong Province (2018KTSCX120), and Foreign Science and Technology Cooperation Plan Project of Guangzhou Science Technology and Innovation Commission (201807010059).

References

1. Sedighi, V., et al.: Content-adaptive steganography by minimizing statistical detectability. IEEE Trans. Inf. Forensics Secur. **11**(2), 221–234 (2015)
2. Holub, V., et al.: Universal distortion function for steganography in an arbitrary domain. EURASIP J. Inf. Secur. **2014**, 1 (2014)
3. Li, B., et al.: A new cost function for spatial image steganography. In: 2014 IEEE International Conference on Image Processing (ICIP) (2014)
4. Holub, V., et al.: Designing steganographic distortion using directional filters. In: 2012 IEEE International Workshop on Information Forensics and Security (WIFS) (2012)
5. Pevný, T., Filler, T., Bas, P.: Using high-dimensional image models to perform highly undetectable steganography. In: Böhme, R., Fong, Philip W.L., Safavi-Naini, R. (eds.) IH 2010. LNCS, vol. 6387, pp. 161–177. Springer, Heidelberg (2010). https://doi.org/10.1007/978-3-642-16435-4_13
6. Guo, L., et al.: Uniform embedding for efficient JPEG steganography. IEEE Trans. Inf. Forensics Secur. **9**(5), 814–825 (2014)
7. Schlegel, D.: Deep machine learning on GPU. University of Heidelber-Ziti, p. 12 (2015)
8. Pevny, T., et al.: Steganalysis by subtractive pixel adjacency matrix. IEEE Trans. Inf. Forensics Secur. **5**(2), 215–224 (2010)
9. Fridrich, J., et al.: Rich models for steganalysis of digital images. IEEE Trans. Inf. Forensics Secur. **7**(3), 868–882 (2012)

10. Kodovsky, J., Holub, V., et al.: Ensemble classifiers for steganalysis of digital media. IEEE Trans. Inf. Forensics Secur. **7**(2), 432–444 (2011)
11. Holub, V., et al.: Random projections of residuals as an alternative to co-occurrences in steganalysis. In: Proceedings SPIE, Electronic Imaging, Media Watermarking, Security, and Forensics XV, San Francisco, CA, vol. 8665 (2013)
12. Holub, V., et al.: Random projections of residuals for digital image steganalysis. IEEE Trans. Inf. Forensics Secur. **8**(12), 1996–2006 (2013)
13. Denemark, T., et al.: Selection-channel-aware rich model for steganalysis of digital images. In: 2014 IEEE International Workshop on Information Forensics and Security (WIFS) (2014)
14. Li, B., et al.: New steganalytic features for spatial image steganography based on derivative filters and threshold LBP operator. IEEE Trans. Inf. Forensics Secur. **13**(5), 1242–1257 (2017)
15. Chen, C., et al.: JPEG image steganalysis utilizing both intrablock and interblock correlations. In: 2008 IEEE International Symposium on Circuits and Systems. IEEE (2008)
16. Fridrich, J., Goljan, M., Hogea, D.: Steganalysis of JPEG images: breaking the F5 algorithm. In: Petitcolas, F.A.P. (ed.) IH 2002. LNCS, vol. 2578, pp. 310–323. Springer, Heidelberg (2003). https://doi.org/10.1007/3-540-36415-3_20
17. Kodovský, J., et al.: Calibration revisited. In: Proceedings of the 11th ACM Workshop on Multimedia and Security. ACM (2009)
18. Liu, Q.: Steganalysis of DCT-embedding based adaptive steganography and YASS. In: Proceedings of the Thirteenth ACM Multimedia Workshop on Multimedia and Security. ACM (2011)
19. Kodovský, J., et al.: Steganalysis in high dimensions: fusing classifiers built on random subspaces. In: Media Watermarking, Security, and Forensics III, vol. 7880. International Society for Optics and Photonics (2011)
20. Kodovský, J., et al.: Steganalysis of JPEG images using rich models. In: Media Watermarking, Security, and Forensics 2012, vol. 8303. International Society for Optics and Photonics (2012)
21. Holub, V., et al.: Low-complexity features for JPEG steganalysis using undecimated DCT. IEEE Trans. Inf. Forensics Secur. **10**(2), 219–228 (2014)
22. Holub, V., et al.: Phase-aware projection model for steganalysis of JPEG images. In: Media Watermarking, Security, and Forensics 2015, vol. 9409. International Society for Optics and Photonics (2015)
23. Song, X., et al.: Steganalysis of adaptive JPEG steganography using 2D Gabor filters. In: Proceedings of the 3rd ACM Workshop on Information Hiding and Multimedia Security. ACM (2015)
24. Denemark, T., et al.: Steganalysis features for content-adaptive JPEG steganography. IEEE Trans. Inf. Forensics Secur. **11**(8), 1736–1746 (2016)
25. Qian, Y., et al.: Deep learning for steganalysis via convolutional neural networks. In: Media Watermarking, Security, and Forensics 2015, vol. 9409. International Society for Optics and Photonics (2015)
26. Krizhevsky, A., et al.: Imagenet classification with deep convolutional neural networks. In: Advances in Neural Information Processing Systems (2012)
27. Pibre, L., et al.: Deep learning is a good steganalysis tool when embedding key is reused for different images, even if there is a cover sourcemismatch. Electron. Imaging **4**(8), 1–11 (2016)
28. Xu, G., et al.: Structural design of convolutional neural networks for steganalysis. IEEE Signal Process. Lett. **23**(5), 708–712 (2016)

29. Xu, G., et al.: Ensemble of CNNs for steganalysis: an empirical study. In: Proceedings of the 4th ACM Workshop on Information Hiding and Multimedia Security. ACM (2016)
30. Qian, Y., et al.: Learning and transferring representations for image steganalysis using convolutional neural network. In: 2016 IEEE International Conference on Image Processing (ICIP) (2016)
31. Ye, J., et al.: Deep learning hierarchical representations for image steganalysis. IEEE Trans. Inf. Forensics Secur. **12**(11), 2545–2557 (2017)
32. Yedroudj, M., et al.: Yedroudj-Net: an efficient CNN for spatial steganalysis. In: 2018 IEEE International Conference on Acoustics, Speech and Signal Processing (ICASSP) (2018)
33. Li, B., et al.: ReST-Net: diverse activation modules and parallel subnets-based CNN for spatial image steganalysis. IEEE Sig. Process. Lett. **25**(5), 650–654 (2018)
34. Zhang, R., et al.: Efficient feature learning and multi-size image steganalysis based on CNN. arXiv preprint arXiv:1807.11428 (2018)
35. Wu, S., et al.: Deep residual learning for image steganalysis. Multimed. Tools Appl. **77**(9), 10437–10453 (2018)
36. Boroumand, M., et al.: Deep residual network for steganalysis of digital images. IEEE Trans. Inf. Forensics Secur. **14**(5), 1181–1193 (2018)
37. Xu, G.: Deep convolutional neural network to detect J-UNIWARD. In: Proceedings of the 5th ACM Workshop on Information Hiding and Multimedia Security. ACM (2017)
38. Chen, M., et al.: JPEG-phase-aware convolutional neural network for steganalysis of JPEG images. In: Proceedings of the 5th ACM Workshop on Information Hiding and Multimedia Security. ACM (2017)
39. Yang, J., et al.: JPEG steganalysis based on densenet. arXiv preprint arXiv:1711.09335 (2017)
40. Zeng, J., et al.: Large-scale JPEG image steganalysis using hybrid deep-learning framework. IEEE Trans. Inf. Forensics Secur. **13**(5), 1200–1214 (2017)
41. Xia, C., et al.: Improved PHARM for JPEG steganalysis: making PHARM more efficient and effective. IEEE Access **7**, 50339–50346 (2019)
42. Feng, G., et al.: Diversity-based cascade filters for JPEG steganalysis. IEEE Trans. Circuits Syst. Video Technol. (2019)
43. Hu, D., et al.: Digital image steganalysis based on visual attention and deep reinforcement learning. IEEE Access **7**, 25924–25935 (2019)
44. Bas, P., Filler, T., Pevný, T.: "Break our steganographic system": the ins and outs of organizing BOSS. In: Filler, T., Pevný, T., Craver, S., Ker, A. (eds.) IH 2011. LNCS, vol. 6958, pp. 59–70. Springer, Heidelberg (2011). https://doi.org/10.1007/978-3-642-24178-9_5
45. Bas, P., et al.: BOWS-2 (2007). http://bows2.ec-lille.fr
46. Russakovsky, O., et al.: Imagenet large scale visual recognition challenge. Int. J. Comput. Vis. **115**(3), 211–252 (2015)

The Design Patent Images Classification Based on Image Caption Model

Hongyu Liu, Qingyun Dai, Ya Li(✉), Chuxin Zhang, Siyu Yi, and Tao Yuan

Guangdong Polytechnic Normal University, Guangzhou 510665, China
liya2829@qq.com

Abstract. Improving the performance of the patented image retrieval system is of great significance in the intellectual property protection. The design patent image has a large amount of data, and how to quickly complete the retrieval is part of the main research issues for the design patent retrieval system. Classification is an effective way to improve the retrieval speed, so some methods of image classification have been proposed before. However, image classification cannot achieve high-level semantic classification. Thus the speed of improvement is very limited. In order to realize the classification effect of high-level semantics, in this paper, we propose a method that uses the image caption model-based to realize the automatic description generation of the design patent image. Experiments show that our method has better classification accuracy and better semantic classification performance than previous image classification methods.

Keywords: Design patent images · Image caption · Image classification

1 Introduction

Intellectual property protection helps to enhance the innovation of enterprises and promote the healthy development of the industrial economy, so it is increasingly valued by enterprises and governments [1]. Design patents as part of intellectual property rights are one of the objects of intellectual property protection. Patent retrieval is the pillar of almost all patent analysis works [2], so the research on design patent image retrieval is of profound significance for intellectual property protection.

The design patent is mainly presented in the form of pictures. Thus the design patent retrieval system is a content-based image retrieval (CBIR) system [3]. The CBIR method uses visual feature vectors to represent images, and the similarity between images is measured by calculating the similarity between visual feature vectors [4]. Although there are many ways to obtain visual feature vectors, in general, visual feature vectors are high-dimensional and there is a semantic gap between them and the upper-level understanding [5]. Moreover, the amount of design patent image data is large. In the retrieval process, if there is no effective indexing mechanism, relying on linear comparison between feature vectors will require a lot of calculation time. Therefore, how to improve the retrieval speed efficiently is one of the main research issues in the current design patent image retrieval.

J. Ren et al. (Eds.): BICS 2019, LNAI 11691, pp. 353–362, 2020.
https://doi.org/10.1007/978-3-030-39431-8_34

Classification is an effective way to improve the speed of retrieval. Classification can complete the order comparison between feature vectors and the corresponding similar distance calculation within the range of similar semantic categories according to semantic requirements. This greatly reduces the scope and number of queries, while classification also eliminates the semantic gap. Therefore, in order to improve the retrieval speed of the design patent image retrieval system, some researchers have proposed image classification methods [6–9]. Li et al. [7] uses the method of edge contour distance and segmentation feature to extract low-level visual features, and combines K-means clustering classification method to achieve the purpose of first classification and retrieval. Wang [8] adopt the support vector machine method to achieve automatic classification of design patent images. Ni et al. [9] proposes a method of using locality-constrained linear (LLC) coding and spatial pyramid matching (SPM) for patent image classification, which proves model based on SPM and LLC have bright future in patent image recognition. The method of image classification greatly reduces the number of matches required for retrieval, and the retrieval speed is significantly improved. However, limited semantic information extracted by image classification has no more detailed expression on the image content. Usually, image classification can only achieve the division between categories, which cannot meet the classification effect of high-level semantics within the same category. In addition, there are still a lot of image data for each category of design patents, and it takes a lot of time to accomplish the sequence comparison among similar semantic categories. Thus, in the long term, the search speed improved by image classification will become more and more limited for the continuous increase of design patent data.

The image captioning is intended to automatically generate a natural language description of an image, which is one of the hot research areas of artificial intelligence [11]. Image captioning is an easy task for humans, but it is a big challenge for the machine. In recent years, deep learning has achieved remarkable success in image captioning tasks [12–17], making it possible for computers to automatically generate high-quality image descriptions. In order to enable the CBIR design patent retrieval system to achieve high-level semantic classification, in this paper we propose a method for automatically generating design patent image text descriptions using image

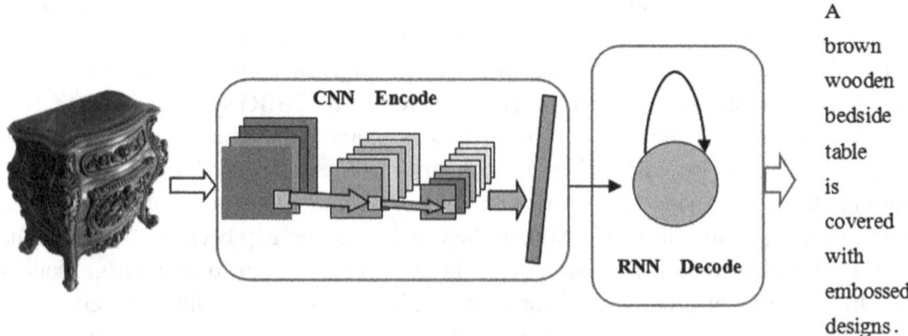

Fig. 1. A convolutional neural network (CNN) as visual encoder to extract visual features and generate captions with a recurrent neural network (RNN).

captioning models, which are shown in Fig. 1. The text generated by the model can correctly describe the patent image while ensuring high class recognition accuracy. The experiment proves that the text description generated by the image captioning model can achieve higher semantic classification effect than image classification method.

2 Method

Vinyals et al. [13] proposed the encode-decode architecture, which is the main model architecture for image captioning tasks. The "encoder" uses a convolutional neural network (CNN) to extract and encode the visual features of image. The "decoder" uses a recurrent neural network (RNN) to translate the image encoding and then generate the relevant text description. Since [14], attention mechanisms have been widely introduced to image captioning model to improve the quality of text description [15–17]. As the first attempt of the image captioning model on the design patent image, for the sake of convenience, this work don't introduced the attention mechanism.

Therefore, the task we have to accomplish is to give a design patent image and then use the image captioning model based on encode-decode framework to generate the maximum probability output description word by word. From the previous work [13, 16] we can know that the encode-decode model can be trained by directly maximizing the following objective given the design patent image:

$$\theta^* = \arg\max_{\theta} \sum_{(I,S)} \log p(S|I;\, \theta) \tag{1}$$

where θ are the parameters of the image captioning model, I is the design patent image, and S is its correct caption. The probability of the corresponding caption S can be obtained as the joint probability distribution over its words $S_0, \ldots, S_T$:

$$\log p(S) = \sum_{t=0}^{T} \log p(S_t|I, S_0, \ldots, S_{t-1}) \tag{2}$$

where T is the length of the caption S. In this encode-decode framework, with RNN, the conditional probability of each step can be modeled from the following equation:

$$\log p(S_t|I, S_0, \ldots, S_{t-1}) = f(W_p h_t) \tag{3}$$

f is a nonlinear function outputs the probability of S_t, W_p is the weight parameters to be learnt, h_t is the hidden state of RNN at time t. In this paper, RNN we use Long-Short Term Memory (LSTM) [18] network, which performs well on a variety of sequence tasks such as machine translation [19], language modeling [20], and text summarization [21]. So h_t is modeled as:

$$h_t = LSTM(x_t, h_{t-1}) \tag{4}$$

$$x_t = W_e S_{t-1} \tag{5}$$

where W_e is the word embedding matrix, we represent each word as one-hot vector S_t of dimension equal to the size of the dictionary. Before that, we need to encode images and words into the same dimensional space, Fig. 2 illustrates the architecture of our method.

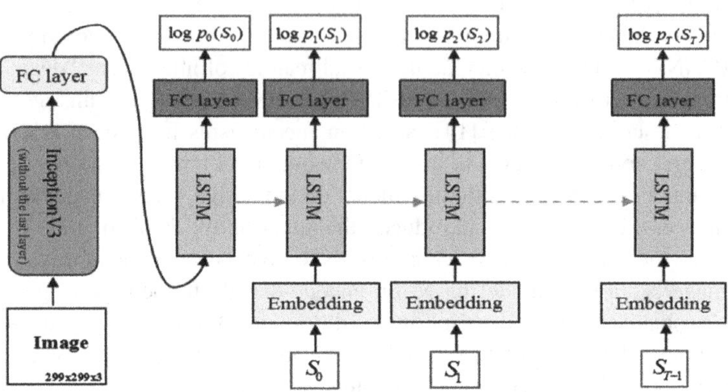

Fig. 2. Illustration of the model. FC layer denote full connection, images and words are mapped to the same dimensional space before being input to LSTM.

3 Experiment

This section describes the preparation of the data set and the specific parameter configuration of the model implementation. Finally, we reported some important relevant results.

3.1 Dataset

In order to speed up the retrieval speed of the system, and in the process of retrieval in line with human cognition and intention. Design Patent Search System creates an index for each category. Usually the category is built to follow a structure of a classification tree that divides the design into several distinct categories. Generally speaking, the amount of data between the same category is still very large. The method of image classification can only establish a category index for patent images without more detailed semantic expression, and cannot achieve semantic classification between the same category.

In this paper, we take the furniture design patent as an example. The furniture design patent usually establishes a classification index for the design patent according to the classification structure of the classification tree in Fig. 3. According to the classification of the classification tree, the image classification method establishes a category index for the design patent image, but cannot establish a classification index of the high-level semantics. However, the same category can be distinguished based on human semantic understanding. For instance, in the sofa category, people can classify the sofa in more detail according to different colors, number of seats, materials, and surface design features.

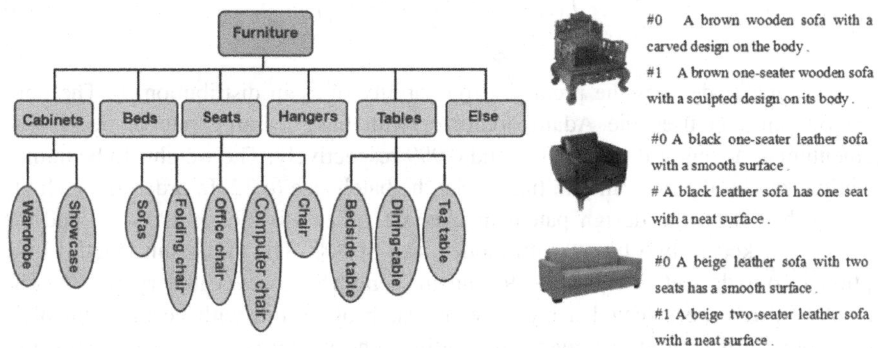

Fig. 3. (Left) Furniture design patent classification tree. (Right) Different sofa design patent images and corresponding image annotation.

In order to let our image caption model realize the description generation of the design patent image, we select 14000 images from the design patent image database to construct our own image captioning model dataset and image classification dataset. Here, each design patent image contains six different perspective images. For the comprehensiveness of the description, we select the stereogram as the description object of the model. After selecting the corresponding image, we manually mark image annotation according to the content of the image. Due to the limited manpower, we only label two different description sentences for each image. Up to now, there are 1,532 image data available for the image captioning model, training data 1056 and testing data 476. We will continue to expand this dataset, more sentences and more data, and hope to make it public in the near future.

3.2 Implementation Details

We embed the design patent image and the word in the same dimension space, the dimension is equal to 300. The CNN uses the model [22] as the image encoder without the top layer, which is pre-trained on ImageNet. The CNN of the part does not participate in the training. Therefore, the CNN will get the code vector of the image, and then convert the image code vector into 300-dimensional through a single-layer fully-connected neural network. Similarly, convert words to the same dimensional space. Words are represented by one-hot encoding, dimensions are equal to the length of the vocabulary, and one-hot encoding is used to obtain an embedded representation of the word through an embedded layer. The converted image code is input to the LSTM to get the hidden state h_0 at time t_0, and h_0 is used to feed to a Softmax layer, which will yield the probability distribution p_0 of the first word. Choose the first word, then feed it into embedding layer which will produce a word embedding of the first world. The embedding of the first will be the input of the LSTM. Above process is repeated until the ending token <end> is predicted, or the maximum length of the sentence is reached.

The loss function for each sentence uses the cross-entropy:

$$L(I,S) = -\sum_{t=0}^{N} \log p_t(S_t) \tag{6}$$

where the $p_t(S_t)$ denotes the prediction probability of S_t in distribution p_t. The optimization function uses the Adam optimizer with base learning rate of 5e−4. The momentum and weight-decay are 0.9 and 0.999 respectively. The weights to be trained are initialized by the randomly initialize. Set the batch size to 32. In order to match the input of the CNN, the design patent images are resized to 299 × 299 × 3, and the LSTM is stacked in two layers with hidden size of 300. The maximum length of the caption in our dataset is equal to 19, and the length of the vocabulary is 776. The predicted words are selected using a beam-search algorithm with beam width of 3. Early stopping was used to prevent over-fitting. The model is implemented in Keras, NVIDIA GTX 1080 GPU.

3.3 Result

In this section, we report the quality of the sentence generated by the model and its performance in the semantic classification.

Sentence Evaluation. We report the sentence generated results using the image captioning evaluation tool [23], which provides the following metrics: Cider, Meteor, Rouge, Bleu, the results are shown in Table 1.

Table 1. Main results for image caption on our dataset and Flickr8k [24]. Bleu-n denotes the Bleu score that uses up to n-grams.

Dataset	Model	Bleu-1	Bleu-2	Bleu-3	Bleu-4	Meteor	Cider
Our dataset	[13]	36.2	28.1	24.9	20.3	16.1	51.1
	Our	**40.3**	**32.2**	**25.1**	**21.1**	**20.2**	**54.4**
Flickr8k	[13]	**63**	**41**	**27**	N/A	N/A	N/A
	Our	61.5	39.9	27.3	19.1	22.1	41.7

As can be seen from Table 1, our model obtains slightly better results on our dataset than [13]. The difference in model structure is that we have two layers of LSTM stacked in our decoding model, [13] using a single layer LSTM. This result is expected because single-layer LSTM has defects in long-sequence modeling [12]. Compared with the performance of the model [13] and ours on the public dataset Flickr8 k, the model has a lot of room for improvement in the evaluation metrics. The reason for this result is largely related to our dataset. Due to our limited staffing, only two different annotation are marked for each design patent image, which may greatly affect the ability of the model to learn. Fortunately, in the continuous expansion of the dataset, we will make relevant improvements to the number of dataset and the quality of the sentences before the data is published.

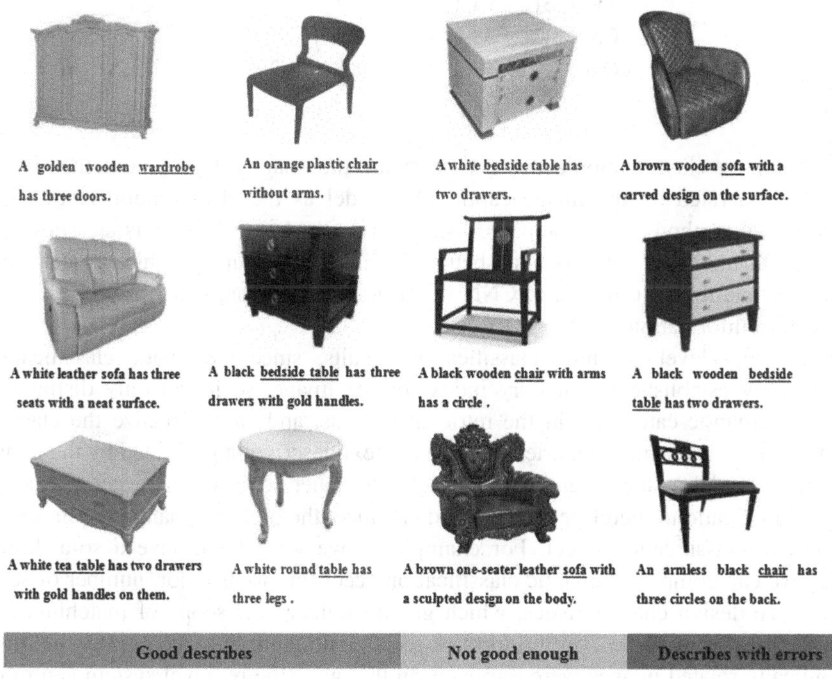

Fig. 4. A selection of evaluation results by human rating.

Figure 4 shown some results based on the person's rating, the model can maintain a high recognition accuracy for the color and category of the design patent image. For each category of features, such as the number of seats in the sofa, the armrests of the chair, the number of drawers in the bedside table, etc. can basically describe accurately, but sometimes make a mistake. In addition, the model is not sensitive enough to the location information in the detailed description of the image.

Classification Performance. We report the results of the model in image classification and high-level semantic classification, all of which are reported in Table 2. The results of the high-level semantic classification are presented using the recall rate (text to image). The recall rate is defined as follows:

$$Recall = \frac{a}{a + b} \tag{7}$$

a is a semantically related image returned, b is a semantically related image that is not returned.

Table 2. Image classification accuracy rate (C) and image-sentence ranking result Recall (R). R@k is the top k results of semantically related.

Model	C	R@1	R@5	R@10
K-mean [7]	91.4	–	–	–
SVM [8]	94.2	–	–	–
CNN [22]	98.8	–	–	–
Our	97.2	15.3	38.8	61.2

In the image classification accuracy, we regard the image category contained in the sentence generated by the image captioning model as the classification result. The previous two methods were compared using our method and the results are shown in Table 2. Our model is able to obtain better classification accuracy, which is attributed to the outstanding performance of CNN in image classification, which can obtain very rich feature information.

In the high-level semantic classification results, since the image classification method only establishes a category index for the image, so it can only distinguish different semantic categories in the retrieval process, and cannot realize the classification between the same categories. We use the text description generated by the image captioning model as the image index, which has richer semantic expression than the image classification. Therefore, our method can meet the higher semantic requirements to improve classification effect. For example, if we want to retrieve a sofa design patent, we can complete semantic classification according to its color, number of seats and surface design characteristics, which greatly reduces the scope of matching. We show the results in Table 2 in the form of recall. The higher the recall rate, the more semantically related images were retrieved. In this way, the retrieval system can more accurately lock the range of data comparison, thus saving a lot of unnecessary comparison time and speeding up the retrieval speed.

4 Conclusion

In this paper, we propose a method to implement automatically generate description of design patent images based on image caption model methods. To train the model, we constructed a design patent image captioning dataset. We have investigated the performance of our model on classification and sentence evaluation, and the results show that our method can obtain better semantic classification performance than the image classification method. However, our model is not sensitive enough to the positional information of the design patent image. Next, we will introduce the attention mechanism or some other methods [25–28] to improve the performance of the model on the design patent image. In addition, we will continue to enrich our dataset and the quality of our annotations until the data is made public. Finally, we will also explore more effective feature extraction and classification approaches including multi-view analysis and image retrieval models in the future [29–33].

Acknowledgements. This work was supported by Research on Optimization Theory and Key Technology of Intelligent Search for Design Patent (1741333) Design Patent Image Retrieval Method and Application (572020144), and Guangdong Provincial Key Laboratory Project (2018B030322016).

References

1. Fang, L., Lerner, J., Wu, C.: Intellectual property rights protection, ownership, and innovation: evidence from China. Rev. Financ. Stud. **30**(7), 2446–2447 (2017)
2. Shalaby, W., Zadrozny, W.: Patent retrieval: a literature review. Knowl. Inf. Syst. 1–30 (2017)
3. Vrochidis, S., Papadopoulos, S., Moumtzidou, A.: Towards content-based patent image retrieval: a framework perspective. World Patent Inf. **32**(2), 94–106 (2010)
4. Rehman, M., Iqbal, M., Sharif, M.: Content based image retrieval: survey. World Appl. Sci. J. **19**(3), 404–412 (2012)
5. Wan, J., Wang, D., Hoi, S.C.H.: Deep learning for content-based image retrieval: a comprehensive study. In: Proceedings of the 22nd ACM International Conference on Multimedia, pp. 157–166. ACM, New York (2014)
6. Csurka, G.: Document image classification, with a specific view on applications of patent images. In: Lupu, M., Mayer, K., Kando, N., Trippe, A. (eds.) Current Challenges in Patent Information Retrieval. TIRS, vol. 37, pp. 325–350. Springer, Heidelberg (2017). https://doi.org/10.1007/978-3-662-53817-3_12
7. Xuming, L., Qingyun, D., Jiangzhong, C., et al.: Design patent image retrieval system based on semantic classification. Comput. Eng. Appl. **48**(16), 202–206 (2012)
8. Senhong, W.: Research on classification methods of design patent image. Guangdong University of Technology, Guangzhou, Guangdong (2013)
9. Ni, H., Guo, Z., Huang, B.: Patent image classification using local-constrained linear coding and spatial pyramid matching. In: 2015 International Conference on Service Science. IEEE, Weihai, China (2015)
10. Vrochidis, S., Moumtzidou, A., Kompatsiaris, I.: Enhancing patent search with content-based image retrieval. In: Paltoglou, G., Loizides, F., Hansen, P. (eds.) Professional Search in the Modern World. LNCS, vol. 8830, pp. 250–273. Springer, Cham (2014). https://doi.org/10.1007/978-3-319-12511-4_12
11. Hossain, M.D., Sohel, F., Shiratuddin, M.F., et al.: A comprehensive survey of deep learning for image captioning. ACM Comput. Surv. CSUR **51**(6), 118 (2019)
12. Peng, Y., Liu, X., Wang, W., Zhao, X., Wei, M.: Image caption model of double LSTM with scene factors. Image Vis. Comput. **86**, 38–44 (2019)
13. Vinyals, O., Toshev, A., Bengio, S., Erhan, D.: Show and tell: a neural image caption generator. In: The IEEE Conference on Computer Vision and Pattern Recognition, CVPR, Boston, USA, pp. 3156–3164 (2015)
14. Xu, K., Ba, J., Kiros, R., Courville, A., et al.: Show, attend and tell: neural image caption generation with visual attention. In: International Conference on Machine Learning 2015, ICML, Lille, France, pp. 2048–2057 (2015)
15. Lu, J., Xiong, C., Parikh, D., et al.: Knowing when to look: adaptive attention via a visual sentinel for image captioning. In: 2017 IEEE Conference on Computer Vision and Pattern Recognition, CVPR, Honolulu, Hawaii, pp. 375–383 (2017)

16. Anderson, P., et al.: Bottom-up and top-down attention for image captioning and visual question answering. In: 2018 Proceedings of the IEEE Conference on Computer Vision and Pattern Recognition, CVPR, pp. 6077–6086 (2018)
17. Gao, L., Li, X., Song, J., et al.: Hierarchical LSTMs with adaptive attention for visual captioning. IEEE Trans. Pattern Anal. Mach. Intell. (2019)
18. Hochreiter, S., Schmidhuber, J.: Long short-term memory. Neural Comput. **9**(8), 1735–1780 (1997)
19. Sutskever, I., Vinyals, O., Le, Q.V.: Sequence to sequence learning with neural networks. In: Advances in Neural Information Processing Systems, pp. 3104–3112 (2014)
20. Sundermeyer, M., Ney, H., Schlüter, R.: From feedforward to recurrent LSTM neural networks for language modeling. IEEE/ACM Trans. Audio Speech Lang. Process. **23**(3), 517–529 (2015)
21. Song, S., Huang, H., Ruan, T.: Abstractive text summarization using LSTM-CNN based deep learning. Multimed. Tools Appl. **78**(1), 857–875 (2019)
22. Szegedy, C., Vanhoucke, V., Ioffe, S., et al.: Rethinking the inception architecture for computer vision. In: Proceedings of the IEEE Conference on Computer Vision and Pattern Recognition, CVPR, LasVegas, Nevada, pp. 2818–2826 (2016)
23. Microsoft COCO caption Evaluation. https://github.com/tylin/coco-caption. 17 Mar 2015
24. Hodosh, M., Young, P., Hockenmaier, J.: Framing image description as a ranking task: data, models and evaluation metrics. J. Artif. Intell. Res. **47**, 853–899 (2013)
25. Zhang, A., Sun, G., Ren, J.: A dynamic neighborhood learning-based gravitational search algorithm. IEEE Trans. Cybern. **48**(1), 436–447 (2016)
26. Zheng, J., Liu, Y., Ren, J., et al.: Fusion of block and keypoints based approaches for effective copy-move image forgery detection. Multidimension. Syst. Signal Process. **27**(4), 989–1005 (2016)
27. Yan, Y., Ren, J., Sun, G., et al.: Unsupervised image saliency detection with Gestalt-laws guided optimization and visual attention based refinement. Pattern Recogn. **79**, 65–78 (2018)
28. Sun, M., Zhang, D., Wang, Z., et al.: Monte Carlo convex hull model for classification of traditional Chinese paintings. Neurocomputing **171**, 788–797 (2016)
29. Ren, J., Wang, D.: Effective recognition of MCCs in mammograms using an improved neural classifier. Eng. Appl. Artif. Intell. **24**(4), 638–645 (2011)
30. Yan, Y., Ren, J., Zhao, H., et al.: Cognitive fusion of thermal and visible imagery for effective detection and tracking of pedestrians in videos. Cogn. Comput. **10**(1), 94–104 (2018)
31. Ren, J., Vlachos, T.: Efficient detection of temporally impulsive dirt impairments in archived films. Signal Process. **87**(3), 541–551 (2007)
32. Zhou, Y., et al.: Hierarchical visual perception and two-dimensional compressive sensing for effective content-based color image retrieval. Cogn. Comput. **8**(5), 877–889 (2016)
33. Ren, J., et al.: Multi-camera video surveillance for real-time analysis and reconstruction of soccer games. Mach. Vis. Appl. **21**(6), 855–863 (2010)

Multi-level Thresholding Using Adaptive Gravitational Search Algorithm and Fuzzy Entropy

Aizhu Zhang[1,2(✉)], Genyun Sun[1,2], Xiuping Jia[3], Chenglong Zhang[1,2], and Yanjuan Yao[4]

[1] China University of School of Geosciences, China University of Petroleum (East China), Qingdao 266580, Shandong, China
zhangaizhu789@163.com

[2] Laboratory for Marine Mineral Resources, National Laboratory for Marine Science and Technology, Qingdao 266071, China

[3] School of Engineering and Information Technology, University of New South Wales, Canberra, ACT 2600, Australia

[4] Satellite Environment Center, Ministry of Environmental protection of China, Beijing 100094, China

Abstract. Conventional multilevel thresholding methods are computationally expensive when applied to color images since they exhaustively search the optimal thresholds by optimizing the objective functions. To address this problem, this paper presents an adaptive gravitational search algorithm (AGSA) based multi-level thresholding for color image. In AGSA, a dynamic neighborhood learning strategy which incorporates the local and global neighborhood topologies is introduced to achieve adaptive balance of exploration and exploitation. Moreover, a sinusoidal chaotic based gravitational constants adjusting operator is embedded to further promote the performance of AGSA. When extending AGSA to solve the multi-level thresholding problem, the fuzzy entropy is adopted as the objective function. Experiments were conducted on two color images to investigate the efficiency of the proposed method. The obtained results are compared with that of the particle swarm optimization (PSO) and *gbest*-guided GSA (GGSA). The experimental results are validated qualitatively and quantitatively by evaluating the mean of the objective function values and the total CPU time required for the execution of each optimization algorithm. Comparison results showed that the AGSA produced superior or comparative segmentation accuracy in almost all of the tested images and the algorithm largely reduce the computational efficiency of GSA.

Keywords: Multi-level thresholding · Fuzzy entropy · Image segmentation · Gravitational search algorithm

1 Introduction

Image segmentation is one of the typical and commonly used image process method in the interpretation of color imagery. Using specific segmentation algorithms, images can be divided into multiple homogenous regions/objects mainly on the basis of two

J. Ren et al. (Eds.): BICS 2019, LNAI 11691, pp. 363–372, 2020.
https://doi.org/10.1007/978-3-030-39431-8_35

properties of pixels, in either gray-level or color vision, i.e. discontinuity around edges and similarity in the same region [1, 19, 20]. One of the most generally utilized proficient is the thresholding technique for it is the least complex approach [1].

The main purpose of image thresholding is to determine one (bi-level thresholding) or m (multi-level thresholding) appropriate threshold values for an image to divide pixels of the image into two or K ($K = m + 1$) different groups [2, 3]. Both the bi-level and multi-level thresholding can be classified into parametric and non-parametric approaches, and the non-parametric approaches have gained much attention because their parameter free property. Particularly, the entropy-based methods have been widely studied and considered effective [4]. Some famous methods includes the maximum entropy method proposed by Kapur et al. [5], the minimum cross-entropy method developed by Li et al. [6], the posteriori entropy based method presented by Sahoo et al. [7], and so on. However, due to there are no clear boundary between regions in complex images, these histogram based segmented leads to some ambiguity. To tackle this problem, Tao et al. [8] designed a new fuzzy entropy based three-level thresholding method for image segmentation.

Exhaustive search algorithm is a kind of typical method for searching the appropriate multi-level thresholds based on specific objective functions or criterion, such as entropy. However, the exhaustive search algorithm will become quiet time-consuming when the number of desired thresholds is increased [9]. Another alternative to fast multi-level thresholding is the incorporation of nature-inspired algorithms (NAs). In the past two decades, many classical NAs, including genetic algorithm (GA), particle swarm optimization (PSO), differential evolution (DE) algorithm, and so on [4, 10–13]. However, the inherent disadvantages of the meta-heuristic algorithms make it still a challenge task to obtain the optimal thresholds rapidly while maintaining high quality capabilities [14].

As one of the outstanding meat-heuristic algorithms, the gravitational search algorithm (GSA), which is inspired by the law of gravity and mass interactions, has proven its promising efficiency for solving complex problems [15]. GSA also has been extended to solve the multi-level thresholding problem. Nevertheless, none of the GSA based thresholding methods have addressed the problems resulted from the K_{best} model where the global property of K_{best} remains unchanged in the evolutionary process. Thus, GSA needs further improvement when utilized to perform segmentation of the complex satellite images.

This paper presents an adaptive GSA (AGSA) based multi-level thresholding method for color image using fuzzy entropy. In AGSA, the neighborhood of each particle is adaptively formed on the basis of evolutionary states. Thereby each particle can learn search information from (i) all the particles in its neighborhood and (ii) the historically best experience of the whole population (***gbest***). The local neighborhood is helpful to decrease the computational complexity and keep search diversity while the global model is beneficial to accelerate the convergence speed. In addition, to further promote the performance of GSA, the sinusoidal chaotic gravitational constants are integrated to further promote the balance of exploration and exploitation of AGSA.

The reminder of this paper is structured as follows. Section 2 describes the proposed AGSA and its implementation in multi-level thresholding. The experiments and comparative evaluation are given in Sect. 3. Finally, the whole paper is concluded in Sect. 4.

2 Methodology

2.1 Dynamic Neighborhood Learning Strategy

The dynamic neighborhood learning strategy is adopted from our previous research [16]. In this strategy, we let $\boldsymbol{X} = [\boldsymbol{x}_1, \boldsymbol{x}_2, \ldots, \boldsymbol{x}_N]$ denote a population, where $x_i = [x_i^1, x_i^2, \ldots, x_i^D]$, i = 1, 2, …, N represents a particle in a D-dimensional search space. In the proposed AGSA, the population is firstly divided into M non-overlapping local neighborhoods randomly, i.e. $\boldsymbol{DN} = \{\boldsymbol{DN}_1, \boldsymbol{DN}_2, \ldots, \boldsymbol{DN}_M\}$. Each local neighborhood has an equal number of particles. Thereby, following the Newton's law of gravity and mass interactions, a particle $\boldsymbol{x}_i$ located in the j-th neighborhood only connects with particles in its local neighborhood $\boldsymbol{DN}_j$ through the gravitational forces as follows.

$$Lv_i^d(t+1) = \sum_{x_p \in DN_j(t), x_p \neq x_i} rand \cdot G(t) \frac{Mass_p(t)}{R_{ip}(t) + \varepsilon} (x_p^d(t) - x_i^d(t)), \tag{1}$$

where *rand* is a uniform random variable in the interval [0, 1], $G(t)$ is the gravitational coefficient in time t, $Mass_p$ is the mass of particle p, R_{ip} is the Euclidean distance between particle i and p, ε is a minimal value which is set to e^{-6} in this paper, $x_p^d(t)$ and $x_i^d(t)$ is the d-th dimensional positions of particle p and i in time t, Lv_i^d is the d-th dimensional velocity of particle $\boldsymbol{x}_i$ generated by the local neighbors in time t.

The mass of particles are calculated from their fitness function values as shown in Eqs. (2)–(5). It is obvious that a heavier particle always represents a better solution with larger or small fitness function value.

$$Mass_i^t = \frac{nmfit_i(t)}{\sum_{j=1}^{N} nmfit_j(t)}, \tag{2}$$

$$nmfit_i(t) = \frac{fit_i(t) - worst(t)}{best(t) - worst(t)}, \tag{3}$$

where $fit_i(t)$ represents the fitness value of particle i at time t. For a minimization problem, the $best(t)$ and $worst(t)$ are defined as follows:

$$best(t) = \min_{j \in \{1,\ldots,N\}} fit_j(t), \tag{4}$$

$$worst(t) = \max_{j \in \{1,\ldots,N\}} fit_j(t). \tag{5}$$

To promote the adaptivity of the neighborhood learning strategy, the local neighborhoods are dynamically adjusted according to the evolutionary state of the population. For a healthy convergence, ***gbest*** can gradually approach the global optimum while other particles get close to the ***gbest*** step by step. If ***gbest*** gets stuck, the ***gbest*** is likely to be a local optimum and leads to population stagnation. Thus the ***gbest*** can be used to evaluate the evolutionary state follows Ref. [16].

For the global neighborhood learning, the particle i also learns from the best experience of the whole population has been found so far, denoted by $\boldsymbol{gbest} = [g^1, g^2, \ldots, g^D]$. Apparently, the ***gbest*** model is a global neighborhood topology [17]. The attraction of the ***gbest*** exerts on the particle i is defined as follow:

$$Gv_i^d(t+1) = rand \cdot (g^d(t) - x_i^d(t)), \tag{6}$$

where $Gv_i^d(t+1)$ is the global velocity produced by the ***gbest***.

Therefore, each particle can simultaneously learning from the local and global neighborhood topologies, and its velocity and position can be updated by:

$$v_i^d(t+1) = rand \cdot v_i^d(t) + c_1 \cdot Lv_i^d(t+1) + c_2 \cdot Gv_i^d(t+1), \tag{7}$$

$$x_i^d(t+1) = x_i^d(t) + v_i^d(t+1). \tag{8}$$

where c_1 and c_2 are acceleration coefficients which are respectively set to $2 - 1.5t/T_{\max}$ and $1.5t/T_{\max}$. The $T_{\max}$ is the minimum iterations.

2.2 Sinusoidal Chaotic Maps Based Gravitational Constants

The sinusoidal chaotic gravitational constants have demonstrated its effectiveness in basic GSA [11]. In this paper, to promote the balance between exploitation and exploration, the sinusoidal chaotic gravitational constants are embedded to AGSA. Specifically, the sinusoidal chaotic gravitational constants are obtained based on the sinusoidal chaotic maps as shown in Eq. (9).

$$C(t) = \eta \cdot C^2(t-1)\sin(\pi \cdot C(t-1)), \tag{9}$$

where $\eta = 2.3$ and the initial value of the sinusoidal chaotic map $C(0) = 0.7$. Moreover, the range of this map lies in the interval of (0, 1).

Accordingly, the range of the chaotic maps, the normalized chaotic values, and the final gravitational constants in time t can be calculated follows Eqs. (10)–(12).

$$W(t) = MAX - \frac{t}{T_{\max}}(MAX - MIN) \tag{10}$$

$$C^{norm}(t) = \frac{(C(t) - a) \times (W(t))}{(b - a)} \tag{11}$$

$$G(t) = G(t) + C^{norm}(t) \tag{12}$$

where [MAX, MIN] represents the adaptive interval, and [a, b] shows the range of chaotic maps. Note that we use $MAX = 20$ and $MIN = e^{-10}$ in our experiments following the set in Ref. [11].

2.3 AGSA Based Multi-level Thresholding

To start the AGSA for multi-level thresholding, initial population should be randomly generated first. Each particle is a candidate solution of the optimal fuzzy parameters. The size of the population (N) is set by users, and dimension (D) of each particle is twice the number of thresholds: $D = 2*m$. In the iteration process, the fitness value of each particle is calculated from the fuzzy entropy follows Ref. [8] and finally the particle with the best fitness value in the last iteration is selected as the optimal thresholds. Segmented image of each channel (Red, Green, and Blue) are then mapped into the RGB space to construct the final segmented color image. The framework of the proposed multi-level image thresholding method is shown in Fig. 1.

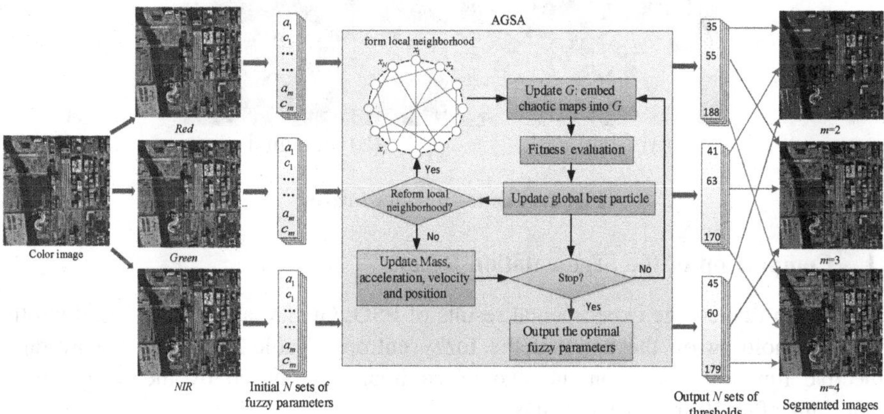

Fig. 1. Framework of the AGSA based satellite image multi-level thresholding. (Color figure online)

3 Experiments and Results

To validate the proposed multi-level thresholding method, we compared the experimental results of AGSA with that of the classical PSO [18] and an excellent improved variant of GSA, i.e. the *gbest*-based GSA (GGSA) [19]. Parameter settings of these four algorithms are listed in Table 1.

Table 1. Parameter settings.

Algorithm	Parameter settings
PSO	$c_1 = c_2 = 2$, $w \in [0.4, 0.9]$, $N = 10*D$, $T_{\max} = 200$;
GGSA	$G_0 = 100$, $\beta = 20$, $c_1 = 2 - 2t^3/T_{\max}^3$, $c_2 = 2t^3/T_{\max}^3$, $k \in [N, 2]$, $N = 10*D$, $T_{\max} = 200$;
AGSA	$G_0 = 100$, $\beta = 20$, $c_1 = 2-1.5t/T_{\max}$, $c_2 = 1.5t/T_{\max}$, $k = 10$, $gm = 5$, $N = 10*D$, $T_{\max} = 200$;

Experimental were conducted on two color images, Grant Park and Shanghai, as shown in Fig. 2. The images are obtained from the Pleiades image Gallery (http://www.satpalda.com/gallery) with the size 583 × 583 and 512 × 512 pixels, respectively. In this paper, the number of thresholds in the range of 4-6 for each tested image. To reduce statistical errors, each test is repeated 10 times independently. The average objective function and CPU time of each algorithm on the two tested images are listed in Table 2. Experiments were conducted on MATLAB R2017b running on an Intel(R) Core™ i3-6100 CPU with 3.70 GHz CPU and 8 GB RAM.

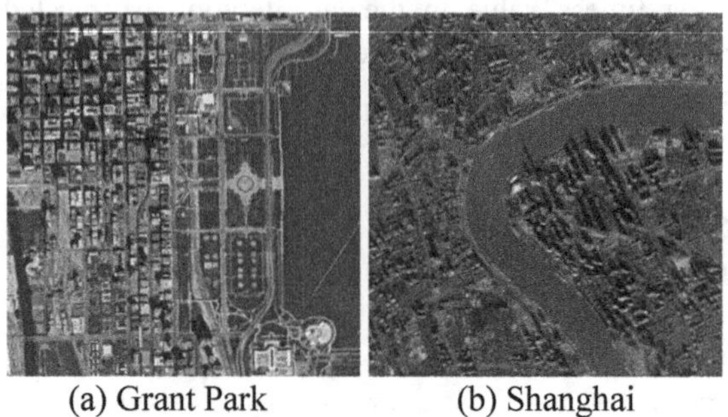

(a) Grant Park (b) Shanghai

Fig. 2. The tested color images.

3.1 Comparison of the Segmentation Results

This section depicts the experimental results of PSO, GGSA, and AGSA based multi-level thresholding on the basis of the fuzzy entropy. Table 2 presents the average objective function values on the two tested images produced by the compared 3 algorithms after 10 independent runs.

Table 2. Comparison of algorithms in terms of best objective function values.

Images	*m*	ch	PSO	GGSA	AGSA
Grant park	4	R	21.718	20.227	**20.101**
		G	21.679	20.228	**20.170**
		B	21.729	20.231	**19.950**
	5	R	24.972	23.410	**23.221**
		G	25.020	23.284	**23.040**
		B	24.977	23.476	**23.280**
	6	R	28.081	26.731	**26.572**
		G	28.017	26.674	**26.376**
		B	28.044	26.373	**26.134**
Shanghai	4	R	21.676	21.386	**21.277**
		G	21.689	21.392	**21.351**
		B	21.693	21.388	**21.261**
	5	R	25.014	24.721	**24.566**
		G	25.056	**24.572**	24.661
		B	25.025	24.696	**24.533**
	6	R	28.090	27.949	**27.927**
		G	27.896	27.958	**27.910**
		B	28.123	27.948	**27.739**

In Table 2, the best results in each row are shown in boldface. As shown, the increase of the thresholds always contribute to the improvement of the objective function values. GGSA performed the best in several cases and obtained better results than that of PSO on all the cases. By contrast, AGSA achieved the best objective function values on the two tested images with different thresholding levels. This may due to the dynamic neighborhood learning strategy and chaotic gravitational constants can effectively improvement the balance of the exploration and exploitation in AGSA. This is also confirmed by the visual interpretation of the segmentation results shown in Figs. 3 and 4. From Figs. 3 and 4 we can find that although the complexity of these images make it hard to compare the segmentation results, the segmented water area in these two tested images shown much better homogeneity.

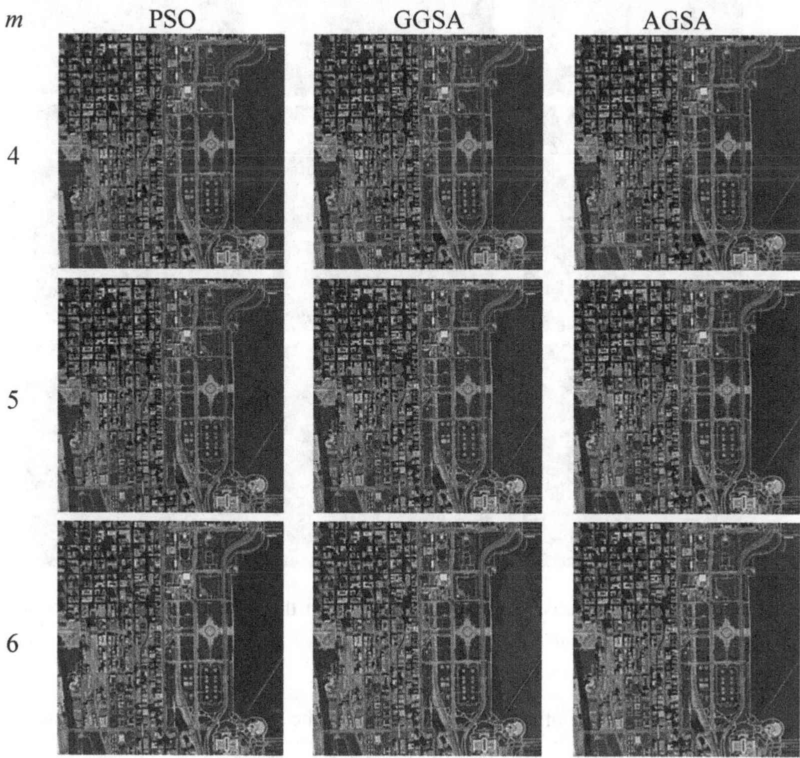

Fig. 3. The segmentation results of Grant Park image with the best fitness values produced by PSO, GGSA, and AGSA with m varies from 4 to 6.

3.2 Comparison of the Computation Efficiency

To statistically analyze the computational efficiency of different methods, the average CPU running times taken by each algorithm on the two tested images are reported in Table 3. As illustrated in Table 3, for all the test images at different thresholding levels, the PSO based method takes the shortest CPU running times, followed by GGSA and AGSA. This is mainly because each particle learns from the least number of particles in PSO, i.e. only leans from the personal and global particles in the iterations. The computational efficiency of AGSA is obviously better than that of the GGSA. This is may come from the utilization of the local neighborhood which effectively decrease the computational complexity of the K_{best} model in GGSA.

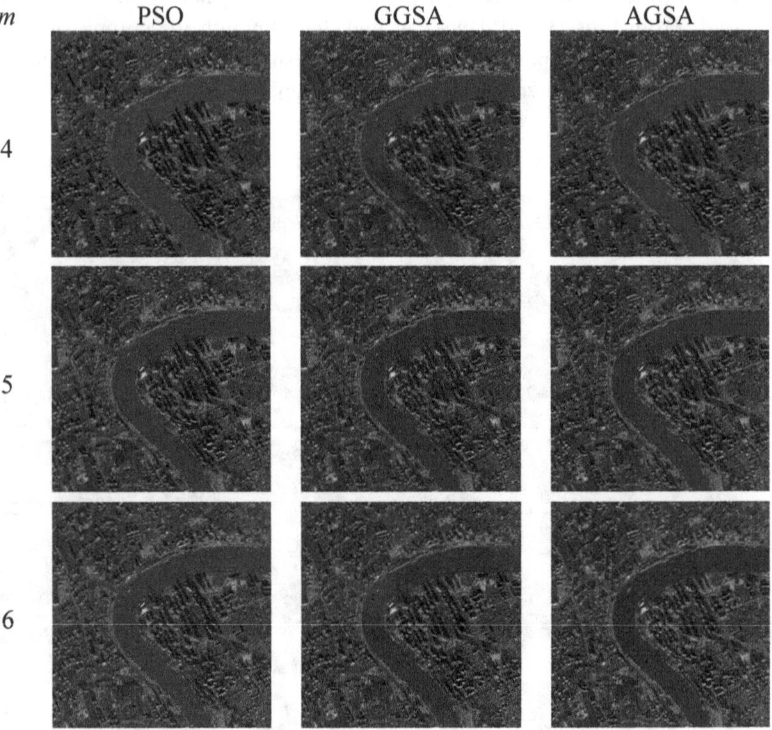

Fig. 4. The segmentation results of Shanghai image with the best fitness values produced by PSO, GGSA, and AGSA with m varies from 4 to 6.

Table 3. Comparison of algorithms in terms of the mean CPU running times.

Images	m	PSO	GGSA	AGSA
Grant park	4	**7.053**	9.995	8.266
	5	**10.230**	14.820	12.096
	6	**14.981**	20.976	16.341
Shanghai	4	**8.423**	10.085	8.263
	5	**10.907**	14.838	12.027
	6	**15.304**	21.672	16.094

4 Conclusions

Multi-level thresholding of color image is still a challenging task. In this paper, we presented a novel multi-level thresholding algorithm for color image segmentation by employing an improved GSA variant, called AGSA. AGSA is characterized by a dynamic neighborhood-based learning strategy, in which the local neighborhood and global neighborhood topologies are combined. More specifically, the local neighborhood of each particle are adaptively formed according to the evolutionary states while the global neighborhood is defined as the historically best experience of the population. The former enables the algorithm to more sufficiently explore the feasible search space while the latter offers the fast convergence toward the global optimum. Moreover, the sinusoidal chaotic gravitational constants are introduced to further promote the performance of AGSA. For multi-level thresholding of color image, the fuzzy entropy is adopted as the objective function. Finally, the particle with the minimum fuzzy entropy is outputted as the optimal thresholds. The experimental results on two tested images verified the superiority and availability of the AGSA compared with PSO, and GGSA. Nevertheless, the qualitative comparison is blurry and the quantitative comparison only based on the objective function values is inefficient. In the future work, we will try to explore more efficient performance evaluation methods for the segmentation of color images.

References

1. Kang, W.-X., Yang, Q.-Q., Liang, R.-P.: The comparative research on image segmentation algorithms, In: First International Workshop on Education Technology and Computer Science, pp. 703–707. IEEE, Wuhan (2009)
2. Horng, M.-H.: Multilevel thresholding selection based on the artificial bee colony algorithm for image segmentation. Expert Syst. Appl. **38**(11), 13785–13791 (2011)
3. Dey, S., Bhattacharyya, S., Maulik, U.: Quantum behaved multi-objective PSO and ACO optimization for multi-level thresholding. In: 2014 International Conference on Computational Intelligence and Communication Networks, pp. 242–246. IEEE, Bhopal (2014)
4. Agrawal, S., Panda, R., Bhuyan, S., Panigrahi, B.K.: Tsallis entropy based optimal multilevel thresholding using cuckoo search algorithm. Swarm Evol. Comput. **11**, 16–30 (2013)
5. Kapur, J.N., Sahoo, P.K., Wong, A.K.: A new method for gray-level picture thresholding using the entropy of the histogram. Comput. Vis. Graph. Image Process. **29**(3), 273–285 (1985)
6. Li, C.H., Tam, P.K.-S.: An iterative algorithm for minimum cross entropy thresholding. Pattern Recogn. Lett. **19**(8), 771–776 (1998)
7. Sahoo, P., Wilkins, C., Yeager, J.: Threshold selection using Renyi's entropy. Pattern Recogn. **30**(1), 71–84 (1997)
8. Tao, W.-B., Tian, J.-W., Liu, J.: Image segmentation by three-level thresholding based on maximum fuzzy entropy and genetic algorithm. Pattern Recogn. Lett. **24**(16), 3069–3078 (2003)

9. Kurban, T., Civicioglu, P., Kurban, R., Besdok, E.: Comparison of evolutionary and swarm based computational techniques for multilevel color image thresholding. Appl. Soft Comput. **23**, 128–143 (2014)
10. Tao, W., Jin, H., Liu, L.: Object segmentation using ant colony optimization algorithm and fuzzy entropy. Pattern Recogn. Lett. **28**(7), 788–796 (2007)
11. Sarkar, S., Paul, S., Burman, R., Das, S., Chaudhuri, S.S.: A Fuzzy Entropy Based Multi-Level Image Thresholding Using Differential Evolution. In: Panigrahi, B.K., Suganthan, P. N., Das, S. (eds.) SEMCCO 2014. LNCS, vol. 8947, pp. 386–395. Springer, Cham (2015). https://doi.org/10.1007/978-3-319-20294-5_34
12. Boussaïd, I., Chatterjee, A., Siarry, P., Ahmed-Nacer, M.: Hybrid BBO-DE algorithms for fuzzy entropy-based thresholding. In: Chatterjee, A., Siarry, P. (eds.) Computational Intelligence in Image Processing, pp. 37–69. Springer, Berlin, Heidelberg (2013). https://doi.org/10.1007/978-3-642-30621-1_3
13. Ali, M., Ahn, C.W., Pant, M.: Multi-level image thresholding by synergetic differential evolution. Appl. Soft Comput. **17**, 1–11 (2014)
14. Rashedi, E., Nezamabadi-pour, H., Saryazdi, S.: GSA: a gravitational search algorithm. Inf. Sci. **179**(13), 2232–2248 (2009)
15. Zhang, A., Sun, G., Ren, J., Li, X., Wang, Z., Jia, X.: A dynamic neighborhood learning-based gravitational search algorithm. IEEE Trans. Cybern. **48**(1), 436–447 (2018)
16. Kennedy, J., Kbehhart, R.: Particle swarm optimization. In: Encyclopedia of Machine Learning, pp. 760–766 (2010)
17. Mirjalili, S., Gandomi, A.H.: Chaotic gravitational constants for the gravitational search algorithm. Appl. Soft Comput. **53**, 407–419 (2017)
18. Mirjalili, S., Lewis, A.: Adaptive gbest-guided gravitational search algorithm. Neural Comput. Appl. **25**(7), 1569–1584 (2014)
19. Sun, G., Ma, P., Ren, J., Zhang, A., Jia, X.: A stability constrained adaptive alpha for gravitational search algorithm. Knowl.-Based Syst. **139**, 200–213 (2018)
20. Tschannerl, J., et al.: MIMR-DGSA: unsupervised hyperspectral band selection based on information theory and a modified discrete gravitational search algorithm. Inf. Fusion **51**, 189–200 (2019)

Detection of Invisible Damage of Kiwi Fruit Based on Hyperspectral Technique

Yanjun Liu, Zhijing Yang(✉), Jiangzhong Cao, Wing-Kuen Ling, and Qing Liu

School of Information Engineering, Guangdong University of Technology, Guangzhou 510006, China
yzhj@gdut.edu.cn

Abstract. In order to study the method of identifying early hidden damage of kiwifruit, near infrared hyperspectral imaging system in the range of 900–1700 nm is used to acquire the near infrared hyperspectral imaging of sound kiwifruits and damage kiwifruits (in three hours). In this research, kernel-based partial least squares (KPLS) method is used to select the effective bands from 224 hyperspectral bands for reducing data dimension. Then principal component analysis (PCA) is applied to extract features from the effective bands. Finally, the classification result is obtained by the support vector machine (SVM), backpropagation neural network (BPNN) and extreme learning machine (ELM). In the experiment section, the proposed method with band selection based on kernel partial least square is compared with the method without band selection. For 69 sound kiwifruits and 69 invisible damaged kiwi fruits, a total of 138 samples were collected. The best accuracy of band selection based on KPLS method is 98.27%, which is obviously better than the result without band selection. The result shows that the near infrared hyperspectral imaging technique can be used to identify early hidden damage of kiwifruit, and the band selection method based on kernel partial least squares is very helpful to improve the recognition accuracy.

Keywords: Hyperspectral imaging · Early hidden damage · Kiwifruit · Kernel-based partial least squares · PCA

1 Introduction

During picking, packaging, storage and transportation of kiwifruits, mechanical damage is often caused by collision or extrusion. Mechanical damage not only reduces the quality of kiwifruit, but also increases the risk of microbial infection, increases the degree of decay and shorten the expiration date. What's more, the damaged tissue can provide a breeding place for the pathogen, and then cause the damage of normal kiwifruits. Because of the dark color and hairy surface of kiwifruit peel, the early hidden damage is difficult to be recognized by naked eyes. Traditional machine vision technology based on RGB imaging system has been successfully applied to identify fruit surface defects [1, 2] and so on. However, it is difficult to identify the early hidden damage of kiwi fruits which are difficult to distinguish by the naked eyes or visible

J. Ren et al. (Eds.): BICS 2019, LNAI 11691, pp. 373–382, 2020.
https://doi.org/10.1007/978-3-030-39431-8_36

imaging. In N. Kotwaliwale's research [3], the internal quality of kiwifruit was examined by x-ray imaging. Because of the high-water content of kiwifruit, the qualitative difference between damage area and normal area was not enough to distinguish the early hidden damage fruit by x-ray imaging. Roberto Moscetti [4] used Near-infrared spectroscopy to detect hailstorm damage on olive fruit, correct recognition rate is around 96%. For test object, the near-infrared spectroscopy only obtains the information of the point rather than comprehensive information which include spectral and spatial information. Therefore, the recognition of the damaged kiwifruit will be affected by this way.

Hyperspectral imaging is a new technique for obtaining both spectral information and spatial information of the objects. It has been widely used in the non-destructive detection of the internal and external quality of agricultural products. Qiao et al. [5] proposed to use singular spectrum analysis to improve beef hyperspectral imaging. Ultra-violet and short-wave infra-red hyperspectral imaging were used to measure the concentration of phenolic flavour compounds on malted barley [6]. For detection of damage fruit, hyperspectral imaging technology has also been greatly developed. Lü et al. [7] studied a method for hidden damage of kiwi fruit based on visible and near infrared (408-117 nm) hyperspectral image, the experimental results show that the error rate of detecting hidden bruises on fruits with hyperspectral imaging was 14.5%. Li [8] utilized PCA to obtain effective PC images, coupled with a novel improved watershed segmentation method (I-WSM). It can identify the bruises on peaches, where 96.5% of the bruises and 97.5% of sound peaches were accurately identified respectively. The hyperspectral image is high-dimensional data, which comprises redundant information. Zabalza et al. [9] proposed using novel segmented stacked autoencoder to reduce dimensions and extract features in hyperspectral imaging. This resulted in reduced complexity but improved efficacy of data abstraction and accuracy of data classification. Segmented PCA can further improve classification accuracy while significantly reducing the computational cost and memory requirement, without requiring prior knowledge [10]. Cen [11] used sequential forward selection with SVM to detect chilling injury in cucumber fruit, yielded the best results. The overall accuracies for two-class and three-class were 100% and 91.6%. Proper feature selection method also improves the recognition accuracy, and requires a robust classifier to recognize and classify sounds and damaged fruit.

To detect the invisible damage of kiwifruit, the commonly used method is to select the spectral band corresponding to the peak point from the weight coefficient of PCA, and use the image processing method after PCA. Therefore, this study aims to develop an automatic feature selection system and attempts to detect invisible damage of kiwifruit using classification algorithm. The specific aims of the paper are:

(1) Obtain hyperspectral images of normal and damage kiwifruits.
(2) Automatically select the effective wavebands from all wavebands.
(3) Use PCA to reduce the dimension of effective wavebands and extract information.
(4) Develop classifier for the classification of sound and damage kiwifruits.

2 Materials and Methods

2.1 Sample Preparation

The kiwi fruit used in this paper is 'CHILE' kiwi fruit, which produced in Chile. A batch of kiwifruit samples are purchased from the market, where the kiwifruits with regular shape, non-destructive, disease-free and non-scrubbing are selected as the experimental sample. The kiwifruit is horizontally placed on a clean platform, and a square plate was placed horizontally near the equator of kiwifruit to exert pressure from top to bottom in order to damage sample. Kiwifruits are divided into two groups with 69 samples each. The first group will not be damaged (normal kiwi fruits), the other one contained bruise kiwi fruits damaged (the early hidden damage is difficult to be distinguished by naked eyes) artificially. Samples of both groups are stored at indoor temperature (27 °C) for 1–3 h before measured by Hyperspectral Imaging System, to ensure that chemical changes occur within the damaged sample. After all samples are measured by Hyperspectral Imaging System, two groups of samples are observed with the naked eyes to confirm that sound and damaged samples could not be distinguished only from the appearance of the samples, and then peeling all samples ensure that the samples are ideal. Images of a kiwifruits before and after peeling skin sound and after damaged in 3 h are shown in Fig. 1.

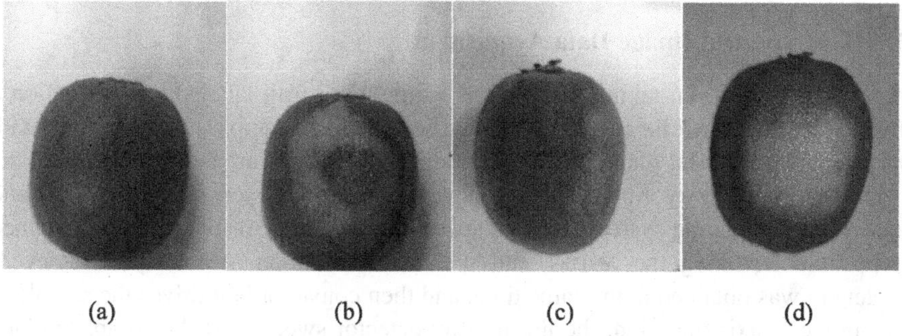

Fig. 1. Images of damage kiwi fruit obtained before (a) and after (b) peeling of skin, images of sound kiwi fruit obtained before (c) and after (d) peeling of skin.

2.2 Hyperspectral Imaging System

The scheme of the hyperspectral imaging system, developed for this research, is shown in Fig. 2. The system consists of hyperspectral camera (SPECIM FX17, Finland), computer (dell), conveyor belt and halogen lamp. With the halogen lamp providing illumination, the conveyor belt and the hyperspectral camera form a push-sweep hyperspectral imaging function. The spectral resolution obtained by hyperspectral camera is 8 nm, the spectral range of the hyperspectral camera is from 900 nm to 1700 nm with 3.5 nm spectral intervals, which resulted in 224 spectral wavebands, the Detector size is 640 pixels by 220 pixels. After a kiwi fruit is fully scanned, a hyperspectral image with spatial and spectral information is obtained.

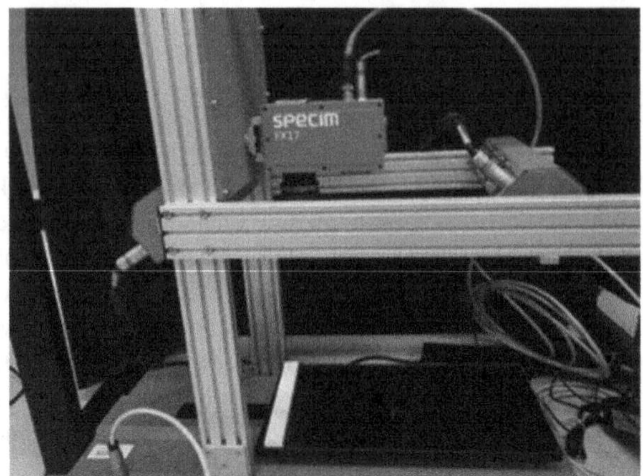

Fig. 2. Hyperspectral imaging system.

For hyperspectral sensor data acquisition, LUMO software was used. Some data processing and analysis procedures are performed using Environment for Visualizing Images (ENVI) V.4.8 (Research Systems Inc., Colorado, USA) and MATLAB 2014a (The MathWorks Inc., US).

2.3 Hyperspectral Image Data Acquisition

When image collection, taking one kiwi at a time, kiwi fruit labeled was placed on a conveyor belt, meanwhile two rows of tungsten halogen lamps at a 45° angle with respect to the horizontal plane provide lighting. LUMO software is used to control the movement of the conveyor belt. The hyperspectral imaging system is a push broom and line-scan based imaging system. A linear space (640 by 1pixel resolution) was obtained by spectrometer along the X-axis, and spectral information of each pixel at every wavelength was obtained at the same time, and then conveyor belt drives the sample to move in the Y-axis direction, the linear array detector sweeps out the complete plane line by line. When the above steps are finished, a three-dimension hyperspectral image with spatial and spectral information is obtained.

2.4 Image Calibration

The heterogeneous intensities of the light source across the whole waveband range and the presence of dark current in the sensor will lead to large noise in the obtained image. Image calibration is performed before measurement by taking the image of a piece of white reference standard with 99% reflectance and a dark frame. When collecting the hyperspectral image of kiwifruit, firstly scanning reference panel to get white image R_{White}, then covering the lens cover for dark image R_{Black}. Finally, the original image $R_{Original}$ is processed to get the Calibration image R_{ref}. The hyperspectral images of the kiwi fruit is calibrated with a white and a dark reference is the following equation:

$$R_{ref} = \frac{R_{Original} - R_{Black}}{R_{White} - R_{Black}} \tag{1}$$

3 The Proposed Framework

3.1 Data Processing

In this research, damage processing was done at the center of kiwifruit (near the equator). In order to reduce the influence of uneven illumination and the difference of tissue composition in different parts on the spectral intensity, the region (50 pixel by 50 pixel) near the equator of sample after image calibration is selected as Region of interest (ROI). Subsequently, the average reflectance spectrum of ROI of each kiwifruit is calculated as a sample. Figure 3 shows the average spectral reflection value of ROI (50 $\times$ 50 pixel) of 40 samples and it shows that the spectral reflection value of the sound region is higher than that of the damaged region in the number 1–63 spectral band region (935 nm–1067 nm). When the spectral number is higher than 63, the spectral curves of the sound kiwifruit and damage kiwifruit are close or even partially mixed, which indicates that the sound samples and the damaged samples can't be well identified in this spectral region. Therefore, in the following research, the hyperspectral images in the band between number 1 and number 63 are processed, it means that the selected effective wavebands in the next step is only in this spectral range.

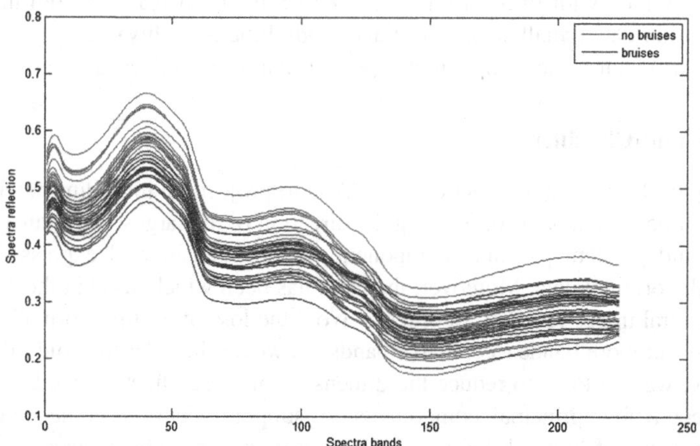

Fig. 3. Reflection spectra (224 bands) of no bruises and hidden bruises kiwifruits.

3.2 Band Selection

Partial least squares is one of the widespread use of a class of multivariate statistical analysis technique [12] and a popular regression technique in chemometrics [13]. In the process of establishing regression, the algorithm not only considers extracting the principal components from matrix Y and matrix X as far as possible (the idea of principal component analysis), but also consider the maximization of the correlation between the principal components extracted from X and Y (the idea of canonical correlation analysis). PLS calculate optimization problem by an iterative method [14], the mathematical expression is as following equation:

$$\underset{t,u}{argmaximize}\ cov(t,u) \tag{2}$$

$$Subject\ to: \|v\| = 1,\ \|c\| = 1$$

Where $t = Xv$ and $u = Yc$, $X \in R^{N \times M}$ represents data matrix of N samples and $Y \in R^{N \times D}$ represents corresponding samples matrix of classes. t is the matrix of X scores, u is the matrix of Y scores. After the first two components, t_1 and u_1 are obtained, p_1 (a vector of loading for the X block) and q_1 (a vector of loading for the Y block) will be calculated. The residuals can be calculated from $E_1 = X - t_1p'$ and $F_1 = Y - u_1q'$. In general,

$$E_n = E_{n-1} - t_np_n' \quad X = E_0 \tag{3}$$

$$F_n = F_{n-1} - u_nq_n' \quad Y = F_0 \tag{4}$$

Repeating above-mentioned steps until the halt condition is satisfied. Kernel partial least squares map the sample data into a higher-dimensional space by kernel function, and then combined with PLS. Sun [15] use KPLS to select features from microarray gene expression data (small sample size and High dimensionality). However, KPLS is rarely used in feature selection of hyperspectral images of hidden damage fruit.

3.3 PCA and Classifier

The principle of dimension reduction of PCA is to project the high-dimensional space to the low-dimensional data space along the direction of the largest covariance, so as to obtain the independent principal component vector and can well express the information of the original data. Moreover, the PCA has been widely used in the processing of hyperspectral image [16, 17]. In order to avoid the loss of useful information, KPLS is used to select more bands as effective bands. However, in order to avoid information redundancy, we use PCA to reduce the dimension of these effective bands again, and finally select a few principal components. A support vector machine constructs a hyperplane or set of hyperplanes in a high or infinite dimensional space, and a good separation is achieved by the hyperplane that has the largest distance to the nearest training data points of any class. In this study, libsvm [18] was used to classify. ELM is a neural network with only one hidden layer and one linear output layer. All the hidden node parameters are independent from the target functions or the training datasets. ELM and improved ELM has successfully been applied to a number of pattern recognition problems [19]. Backpropagation neural network is a common method of teaching artificial neural networks how to perform a given task. The above three methods are used in this experiment.

4 Results and Discussion

The above algorithm was used to identify 69 sound samples and 69 hidden damage samples. 60% samples are randomly selected from all samples as the training set, and the rest as the verification set. The experiment is repeated 20 times and the average accuracy is obtained. The result is compared with the results without KPLS. In this paper, three methods are used for comparisons. The first one is SVM with KPLS and PCA (SKP); the second one is SVM with PCA (SP); and the third one only uses SVM. In the same way, BPNN with KPLS and PCA (BKP), BPNN with PCA (BP), ELM with KPLS and PCA (EKP), ELM with PCA (EP). Results obtained by the system are given in Table 1. Table 1 shows that the recognition accuracy rate of methods with KPLS is superior to the methods without band selection. SKP obtains the best result as 98.27%, which is 2.73% and 6.27% higher than PS method and SVM method respectively.

In this research, the confusion matrix is introduced to measure the performance of the classifier, because accuracy cannot fully measure it. The classification problem of distinguishing between hidden damaged kiwi fruits and sound kiwi fruits is treated as a binary problem. In the experiment, hidden damaged kiwi fruit is a positive class and sound kiwi fruit is a negative class. The four results will be output after the classifier which has been tested on samples. If a sample is a positive class and is also predicted as a positive class, it is called a true positive (TP), and if it is classified as negative class, it is counted as false negative (FN). In the same way, if a sample is a negative class and is also predicted as a negative class, it is called a true negative (TN), and if it is classified as positive class, it is counted as false positive (FP). The true positive rate (TPR) which is also called a recall is estimated as:

$$\mathrm{TPR} = \frac{\mathrm{TP}}{\mathrm{TP} + \mathrm{FN}} \tag{5}$$

The false positive rate (FPR) of the classifier is:

$$\mathrm{FPR} = \frac{\mathrm{FP}}{\mathrm{TN} + \mathrm{FP}} \tag{6}$$

The precision of the classifier is:

$$Precision = \frac{\mathrm{TP}}{\mathrm{TP} + \mathrm{FP}} \tag{7}$$

F-measure is the weighted harmonic mean of precision and recall, and β is the weight coefficient. In this paper, β is set to 1, the F-measure of the classifier is:

$$F - measure = \left(1 + \beta^2\right)\frac{Precision \times recall}{\beta^2 \times Precision + recall} \quad (8)$$

To analyze the performance of the classifiers, the results of the analysis of the accuracy by different methods are presented in Table 1. It shows that the model with the best performance is the SKP. It has the highest values of the F-measure (0.9803) and TPR (0.9831), a smallest FPR (0.0211). Above three methods show that the indicators of methods with KPLS are superior to that of methods without band selection.

Table 1. The analysis of indicators by different methods

Classification model	TPR	FPR	Precision	F-measure ($\beta = 1$)	Accuracy
SKP	0.9831	0.0211	0.9776	0.9803	98.27%
SP	0.9492	0.0387	0.9583	0.9537	95.54%
SVM	0.9191	0.1004	0.8956	0.9072	92.00%
BKP	0.9628	0.0196	0.9827	0.9726	97.09%
BP	0.9054	0.0393	0.9640	0.9337	93.09%
BPNN	0.9493	0.0393	0.9656	0.9573	95.45%
EKP	0.9790	0.0833	0.9144	0.9455	94.64%
EP	0.9147	0.0781	0.9147	0.9147	92.18%
ELM	0.9522	0.0954	0.9007	0.9257	92.73%

5 Conclusion

This paper shows that, a near infrared hyperspectral imaging system can be used to identify early hidden injury kiwi in the wavelength range from 900 nm and 1700 nm. Data processing algorithm uses KPLS to select the bands as the effective bands. Even if the number of samples is small, the effective bands can be extracted and achieve a high recognition accuracy. Then PCA is used to conduct dimensionality reduction processing for the effective bands. Finally, three classifiers are used to classify after processed samples. The best detection accuracy of the proposed method is 98.27%, which is significantly better than other methods. The F-measure (0.9803) and TPR (0.9831) of SKP also indicate the superiority of the proposed model. This research provides a basis for the development of a rapid and accurate detection system for kiwifruit with hidden damage. Future work includes exploration of new approaches for feature extraction [20–22], feature fusion [23], band selection [24] and classification as well as new application areas [25].

Acknowledgement. This work is supported in part by the National Nature Science Foundation of China (nos. U1701266, 61471132), the Innovation Team Project of Guangdong Education Department (no. 2017KCXTD011), Natural Science Foundation of Guangdong Province China (no. 2018A030313751), and Science and Technology Program of Guangzhou, China (nos. 201803010065, 201802020010).

References

1. Hassankhani, R., Navid, H., Sayedarabi, H.: Potato surface defect detection in machine vision system. Afr. J. Agric. Res. **7**(5), 844–850 (2012)
2. Throop, J.A., Aneshansley, D.J., Anger, W.C., Peterson, D.L.: Quality evaluation of apples based on surface defects: development of an automated inspection system. Postharvest Biol. Technol. **36**(3), 281–290 (2005)
3. Kotwaliwale, N., Weckler, P.R., Brusewitz, G.H., Kranzler, G.A., Maness, N.O.: Non-destructive quality determination of pecans using soft X-rays. Postharvest Biol. Technol. **45** (3), 372–380 (2007)
4. Moscetti, R., Haff, R.P., Monarca, D., Cecchini, M., Massantini, R.: Near-infrared spectroscopy for detection of hailstorm damage on olive fruit. Postharvest Biol. Technol. **120**, 204–212 (2016)
5. Qiao, T., Ren, J., Craigie, C., Zabalza, J., Maltin, C., Marshall, S.: Singular spectrum analysis for improving hyperspectral imaging based beef eating quality evaluation. Comput. Electron. Agric. **115**, 21–25 (2015)
6. Tschannerl, J., Ren, J., Jack, F., et al.: Potential of UV and SWIR hyperspectral imaging for determination of levels of phenolic flavour compounds in peated barley malt. Food Chem. **270**, 105–112 (2019)
7. Lü, Q., Tang, M.: Detection of hidden bruise on kiwi fruit using hyperspectral imaging and parallelepiped classification. Proc. Environ. Sci. **12**(B), 1172–1179 (2012)
8. Li, J., Chen, L., Huang, W.: Detection of early bruises on peaches (Amygdalus persica L.) using hyperspectral imaging coupled with improved watershed segmentation algorithm. Postharvest Biol. Technol **135**, 104–113 (2018)
9. Zabalza, J., et al.: Novel segmented stacked autoencoder for effective dimensionality reduction and feature extraction in hyperspectral imaging. Neurocomputing **185**, 1–10 (2016)
10. Ren, J., Zabalza, J., Marshall, S., Zheng, J.: Effective feature extraction and data reduction in remote sensing using hyperspectral imaging [applications corner]. IEEE Signal Process. Mag. **31**(4), 149–154 (2014)
11. Cen, H., Lu, R., Zhu, Q., Mendoza, F.: Nondestructive detection of chilling injury in cucumber fruit using hyperspectral imaging with feature selection and supervised classification. Postharvest Biol. Technol. **111**, 352–361 (2016)
12. Wold, H.: Estimation of principal components and related models by iterative least squares. Multivariate Anal. **1**, 391–420 (1966)
13. Nissen, L.R., Byrne, D.V., Bertelsen, G., Skibsted, L.H.: The antioxidative activity of plant extracts in cooked pork patties as evaluated by descriptive sensory profiling and chemical analysis. Meat Sci. **68**(3), 485–495 (2004)
14. Geladi, P., Kowalski, B.R.: Partial least-squares regression: a tutorial. Anal. Chim. Acta **185**, 1–17 (1986)
15. Sun, S., Peng, Q., Shakoor, A.: A kernel-based multivariate feature selection method for microarray data classification. PLoS One **9**(7), e102541 (2014)
16. Farrell, M.D., Mersereau, R.M.: On the impact of PCA dimension reduction for hyperspectral detection of difficult targets. IEEE Geosci. Remote Sens. Lett. **2**(2), 192–195 (2005)
17. Agarwal, A., El-Ghazawi, T., El-Askary, H., Le-Moigne, J.: Efficient hierarchical-PCA dimension reduction for hyperspectral imagery. In: 2007 IEEE International Symposium on Signal Processing and Information Technology, pp. 353–356 (2007)

18. Chang, C.C., Lin, C.J.: LIBSVM: a library for support vector machines. ACM Trans. Intell. Syst. Technol **2**, 27:1–27:2 (2011)
19. Cao, F., et al.: Sparse representation-based augmented multinomial logistic extreme learning machine with weighted composite features for spectral-spatial classification of hyperspectral images. IEEE Trans. Geosci. Remote Sens. **56**(11), 1–17 (2018)
20. Zabalza, J., et al.: Novel two-dimensional singular spectrum analysis for effective feature extraction and data classification in hyperspectral imaging. IEEE Trans. Geosci. Remote Sens. **53**(8), 4418–4433 (2015)
21. Zabalza, J., et al.: Novel folded-PCA for improved feature extraction and data reduction with hyperspectral imaging and SAR in remote sensing. ISPRS J. Photogr. Remote Sens. **93**, 112–122 (2014)
22. Qiao, T., Yang, Z., Ren, J., et al.: Joint bilateral filtering and spectral similarity-based sparse representation: a generic framework for effective feature extraction and data classification in hyperspectral imaging. Pattern Recogn. **77**, 316–328 (2018)
23. Sun, H., Ren, J., Zhao, H., et al.: Superpixel based feature specific sparse representation for spectral-spatial classification of hyperspectral images. Remote Sens. **11**(5), 536 (2019)
24. Tschannerl, J., et al.: Unsupervised hyperspectral band selection based on information theory and a modified discrete gravitational search algorithm. Inform. Fusion **51**, 189–200 (2019)
25. Qiao, T., et al.: Quantitative prediction of beef quality using visible and NIR spectroscopy with large data samples under industry conditions. J. Appl. Spectrosc. **82**(1), 137–144 (2015)

Forensic Detection Based on Color Label and Oriented Texture Feature

Tingge Zhu[1(✉)], Jiangbin Zheng[1], Mingchen Feng[1], Ying Liu[2,3], Wei Liu[2], Nailiang Kuang[4], and Chao Zhao[4]

[1] Department of Computer Science and Engineering, School of Computers, Northwestern Polytechnical University, Xi'an, China
tgzhu@xupt.edu.cn, zhengjb0163@163.com, mingchen@mail.nwpu.edu.cn

[2] School of Telecommunication and Information Engineering, Xi'an University of Posts and Telecommunications, Xi'an, Shaanxi, China
ly_yolanda@sina.com, bme_liuwei@163.com

[3] Key Laboratory of Electronic Information Processing Technology for Crime Scene Investigation Application, Ministry of Public Security, Xi'an, China

[4] Xi'an Microelectronics Technology Institute, Xi'an, China

Abstract. Copy-move forgery is one of the most tampered means. In this paper, we propose a blind method based on the color label and oriented color texture feature for copy-move detection. Firstly, we compute local color entropy of every pixel, which is grouped into several categories as color labels. Then an image is divided into overlapping blocks, oriented color texture feature of which is extracted. Similar blocks are searched in these blocks with the same color label, and then we fuse these similar block pairs into several regions. According to the linkage relation of these regions, the tampered regions are located. Experiment results have demonstrated that the proposed algorithm has good performance in terms of improved detection accuracy and reduced execution time, at the same time, it also can detect these tampered images inpainted by exemplar-based inpainting technique.

Keywords: Digital image forensic · Forged region detection · Color label · Oriented texture feature

1 Introduction

With the development of image processing and editing techniques, it has become easier and easier to tamper with an image, which will bring bad effects to the society, judiciary, news reports and so on [1]. So, it has become a hot topic for digital forgery detection in recent years [2–6]. Now, tampering detection techniques are categorized as active techniques [7] and passive techniques [8, 9]. Active techniques include digital watermark and signature, which is embedded into an image in advance. In fact, most images don't carry watermarks, so its constraints adjured the evolution of passive techniques. Copy-move forgery (CMF) is the most tampered means. To some extent, image inpainting [10, 11] can also be thought of as a copy-paste. Two tampered

J. Ren et al. (Eds.): BICS 2019, LNAI 11691, pp. 383–395, 2020.
https://doi.org/10.1007/978-3-030-39431-8_37

examples are shown in Fig. 1. Figure 1b is an example of removing object and image inpainting. Figure 1d is an example of adding an object.

(a) Original image

(b)Tampered image

(c) Original image

(d) Tampered image

Fig. 1. Two examples of tampered image

Over the last decade or so, there are several kinds of approaches for forgery detection, but the most popular approaches are block-based and keypoint-based [12]. In the early, Fridrich proposed a block-based technique to detect CMF [13], which extracts DCT features of every overlapping image blocks, and these features are sorted lexicographically to search similar blocks, then the tampered region is located. Later, many methods based on block matching are proposed [2, 4, 6, 14–16]. The biggest difference between them is the feature of the overlapping block, and most of them have very high characteristic dimensions. So, in [15, 16], principal components analysis (PCA) is utilized to reduce the characteristic dimension for CMF detection. However, because of the exhaustive search, they are still computationally intensive.

In order to solve this problem, keypoint-based methods are employed because of their robust performance and relatively low computational costs, such as scale invariant feature transform (SIFT) [3] and speeded-up robust features (SURF) [17, 18], or their fusion [19, 20]. However, in terms of accuracy, they are weaker than block-based methods. That is because it is difficult to extract feature points in the uniform area of an image. But such block pairs with high similarity can be easily found in uniform regions, which will inevitably interfere with the detected forged regions.

In this paper, we propose a blind method based on the color label and oriented color texture feature. Firstly, local color entropy is computed and clustered, we get color labels. Then oriented color texture feature of every overlapping block is extracted. Similar blocks are searched in these blocks with the same color label, and then we fuse these similar block pairs into several regions. According to the linkage relation of these regions and post-processing, the tampered regions are located.

The remaining part of this paper is organized as follows. In Sect. 2, the proposed algorithm is presented. In Sect. 3, we evaluate the experimental results and performance in comparison with other benchmarking algorithms. Finally, some concluding remarks are drawn in Sect. 4. The details are discussed below.

2 The Proposed Algorithm

In general, an image is divided into overlapping blocks in block-based method, and feature of every block is extracted, then similar blocks are searched in these blocks. The majority of these methods extract the features of the image block based on greyscale. So the color feature is discarded, which affects detection accuracy. This paper proposes a method based on the color label and oriented local color texture feature (See Fig. 2). Firstly, local color entropy is computed, then which is clustered. Oriented local color texture feature of every overlapping block is extracted. Similar blocks are searched in these blocks with the same color label, and then similar block pairs are fused into several regions based on 8-connect. According to the linkage relation of these regions. Then we apply the morphology closing to filter out small islands within the detected regions, and the tampered regions are located. A detailed discussion of the proposed approach is presented as follows.

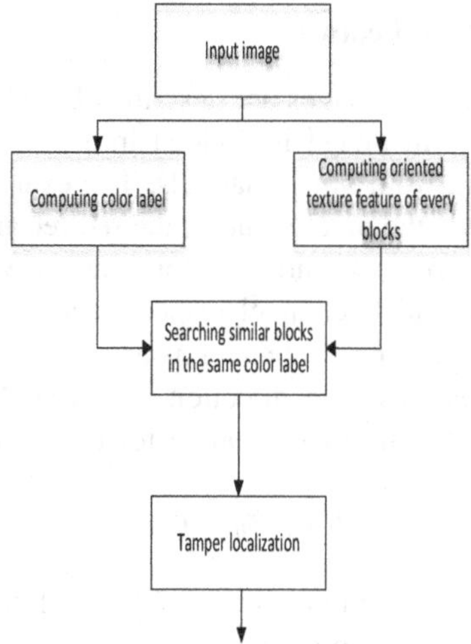

Fig. 2. Workflow of the proposed algorithm.

2.1 Color Label

Whether inpainting or copy-move, in general, tampered regions are covered with other regions in the image, so they are similar in term of color and texture. Based on this, we search similar blocks in these blocks with the same color. Therefore, we divide the image into regions based on the combined color features. Unlike the RGB and CMYK color models, the main advantage of Lab color space is that it is very similar to the perception of human eyes [15]. We convert the input image I into the Lab color space. According to the color distribution in the a and b channels, we compute the entropy for each pixel on the image I as follows.

For each pixel q, in consideration of its $t \times t$ neighborhood U_q centered at q, we define a variable $S(q)$ denoting the local entropy of q by

$$Entropy_a(q) = -\sum_{q \in U_q} \mathrm{P}(I_a(q)) \log_2 \mathrm{P}(I_a(q)) \quad (1)$$

$$Entropy_b(q) = -\sum_{q \in U_q} \mathrm{P}(I_b(q)) \log_2 \mathrm{P}(I_b(q)) \quad (2)$$

$$S(q) = Entropy_a(q) + Entropy_b(q) \quad (3)$$

where $\mathrm{P}(I_a(q))$ is the probability of channel a value in U_q.

We normalize $S(q)$ within the interval [0, 1] and cluster the image into k groups according to the determined local entropy of each pixel [31], which is considered as color labels, so we get k color labels.

2.2 Oriented Local Texture Feature

Generally, the texture features of images are described based on gray images. Hereon, we consider every channel. An image is divided into overlapping blocks, and their texture features are extracted from three channels. The example of an image block is shown in Fig. 3, which shows the pixel value of the red rectangle in Fig. 3(a) for R, G and B channel respectively. r_{00}, g_{00} and b_{00} represent the values of the center pixel from R channel, G channel and B channel respectively, Accordingly, r_{ij}, g_{ij} and b_{ij} represent other pixel values. Taking R channel as an example, we use local difference to calculate local texture features with direction (See Fig. 4). We use the following formula to get local texture feature of R channel for this block (See Fig. 4a)

$$dr_{ij} = r_{ij} - r_{00} \quad (4)$$

Figure 4b and c are the direction and amplitude of texture feature in Fig. 4a respectively. Let the maximum and minimum amplitude of local texture feature of the kth block be $Ar^k_{\max}$ and $Ar^k_{\min}$, $k = 1, \ldots (M - b + 1)(N - b + 1)$, the angle between them is θr^k. Their ratio is defined as follows.

$$ratior^k = \frac{Ar^k_{\max}}{Ar^k_{\min}} \quad (5)$$

According to this, we get We can get $ratiog^k$ and $ratiob^k$, θg^k and θb^k, which represent the ratios and angels of the other two channels for the kth block. Then we normalize $(ratior^k, ratiog^k, ratiob^k)$ and $(\theta r^k, \theta g^k, \theta b^k)$ separately.

Let BF^k represent the feature vector of the kth block, as shown below.

$$BF^k = (ratiorN^k, ratiogN^k, ratiobN^k, \theta rN^k, \theta gN^k, \theta bN^k) \quad (6)$$

Where $(ratiorN^k, ratiogN^k, ratiobN^k)$ and $(\theta rN^k, \theta gN^k, \theta bN^k)$ represent the normalized value.

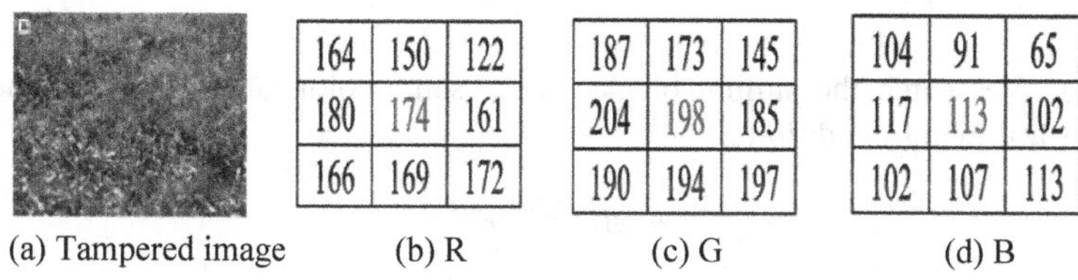

Fig. 3. An example for three channels of a block (Color figure online)

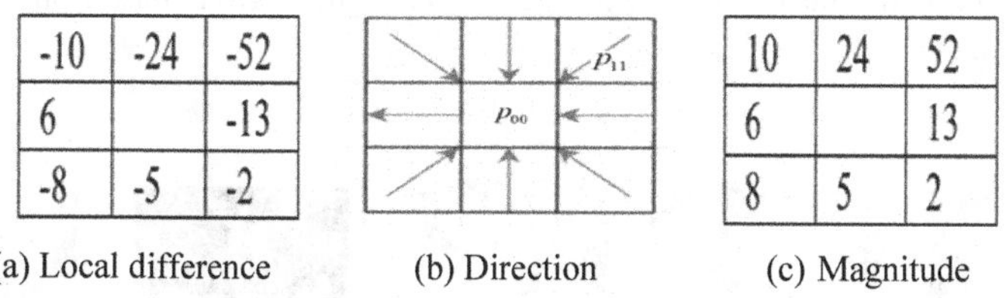

Fig. 4. Oriented local texture feature of a block in Fig. 3b

2.3 Similarity Matching

Unlike exhaustive search, our approach supposes that similar blocks are searched in the same color Label, rather than in all overlapping blocks. The details of the similarity search are described as follows.

Step 1. The local color entropy in the neighborhood of each pixel is computed, and a color entropy image is obtained, then we cluster the image into k groups according to the determined local color entropy of each pixel.

Step 2. An image is divided into overlapping blocks of $b \times b$, so there are $(M - b + 1) \times (N - b + 1)$ blocks.

Step 3. To count oriented local texture feature of every block, and which are is normalized. We use the ratio of the maximum to the minimum value of the local difference and the angle between them to characterize the block, which is denoted by $BF^k, k = 1, 2...(M - b + 1) \times (N - b + 1)$.

Step 4. Suppose BF^k and $BF^{k'}$ be two different block feature. $disBF$ is defined as the distance between the two block feature, as follows.

$$disBF = |BF^k - BF^{k'}|, k \neq k' \tag{7}$$

Step 5. Let (x_k, y_k) and $(x_{k'}, y_{k'})$ represent the coordinates of the first pixel in the upper left corner in $Block_k$ and $Block_{k'}$ respectively. The distance *disB* between them is defined as follows.

$$disB = \sqrt{(x_k - x_{k'})^2 + (y_k - y_{k'})^2} \tag{8}$$

Step 6. We search the similar blocks in the same color label. If *disBF* and *disB* satisfy the following conditions,

$$disBF < ThBF \tag{9}$$

$$disB < ThB \tag{10}$$

Thus, the two blocks are similar(See Fig. 5c).

Step 7. These similar blocks are merged into several regions based on 8-connected (See Fig. 5d).

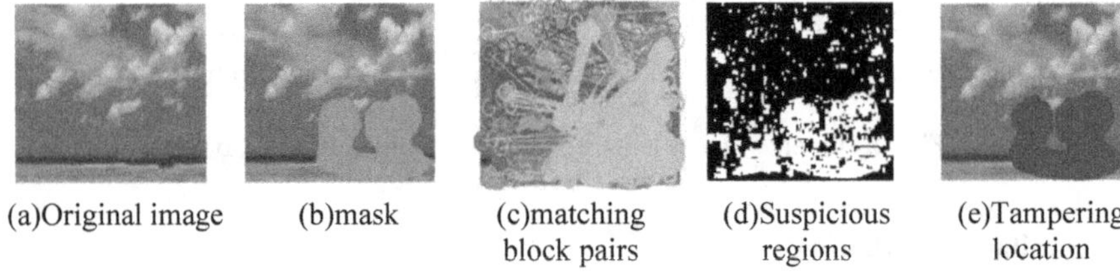

(a)Original image (b)mask (c)matching block pairs (d)Suspicious regions (e)Tampering location

Fig. 5. A detection example

2.4 Tampering Location

A suspicious region contains a certain number of small blocks. According to the characteristics of tampering, a suspicious block in a region always accompanies with its corresponding block in another region. If two suspicious regions have the amount of matched block pairs, we think that there a strong region linkage between the two regions, which can be categorized into three classes: many-to-one linkage, one-to-one linkage, and self-linkage [11].

In general, self-linkage always occurs in these areas with smooth texture and the same color, in fact, which is genuine. So mismatching is always in these areas. According to it, we can filter out error detection. One-to-one linkage happens in an image tampered by means of copy-move and many-to-one linkage is caused by image inpainting.

$Linknum_{ij}$ denotes the number of matching block pairs between two regions, $Linknum_i$ denotes the number of linkage relation with other regions. S_i denotes the number of pixels in the region. Tampering location is described as follows.

Step 1. When a region satisfies the following condition,

$$Linknum_i \geq \gamma \tag{11}$$

$$S_i > 5S_j, i \neq j \tag{12}$$

The region belongs to these regions with many-to-one linkage relation. The region is retained as a tamper region, accordingly, other regions associated with it are discarded.

Step 2. When a region satisfies the following condition,

$$Linknum_i < \gamma \tag{13}$$

$$Linknum_{ij} > \tau \tag{14}$$

The region belongs to these regions with one-to-one linkage relation. There are at least two matching regions in the image. So τ is not too small to filter out mismatching in uniform areas.

Finally, we apply the morphology closing to filter out small islands within the detected regions, (See Fig. 5e).

3 Experiment Results

Our algorithm was implemented on a computer (Intel 2.10 GHz processor, 16 GB RAM) using Matlab2016a. In this section, we introduce the database, evaluation metrics, and performance of the proposed scheme under different circumstances.

3.1 Databases

In this section, we use three databases to evaluate the performance of the proposed scheme. The first database is the CoMoFoD_small_v2 database presented in [21]. The second database is provided by Christlein et al. [22], which can be downloaded from [23]. The third database is produced by Criminisi's inpainting algorithm [10, 11]. We choose some image from three databases to test the performance of the proposed method.

3.2 Evaluation Metrics

For quantitative evaluation, the recall and precision rates and F1 measurement, as defined below, are employed for pixel-level performance assessment:

$$Precision = \frac{T_p}{T_p + F_p} \times 100\% \tag{15}$$

$$Recall = \frac{T_p}{T_p + F_N} \times 100\% \tag{16}$$

$$F_1 = \frac{2 \times Precision \times Recall}{precision + Recall} \tag{17}$$

Where T_p, F_p and F_N are the number of correctly identified pixels, the number of mistakenly detected pixels and the number of missed pixels, respectively. F_1 is a trade-off between precision and recall. The higher Precious, Recall and F_N, the more superior performance.

3.3 Several Parameters

There are three parameters including k, γ and τ in this proposed method. The first step is to segment the input image into k parts based on local entropy measurement as discussed in Sect. 2.1. Compared with exhaustive search, if k is too large, the calculation amount will not be significantly reduced, and if k is too small, the lost detection will increase, thus the detection accuracy will decrease. Here, the parameter k is determined by the size of the input image as follows.

$$k = \max(M, N)/200 \tag{18}$$

The second parameter is γ, which represents the number of linkage relation with other suspicious regions. Because their features between image blocks are similar in the smooth region, so some matching pairs occur in the smooth region. So γ is empirically set as 6 to avoid mismatching.

The third parameter is τ, which represents the number of matching pairs between the two regions. Because tampered regions are not so small, and there are matching pairs in smooth areas. τ is empirically set to 10 to filter out mismatching.

3.4 Detection Results and Discussions on the Three Databases

In the section, we perform our method on these data selected from three databases mentioned above to evaluate the performance, including post-processing operations and no post-processing operations. Most of the tampered image are impressively realistic, so it is difficult to distinguish true or false. The test images contain smooth or textured regions.

We choose some data from the first two databases. Since original images in the second database have a large size, block-based methods don't work on the second database. So the proposed method is just compared with method [3] and [19]. We test our method without post-processing. Part of detection results is shown in Fig. 6. When the forgeries occurred in a smooth region, the method proposed in [3] can detect a portion of tampered regions (such as Fig. 6a3, c3, d3 and d4), which is the reason that few feature points can be extracted from smooth regions. The proposed method correctly detected the copy-move forgeries in these images. The proposed method has better detect results than [3] and [19] as shown in Table 1. But in terms of time-consuming, the proposed method is much weaker.

We compare the performance of the proposed method and [11] on the third database. Partial detection results are shown in Fig. 7. In term of accuracy and time-consuming, the proposed method is superior to the method proposed in [11], because they have different search ranges for similar blocks, the proposed method employs searching in the same color label. However, the method proposed in [11] employs exhaustive searching.

Here, we test these images with post-processing on the first database, including brightness changes, blur, and contrast adjustments. Table 3 presents the details of the parameters used for three post-processing operations. Detection performances are shown in Table 4. The proposed method can detect three post-processing (Table 2).

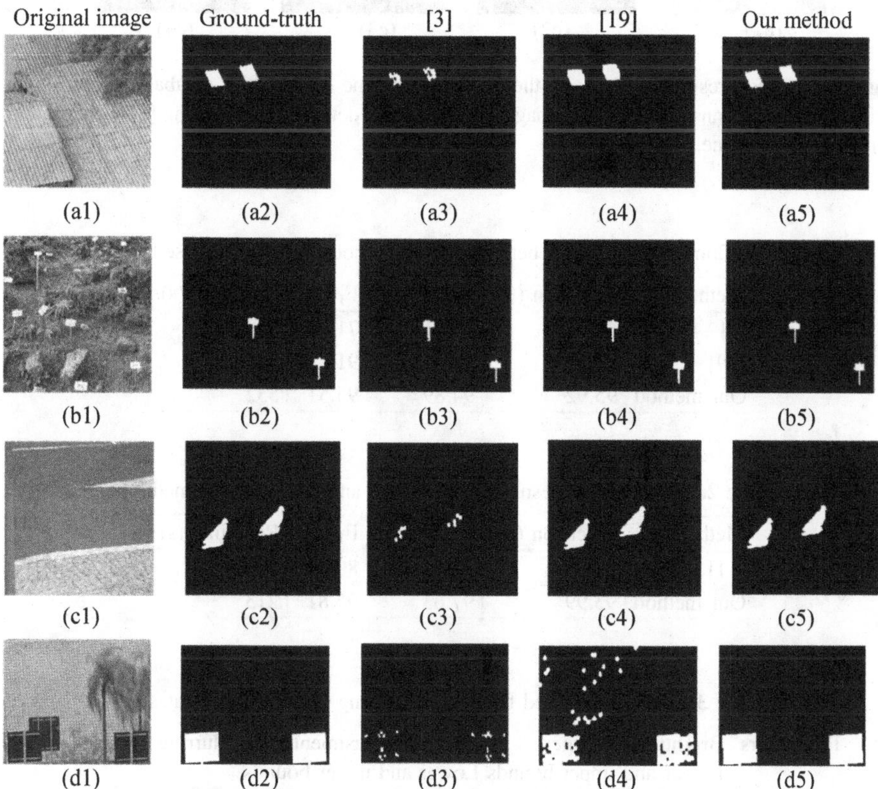

Fig. 6. Detection results of [3, 19] and the proposed scheme. From left to right, the four columns show the test images, ground truth, and detected results using [3] scheme, [19] scheme and our proposed scheme, respectively.

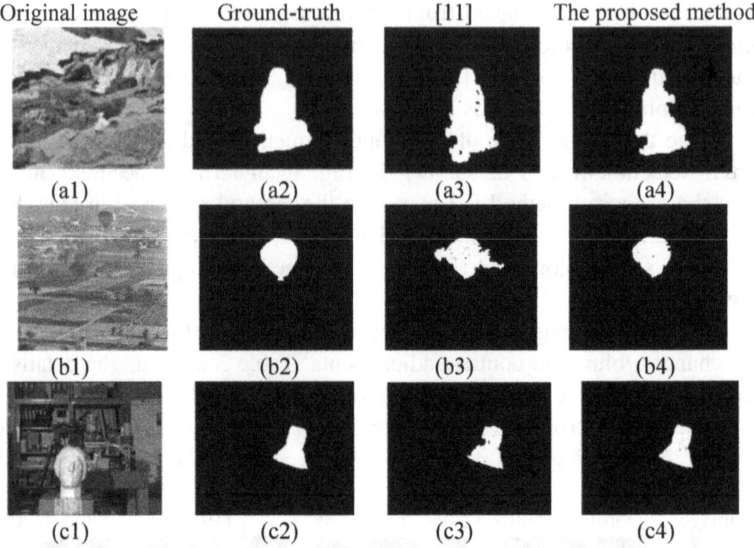

Fig. 7. Detection results of [11] and the proposed scheme on the third database. From left to right, the four columns show the test images, ground truth, detected results using [11] scheme and our proposed scheme, respectively.

Table 1. Comparative results between other methods and the proposed method

Methods	Precision (%)	Recall (%)	F_1 (%)	Run time (s)
[3]	65.81	75.61	71.27	109
[19]	93.21	90.37	91.82	138
Our method	95.92	94.89	95.51	532

Table 2. Comparative results between [11] and the proposed method

Methods	Precision (%)	Recall (%)	F_1 (%)	Run time (s)
[11]	90.47	88.75	89.73	296
Our method	93.99	97.63	95.81	213

Table 3. Parameters used for post-processing in CoMoFoD dataset

Parameters	Brightness changes Lower and upper bounds	Contrast adjustments Lower and upper bounds	Blurring variance
Level 1	0.01, 0.95	0.01, 0.95	0.009
Level 2	0.01, 0.9	0.01, 0.9	0.005
Level 3	0.01, 0.8	0.01, 0.8	0.0005

Table 4. Performance for post-processing in CoMoFoD dataset

Post-processing	Precision (%)	Recall (%)	F_1 (%)
Brightness changes Lower and upper bounds	91.31	84.73	86.95
Contrast adjustments Lower and upper bounds	95.47	89.01	91.58
Blurring variance	69.98	67.15	68.17

(a)Original image (b)Tampering image (c)Detection result

Fig. 8. Two examples of detection for these images based on deep learning

4 Conclusion and Future Works

In this paper, a fast and effective forensic method is proposed. Because local color entropy of every pixel is computed, and then we group into several color labels. By oriented color texture feature of every block, similar blocks are searched in these blocks with the same color label. and then these similar blocks are fused. Based on the link relationships between regions, the tampered regions are located. Experimental results show that the proposed algorithm is better than the general block-based algorithm in term of time but worse than the point-based method. The proposed algorithm is superior to these proposed in [3, 11, 19].

In recent years, image tampering based on deep learning is a new tampering method. The existing algorithms detect the tampering images from standard databases, which don't work on the tampering images based on deep learning (See Fig. 8) [24]. Therefore, in the future work, we will study about this kind of tamper detection.

Acknowledgement. This authors would like to acknlowledge the financial support of the following research grants: Grant No. 2018GY-135 from Key Research and Development Project of Shaanxi Science and Technology.

References

1. Farid, H.: Image forgery detection. IEEE Signal Process. Mag. **26**(2), 16–25 (2009)
2. Dixit, R., Naskar, R.: Review, analysis and parameterization of techniques for copy-move forgery detection in digital images. IET Image Process. **11**(9), 746–759 (2017)
3. Amerini, I., Ballan, L., Caldelli, R., et al.: A sift-based forensic method for copy–move attack detection and transformation recovery. IEEE Trans. Inf. Forensics Secur. **6**(3), 1099–1110 (2011)
4. Hayat, K., Qazi, T.: Forgery detection in digital images via discrete wavelet and discrete cosine transforms. Comput. Electr. Eng. **62**, 448–458 (2017)
5. Ferreira, A., Felipussi, S., Alfaro, C., Fonseca, P., Vargas-Muñoz, J., dos Santos, J., et al.: Behavior knowledge space-based fusion for copy-move forgery detection. IEEE Trans. Image Process. **25**(10), 4729–4742 (2016)
6. Al-Qershi, O.M., Khoo, B.E.: Comparison of matching methods for copy-move image forgery detection. In: Ibrahim, H., Iqbal, S., Teoh, S.S., Mustaffa, M.T. (eds.) 9th International Conference on Robotic, Vision, Signal Processing and Power Applications. LNEE, vol. 398, pp. 209–218. Springer, Singapore (2017). https://doi.org/10.1007/978-981-10-1721-6_23
7. Fadl, S., Semary, N.: Robust copy-move forgery revealing in digital images using polar coordinate system. Neurocomputing **265**, 57–65 (2017)
8. Mahmood, T., Nawaz, T., Ashraf, R., Shah, M., Khan, Z., Irtaza, A., et al.: A survey on block based copy move image forgery detection techniques. In: 2015 11th International Conference on Emerging Technologies (ICET), Peshawar, Pakistan, pp. 1–6 (2015)
9. Asghar, K., Habib, Z., Hussain, M.: Copy-move and splicing image forgery detection and localization techniques: a review. Aust. J. Forensic Sci. **49**, 281–307 (2017)
10. Criminisi, A., Perez, P., Toyama, K.: Region filling and object removal by exemplar-based image inpainting. IEEE Trans. Image Process. **13**(9), 1200–1212 (2004)
11. Chang, I., Yu, J., Chang, C.: A forgery detection algorithm for exemplar-based inpainting images using multi-region relation. Image Vis. Comput. **31**(1), 57–71 (2013)
12. Soni, B., Das, P.K., Thounaojam, D.M.: CMFD: a detailed review of block-based and key feature based techniques in image copy-move forgery detection. IET Image Process. **12**(2), 167–178 (2018)
13. Fridrich, A., Soukal, B., Lukáš, A.: Detection of copy-move forgery in digital images. Comput. Sci. **3**, 55–61 (2003)
14. Zhao, J., Guo, J.: Passive forensics for copy-move image forgery using a method based on DCT and SVD. Forensic Sci. Int. **233**(1), 158–166 (2013)
15. Popescu, A., Farid, H.: Exposing digital forgeries in color filter array interpolated images. IEEE Trans. Signal Process. **53**(10), 3948–3959 (2005)
16. Toqeer, M., Tabassam, N., Aun, I., Rehan, A., Mohsin, S., Tariq, M.: Copy-move forgery detection technique for forensic analysis in digital images. Math. Probl. Eng. **2016**, 1–13 (2016)
17. Shivakumar, B., Baboo, L.: Detection of region duplication forgery in digital images using SURF. Int. J. Comput. Sci. Issues **8**(4), 199–205 (2011)
18. Manu, V.T., Mehtre, B.M.: Detection of copy-move forgery in images using segmentation and SURF. Advances in Signal Processing and Intelligent Recognition Systems. AISC, vol. 425, pp. 645–654. Springer, Cham (2016). https://doi.org/10.1007/978-3-319-28658-7_55
19. Emam, M., Han, Q., Zhang, H.: Two-stage keypoint detection scheme for region duplication forgery detection in digital images. J. Forensic Sci. **63**(1), 101–111 (2018)

20. Yu, L., Han, Q., Niu, X.: Feature point-based copy-move forgery detection: covering the non-textured areas. Multimedia Tools Appl. **75**(2), 1159–1176 (2016)
21. Tralic, D., Zupancic, I., Grgic, S.: CoMoFoD-new database for copy-move forgery detection. In: IEEE International Symposium, pp. 49–54 (2013)
22. Christlein, V., Riess, C., Jordan, J., Angelopoulou, E.: An evaluation of popular copy-move forgery detection approach. IEEE Trans. Inf. Forensics Secur. **7**(6), 1841–1854 (2012)
23. http://www5.cs.fau.de/research/data/image-manipulation/
24. Zheng, C., Cham, T., Cai, J.: Pluralistic image completion. In: CVPR, Los Angeles, USA, pp. 1–21 (2019)

Salient Object Detection via Graph-Based Flexible Manifold Ranking

Ying Yang[1], Bo Jiang[2], Yun Xiao[2], and Jin Tang[2](✉)

[1] School of Computer and Information Engineering, Fuyang Normal University, Fuyang 236037, China
yyang@fynu.edu.cn

[2] School of Computer Science and Technology, Anhui University, Hefei 230601, China
{jiangbo,xiaoyun,tj}@ahu.edu.cn

Abstract. The task of saliency detection is to segment salient objects in natural scenes. Simple and effective saliency detection model has always been a challenging problem. We explore a graph-based flexible manifold ranking approach for single image saliency detection. An input image is represented as an undirected graph. Feature vectors are extracted covering regional color and texture. An optimal function is used to infer the labels based on linear classification projection and manifold ranking in our work. The optimal function further ensures the reliability of the prediction results. Extensive experiments on four benchmark datasets show that our method is better than the other eight classic methods. So the proposed method is a competitive method.

Keywords: Salient object detection · Bottom-up approach · Background prior · Flexible Manifold Ranking

1 Introduction

Salient object detection, which aims to detect and segment automatically salient objects in natural scenes, is an important research branch in computer vision. Since Itti et al. [8] proposed a saliency-based visual attention computing model in 1998, salient object detection has been greatly developed in the past twenty years. However, a model for good saliency detection, which meets accurate segmentation, computational efficiency, and good generalization, has always been a challenging problem. Existing saliency detection methods are divided into classic models [1–4, 6, 8–13, 15, 20–25] and deep learning based models [7]. Comparing with deep learning based models, the classic models are simple, easy-to-understand. Classic models are divided into bottom-up models [1–4, 9, 10, 13, 20, 21, 23–27] and top-down models [11]. A combined model can be found in [28], and even for video saliency detection [29]. In this paper, we focus on the bottom-up graph-based model for saliency detection.

Due to simplicity and efficiency, graph-based models [1, 3, 4, 9] have attracted much attention for saliency detection recently. These methods generally construct a

J. Ren et al. (Eds.): BICS 2019, LNAI 11691, pp. 396–405, 2020.
https://doi.org/10.1007/978-3-030-39431-8_38

graph or many graphs to get image structure, and then design kinds of propagation mechanism or ranking model to generate saliency maps. Harel et al. [9] propose the graph-based visual saliency (GBVS) model. Jiang et al. [1] design a novel propagation model via absorbing Markov Chain (MC) for saliency detection. Li et al. [3] develop a regularized random walks ranking model (RRWR) for saliency detection. Yang et al. [4] propose a graph-based manifold ranking (GMR) method, which is an efficient model. A lot of follow-up works have focused on improving the GMR method. From the existing related literature [2, 13, 21], there are several views to improve the GMR method: reconstructing graph structure, introducing multi-feature descriptors or multi-scale segmentation images, and incorporating external cues and so on. Wang et al. [13] propose a visual saliency model that fuses three features and the L-layer Gaussian pyramid multiple scales based on a novel graph structure. Lin et al. [21] attempt to study saliency detection by incorporating multi-scale global cues. Li et al. [2] integrate thermal information into a RGB image.

In this paper, we propose to explore Graph based Flexible Manifold Ranking (GFMR) for single image saliency detection problem. Specifically, we have made three main improvements based on [4]. Firstly, we propose an objective function that incorporates a linear classification projection into manifold ranking to infer the prediction labels of all nodes. Secondly, we extract multi-feature descriptors that cover regional color and texture. Thirdly, instead of generating four initial background saliency maps with four borders (top, bottom, left and right) of an image separately in [4], we gain one background saliency map with all four borders of an image together. Flexible Manifold Ranking (FMR) has been explored in data learning and co-saliency detection tasks [5, 16]. Differently, we focus on single image saliency detection. Experimental results demonstrate that our method is superior to the GMR method particularly in multi-object scene, so it is a competitive bottom-up solution.

2 The Proposed Method

First, we segment an input image into superpixels by the Simple Linear Iterative Clustering (SLIC) algorithm [14]. Next, we extract features and construct an undirected weighted graph. Then we calculate ranking scores by the GFMR algorithm with background queries, and a rough background saliency map is gained. According to the ranking scores, the foreground queries are determined by adaptive threshold and binarization. Last, we calculate ranking scores by the GFMR algorithm with foreground queries, and the refined saliency map is obtained. Figure 1 shows the main steps of the proposed method.

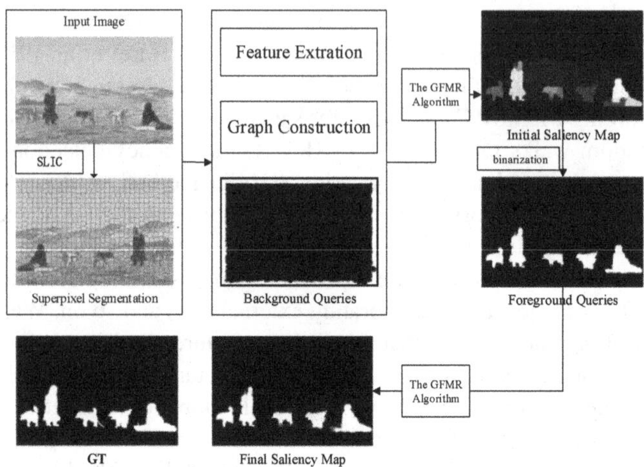

Fig. 1. Pipeline of the proposed method

2.1 The Graph Construction

We construct an undirected weighted graph $\mathrm{G} = (\mathrm{V}, \mathrm{E}, \mathbf{A})$. An image is segmented into superpixels. All superpixels of the image are viewed as V, a set of nodes of the graph. E, a set of undirected edges of the graph, which connects all related superpixels. **A**, a set of weights on edges, which measures the similarities among superpixels. **A** is called an affinity matrix. We adopt the method in [4] to build the graph. First, we connect each node with its spatial neighbors as well as the neighbors of its neighbors. Then, any pair of boundary nodes on the four sides of an image is connected. Thus, the close-loop graph is finished. Next, we in detail introduce how to get the affinity matrix **A**.

In our work, $\mathbf{A} = \left[a_{ij}\right]_{n\times n}$ is calculated using distances among feature descriptors of the nodes. We adopt color and texture features. For color features, we use mean values in Lab and RGB color space. For texture feature, we calculate the normalized LBP histograms, i.e., a vector of 59 dimensions [11]. Denote $v^{lab}, v^{rgb}, h^{lbp}$ be the mean values of Lab color, RGB color and LBP histogram of a node. The weight a_{ij} is defined by the Gaussian similarity function as follow:

$$a_{ij} = \exp(-(\lambda_1\left(\left\|v_i^{lab} - v_j^{lab}\right\|\right) + \lambda_2\left(\left\|v_i^{rgb} - v_j^{rgb}\right\|\right) + \lambda_3\left(\chi^2\left(h_i^{lbp}, h_j^{lbp}\right)\right))/\delta^2). \quad (1)$$

In Eq. (1), λ_1, λ_2 *and* λ_3 are weighting parameters. In our experiments, setting $\lambda_1 = 0.65, \lambda_2 = 0.1, \lambda_3 = 0.25$ and $\delta^2 = 0.05$. $\chi^2\left(h_i, h_j\right)$ is the chi-squared distance. The value of $\chi^2\left(h_i, h_j\right)$ is calculated by the following formula:

$$\chi^2\left(h_i, h_j\right) = \sum\nolimits_{l=1}^{B} \frac{2\left(h_i(l) - h_j(l)\right)^2}{h_i(l) + h_j(l)}, \quad (2)$$

where B is the number of bins and B is 59. It is clear that the affinity matrix **A** is a sparse matrix, and it is also a symmetric matrix.

2.2 The Graph-Based Flexible Manifold Ranking Algorithm

Now, we partition all nodes into the background and the object(s) based on $G = (V, E, \mathbf{A})$. To accurately partitioning the background and the object(s), we explore a GFMR algorithm for the graph labeling problem. In general, the graph labeling problem is regarded as a graph-based manifold ranking problem. In traditional manifold ranking algorithm [4], objective function focus on the manifold smoothness and label fitness. When the queries are fixed, the ranking scores of nodes just depend on the affinity matrix [4]. Inspired by [5, 16], we incorporate a linear classification projection into manifold ranking to infer the labels of all nodes. The linear classification projection can directly map the original image features to the prediction labels. Experiments show that the dual constraint further ensures the reliability of the prediction results. The GFMR algorithm is described as follows.

Feature vector of 65 dimensions is extracted from Lab (3 dimensions), RGB (3 dimensions) and LBP (59 dimensions) spaces of each node. Denote $\mathbf{X} = [\mathbf{x}_1, \mathbf{x}_2, \ldots, \mathbf{x}_n] \in \mathbb{R}^{m \times n}$, $i = 1, 2, \ldots, n$, where $\mathbf{x}_i$ corresponds to a node, m is the feature dimensions and n is the number of all nodes. $\mathbf{y} = [y_1, y_2, \ldots, y_n]^T \in \mathbb{R}^{n \times 1}$ is a binary indicator vector, in which $y_i = 1$ if x_i is labeled query, otherwise $y_i = 0$. Denote $\mathbf{f} = [f_1, f_2, \ldots, f_n]^T \in \mathbb{R}^{n \times 1}$ as the prediction labels of all nodes. Then the prediction labels $\mathbf{f}$ are computed by solving the following objective function [5, 16]:

$$(\mathbf{f}^*, \mathbf{w}^*, b^*) = \arg\min(\frac{1}{2}\sum_{i,j}(f_i - f_j)^2 a_{ij} + \sum_i k_{ii}(f_i - y_i)^2) + \mu\|\mathbf{f} - (\mathbf{X}^T\mathbf{w} + \mathbf{1}b)\|^2. \tag{3}$$

In the second term of Eq. (3), $\mathbf{K} = [k_{ij}]_{n \times n}$ is a diagonal matrix whose elements are set as follow:

$$k_{ij} = \begin{cases} 1, & \textit{if } i = j \textit{ and } \mathrm{x}_i \textit{ is labeled}, \\ 0.001, & \textit{if } i = j \textit{ and } \mathrm{x}_i \textit{ is unlabeled}, \\ 0, & \textit{if } i \neq j. \end{cases} \tag{4}$$

In the third term of Eq. (3), $\mathbf{X}^T\mathbf{w} + \mathbf{1}b$ is a linear projection function of **X**, which maps the original image features **X** to the prediction labels **f**.

Equation (3) is jointly convex function, so there exists the optimal solution. The optimal solution **f** can be written as [5, 16]:

$$\mathbf{f} = (\mathbf{K} + \mathbf{L} + \mu\mathbf{H}_c + \mu\mathbf{N})^{-1}\mathbf{K}\mathbf{y}. \tag{5}$$

In Eq. (5), $\mathbf{L} \in \mathbb{R}^{n \times n}$ is the graph Laplacian matrix and **L** is defined as **D** minus **A**. **D** is the degree matrix of **A**, setting $\mathbf{D} = \mathrm{diag}\{d_{11}, d_{22}, \ldots, d_{nn}\}$ and $d_{ii} = \sum_j a_{ij}$. $\mathbf{H}_c = \mathbf{I} - (1/n)\mathbf{1}\mathbf{1}^T$, where $\mathbf{I} \in \mathbb{R}^{n \times n}$ is an identity matrix. If we define $\mathbf{X}_c = \mathbf{X}\mathbf{H}_c$, then

$\mathbf{N} = \mathbf{X}_c^T(\mathbf{X}_c\mathbf{X}^T)^{-1}\mathbf{X}_c\left[\mathbf{X}^T(\mathbf{X}_c\mathbf{X}^T)^{-1}\mathbf{X}_c - 2\mathbf{I}\right]$. In our experiments, set parameter $\mu = 0.01$. So far, we can gain the prediction label (ranking score) of each node using formula (5) with the given queries.

2.3 Two-Stage Saliency Detection Framework

Similar to previous works [4] and [16], in our method, the result is obtained by two stages. The first stage is to get the initial rough saliency map with background queries. The second stage is to obtain the refined saliency map with foreground queries.

First Stage. We initialize background queries based on the boundary prior [4, 23]. The four-edge superpixels of an image are regarded as background queries, and other superpixels are used as unlabeled data. Using the GFMR algorithm, we calculate ranking scores of all superpixels, i.e. vector **f**. The ranking scores represent the similarity between superpixels and background seeds. The larger the score, the more similar it is to the background. The vector **f** is normalized to the range in [0, 1]. The saliency value can be written as:

$$\bar{\mathbf{f}}^{(1)} = 1 - \mathbf{f}^{(1)}, \tag{6}$$

where $\mathbf{f}^{(1)}$ represents the normalized value and $\bar{\mathbf{f}}^{(1)}$ indexes the saliency values of all superpixels in the first stage. Because $\mathbf{f}^{(1)}$ is gained based on background queries, it represents consistency with the background. So the $\bar{\mathbf{f}}^{(1)}$ represents consistency with the foreground. The larger the saliency value of a superpixel, the more likely it is a salient object. If we assign the saliency value of a superpixel to its each pixel to the range in [0, 255], the initial rough saliency map is obtained.

Second Stage. The initial saliency map is rough. It is necessary to refine the background and object(s) again. Considering that the adaptive threshold is more conducive to select the foreground queries, we select the foreground queries from the prediction label $\bar{\mathbf{f}}^{(1)}$, which is generated by the first stage as:

$$\mathbf{y} = [y_1, y_2, \ldots, y_n]^T = \left(\bar{\mathbf{f}}^{(1)} \geq \theta * mean\left(\bar{\mathbf{f}}^{(1)}\right)\right), \tag{7}$$

where θ is a control parameter. In our experiments, θ is equal to 2. If the i-th superpixel is labeled to foreground queries, $y_i = 1$, otherwise $y_i = 0$. We use the GFMR algorithm with $\mathbf{y}$ to calculate the final labels (denoted with $\mathbf{f}^{(2)}$) of all superpixels. In the second stage, the saliency values are equal to $\mathbf{f}^{(2)}$. Each pixel belonging to the same superpixel is assigned the same saliency value and the final refined saliency map is obtained.

3 Experiments

3.1 Datasets

We evaluate our method on four datasets. The ECSSD dataset [12] contains of 1000 natural images with complex structure. The Pascal-S dataset [22] have 850 natural images and it is a challenging dataset. The SOD dataset [19] including 300 images is also a challenging dataset and some images have multiple objects. The SED2 dataset [17] with 100 images is challenging because every image has two salient objects.

3.2 Evaluation Criterions

P-R curve is used to evaluate the performance for saliency detection method. F-measure is another important quantitative indicator, and it is computed as follow [4]:

$$F_{\beta} = \frac{\left(1+\beta^2\right) \times Precision \times Recall}{\beta^2 \times Precision + Recall}. \tag{8}$$

In Eq. (8), we set $\beta^2 = 0.3$. Similar to work [4], an adaptive threshold strategy is adopted to compute precision, recall, and F-measure scores. In addition to quantitative indicators, we also select some saliency maps for qualitative evaluation.

3.3 Comparison with Other Methods

We don't have a comparison with the deep-learning based approaches which has been focused since 2015 for saliency detection. Therefore, we evaluate the proposed method and eight classic state-of-the-art methods, including CA [18], FT [15], GS [23], GMR [4], HS [12], RRWR [3], SF [6], and wCO [20].

Quantitative Results. The P-R curves show that our method is better than the others, as shown in column (a) of Figs. 2, 3, 4 and 5. Compared with the GMR method, the P-R curves generated by our method are advantageous on all four datasets.

Column (b) of Figs. 2, 3, 4 and 5 shows F-measure curves. Overall, the maximum F-measure of our model at different threshold is advantageous. When the threshold changes in a wide range, the corresponding F-measure value is always near to the maximum value, which proves the stability of our model.

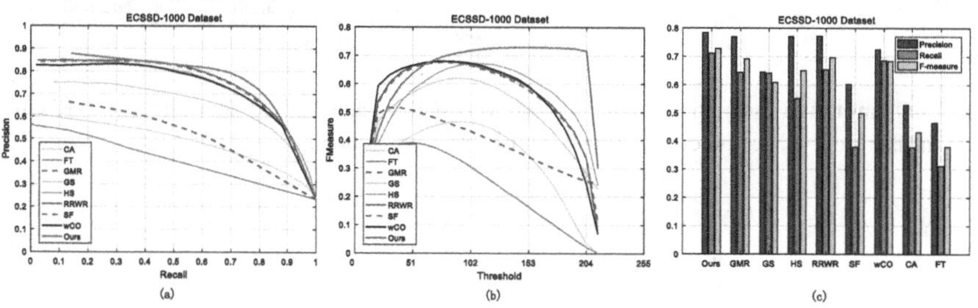

Fig. 2. Quantitative evaluation of 9 methods on ECSSD dataset. Left to right: (a) P-R curve, (b) F-measure curve, (c) precision, recall, and F-measure scores.

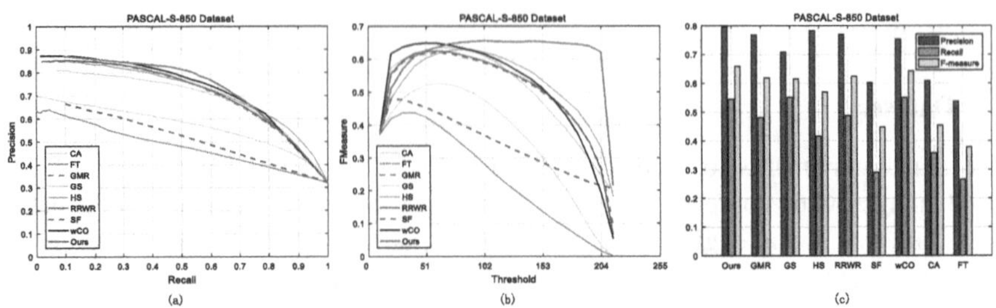

Fig. 3. Quantitative evaluation of 9 methods on PASCAL-S dataset. Left to right: (a) P-R curve, (b) F-measure curve, (c) precision, recall, and F-measure scores.

Column (c) of Figs. 2, 3, 4 and 5 reflect precision, recall and F-measure scores of 9 approaches on different dataset. Our method achieves an improvement of 2%–4% in comparison with the GMR model. Our precision, recall, and F-measure scores exceed the baseline GMR model 6.01%, 9.71% and 7.69% on the SED2 dataset, respectively.

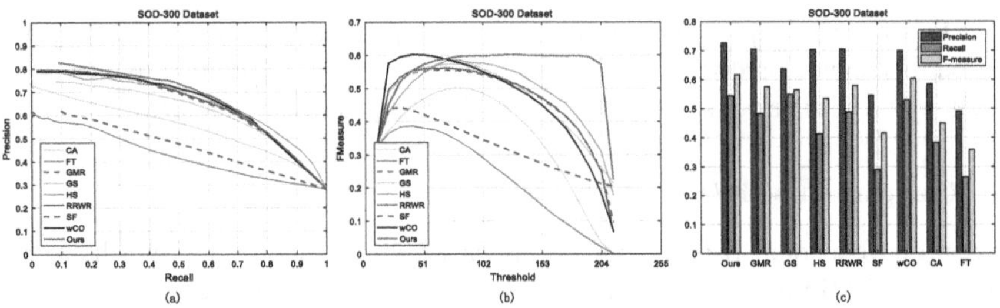

Fig. 4. Quantitative evaluation of 9 methods on SOD dataset. Left to right: (a) P-R curve, (b) F-measure curve, (c) precision, recall, and F-measure scores.

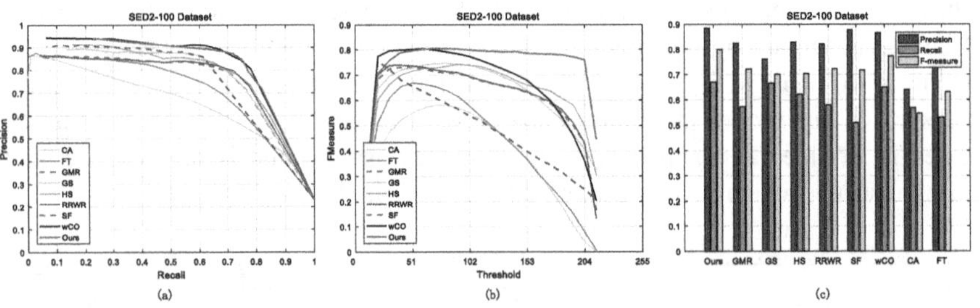

Fig. 5. Quantitative evaluation of 9 methods on SED2 dataset. Left to right: (a) P-R curve, (b) F-measure curve, (c) precision, recall, and F-measure scores.

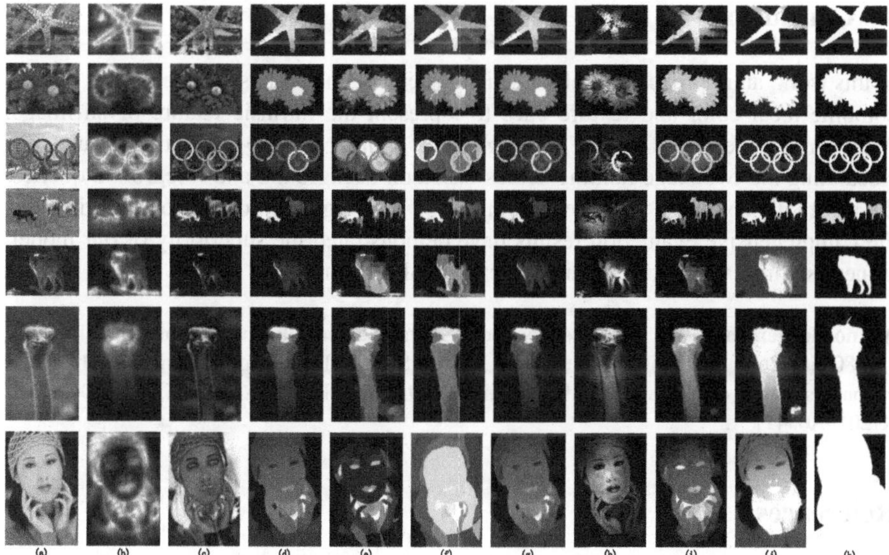

Fig. 6. Qualitative evaluation. Comparison of our method with other eight methods. Left to right: (a) Input image, (b) CA [18], (c) FT [15], (d) GMR [4], (e) GS [23], (f) HS [12], (g) RRWR [3], (h) SF [6], (i) wCO [20], (j) Ours, (k) GT. Our method is able to detect both the foreground and background uniformly.

Qualitative Results. Figure 6 shows a group of saliency maps. In first column of Fig. 6, the first, third and seventh images are from the ECSSD dataset, the second, fifth and sixth images are from the SOD dataset, and the fourth image is from the PASCAL-S dataset. Obviously, our saliency maps have the highest quality and our method effectively suppresses background and highlights the object(s). As shown in the first row of Fig. 6, when a single object and background have obvious contrast, our result is almost consistent with the ground-truth. If the image is with multiple objects (2th, 3th and 4th rows of Fig. 6), our saliency maps are far superior to other saliency maps in vision. Due to the contribution of the LBP texture feature, the proposed method can detect salient object with a similar appearance to the background regions, as shown in line 5 of Fig. 6. In line 6 of Fig. 6, our saliency map is better than the others, but a small region of background is mistakenly counted to the foreground. The color feature is dominant and the texture feature is accessory in the proposed algorithm. The color and texture of the small region are highly similar to the foreground, so the small region is mistaken to the foreground. The object is too big and heterogeneous in the last row of Fig. 6. Although all the results are not ideal, ours is closest to the ground-truth. All of these facts imply that the proposed model is a competitive and attractive solution.

4 Conclusion

In this work, an improved model for saliency detection is proposed. The feature metrics combine local color and texture cues to represent the intrinsic feature of an image. Afterward, we explore the GFMR algorithm to improve the prediction results. By calculating the two-stage ranking scores based on background and foreground queries, the ideal saliency map is obtained. Comparison with eight approaches on four datasets, the comprehensive evaluation results have demonstrated the superiority of our model. In next studies, we prepare to integrate thermal information.

Acknowledgement. This work is supported by Natural Science Foundation of Anhui Province (1908085QF264, 1808085QF209) and the Natural Science Foundation of Anhui Higher Education Institution of China (KJ2019A0536, KJ2019A0532, KJ2019A0529, KJ2019A0026 and KJ2019A0541).

References

1. Jiang, B., Zhang, L., Lu, H., Yang, C., Yang, M.-H.: Saliency detection via absorbing markov chain. In: IEEE International Conference on Computer Vision (ICCV), pp. 1665–1672 (2013)
2. Li, C., Wang, G., Ma, Y., Zheng, A., Luo, B., Tang, J.: A unified RGB-T saliency detection benchmark: dataset, baselines, analysis and a novel approach. arXiv:1701.02829 (2017)
3. Li, C., Yuan, Y., Cai, W., Xia, Y., Feng, D.D.: Robust saliency detection via regularized random walks ranking. In: IEEE Conference on Computer Vision and Pattern Recognition (CVPR), pp. 2710–2717 (2015)
4. Yang, C., Zhang, L., Lu, H., Ruan, X., Yang, M.-H.: Saliency detection via graph-based manifold ranking. In: IEEE Conference on Computer Vision and Pattern Recognition (CVPR), pp. 3166–3173 (2013)
5. Nie, F., Xu, D., Tsang, I.W.-H., Zhang, C.: Flexible manifold embedding: a framework for semi-supervised and unsupervised dimension reduction. IEEE Trans. Image Process. **19**(7), 1921–1932 (2010)
6. Perazzi, F., Krahenbuhl, P., Pritch, Y., Hornung, A.: Saliency filters: contrast based filtering for salient region detection. In: IEEE Conference on Computer Vision and Pattern Recognition (CVPR), pp. 733–740 (2012)
7. Li, G., Yu, Y.: Visual saliency based on multiscale deep features. In: IEEE Conference on Computer Vision and Pattern Recognition (CVPR), pp. 5455–5463 (2015)
8. Itti, L., Koch, C., Niebur, E.: A model of saliency-based visual attention for rapid scene analysis. IEEE Trans. Pattern Anal. Mach. Intell. **20**(11), 1254–1259 (1998)
9. Harel, J., Koch, C., Perona, P.: Graph-based visual saliency. In: Advances in Neural Information Processing Systems (NIPS), pp. 545–552 (2006)
10. Cheng, M.-M., Mitra, N.J., Huang, X., Torr, P.H.S., Hu, S.-M.: Global contrast based salient region detection. IEEE Trans. Pattern Anal. Mach. Intell. **37**(3), 569–582 (2015)
11. Tong, N., Lu, H., Ruan, X., Yang, M.: Salient object detection via bootstrap learning. In: IEEE Conference on Computer Vision and Pattern Recognition (CVPR), pp. 1884–1892 (2015)
12. Yan, Q., Xu, L., Shi, J., Jia, J.: Hierarchical saliency detection. In: IEEE Conference on Computer Vision and Pattern Recognition (CVPR), pp. 1155–1162 (2013)

13. Wang, Q., Zheng, W., Piramuthu, R.: GraB: visual saliency via novel graph model and background priors. In: IEEE Conference on Computer Vision and Pattern Recognition (CVPR), pp. 535–543 (2016)
14. Achanta, R., Shaji, A., Smith, K., Lucchi, A., Fua, P., Süsstrunk, S.: Slic superpixels. EPFL Technical report no. 149300 (2010)
15. Achanta, R., Hemami, S., Estrada, F., Süsstrunk, S.: Frequency-tuned salient region detection. In: IEEE Conference on Computer Vision and Pattern Recognition (CVPR), pp. 1597–1604 (2009)
16. Quan, R., Han, J., Zhang, D., Nie, F.: Object co-segmentation via graph optimized-flexible manifold ranking. In: IEEE Conference on Computer Vision and Pattern Recognition (CVPR), pp. 687–695 (2016)
17. Alpert, S., Galun, M., Brandt, A., Basri, R.: Image segmentation by probabilistic bottom-up aggregation and cue integration. IEEE Trans. Pattern Anal. Mach. Intell. **34**(2), 315–327 (2012)
18. Goferman, S., Zelnik-Manor, L., Tal, A.: Context-aware saliency detection. IEEE Trans. Pattern Anal. Mach. Intell. **34**(10), 1915–1926 (2010)
19. Movahedi, V., Elder, J.H.: Design and perceptual validation of performance measures for salient object segmentation. In: Computer Vision and Pattern Recognition Workshops (CVPR), pp. 49–56 (2010)
20. Zhu, W., Liang, S., Wei, Y., Sun, J.: Saliency optimization from robust background detection. In: IEEE Conference on Computer Vision and Pattern Recognition (CVPR), pp. 2814–2821 (2014)
21. Lin, X., Wang, Z., Ma, L., Wu, X.: Saliency detection via multi-scale global cues. IEEE Trans. Multimed. (2018). https://doi.org/10.1109/2884474
22. Li, Y., Hou, X., Koch, C., Rehg, J., Yuille, A.: The secrets of salient object segmentation. In: IEEE Conference on Computer Vision and Pattern Recognition (CVPR), pp. 280–287 (2014)
23. Wei, Y., Wen, F., Zhu, W., Sun, J.: Geodesic saliency using background priors. In: Fitzgibbon, A., Lazebnik, S., Perona, P., Sato, Y., Schmid, C. (eds.) ECCV 2012. LNCS, vol. 7574, pp. 29–42. Springer, Heidelberg (2012). https://doi.org/10.1007/978-3-642-33712-3_3
24. Jiang, B., He, Z., Ding, C., et al.: Saliency detection via a multi-layer graph based diffusion model. Neurocomputing (2018). https://www.sciencedirect.com/science/article/abs/pii/S0925231218308026
25. Xiao, Y., Wang, L., Jiang, B., et al.: A global and local consistent ranking model for image saliency computation. J. Vis. Commun. Image Represent. **46**, 199–207 (2017)
26. Han, J., Zhang, D., Cheng, G., Guo, L., Ren, J.: Object detection in optical remote sensing images based on weakly supervised learning and high-level feature learning. IEEE Trans. Geosci. Remote Sens. **53**(6), 3325–3337 (2014)
27. Han, J., Zhang, D., Hu, X., Guo, L., Ren, J., Wu, F.: Background prior-based salient object detection via deep reconstruction residual. IEEE Trans. Circ. Syst. Video Technol. **25**(8), 1309–1321 (2014)
28. Yan, Y., et al.: Unsupervised image saliency detection with Gestalt-laws guided optimization and visual attention based refinement. Pattern Recogn. **79**, 65–78 (2018)
29. Wang, Z., et al.: A deep-learning based feature hybrid framework for spatiotemporal saliency detection inside videos. Neurocomputing **287**, 68–83 (2018)

Deep Neural Network for Pancreas Segmentation from CT Images

Zhanlan Chen and Jiangbin Zheng(✉)

Northwestern Polytechnical University, Xi'an, China
zhengjb@nwpu.edu.cn

Abstract. Automatic pancreas segmentation from Computed Tomography (CT) images is a prerequisite of clinical practices such as cancer detection, yet challenging due to the variability in shape. To address this challenge, we propose a Hierarchical Convolutional Neural Network (H-CNN) to fuse multi-scale features, which could remedy the lost image details in progressive convolutional and pooling layers. In our proposed H-CNN, a hierarchical fusion block is designed to fuse low-level and high-level features across different layers. The H-CNN is evaluated on NIH pancreas dataset and outperforms the current state-of-art methods by achieving 86.59% ± 4.33% in terms of DSC. The experimental results confirm the effectiveness of the proposed H-CNN.

Keywords: Pancreas segmentation · Convolutional Neural Network · Medical image segmentation

1 Introduction

Pancreas segmentation from CT images is an important step in computer-aided diagnosis and treatment such as cancer detection [1]. In practice, to reduce the damage to other adjacent tissues and save human surgery, it is worthwhile [2] to explore an automated and precise method for pancreas segmentation from medical images. As segmentation from CT images is still a challenging task in pancreas diagnoses [3], we focus on pancreas segmentation from CT images in this paper.

1.1 Challenges and Motivations

There are two main challenges for automated CT pancreas segmentation. Firstly, the greatly irregular boundary of pancreas across different diseases (as shown in Fig. 1). Secondly, the inherent image noise and distortions in CT images. Convolutional Neural Networks (CNNs) [4] are formed by consecutive convolutional layers [4] and pooling layers [5], which have shown excellence in image segmentation. However, since pooling layers [6] in CNNs inevitably loss information details when applied to CT images, it is difficult to precisely delineate the variant boundary of the pancreas. To overcome the limitation [7, 9] of CNNs, there are effective methods proposed. For example, Deeplab [8] designed dilated convolution to replace pooling layer, which can enlarge the receptive field without down-scaling feature maps. Other methods such as SegNet [10] progressively up-sample the convolved feature maps from previous layers

J. Ren et al. (Eds.): BICS 2019, LNAI 11691, pp. 406–413, 2020.
https://doi.org/10.1007/978-3-030-39431-8_39

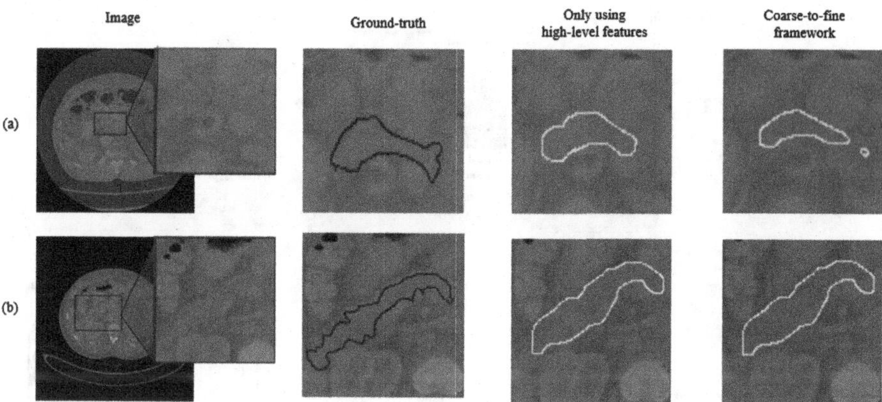

Fig. 1. Examples of current CNN based pancreas segmentation methods: segmentation results are marked as yellow, while the ground-truth is marked as red. (Color figure online)

to improve the image details. These methods made use of the enlarged convolved features from penultimate layers to retain more local image details.

The aforementioned methods showed improvements for three-channel color images, yet failing to achieve great performance on single-channel CT images to segment the pancreas. To more effectively make use of the convolved features from different layers in CNNs, Yu et al. [11] have proved the effectiveness of combining multi-scale features to retain local image details which are important to delineate boundary. Therefore, in this paper, we take the advantages of CNNs in a deep fusion of multi-scale features to remedy boundary information and improve pancreas segmentation from CT images.

1.2 Related Work

Earlier pancreas segmentation methods for CT images, can be mainly grouped into probabilistic atlas and statistical shape modeling [13, 14]. For example, Suzuki et al. [12] incorporated the spatial interrelations into a statistical atlas for pancreas segmentation. However, as it is difficult to find a model which covers all possible variabilities, these shape-based methods commonly fail to solve the challenge that the variant boundary shape of different pancreas.

More recently, some investigators have proposed CNNs based methods for pancreas segmentation. As the highly convolved features are produced from a set of layers in CNNs, they can be treated as high-level features. Roth et al. [17] learned high-level features from a holistically-nested network to further refine them with a random forest. Ronneberger et al. [18] proposed a popular model (U-Net) for medical image segmentation. Milletari et al. [19] extended U-Net into a 3D model (V-Net) and achieved improvement. Zhou et al. [20] suggested to find a rough pancreas region and refined the

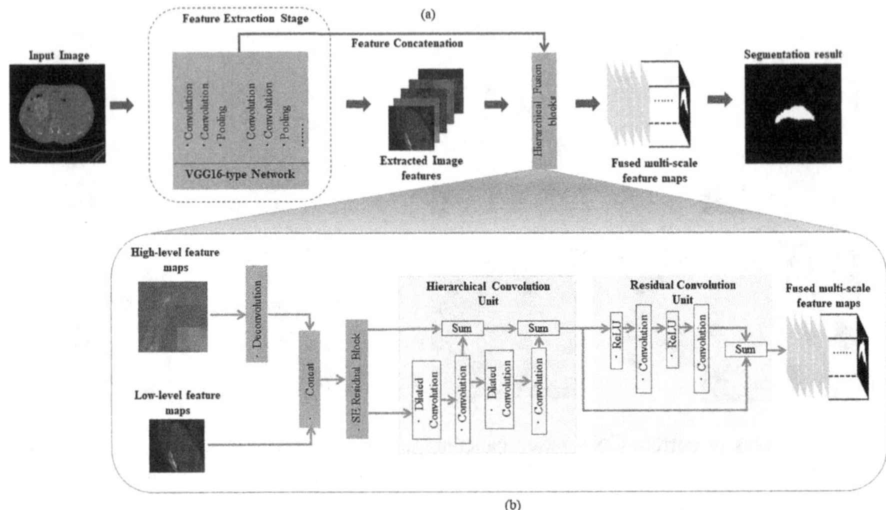

Fig. 2. Overview of the proposed H-CNN for pancreas segmentation. (a): the architecture of H-CNN. The H-CNN adopts VGG16 for feature extraction. Finally, H-blocks perform multi-scale feature fusion on the top of VGG. (b): detailed structure of a Hierarchical fusion block which fuses multi-scale features to remedy the local details from the feature extraction stage.

region through learning an FCN based fixed-point model iteratively. Although high-level features can contain more semantic information, relying on these features may limit the segmentation performance of CNNs – because of the lost boundary information obtained from low-level layers in CNNs.

1.3 Contribution

The main contribution of this paper is fusing multi-scale features for pancreas segmentation from CT images. Firstly, alternative to generating segmentation maps from high-level features, our H-CNN hierarchically extracts and fuse high-level and low-level features to address the challenge of irregular pancreas boundary. The proposed Hierarchical Fusion Block (H-block) can hierarchically refine different level features, especially the proposed H-block can capture context from a larger image region to better make use of features. Secondly, we used residual connections [21] in H-block to propagate gradients throughout different layers.

2 Method

As shown in Fig. 2, H-CNN is built upon encoder-decoder architecture. The encoder sub-network is a VGG16-type network to extract image features in different resolution. Then, the Hierarchical Fusion Block (H-block) in the decoder sub-network fuses high-level features convolved from the encoder with low-level features to retain local details.

2.1 Convolution-Pooling Block

Convolution-pooling blocks (CP-block) lies in the encoder sub-network, where each of them has two convolutional layers and one pooling layers. The convolutional layers convolve input image to extract features, while the pooling layers enlarge the receptive field and reduce the sensitivity of features to shift and distortion.

2.2 Hierarchical Fusion Block

Due to the lost local details in encoder sub-network are important for boundary delineation, we propose a hierarchical fusion block (H-block) to fuse multi-scale features so as to remedy the local details. As shown in Fig. 2(b), each H-block has three main components: *multi-scale fusion block, hierarchical convolution block* and *residual convolution block.*

Multi-scale Fusion. This block first up-samples the high-level features for input adaptation, which generates feature maps at the same feature dimensions as the low-level features. Then, all feature maps are fused by concatenation.

Hierarchical Convolution Block. The output features then are fed into the hierarchical convolution block. The proposed hierarchical convolution block aims to capture features from a larger image region. In particular, this part has a set of convolution blocks, each having a dilated convolution layer and a convolution layer. The dilated convolution layer could generate features from an enlarged receptive filed without losing feature details. Note that each dilated convolution is followed by a convolution layer which servers as cross-channel interaction and information aggregation. The output features of all hierarchical convolution blocks are fused together with the input features through summation.

3 Data and Experiment

3.1 Data and Evaluation Metrics

The NIH pancreas segmentation dataset [3] containing 82 CT samples, is used to evaluate the proposed model. The resolution of each sample is $512\times$ $512\times$ D, where $\mathrm{D} \in [181, 466]$. Manual ground-truths for the samples are also supplied.

Dice Srensen Coefficient (DSC) and Volumetric overlap error (VOE) are two common evaluation metrics in pancreas segmentation [17, 22]. In this paper, we used these two metrics to evaluate our model. Denote P and G as the segmentation result and ground-truth mask, DSC is formulated as $DSC(\mathrm{P},\mathrm{G}) = \frac{2*|P\cap G|}{|P|+|G|}$. The value of DSC ranges in [0, 1], where a good segmentation method should have a high DSC. VOE is defined as $VOE(\mathrm{P},\mathrm{G}) = 1 - \frac{|P\cap G|}{|P\cup G|}$, which represents the error rate of segmentation result.

3.2 Implementation

All experiments were run on an NVIDIA TITAN GPU to boost the training. For the data augmentation, we utilized rotation (90°, 180° and 270°) and flip in all three planes, to increase the number of training samples. We then trained H-CNN by SGD optimizer with a 10 mini-batch and a base learning rate to be 0.001 via polynomial decay in a total 80000 iterations. Following the training protocol [9], we performed 4-fold cross-validation to validate our model. The H-CNN is compared with four state-of-art pancreas segmentation methods, including Fixed-Point [20], Hierarchical FCN [23, 24], Holistically-Nested [17] and DeepOrgan [3].

4 Results

Overall Performance. The experimental results (DSC) of H-CNN and comparison methods on the NIH pancreas segmentation dataset are listed in Table 1. The comparison with previous methods showed that our method achieved a better segmentation result. To quantify the improvements in terms of statistical significance, we tested the p-value whose value $\leq$ 0.05 indicates a significant difference.

Evaluation of Hierarchical Fusion Block (H-Block). After high-level features obtained from the encoder sub-network, we fused multi-scale features via H-block. To provide a clear pattern about the effect of this block, we removed the H-block and directly used original decoder structure in U-Net to produce the final segmentation maps. As shown Fig. 4, the proposed H-block can optimize pancreas segmentation compared to the baseline model U-Net. To quantify these improvements in terms of statistical significance we performed student t-tests, where the p-value $\leq$ 0.05 (DSC: p-value = 0.004 and VOE: p-value = 0.017).

5 Discussion

H-CNN Segmentation. The advantage of using H-CNN for pancreas lies in designing a Hierarchical Fusion Block (H-block) which fuses multi-scale features to remedy the lost local details brought by pooling. Although the location of pancreas can be predicted using the high-level features obtained from the down-sampling procedure, the

Table 1. Quantitative results of different methods on NIH pancreas dataset.

Method	DSC [%]	VOE [%]
DeepOrgan	71.08 ± 8.20	47.50 ± 18.51
Holistically-Nested	81.30 ± 6.30	34.57 ± 16.73
Hierarchical FCN	82.20 ± 10.20	28.90 ± 10.23
Fixed-Point	82.37 ± 5.68	34.57 ± 16.73
H-CNN	**86.59 ± 4.33**	**24.05 ± 5.73**

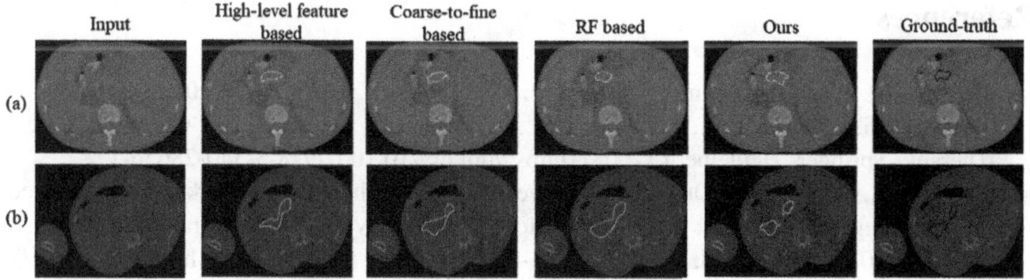

Fig. 3. Comparison of generated pancreas segmentation maps between our proposed model and state-of-art methods (RF, coarse-to-fine and high-level feature based methods) in two pancreas CT cases; segmentation results are shown in yellow and the ground-truth is shown in red. (Color figure online)

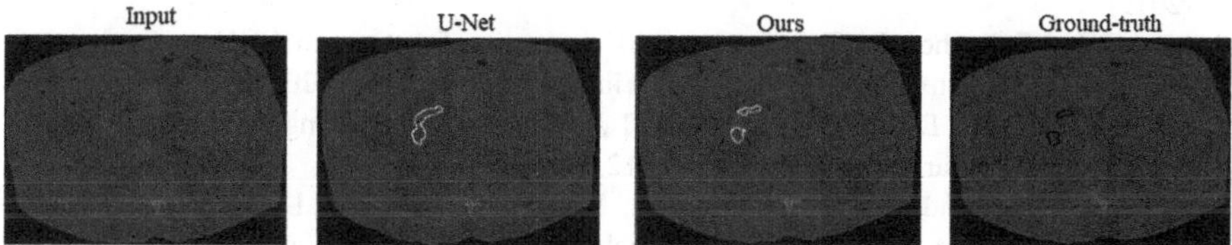

Fig. 4. An example of axial pancreas CT images compares the delineation results of U-Net baseline and ours: segmentation results are shown in yellow and the ground-truth is shown in red (Best viewed in color).

pancreas boundary cannot be precisely delineated. Some CNNs for segmentation such as FCN and U-Net, also fuse low-level and high-level features. However, these networks just simply fuse corresponding features directly from encoder with up-sampled decoder output through skip connection, which may not efficiently use different level features. By contrast, the proposed Hierarchical Fusion block (H-block) can hierarchically refine different level features, especially the proposed H-block can capture context from a larger image region to better make use of features.

H-CNN and the State-of-Art Methods. DeepOrgan segmented pancreas by classifying the candidate regions with random forest. Hierarchical FCN purely used high-level features for segmentation. However, as these two methods purely relied on high-level features which failed to delineate complex boundary (Fig. 3). Holistically-Nested FCN and Fixed-point methods are not end-to-end models, thus, the trained models may not be suboptimal. By contrast, our H-CNN fused multi-scale features to more precisely delineate the pancreas segmentation.

6 Conclusion

In this paper, we proposed a CNN based model, H-CNN, for CT pancreas segmentation. Motivated by the high relevance of low-level features and boundary delineation, we fused low-level images cues and high-level convolved features to delineate the pancreas boundary. Our H-CNN outperformed the existing popular CNN models.

References

1. Hidalgo, M.: Pancreatic cancer. N. Engl. J. Med. **362**(17), 1605–1617 (2010)
2. Beger, H.G., Matsuno, S., Cameron, J.L.: Diseases of the Pancreas: Current Surgical Therapy. Springer, Heidelberg (2008). https://doi.org/10.1007/978-3-540-28656-1
3. Roth, H.R., et al.: DeepOrgan: multi-level deep convolutional networks for automated pancreas segmentation. In: Navab, N., Hornegger, J., Wells, W.M., Frangi, A.F. (eds.) MICCAI 2015. LNCS, vol. 9349, pp. 556–564. Springer, Cham (2015). https://doi.org/10.1007/978-3-319-24553-9_68
4. Shin, H.-C., et al.: Deep convolutional neural networks for computer-aided detection: CNN architectures, dataset characteristics and transfer learning. IEEE Trans. Med. Imaging **35**(5), 1285–1298 (2016)
5. Krizhevsky, A., Sutskever, I., Hinton, G.E.: ImageNet classification with deep convolutional neural networks. In: Advances in Neural Information Processing Systems, pp. 1097–1105 (2012)
6. Lee, C.-Y., Gallagher, P., Tu, Z.: Generalizing pooling functions in CNNs: mixed, gated, and tree. IEEE Trans. Pattern Anal. Mach. Intell. **40**(4), 863–875 (2017)
7. Springenberg, J.T., Dosovitskiy, A., Brox, T., Riedmiller, M.: Striving for simplicity: the all convolutional net. arXiv preprint arXiv:1412.6806 (2014)
8. Chen, L.-C., Papandreou, G., Kokkinos, I., Murphy, K., Yuille, A.L.: DeepLab: semantic image segmentation with deep convolutional nets, atrous convolution, and fully connected CRFs. IEEE Trans. Pattern Anal. Mach. Intell. **40**(4), 834–848 (2017)
9. Noh, H., Hong, S., Han, B.: Learning deconvolution network for semantic segmentation. In: Proceedings of the IEEE International Conference on Computer Vision, pp. 1520–1528 (2015)
10. Badrinarayanan, V., Kendall, A., Cipolla, R.: SegNet: a deep convolutional encoder-decoder architecture for image segmentation. IEEE Trans. Pattern Anal. Mach. Intell. **39**(12), 2481–2495 (2017)
11. Yu, F., Wang, D., Shelhamer, E., Darrell, T.: Deep layer aggregation. In: Proceedings of the IEEE Conference on Computer Vision and Pattern Recognition, pp. 2403–2412 (2018)
12. Suzuki, Y., et al.: Automated segmentation and anatomical labeling of abdominal arteries based on multi-organ segmentation from contrast-enhanced CT data. In: Drechsler, K., et al. (eds.) CLIP 2012. LNCS, vol. 7761, pp. 67–74. Springer, Heidelberg (2013). https://doi.org/10.1007/978-3-642-38079-2_9
13. Shimizu, A., Kimoto, T., Kobatake, H., Nawano, S., Shinozaki, K.: Automated pancreas segmentation from three-dimensional contrast-enhanced computed tomography. Int. J. Comput. Assist. Radiol. Surg. **5**(1), 85 (2010)
14. Wolz, R., Chu, C., Misawa, K., Fujiwara, M., Mori, K., Rueckert, D.: Automated abdominal multi-organ segmentation with subject-specific atlas generation. IEEE Trans. Med. Imaging **32**(9), 1723–1730 (2013)
15. Dmitriev, K., Gutenko, I., Nadeem, S., Kaufman, A.: Pancreas and cyst segmentation. In: Medical Imaging 2016: Image Processing. International Society for Optics and Photonics, p. 97842C (2016)
16. Grady, L.: Random walks for image segmentation. IEEE Trans. Pattern Anal. Mach. Intell. **11**, 1768–1783 (2006)
17. Roth, H.R., Lu, L., Farag, A., Sohn, A., Summers, R.M.: Spatial aggregation of holistically-nested networks for automated pancreas segmentation. In: Ourselin, S., Joskowicz, L., Sabuncu, M.R., Unal, G., Wells, W. (eds.) MICCAI 2016. LNCS, vol. 9901, pp. 451–459. Springer, Cham (2016). https://doi.org/10.1007/978-3-319-46723-8_52

18. Ronneberger, O., Fischer, P., Brox, T.: U-Net: convolutional networks for biomedical image segmentation. In: Navab, N., Hornegger, J., Wells, W.M., Frangi, A.F. (eds.) MICCAI 2015. LNCS, vol. 9351, pp. 234–241. Springer, Cham (2015). https://doi.org/10.1007/978-3-319-24574-4_28
19. Milletari, F., Navab, N., Ahmadi, S.-A.: V-Net: fully convolutional neural networks for volumetric medical image segmentation. In: 2016 Fourth International Conference on 3D Vision (3DV). IEEE, pp. 565–571 (2016)
20. Zhou, Y., Xie, L., Shen, W., Wang, Y., Fishman, E.K., Yuille, A.L.: A fixed-point model for pancreas segmentation in abdominal CT scans. In: Descoteaux, M., Maier-Hein, L., Franz, A., Jannin, P., Collins, D.L., Duchesne, S. (eds.) MICCAI 2017. LNCS, vol. 10433, pp. 693–701. Springer, Cham (2017). https://doi.org/10.1007/978-3-319-66182-7_79
21. He, K., Zhang, X., Ren, S., Sun, J.: Deep residual learning for image recognition. In: Proceedings of the IEEE Conference on Computer Vision and Pattern Recognition, pp. 770–778 (2016)
22. Mahapatra, D., et al.: Automatic detection and segmentation of Crohn's disease tissues from abdominal MRI. IEEE Trans. Med. Imaging **32**(12), 2332–2347 (2013)
23. Roth, H.R., et al.: Hierarchical 3D fully convolutional networks for multi-organ segmentation. arXiv preprint arXiv:1704.06382 (2017)
24. Ren, J., Wang, D., Jiang, J.: Effective recognition of MCCs in mammograms using an improved neural classifier. Eng. Appl. Artif. Intell. **24**(4), 638–645 (2011)

Semantical Knowledge Guided Salient Object Detection with Multiple Proposals

Xue Zhang, Zheng Wang(✉), and Meijun Sun

Tianjin University, Tianjin 300350, China
Dorothyzhx@foxmail.com, {wzheng,sunmeijun}@tju.edu.cn

Abstract. In recent years, the area of salient object detection has developed rapidly duo to the revival of deep learning techniques, especially the emergence of deep Convolutional Neural Networks (CNNs), which has greatly boosted the detection result. Although CNNs can be used to perceive the salient objects, it is difficult to work for images with complex background, which is also a major problem faced by most work. In this paper, we introduce a salient object detection method using high-level features with semantic meaning. In order to obtain the accurate region and edge of all the salient objects in an image, our model has two designs: (1) utilizing multiple proposals as the semantical knowledge prior to enhance the power of locate objects, that are most likely to cover the entire salient regions of an image, and (2) using several attention modules to improve the representation ability of our model, and using abundant low-level feature information extracted by the encoder of the network to assist its decoder to obtain the precise saliency map relatively. In addition, our model can make full use of multi-level features and semantical knowledge, so the saliency map we got is very excellent. The experiments shows that our approach achieves state-of-the-art performance on four public benchmarks, and produces significant improvements over existing well-known methods.

Keywords: Salient object detection · Object proposals · Semantical knowledge

1 Introduction

Salient object detection (SOD) aims to highlight the most conspicuous regions in images. With the development of deep learning, SOD can be greatly applied to other tasks as a preprocessing procedure, such as image captioning [3,16], image matching [30,31], visual question answering [14], object detection [6,12], person re-identification [36], *etc.*

In the past decades, SOD technology has been dramatically evolved. Previous SOD methods utilize hand-craft visual features [27,37] and heuristic priors [1,32] to detect salient objects. However, most of them focus on low-level features and can not fully catch high-level semantic features, so that the saliency maps got

J. Ren et al. (Eds.): BICS 2019, LNAI 11691, pp. 414–422, 2020.
https://doi.org/10.1007/978-3-030-39431-8_40

by them are not to our satisfactory. Recently, the emergence of deep CNNs has opened the door of the rapid development of SOD. Deep CNNs [22] extract image features in an end-to-end manner and then get salient objects after training the model. Convolution operations near the bottom of the network can obtain low-level feature information. With the deepening of the network, high-level semantic information becomes stronger. Therefore, deep CNNs can automatically locate the salient objects more accurate than most detection methods used before the age of deep CNNs.

In order to make full use of the low-level information which is sensitive to edges and the high-level semantic information which is sensitive to salient objects, we extract the feature maps from the encoder of the network and fuse them into the decoding stage, so that the model can make the best of the different level features in every stage. What's more, we also import several attention modules to make full use of the spatial and channel features transferring between the adjacent layers. More importantly, for the purpose of perceiving the salient objects that are most likely cover all the salient regions quickly and accurately, we use multiple object proposals as semantical knowledge prior to guide the model. Our experimental results clearly demonstrate the effectiveness of the proposed method on four well-known benchmark datasets.

In summary, the main contributions of our work are as follows:

- We propose a method to detect salient objects in images using multiple proposals as semantical knowledge. With rich information of semantics about proposals, the model can perceive all salient regions faster and better.
- Our model makes the most of the multi-level features extracted at every stage of the model by integrating the low-level features got at the bottom of the model with the high-level features got at the top of the model. In addition, we are the first to use attention modules in the saliency detection, and we put several attention modules into the model to optimize features transferring between layers to get a better result.
- Our method shows good generalization and yields comparable even better performance than the state-of-the-art SOD methods on several public datasets.

2 Related Work

SOD technology has attracted lots of interests among the computer vision scholars. Unlike fixation [4], one of the attention mechanism work, SOD aims at extracting all the salient regions with clear contour and represents them using a binary graph. SOD methods can be mainly divided into hand-craft features based approach and learning based approach according to the way to get features of images. For the hand-crafted methods [9,29], they can be traced back to [20], Treisman proposed a feature-integration model of attention. The model selects the most important visual features and combines them to get the salient objects. Wang *et al.* [21] treated the saliency computation as the regression problem. Lee *et al.* [11] proved that the hand-crafted features can provide additional information to boost the performance of saliency detection, which depends on high-level features only. Xie *et al.* [26] proposed a new computational saliency detection model which is implemented with a coarse to fine strategy under the Bayesian framework. Although the hand-craft SOD methods can achieve a nice detection, they are not robust enough to deal with the complex scenarios. Thus, more and more researcher pay attention to learning based approach [13,22] to bring an accurate result. Hou *et al.* [7] introduced a series of short connections between deeper and shallower layers, and the activation of each layer can highlight the corresponding objects and detect their boundaries accurately. Liu *et al.* [15] solved the SOD problem by expanding the pooling part of the convolutional neural network. Zhang *et al.* [35] integrated multi-level feature maps into multiple resolution at first, which includes rough semantics and fine details and then learned to combine these feature maps at each resolution adaptively. Finally, the results were fused effectively to generate the final saliency map. Particularly, Guo *et al.* [5] utilized the object porposals to detect salient objects, and they considered the SOD as the ranking and voting strategy to object proposals. Different from using the object proposals to make up the saliency map, we use multiple object proposals as semantical knowledge to assist the model in perceiving the most conspicuous regions in images quickly and exactly.

3 Approach

3.1 Overview

In this work, we describe a procedure for building and learning deep image saliency detection networks using the multiple objects proposals as high-level prior. An overview of our method is presented in Fig. 1. From the macro point of view, the process for our method to detect salient objects can be divided into to two main steps roughly. Firstly, we put an image I into the proposal extractor and get a lot of object proposals. Then we calculate a score for each object proposal and order them according to the score. We chose top 10 as the final proposals used in our model which are most likely to cover all the salient regions of an image. Secondly, the 10 object proposals P are thrown into the network to catch the saliency map F after the encoding-decoding operations. The training of our model can be achieved by minimizing the following objective function:

$$\min_{\theta} \sum_{k} Loss(L(I_k), F_k(I_k; \theta)) \tag{1}$$

where $L(I_k)$ represents the label of the *k-th* image I_k, and F_k is the saliency map got by our method. θ denotes the model parameter. $Loss(\cdot)$ is the per-pixel loss function.

In the rest of this section, we explain the procedure of data preprocessing and the prediction network in detail.

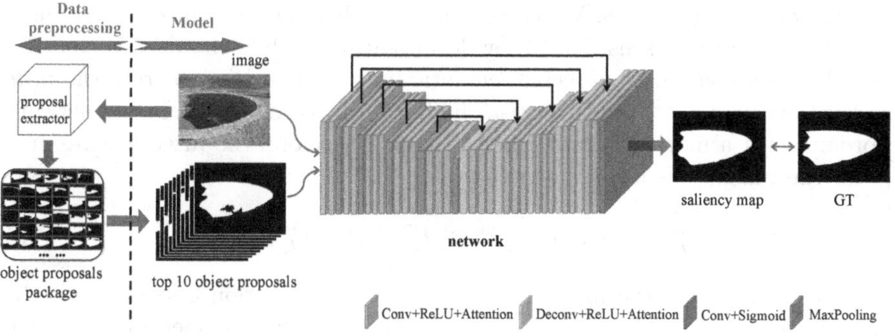

Fig. 1. The overview of our approach. To understand the work procedure better, we also place the data preprocessing pipeline on the left of the figure.

3.2 Data Preprocessing

The multiple proposals used in our method are obtained from the proposal extractor [8]. Given an image I_i, the extractor can produce hundreds of object proposals. Here we represent them with P. However, not all of these proposals are useful for our methods, because lots of them are mixed with much noise strongly. The working principle of the proposal extractor is to generate a set of segmentations by performing graph cuts, and rank them according to their importance. To get the object proposals which are most likely to cover all the salient regions, we rank them again by computing the new Intersection-over-Union (IoU) score τ, which are modified by our method, between all of the extracted proposals and the label of image. Then we select top 10 of them with the score greater than 3 as the high-level semantic knowledge experimentally. The new IoU score can be written as Eq. (2):

$$\tau = \frac{P_j(I_i) \bigcap L(I_i)}{P_j(I_i) \bigcup L(I_i) - P_j(I_i) \bigcap L(I_i)} \tag{2}$$

where $P_j(I_i)$ is the *j-th* proposal got by the extractor for the *i-th* image I_i.

3.3 Network Structure

Our network is rooted in VGG-16 model [18], which is pre-trained on the ImageNet, but we have improved it by adding several attention modules proposed in [25] between adjacent convolutional layers. We also integrate the low-level features of the encoder into the high-level features of the decoder by concatenating each pair of them. What needs to be added is that the attention module has two sequential sub-modules, channel attention module and spatial attention module. Because of the outstanding performance of attention modules for feed-forward convolutional networks, we use them behind every convolutional layer to transfer features more efficiently. Thus, the useful features can be fully utilized to perceive the salient regions. Moreover, we know that the convolution layers near the bottom are more sensitive to low-level features, while the deeper convolutional layers are easier to perceive semantic information. We integrate the *m-th* low-level features $f_{I_i}^{m_{low}}$ and the *m-th* high-level features $f_{I_i}^{m_{high}}$ in the network in order to get a more accurate saliency map. Therefore, the fused feature map $\tilde{f}_{I_i}^{m}$ for the image I_i is formally written as:

$$\tilde{f}_{I_i}^{m} = \sigma(Concat(f_{I_i}^{m_{low}}, f_{I_i}^{m_{high}}) \otimes w_{I_i}^{m} + b_{I_i}^{m}) \tag{3}$$

where $w_{I_i}^{m}$ represents the filters for the *m-th* de-convolution operation for the image I_i, and b_i^m is its biases. $Concat(\cdot)$ is the concatenate operation between the two features, and $\otimes$ represents convolution operation. $\sigma(\cdot)$ refers to ReLU, a kind of non-linear activation function.

4 Experiments

4.1 Experimental Setup

Datasets and Evaluation Metrcis: We evaluate our method on four public benchmark datasets. **HKU-IS** [17] consists of 4,447 images including multiple disconnected objects. **ECSSD** [28] has 1,000 natural images with complex structures. **PASCAL-S** [33] comes from the PASCAL VOC [2] and contains 850 images. **MSRA5K** [19] has 5,000 images of all kinds.

We evaluate the performance of our model and compare with other works by four widely used metrics, i.e., Precision-Recall Curve (PR Curve), Area Under Curve (AUC) score, F-measure and Mean Absolute Error (MAE). F-measure, which we denotes as F_β, is an overall performance measure. It can be computed by the weighted harmonic mean of the precision and recall:

$$F_\beta = \frac{(1+\beta^2) \times Precision \times Recall}{\beta^2 \times Precision + Recall} \tag{4}$$

where β^2 is set to 0.3 following [15]. MAE is the similarity between a saliency map S and ground truth G:

$$MAE = \frac{1}{W \times H} \sum_{x=1}^{W} \sum_{y=1}^{H} |S(x,y) - G(x,y)| \tag{5}$$

where S is the saliency map and G represents the ground truth. W and H denote the width and height of S respectively.

Implementation: Our experiments are conducted with a NVIDIA GTX 1080Ti GPU. The code is based on Python with the Keras toolbox. Our method is rooted in the VGG-16 model and parameters in other layers are initialized randomly. In the training stage, all the images are resized to 224×224 and we use Adam optimizer and the learning rate is set to 10^{-6}.

4.2 Performance Comparison

We compare our method with three state-of-the-art deep learning based SOD approaches including RFCN [23], C2SNet [13], WSS [22], and five conventional counterparts including HS [28], MBS [34], SF [10], wCtr [37] and GS [24]. As shown in Fig. 2 and Table 1, our proposed method outperform existing works across almost all the datasets according to the evaluation metrics, and they demonstrate the effectiveness of our proposed method strongly.

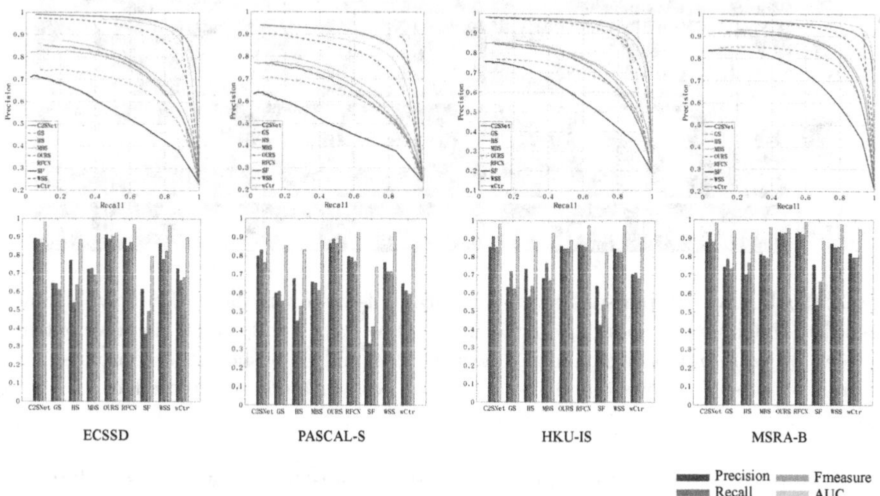

Fig. 2. The PR curves and bar graphs show the comparison of nine saliency maps on four popular salient object datasets.

Table 1. Quantitative evaluations. The best three scores are shown in red, blue, green, respectively

Methods	MSRA-B		PASCAL-S		HKU-IS		ECSSD	
	F-measure	MAE	F-measure	MAE	F-measure	MAE	F-measure	MAE
HS	0.7669	0.1621	0.5272	0.2625	0.6377	0.2150	0.6347	0.2274
MBS	0.7922	0.1116	0.6126	0.1964	0.6678	0.1503	0.6903	0.1707
SF	0.6640	0.1660	0.4187	0.2358	0.5347	0.1744	0.4921	0.2187
wCtr	0.7959	0.1106	0.5935	0.1986	0.6770	0.1424	0.6762	0.1712
GS	0.7348	0.1445	0.5553	0.2209	0.6213	0.1681	0.6080	0.2058
RFCN	0.9211	0.0346	0.7685	0.1036	0.8564	0.0546	0.8714	0.0667
C2SNet	0.8765	0.0478	0.7632	0.0805	0.8534	0.0460	0.8666	0.0535
WSS	0.8535	0.0763	0.7151	0.1395	0.8237	0.0790	0.8233	0.1039
OURS	0.9267	0.0287	0.8678	0.0544	0.8455	0.0555	0.9002	0.0451

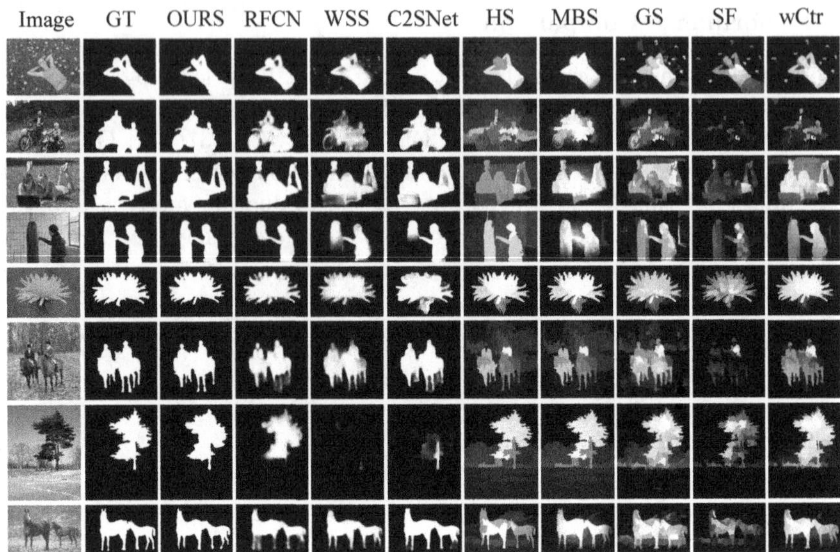

Fig. 3. Qualitative comparisons to previous state-of-the-art methods. The rows 1 shows the object touching the boundary of the image. The rows 2 and 6 show the low contrast between objects and backgrounds. The rows 2–4 and 6, 8 show the comparison in multiple objects. The rows 5 and 7 show the objects with complicated edges.

From the performance comparison with the state-of-the-art, we can see that our method can largely outperform other leading methods on MSRA-B, PASCAL-S and ECSSD. Particularly, our method increases the highest F-measure score by 0.61%, 12.92%, 3.31% and decreases the lowest MAE score by 17.05%, 32.42%, 15.70%, respectively.

We also visualize some example saliency maps of our model in Fig. 3. From the picture we can see that our method can achieve more accurate results.

5 Conclusions

In this paper, we propose a new method to detect salient objects by using multiple proposals as semantical knowledge. We first use the proposal extractor to acquire hundreds of object proposals, and then rank them using the method we mentioned earlier. To avoid too much computation, we chose top 10 of them as the most semantical knowledge. Moreover, we are the first to insert attention modules into VGG-16 model to detect salient objects, and we also mix the low-level features of the encoder with the high-level features of the decoder to get a much better saliency map. Extensive evaluations demonstrate that our method can improve the performance of SOD significantly and show nice generalization of our model.

References

1. Cheng, M.M., Mitra, N.J., Huang, X., Torr, P.H., Hu, S.M.: Global contrast based salient region detection. In: Computer Vision and Pattern Recognition (2011)
2. Everingham, M., Van Gool, L., Williams, C.K.I., Winn, J., Zisserman, A.: The pascal visual object classes (VOC) challenge. Int. J. Comput. Vis. **88**(2), 303–338 (2010)
3. Fang, H., Gupta, S., Iandola, F., Srivastava, R., Zweig, G.: From captions to visual concepts and back. In: IEEE Conference on Computer Vision and Pattern Recognition (2014)
4. Gorji, S., Clark, J.J.: Attentional push: a deep convolutional network for augmenting image salience with shared attention modeling in social scenes. In: IEEE Conference on Computer Vision and Pattern Recognition (2017)
5. Guo, F., et al.: Video saliency detection using object proposals. IEEE Trans. Cybern. **PP**(99), 1–12 (2017)
6. Hou, Q., Cheng, M.M., Hu, X., Borji, A., Torr, P.: Deeply supervised salient object detection with short connections. In: IEEE Conference on Computer Vision and Pattern Recognition (2017)
7. Hou, Q., Cheng, M.M., Hu, X., Borji, A., Tu, Z., Torr, P.H.S.: Deeply supervised salient object detection with short connections. In: IEEE Conference on Computer Vision and Pattern Recognition, pp. 5300–5309 (2017)
8. Endres, I., Hoiem, D.: Category independent object proposals. In: Daniilidis, K., Maragos, P., Paragios, N. (eds.) ECCV 2010. LNCS, vol. 6315, pp. 575–588. Springer, Heidelberg (2010). https://doi.org/10.1007/978-3-642-15555-0_42
9. Itti, L., Koch, C., Niebur, E.: A model of saliency-based visual attention for rapid scene analysis. IEEE Trans. Pattern Anal. Mach. Intell. **20**, 1254–1259 (1998). https://doi.org/10.1109/34.730558
10. Krahenbuhl, P.: Saliency filters: contrast based filtering for salient region detection. In: IEEE Conference on Computer Vision and Pattern Recognition (2012)
11. Lee, G., Tai, Y.W., Kim, J.: Deep saliency with encoded low level distance map and high level features. In: IEEE Conference on Computer Vision and Pattern Recognition (2016)
12. Li, G., Yu, Y.: Deep contrast learning for salient object detection. In: IEEE Conference on Computer Vision and Pattern Recognition (2016)
13. Li, X., Yang, F., Cheng, H., Liu, W., Shen, D.: Contour knowledge transfer for salient object detection. In: Europeon Conference on Computer Vision (2018)
14. Lin, Y., Pang, Z., Wang, D., Zhuang, Y.: Task-driven visual saliency and attention-based visual question answering. CoRR abs/1702.06700 (2017)
15. Liu, J., Hou, Q., Cheng, M.M., Feng, J., Jiang, J.: A simple pooling-based design for real-time salient object detection. CoRR abs/1904.09569 (2019)
16. Ramanishka, V., Das, A., Zhang, J., Saenko, K.: Top-down visual saliency guided by captions. In: IEEE Conference on Computer Vision and Pattern Recognition (2016)
17. Rui, Z., Ouyang, W., Li, H., Wang, X.: Saliency detection by multi-context deep learning. In: IEEE Conference on Computer Vision and Pattern Recognition (2015)
18. Simonyan, K., Zisserman, A.: Very deep convolutional networks for large-scale image recognition. CoRR abs/1409.1556 (2015)
19. Tie, L., et al.: Learning to detect a salient object. IEEE Trans. Pattern Anal. Mach. Intell. **33**(2), 353–367 (2011)

20. Treisman, A.M., Gelade, G.: A feature-integration theory of attention. Cogn. Psychol. **12**(1), 97–136 (1980)
21. Wang, J., Jiang, H., Yuan, Z., Cheng, M.M., Hu, X., Zheng, N.: Salient object detection: a discriminative regional feature integration approach. Int. J. Comput. Vis. **123**(2), 251–268 (2017)
22. Wang, L., Lu, H., Wang, Y., Feng, M., Xiang, R.: Learning to detect salient objects with image-level supervision. In: IEEE Conference on Computer Vision and Pattern Recognition (2017)
23. Wang, L., Wang, L., Lu, H., Zhang, P., Ruan, X.: Saliency detection with recurrent fully convolutional networks. In: Leibe, B., Matas, J., Sebe, N., Welling, M. (eds.) ECCV 2016. LNCS, vol. 9908, pp. 825–841. Springer, Cham (2016). https://doi.org/10.1007/978-3-319-46493-0_50
24. Wei, Y., Wen, F., Zhu, W., Sun, J.: Geodesic saliency using background priors. In: Fitzgibbon, A., Lazebnik, S., Perona, P., Sato, Y., Schmid, C. (eds.) ECCV 2012. LNCS, vol. 7574, pp. 29–42. Springer, Heidelberg (2012). https://doi.org/10.1007/978-3-642-33712-3_3
25. Woo, S., Park, J., Lee, J.Y., Kweon, I.S.: CBAM: convolutional block attention module. In: Europeon Conference on Computer Vision (2018)
26. Xie, Y., Lu, H.: Visual saliency detection based on Bayesian model. In: IEEE International Conference on Image Processing (2011)
27. Xin, L., Fan, Y., Chen, L., Cai, H.: Saliency transfer: an example-based method for salient object detection. In: International Joint Conference on Artificial Intelligence (2016)
28. Yan, Q., Li, X., Shi, J., Jia, J.: Hierarchical saliency detection (2013)
29. Yang, C., Zhang, L., Lu, H., Xiang, R., Yang, M.H.: Saliency detection via graph-based manifold ranking. In: IEEE Conference on Computer Vision and Pattern Recognition (2013)
30. Yang, T.Y., Hsu, J.H., Lin, Y.Y., Chuang, Y.Y.: DeepCD: learning deep complementary descriptors for patch representations. In: IEEE International Conference on Computer Vision (2017)
31. Yang, T.Y., Lin, Y.Y., Chuang, Y.Y.: Accumulated stability voting: a robust descriptor from descriptors of multiple scales. In: IEEE Conference on Computer Vision and Pattern Recognition (2016)
32. Yao, Q., Lu, H., Xu, Y., He, W.: Saliency detection via cellular automata. In: IEEE Conference on Computer Vision and Pattern Recognition (2015)
33. Yin, L., Hou, X., Koch, C., Rehg, J.M., Yuille, A.L.: The secrets of salient object segmentation (2014)
34. Zhang, J., Sclaroff, S., Zhe, L., Shen, X., Price, B., Mech, R.: Minimum barrier salient object detection at 80 fps. In: IEEE International Conference on Computer Vision (2015)
35. Zhang, P., Wang, D.K., Lu, H., Wang, H., Ruan, X.: Amulet: aggregating multi-level convolutional features for salient object detection. In: IEEE International Conference on Computer Vision, pp. 202–211 (2017)
36. Zhao, R., Ouyang, W., Wang, X.: Person re-identification by saliency learning. IEEE Trans. Pattern Anal. Mach. Intell. **39**(2), 356–370 (2017)
37. Zhu, W., Shuang, L., Wei, Y., Jian, S.: Saliency optimization from robust background detection. In: IEEE Conference on Computer Vision and Pattern Recognition (2014)

Combining Multi-level Loss for Image Denoising

Fei Li[1(✉)], Nailiang Kuang[3], Jiangbin Zheng[1,2(✉)], Qianru Wei[1], Yue Xi[2], and Yanrong Guo[3]

[1] School of Microelectronics and Software, Northwestern Polytechnical University, Xi'an, People's Republic of China
lflovelife@mail.nwpu.edu.cn

[2] School of Computer Science, Northwestern Polytechnical University, Xi'an, People's Republic of China
zhengjb@nwpu.edu.cn

[3] Xi'an Microelectronics Technology Institute, Xi'an, China

Abstract. The image processing has witnessed remarkable progress in image denoising. Nevertheless, restoring the visual quality of the image remains a great challenge. Existing methods might fail to obtain the denoised images with high visual quality since they ignore the potential connection with the high-level feature and result in over-smoothing results. Aiming to research whether high-level feature could influence the performance of denoising task, we propose an end-to-end multi-module neural network architecture, which introduces the combination of the high-level and low-level feature in the training process, for image denoising. In order to guide model preserve structural information efficiently, we introduce a hybrid loss, which is designed to restore details from both pixel and feature space. The experimental results show our method improves the visual quality of images and performs well compared with state-of-the-art methods on three benchmarks.

Keywords: Image denoising · Edge loss · Hybrid loss function

1 Introduction

Image denoising is a fundamental but challenging task in computer vision field. It aims to recover the clean image X from its noisy observation Y. Generally, the real noisy image can be formulated as follows

$$Y = X + \sigma(x), \tag{1}$$

where $\sigma(x)$ is the corrupted noise. And additive white Gaussian noise (AWGN) is the hot topic in image denoising. We focus on the color image denoiser of AWGN.

There are several traditional denoising algorithms for AWGN in early studies [3,6], each of which serves as a prior for efficiently solving denoising issues. However, these existing classical methods contain several drawbacks. Compared with

J. Ren et al. (Eds.): BICS 2019, LNAI 11691, pp. 423–432, 2020.
https://doi.org/10.1007/978-3-030-39431-8_41

methods based on the artificial neural network, these methods require higher time complexity and rely on hand-crafted prior largely.Therefore, with the great breakthrough of artificial neural networks, a lot of progress for image denoising has been made in recent year [7,13,22,25]. In contrast to the extensive literature describing, little attention has been paid to context detail and visual semantic information of images. Convolution neural networks (CNNs) methods focus on improving the image peak signal to noise ratio (PSNR) and minimize the mean square error (MSE). A major issue toward MSE just is the lack of context detail and semantic information, which results in blurred regions and over-smoothing mostly. The strategy obtains the average solution rather than the optimum solution. This is why the output image after losing a lot of details still gets a higher PSNR score. In addition, existing CNNs methods are insensitive to pixels near image edges, which because of the unbalanced sample amount of edge and unedge region. As shown in Fig. 1, both CBM3D [3] and Dn-CNN [25] introduce over-smoothing regions and drop structural detail clearly in the zoom-in region.

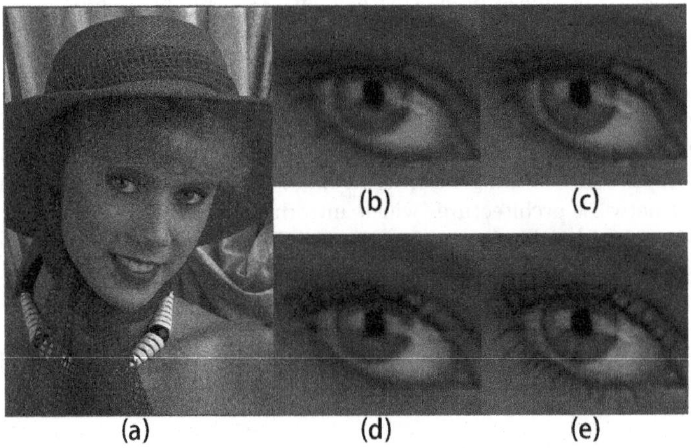

Fig. 1. (a) Input image with noise $\sigma = 25$. Denoised by (b) CBM3D, (c) Dn-CNN and (d) our method. (e) Ground truth.

To rectify these weakness, we present the attempt in combination of high-level and low-level feature in CNN for image denoising, and propose a new multi-module framework for image denoising. First of all, we propose an end-to-end multi-module network to produce feature with different spatial character. The backbone of network uses dilated convolutions [21] instead of traditional convolutions to avoid the dilemma of gradient vanishing and exploding. Dilated convolutions owns bigger receptive field size within same setting and are effective ways to increase receptive field size, which influence obtained features and model capability significantly. More importantly, we design reconstruction module, which is motived by [20] and residual learning [7], to acquire various scale semantic detail by kernels of different size. Second, in order to emphasize the potential connection between low-level and high-level tasks, we introduce the combination of these tasks together to guide image denoising in both pixel and feature space. Specificity, we investigate the characteristics of different losses and adopt the perceptual loss [9,23], which compares difference of images in feature space, to final hybrid loss to maintain semantic-aware details of image sample. Model jointly minimizes the pixel-level image reconstruction loss and the high-level feature loss together. In addition, considering that these methods are insensitive to pixels near image edges and cause over-smoothing region universally, the edge loss is designed to increase the weight of edge loss and reserve edge details efficiently. The hybrid loss ensures model not only removes noise but also remains textural information. So we can observe in Fig. 1 that our methods restores more structural details.

In summary, our main contribution can be summarized as follows. First, an end-to-end framework has been proposed, which contains a larger receptive field size and provides features of different scales. Second, we introduce a hybrid loss, consisting of reconstruction, edge and perceptual loss, to preserve the context details and edge information. More importantly, the hybrid loss guides model pay more attention to edge region reconstruction.

2 Related Work

Existing denoising methods can be broadly categorized as methods based on handcrafted feature [1,3,6,12,27] and artificial natural networks (ANNs) methods [2,8,13,21,24–26].

Most of methods based structural prior take advantage of local and non-local structures in images. [1,27] encode local structures and remove noise by coefficient shrinkage for image denoising. As for the non-local methods, these methods including non-local sparse (LSSC) [12], weighted norm minimization (WNNM) [6], and block-matching and 3D filtering (BM3D) [3] achieve improvement. Conventional methods mostly follow the strategy of group match or cluster to the same patch in the image, and apply local and non-local structural prior to these groups. These methods lack of versatility and produce unsatisfied results mostly.

More recently, a number of ANN-based methods have been developed for image denoising, including multilayer perception (MLP) and CNNs based methods. The MLP is the model of stacking hidden layers [2], which is the first learning method and compares performance with BM3D [3]. The CNNs based methods are utilized for denoising task in [8] firstly. A very deep networks designed with skip connection and residual module for image restoration [7,13] achieve better performance. [21] replaces regular convolution with dilated layer, which is used to expand the receptive field size [24] to denoise image. Besides, recent approaches have been transferred to the flexibility and speed of model. FFDNet [26] processes on down-sampled images patches to reduce the feature time significantly and obtains a fast and flexible denoising framework. However, above methods resolve noise in the low-level pixel space and minimize MSE error between predicted noise and AWGN noise. So related works [11,14,16] combine low-level pixel space and high-level vision tasks for image denoising.

3 Proposed Method

In this section, we first propose our network architecture and each module utilized in our model (Sect. 3.1), and then present the component of the hybrid loss (Sect. 3.2).

3.1 Network Architecture

We propose an end-to-end multi-module network to recover the clean image from the noisy input. Model takes the noisy color image as input and its output is the denoising color image of the same size. The overall network structure and the data process flow are presented in Fig. 2. These modules feature extraction module **(FEM)**, inception reconstruction module **(IRM)** and feature combining module **(FCM)** in this network will be elaborated as follows respectively.

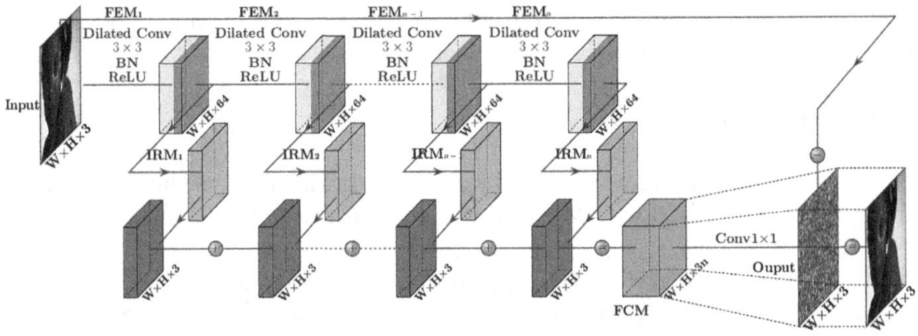

Fig. 2. The framework of our proposed end-to-end multi-module network for image denoising.

FEM. The module adopts the dilated convolution layer to replace all common convolutions. Because dilated convolutions own the same or bigger receptive field as corresponding units in the original model, which could expand the receptive field without increasing the number of the filter kernel. Besides, our model extracts feature map on different depth of the network to ensure these features contain different spatial characteristics. Each module consists of a dilated convolution layer, a batch normalization and a *ReLU* neuron. The output of each module is both the input to the next FEM and the corresponding IRM.

IRM. The module aims to realize the reconstruction of the different feature from each FEM. Its detail is illustrated in Fig. 2. Each IRM contains 5 convolutions of different size, aims for acquiring feature of different scales. Feature map is forwarded across two separated branches after first convolution, the above convolution with the size of 1×1, and the below is 3×3. And output features from two branches are summed and sent to subsequent layers. Finally, we adopt

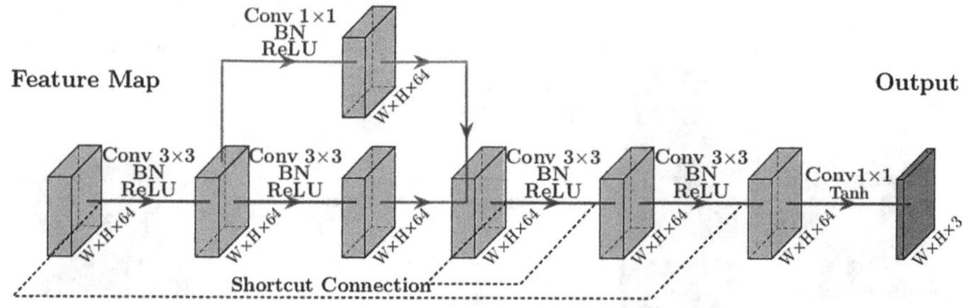

Fig. 3. The detail of inception reconstruction module.

convolution with 1×1 to transfer feature size from $W \times H \times 64$ to $W \times H \times 3$. And we adopt $Tanh$ to replace $ReLU$ to simulate the distribution of estimated noise. Meanwhile, the module also takes shortcut connection for the paired layers (Fig. 3).

FCM. The input of the module is the combined feature from each IRM, and we concatenate all the outputs and take convolution with a size of 1×1 to transfer the feature dimension from $W \times H \times 3n$ to $W \times H \times 3$. The output is noise estimation. Finally, the clean image could be obtained by the noisy input subtracts the model's output.

3.2 Robust Hybrid Loss Function

Inspired by the advantages of previous approaches [11,14,16], we propose a new hybrid loss function to enhance the quality of the denoised results. The loss focuses on the combination of high-level visual semantic features and pixel-wise loss and is adopted to guide our model training. As shown in Fig. 4, three loss components **Reconstruction loss**, **Edge loss** and **Perceptual loss** have been adopted in our model, and we describe them sequentially as follows.

Reconstruction Loss. L_{mse} is the MSE loss between the denoised results and ground truth, which is represented as

$$\mathrm{L}_{mse} = \frac{1}{HW} \sum_{i=1}^{H} \sum_{j=1}^{W} \left((x_g)_{i,j} - (x_c)_{i,j} \right)^2 \tag{2}$$

where x_g, x_c denotes the ground truth and denoised results form proposed network, and W, H indicates size of image.

Perceptual Loss. In order to obtain realistic images, we introduce the perceptual loss based on the pre-trained VGG features to constrain the denoiser, which is defined as

$$\mathrm{L}_{per} = \frac{1}{HW} \sum_{i=1}^{H} \sum_{j=1}^{W} \| \phi_H (x_g)_{i,j} - \phi_H (x_c)_{i,j} \|_2^2 \tag{3}$$

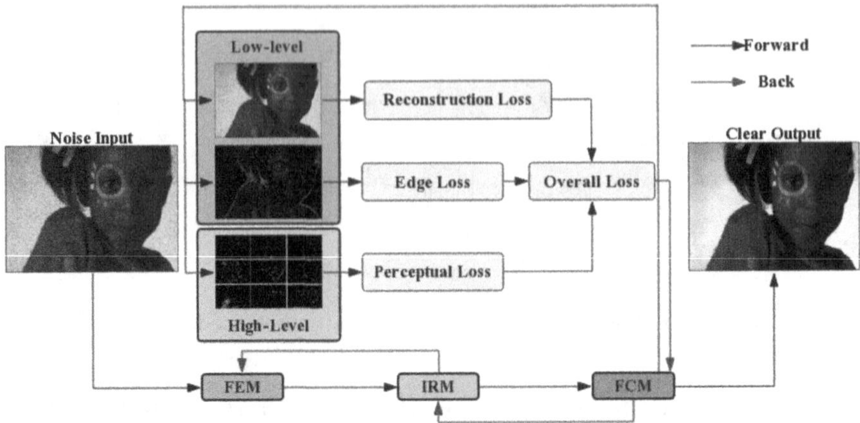

Fig. 4. The hybrid loss function consists of three parts.

where $\phi_H(\cdot)$ represents the feature extractor and $\phi_H(\cdot)_{i,j}$ indicates pixel in the i-th column and j-th row of the network feature, each of which is of size $H \times W$. Usually, we adopt VGG [19] network which is pre-trained on ImageNet [17] as extractor. The key function of $\mathcal{L}_{per}$ is measuring the difference between images in the feature space rather than pixel space. We find that using Eq. (3) is efficient to the details restoration and noise removing but it accordingly introduces artifacts in the denoised results. This inevitably degrades quality of the recovered images.

Edge Loss. To remove these artifacts and preserve structures information, we introduce L_{edge} to enhance the influence of edge structure in the training process. L_{edge} is defined as

$$\mathcal{L}_{edge} = \mathcal{L}_{edge.g} + \mathcal{L}_{edge.f} \tag{4}$$

Here, $\mathcal{L}_{edge}$ is subdivided into two parts, $\mathcal{L}_{edge.g}$ indicates the two-directional (i.e., horizontal and vertical direction) gradient loss and $\mathcal{L}_{edge.f}$ represents the low-level loss extracted by network. The $\mathcal{L}_{edge.g}$ detail is given as

$$\begin{aligned} \mathcal{L}_{edge.g} = \frac{1}{HW} \sum_{i=1}^{H} \sum_{j=1}^{W} & \left(H_r\left(x_g\right)_{i,j} - H_r\left(x_c\right)_{i,j} \right)^2 \\ & + \left(H_c\left(x_g\right)_{i,j} - H_c\left(x_c\right)_{i,j} \right)^2 \end{aligned} \tag{5}$$

where H_r and H_c denotes methods to compute gradients of images along rows and columns respectively. As for the $\mathcal{L}_{edge.f}$ is designed as

$$\mathcal{L}_{edge.f} = \frac{1}{HW} \sum_{i=1}^{H} \sum_{j=1}^{W} \| \phi_L\left(x_g\right)_{i,j} - \phi_L\left(x_c\right)_{i,j} \|_2^2 \tag{6}$$

where the $\phi_L(\cdot)$ indicates the pre-trained VGG network as well as $\phi_H(\cdot)$. Specifically, We pick layer $relu1\_1$ and $relu2\_2$ to extract low-level feature.

Overall Loss. The overall loss function is composed of above three parts and defined as

$$\text{Ł}_{total} = \lambda_{mse}\text{Ł}_{mse} + \lambda_{per}\text{Ł}_{per} + \lambda_{edge}\text{Ł}_{edge} \tag{7}$$

where the λ are positive weights and the whole network is trained by minimizing Eq. (7).

Table 1. Color image denoising results. Average **PSNR/SSIM** for various level noise on CBSD68, Kodak24, and LIVE1. The best performance is red and second is green.

Databases	Noise	Methods				
		CBM3D	Dn-CNN	FFDNet	UDNet	Ours
CBSD68	$\sigma = 25$	30.69/0.8674	31.23/0.8835	31.20/0.8828	31.16/0.8804	31.29/0.8841
	$\sigma = 50$	27.37/0.7624	27.92/0.7925	27.96/0.7910	27.86/0.7873	28.05/0.7937
	$\sigma = 75$	25.73/0.6954	24.47/–	26.24/0.7240	24.99/0.6541	26.29/0.7250
Kodak24	$\sigma = 25$	31.81/0.8667	32.35/0.8808	32.25/0.8797	32.22/0.8766	32.39/0.8813
	$\sigma = 50$	28.62/0.7768	29.16/0.7989	29.10/0.7976	29.00/0.7932	29.28/0.8019
	$\sigma = 75$	26.82/0.7193	25.04/–	27.27/0.7396	25.83/0.6454	27.52/0.7419
LIVE1	$\sigma = 25$	30.89/0.8739	31.49/0.8877	31.39/0.8866	31.21/0.8836	31.49/0.8890
	$\sigma = 50$	27.55/0.7776	28.17/0.8023	28.11/0.8010	27.99/0.7962	28.24/0.8053
	$\sigma = 75$	25.85/0.7125	–/–	26.31/0.7363	25.03/0.6580	26.41/0.7389

4 Experiments

4.1 Datasets

Our model takes RGB images as input and rebuilds color images directly. We generate training and testing dataset by adding the AWGN with zero mean to the original image, which is viewed as the ground truth. For training, we produce synthesized sample over the test dataset of Pascal Visual Object Classes (VOC) challenge [5], which consists of 1,449 images. For testing, we evaluate our network over three popular benchmarks: (1) the Kodak24[1], which is the standard denoising dataset; (2) the CBSD68 dataset, which contains 64 color images in [26]; (3) the LIVE1 dataset [18] (29 images) contains images with diverse properties.

4.2 Implementation Details

We specify the implementation details of our proposed method. For network architecture, the number of FEM and IRM is 10 respectively. The size of each dilated convolution of FEM is 3×3 and the corresponding dilated factor is set as $[1, 1, 2, 2, 3, 3, 2, 2, 1, 1]$ respectively from top to bottom. In training process,

[1] http://r0k.us/graphics/kodak/.

128 random crop patches with the size of 40×40 mean obtained as inputs. We use the ADAM optimizer algorithm [4] to train our model, whose initial learning rate is set as 0.001, and decreased by 20% when the training loss stops decreasing, until 0.0001. We adopt a weight decay of 0.0001 and a momentum of 0.9. The loss of separately training model is equivalent to Eq. (4) as $\lambda_{mse} = 0.8$, $\lambda_{edge} = \lambda_{per} = 0.1$. The proposed algorithm is implemented in Pytorch library [15] on a computer with 2 NVIDIA 1080Ti GPUs.

4.3 Results and Discussion

We evaluate the proposed method on three datasets across two metrics PSNR and structural similarity index (SSIM). We compare our model with state-of-the-art denoising methods, including CBM3D [3], Dn-CNN [25], FFDNet [26] and UDNet [10]. All implementation codes of above methods are all from its public websites and the default parameter settings are consistent to its papers. Image with noise of different levels (e.g., 25, 50 and 75) are fed into all models. Compared with the single metric PSNR, higher SSIM means image contains more structural detail and model restores textural detail better. Table 1 summarises the performance concerning average PSNR and SSIM.

Quantitative Analyse. Table 1 summarizes the performance in terms of average PSNR and SSIM. We could observe that our method achieves the almost best denoising performance on these datasets under different level noises situation. And we take noise level $\sigma = 50$ on dataset LIVE1 as an example, and find that our methods achieves better results, 0.69, 0.07, 0.13 and 0.25 dB PSNR, 0.0277, 0.0030, 0.0043 and 0.0091 SSIM, gains over with other methods respectively. High SSIM means our model could recover textural detail effectively.

Qualitative Analyse. To have a qualitative comparisons, several recovered images from above methods on the LIVE1 are shown in Fig. 5. As can be found, our method can remain more semantic regions compare with others.

We could observe that our method achieves the best denoising performance on three datasets under noises situation at different level. And we can conclude that our way is more appropriate for the image with high-level noise clearly. The higher the noise level, the more advantages this method has been better than other methods.

4.4 Extension

Our model can be easily extended to other reconstructed tasks, e.g. inpainting or low-light enhancement. Specificly , we transformed our model for low-light enhancement task and the result represented this model contains strong extensibility and capability.

Fig. 5. Noise Level ($\sigma = 25$) Denoising examples from LIVE1. PSNR and SSIM values appear below each of the image.

5 Conclusion

In this paper, we introduce an end-to-end multi-module framework to resolve the challenge of image denoising with AWGN, and proposed method achieves state-of-the-art performance over three public benchmarks. Our network is modularized and all its intermediate layers are utilized to extract features of different scales and contribute to the noise estimation directly. Furthermore, a hybrid robust loss has been designed to overcome the over-smoothing and pay more attention on edge region. This work allows us to gain several exciting insights into the denoising task. In our future research, we plan to characterize the real world image denoising and adopt the generative adversarial network (GAN) to simulate the real noise distribution.

Acknowledgement. This work has been supported by HGJ, HJSW and Research & Development plan of Shaanxi Province (Program No. 2017ZDXM-GY-094, 2015KTZDGY04-01).

References

1. Aharon, M., Elad, M., Bruckstein, A.: *rmk*-SVD: an algorithm for designing overcomplete dictionaries for sparse representation. TSP **54** (2006)
2. Burger, H.C., Schuler, C.J., Harmeling, S.: Image denoising: can plain neural networks compete with BM3D? In: CVPR, June 2012
3. Dabov, K., Foi, A., Katkovnik, V., Egiazarian, K.: Color image denoising via sparse 3D collaborative filtering with grouping constraint in luminance-chrominance space. In: ICIP, September 2007
4. Duchi, J., Hazan, E., Singer, Y.: Adaptive subgradient methods for online learning and stochastic optimization. JMLR **12**(7), 2121–2159 (2011)
5. Everingham, M., Eslami, S.M.A., Van Gool, L., Williams, C.K.I., Winn, J., Zisserman, A.: The pascal visual object classes challenge: a retrospective. IJCV **111**, 98–136 (2015)
6. Gu, S., Zhang, L., Zuo, W., Feng, X.: Weighted nuclear norm minimization with application to image denoising. In: CVPR, June 2014
7. He, K., Zhang, X., Ren, S., Sun, J.: Deep residual learning for image recognition. In: CVPR, June 2016

8. Jain, V., Seung, H.S.: Natural image denoising with convolutional networks. In: NIPS (2008)
9. Johnson, J., Alahi, A., Li, F.: Perceptual losses for real-time style transfer and super-resolution. CoRR (2016)
10. Lefkimmiatis, S.: Universal denoising networks: a novel CNN architecture for image denoising. In: CVPR (2018)
11. Liu, D., Wen, B., Liu, X., Wang, Z., Huang, T.S.: When image denoising meets high-level vision tasks: a deep learning approach. In: IJCAI (2018)
12. Mairal, J., Bach, F., Ponce, J., Sapiro, G., Zisserman, A.: Non-local sparse models for image restoration. In: ICCV. IEEE (2009)
13. Mao, X.J., Shen, C., Yang, Y.B.: Image restoration using very deep convolutional encoder-decoder networks with symmetric skip connections. CoRR (2016)
14. Niknejad, M., Bioucas-Dias, J.M., Figueiredo, M.A.T.: Class-specific poisson denoising by patch-based importance sampling. arXiv preprint arXiv:1706.02867 (2017)
15. Paszke, A., et al.: Automatic differentiation in PyTorch (2017)
16. Remez, T., Litany, O., Giryes, R., Bronstein, A.M.: Class-aware fully convolutional gaussian and poisson denoising. TIP **27**(11), 5707–5722 (2018)
17. Russakovsky, O., et al.: ImageNet large scale visual recognition challenge. IJCV **115**(3), 211–252 (2015)
18. Sheikh, H.R., Sabir, M.F., Bovik, A.C.: A statistical evaluation of recent full reference image quality assessment algorithms. TIP **15**(11), 3440–3451 (2006)
19. Simonyan, K., Zisserman, A.: Very deep convolutional networks for large-scale image recognition. In: ICLR (2015)
20. Szegedy, C., et al.: Going deeper with convolutions. In: CVPR, pp. 1–9 (2015)
21. Wang, T., Sun, M., Hu, K.: Dilated deep residual network for image denoising. In: ICTAI, November 2017
22. Xie, J., Xu, L., Chen, E.: Image denoising and inpainting with deep neural networks. In: NIPS (2012)
23. Yang, Q., et al.: Low-dose CT image denoising using a generative adversarial network with wasserstein distance and perceptual loss. T-MI **37**(6), 1348–1357 (2018)
24. Yu, F., Koltun, V., Funkhouser, T.: Dilated residual networks. In: CVPR, July 2017
25. Zhang, K., Zuo, W., Chen, Y., Meng, D., Zhang, L.: Beyond a gaussian denoiser: residual learning of deep CNN for image denoising. TIP **26**, 3142–3155 (2017)
26. Zhang, K., Zuo, W., Zhang, L.: FFDNet: toward a fast and flexible solution for CNN-based image denoising. TIP **27**(9), 4608–4622 (2018)
27. Zoran, D., Weiss, Y.: From learning models of natural image patches to whole image restoration. In: ICCV. IEEE (2011)

A Contour-Based Multi-scale Vision Corner Feature Recognition Using Gabor Filters

Jie Ren(✉), Nannan Chang, and Weichuan Zhang

College of Electronics and Information, Xi'an Polytechnic University, Xi'an, Shanxi 710048, People's Republic of China
renjie@xpu.edu.cn

Abstract. This paper proposes a corner detection algorithm based on the correlation matrices, in which the combination of edge shapes and gray variations in multiple scalars are used. First, a Canny edge detector is used to detect the edge contours of an input image. In each scale, the direction derivative of each pixel on the edge curves and its surrounding pixels are extracted by using Gabor filters with imaginary parts (IPGFs), which are further used to construct the correlation matrices. Then, the sum of normalized eigenvalues of the correlation matrices at different scales is computed to extract potential corners. Finally, non-maximum suppression and a threshold are used to extract final corners. The experimental results show that the proposed method improves the detection accuracy and is noise resistance compared with Harris algorithm.

Keywords: Corner detection · The imaginary parts of the gabor filters (IPGFs) · Multiple scale

1 Introduction

In computer vision, feature extraction of images is an important research topic. The features include colors, corners, textures, edges and shapes of a given image. Corners, which determines the shape of the target in the image, is one of the main features. Therefore, Corner detection is a preliminary stage in a variety of image processing and computer vision applications, such as the target recognition [1, 33, 34], camera calibration [2], three-dimensional reconstruction [3, 35, 36], image matching [4], etc.

The position of the corner is the intersection of more than two edges. The existing methods can be generally divided into three categories: intensity-based methods [5], template-based methods [6] and contour-based methods [7]. Considering that the Corner not only reflects the shape information of edge contour in the image, but also is the point with the greatest change of the gray values, it mainly exists in the edge part. In this paper, the corner detection is based on the extraction of edge contours.

After observing the shape of the edge contour, Attneave found that the curvature at the corner was large [8]. Freeman chain codes are extracted from the boundary of the segmented image. Then, the gradient and angle of the boundary pixels are calculated according to freeman chain codes of each contour [9]. This method is improved by using the local maximum point of curvature [10], local histogram of chain codes [11], resolution coupling technology [12].

J. Ren et al. (Eds.): BICS 2019, LNAI 11691, pp. 433–442, 2020.
https://doi.org/10.1007/978-3-030-39431-8_42

Since some significant corners are missing and some points are false detected as corner points when the features are within the different sizes, many multi-scale corner detection algorithms are proposed to instead of single-scalar methods. The core idea of multi-scale is to simulate the characteristics of image data. The input image is present in a range of scales [13], then potential corners are detected in each scale, followed by a combination method.

Asada and Brady [14] use multi-scale technology to find curvature changes of edge pixels to detect corner points. Mokhtarian and Macworh [15] proposed curvature scale space (CSS) technology to detect corners in the entire scale space. In 2001, Mokhtarian and Mokhanna [16] improved CSS algorithm [17] by smoothing edge curves of different lengths with different scales of Gaussian kernels. It can extract edge structure information more accuracy and suppress noise better. Gao et al. [18] presented a multi-scale corner detection algorithm based upon the local natural scale. Awrangjeb et al. [19] proposed multi-chord corner detection based upon the chord-to-point distance accumulation (CPDA) discrete curvature estimation technique [20]. In [21], a polygon is used to approximate a shape contour, and then the polygon vertices are extracted from the curvature extremes through scale space. Recently, the combination of contour shape and intensity variation information had been considered [22] to extract corners. Zhang and Shui [23] presented a contour-based corner detector using angle difference of the principal directions of anisotropic Gaussian directional derivatives. Although these methods have offered the better detection performance than the previously detectors, there is much room for improvement.

In [24], Gabor filters are proved to be used as the model of human visual system. Gabor filters [25] are demonstrated as the optimal filters to extract local feature, such as edge/corner detection. However, the most important properties [26] of the Gabor filters are related to invariance to illumination, rotation, scale, and translation, which are especially useful in feature extraction. It is indicated whether a pixel is corner or not depends upon the gray values of that pixel and its surrounding pixels.

Nowadays, many researches use Convolutional-Neural-Network (CNN) to learn the corners and other features. In [27], a fully-convolutional model is applied to computes pixel-level interest point locations and associated descriptors in one forward pass.

In this paper, a multiple scalar contour-based corner detection algorithm is proposed. Firstly, the Canny [28] edge detector is used to extract the edge of the image. Then the gap between the extract edge contour are filled. The multi-scale local curvature estimation is obtained by filtering the edges with imaginary parts of Gabor filters (IPGFs) at different scales. Finally, the sum of normalized eigenvalues at different scales is computed to extract potential corners and non-maximum suppression is used to extract final corners. This method used the combination of edge shapes and gray variations in multiple scalars. It can improve the robustness of the corner detection algorithm. The comparison between the proposed method and Harris [29] methods show that our approach is more competitive with respect to detection accuracy and noise robustness.

This following is the organization of the remainder of this paper. Section 2 introduces the IPGFs and its properties. Section 3 presents a new corner measure and its corresponding corner detector. Simulation results of the proposed methods are presented in Sect. 4, followed by a conclusions and discussions.

2 Corner Extraction with IPGFs

IPGFs are proved [22] to have the ability to extract the fine intensity variation information, which provide intuitive and useful information to describe the shape of the 2-D structures. In this section, we describe the property of IPGFs for corner extraction.

2.1 Imaginary Parts of Gabor Filters

In the continuous spatial domain, the IPGFs are expressed as [26]:

$$\begin{aligned} \psi(x,y;f,\theta) &= \frac{1}{2\pi\gamma\eta}\exp\left(-\left(\frac{u^2}{\gamma^2}+\frac{v^2}{\eta^2}\right)\right)\sin(2\pi f u), \\ u &= x\cos\theta + y\sin\theta, \\ v &= -x\sin\theta + y\cos\theta. \end{aligned} \tag{1}$$

where f is the central frequency of the filter, θ is the anti-clockwise rotation of the Gaussian major and the plane wave, γ is the spatial width of the filter along the plane wave, and η the spatial width perpendicular to the wave. Figure 1 shows a 2-D IPGF in spatial domain.

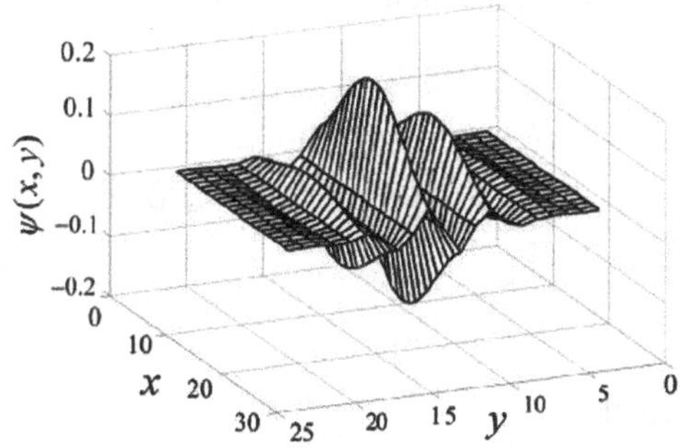

Fig. 1. A 2-D IPGF in spatial domain with$f_0 = 0.24$, $\theta = 0^o$, $\gamma = 1$, $\eta = 2$.

The IPGFs response at any location (x, y) for an input image $I(x, y)$ can be calculated with the convolution

$$\begin{aligned} \varsigma_I(x,y;f,\theta) &= I(x,y) * \psi(x,y;f,\theta) \\ &= \int\int_{-\infty}^{\infty} I(x_\tau,y_\tau)\psi(x-x_\tau,y-y_\tau;f,\theta)dx_\tau dy_\tau. \end{aligned} \tag{2}$$

It is easy to prove that the magnitude response of the IPGFs is a periodic function with a period π and thus the IPGFs in the interval [0, π] are enough to describe the directional intensity variation at a pixel. The magnitude response of the IPGFs along the orientation θ reflects the image intensity variation along the orientation $\theta + \pi/2$. Under this way, a set of IPFGs along different orientations can be used to distinguish different types of corners and edge pixels completely.

2.2 Discrete Multi-scale IPGFs

Images are two-dimensional discrete signals in the integer lattice Z^2. So, the continuous IPGFs in (1) must be transferred to their discrete forms. Furthermore, most of the input images contain multiple size features. To extract local intensity variation information around a pixel, various filters along different orientations and scales need to be used. Given a scale factor, a central frequency f_0, the width of the major axis γ and the minor axis η, the discrete multi-scale IPGFs are derived

$$\begin{aligned} \psi(m,n;f_0,k,s) &= \frac{a^{-s}}{2\pi\gamma\eta}\exp\left(-\left(\frac{u^2}{\gamma^2}+\frac{v^2}{\eta^2}\right)\right)\sin(2\pi f_0 u), \\ u &= a^{-s}(m\cos\theta_k + n\sin\theta_k), \\ v &= a^{-s}(-m\sin\theta_k + n\cos\theta_k). \end{aligned} \tag{3}$$

Here, $\theta_k = \pi k/K$ is the orientation for $k = 0, 1, \ldots, K-1$, where K is the total number of orientations. $a^{-s}(a > 1)$, $s = 0, 1, \ldots, S-1$ is the scale factor. For a discrete image $I(m,n)$, the discrete magnitude responses of IPGFs along different directions at each scale are

$$\begin{aligned} \zeta(m,n;k,s) &= I(m,n) * \psi(m,n;k,s) \\ &= \sum_{m_x}\sum_{n_y} I(m-m_x, n-n_y)\psi(m_x,n_y;k,s)\cdot \end{aligned} \tag{4}$$

3 Proposed Method

In this paper, a multiple scalar contour-based corner detection algorithm is proposed. Firstly, the edge map is detected from the input image using the Canny edge detector. The gaps within a range on edge contour are filled in the edge image. Then, for each point of edge contour and its surrounding points, their response at different scalars are computed. The normalized multiplication of multi-scale responses is applied to generated the final corner responses. Finally, the non-maximum suppression is utilized to remove false detection.

After edge detection, let $P^j = \{P_1^j, P_2^j, \ldots, P_N^j\}$ be the $j-th$ extracted contour. The $q-th$ pixel on the $j-th$ contour is denoted as $P_q^j(m_q, n_q)$. Its direction derivative vector at scale s is $\zeta(m_q, n_q; k, s)$, where $s = 0, 1, \ldots, S-1$, $k = 0, 1, \ldots, K-1$. $P_q^j(m_q, n_q)$ and its neighborhood pixels are:

$$P_{q,8}^{j} = \begin{bmatrix} P_q^j(m_q-1,n_q-1) & P_q^j(m_q-1,n_q1) & P_q^j(m_q-1,n_q+1) \\ P_q^j(m_q,n_q-1) & P_q^j(m_q,n_q) & P_q^j(m_q,n_q+1) \\ P_q^j(m_q+1,n_q-1) & P_q^j(m_q+1,n_q) & P_q^j(m_q+1,n_q+1) \end{bmatrix} \tag{5}$$

Their corresponding direction derivative vectors can construct a derivative matrix:

$$M_q^j(k,s) = \begin{bmatrix} \zeta(m_q-1,n_q-1;k,s) & \zeta(m_q-1,n_q;k,s) & \zeta(m_q-1,n_q+1;k,s) \\ \zeta(m_q,n_q-1;k,s) & \zeta(m_q,n_q;k,s) & \zeta(m_q,n_q+1;k,s) \\ \zeta(m_q+1,n_q-1;k,s) & \zeta(m_q+1,n_q;k,s) & \zeta(m_q+1,n_q+1;k,s) \end{bmatrix} \tag{6}$$

In each scale, the derivative matrix of P_q^j for the $k-th$ directions are calculated. Then, all K derivative matrices are summed and normalized with max value of each element in the matrices.

$$M_q^j(s) = \sum_{k=0}^{K-1} \frac{M_q^j(k,s)}{\max\left(\left|M_q^j(k,s)\right|\right)} \tag{7}$$

Then the correlation matrix of the edge pixel P_q^j, at scale s, is defined as

$$C_q^j(s) = (M_q^j(s))^T M_q^j(s). \tag{8}$$

The eigenvalues of $C_q^j(s)$ is calculated and denoted as $E_q^j(s)$, which indicates the intensity variation of pixel at each direction. Then, the sum of each elements in $E_q^j(s)$ are calculated and normalized as the single-scale response at the point P_q^j.

$$T_q^j(s) = \frac{\sum_{k=1}^{K} E_q^j(s)}{\max_k\left(\left|E_q^j(s)\right|\right)}. \tag{9}$$

Finally, the response at the point P_q^j in all scales is the multiplication of all single-scale responses:

$$T_q^j = \prod_{s=1}^{S} T_q^j(s). \tag{10}$$

The use of the above multiplication has an additional advantage. On the same edge contour, the normalized magnitude response of corners should be larger than that of edge pixels; multiplication makes the corners more distinguishable. When the corner response for each point on the edge contour is calculated, non-maximum suppression [30] is applied to the corner response. A local window is used to slide through all the pixels of the edge contour. If the center pixel of the window is the local maxima within the window, the central pixel scale-product is kept; otherwise, it would be set to zero. Finally, a global threshold T_h is used to further remove false detection and extract corners.

4 Performance Evaluation

To evaluate the performance of the proposed method, six images (see Fig. 2) with different scenes, collected from standard databases [31] are used for the robustness evaluation. The test results are compared with the Harris corner detection method. The new corner measure is computed using the IPGFs with $f_0 = 0.24, \gamma^2 = 4, \eta^2 = 16, K = 8$.

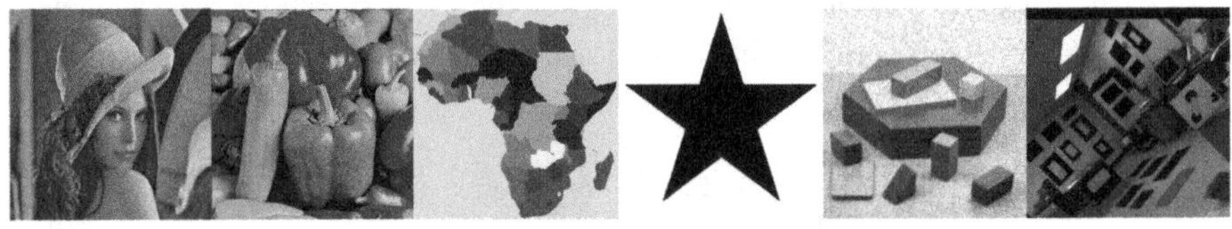

Fig. 2. Six test images for computation of the average repeatability and noise degradation.

Other parameters for Canny edge detection, edge gaps filling, the window size of non-maxima suppression and local threshold were decided by experimentation. In this paper, the low and upper threshold of Canny edge detector is [0.15 0.35], the fill gap size is 1, the size of non-maxima suppression window is 7×7, the threshold $T_h = 0.1$. The corner detection results of proposed method and Harris method are shown in Fig. 3.

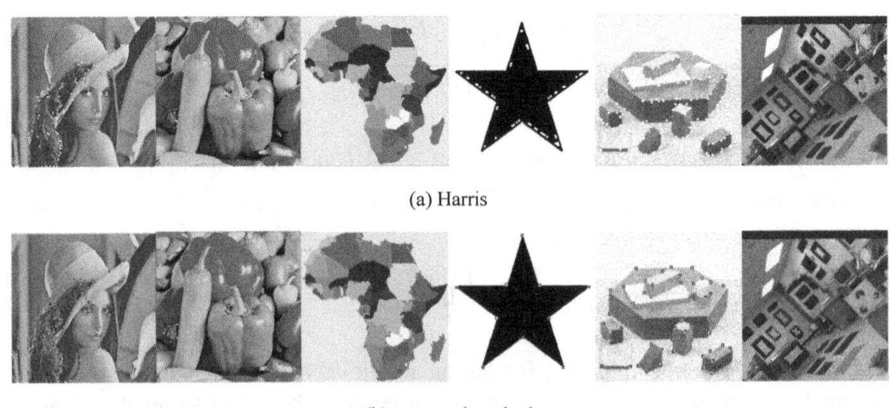

(a) Harris

(b) proposed method

Fig. 3. Corner detection results compared with Harris method.

To evaluate the robustness of the proposed method, the test images are obtained by applying the rotations and Gaussian noise attacks on each original image. Average repeatability and localization error [32] are uses in this paper. The average repeatability R_{avg} explicitly measures the stability of the detected corners between original and test images.

$$R_{avg} = \frac{N_r}{2}(\frac{1}{N_o} + \frac{1}{N_t}) \tag{13}$$

where N_o and N_t are the number of detected corners from original and test images by a detector, and N_r is the number of repeated corners between them. It is noted that a corner p_i is detected in original image and its corresponding position is point q_j after image rotation. If a corner is detected in the rotated image, which is in the neighborhood of q_j (within 4 pixels), then a repeated corner is achieved.

The localization error *Le* is defined as the average distance on all the matched pairs. Let $\{(\mathbf{IP}_k, \widehat{\mathbf{IP}}_k), k = 1, 2, \cdots, N_r\}$ be the matched corner pairs in the original and test images. Then, the localization error is calculated by

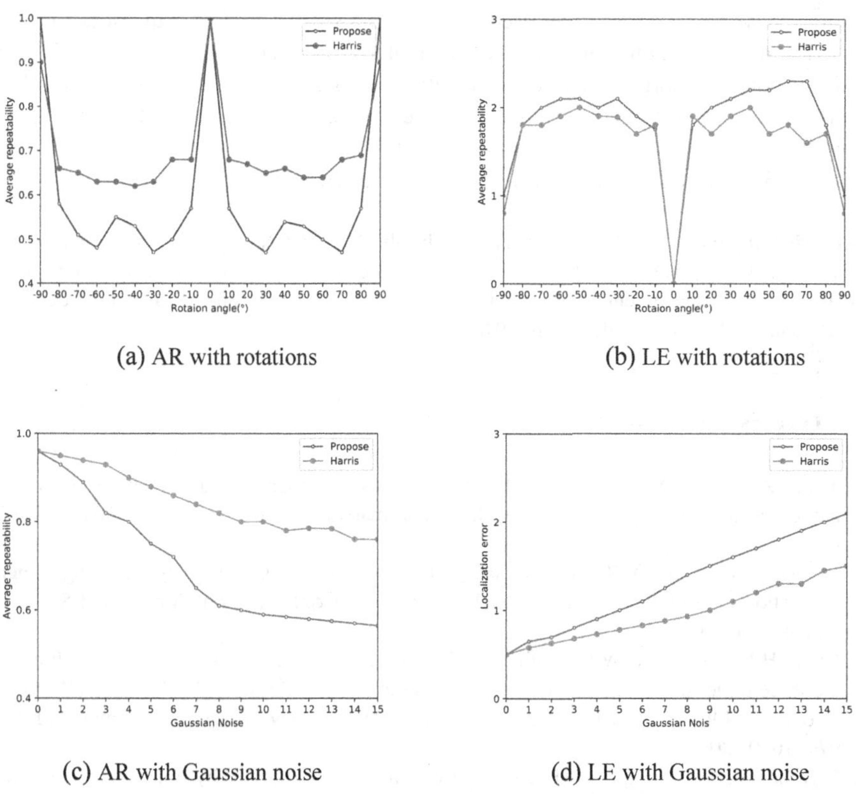

(a) AR with rotations (b) LE with rotations

(c) AR with Gaussian noise (d) LE with Gaussian noise

Fig. 4. Average repeatability (AR) and localization error (LE) under the rotations and Gaussian noise.

$$Le = \sqrt{\frac{1}{N_r}\sum\nolimits_{k=1}^{N_r} \left\| \mathbf{IP}_k - \widehat{\mathbf{IP}}_k \right\|_2^2}. \tag{14}$$

Figure 4 shows the average repeatability (AR) and localization error (LE) under the rotations and Gaussian noise. The standard deviation of Gaussian noise is from 1 to 15 at 1 apart. The proposed method has better performance because the local intensity variation information is embedded into the contour-based corner detection framework. The contour extraction can greatly reduce the occurrence probability of false corners and the IPGFs are robust to the image rotation. Furthermore, the multiplication can suppress the false corners and detect real corners exactly.

5 Conclusion

In this paper, the local intensity variation information is used to improve the contour-based corner detection. First, the edge contours of an input image are extracted. For each point in the edge contour and its surrounding points, a set of imaginary parts Gabor filters (IPGFs) with different scales are applied to extract the direction derivative vectors. These vectors are further used to generate a set of correlation matrices for each point. The multiplication of normalized eigenvalues of each correlation matrices is used to detect potential corners. The experimental results show that the proposed method improves the detection accuracy and is noise resistance compared with Harris algorithm. For future work, new feature extraction, tracking and learning approaches will be explored [37, 38], especially deep learning and saliency detection [39, 40].

Acknowledgments. This work was supported by the National Natural Science Foundation of China (No. 61401347), the Shaanxi natural science basic research project under Grant 2017JQ6058, and the Scientific Research Program funded by Shaanxi Provincial Education Department, P. R. China, under Grant 19JK0364.

References

1. Yang, Z.G., Liu, X.J., Zhang, Q.W.: Moving target recognition and tracking techniques based on infrared image, applied mechanics and materials. Trans. Tech. Publ. **608**, 473–477 (2010)
2. Huang, G.S., Tseng, Y.Y.: Application of stereo vision 3D target recognition using camera calibration algorithm. In: 2015 AASRI International Conference on Circuits and Systems. Atlantis Press (2015)
3. Cline, H.E., Lorensen, W.E., Ludke, S., Crawford, C.R., Teeter, B.C.: Two algorithms for the three-dimensional reconstruction of tomograms. Med. Phys. **15**(3), 320–327 (1988)
4. Zitova, B., Flusser, J.: Image registration methods: a survey. Image Vis. Comput. **21**(11), 977–1000 (2003)
5. Myronenko, A., Song, X.: Intensity-based image registration by minimizing residual complexity. IEEE Trans. Med. Imag. **29**(11), 1882–1891 (2010)

6. Mignotte, M., Meunier, J.: A multiscale optimization approach for the dynamic contour-based boundary detection issue. Comput. Med. Imag. Graph. **25**(3), 265–275 (2001)
7. Liu, Y., Goto, S., Ikenaga, T.: A contour-based robust algorithm for text detection in color images. IEICE Trans. Inf. Syst. **89**(3), 1221–1230 (2006)
8. Ryu, J.B., Park, H.H.: Log-log scale Harris corner detector. Electron. Lett. **46**(24), 21–22 (2010)
9. Rosenfeld, A., Weszka, J.S.: An improved method of angle detection on digital curves. IEEE Trans. Comput. **24**(9), 940–941 (1975)
10. Cooper, J., Venkatesh, S., Kitchen, L.: Early jump-out corner detectors. IEEE Trans. Pattern Anal. Mach. Intell. **15**(8), 823–828 (1993)
11. Arrebola, F., Bandera, A., Camacho, P., Sandoval, F.: Corner detection by local histograms of contour chain code. Electron. Lett. **32**(21), 1771–1796 (1997)
12. Arrebola, F., Sandoval, F.: Corner detection and curve segmentation by multi-resolution chain-code linking. Pattern Recogn. **38**(7), 1596–1614 (2005)
13. Lindeberg, T.: Scale-Space Theory in Computer Vision. Kluwer Academic Publishers (1994)
14. Asada, H., Brady, M.: The curvature primal sketch. IEEE Trans. Pattern Anal. Mach. Intell. **1**, 2–14 (1986)
15. Mokhtarian, F., Mackworth, A.: Scale-based description and recognition of planar curves and two-dimensional shapes. IEEE Trans. Pattern Anal. Mach. Intell. **1**, 34–43 (1986)
16. Mokhtarian, F., Mohanna, F.: Enhancing the curvature scale space corner detector. In: Proceedings of Scandinavian Conference on Image Analysis, pp. 145–152 (2001)
17. Mokhtarian, F., Suomela, R.: Robust image corner detection through curvature scale space. IEEE Trans. Pattern Anal. Mach. Intell. **20**(12), 1376–1381 (1998)
18. Gao, X., Sattar, F., Quddus, A., Venkateswarlu, R.: Multiscale contour corner detection based on local natural scale and wavelet transform. Image Vis. Comput. **25**(6), 890–898 (2007)
19. Awrangjeb, M., Lu, G.: Robust image corner detection based on the chord-to-point distance accumulation technique. IEEE Trans. Multimed. **10**(6), 1059–1072 (2008)
20. Han, J.H., Poston, T.T.: Chord-to-point distance accumulation and planar curvature: a new approach to discrete curvature. Pattern Recogn. Lett. **22**(7), 1133–1144 (2001)
21. Pinheiro, A.M., Ghanbari, M.: Piecewise approximation of contours through scale-space selection of dominant points. IEEE Trans. Image Process. **19**(6), 1442–1450 (2010)
22. Zhang, W.C., Wang, F.P., Zhu, L., Zhou, Z.F.: Corner detection using Gabor filters. IET Image Process. **8**(11), 639–646 (2014)
23. Zhang, W.C., Shui, P.L.: Contour-based corner detection via angle difference of principal directions of anisotropic Gaussian directional derivatives. Pattern Recogn. **48**(9), 2785–2797 (2015)
24. Manjunath, B.S., Ma, W.Y.: Texture feature for browsing and retrieval of image data. IEEE Trans. PAMI **18**(8), 837–842 (1996)
25. Daugman, J.G.: Uncertainty relation for resolution in space, spatial frequency, and orientation optimized by two-dimensional visual cortical filters. J. Opt. Soc. Am. A **2**(7), 1160–1169 (1985)
26. Kamarainen, J.K., Kyrki, V., Kälviäinen, H.: Invariance properties of Gabor filter-based features–overview and applications. IEEE Trans. Image Process. **15**(5), 1088–1099 (2006)
27. DeTone, D., Malisiewicz, T., Rabinovich, A.: Superpoint: self-supervised interest point detection and description. In: Proceedings of the IEEE Conference on Computer Vision and Pattern Recognition Workshops, pp. 224–236 (2018)
28. Canny, J.: A computational approach to edge detection. In: Readings in Computer Vision, pp. 184–203. Morgan Kaufmann (1987)

29. Harris, C.G., Stephens, M.: A combined corner and edge detector. In: Alvey Vision Conference, vol. 15, no. 50, pp. 10–5244 (1988)
30. Kitchen, L., Rosenfeld, A.: Gray-level corner detection. Pattern Recogn. Lett. **1**(2), 95–102 (1982)
31. The Image Database. http://figment.csee.usf.edu/edge/roc
32. Schmid, C., Mohr, R., Bauckhage, C.: Evaluation of interest point detectors. Int. J. Comput. Vis. **37**(2), 151–172 (2000)
33. AlKhateeb, J.H., Pauplin, O., Ren, J., Jiang, J.: Performance of hidden Markov model and dynamic Bayesian network classifiers on handwritten Arabic word recognition. Knowl.-Based Syst. **24**(5), 680–688 (2011)
34. AlKhateeb, J.H., Ren, J., Jiang, J., Al-Muhtaseb, H.: Offline handwritten Arabic cursive text recognition using Hidden Markov Models and re-ranking. Pattern Recogn. Lett. **32**(8), 1081–1088 (2011)
35. Han, J., Zhang, D., Hu, X., Guo, L., Ren, J., Wu, F.: Background prior-based salient object detection via deep reconstruction residual. IEEE Trans. Circ. Syst. Video Technol. **25**(8), 1309–1321 (2014)
36. Tschannerl, J., et al.: Unsupervised hyperspectral band selection based on information theory and a modified discrete gravitational search algorithm. Inf. Fus. **51**, 189–200 (2019)
37. Feng, Y., et al.: Object-based 2D-to-3D video conversion for effective stereoscopic content generation in 3D-TV applications. IEEE Trans. Broadcast. **57**(2), 500–509 (2011)
38. Ren, J., et al.: Multi-camera video surveillance for real-time analysis and reconstruction of soccer games. Mach. Vis. Appl. **21**(6), 855–863 (2010)
39. Yan, Y., et al.: Cognitive fusion of thermal and visible imagery for effective detection and tracking of pedestrians in videos. Cogn. Comput. **10**(1), 94–104 (2018)
40. Yan, Y., et al.: Unsupervised image saliency detection with Gestalt-laws guided optimization and visual attention based refinement. Pattern Recogn. **79**, 65–78 (2018)

Multi-layer Weight-Aware Bilinear Pooling for Fine-Grained Image Classification

Fenglei Li, Qin Xu(✉), Zehui Sun, Yiming Mei, Qiang Zhang, and Bin Luo

Key Laboratory of Intelligent Computing and Signal Processing of Ministry of Education, School of Computer Science and Technology, Anhui University, Hefei 230601, China
lifenglei1014@163.com, {xuqin,luobin}@ahu.edu.cn, cvsunzehui@163.com, yimingmeiahu@163.com, zhangqiangahu@163.com

Abstract. Fine-grained images have similar global structure but exhibit variant local appearance. Bilinear pooling models have been proven to be effective in modeling different semantic parts and capturing the effective feature learning for fine-grained image classification. However, the bilinear models do not consider that convolutional neural networks (CNNs) may lose important semantic information during forward propagation, and feature interactions of different convolutional layers enhance feature learning which improves classification performance. Therefore, we propose a multi-layer weight-aware bilinear pooling method to model cross-layer object parts feature interaction as the feature representation, and different weights are assigned to each convolutional layer to adaptively adjust the outputs of the convolutional layers to highlight more discriminative features. The proposed method results in great performance improvement compared with previous state-of-the-art approaches. We demonstrate the effectiveness of our method on the CUB-200-2011 and FGVC-Aircraft datasets.

Keywords: Fine-grained image classification · Multi-layer weight-aware model · Multi-layer Weight-Aware Bilinear Model

1 Introduction

Fine-grained image classification is a subtask of traditional image classification. The purpose of fine-grained image classification is to recognize different subcategories of the same basic-level category which have similar appearance, such as recognizing species of birds [9] or identifying particular models of aircraft [10]. Fine-grained image classification is more difficult than traditional image classification, the reason is that fine-grained images have slight inter-class differences and large intra-class differences. Moreover, fine-grained image classification is extremely challenging due to the large number of categories and lack of training data.

J. Ren et al. (Eds.): BICS 2019, LNAI 11691, pp. 443–453, 2020.
https://doi.org/10.1007/978-3-030-39431-8_43

The widely used convolutional neural network (CNNs) models for fine-grained image classification have made great progress. These models usually use the output of the last convolutional layer as the feature representation. However, there is some information loss in the forward propagation of CNNs. The information in the last layer is too coarse to allow precise fine-grained image classification and insufficient to describe various semantic parts of object. In fact, the intermediate convolution activations provide important discriminative information for fine-grained classification. It is essential to use the features of multiple convolution layers to acquire more discriminative semantic information.

Motivated by the above observations, we propose a novel approach that uses multi-layer weight-aware feature interaction to obtain different layers of object parts feature relations of fine-grained image. Local parts relations of object are captured by bilinear pooling model [1], which is particularly effective for fine-grained image classification. Architecture of the model consists of two stream CNNs whose outputs are multiplied using outer product at each location of an image, then bilinear pooling is used to obtain image descriptor. Most existing bilinear pooling based models [1,3,5] only take activations of the last convolution layer as representation of an image. The intermediate convolution activations are neglected, which result in the loss of discriminative information of fine-grained image classification. Therefore, we use the features of multiple convolution layers and assign adaptive weights to the feature of each layer in order to minimize the loss of useful discriminative information for fine-grained classification.

We summarize our contributions to fine-grained image classification as follows. First, we propose a novel approach for efficient interaction of different convolutional layer features, and assign adaptive weights to the features of each layer for the first time. Second, we integrate multiple convolution layers to obtain more semantic information, which is especially important for fine-grained image classification. Third, the evaluation and discussions on widely used datasets demonstrate the effectiveness of the proposed method.

2 Related Work

2.1 Fine-Grained Image Classification

Fine-grained images usually have a similar global appearance structure. According to different supervised information, fine-grained image classification is divided into strongly supervised classification model and weakly supervised classification model. Many supervised learning based image classification algorithms [2,27,28,30] have been proposed, which refer to the use of additional manual annotation information, such as bounding box and parts annotations in addition to the category labels of the images during model training. However, these methods have a drawback that annotations of location of discriminative parts and bounding box within an image are not obtained easily. On the other hand, weakly supervised classification methods [1,3–7,14–16,25] have received increasing attention, and image classification based only on category labels is a major trend in fine-grained image research in recent years. Xiao et al. [4]

propose two levels of attention mechanism, which is the first attempt to complete fine-grained image classification without relying on additional annotation information. The model mainly focuses on two different levels of features, namely Object-Level and Part-Level, which are the two layers of information used in the previous strongly supervised work, such as bounding box and location information. Lin et al. [1] design a novel bilinear CNN model in which two networks coordinate with each other to complete fine-grained image classification. Recently, some variants of bilinear models [3,5,7,8] have achieved good performance. Kong et al. [3] propose a low-rank bilinear pooling that greatly reduced computational complexity and the size of the bilinear model. Kim et al. [8] perform low-rank approximation on parameter matrices for bilinear pooling.

2.2 Feature Interaction

Many methods [17–19] have been proposed to fuse multiple features to enhance the performance of specific tasks. Yan et al. [18] propose to adaptive fusion of color and spatial descriptors for color-coded/trademark image retrieval. Recent work by Hariharan et al. [21] has shown that the early and middle layers of CNNs promote precise localization of objects. So taking only the feature of a single convolutional layer as the feature representation is not enough for fine-grained images. Qi et al. [20] propose to exploit convolutional activations of spatial relation to improve fine-grained image performance. The method regards each convolution activation as a potential object part feature while utilizing the spatial distance relationship between the object parts to select superior object part pairs for classification. However, it only considers the feature interaction between the last layer of convolutional activations. Features from different convolutional layers are integrated by [22,24–26]. Cai et al. [22] propose to integrate convergence response of different layers to model the interaction of part features. However, only cascading multiple convolution features fails to result in the feature interaction between convolutional layers. Yu et al. [25] significantly improve classification performance using the hierarchical bilinear pooling method. Li et al. [26] propose to adaptively learn channel weights through multiple different convolution kernel sizes.

3 Proposed Method

In this section, the multi-layer weight-aware model (WAM) where adaptive weights are learned and assigned to different convolutional layers to balance the output of the convolutional layer is proposed. Then the feature interaction between multiple convolutional layers and the bilinear pooling are utilized to get the final image descriptor. The WAM is introduced in Sect. 3.1. The overall framework is described in Sect. 3.2.

3.1 Multi-layer Weight-Aware Model

In order to capture the feature interactions of different convolutional layers to obtain more semantic information for fine-grained image classification. We fuse

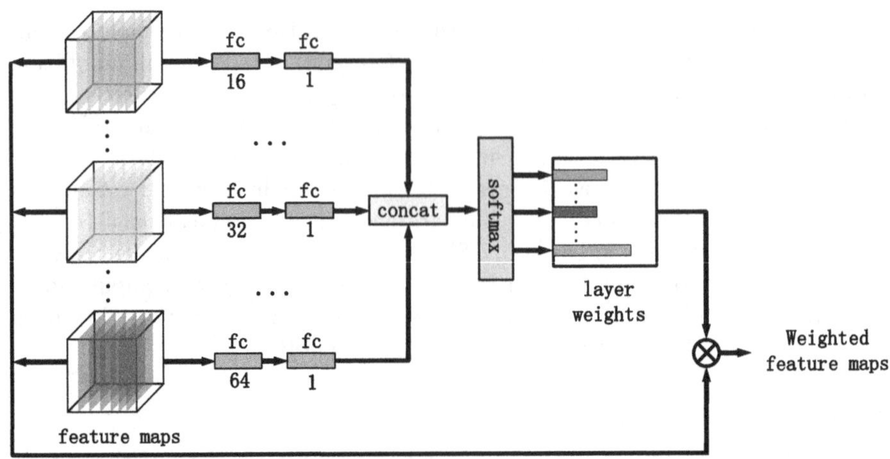

Fig. 1. Illustration of our Weight-Aware Model (WAM). The left column represents the feature maps of multiple convolutional layers of an image.

multiple convolutional layer features and assign different weights to each convolutional layer feature. The learned weights of different convolutional layers adaptively integrate hierarchical features to highlight more discriminative features, thereby significantly improving classification performance. First, We combine multi-layer convolutional features, adaptively adjust the weight of each convolution layer by utilizing softmax function. Second, the feature maps of each convolution layer is multiplied by this weight. Finally, the feature maps of each convolution layer is weighted. As shown in Fig. 1.

Given an image I with height H and width W as input, it is forwardly propagated through a CNN model. Suppose the feature maps of i-th convolutional layer is considered as $X_i \in R^{w_i \times h_i \times c_i}$, where w_i, h_i, c_i denote width, height, channels respectively. $i \in \{1, 2, \ldots, l\}$, and l is the number of convolutional layers. Then the proposed multi-layer weight-aware model is defined by

$$\begin{aligned} X^i &= fc^{i2}(fc^{i1}(X_i)) \\ X^{concat} &= X^1 \oplus X^2 \oplus \cdots \oplus X^l \\ m &= softmax(X^{concat}) \\ X &= m \otimes X^{concat} \end{aligned} \tag{1}$$

where fc^{i1} and fc^{i2} denote the fully connected operation i-th convolutional layer which consist of dropout, fully connected and ReLU, X^i denotes the features the i-th convolutional layer after transforming. $\oplus$ and $\otimes$ represent the operations of concatenation and weighting respectively. m indicates the layer weight, and $softmax(\cdot)$ is the softmax function. X denotes the output of weighted feature maps, which is applied to the bilinear model for fine-grained image classification.

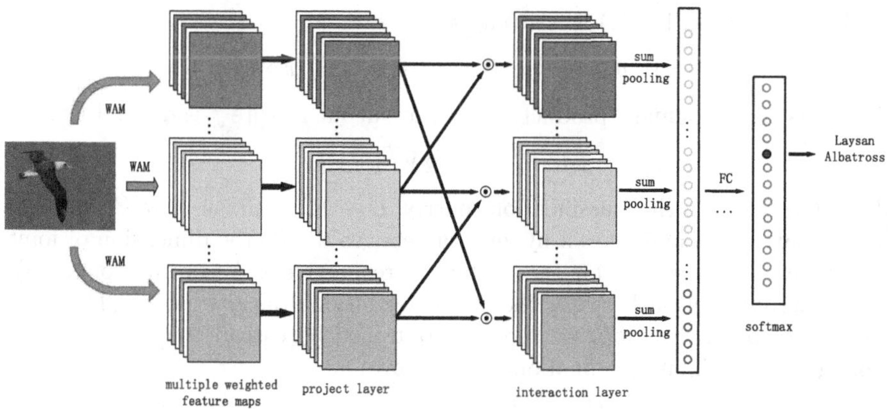

Fig. 2. Framework of our Multi-Layer Weight-Aware Bilinear Model for fine-grained image classification. Input image on the left, multiple weighted feature maps are generated by Weight-Aware Model (WAM) as shown in Fig. 1. The multiple weighted feature maps are sent to high-dimensional mapping spaces to obtain attributes of multiple object parts, and element-wise multiplication is used to get the interaction of multiple object part attributes. Then the high-dimensional features are integrated through the sum pooling. The output of feature is sent to fully connected layer and softmax layer to obtain the final classification result.

3.2 Multi-layer Weight-Aware Bilinear Model

Bilinear model [1] has made great progress in fine-grained image classification. However, the bilinear model has a high dimension due to the feature outer product. Recently, Kim et al. [8] propose to use Hadamard product for low-rank bilinear pooling. Compared with the traditional bilinear model, it does not increase the training parameters, but reduces the dimension of the feature. Yu et al. [25] propose a hierarchical bilinear pooling model, which further captures more semantic part interactions by cascading multiple bilinear modules. On this basis, we utilize a multi-layer weight-aware model to improve fine-grained image classification performance. The overall frame is shown in Fig. 2.

Specifically, suppose a weighted feature maps is considered as $X \in R^{w \times h \times c}$, where w, h, c denote width, height and channels of feature maps respectively, and another weighted feature maps is $Y \in R^{w_1 \times h_1 \times c_1}$ with width w_1, height h_1, channels c_1. According to Kim et al. [8], considering every pair features, the bilinear model is formulated by

$$f_i = x^T W_i y + b_i \tag{2}$$

where $x = [x_1, x_2, ..., x_c]^T$ and $y = [y_1, y_2, ..., y_{c_1}]^T$ denote the input vectors at the same spatial location on X and Y respectively. $W_i \in R^{c \times c_1}$ is a weight matrix and b_i is the bias. $W = [W_1, W_2, \ldots, W_n]$ is learned in order to get the total output $f \in R^n$, where $W \in R^{c \times c_1 \times n}$. The work by [11] proposes the weight matrix is factorized into two one-rank vectors, ie, $W_i = U_i V_i^T$ where $U_i \in R^c$

and $V_i \in R^{c_1}$. Then Eq. (2) is written as

$$f_i = x^T W_i y + b_i = x^T U_i V_i^T y + b_i = U_i^T x \circ V_i^T y + b_i \tag{3}$$

where $\circ$ is the Hadamard product. Thus the output feature f is defined by

$$f = P^T(U^T x \circ V^T y) + b \tag{4}$$

where $P \in R^{d \times n}$ is the classification matrix, $U \in R^{c \times d}$ and $V \in R^{c \times d}$ are projection matrices. d and b are a hyperparameter to decide the dimension of joint embeddings and the bias for the output f, respectively. According to Eq. (4), we get the interaction between the two convolutional layer features. Then the bilinear vector of the proposed model is obtained by cascade multiple bilinear pooling outputs. Thus the final output is shown as

$$F = P^T concat(U^T x \circ V^T y, U^T x \circ Q^T z, \cdots, V^T y \circ Q^T z) + b \tag{5}$$

where Q is the projection matrix corresponding convolution layer feature z.

4 Experiments

4.1 Experimental Setups

Datasets: Our algorithm is evaluated on two widely used datasets: CUB-200-2011 [9] and FGVC-Aircraft [10]. CUB-200-2011 includes 200 category numbers with 11788 images in total, and FGVC-Aircraft includes 100 category numbers with 10000 images in total. Part bounding box and annotations are not utilized, and category labels are only used in our experiments. The detailed statistics are summarized in Table 1.

Table 1. Summary statistics of datasets

Dataset	#Class	#Training	#Testing
CUB-200-2011	200	5994	5794
FGVC-Aircraft	100	6667	3333

Implementation Details: We evaluate our method with VGG-16 [12] model pretrained on ImageNet classification dataset. Our model can be also applied to other widely used networks, such as ResNet [13]. We select the last three convolutional layer outputs as feature representations. The training process is divided into two steps. The first step is to train the parameters of the full connection layer and save them. The second step fine-tunes the parameters of the entire model. The size of input image is 448×448. We train our model using stochastic gradient descent with a batch size of 24, momentum of 0.9, weight decay of 5×10^{-4}, learning rate of 10^{-3}, adaptive adjustment of learning rate with factor of 0.1 and patience of 5. We implement our experiments in PyTorch on a server with Tian XP GPUs. Furthermore, all the parameter settings are available in the source code to be released for accessible reproducible research.

4.2 Model Analysis

In our model, there is a manually defined hyperparameter d in Eq. (4) and the impact of selecting convolutional layer on classification. We use the last three convolutional layer outputs of the VGG-16 model [12] as a feature representation, which are represented as $relu5\_1, relu5\_2, relu5\_3$. The HBP model proposed by Yu et al. [25] explores the impact of these two factors on classification. The model achieves the best results when d=8192 and convolutional layer selection as $relu5\_3 * relu5\_2 + relu5\_3 * relu5\_1 + relu5\_2 * relu5\_1$. Therefore, we use the same settings in our experiment.

Table 2. Comparison accuracy (%) on CUB-200-2011 testing dataset. Anno. represents using extra bounding box or parts annotation information.

Method	Anno.	Accuracy
Part-RCNN [2]	√	76.4
PA-CNN [30]	√	82.8
DeepLAC [27]	√	80.3
VGG-19 [12]		77.8
TLAN [4]		77.9
DVAN [23]		79.0
NAC [29]		81.0
MG-CNN [28]		81.7
LRBP [3]		84.2
B-CNN [1]		84.0
our($relu5\_1 + relu5\_2 + relu5\_3$)		83.8
our(WAM)		82.4
our(relu5_1+relu5_2+relu5_3+WAM)		**84.2**

4.3 Comparison Results and Discussion

Evaluation on CUB-200-2011: We first evaluate our method on CUB-200-2011 dataset, the classification accuracy is summarized in Table 2. As can be seen from the table, We compare three strongly supervised baselines, in which the best result($relu5\_1$+$relu5\_2$+$relu5\_3$+WAM) of our method exceeds Part-RCNN [2] 7.8%, DeepLAC [27] 3.9%, PA-CNN [30] 1.4%, respectively. The fact that our method exceeds the strongly supervised methods even if extra bounding box or parts annotation are not utilized. For the weakly supervised methods without extra annotation, we first evaluate base network, such as VGG-19 [12]. Second, we compare the state-of-the-art methods, which are TLAN [4], DVAN [23], NAC [29], MG-CNN [28]. Finally, bilinear pooling based approaches are evaluated. Our model outperforms all of the above methods, Where the LRBP [3] method is very close to our performance. Compared with the B-CNN [1], we significantly reduce the feature dimension, and the proposed method has higher accuracy. We also conduct a comparative experiment on convolution weights. First, when convolutional layer weights are not utilized and only use the interactions of different layer convolution features, we get an accuracy of 83.8%. Second, weighted convolution features is only used as feature outputs, we have an accuracy of 82.4%. However, we get an accuracy of 84.2% when the two factors are combined. It can be seen that when the convolution layer weights are adopted, it improves classification performance.

Evaluation on FGVC-Aircraft: We further conduct experiments on the public FGVC-Aircraft dataset. The classification accuracy is summarized in Table 3. According to the experiment of CUB-200-2011, we get the best performance on the method of $relu5\_1 + relu5\_2 + +relu5\_3$+WAM. Therefore, we conduct evaluation experiments on this basis. The baselines which we compare include FV-CNN [33], FC-VGG16 [12], ResNet-50 [13], Chai et al. [31], Fisher [32], MG-CNN [28], and B-CNN [1]. Our experimental results have significant performance improvements, achieving 85.3% classification accuracy.

Table 3. Comparison accuracy (%) on FGVC-Aircraft testing dataset. Anno. represents using extra bounding box or parts annotation information.

Method	Anno.	Accuracy
FV-CNN [33]		81.5
FC-VGG16 [12]		74.1
ResNet-50 [13]		81.2
Chai et al. [31]		72.5
Fisher [32]		77.6
MG-CNN [28]		82.5
B-CNN [1]		84.1
our(relu5_1+relu5_2+relu5_3+WAM)		**85.3**

5 Conclusion

In this paper, we propose a novel multi-layer weight-aware bilinear model for fine-grained image classification. We combine the convolutional features of different layers which denote different object parts, and the interactions of different layers of object parts are obtained by the Hadamard product. We demonstrate the performance of our model on different fine-grained image classification datasets. In the future, we will utilize the attention mechanism to capture parts localization and interaction of different object parts.

Acknowledgments. The authors would like to thank the anonymous referees for their constructive comments which have helped improve the paper. This work was supported by National Natural Science Foundation of China (61502003, 71501002, 61472002, 61671018, 61860206004), by the Key Research Project of Humanities and Social Sciences in Colleges and Universities of Anhui Province under Grant SK2019A0013.

References

1. Lin, T.Y., RoyChowdhury, A., Maji, S.: Bilinear cnn models for fine-grained visual recognition. In: Proceedings of the IEEE International Conference on Computer Vision, pp. 1449–1457 (2015)
2. Zhang, N., Donahue, J., Girshick, R., Darrell, T.: Part-based R-CNNs for fine-grained category detection. In: Fleet, D., Pajdla, T., Schiele, B., Tuytelaars, T. (eds.) ECCV 2014. LNCS, vol. 8689, pp. 834–849. Springer, Cham (2014). https://doi.org/10.1007/978-3-319-10590-1_54
3. Kong, S., Fowlkes, C.: Low-rank bilinear pooling for fine-grained classification. In: Proceedings of the IEEE Conference on Computer Vision and Pattern Recognition, pp. 365–374 (2017)
4. Xiao, T., Xu, Y., Yang, K., Zhang, J., Peng, Y., Zhang, Z.: The application of two-level attention models in deep convolutional neural network for fine-grained image classification. In: Proceedings of the IEEE Conference on Computer Vision and Pattern Recognition, pp. 842–850 (2015)
5. Gao, Y., Beijbom, O., Zhang, N., Darreel, T.: Compact bilinear pooling. In: Proceedings of the IEEE Conference on Computer Vision and Pattern Recognition, pp. 365–374 (2016)
6. Zhang, X., Xiong, H., Zhou, W., Lin, W., Tian, Q.: Picking deep filter responses for fine-grained image recognition. In: Proceedings of the IEEE Conference on Computer Vision and Pattern Recognition, pp. 1134–1142 (2016)
7. Lin, T.Y., Maji, S.: Improved bilinear pooling with cnns. arXiv preprint arXiv:1707.06772 (2017)
8. Kim, J.H., On, K.W., Lim, W., Kim, J., Ha, J.W., Zhang, B.T.: Hadamard product for low-rank bilinear pooling. arXiv preprint arXiv:1610.04325 (2016)
9. Wah, C., Branson, S., Welinder, P., Perona, P., Belongie, S.: The Caltech-UCSD birds-200-2011 dataset. Technical report CNS-TR-2011-001, California Institute of Technology (2011)
10. Maji, S., Rahtu, E., Kannala, J., Blaschko, M., Vedaldi, A.: Fine-grained visual classification of aircraft. arXiv preprint arXiv:1306.5151 (2013)
11. Pirsiavash, H., Ramanan, D., Fowlkes, C.C.: Bilinear classifiers for visual recognition. In: Advances in Neural Information Processing Systems, pp. 1482–1490 (2009)
12. Simonyan, K., Zisserman, A.: Very deep convolutional networks for large-scale image recognition. arXiv preprint arXiv:1409.1556 (2014)
13. He, K., Zhang, X., Ren, S., Sun, J.: Deep residual learning for image recognition. In: Proceedings of the IEEE Conference on Computer Vision and Pattern Recognition, pp. 770–778 (2016)
14. Fu, J., Zheng, H., Mei, T.: Look closer to see better: recurrent attention convolutional neural network for fine-grained image recognition. In: Proceedings of the IEEE Conference on Computer Vision and Pattern Recognition, pp. 4438–4446 (2017)

15. Zheng, H., Fu, J., Mei, T., Luo, J.: Learning multi-attention convolutional neural network for fine-grained image recognition. In: Proceedings of the IEEE International Conference on Computer Vision, pp. 5209–5217 (2017)
16. Sun, M., Yuan, Y., Zhou, F., Ding, E.: Multi-attention multi-class constraint for fine-grained image recognition. In: Ferrari, V., Hebert, M., Sminchisescu, C., Weiss, Y. (eds.) ECCV 2018. LNCS, vol. 11220, pp. 834–850. Springer, Cham (2018). https://doi.org/10.1007/978-3-030-01270-0_49
17. Zheng, J., Liu, Y., Ren, J., Zhu, T., Yan, Y., Yang, H.: Fusion of block and keypoints based approaches for effective copy-move image forgery detection. Multidimension. Syst. Signal Process. **27**(4), 989–1005 (2016)
18. Yan, Y., Ren, J., Li, Y., Windmill, J.F., Ijomah, W., Chao, K.M.: Adaptive fusion of color and spatial features for noise-robust retrieval of colored logo and trademark images. Multidimension. Syst. Signal Process. **27**(4), 945–968 (2016)
19. Ren, J., Jiang, J., Wang, D., Ipson, S.S.: Fusion of intensity and inter-component chromatic difference for effective and robust colour edge detection. IET Image Proc. **4**(4), 294–301 (2010)
20. Qi, L., Lu, X., Li, X.: Exploiting spatial relation for fine-grained image classification. Pattern Recogn. **91**, 47–55 (2019)
21. Hariharan, B., Arbelez, P., Girshick, R., Malik, J.: Hypercolumns for object segmentation and fine-grained localization. In: Proceedings of the IEEE Conference on Computer Vision and Pattern Recognition, pp. 447–456 (2015)
22. Cai, S., Zuo, W., Zhang, L.: Higher-order integration of hierarchical convolutional activations for fine-grained visual categorization. In: Proceedings of the IEEE Conference on Computer Vision and Pattern Recognition, pp. 511–520 (2017)
23. Zhao, B., Wu, X., Feng, J., Peng, Q., Yan, S.: Diversified visual attention networks for fine-grained object classification. IEEE Trans. Multimedia **19**(6), 1245–1256 (2017)
24. Liu, L., Shen, C., van den Hengel, A.: The treasure beneath convolutional layers: cross-convolutional-layer pooling for image classification. In: Proceedings of the IEEE Conference on Computer Vision and Pattern Recognition, pp. 4749–4757 (2015)
25. Yu, C., Zhao, X., Zheng, Q., Zhang, P., You, X.: Hierarchical bilinear pooling for fine-grained visual recognition. In: Ferrari, V., Hebert, M., Sminchisescu, C., Weiss, Y. (eds.) ECCV 2018. LNCS, vol. 11220, pp. 595–610. Springer, Cham (2018). https://doi.org/10.1007/978-3-030-01270-0_35
26. Li, X., Wang, W.H., Hu, X.L., Yang, J.: Selective kernel networks. arXiv preprint arXiv:1903.06586 (2019)
27. Lin, D., Shen, X., Lu, C., Jia, J.: Deep lac: Deep localization, alignment and classification for fine-grained recognition. In: Proceedings of the IEEE Conference on Computer Vision and Pattern Recognition, pp. 1666–1674 (2015)
28. Wang, D., Shen, Z., Shao, J., Zhang, W., Xue, X., Zhang, Z.: Multiple granularity descriptors for fine-grained categorization. In: Proceedings of the IEEE International Conference on Computer Vision, pp. 2399–2406 (2015)
29. Simon, M., Rodner, E.: Neural activation constellations: unsupervised part model discovery with convolutional networks. In: Proceedings of the IEEE International Conference on Computer Vision, pp. 1143–1151 (2015)
30. Krause, J., Jin, H., Yang, J., Fei-Fei, L.: Fine-grained recognition without part annotations. In: Proceedings of the IEEE Conference on Computer Vision and Pattern Recognition, pp. 5546–5555 (2015)

31. Chai, Y., Lempitsky, V., Zisserman, A.: Symbiotic segmentation and part localization for fine-grained categorization. In: Proceedings of the IEEE International Conference on Computer Vision, pp. 321–328 (2013)
32. Cimpoi, M., Maji, S., Vedaldi, A.: Deep filter banks for texture recognition and segmentation. In: Proceedings of the IEEE Conference on Computer Vision and Pattern Recognition, pp. 3828–3836 (2015)
33. Gosselin, P.H., Murray, N., Jgou, H., Perronnin, F.: Revisiting the fisher vector for fine-grained classification. Pattern Recogn. Lett. **49**, 92–98 (2014)

Data Analysis and Natural Language Processing

Offline Arabic Handwriting Recognition Using Deep Machine Learning: A Review of Recent Advances

Rami Ahmed[1], Kia Dashtipour[2(✉)], Mandar Gogate[7], Ali Raza[3], Rui Zhang[4], Kaizhu Huang[4], Ahmad Hawalah[5], Ahsan Adeel[6], and Amir Hussain[7]

[1] Sudan University of Science and Technology, Khartoum, Sudan
ramisaad@sustech.edu

[2] University of Stirling, Stirling FK9 4LA, Scotland, UK
kd28@cs.stir.ac.uk

[3] Department of Electrical Engineering and Computing, Rochester Institute of Technology, Dubai, UAE
axrcada@rit.edu

[4] Electrical and Electronic Engineering, Xi'an Jiaotong Liverpool University, Suzhou, China
{rui.zhang02,Kaizhu.Huang}@xjtlu.edu.cn

[5] College of Computer Science and Engineering, Taibah University, Medina, Saudi Arabia
ahawalah@taibahu.edu.sa

[6] School of Mathematics and Computer Science, University of Wolverhampton, Edinburgh EH16 5XW, UK
a.adeel@wlv.ac.uk

[7] School of Computing, Edinburgh Napier University, Merchiston Campus, Edinburgh EH10 5DT, Scotland, UK
A.Hussain@napier.ac.uk

Abstract. In pattern recognition, automatic handwriting recognition (AHWR) is an area of research that has developed rapidly in the last few years. It can play a significant role in broad-spectrum of applications rending from, bank cheque processing, application forms processing, postal address processing, to text-to-speech conversion. However, most research efforts are devoted to English-language only. This work focuses on developing Offline Arabic Handwriting Recognition (OAHR). The OAHR is a very challenging task due to some unique characteristics of the Arabic script such as cursive nature, ligatures, overlapping, and diacritical marks. In the recent literature, several effective Deep Learning (DL) approaches have been proposed to develop efficient AHWR systems. In this paper, we commission a survey on emerging AHWR technologies with some insight on OAHR background, challenges, opportunities, and future research trends.

Keywords: Offline Arabic Handwritten Recognition · Offline Arabic database · Deep Learning

J. Ren et al. (Eds.): BICS 2019, LNAI 11691, pp. 457–468, 2020.
https://doi.org/10.1007/978-3-030-39431-8_44

1 Introduction

Handwriting recognition task is considered as a sub-problem of the Optical Character Recognition OCR domain [1, 2] which i's an automatic process for reading handwriting or machine printed scripts [1, 3]. Handwritten Character Recognition System (HCR) can be categorized into two types of approaches, online and offline [2, 4, 5]. Online type is applied to digital appliances such as personal data assistants for the sequence of points traced out by the pen. Offline type is applied to already written scripts like text in scanned documents. Offline type is originally classified as a harder task than online task [1, 3, 4, 38–41]. OAHR system is an automatic process of recognizing the offline human handwritten Arabic scripts in digital images. Arabic is world's fifth most spoken language and the Modern Standard Arabic (MSA) is being used by population more than 313 million people [2, 6]. OAHR has approached a variety of major challenges, particularly, those related to the variation in writing within human handwriting qualities and styles [2, 7]. In addition, there are many difficulty factors those linked to the Arabic writing mechanism such as cursive nature, the presence of diacritical dots and marks, similarities between letters, overlapping and elongation characters [1, 8–11].

In recent years, deep learning has developed as a part of the machine learning algorithms and it has become much popular for many researchers and applied to many fields, such as computer vision and natural language processing [7, 10, 12, 13, 34, 35]. DL techniques have effectively applied for Arabic/Latin text handwritten scripts recognition and they have achieved state-of-the-art performance in the field [7, 10, 14].

This review is restricted to OAHR systems and the recent used DL approaches. Specifically, OAHR has lack of reviews and surveys. The majority of explored reviews covered the characteristics of Arabic writing script and overviewed the OAHR and most related general model and its effective methods for each phase. Khorsheed et al. [15] and Lorigo et al. [2] are provided comprehensive review of the domain's fundamentals and analyzed the most used methods in all stages of the generalized framework for OAHR system. In Asebriy et al. [1], introduced an overview and performance evaluation of some OAHR systems based on IFN/ENIT database benchmarking. El Moubtahij et al. and El Qacimy et al. [17] are presented reviews of feature extraction techniques for OAHR systems and their recognition rates.

The contribution of this review is worthy for many reasons. First, to the best of our knowledge this is first paper for reviewing deep learning for handwriting recognition. Second, it provides a distinguished comprehensive of the Arabic script writing characteristics with oriented classification and extended properties will help researchers to be more familiar with the field. Third, the available Arabic benchmarks database are specified and summarized according to their most common characteristics. Finally, the review is improved by providing the literature, discussion and comparative results for the recent DL approaches that have been used in OAHR systems. The remainder of this paper is structured as follows: Sect. 2 introduces the background on the field including Arabic script characteristics, handwriting applications and most common available datasets will be conducted. Section 3 presents a literature review on recent DL advances in the field. Section 4 presents an experimental comparison of selected OAHR Deep CNN approaches. Last, Sect. 5 concludes the paper.

2 Arabic Handwriting Recognition Background

2.1 Arabic Script Writing Characteristics

- The Arabic alphabet basic set consists of 28 letters [2–4, 8, 15] and it contains additional Arabic alphabet set (e.g.; ء, أ, إ, ؤ, ئ, ى, لا, ة) [15, 16] they have different shapes for each character based on its position in the word (isolated, start, middle and ending forms) [3, 8].
- Some of the Arabic script characters have a cursive nature such as (ب, ت, ث, ج, ح, خ, س, ش, ص, ض, ط, ظ, ع, غ, ف, ق, ك, ل, م, ن, ه, ي, ئ) [3, 4, 8].
- The dots existence are sensitive characteristic that have been used for distinguishing between letters (ب, ت, ث, ج, خ, ذ, ز, ش, ض, ظ, غ, ف, ق, ن, ي, ة) [3, 8] and their counts are (1, 2, 3, 1, 1, 1, 1, 3, 1, 1, 1, 1, 2, 1, 2, 2) respectively.
- Some characters' shapes have loops (ص, ض, ط, ظ, ف, ق, م, ه, و, ؤ).
- There are no different cases (such as upper case and lower case) for the letters, just only one case [2, 4].
- The non-cursive letters (ا, د, ذ, ر, ز, و) can divide a single word into one or many sub-words or pieces of Arabic words (PAW) [3, 4]. Figure 1 shows samples of PAWs.

Fig. 1. Words showing one, two, three, and four PAWs respectively.

- Alphabet set is used in many other languages such as Dari, Urdu, Pashto, Farsi (Persian), and Jawi [2, 8, 16].
- In contrast to Latin text, Arabic writing direction is from right to left in a cursive manner [2–4, 8, 17].
- Arabic writing styles can be classified into three classes based on their difficulty, namely: typewritten or machine-printed (easier), typeset style (difficult), handwritten or human-generated (most difficult) [15, 17].
- The baseline or horizontal line that runs through the text's connected [2, 8, 15].
- Arabic script consists of different font types with distinctive properties for each one [3].
- Automatic recognition of the Arabic text is very sophisticated process due to the connectivity, cursive nature, similarity and variety of writing widths of the characters. Dots, diacritics (e.g.; Nunation/Tanween Fat-ha, Dumma, etc.), ligature and overlaps (as shown in Fig. 2) characteristics have added more challenges.

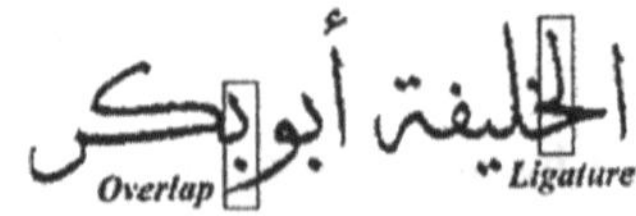

Fig. 2. A sample of the ligature and overlap.

2.2 Handwriting Applications

The automatic recognition of handwriting script from textual image format has a significant role in vast range of human computer interaction applications which they span across the wide domain, including bank cheque processing [1, 4, 5, 8, 15–18], signature verification [5, 15], postal processing (automatic reading for postal address and pin code [1, 5, 8, 16, 18], automatic postal mail sorting [1, 2, 4, 15, 17]), document processing (automatic processing of old manuscripts and documents [4], document editing or convenient editing of previously printed documents [1, 2, 33], machine processing and reading customer-filled forms such as government, insurance claims and application forms [4, 15, 18], document archiving and content Based Image Retrieval [19], searching and keyword spotting for words in large volumes of documents [2]), zip code recognition [8, 16], digital character conversion and identification [5, 19], meaning translation system [5, 19], and text-to-speech conversion system (one of its most helpful uses in the real-world the reading aids for the blind [5, 19]). The most recent trend in OAHR applications is the of the handwritten text spotting in scene images [19].

2.3 OAHR Benchmark Datasets

There are several Arabic handwritten datasets types including characters, words, subwords, pages (text, forms, manuscripts), lines, paragraphs, signatures, cheques, and digits [20] and they developed for specific domains like financial use and postal addresses [21]. Ideally, a big dataset for training and testing is highly required for building good recognition systems those can able to yield high accuracy despite the handwriting challenges such as ligature and overlapping. However, the number of the publicly available Arabic handwriting datasets is still limited and domain-specific [21]. Most of the current handwritten Arabic benchmark databases those have been introduced by [16, 20, 21] are IFN/ENIT, ADBase (MADbase), HACDB, CENP ARMI, IESK-arDB, AHDB, APTI, SUST- ALT, Arabic checks, ARABASE, IBN-E-SINA, KHATT and QUWI.

2.4 OAHR Framework

The overall architecture of OAHR general framework includes the frequent stages, namely Data Acquisition, Pre-Processing, Segmentation, Feature Extraction, Classification, and Post-Processing. Usually, researchers' approaches have used all/a subset/merged stages [2, 4]. Each stage (in order) is further described in brief as below:

- *Data Acquisition:* Usually, cameras and scanners (most convenient tool) are used for acquiring text images [15].
- *Pre-Processing:* The major objective of this phase is to improve the quality of original acquired text image by removing the irrelevant information and then to produce a clean text image that can be suitable for future processing [4, 20, 22, 23]. Applying such pre-processing techniques (e.g.; noise removal and thinning) to the Arabic language has a little difference compared with other languages [20]. For example, in conventional noise algorithms proposed for Latin scripts, Arabic characters dots can be viewed as a noise, which makes the noise removal process more difficult [24].
- *Segmentation:* It is the segmentation of a text image into pixel segments, the piece of Arabic words (PAWs) or line segments [20]. Many segmentation algorithms are not adequate for offline Arabic handwriting tasks and accordingly, modifications are required by researchers in order to be suitable for such ones [4].
- *Feature Extraction:* is the process of retrieving and measurement of the most pertinent, informative and non-redundant attributes from the text image raw data [4, 18, 22, 23] and then transform them into a vector of features [11]. There are three categories of features methods which are structural features, statistical features [4, 18], and feature space transformations [15].
- *Classification:* The purpose of classification phase is to identify and assign each observation (input feature) with a class label or membership scores [4] (character/word) to the correct related defined classes [4, 18, 22], so that texts in images are transformed in to computer understandable form [22, 36].
- *Post-Processing:* This final phase is dedicated for minimizing error rate of output word recognition phase by using the Arabic linguistic knowledge level which could be either on character level, lexical level, morphological level, the syntactic, higher semantic level or discourse levels [20].

3 Deep Learning Recent Advances for OAHR

Recently, DL approach is becoming the new trend in the offline handwriting recognition field [10, 25] due to its hierarchical structure network that simulates the human brain's structure in terms of extracting the internal and external features of input data [3]. The available large-scale data (images datasets) are required and appropriate for the DL which will lead to good performance and accuracy in their recognition decisions. DL has many architectures that have been employed in handwriting recognition applications such as Deep Boltzmann Machine (DBM), Stacking Auto-Encoder (SAE), Deep Neural Networks (DNN), Deep Belief Network (DBN), Long Short-Term Memory (LSTM) and Convolutional Neural Networks (CNN) [10, 14, 26, 37].

Elleuch et al. [25] proposed an approach based on an unsupervised feature learning approach using Deep Belief Neural Network (DBNN) and two different offline databases used to evaluate the performance of the approach. The first database is the HACDB for Arabic characters which it is split into a training set of 5,280 images and a testing set of 1,320 images. The second one is the ADAB database for Tunisian town's names, in which the dataset 1, 2 and 3 are used in training phase and the rest 4, 5 and 6 in the testing phase. An error classification rate of 2.1% was achieved on the HACDB database and 41% on ADAB database. Elleuch et al. [23] presented two deep learning approaches, namely: DBN and CDBN which are experimented on HACDB and IFN/ENIT databases. For the HACDB with the same splitting settings that have been used in the first study, the DBN and CDBN have achieved promising results with an ECR of 2.1% and 1.82% respectively. For IFN/ENIT, the CDBN is only applied for the high-level dimension data and it scored a WER of 16.3%. Additionally, in 2015, Elleuch et al. [14] investigated two Deep Learning architectures with a greedy layer-wise unsupervised learning algorithm, namely: Deep Belief Network (DBN) and Convolutional Neural Networks (CNN). Both classifiers were tested on HACDB database and the results show that the ECR of the DBN (1.67% and 3.64%) outperforms the CNN (5% and 14.71%) using (24 and 66) class labels of character patterns in order.

ElAdel et al. [27] presented a Deep Convolutional Neural Wavelet Network (DCNWN) based on the Neural Network (NN) architecture, the Fast Wavelet Transform (FWT) and the Adaboost algorithm, in which the FWT based on Multi-Resolution Analysis (MRA) at different levels of abstraction is used to extract character's features. A classification rate of 93.92% has been achieved for different groups of the IESK-arDB database with 6000 characters. In 2016, Elleuch et al. [28] proposed a robust model that integrated two architectures; Convolutional Neural Network (CNN) as features extractor and Support Vector Machine (SVM) as a recognizer, in addition to the dropout technique for protecting the model from over-fitting. The evaluation of the model is conducted on HACDB and IFN/ENIT databases and it is achieved higher recognition rates with an ECR of (5% and 5.83%) for HACDB classes (24 and 66) respectively and a WER of 7.05% for IFN/ENIT using 56 classes. In 2016, El-Sawy et al. [10] provided a Convolutional Neural Network (CNN) technique which it is implemented using LeNet-5 architecture and were evaluated on a large Arabic digits database (MADBase). The MADBase is divided into 60,000 images for training and 10,000 images for testing. The approach is achieved an ECR of 12%. In 2016, Elleuch et al. [26] presented a deep networks model based on Support Vector Machine (SVM) named Deep SVM (DSVM) and this model is protected against over-fitting by using dropout technique. This approach was tested on HACDB (66 classes) database and an ECR of 5.68% has been achieved. In 2017, Loey et al. [7] provided a new unsupervised deep learning approach with Stacked Auto-encoder (SAE) and demonstrated its effectiveness over the MADBase Arabic handwritten digits (60,000 training images and 10,000 testing images), in which the testing process of the robust approach showed a promising results of average classification accuracy of 98.5%. In 2017, Ashiquzzaman et al. [29] proposed a novel algorithm based on Convolutional Neural Network (CNN) and it is used the Rectified Linear Unit (ReLU) activation function with the dropout technique as a regularization layer. The algorithm is tested against the CMATERDB (2,000 training samples and 1,000 test samples) Arabic handwritten digit dataset and it is achieved a classification accuracy of 97.4%.

3.1 Comparative Study

Table 1 displays a precise summary of a comparative study of the discussed recent DL of OAHR approaches.

Table 1. Comparative study of OAHR approaches performance

Ref.	Year	Algorithm(s)	Offline Arabic dataset(s)		Recognition evaluation		
			Name (class)	Type	ECR	WER	CA
[25]	2015	DBNN	HACDB (66)	Characters	2.1%	–	–
			ADAB	Words	–	41%	–
[30]	2015	DBN	HACDB	Characters	2.1%	–	–
		CDBN	HACDB	Characters	1.82%	–	–
			IFN/ENIT	Words	–	16.3%	–
[27]	2015	DCNWN	IESK-arDB	Characters	–	–	93.92%
[14]	2015	CNN	HACDB (24)	Characters	5%	–	–
			HACDB (66)		14.71%	–	–
		DBN	HACDB (24)		1.67%	–	–
			HACDB (66)		3.64%	–	–
[28]	2016	CNN based-SVM with dropout	HACDB (24)	Characters	2.09%	–	–
			HACDB (66)		5.83%	–	–
			IFN/ENIT (56)		7.05%	–	–
[10]	2016	CNN	MADBase	Digits	–	–	88%
[7]	2016	Deep SVM with dropout	HACDB (66)	Characters	5.68%	–	–
[26]	2017	SAE	MADBase	Digits	–	–	98.5%
[29]	2017	CNN	CMATERDB	Digits	–	–	97.4%

4 Comparison of OAHR Deep CNN Approaches

The comparison task between the approaches is complex and hard to achieve, because it is influenced by two major difficulty factors: the benchmark datasets specifications, such as diversity [31] and preprocessing, and the reported models' technical specifications, such as model description precision [31] and tools. To highlight and remedy these difficulty factors, we selected among the state-of-art OAHR techniques in the papers discussed earlier, majorly the basic deep CNN approaches [10, 14] and [29] for experimental comparison with their completely different datasets: HACDB (66), MADBase and CMATERDB, respectively.

4.1 Benchmark Datasets Specifications

The analysis of the DL approaches' accuracy comparison in Table 1 demonstrates two types of results: reasonable and unreasonable quantitative results. First, the quantitative comparison between methods' performance, such as [7, 14, 25, 28, 30] on the same

HACDB dataset is reasonable and straightforward. More importantly, the measurement of the authors' models' performance on different datasets with different characteristics, such as [10, 14, 29], as well as the comparison of specific domain approaches on one common dataset that are not designed for [31] are unreasonable. In our implementation, we categorized the selected approaches into two groups based on datasets types: variant datasets that include Arabic characters and numbers, and similar datasets that include Arabic numbers only. First, the experiment was based on the variant datasets dedicated to the original methods datasets. It demonstrates the actual results of the reducible methods compared to the authors' reported ones, and it resolves the deficiency of the methods' technical specifications and the dataset preprocessing task details by predicting such information. Second, the experiment based on the similar datasets showed the performance and generalization of these models over the OAHR domain, and it resolves the issue of the comparison between the approaches on different datasets. Moreover, preprocessing posed a greater challenge in reproducing the authors' works. For example, Elleuch et al. [14] expanded the size of the training set ten times by using the elastic deformation technique, but the authors did not provide the values of σ and α. In our experiment, we used common elastic transformation implementation [32] with default values, and this may address one of the reasons of the low accuracy. Furthermore, Ashiquzzaman et al. [29] split up the CMATERDB dataset into 2,000 training samples and 1,000 test samples without specifying the way they achieved this. Here, we employed an automatic process called the 'train_test_split' function to split the dataset with the 'train_size' value = 0.656 and 'Seed' value = 7.

4.2 Approaches Technical Specifications

During the process of reproducing the selected approaches in the respective papers, we attempted to follow the authors models' technical specifications as precisely as possible, and we did our best to overcome the lack of descriptions, and this in turn resulted in unexpected outcomes in the implementation. For example, El-Sawy et al. [10] and Elleuch et al. [14] did not specify the following sensitive specifications:

- The activation function type for the convolutional layers (We used the ReLU function)
- The subsampling layer type (We used AveragePooling2D as the best value)
- The activation function type of the output layer (W used Softmax as the best value)
- Batch size (We used size = 128)
- Model's compilation parameters, such as optimizing and loss calculation functions (We used categorical_crossentropy for loss parameter and 'Adam' optimizer)
- Seed value for environment randomization (We used seed = 7)

In addition to all these missing specifications' values, El-Sawy et al.'s [10] model reproduction process failed when we used kernel size = 6×6 for the fifth layer as reported, so we conducted the experiment using the original LeNet-5 CNN architecture kernel size (5×5).

The experimental approaches were implemented using Keras Library with the TensorFlow backend and Python. All our experiments' results were calculated from the Confusion Matrix in order to obtain the actual accuracy. We stored the best epoch's value and then it was used, and this is because the last epoch does not usually have the best score. Due to all the previous difficulty factors, our experiments' accuracy results based on different datasets as shown in Table 2 vary from the ones reported by the respective authors. For example, Elleuch et al. [14] reported 14.71% ECR, however we obtained a very low ECR of 59.69%; El-Sawy et al. [10] reported 88% accuracy, but we obtained a very good accuracy of 98.84%; Ashiquzzaman et al. [29] reported 97.4% accuracy and we obtained exactly the same accuracy of 97.48%, and this is because of the precise and accurate details in the corresponding original publication. We conducted our second set of experiments based on similar datasets, as shown in Table 3, where they provided a reasonable result and demonstrated that Ashiquzzaman et al.'s [29] approach has outperformed the El-Sawy et al. [10] approach.

Table 2. Quantitative comparison of OAHR deep CNN approaches using different datasets

Paper	DL technique	Offline Arabic dataset(s)		Reported results	Results in our tests
		Name (class)	Type		
Elleuch et al. [14]	CNN	HACDB (66)	Characters	14.71% ECR	59.69% ECR
El-Sawy et al. [10]	CNN	MADBase	Digits	88% accuracy	98.84% accuracy
Ashiquzzaman et al. [29]	CNN	CMATERDB	Digits	97.4% accuracy	97.48% accuracy

Table 3. Quantitative comparison of OAHR Deep CNN approaches using similar datasets

Paper	DL technique	Accuracy in our tests	
		MADBase (Digits Dataset)	CMATERDB (Digits Dataset)
El-Sawy et al. [10]	CNN	98.84% accuracy	95.16% accuracy
Ashiquzzaman et al. [29]	CNN	98.95% accuracy	97.48% accuracy

5 Conclusion

This paper has introduced a comprehensive review of offline Arabic handwriting recognition, including Arabic script writing characteristics and challenges, applications, description of the publicly available bench mark databases. recognition system framework. This work has reviewed the most current DL state-of-art approaches on OAHR systems and concluded with a summary of the comparative study of OAHR approaches performance. Therefore, this area of research is still open for further exploring and enhancement and extensive research need to be conducted. Moreover, many of recent OAHR applications such as meaning translation system, text-to-speech conversion system and handwritten text spotting in scene images are considered as hot topics and extremely challenging. More novel approaches and more comprehensive and large databases, taking into consideration the challenging characteristics of Arabic text, are highly required. In our future work, we are aiming to create a more inclusive off-line Arabic handwritten characters dataset which will cover all characters' shapes and compare corresponding DL state-of-art approaches by applying them to this dataset and make it publicly available for the research community.

References

1. Asebriy, Z., Raghay, S., Bencharef, O., Chihab, Y.: Comparative systems of handwriting Arabic character recognition. In: 2014 Second World Conference on Complex Systems (WCCS), pp. 90–93 (2014)
2. Lorigo, L., Govindaraju, V.: Offline Arabic handwriting recognition: a survey. IEEE Trans. Pattern Anal. Mach. Intell. **28**, 712–724 (2006)
3. Bahashwan, M.A., Bakar, S.A.A.: A database of Arabic handwritten characters. In: 2014 IEEE International Conference on Control System, Computing and Engineering (ICCSCE 2014), pp. 632–635 (2014)
4. Qacimy, B.E., Hammouch, A., Kerroum, M.A.: A review of feature extraction techniques for handwritten Arabic text recognition. In: 2015 International Conference on Electrical and Information Technologies (ICEIT), pp. 241–245 (2015)
5. Patel, S.R., Jha, J.: Handwritten character recognition using machine learning approach - a survey. In: 2015 International Conference on Electrical, Electronics, Signals, Communication and Optimization (EESCO), pp. 1–5 (2015)
6. Ethnologue: Languages of the World, 21th ed. SIL Int'l (2018). https://www.ethnologue.com/21/country/SA/languages/. Accessed 01 Apr 2019
7. Elleuch, M., Mokni, R., Kherallah, M.: Offline Arabic Handwritten recognition system with dropout applied in Deep networks based-SVMs. In: 2016 International Joint Conference on Neural Networks (IJCNN), pp. 3241–3248 (2016)
8. Alkhateeb, J.H.: A database for arabic handwritten character recognition. Proc. Comput. Sci. **65**, 556–561 (2015)
9. Chammas, E., Mokbel, C., Likforman-Sulem, L.: Arabic handwritten document preprocessing and recognition. In: 2015 13th International Conference on Document Analysis and Recognition (ICDAR), pp. 451–455 (2015)
10. El-Sawy, A., El-Bakry, H., Loey, M.: CNN for handwritten arabic digits recognition based on LeNet-5. In: Advances in Intelligent Systems and Computing Proceedings of the International Conference on Advanced Intelligent Systems and Informatics 2016, pp. 566–575 (2016)
11. Meddeb, O., Maraoui, M., Aljawarneh, S.: Hybrid modeling of an OffLine Arabic Handwriting Recognition System AHRS. In: 2016 International Conference on Engineering & MIS (ICEMIS), pp. 1–8 (2016)
12. Gogate, M., Adeel, A., Hussain, A.: A novel brain-inspired compression-based optimised multimodal fusion for emotion recognition. In: 2017 IEEE Symposium Series on Computational Intelligence (SSCI), pp. 1–7. IEEE, November 2017
13. Gogate, M., Adeel, A., Hussain, A.: Deep learning driven multimodal fusion for automated deception detection. In: 2017 IEEE Symposium Series on Computational Intelligence (SSCI), pp. 1–6. IEEE, November 2017

14. Elleuch, M., Tagougui, N., Kherallah, M.: Towards unsupervised learning for Arabic handwritten recognition using deep architectures. In: Arik, S., Huang, T., Lai, W.K., Liu, Q. (eds.) ICONIP 2015. LNCS, vol. 9489, pp. 363–372. Springer, Cham (2015). https://doi.org/10.1007/978-3-319-26532-2_40
15. Khorsheed, M.S.: Off-line arabic character recognition – a review. Pattern Anal. Appl. **5**, 31–45 (2002)
16. Hussain, R., Raza, A., Siddiqi, I., Khurshid, K., Djeddi, C.: A comprehensive survey of handwritten document benchmarks: structure, usage and evaluation. EURASIP J. Image Video Process. **2015**, 46 (2015)
17. El Moubtahij, H., Halli, A., Satori, K.: Review of feature extraction techniques for offline handwriting Arabic text recognition. Int. J. Adv. Eng. Technol. **7**(1), 50 (2014)
18. Qacimy, B.E., Kerroum, M.A., Hammouch, A.: Word-based Arabic handwritten recognition using SVM classifier with a reject option. In: 2015 15th International Conference on Intelligent Systems Design and Applications (ISDA), pp. 64–68 (2015)
19. Manisha, C.N., Reddy, E.S., Krishna, Y.S.: Role of offline handwritten character recognition system in various applications. Int. J. Comput. Appl. **135**, 30–33 (2016)
20. Alsanousi, W.A., Adam, I.S., Rashwan, M., Abdou, S.: Review about off-line handwriting Arabic text recognition. Int. J. Comput. Sci. Mob. Comput. **6**, 4–14 (2017)
21. Lawgali, A.: A survey on Arabic character recognition. Int. J. Sign. Process. Image Process. Pattern Recogn. **8**, 401–426 (2015)
22. Manwatkar, P.M., Singh, K.R.: A technical review on text recognition from images. In: 2015 IEEE 9th International Conference on Intelligent Systems and Control (ISCO), pp. 1–5 (2015)
23. Arif, M., Hassan, H., Nasien, D., Haron, H.: A review on feature extraction and feature selection for handwritten character recognition. Int. J. Adv. Comput. Sci. Appl. **6**, 204–212 (2015)
24. Boukerma, H., Farah, N.: Preprocessing algorithms for Arabic handwriting recognition systems. In: 2012 International Conference on Advanced Computer Science Applications and Technologies (ACSAT), pp. 318–323 (2012)
25. Elleuch, M., Tagougui, N., Kherallah, M.: Arabic handwritten characters recognition using Deep Belief Neural Networks. In: 2015 IEEE 12th International Multi-Conference on Systems, Signals & Devices (SSD 2015), pp. 1–5 (2015)
26. Loey, M., El-Sawy, A., EL-Bakry, H.: Deep Learning Autoencoder Approach for Handwritten Arabic Digits Recognition. arXiv preprint arXiv:1706.06720. (2017)
27. Eladel, A., Ejbali, R., Zaied, M., Amar, C.B.: Dyadic multi-resolution analysis-based deep learning for arabic handwritten character classification. In: 2015 IEEE 27th International Conference on Tools with Artificial Intelligence (ICTAI), pp. 807–812 (2015)
28. Elleuch, M., Maalej, R., Kherallah, M.: A new design based-SVM of the CNN classifier architecture with dropout for offline arabic handwritten recognition. Proc. Comput. Sci. **80**, 1712–1723 (2016)
29. Ashiquzzaman, A., Tushar, A.K.: Handwritten Arabic numeral recognition using deep learning neural networks. In: 2017 IEEE International Conference on Imaging, Vision & Pattern Recognition (icIVPR), pp. 1–4 (2017)
30. Elleuch, M., Tagougui, N., Kherallah, M.: Deep learning for feature extraction of Arabic handwritten script. In: Azzopardi, G., Petkov, N. (eds.) CAIP 2015. LNCS, vol. 9257, pp. 371–382. Springer, Cham (2015). https://doi.org/10.1007/978-3-319-23117-4_32
31. Dashtipour, K., et al.: Erratum to: multilingual sentiment analysis: state of the art and independent comparison of techniques. Cogn. Comput. **8**, 772–775 (2016)
32. Spatial Transformer Network with Affine, Projective and Elastic Transformations. https://github.com/dantkz/spatial-transformer-tensorflow. Accessed 01 Apr 2019

33. Ieracitano, C., Mammone, N., Bramanti, A., Hussain, A., Morabito, F.C.: A Convolutional Neural Network approach for classification of dementia stages based on 2D-spectral representation of EEG recordings. Neurocomputing **323**, 96–107 (2019)
34. Ahmad, I., Fink, G.A.: Class-based contextual modeling for handwritten Arabic text recognition. In: 2016 15th International Conference on Frontiers in Handwriting Recognition (ICFHR), pp. 554–559 (2016)
35. Du, X., Cai, Y., Wang, S., Zhang, L.: Overview of deep learning. In: 2016 31st Youth Academic Annual Conference of Chinese Association of Automation (YAC), pp. 159–164 (2016)
36. Dashtipour, K., Hussain, A., Gelbukh, A.: Adaptation of sentiment analysis techniques to Persian language. In: Gelbukh, A. (ed.) CICLing 2017. LNCS, vol. 10762, pp. 129–140. Springer, Cham (2018). https://doi.org/10.1007/978-3-319-77116-8_10
37. Dashtipour, K., Gogate, M., Adeel, A., Hussain, A., Alqarafi, A., Durrani, T.: A comparative study of persian sentiment analysis based on different feature combinations. In: Liang, Q., Mu, J., Jia, M., Wang, W., Feng, X., Zhang, B. (eds.) CSPS 2017. LNEE, vol. 463, pp. 2288–2294. Springer, Singapore (2019). https://doi.org/10.1007/978-981-10-6571-2_279
38. AlKhateeb, J.H., Pauplin, O., Ren, J., Jiang, J.: Performance of hidden Markov model and dynamic Bayesian network classifiers on handwritten Arabic word recognition. Knowl.-Based Syst. **24**(5), 680–688 (2011)
39. AlKhateeb, J.H., Ren, J., Jiang, J., Al-Muhtaseb, H.: Offline handwritten Arabic cursive text recognition using Hidden Markov Models and re-ranking. Pattern Recogn. Lett. **32**(8), 1081–1088 (2011)
40. AlKhateeb, J.H., et al.: Knowledge-based baseline detection and optimal thresholding for words segmentation in efficient pre-processing of handwritten Arabic text. In: Fifth International Conference on Information Technology: New Generations, pp. 1158–1159 (2018)
41. AlKhateeb, J.H., et al.: Word-based handwritten Arabic scripts recognition using DCT features and neural network classifier. In: 5th International Multi-Conference on Systems, Signals and Devices, pp. 1–5 (2008)

A Study of Balance Ability for Children Between 5–6 Years Using Data Mining Techniques

Mingchen Feng[1(✉)] and Yanqin Liu[2]

[1] School of Computer Science, Northwestern Polytechnical University, Xi'an, China
mingchen@mail.nwpu.edu.cn

[2] Department of Sports, Xi'an Fanyi University, Xi'an, China
xiaojingcomeon@163.com

Abstract. In kindergarten, pediatric head injuries occur commonly and are being reported in increasing numbers. Among multiple reasons that caused them, balance ability is considered the critical one. In this paper we conduct a study to describe factors that related to balance ability. First we conduct Movement Assessment Battery for Children (M-ABC) tests on children between 5–6 from urban and rural areas to collect data, and then we visualize and perform data mining techniques to further explore the data, we utilized state-of-the-art classification models to highlight key factors that influence children balance ability. Experimental results show that balance ability is closely related to the performance of catching beanbag and walking with heels raised. We also found that for balance ability prediction using our dataset, XGBoost and BP neural network perform better than decision tree. The promising results will undoubtedly provide guidance on how to improve children motor skills and assist teachers for reducing injures.

Keywords: Children balance ability analysis · Data mining · M-ABC

1 Introduction

Body balance refers to a person's ability to be aware and control his body posture in the air in order to maintain orthostatic position in statics and dynamics [1]. Assessing balance is included in the complex process of kinesic testing and children's psychomotor development. Researchers [2] has found that children show decreased dynamic balance after mild traumatic brain injury, but unfortunately, according to Stanford Children's Health [3], head injuries are one of the most common causes of disability and death in children. As such we conduct a study aiming at discovering key factors that effect children's balance ability.

Movement Assessment Battery for Children (M-ABC) [4] assessment is paralleled by an observational approach to perceptual-motor aspects and emotional and motivational difficulties the child may have in relation to motor tasks. Its tasks cover three areas: Manual Dexterity, Ball Skills, Static and Dynamic Balance. With the help of M-ABC testing, we can identify delay or impairment in motor development, assess groups

J. Ren et al. (Eds.): BICS 2019, LNAI 11691, pp. 469–478, 2020.
https://doi.org/10.1007/978-3-030-39431-8_45

of children in classroom situations, and measure the extent to which a child's attitudes and feelings about motor tasks are situation specific or more generalized. So we choose M-ABC to collect the original data.

In this paper, we study and analyze children's balance ability between rural and urban areas using M-ABC testing data. We first collect data from two kindergartens in urban and rural areas using M-ABC assessments. Then we process and visualize the data to explore the structure of the dataset and identify potential patterns. Finally, we perform data mining techniques to uncover critical factors that determine a child's balance ability and obtain a model to classify whether a child has good balance ability given some testing parameters. We tried different widely adapted classification models that are specifically used for big data analysis.

2 Related Work

In the literature researchers have devoted attention to study factors that related to children's balance. Libardoni et al. [5] established the reference ranges for balance scores and developed prediction equations for estimation of balance scores in children aged 8 to 12 years old. Moraru et al. [1] compared the balance ability in sporty and unsporty children and found that children in the sporty group obtained higher values in balance ability test compared to the unsporty group. Walicka-Cupryś et al. [6] assessed balance ability in hearing-impaired children, and found that deaf children had higher static balance parameters than their peers without hearing problems. Patikas et al. [7] explored the impact of obesity on plantar pressure and balance ability in children. Mitsiou et al. [8] examined the disorders in motor coordination of 8/9-year-old school aged children and detected the possible differences in balance performance between those children assessed with Developmental Coordination Disorder. Humphriss et al. [9] described and analyzed balance test results in children between 7 to 10 years old from a large UK data. de Souza Melo et al. [10] compared the balance performance between normal hearing children and those with sensorineural hearing loss considering the sex and age range of the sample, and analyze balance performance according to the degrees of hearing loss and etiological factors in the latter group. Eshraghi et al. [11] conducted a review to illustrate the relationship between walking and balance in children.

However previous study mainly focus on using traditional analytics methods, few works consider analyze children's balance ability using data mining techniques as they have achieved great success in many fields [12, 13]. Moreover, the majority of these studies merely focused on the balance ability of children with physical defects, but did not consider what factors affecting the balance ability of healthy children. In this paper, we collect, visualize and analyze M-ABC data to uncover potential factors that related to children's balance ability and proposed novel models to predict balance level for children.

3 Methodology

We explored 3 data mining algorithms, i.e. C 4.5, XGBoost and BP Neural Network.

3.1 C 4.5

C 4.5, one of the well-known data mining algorithms, is used to generate decision trees. It is developed base on the decision tree algorithm ID3 [14], but it extends ID3 by guarantee an optimal solution to analyze continuous data as shown below:

$$\mathrm{GainRatio}(A) = \frac{Gain(A)}{SplitInfo(A)} \quad (1)$$

$$\mathrm{SplitInfo_A(D)} = -\sum_{j=1}^{y} \frac{|D_j|}{|D|} \times \log_2\left(\frac{|D_j|}{|D|}\right) \quad (2)$$

$$\mathrm{Gain}(A) = Info(D) - Info_A(D) \quad (3)$$

$$\mathrm{Info}(D) = -\sum_{i=1}^{m} p_i \log_2(p_i) \quad (4)$$

Where D is the data set and A is an attribute in D.

3.2 XGBoost

XGBoost [15] (eXtreme Gradient Boosting) is a scalable end-to-end tree boosting system, which is used widely by data scientists to achieve state-of-the-art results on many machine learning challenges. The target function of XGBoost is defined below:

$$\mathrm{F_{obj}}(\theta) = \mathrm{L}(\theta) + \Omega(\theta) \quad (5)$$

$$\Omega(\theta) = \gamma T + \frac{1}{2}\lambda\|\omega\|^2 \quad (6)$$

$$\mathrm{L}(\theta) = \sum_{i=1}^{n} \left[l(y_i, \hat{y}^{(t-1)}) + g_i S_t(T_i) + \frac{1}{2} h_i S_t^2(T_i) \right] \quad (7)$$

Where $L(\theta)$ is mean square loss function, γ is the learning rate, T is the number of leaves, g_i, h_i refer to two order Taylor expansion.

3.3 BP Neural Network

The back propagation (BP) neural network algorithm is a multi-layer feed-forward network trained according to error back propagation algorithm and is one of the most widely applied neural network models. BP network can be used to learn and store a great deal of mapping relations of input-output model, and no need to disclose in advance the mathematical equation that describes these mapping relations. A 3-layer BP network is described below:

Given X_i as the input node, Y_i as the hidden node, and Z_i as the output node.

Where,

$$Y_i = f(\sum_i w_{ji}x_i - \theta_i) \tag{8}$$

$$Z_i = f(\sum_j v_{lj}y_j - \theta_l) \tag{9}$$

Where w, v are weight value of input and hidden nodes.

Error of output node is computed as

$$E = \frac{1}{2}\sum_l (t_l - f(\sum_j v_{lj}f(\sum_i w_{ji}x_i - \theta_j) - \theta_l))^2 \tag{10}$$

4 Experimental Results

4.1 Data Acquisition

In order to obtain the data, we conduct M-ABC tests in two kindergartens in Xi'an, one from rural and the other from urban area. In each area, we tested 60 children aged 5–6 years, to be specific it includes the following programs:

(1) Posting Coins: Testers throw 12 coins using their habitual and non-habitual hands respectively, and then record time they used;
(2) Threading Beads: Testers thread 12 beads and record time used;
(3) Catching Beanbag: The activities in this section utilize a beanbag and testers catch it in 10 times and record numbers of success;
(4) One-leg balance: Participants stand on one leg and record the time;
(5) Walking Heels Raised: Testers walk with their heels raised, and count the number of steps, 15 steps at most;

Based on one-leg balance results, gender and age, through a series of computing we obtain three level of balance ability: High, Medium, and Low. Thus, the data collected is organized as follows (Table 1):

Table 1. A sample of the dataset.

Sex	Age	Posting coins	One-leg balance	Threading beads	Catching beanbag	Walking Heels Raised	Area	Level
M	5	Habi: 14 Non: 18	Left: 28 Right: 34	38	9	12	Rural	High
F	6	Habi: 16 Non: 19	Left: 28 Right: 34	46	7	9	Rural	Medium
M	6	Habi: 20 Non: 26	Left: 15 Right: 19	49	3	4	Urban	Low
F	5	Habi: 17 Non: 18	Left: 24 Right: 30	42	8	6	Urban	Medium

4.2 Statistical Visualization

Figure 1 shows the distribution of balance ability between different genders. There are 55 girls and 65 boys in our dataset. We can calculate that there are 73% girls whose balance ability is above medium and the index is 63% in boys. This indicates that for children between 5–6, girls have better balance ability than boys, as we can see from the figure that there are more boys whose balance level is lower than that of girls'.

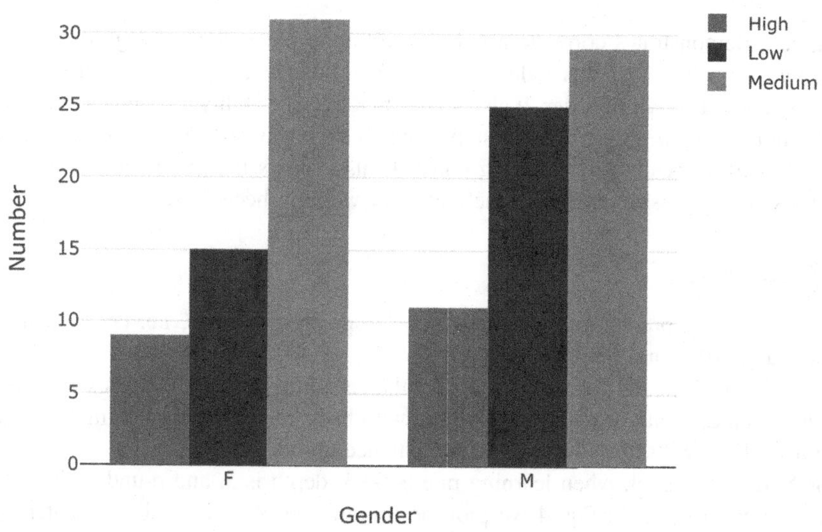

Fig. 1. The differences of balance ability between boys and girls.

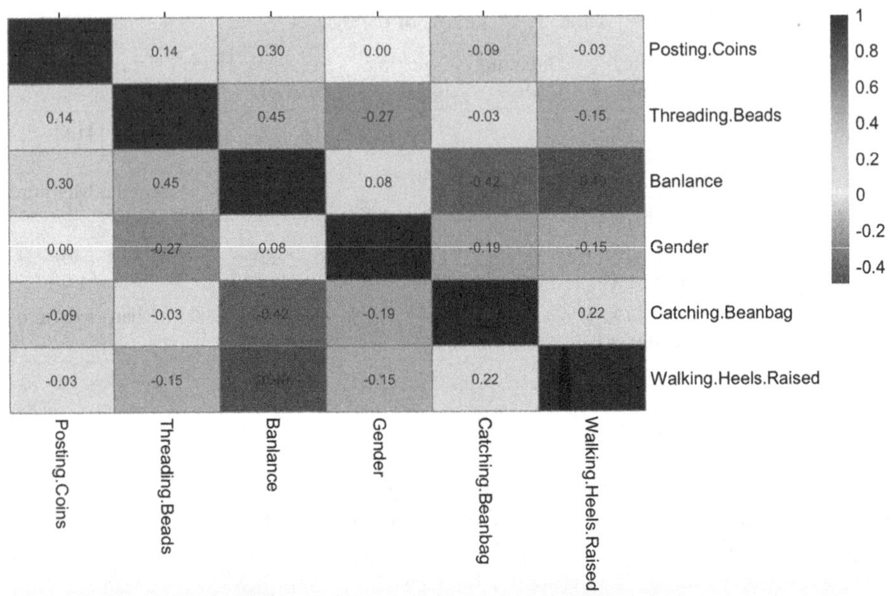

Fig. 2. Heatmap of correlation between different parameters.

Figure 2 demonstrates correlation between different parameters, this graph proves our views that girls have better balance ability than boys as most of the attributes are negatively correlated with gender. It also shows that balance ability has high correlation with the number of beanbag caches, steps when walking with heels raised, and time used by threading beads and throwing coins. It also shows that the skill of catching beanbag is strongly associated with the ability of walking heels raised.

4.3 Classification

For balance ability prediction, we applied 3 classification models, i.e. decision tree, XGBoost and BP neural network.

Figure 3 displays the decision tree of balance ability, which indicates that, for example, when catching beanbag >7, walking with heels raised >6 or catching beanbag ≥ 7 and walking with heels raised >12 the balance ability is high.

For XGBoost model, when learning rate is 0.95, depth is 5, and round is 500, we obtain the lowest rmse. In Fig. 4 we plot the importance of each attributes. Catching beanbag and walking with heels raised are two most important parameters.

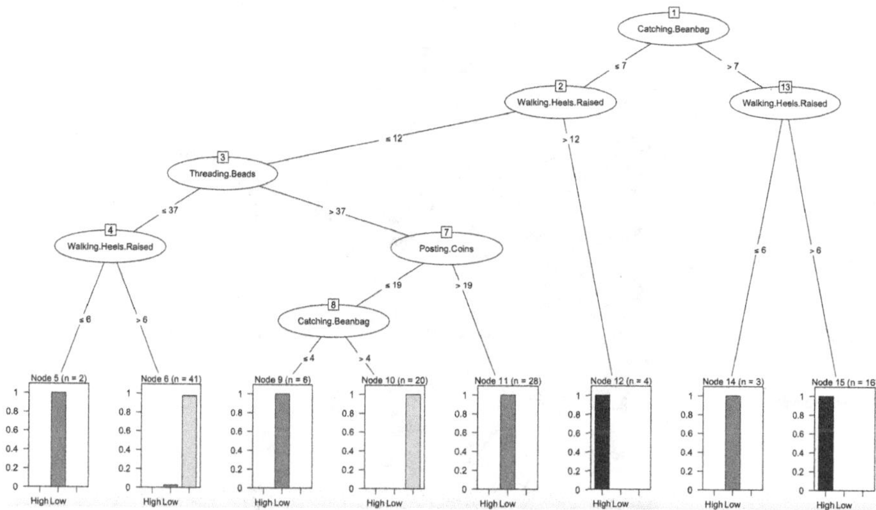

Fig. 3. Decision tree of Balance ability.

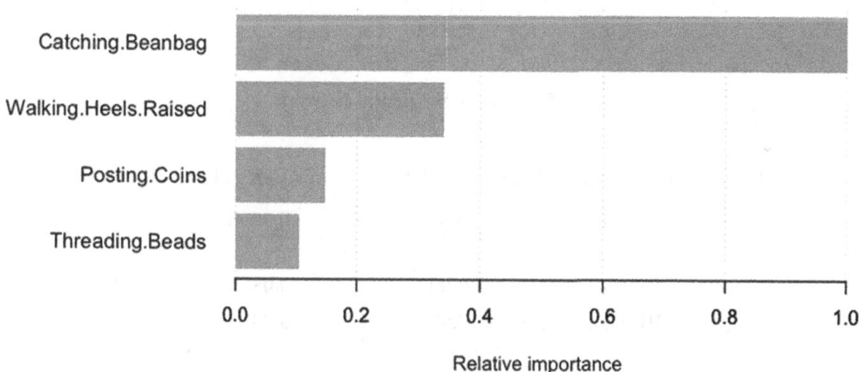

Fig. 4. Importance of each parameter in XGBoost.

For BP neural network, we set hidden layer 20, learning rate 0.9 and threshold 0.5, and then in Fig. 5 we plot the network.

After training the model, we test the models using testing data, by exploring accuracy, recall and F_1-Score, we evaluate each model. The results are shown in Table 2, we can conclude that XGBoost and BP neural network perform better than decision tree and XGBoost is the most stable one.

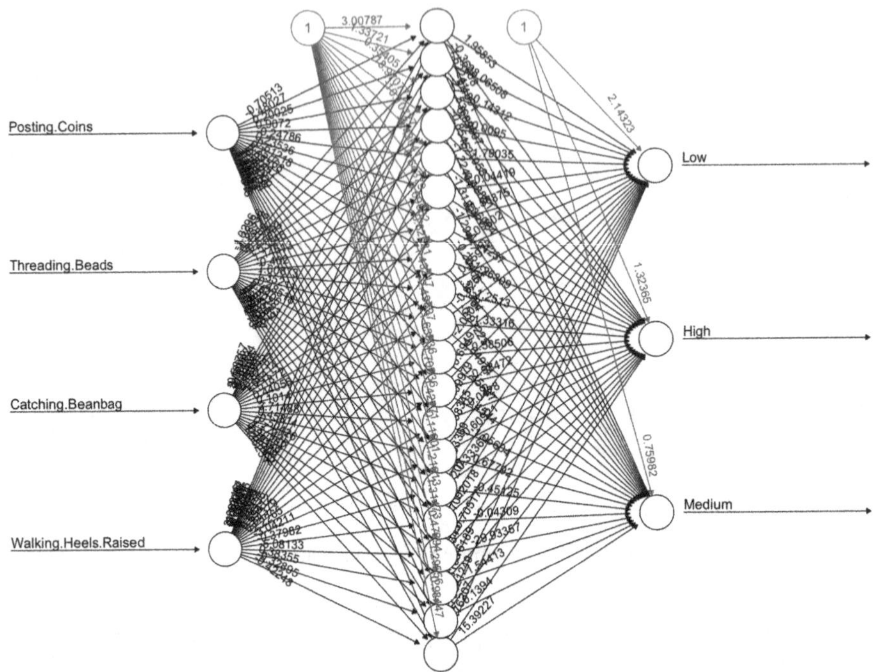

Fig. 5. Plot of BP neural network.

Table 2. Comparison of different models by accuracy, recall and F1-score.

Model	Accuracy	Recall	F_1-score
C4.5	0.975	0.88	0.925
XGBoost	0.992	0.92	0.955
BP neural network	0.984	0.91	0.945

5 Conclusion and Future Work

In this paper we analyzed M-ABC testing data to study children's balance ability with two purpose: visualizing the data to find essential factors related to balance ability and predict balance level using data mining techniques. We visualize the data to uncover some interesting patterns and attributes that associate with balance ability. We also explore 3 classification models to predict balance ability. We found that XGBoost and BP neural network models performed better than decision tree. In the future, we plan to add more features that related to children motor skills and using more state-of-the-art algorithms to get higher accuracy for this problem. Besides, as Deep Learning [16–18, 22] and Artificial Intelligence [19, 20] has achieved big success in computer vision, we also want to perform deep learning models and other learning algorithms [21] on our dataset.

Acknowledgments. This work has been supported by The 13th Five-Year Plan of Education Science in Shaanxi Province (Program No. SGH18H457) and Key Project in Xi'an Fanyi University (Program No. J18A07).

References

1. Moraru, C., Neculaeş, M., et al.: Comparative study on the balance ability in sporty and unsporty children. Procedia-Soc. Behav. Sci. **116**, 3659–3663 (2014)
2. Gagnon, I., Swaine, B., et al.: Children show decreased dynamic balance after mild traumatic brain injury. Arch. Phys. Med. Rehabil. **85**(3), 444–452 (2004)
3. Head Injury in Children. https://www.stanfordchildrens.org/en/topic/default?id=head-injury-in-children-90-P02604
4. Brown, T., Lalor, A.: The movement assessment battery for children-2nd edition (MABC-2): a review and critique. Phys. Occup. Ther. Pediatr. **29**(1), 86–103 (2009)
5. de Cássia Libardoni, T., da Silveira, C.B., et al.: Reference values and equations reference of balance for children of 8 to 12 years. Gait Posture **60**, 122–127 (2018)
6. Walicka-Cupryś, K., Przygoda, Ł., et al.: Balance assessment in hearing-impaired children. Res. Dev. Disabil. **35**(11), 2728–2734 (2014)
7. Patikas, D., Bilili, E., et al.: The impact of obesity on plantar pressure and balance ability in children. Gait Posture **1**(42), S26–S27 (2015)
8. Mitsiou, M., Giagazoglou, P., et al.: Static balance ability in children with developmental coordination disorder. Eur. J. Phys. Educ. Sport **11**, 17–23 (2016)
9. Humphriss, R., Hall, A., et al.: Balance ability of 7 and 10 year old children in the population: results from a large UK birth cohort study. Int. J. Pediatr. Otorhinolaryngol. **75**(1), 106–113 (2011)
10. de Souza Melo, R., Lemos, A., et al.: Balance performance of children and adolescents with sensorineural hearing loss: repercussions of hearing loss degrees and etiological factors. Int. J. Pediatr. Otorhinolaryngol. **110**, 16–21 (2018)
11. Eshraghi, A., Safaeepour, Z., et al.: Walking and balance in children and adolescents with lower-limb amputation: a review of literature. Clin. Biomech. **59**, 181–198 (2018)
12. Feng, M., Zheng, J., Han, Y., Ren, J., Liu, Q.: Big data analytics and mining for crime data analysis, visualization and prediction. In: Ren, J., et al. (eds.) BICS 2018. LNCS (LNAI), vol. 10989, pp. 605–614. Springer, Cham (2018). https://doi.org/10.1007/978-3-030-00563-4_59
13. Li, N., Zheng, J., Feng, M.: A big data analytics platform for information sharing in the connection between administrative law and criminal justice. In: Ren, J., et al. (eds.) BICS 2018. LNCS (LNAI), vol. 10989, pp. 654–662. Springer, Cham (2018). https://doi.org/10.1007/978-3-030-00563-4_64
14. Ruggieri, S.: Efficient C4. 5 [classification algorithm]. IEEE Trans. Knowl. Data Eng. **14**(2), 438–444 (2002)
15. Chen, T., Guestrin, C.: XGBoost: a scalable tree boosting system. In: Proceedings of the 22nd ACM SIGKDD International Conference on Knowledge Discovery and Data Mining, pp. 785–794. ACM, San Francisco (2016)
16. Ren, J., Jiang, J.: Hierarchical modeling and adaptive clustering for real-time summarization of rush videos. IEEE Trans. Multimedia **11**(5), 906–917 (2009)
17. Xi, Y., Zheng, J., et al.: Beyond context: exploring semantic similarity for small object detection in crowded scenes. Pattern Recogn. Lett. (2019, in press)
18. Chen, J., Ren, J.: Modelling of content-aware indicators for effective determination of shot boundaries in compressed MPEG videos. Multimedia Tools Appl. **54**(2), 219–239 (2011)

19. Ren, J., Vlachos, T.: Immersive and perceptual human-computer interaction using computer vision techniques. In: 2010 IEEE Computer Society Conference on Computer Vision and Pattern Recognition Workshops, pp. 66–72. IEEE (2010)
20. Yan, Y., Ren, J., et al.: Cognitive fusion of thermal and visible imagery for effective detection and tracking of pedestrians in videos. Cogn. Comput., 1–11 (2017)
21. Yan, Y., Ren, J., et al.: Unsupervised image saliency detection with Gestalt-laws guided optimization and visual attention based refinement. Pattern Recogn. **79**, 65–78 (2018)
22. Wang, Z., Ren, J., Zhang, D., et al.: A deep-learning based feature hybrid framework for spatiotemporal saliency detection inside videos. Neurocomputing **287**, 68–83 (2018)

Analysis of SDN Attack and Defense Strategy Based on Zero-Sum Game

Rongfu Zhou[1], Jun Lin[2(✉)], Lan Liu[1], Min Ye[3], and Shunhe Wei[3]

[1] College of Electronic and Information, Guangdong Polytechnic Normal University, Guangzhou, China
1141689193@qq.com

[2] China Electronic Product Reliability and Environmental Testing Research Institute, Guangzhou, China
linjun@ceprei.com

[3] Guangdong Overseas Chinese Vocational School, Guangzhou, China
ym@gdhqzz.cn

Abstract. Software Defined Network is a huge innovation in the field of computer networks. This technology implements software to control forwarding routing packets. The SDN controller can realize the use of the control plane, to manage various virtual exchange forwarding devices, thereby saving a lot of money, and shortening the development test cycle of SDN. However, with the advent of SDN-related network equipment, security issues have become an important factor constraining its development. This paper designs and simulates an SDN packet sampling strategy, using zero-sum game and analyzing the security of multiple SDN topology networks. The SDN packet sampling problem is modeled as a zero-sum security game, in which both attackers and defenders participate, and the importance of each point is quantified into the income value. The income of the attackers and defenders are determined according to the income value. Under the knowledge of incomes of attack and defense, we determine the SDN topology with the highest security performance and security defense strategy.

Keywords: Security · Zero-sum game · SDN · Packet sampling strategy

1 Introduction

The software defined network originated from the Clean State research project of Stanford University in 2006 [1]. In 2009, Mckeown teachers formally proposed the concept of software-defined network. Its core technology, OpenFlow, separates the control plane of the network device from the data plane, thus achieving flexible control of network traffic, making the network more intelligent as a pipeline, providing a good platform for innovation of core networks and applications. Using layered thinking, SDN separates data from control. At the control level, including a logically centralized and programmable controller, the global network information can be mastered, allowing operators and researchers to manage the configuration network and deploy new protocols. At the data layer, including switches (unlike traditional two-layer

J. Ren et al. (Eds.): BICS 2019, LNAI 11691, pp. 479–485, 2020.
https://doi.org/10.1007/978-3-030-39431-8_46

switches, specifically for devices that forward data), only a simple data forwarding function is provided, which can quickly process matching data packets to meet the increasing demands of traffic. The two layers interact with an open unified interface (such as OpenFlow). The controller sends a unified standard rule to the switch through the standard interface. The switch only needs to perform corresponding actions according to these rules [2].

In recent years, SDN has been increasingly valued by Internet companies. Major mainstream manufacturers have begun to deploy SDN networks. Many commercial cases have been applied. For example, Google built a B4 [3] network based on SDN to transform its WAN network. Cimorelli et al. [4] proposes a distributed load balancing algorithm based on game theory to balance the traffic of the controller cluster. Abraxas of Switzerland adopted Huawei's SDN-based data center network solution to build a virtualized multi-tenant cloud data center network. In order to provide users with a better experience, Tencent use SDN to achieve differentiated path differentiation calculation and flow control. And in the development of Internet communication technology in the coming decades, SDN also has broad prospects for development. For example, in the 5G era, there will be scenarios such as massive communication and tens of billions of devices accessing. These scenarios are incomparably demanding networks. Architecture, flexible services and high-performance networks, software-defined network will be the key technology to promote the development of 5G networks in a distributed and intelligent way.

SDN is based on the granularity of data flow control, so that it does not understand the internal information of the data stream, which makes SDN vulnerable to attacks by Trojan horses, worms, spam, DDos, etc. [5]. Li and Ren [6] proposed a method for intrusion detection using Snort system. Jiang et al. [7] proposed a method of real-time feedback. In order to ensure the security of the network, it is necessary to detect the data packet. However, due to the upper limit of network performance, detecting all data packets in a high-speed transmission network will cause a large delay, which will seriously affect the transmission capacity of the network. Therefore, random extraction of data packets under limited network resources will occur. Reduce latency, increase network bandwidth, and at the same time ensure network security to a certain extent.

Zero-sum game is a concept of game theory and is a non-cooperative game. The parties involved in the game, under strict competition, the gain of one party necessarily means the loss of the other party. The sum of the gains and losses of the parties to the game is always "zero", and there is no possibility of cooperation between the two parties [7]. In the network, the attack and defense model between the attacker and the defender is built into a zero-sum game [8]. When the attacker successfully attacks, the attacker scores positive and the defense battle scores negative. The sum of the two is still zero.

2 SDN Packet Sampling Problem Zero-Sum Game Model

The attacker's behavior can be seen as sending a malicious packet from a controlled computer to one or more network devices. When the defender checks the data packet, if the malicious packet is sampled, the attack fails, and the defender scores positive. Otherwise, the attack succeeds and the defender scores negative.

The attacker sends a packet from one network device to one or more network devices. If the defender is not intercepted, the attack is successful and the score is positive. Otherwise, even if the attack fails, the score is negative.

Based on the above background, the hypothesis is:

Hypothesis 1: Under the limited defensive resource constraints, the probability that a defender detects a packet is directly proportional to its importance.
Hypothesis 2: attackers always pursue maximum revenue, so they will prioritize attacks on network devices of high importance.

In the offensive and defensive game project, both the attacker and the defender will maximize their own revenues with the optimal strategy, and imitate the SDN data packet raising problem into a zero-sum game in which both offense and defense participate.

The SDN network is constructed into a phaseless graph, and the set of vertices is V, the graph of the edge set E is recorded as G = (V, E), and the number of vertices and the number of edges of G = (V, E) are respectively |V| and |E|. Connect two vertices u, the edges of v are denoted as e = (u, v).

When an attacker launches an attack, the probability of sending a malicious packet is proportional to the importance. It is assumed that k packets are extracted for every n packets of the network device of importance x, and m packets are included in the n packets. Then, the probability of extracting k out of n packets in n packets is $\frac{c_{n-m}^{k}}{C_n^k}$, then this is the probability that no malicious packets are detected.

For the attacker, the revenue is

$$U_a = \frac{c_{n-m}^{k}}{C_n^k} * \mathrm{x}$$

For the defender, the benefit is

$$U_X = -\frac{c_{n-m}^{k}}{C_n^k} * \mathrm{x}$$

3 Node Importance Calculation

When an attacker successfully attacks the network node v_t, the gain that can be obtained is the importance $\varphi(v_t)$ corresponding to the node v_t, and the attacker tends to attack the higher-priority nodes in the network, to cause greater impact on the network. Damage, so the network node income value is quantified according to the importance of the network node, and the higher value is given to the more important network nodes. The nodes in the network are divided into switch nodes $S_k \in$ S, S is contained in N and the host node $H_k \in$ H, and H is included in N. For the normal operation of the network, the importance of the switch node (switching device) is equal to the sum of the importance of all the host nodes (terminal devices) connected to it. The importance of different switches in the network may be different, such as the core switch is more important than the edge switch; there is no difference between different hosts. In summary, Theorems 1 and 2 are proposed.

Theorem 1: The importance of each switch node is divided into direct importance and indirect importance.

Theorem 2: The direct importance of a switch node is equal to the sum of the importance of the host nodes to which it is connected, and the indirect importance is equal to the direct importance of the switch to which it is connected.

Theorem 3: The importance of each switch node may be different, and each host node is of equal importance.

According to Theorems 1, 2, the importance level of the switch node and the host node is divided. The importance level SIValue of the switch node is often higher than the importance level HIValue of the host node. The specific values can be used to represent different network nodes according to different network scenarios. The importance level, such as HIValue, can take a value of 1. When taking values, pay attention to the size relationship between them, that is, $\mathrm{SI} = \sum_{i=1}^{n} HI$ Value.

According to Theorem 2, assuming that the importance of each host is 1, then the importance of a switch is equal to the sum of the importance of all the hosts connected to it, which is of direct importance, plus the direct importance of all switches connected to it.

4 Analysis of Offensive and Defensive Strategy Game Model

For an attacker, there are two main attack strategies:

1. Send malicious packets to the defender network device on average if the unknown network device is important.
2. Send malicious packets to the defender network device in an important proportion, given the importance of the network device.

Suppose an attacker uses attack strategy 1 to distribute malicious packets evenly to n network devices, and this n is exactly equal to the number of defender network devices. It is assumed that when an attacker uses an attack strategy, it may be randomly assigned to a network device of high importance to the defender, or may be randomly assigned to a network device of low importance.

When defenders deal with attackers, there are two main defense strategies:

(1) The probability of network device packet detection is equal.
(2) The probability of network device packet detection is directly proportional to its importance.

5 Modeling Simulation

In order to verify the difference of the above strategies, the Matlab and graph theory methods were used to build the model. Four groups of topologies and four offensive and defensive strategies were used to perform 16 sets of simulations. Each set of simulations was repeated 10 times, and then each set of simulations was averaged. Under the combination of different attack strategies and topologies, the SDN packet and random sampling strategy based on zero-sum game are compared. The experimental topology is shown in Table 1. The defender's detection success rate and attacker's benefit are shown in Table 2. The income value is in US dollars in the financial currency.

Table 1. Network topology

	Topology 1	Topology 2	Topology 3	Topology 4
#switches	3	1	5	3
#hosts	4	4	5	5
#links	7	4	9	7
Topology	Tree type	Star type	Line type	Hybrid type

Table 2. Defender's detection success rate of attack and the profit of the attacker

Experimental method		Defensive detection success rate	Attacker gain
Topology 1	Attack strategy 1VS defensive strategy 1	0.41	7.2
	Attack strategy 1VS defensive strategy 2	0.75	6.8
	Attack Strategy 2VS Defensive Strategy 1	0.75	6.3
	Attack Strategy 2VS Defensive Strategy 2	0.98	5.7
Topology 2	Attack strategy 1VS defensive strategy 1	0.62	3.1
	Attack strategy 1VS defensive strategy 2	0.96	2.1
	Attack Strategy 2VS Defensive Strategy 1	0.96	2.2
	Attack Strategy 2VS Defensive Strategy 2	0.99	2.4

(*continued*)

Table 2. (*continued*)

Experimental method		Defensive detection success rate	Attacker gain
Topology 3	Attack strategy 1VS defensive strategy 1	0.19	16.1
	Attack strategy 1VS defensive strategy 2	0.29	17.1
	Attack Strategy 2VS Defensive Strategy 1	0.29	17.1
	Attack Strategy 2VS Defensive Strategy 2	0.39	13.7
Topology 4	Attack strategy 1VS defensive strategy 1	0.41	8.5
	Attack strategy 1VS defensive strategy 2	0.75	7.3
	Attack Strategy 2VS Defensive Strategy 1	0.75	7.3
	Attack Strategy 2VS Defensive Strategy 2	0.98	6.1

In the experiment, there is only one malicious host, and the malicious data sent to the network every second is 20 per second. Each network device can receive 20 packets per second, and the total number of samplings per network device of the entire topology per second. For 20, the attack proceeds retain a decimal.

The experimental data shows that compared with attack strategy 1, attack strategy 2 will improve the defensive success rate and reduce the attack revenue. It indicates that in the network attack, the malicious power of the malicious packet is increased to the target host, which will make the target host easy to find the attack. And take the initiative to defend. Compared with defensive strategy 1, defensive strategy 2 will improve the detection success rate and reduce the attack benefit. The reason is that the SDN packet detection strategy based on zero-sum game tends to protect important nodes, so the strategy is effective.

6 Summary

SDN flow-based control granularity makes it vulnerable to worms, Trojan horses, spam, etc., so it is necessary and important to detect packets in SDN. In order to optimize the network security resource configuration in the SDN packet sampling problem, this paper proposes the SDN packet sampling problem zero-sum game model and the network node revenue value quantification method. The defender adopts active defense and pays attention to protecting important nodes to improve the network defense performance. The simulation results show that the SDN packet sampling strategy based on zero-sum game is effective.

Future work will focus on extended cybersecurity applications [10], especially using machine learning and optimization approaches [11, 12]. Deep learning and compressed sensing may be also focused, where the challenges in cloud enabled big data analytics can be targeted [13–15].

Acknowledgment. This research is supported by Special project for research and development in key areas of Guangdong Province (2019B010121001), Guangdong Provincial Department of Education Innovation Project (2016KTSCX078) and Science & Technology Projects of Guangdong Province (2018a070717021).

References

1. Zhang, C., Cui, Y., Tang, W., Wu, J.: Research progress in Software Defined Network (SDN). J. Softw. (2015)
2. Zhang, W.: Depth Analysis SDN, Benefits, Strategy, Technology, Practice. Publishing House of Electronics Industry, Beijing (2014). ISBN 978-7-121-21821-7
3. Jain, S., Kumar, A., Mandal, S., et al.: B4: experience with a globally-deployed software defined WAN. In: Association for Computing Machinery's Special Interest Group on Data Communications, vol. 43, no. 4, pp. 3–14 (2013)
4. Cimorelli, F., Priscoli, F.D., Pietrabissa, A., et al.: A distributed load balancing algorithm for the control plane in software defined networking. In: Proceedings of 24th Mediterranean Conference on Control and Automation, pp. 1033–1040. IEEE (2016)
5. Zhang, W., Wang, X., Zhang, S., Huang, M.: SDN data packet sampling strategy based on security game. J. Zhengzhou Univ. (Sci. Ed.) **50**(01), 15–19 (2018)
6. Gao, P., et al.: Analysis and realization of snort-based intrusion detection system. J. Comput. Appl. Softw. **23**(8), 134–135 (2006)
7. Jiang, J., et al.: Live: an integrated production and feedback system for intelligent and interactive tv broadcasting. IEEE Trans. Broadcast. **57**(3), 646–661 (2011)
8. Zhou, H.: Zero-sum game and H_∞ control for discrete random singular systems. J. Nanchang Univ. (Sci. Technol.) **41**(06), 519–523 (2017)
9. Meng, F., Lan, J., Hu, Y.: Bandwidth allocation strategy of data center backbone based on cooperative game. Comput. Res. Dev. **53**(06), 1306–1313 (2016)
10. Wang, X., et al.: TKRD: trusted kernel rootkit detection for cybersecurity of VMs based on machine learning and memory forensic analysis. Math. Biosci. Eng. **16**(4), 2650–2667 (2019)
11. Feng, W., Huang, W., Ren, J.: Class imbalance ensemble learning based on margin theory. Appl. Sci. **8**(5), 815(2018)
12. Sun, G., Ma, P., et al.: A stability constrained adaptive alpha for gravitational search algorithm. Knowl.-Based Syst. **139**, 200–213 (2018)
13. Feng, M., et al.: Big data analytics and mining for effective visualization and trends forecasting of crime data. IEEE Access **7**, 106111–106123 (2019)
14. Zhao, H., et al.: Compressive sensing based secret signals recovery for effective image Steganalysis in secure communications. Multimedia Tools Appl. **78**(20), 29381–29394 (2019)
15. Wang, Z., et al.: A deep-learning based feature hybrid framework for spatiotemporal saliency detection inside videos. Neurocomputing **287**, 68–83 (2018)

The Research and Application of Mathematical Morphology in Seismic Events Edge Detection and Machine Vision

Jing Zhao[1(✉)], Cailing Wang[2], Ni'na Chang[1], Qiyu Yuan[1], Yan Zhao[1], Yifan Wu[1], Tongtong Han[1], Sifan Jia[1], and Daxing Wang[3]

[1] School of Earth Science and Engineering, Xi'an Shiyou University, Xi'an 710065, China
zhaojing@xsyu.edu.cn
[2] School of Computer Science, Xi'an Shiyou University, Xi'an 710065, China
[3] Research Institute of E&D, Changqing Oil-Field Company of CNPC, Xi'an 710065, China

Abstract. The event represents the formation interface with different lithology, namely sediment interface. It can also represent the geochronologic isochronous stratigraphic interfaces. This is the basis of the seismic interpretation, including the research of sequence stratigraphy, reservoir prediction and characterization. Events picking play a decisive role in the determination of the reflection interface. This paper is a research on the events extraction from pre/post stack reflection seismic data. The mathematical morphology is widely used in denoising, feature extraction, edge detection and other fields. In this paper, we proposed a mathematical morphology algorithm that is suitable for the seismic events picking. Based on cognitive computing, the mathematical morphology was applied to the SSPA section to reduce the noise, where eight structure elements with the size of 5×5 and weighing fusion based on the theory of entropy were proposed to improve the accuracy and computational efficiency. The proposed structure elements can approximate the shape of the events which are hyperbolic curve in pre-stack seismic data, VSP data and the crosswell seismic data. The event curves obtained by applying the proposed method to the synthetic layered model and field record is continuous and correspond to the events in the original data. The results indicate the high accuracy and efficiency of the proposed method.

Keywords: Cognitive model · Mathematical morphology · Events extraction · Pre/post reflection data

1 Introduction

The events are the link of the phase peak (crests or troughs). When we interpret the seismic record, the events are marked out according to vibration which have similar shape and occur regularly. These events indicate seismic waves with different category

J. Ren et al. (Eds.): BICS 2019, LNAI 11691, pp. 486–496, 2020.
https://doi.org/10.1007/978-3-030-39431-8_47

or stratum. The events picking of seismic record play a fundamental role, the accuracy of the result is directly related to the subsequent seismic data processing.

So far, there are lots of efficient events picking methods, but most of them divide up into four types. One is picked according to the instantaneous feature of the seismic record, such as maximum amplitude method and energy ratio method. The second type is picking events according to the global feature of the record, such as correlation method and constrained first arrival method. The third type is picking events by artificial intelligence method, such as artificial neural network method and fractal method. The last type is according to the edge detection method based on the principle of digital image processing.

Applying mathematical morphology to extract the events fall into the last category. The mathematical morphology is widely used in denoising, feature extraction, edge detection, image segmentation, object recognition, image restoration and reconstruction and other fields. It is based on the foundation of set theory. Its basic idea is to construct structure elements which have certain forms to match and extract the position of the corresponding shape in the image, and then analyze and identity the image. The mathematical morphology use the structure elements to 'detect' the signals, remain the main shape and delete the incoherent shapes. Mathematical morphology is based on the probe, which is similar to the human visual characteristics. The structure elements used as probes can carry the knowledges (shape, size, etc.) directly to detect the structure feature of the images.

The mathematical morphology is proposed by J. Serra and G. Matheron [1], which is named as 'Hit-or-Miss Transform'. Li [2] proposed the morphology operators introduced by threshold decomposition. This method processed the gray value image using the binary morphology, and constructed the morphology factors which have better real-time processing capability. Russo [3] proposed a color edge detection method. This method used different series structures in the color images to generate different color morphology. Sinha and Dougherty [4] introduced fuzziology into morphology to form fuzzy mathematical morphology. The images have complication and correlation, so it will occur imperfection and inaccuracy when processing the images. It will have better result in some cases when applying fuzzy set theory to the image processing. Koskinen [5] proposed soft morphological for filtering. This method introduced order statistics into morphology, instead the maximum minimum method using the sort weighted statistical method. Gasteratos [6] introduced fuzzy set theory into soft mathematical morphology and proposed fuzzy soft mathematical morphology. This method chosen fuzzy set operator, structure element corn and soft boundary definition domain according to image topological structure. Fabio [7] proposed non-linearity multiresolution analysis method which combining mathematical morphology and wavelet transformation. This method have better multiresolution analysis feature and anti-noise performance.

Mathematical morphology have applied to seismic exploration. Xie [8] studied mathematical morphology to suppress surface wave. After median filtering to original data, then suppressing surface wave with the proposed method, the noisy section became clean and the events of the reflection became more continuous. Li [9] proposed a method for noise attenuation by reducing the effect of noise using multiscale morphology. Features at various scales are extracted by means of morphological filtering.

Lu [10] applied the multi-structure adaptive morphological filter in the processing of seismic images. A research in using the technology of mathematical morphology filtering to improve SNR and resolution of the seismic data is carried out. Huang [11] studied image edge detection based on mathematical morphology and fuzzy mathematics. A new multiple order morphology edge detection algorithm based on partial fuzzy enhancement is proposed.

Events picking method using edge detection algorithm cannot use characteristics of wave motion. In this paper, we derive a multi-scale morphology to detect events of the pre/post-stack seismic data. The morphology is applied to the slant stacked peak amplitude (SSPA) section. The SSPA section make use of the instantaneous amplitude and can filter noise. The result can be used for tomography and interpretation. Another innovation is that comentropy and entity weighting are introduced to the image edge fusion. The picked events are more continuous and accurate than the existing method.

2 The Proposed Morphology Approach for Events Picking

The interpretation of 'visibility' and 'invisibility' standing on the angle of human biological vision and mentality can be understood as 'union' and 'intersection'. That is to say, we can understand the all visible things in reality as the set union of the things and the invisible things as the intersection of the things. Set-based is more appropriate than the analytic theory for the analysis and processing of the visual image. Mathematics morphology is based on the sets theory, so all the operation of the mathematics morphology is defined by union, intersection and complement. Define $f(x, y)$ as the input image, $g(i,j)$ is the structure element, $\oplus$ and Θ are the signs of the dilation and erosion operations individually. The dilation operation of the gray image is defined as:

$$f \oplus g = \max_{(i,j)}[f(x - i, y - j) + g(i,j)] \tag{1}$$

The erosion operation of the gray image is defined as:

$$f \Theta g = \min_{(i,j)}[f(x + i, y + j) - g(i,j)] \tag{2}$$

Dilation and erosion are not inverse, so they can be used in combination. Operating the erosion to the image and then operating the dilation to the image is called the unlock operation of the gray image, which is defined as:

$$f \circ g = (f \Theta g) \oplus g \tag{3}$$

Conversely, dilating the image and then eroding the image is called the close operation of the gray image, which is defined as:

$$f \bullet g = (f \oplus g) \Theta g \tag{4}$$

The unlock and close operation all can remove special image details which are smaller than the structure elements. The unlock operation can separate the images and the close operation can continue the images. The shape of the structure elements will affect the accuracy of the matching objective. For a given structure element g, it can be designed as eight matrix which is 5 × 5. The eight matrix $g_1 \sim g_8$ are:

$$\begin{bmatrix} 0 & 0 & 1 & 0 & 0 \\ 0 & 0 & 1 & 0 & 0 \\ 0 & 0 & 1 & 0 & 0 \\ 0 & 0 & 1 & 0 & 0 \\ 0 & 0 & 1 & 0 & 0 \end{bmatrix}, \begin{bmatrix} 0 & 0 & 0 & 0 & 0 \\ 0 & 0 & 0 & 0 & 0 \\ 1 & 1 & 1 & 1 & 1 \\ 0 & 0 & 0 & 0 & 0 \\ 0 & 0 & 0 & 0 & 0 \end{bmatrix}, \begin{bmatrix} 0 & 0 & 0 & 0 & 1 \\ 0 & 0 & 0 & 1 & 0 \\ 0 & 0 & 1 & 0 & 0 \\ 0 & 1 & 0 & 0 & 0 \\ 1 & 0 & 0 & 0 & 0 \end{bmatrix}, \begin{bmatrix} 1 & 0 & 0 & 0 & 0 \\ 0 & 1 & 0 & 0 & 0 \\ 0 & 0 & 1 & 0 & 0 \\ 0 & 0 & 0 & 1 & 0 \\ 0 & 0 & 0 & 0 & 1 \end{bmatrix}, \begin{bmatrix} 0 & 0 & 1 & 0 & 0 \\ 0 & 0 & 1 & 0 & 0 \\ 1 & 1 & 1 & 1 & 1 \\ 0 & 0 & 1 & 0 & 0 \\ 0 & 0 & 1 & 0 & 0 \end{bmatrix},$$
$$\begin{bmatrix} 1 & 1 & 1 & 1 & 0 \\ 0 & 0 & 0 & 0 & 1 \\ 0 & 0 & 0 & 0 & 0 \\ 0 & 0 & 0 & 0 & 0 \\ 0 & 0 & 0 & 0 & 0 \end{bmatrix}, \begin{bmatrix} 1 & 1 & 1 & 0 & 0 \\ 0 & 0 & 0 & 1 & 0 \\ 0 & 0 & 0 & 0 & 1 \\ 0 & 0 & 0 & 0 & 0 \\ 0 & 0 & 0 & 0 & 0 \end{bmatrix}, \begin{bmatrix} 1 & 1 & 0 & 0 & 0 \\ 0 & 0 & 1 & 0 & 0 \\ 0 & 0 & 0 & 1 & 0 \\ 0 & 0 & 0 & 0 & 1 \\ 0 & 0 & 0 & 0 & 0 \end{bmatrix} \tag{5}$$

$g_1 \sim g_5$ can match the horizontally layered medium and the fault, $g_6 \sim g_8$ can match the events with hyperbolic trend. Multi-scale structure element is defined as:

$$ng = g \oplus g \oplus \cdots \oplus g \tag{6}$$

Where, n is the scale parameter.

To reduce the influence of noise and improve the accuracy of the edge detection, it's necessary to detect the edge by applying structure elements with different scales and integrate the detected edges by weighting fusion. Multiscale edge detection formula is:

$$G_i^n = (f \circ ng_i) \oplus ng_i - (f \bullet ng_i)\Theta ng_i \tag{7}$$

Multiscale edge fusion formula is:

$$Gf^n = \sum_{i=1}^{K} u_i G_i^n \tag{8}$$

Where, u_i is the weighting coefficient used to fuse the edge detection images with different scales.

Information entropy can indicate the complexity and richness of the images, and can indicate the percentage of different edges. We can calculate the weighting and determine the fusion of the edge images by calculating the entropy contained in different scale edge images according to the principle of the weighting fusion. The quantity of information is:

$$-\log_2(P_0), -\log_2(P_1), \cdots, -\log_2(P_{L-1}) \tag{9}$$

Where, $P_0, P_1, \cdots, P_{L-1}$ is the probability of different level of gray image. The entropy of the record is:

$$H = -\sum_{i=0}^{L-1} P_i \log_2(P_i) \tag{10}$$

Distance can be taken to measure the similarity degree of the entities. The smaller the distances are, the more similar the two entities are. The entropy and the entity weighting are chosen to operate the edge fusion. The similarity degree of each entity is obtained by calculating the difference value (which is taken as the distance) of the entropy of each edge section. The difference value of edge section f_a and f_b is:

$$D(f_a, f_b) = |H(a) - H(b)| \quad a, b = 1, 2, 3, \cdots, n \tag{11}$$

Where, n is the number of scales. The function of difference values is:

$$FD(f_a, f_b) = \sum_{b=1}^{n} |H(a) - H(b)| \quad a, b = 1, 2, 3, \cdots, n \tag{12}$$

The inverse support function is:

$$SF(f_a) = \sum_{b=1}^{n} FD(f_a, f_b) \quad a, b = 1, 2, 3, \cdots, n \tag{13}$$

The real seismic record has lower signal to noise ratio, especially for pre-stacked data. We have proposed an edge detection analysis based on SSPA profiles for events picking in seismic data. Slant-stack is carried out because it serves as a filter and can reduce the noise. Because the instantaneous amplitude (IA) section has better quality than the seismic record, we obtain the SSPA profile by implying slant-stack transformation on the IA section [12, 13]. The IA section is calculated as follow:

$$a(t) = \|s(t) + i \cdot H[s(t)]\| \tag{1}$$

where $a(t)$ is instantaneous amplitude, $s(t)$ the trace of seismic data and $H[s(t)] = \mathrm{Im}[C_g^{-1} \int_{-\infty}^{+\infty} S(b, a) s^{-1} ds$ the Hilbert signal obtained from wavelet transformation (WT). Slant-stack is carried out using the local Radon transformation. It is applied on the IA section to stack several traces nearby the reference trace. In this way, we can construct a super-gather to increase the SNR. Calculate the sum of IA under different directions and record the results on the corresponding positions in the τ-p domain. When the chosen gradient for adding up is close or equal to the gradient of the event of the observed record, the added value is maximum in τ-p domain. Pick the maximal value of the slant stack amplitude data, which is called the SSPA, and record it on the corresponding position in t-x domain.

The flowchart of the proposed method is:

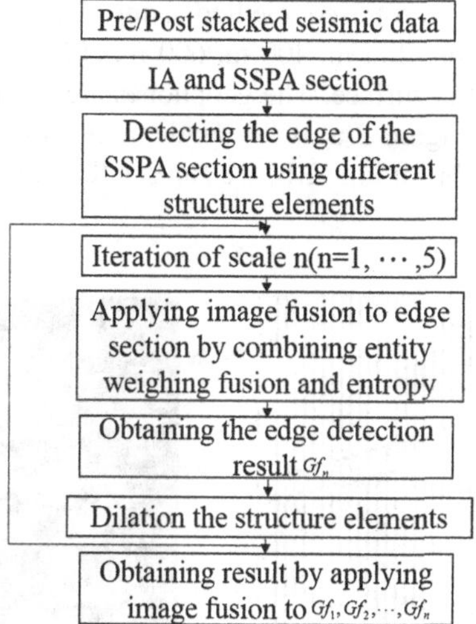

3 Experiments and Results

3.1 Synthetic Model

We test the proposed method using a synthetic model as shown in Fig. 1(a). Figure 1(b) is the result of edge detection. As shown in the figure, the mathematical morphology can precisely detect the edge line in different directions.

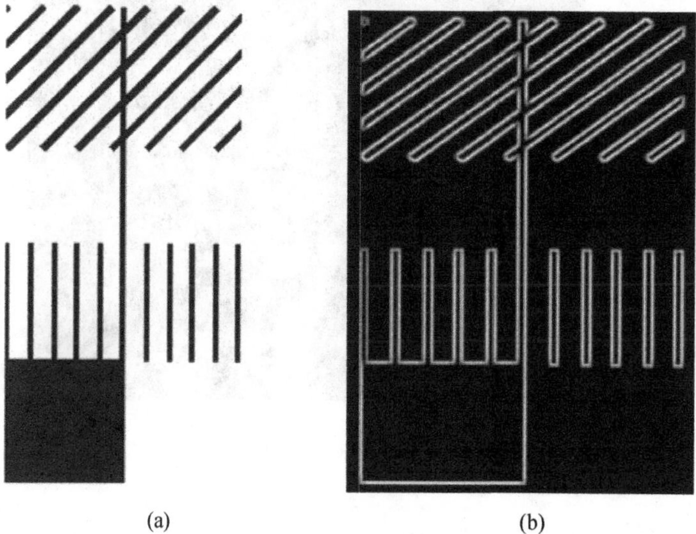

Fig. 1. (a) Original composite diagram; (b) Detected edge.

3.2 The Pre-stack Noisy Common Shotpoint (CSP) Gather Model

We test the validity of the proposed method using a pre-stack noisy CSP model. The SNR is 5. The depths are 200 m, 400 m, 600 m, 800 m, and 1000 m. The source is located at the origin of the surface. The geophones are located from 20 m to 500 m with the interval of 10 m. Figure 2(a) is the synthetic record of the 5 layers media and Fig. 2(b) is SSPA section. From Fig. 2(b) we can see that the SSPA section has higher

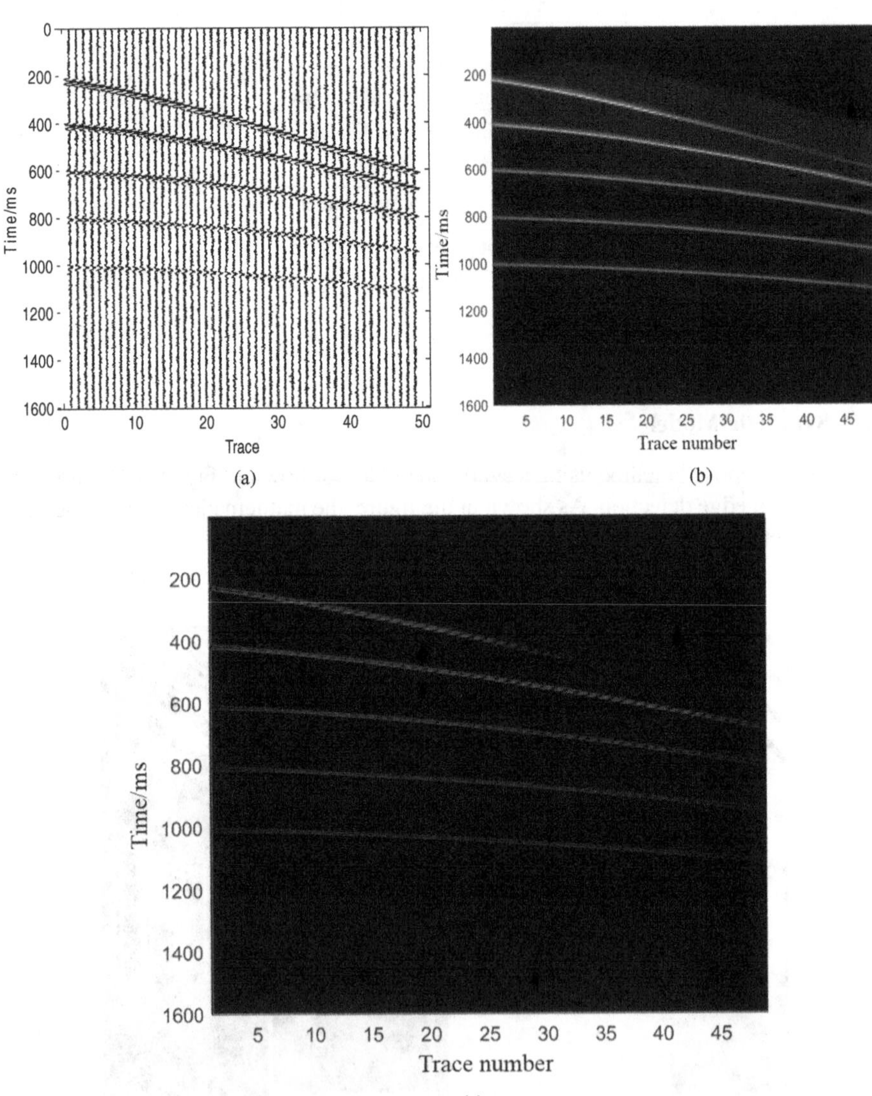

Fig. 2. (a) The synthetic pre-stack seismic data; (b) The SSPS section; (c) The events picking result by mathematical morphology.

SNR. This is because SSPA like a low-pass filter which can filter the high frequency noisy. Figure 2(c) is the detected events from SSPA section which is accurate and continuous, and correspond to the position of the events of the original data.

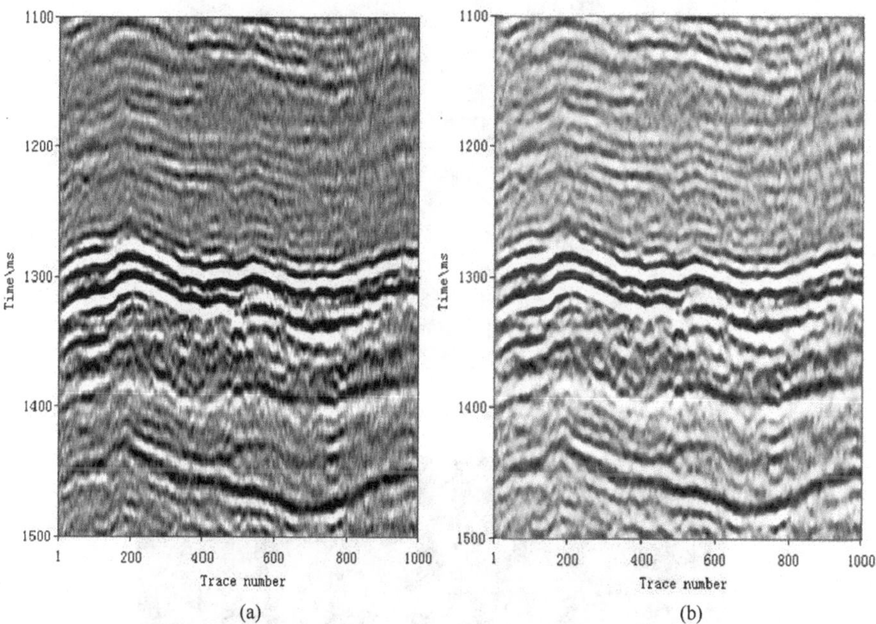

Fig. 3. (a) The real post-stack seismic data of oilfield; (b) The result by median filtering.

3.3 The Real Post-stack Seismic Reflection Record of the Oilfield

The last example is the real post-stack seismic data as shown in Fig. 3(a). The median filtering is operated firstly to reduce the noise. The filtering result is shown in Fig. 3(b) which indicate that partial noise is filtered. To improve the SNR further, we applied wavelet transform and Radon transform to the original data to obtain the SSPA section as shown in Fig. 4(a) which indicate that the section has higher SNR. Figure 4(b) is the detected events by mathematical morphology method. As can be seen from the diagram, the events near 1300 ms and 1450 ms can be detected accurately. The detected events are continuous and correspond to the original seismic record.

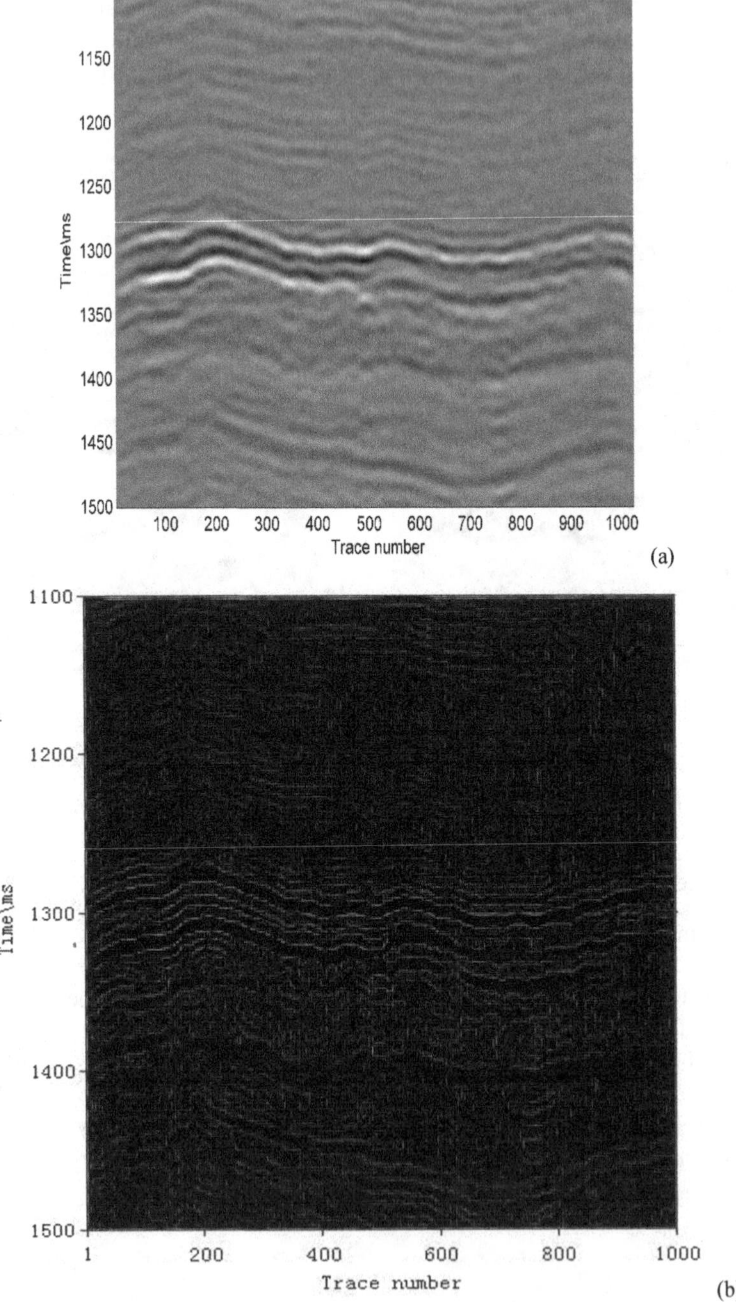

Fig. 4. (a) The SSPA section of the real record; (b) The detected events section based the SSPA section by mathematical morphology algorithm.

4 Conclusion

In this paper, we proposed a mathematical morphology algorithm that is suitable for the seismic events picking. Based on cognitive computing, the mathematical morphology was introduced into the SSPA section to reduce the noise, where eight structure elements with the size of 5×5 and weighing fusion based on the theory of entropy were proposed to improve the accuracy and computational efficiency. The proposed method was applied to events extraction for seismic interpretation and travel time picking. The new method has good feasibility, fast computation and high accuracy. Test results on three synthetic record and the real data indicate that this method has great potential to derive reliable seismic events, which may speed up the tomography and seismic interpretation. Compared with other classical events detection methods, our approach will be further improved along with the development of high performance computing.

For future work, we will explore new techniques for more reliable event extraction. These include approaches for image retrieval [14], spatiotemporal detection [15], optimization [16] and tracking [17]. In addition, deep learning models and saliency detection will also be investigated, following similar techniques as suggested in [18–20].

Acknowledgment. We thank National Natural Science Foundation of China (41604113), National Nature Science Foundation Project of International Cooperation (41711530128) and National Innovation and Entrepreneurship Training Program for College Students (201810705050) for their support.

References

1. Serra, J.: Image Analysis and Mathematical Morphology (1982). ISBN 0-12-637240-3
2. Li, L., Gao, Z., Huang, W.P.: A novel kind of morphological operators induced by threshold decomposition. Opt. Tech. **27**(1), 74–81 (2001)
3. Russo, F., Lazzari, A.: Color edge detection in presence of Gaussian noise using nonlinear prefiltering. IEEE Trans. Instrum. Meas. **54**(1), 352–358 (2005)
4. Sinha, D., Dougherty, E.R.: Fuzzy mathematical morphology. J. Vis. Commun. Image Represent. **3**(3), 286–302 (1992)
5. Koskinen, L., Astola, J.T., Neuvo, Y.A.: Soft morphological filters. In: Proceedings of SPIE - The International Society for Optical Engineering, vol. 1568 (1991)
6. Gasteratos, A., Andreadis, I., Tsalides, P.: Fuzzy soft mathematical morphology. In: IEE Proceedings of Vision, Image and Signal Processing, vol. 145, no. 1, p. 41 (1998)
7. Lazzaroni, F., Leonardi, R., Signoroni, A.: High-performance embedded morphological wavelet coding. IEEE Signal Process. Lett. **10**(10), 293–295 (2003)
8. Xie, J.: Several digital techniques and their application for optimizing quality of seismic data. Ph.D. thesis, Jilin University (2009)
9. Li, L.: The application of mathematical morphology in seismic data processing. Ph.D. thesis, China University of Petroleum (2005)
10. Lu, H.: The application of multi-structure adaptive morphological filter in processing of seismic images. Ph.D. thesis, Chengdu University of Technology (2012)

11. Huang, H.: The research and application of mathematical morphology in image edge detection and machine vision. Ph.D. thesis, Dongbei University (2012)
12. Zhao, J., Ren, J., Gao, J., et al.: Automatic events extraction in pre-stack seismic data based on edge detection in slant-stacked peak amplitude profiles. J. Petrol. Sci. Eng. **178**, 459–499 (2019)
13. Zhao, J., Ren, J., et al.: Cognitive seismic data modelling based successive differential evolution algorithm for effective exploration of oil-gas reservoirs. J. Petrol. Sci. Eng. **171**, 1159–1170 (2018)
14. Zhou, Y., et al.: Hierarchical visual perception and two-dimensional compressive sensing for effective content-based color image retrieval. Cogn. Comput. **8**(5), 877–889 (2016)
15. Ren, J., Vlachos, T.: Efficient detection of temporally impulsive dirt impairments in archived films. Sig. Process. **87**(3), 541–551 (2007)
16. Sun, G., et al.: A stability constrained adaptive alpha for gravitational search algorithm. Knowl. Based Syst. **139**, 200–213 (2018)
17. Ren, J., et al.: Multi-camera video surveillance for real-time analysis and reconstruction of soccer games. Mach. Vis. Appl. **21**(6), 855–863 (2010)
18. Wang, Z., et al.: A deep-learning based feature hybrid framework for spatiotemporal saliency detection inside videos. Neurocomputing **287**, 68–83 (2018)
19. Han, J., et al.: Background prior-based salient object detection via deep reconstruction residual. IEEE Trans. Circuits Syst. Video Technol. **25**(8), 1309–1321 (2014)
20. Yan, Y., et al.: Unsupervised image saliency detection with Gestalt-laws guided optimization and visual attention based refinement. Pattern Recogn. **79**, 65–78 (2018)

PerSent 2.0: Persian Sentiment Lexicon Enriched with Domain-Specific Words

Kia Dashtipour[1](✉), Ali Raza[2], Alexander Gelbukh[3], Rui Zhang[4], Erik Cambria[5], and Amir Hussain[6]

[1] Department of Computing Science and Mathematics, Faculty of Natural Sciences, University of Stirling, Stirling FK9 4LA, UK
kd28@cs.stir.ac.uk

[2] Department of Electrical Engineering and Computing, Rochester Institute of Technology, Dubai, UAE

[3] Instituto Politécnico Nacional, Mexico City, Mexico

[4] Electrical and Electronic Engineering, Xi'an Jiaotong Liverpool University, Suzhou, China

[5] School of Computer Science and Engineering, Nanyang Technological University, 50 Nanyang Drive, Singapore, Singapore

[6] School of Computing, Edinburgh Napier University, Merchiston Campus, Edinburgh EH10 5DT, Scotland, UK

Abstract. Sentiment analysis is probably the most actively growing area of natural language processing nowadays, which leverages huge amount of user-contributed data on Internet to improve income of businesses and quality of life of consumer. The majority of existent sentiment-analysis systems is focused on English, due to lack of resources and tools for other languages. To fill this gap for Persian language, in our previous work we have compiled the first version of PerSent Persian sentiment lexicon, which was small and included only words and phrases from general domain. In this paper, we present its extension with words from three different domains and evaluate its performance on polarity classification task using various machine learning-based classifiers. We use a multi-domain dataset to evaluate the performance of our new lexicon on various domains. Our results demonstrate usefulness of the new lexicon for analysis of product and movie reviews and especially of political news in Persian language.

Keywords: Persian · Sentiment analysis · Machine learning

1 Introduction

The advent of the social networks, blogs and websites allows Internet users to share their views, content, ideas and opinions with millions of people connected to the World Wide Web [7,11]. This information has benefits for companies, because they can understand the public opinion about their products and services. It is also in the interest of large public institutions to collect, retrieve and

J. Ren et al. (Eds.): BICS 2019, LNAI 11691, pp. 497–509, 2020.
https://doi.org/10.1007/978-3-030-39431-8_48

correctly interpret user-contributed information [16,20]. Most importantly, the huge amount of user-generated contents in Internet is successfully exploited to help the consumers to make informed buying decisions: when we want to buy a product, we need to know what experience other users had with this product. According to a research on the buying behaviour of Internet users, 60% of American users search for product reviews before buying [9,22].

To use this information, we need to be able to distinguish what is important and interesting. In the new information age, where opinion and thoughts are shared through social networks, tools which can understand the content are becoming important [12,13].

Sentiment analysis a set of techniques used to analyse people's opinions, views, sentiments, evaluations, appraisals, behaviour and emotions towards entities such as the product or services. Sentiment analysis is mainly focused on detection of polarity: whether the user's opinion towards the product is positive or negative [21]. Using sentiment analysis technology, it is possible to classify the reviews basing on their polarity or even specific emotions expressed in the review, such as anger, happiness, or sadness [19].

A wide range of tools and resources for sentiment analysis have been developed. However, the majority of these resources are for the English language, while considerably smaller amount of resources is available for other languages. Specifically, until recently there were no sentiment analysis resources available for Persian language, one of major languages with 54 million speakers. To fill this gap, we have developed the Persian lexicon called PerSent. In its first version, the lexicon contained has 1500 Persian words, along with their part-of-speech (POS) tag and sentiment polarity [15]. The polarity of each word was set manually as a real number in the interval from -1 to $+1$, where -1 corresponds to very negative polarity and $+1$ corresponds to very positive polarity.

A disadvantage of the first version of the PerSent lexicon was its small size: for the Persian language, with its various dialects, 1500-word lexicon is far too small. In addition, that version included only words of general domain, which did not reflect the lexicon used in domains for which sentiment analysis is typically used. Accordingly, in this paper we present an extended version of the PerSent Persian sentiment lexicon, PerSent 2.0, and evaluate its performance on different datasets and different domains. Specifically, this new version includes a large number of entries from the news, product, and movie domains.

The paper is organised as follows. Section 2 discusses the related work on sentiment lexicons for English and for other languages. Section 3 describes the methodology we followed to extend our lexicon. Section 4 presents our evaluation methodology. Section 5 gives the experimental results. Finally, Sect. 6 concludes the paper.

2 Related Work

Sentiment analysis techniques can be classified into lexicon-based techniques, machine learning-based techniques, and hybrid techniques. In this paper, we are interested in lexicon-based techniques and, specifically, in lexicons available for sentiment analysis of English and other languages.

2.1 English Lexicons

When people communicate, they share their background knowledge to understand each other more effectively. This is called common-sense knowledge. The Open Mind corpus project has been collecting this kind of information from volunteers to use it for research purposes. The resulting corpus is called ConceptNet [7]. In ConceptNet network, nodes are connected by edges which are labelled with common-sense assertions: for example, the concepts "person" and "cook" are connected by the assertion "capable of cooking".

SenticNet [10] is a sentiment resource based on a multi-disciplinary approach involving common-sense information, which is used for sentiment analysis and opinion mining. It provides positive or negative polarity for concepts (multi-word expressions) in the form of a real number. Unlike other lexicons, it does not have a label for neutral polarity. SenticNet has been used for sentiment analysis at sentence and document levels [8].

SentiSense [3] is a lexicon for polarity and intensify classification and emotion detection, where words are labelled basing on the emotions associated with them. Since words can act as subjective or objective depending on the sense, which is determined by the context, SentiSense associates polarity with a specific sense of the word, corresponding to a WordNet synset. WordNet-affect [6] is a small lexical resource that contains details about the emotions expressed by words and phrases. WordNet-affect presents a hierarchy for labels of the domain. It also uses WordNet synsets to denote the affective concepts, which are the words of phrases that express some emotion. Some of them express the emotions directly, such as "sad", "happy", etc., while other words express emotions implicitly through mentions of attitude, behaviour, physical states, etc. WordNet-affect uses six different emotion labels (joy, anger, fear, sadness, disgust and surprise) to classify words and phrases.

SentiWordNet [4] is a large lexicon, also based on WordNet synsets, which classifies the words and phrases into positive, negative, or objective. Table 1 summarizes notable lexicons available for the English language.

2.2 Lexicons for Other Languages

Urdu is becoming popular in Internet as more people share their opinion and sentiment in this language. Syed et al. [28] introduced a lexicon for the Urdu language. In the lexicon, they considered single words and multiword expressions such as "nice boy". It was evaluated on online reviews, achieving overall accuracy of 72%.

Al-Moslmi et al. [2] developed a lexicon for Arabic language. The lexicon contains 8860 positive and negative words and phrases along with their POS tag and manually assigned positive or negative sentiment score. Various machine learning-based classifiers were used to evaluate the performance of this lexicon,

Table 1. English lexicons

Reference	Name	Domain	Comments
[9]	SenticNet	Multi-domain	100,000 words and phrases annotated with polarity and emotion
[3]	SentiSense	Multi-domain	5,496 words annotated with emotions
[6]	WordNet-affect	Multi-domain	Only emotion labels
[25]	Opinion Observer	Multi-domain	It contains 6,8000 positive and negative words
[3]	SentiWordNet	Multi-domain	117,695 words and phrases labelled as positive, negative, or objective
[24]	AFINN	Multi-domain	It contains 2,477 word forms, which were converted into positive and negative
[17]	Hedonomete	Multi-domain	It contains 10,000 words extracted from tweets

SVM providing better results in comparison with other classifiers. The overall performance of a system based on this lexicon was 86.87%.

Abdulla et al. [1] automatically developed a lexicon for Arabic language. The lexicon was developed for standard language such as Arabic language used in newspaper and media. First 300 words were collected from SentiWordNet; then the new words are added automatically, with polarity set based on the existing words. The overall performance of the approach was 74.6%.

Sharma et al. [27] developed a sentiment lexicon for Hindi. The lexicon contains nouns, verbs, adjectives and adverbs along with polarity assigned manually. A method has been proposed to detect words with incorrect polarity orientation, because some words are associated with both positive and negative sentiment. The overall performance of this approach was 87%.

Remus et al. [26] developed a German lexicon, which lists words along their polarity, POS tag and infections. In this German lexicon, the adjectives and adverbs are assigned polarity labels, but nouns and verbs are not considered to imply any polarity. In order to calculate the polarity of a word, the following equation was used:

$$SO - A(w) = \sum_{(p \in P)} A(w,p) \sum_{(n \in N)} A(w,n). \tag{1}$$

where SO-A(w) is the semantic orientation of the word w measured via association, A(w,n) is association between two words, and P and N are manually selected sets of positive and negative words, respectively. The proposed lexicon was shown to have high accuracy and to give good results.

Yang et al. [29] developed a lexicon for Chinese sentiment analysis. They developed a new algorithm to detect the polarity of Chinese words in the sentence. The lexicon provided performance of 92.40%. Table 2 summarizes major sentiment lexicons available for languages other than English.

Table 2. Non-English lexicons

Reference	Name	Domain	Language	Comments
Syed et al. [28]	SentiUnits	Multi-domain	Urdu	Only nouns and adjectives
Al-Moslmi et al. [2]	Arabic Senti	Multi-domain	Arabic	Different domains: fashion, hotels, restaurants, politics etc.
Abdulla et al. [1]	Automatic Arabic lexicon	Multi-domain	Arabic	300 words and phrases translated
Sharma et al. [27]	Hindi Senti	Products and movies reviews	Hindi	8706 words and phrases along with POS tag and polarity
Remus et al. [26]	SentiWS	Multi-domain	German	1,818 positive and 1,650 negative words
Yang et al. [29]	Chinese Sentiment	Multi-domain	Chinese	4,000 words

3 PerSent 2.0 Persian Sentiment Lexicon

The main problem of the first version of the PerSent Persian sentiment lexicon was its small size and the lack of words specific for those domains for which sentiment analysis is especially useful. To overcome this issue, we developed a next version of PerSent, enriched with words and phrases from three domains: news, movies, and products. The POS tags such as adjective, adverb, verb and noun are also important to process sentences in Persian language, so in our lexicon we give the POS tags for its entries.

We collected words and phrases from different online sources, which reflect different domains such as news, movies and products. For the news domain, we used more than one hundred news articles from www.bbc.com/persian to collect words and phrases from both headlines of news and the main content of the articles. For the movie domain, we used one hundred articles from the site www.caffecinema.com, where different writers present articles about movies they have watched. For the product domain, we used the contents of the site www.mobile.ir, which provides latest technology news about mobile phones and updated daily with new articles.

We processed the articles from these websites with JHAZM, a Java toolkit for stemming, normalisation, POS tagging and dependency parsing [23]. This toolkit is available online to download (https://libraries.io/github/mojtaba-khallash). Specifically, we used the JHAZM POS tagger to tag adjectives, adverbs, nouns and verbs; words of other parts of speech such as determiners were discarded because we do not include them in PerSent.

At the next step, three annotators manually assigned polarity to the new words and phrases. The annotators were educated native speakers of Persian speakers; two of them were 50 to 60 years old and one was 30 years old. They assign polarity to words and phrases as a real number between −1 and +1. Initially, only two annotators assigned the polarity to each word or phrase. Then the cases when these two annotators significantly disagreed were detected, as well as the cases when words or phrases similar in their meaning were assigned significantly different values. For these words, the third annotator assigned the final polarity. For example, the two annotators did not agree on the polarity of the words ضعیف (poor) and بد (bad); then the third annotator decided that the word is ضعیف (poor) is more negative in comparison with the word بد (bad).

The final lexicon gives for each word or phrase its POS tag, polarity sign, and polarity score. Table 3 provides examples of entries of the PerSent 2.0 lexicon (translation is added to the table for convenience of the reader and is not part of the PerSent lexicon).

Table 3. Sample entries of PerSent 2.0

Word	Translation	POS	Polarity	Score	Domain
لحضه خوش	Good time	Noun	POS	+0.7	Movie
فیلم درجه سوم	Third class movie	ADJ	Neg	–0.5	Movie
اسان براي استفاده	Easy to use	ADJ	POS	+0.4	Product
کیفیت تصویري بد	Poor Quality	ADJ	Neg	-0.6	Product
پیسرفت سیاسي	Political Progress	Noun	POS	+0.5	News
شکنجه	Torture	Noun	Neg	–0.6	News

Tables 4 and 5 show the distribution of entries of the lexicon by POS tags and domains, correspondingly. In the latter table, general-domain entries are the entries from the first version of our lexicon and other domains are new in this version. As to the language register, 94% of entries of our lexicon are formal words, for example, زیبا (beautiful), خوب (nice), and 6% are informal, such as جالب (cool), ارزان (cheap).

Table 4. Statistics of POS tags in our lexicon

POS tag	Entries
Adjectives	1483
Nouns	856
Verbs	456
Adverbs	205

Table 5. Statistics of the entries of our lexicon by domain

Domain	Enteries	Example
General	1500	زیبا Beatiful
News	840	شکنجه Torture
Movies	430	فیلم درجه سوم Third Class movie
Products	230	آسان برای استفاده کردن Easy to use

4 Evaluation Methodology

In order to evaluate the performance of the new PerSent 2.0 lexicon, we used two different machine-learning algorithms: SVM and Naïve Bayes. Figure 1 shows our evaluation framework, which consists of the following processing steps.

Pre-processing included various stages, such as tokenisation, normalisation, stemming and stop-words removal:

- Tokenisation: Tokenisation is the process of breaking the text into individual tokens, such as words, numbers etc. For example, فیلم زیبای بود (it was nice movie) was broken down to بود (was), زیبای (beauty) فیلم (movie).
- Normalisation: Text normalisation is used to convert numbers, dates and abbreviations into a standard form, in our case textual strings. For example, من ۲۰۰۰ تا بلیط خریدم (I bought 2000 tickets) was converted into من دو هزار تا بلیط خریدم (I bought two thousand tickets).
- Stemming: Stemming is the process of reducing various morphological forms of words to the main dictionary form. For example, رفتن (going) was changed to رفت (go); خودرو زیبای داشتید (your car was beautiful) was changed to خودرو زیبا داشت (your car is beautiful) (Dickinson et al. 2015).
- Stop-word removal: It is important to remove some words before processing the text: some words are too common and at the same time they do not

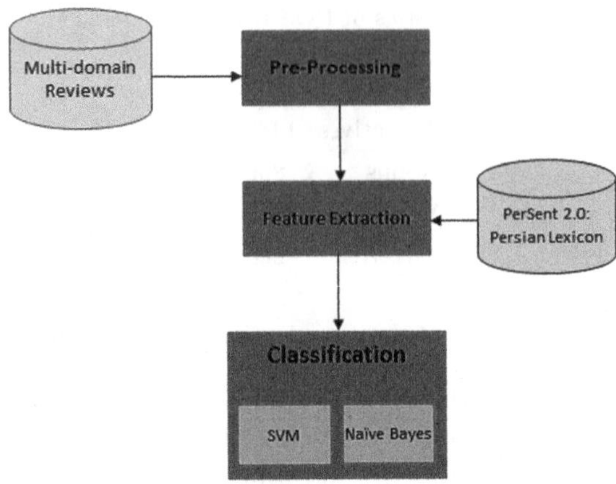

Fig. 1. Persian framework

express any polarity, for example, به (to), از (from), etc. Filtering these words out has positive impact on the overall performance of the system [14].

Feature Selection: Feature selection or variable selection is the process of selecting appropriate features to build the model for machine-learning methods in order to save training time, to reduce overfitting and to simplify the model to make it easier for research and interpretation. Table 6 presents the features we used. The PerSent lexicon gives the POS for the entries as well as their polarity.

Table 6. Feature selection

Category	Features
POS-specific features	Frequency of positive and negative nouns
	Frequency of positive and negative adjectives
	Frequency of positive and negative adverbs
	Frequency of positive and negative verbs
Presence and frequency of words	Frequency of positive words
	Frequency of negative words
	Presence of positive words
	Presence of negative words
Polarity of words	Overall polarity of positive words
	Overall polarity of negative words

5 Results and Discussion

We evaluated our lexicon on three different datasets. The first one was a Persian movie review dataset. To compile this dataset, we collected 500 positive and 500 negative movie reviews from the sites www.cinematicket.org and www.caffecinema.com, for the period from 2012 to 2016. The second one was the Voice of America (VOA) Persian headline news. The dataset, belonging to the Voice of America's Persian service, is available online; it also contains 500 positive and 500 negative headline news [5]. The third one was a dataset of cell-phone reviews, also of 500 positive and 500 negative reviews [5].

As the measure of the performance of the system we used accuracy:

$$Accuracy = \frac{Number\ of\ correctly\ classified\ instances}{Total\ number\ of\ instances\ to\ classify} \tag{2}$$

Table 7. Evaluation results

Features used	Naive Bayes			SVM		
	News	Movie	Phone	News	Movie	Phone
Freq. of positive and negative nouns	74.20	69.70	64.20	75.50	70.90	66.80
Freq of positive and negative adjectives	76.30	70.10	66.30	78.60	71.50	68.40
Freq. of positive and negative verbs	71.60	67.30	63.50	74.20	68.90	65.20
Freq. of positive and negative adverbs	72.60	63.80	63.10	70.20	65.40	64.70
All POS-specific features	77.50	64.20	67.40	79.70	72.10	69.60
Freq. of positive words	69.50	61.80	63.80	70.20	64.80	64.20
Freq. of negative words	67.40	61.40	62.70	68.70	63.70	63.10
Presence of positive words	72.60	68.20	65.80	74.40	69.50	67.30
Presence of negative words	70.20	65.30	63.50	71.50	68.30	64.60
All frequency-related features	73.90	70.60	67.70	75.30	71.30	69.10
Overall polarity	79.60	71.40	69.80	**81.30**	**74.50**	**70.80**

To evaluate the performance of the PerSent 2.0 lexicon, we trained SVM and Naïve Bayes classifiers. To train a classifier, the features listed in Table 6 were extracted from each document in the dataset and fed into classifier along with the polarity indicated in the dataset for the given document. Evaluation was conducted with tenfold cross-validation. Table 7 shows the results for different datasets.

As expected, SVM obtained better accuracy than Naïve Bayes. Our results also show that on the VOA Persian headline news dataset we obtained better results in comparison with product reviews and movie reviews datasets. The VOA Persian headline news mostly contains words of formal register. In contrast, the Persian movie reviews and product reviews contain words from many dialects, slang and informal words. The current version of our lexicon does not contain these types of words. Still, the new version of our Persian lexicon gave better results in comparison with previous versions of the lexicon. Table 8 shows the results for different datasets using PerSent lexicon (Previous version). The result shows the PerSent lexicon received lower accuracy in compare with PerSent 2.0 (Table 8).

Table 8. Comparison results

Features used	Naive Bayes			SVM		
	News	Movie	Phone	News	Movie	Phone
Freq. of positive and negative nouns	65.40	63.40	58.70	67.30	65.60	64.10
Freq. of positive and negative adjectives	65.70	64.50	59.30	68.70	66.50	65.90
Freq. of positive and negative verbs	63.90	62.70	56.10	66.50	64.20	63.40
Freq. of positive and negative adverbs	64.20	63.10	57.60	66.90	63.80	63.30
All POS-specific features	66.10	65.20	60.30	70.10	66.90	66.30
Freq. of positive words	63.20	61.30	54.20	65.30	63.10	62.80
Freq. of negative words	61.50	60.90	53.60	64.10	62.70	62.50
Presence of positive words	63.50	61.80	56.70	65.80	63.60	63.10
Presence of negative words	62.80	61.30	56.10	65.20	63.40	62.90
All frequency-related features	64.20	62.90	57.90	66.40	63.90	63.90
Overall polarity	68.70	65.30	61.50	72.60	70.30	69.80

Adjectives gave better results in comparison with words of other parts of speech such as nouns, verbs and adverbs, because in Persian language adjectives more typically express polarity in comparison with adverbs, nouns and verbs.

Some sentences in the datasets contained English adjectives and abbreviations, especially in the product review and movie review datasets. Our lexicon does not contain any English words and phrases, and in our implementation, we did not use English lexicons to handle such cases, though a system based on lexicons for several languages could correctly process such sentences. In addition, in these experiments we did not handle negation and other valence shifters. There were some sentences in the datasets that contained negation, for example, امروز روز خوبي براي خط هواي نبود (Today, it was not good day for airline), so our system classified this sentence wrongly. These issues are limitations not of the lexicon itself but only of our evaluation procedure.

However, in addition to English words, the cell-phone reviews contain many technical words and abbreviations, for example, "finger touch feature", which are absent in our lexicon. We plan to extend our lexicon with such expressions in our future work.

6 Conclusion

We have presented an extended version of our PerSent sentiment lexicon, enriched with words and phrases specific for three different domains. This new version of the lexicon contains 3000 words and phrases along with their polarity between -1 to $+1$ as well as their part-of-speech tag.

We evaluated our new lexicon on three datasets belonging to three different domains. We obtained better results on the dataset of Persian headline news. Our experimental results show that the new lexicon is a useful tool for analysing Persian political news and gives good results when used to analyse product and movie reviews. In our experiments, we used two different classifiers: SVM and Naïve Bayes; as expected, SVM gave better results. The new lexicon is freely available for download once the paper has been accepted from the URL http://www.gelbukh.com/resources/persent.

In our future work, we plan to develop a multilingual lexicon, since some reviews from our test datasets contain code-mixed text, such as a mixture of Persian and English words. We also plan to extend our lexicon with additional words and domains, and employ sparse deep learning [18]s and reinforcement learning algorithms to compare with current benchmarks.

References

1. Abdulla, N., Mohammed, S., Al-Ayyoub, M., Al-Kabi, M., et al.: Automatic lexicon construction for Arabic sentiment analysis. In: 2014 International Conference on Future Internet of Things and Cloud (FiCloud), pp. 547–552. IEEE (2014)
2. Al-Moslmi, T., Albared, M., Al-Shabi, A., Omar, N., Abdullah, S.: Arabic senti-lexicon: constructing publicly available language resources for Arabic sentiment analysis. J. Inf. Sci. **44**(3), 345–362 (2018)
3. de Albornoz, J.C., Plaza, L., Gervás, P.: SentiSense: an easily scalable concept-based affective lexicon for sentiment analysis. In: LREC, pp. 3562–3567 (2012)
4. Baccianella, S., Esuli, A., Sebastiani, F.: SentiWordNet 3.0: an enhanced lexical resource for sentiment analysis and opinion mining. In: LREC, vol. 10, pp. 2200–2204 (2010)
5. Basiri, M.E., Naghsh-Nilchi, A.R., Ghassem-Aghaee, N.: A framework for sentiment analysis in Persian. Open Trans. Inf. Process. **1**(3), 1–14 (2014)
6. Bobicev, V., Maxim, V., Prodan, T., Burciu, N., Angheluş, V.: Emotions in words: developing a multilingual wordnet-affect. In: Gelbukh, A. (ed.) CICLing 2010. LNCS, vol. 6008, pp. 375–384. Springer, Heidelberg (2010). https://doi.org/10.1007/978-3-642-12116-6_31
7. Cambria, E., Havasi, C., Hussain, A.: SenticNet 2: a semantic and affective resource for opinion mining and sentiment analysis. In: FLAIRS Conference, pp. 202–207 (2012)
8. Cambria, E., Poria, S., Bajpai, R., Schuller, B.: SenticNet 4: a semantic resource for sentiment analysis based on conceptual primitives. In: Proceedings of COLING 2016, the 26th International Conference on Computational Linguistics: Technical Papers, pp. 2666–2677 (2016)

9. Cambria, E., Poria, S., Hazarika, D., Kwok, K.: SenticNet 5: discovering conceptual primitives for sentiment analysis by means of context embeddings. In: Proceedings of AAAI (2018)
10. Cambria, E., Speer, R., Havasi, C., Hussain, A.: SenticNet: a publicly available semantic resource for opinion mining. In: AAAI Fall Symposium: Commonsense Knowledge, vol. 10 (2010)
11. Dashtipour, K., Gogate, M., Adeel, A., Algarafi, A., Howard, N., Hussain, A.: Persian named entity recognition. In: 2017 IEEE 16th International Conference on Cognitive Informatics & Cognitive Computing (ICCI* CC), pp. 79–83. IEEE (2017)
12. Dashtipour, K., Gogate, M., Adeel, A., Hussain, A., Alqarafi, A., Durrani, T.: A comparative study of Persian sentiment analysis based on different feature combinations. In: Liang, Q., Mu, J., Jia, M., Wang, W., Feng, X., Zhang, B. (eds.) CSPS 2017. LNEE, vol. 463, pp. 2288–2294. Springer, Singapore (2019). https://doi.org/10.1007/978-981-10-6571-2_279
13. Dashtipour, K., Gogate, M., Adeel, A., Ieracitano, C., Larijani, H., Hussain, A.: Exploiting deep learning for Persian sentiment analysis. In: Ren, J., et al. (eds.) BICS 2018. LNCS (LNAI), vol. 10989, pp. 597–604. Springer, Cham (2018). https://doi.org/10.1007/978-3-030-00563-4_58
14. Dashtipour, K., Hussain, A., Gelbukh, A.: Adaptation of sentiment analysis techniques to Persian language. In: Gelbukh, A. (ed.) CICLing 2017. LNCS, vol. 10762, pp. 129–140. Springer, Cham (2018). https://doi.org/10.1007/978-3-319-77116-8_10
15. Dashtipour, K., Hussain, A., Zhou, Q., Gelbukh, A., Hawalah, A.Y.A., Cambria, E.: PerSent: a freely available Persian sentiment lexicon. In: Liu, C.-L., Hussain, A., Luo, B., Tan, K.C., Zeng, Y., Zhang, Z. (eds.) BICS 2016. LNCS (LNAI), vol. 10023, pp. 310–320. Springer, Cham (2016). https://doi.org/10.1007/978-3-319-49685-6_28
16. Dashtipour, K., et al.: Multilingual sentiment analysis: state of the art and independent comparison of techniques. Cogn. Comput. **8**(4), 757–771 (2016)
17. Dodds, P.S., Harris, K.D., Kloumann, I.M., Bliss, C.A., Danforth, C.M.: Temporal patterns of happiness and information in a global social network: hedonometrics and Twitter. PloS One **6**(12), e26752 (2011)
18. Gogate, M., Adeel, A., Hussain, A.: Deep learning driven multimodal fusion for automated deception detection. In: 2017 IEEE Symposium Series on Computational Intelligence (SSCI), pp. 1–6. IEEE (2017)
19. Gogate, M., Adeel, A., Hussain, A.: A novel brain-inspired compression-based optimised multimodal fusion for emotion recognition. In: 2017 IEEE Symposium Series on Computational Intelligence (SSCI), pp. 1–7. IEEE (2017)
20. Ieracitano, C., et al.: Statistical analysis driven optimized deep learning system for intrusion detection. In: Ren, J., et al. (eds.) BICS 2018. LNCS (LNAI), vol. 10989, pp. 759–769. Springer, Cham (2018). https://doi.org/10.1007/978-3-030-00563-4_74
21. Ieracitano, C., Mammone, N., Bramanti, A., Hussain, A., Morabito, F.C.: A convolutional neural network approach for classification of dementia stages based on 2D-spectral representation of EEG recordings. Neurocomputing **323**, 96–107 (2019)
22. Ieracitano, C., Panto, F., Mammone, N., Paviglianiti, A., Frontera, P., Morabito, F.C.: Towards an automatic classification of SEM images of nanomaterial via a deep learning approach. In: Multidisciplinary Approaches to Neural Computing, in press

23. Khallash, M., Hadian, A., Minaei-Bidgoli, B.: An empirical study on the effect of morphological and lexical features in Persian dependency parsing. In: Proceedings of the Fourth Workshop on Statistical Parsing of Morphologically-Rich Languages, pp. 97–107 (2013)
24. Koto, F., Adriani, M.: A comparative study on twitter sentiment analysis: which features are good? In: Biemann, C., Handschuh, S., Freitas, A., Meziane, F., Métais, E. (eds.) NLDB 2015. LNCS, vol. 9103, pp. 453–457. Springer, Cham (2015). https://doi.org/10.1007/978-3-319-19581-0_46
25. Liu, B., Hu, M., Cheng, J.: Opinion observer: analyzing and comparing opinions on the web. In: Proceedings of the 14th International Conference on World Wide Web, pp. 342–351. ACM (2005)
26. Remus, R., Quasthoff, U., Heyer, G.: SentiWS - a publicly available German-language resource for sentiment analysis. In: LREC (2010)
27. Sharma, R., Bhattacharyya, P.: A sentiment analyzer for Hindi using Hindi senti lexicon. In: Proceedings of the 11th International Conference on Natural Language Processing, pp. 150–155 (2014)
28. Syed, A.Z., Aslam, M., Martinez-Enriquez, A.M.: Lexicon based sentiment analysis of Urdu text using SentiUnits. In: Sidorov, G., Hernández Aguirre, A., Reyes García, C.A. (eds.) MICAI 2010. LNCS (LNAI), vol. 6437, pp. 32–43. Springer, Heidelberg (2010). https://doi.org/10.1007/978-3-642-16761-4_4
29. Yang, C., Lin, K.H.Y., Chen, H.H.: Building emotion lexicon from weblog corpora. In: Proceedings of the 45th Annual Meeting of the ACL on Interactive Poster and Demonstration Sessions, pp. 133–136. Association for Computational Linguistics (2007)

Real Time Detection of Surface Defects with Inception-Based MobileNet-SSD Detection Network

Jianwen Zhou[1,2,3], Wenjing Zhao[4], Lei Guo[5], Xinying Xu[1], and Gang Xie[1,6(✉)]

[1] College of Electrical and Power Engineering, Taiyuan University of Technology, Taiyuan 030024, China
xiegang@tyut.edu.cn

[2] Shanxi Key Laboratory of Advanced Control and Intelligent Information System, Taiyuan 030024, China

[3] Engineering Research Center for Key Technologies of Flat Panel Display Intelligent Manufacturing Equipment, Taiyuan University of Science and Technology, Taiyuan 030024, China

[4] Engineering Training Center, Taiyuan University of Technology, Taiyuan 030024, China

[5] College of Information and Computer, Taiyuan University of Technology, Taiyuan 030024, China

[6] College of Electronic Information Engineering, Taiyuan University of Science and Technology, Taiyuan 030024, China

Abstract. Effective surface defect detection are of great significance for the production of high quality products. Aiming at real-time detection of surface defect, we propose a reusable and high-efficiency Inception-based MobileNet-SSD method for surface defect inspection in industrial environment. First, convolutional layers for feature extraction used in SSD were replaced by depthwise separable convolutions utilized in MobileNet so that the speed of the network can be faster. Then, the layer in the base network as convolutional feature layer is constructed as Inception which can extract more rich features through multiple convolution combinations of different scales. Finally, predictions from multiple feature maps with different resolutions are combined by the network to naturally handle objects of various sizes. Experimental results on a surface defect dataset containing 2750 images of 5 classes we established confirm that our network has competitive accuracy and is much faster. For 300 × 300 input, ours network achieves 96.1% mAP on DAGM 2007 test at 73FPS on a NVIDIA GTX 1080Ti, outperforming a comparable state-of-the-art FCN model.

Keywords: Surface defect · Real time detection · Inception · MobileNet-SSD

1 Introduction

Visual analysis for product surface is a common computer vision application. However, due to the harsh and volatile environment in the actual production, product surface defect are diverse, such as scars, scratches, inclusions, black burn and so on. This poses

J. Ren et al. (Eds.): BICS 2019, LNAI 11691, pp. 510–519, 2020.
https://doi.org/10.1007/978-3-030-39431-8_49

a challenge to high quality products. Therefore, effective surface defect detection methods are of great significance for improving production efficiency.

The traditional method relies on the features of hand-designed. The selection of these features depends on the designer's experience, so it is not satisfactory in terms of the mobility and accuracy of the model. To overcome such drawbacks, a novel framework was proposed for saliency detection by first modeling the background and then separating salient objects from the background [1]. On the other hand, since AlexNet [2] won the ImageNet competition in 2012, the deep learning method has been widely used in visual tasks such as classification, detection, and tracking because of its powerful feature extraction capabilities. However, surface defect detection has unusual requirements for the real-time performance of the network in industrial environment, and the current network has room for further improvement.

In this paper, we propose a new method to detect surface defects by combining SSD, MobileNet and Inception, an effective method to compress convolutional layers with little accuracy dcline. The new method utilizes two new operations, depthwise convolution and pointwise convolution, to greatly reduce computation cost while almost maintaining accuracy. Meanwhile, in order to overcome the shortcoming that the poor feature extraction ability while using MobileNet as base network, the layer in MobileNet as feature layer is replaced by the Inception to achieve a balance between accuracy and speed.

The remainder of this paper is organized as follows. Section 2 reviews related work. Section 3 describes the architecture of our method in detail. Section 4 presents experiments and discussions, followed by conclusions and future work in Sect. 5.

2 Related Work

The traditional defect detection methods based on the classical image processing algorithm, which is mainly divided into three stages, image preprocessing, feature extraction and classification. Hu et al. [3] proposed a hybrid chromosome optimization algorithm to optimize the detection of steel surface defects by SVM. An adaptive segmentation algorithm based on the grayscale features of the surface of the defect region is proposed in [4], but the category of the defect cannot be distinguished. Statistical methods proposed by [5] are used to detect defects on metal surfaces, the method analyzes wavelet image information of infrared imaging and grayscale changes in defect regions. Xu et al. [6] extracted the sub-band characteristics of different scales and directions of the surface defect of the steel strip through Tetrolet-based method, then classify the defects by SVM. A novel animal detection method is introduced, based on a top view 3-D point cloud data obtained by using the Kinect sensor [7]. In [8], based on fusing visible and thermal images, a cognitive model along with an improved mean-shift method is proposed for tracking the pedestrians in the videos. In Zheng et al. [9], fusion of two approaches is proposed for effective copy-move forgery detection, where SIFT was used to extract feature points as keypoints and Zernike moments was used as block features to detect forgery in smooth regions. Other well-known methods include based on histogram, co-occurrence matrices, spatial domain and frequency domain filtering design [10–12].

In recent few years, deep learning has performed well in many fields, such as natural language processing, speech recognition, and computer vision. Wu et al. [13] used CNN to complete image patch classification and automatically extract features, then builded a voting mechanism to do classification and location. Wang et al. [14] introduced a deep learning framework based hybrid spatiotemporal saliency feature extraction, which extracted high-level features from raw video data, and then integrated with other high-level features for saliency detection from video footages. The R-CNN family [15–18] and the YOLO family [19, 20] are representatives of the object detection ConvNets. [21] combined Fast R-CNN with depthwise separable convolution to meet the real-time requirements of detection, then added center loss to improve detection accuracy. Li et al. [22] detected the surface defects of steel strip by constructing an all convolutional YOLO detection network. SSD [23] is a new proposed method different from the above two methods. Although Fast YOLO can run at 155 FPS on Pascal VOC2007, it has lower accuracy by almost 22% mAP. And not only SSD300 but also SSD512 method outperforms Faster R-CNN in both speed and accuracy. The trade-off between accuracy and speed can be achieved by some optimization algorithms. For example, Zhang et al. [24] integrated a dynamic neighborhood learning (DNL) with GSA to provide better trade off between exploration and exploitation based on the evolutionary states. We need to know that about 80% of the forward time is spent on the base network (VGG16 [25]). Therefore, using a faster base network could even further improve the speed. In this paper, we increase the speed of SSD by combining them with MobileNet and Inception [26] to meet the speed and accuracy requirements of industrial production.

3 Method

The early network layers are based on depthwise separable convolution utilized in MobileNet and Inception for high quality image classification, which is called the base network. Five convolutional feature layers are added to the end of the base network. The network combines predictions from multiple feature maps with different resolutions to naturally handle objects of various sizes. The overall detection procedure is shown in Fig. 1.

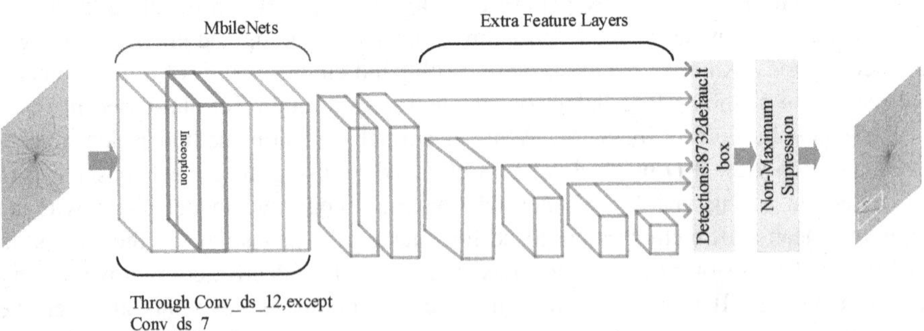

Fig. 1. The overall detection procedure. The convolution layers for base network are standard convolutions in original SSD and they are MobileNet and Inception in our MobileNet-SSD, which we will discuss in the next subsection.

3.1 MobileNet-SSD

The SSD method bases on a feedforward convolution network, which generates a set of bounding boxes of fixed size and scores of object class instances in these boxes, followed by a non-maximum suppression step to generate final detection. In the original paper, the author used VGG as the base network. In this paper, we construct the base network in SSD as 3 × 3 depthwise separable convolution and Inception. The base network consists of the first 12 layers of MobileNet and replaces Conv_ds_7 with Inception. And detailed network structure is show in Table 1 (Each line describes repeated *n* times, number *c* of output channels, and stride s). These layers are gradually reduced in size and can be used to predict at multiple scales. Each added feature layer (or optionally an existing feature layer from the base network) can produce a fixed set of detection predictions using a set of 3 × 3 convolutional filters.

In this paper, we increase the speed of SSD by combining them with depthwise separable convolution [27] to meet the speed requirements of industrial production. According to [28], we know that MobileNet only needs 1/33 of the parameters of Visual geometry group-16 (VGG-16) to achieve the same classification accuracy. There is a batchnorm and ReLU nonlinearity behind each layer to increase the convergence speed of the network during training and the stability of the extracted features. In addition, adding ReLU nonlinearity to improve the representation ability of the feature map after filtering ends. Thanks to the convolutional computational savings, the SSD is accelerated by approximately 1.3 times with only 0.1% loss of accuracy, making the network more responsive to real-time defect detection.

Table 1. Detailed base network structure

Input	Operator	c	n	s
$300^2 \times 3$	conv2d	32	1	2
$150^2 \times 32$	conv_ds	64	1	1
$150^2 \times 64$	conv_ds	128	2	2
$38^2 \times 128$	conv_ds	256	1	1
$38^2 \times 256$	conv_ds	256	1	2
$38^2 \times 256$	Inception	512	1	*
$38^2 \times 512$	conv_ds	512	4	1
$38^2 \times 512$	conv_ds	512	1	2

3.2 Inception

One particular structure used in GoogLeNet is called Inception, which was responsible for setting the new state of the art for classification and detection in the ImageNet Large-Scale Visual Recognition Challenge 2014 (ILSVRC14). The main hallmark of this architecture is the improved utilization of the computing resources inside the network. This was achieved by a carefully crafted design that allows for increasing the depth and width of the network while keeping the computational budget constant. The Inception in our network is shown in Fig. 2. Figure 2 shows that there are 4 branches for the input, which are convolved or pooled with filters of different sizes, and finally stitched together in the feature dimension. In this way, convolution is performed simultaneously on multiple scales, and features of different scales can be extracted. More feature richness also means more accurate judgment in the final classification. 1×1 convolutions are used to compute reductions before the expensive 3×3 and 5×5 convolutions. Besides being used as reductions, they also include the use of rectified linear activation which makes them dual-purpose.

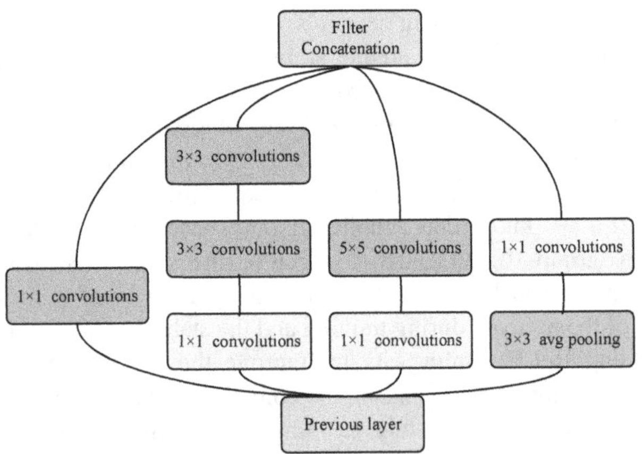

Fig. 2. The Inception in our network.

SSD network combines predictions from multiple feature maps with different resolutions to naturally handle objects of various sizes. Each added feature layer (or optionally an existing feature layer from the base network) can produce a fixed set of detection predictions using a set of convolutional filters. Although in order to increase the speed of the network, we replaced the base network with a set of depthwise separable layers, but this structure sacrifices feature extraction ability for computational savings. For the actual production in the factory, the detection speed is as important as the detection accuracy, so optionally an existing feature layer from the base network is replaced by the Inception to keep a balance between accuracy and speed.

4 Experiment

4.1 Dataset

The performance of our method uses the DAGM 2007 [29] dataset for verification, which is the official usage dataset of the Competition at DAGM 2007 symposium. The competition was inspired by the fact that automated optical inspection allows to reduce the cost of industrial quality control significantly. The data is artificially generated, but similar to real world problems. Firstly, we obtained 750 surface defect images, which were classified into five categories according to the defect types, and each defect was a part of the unique texture background. Then we expanded the data set by several methods, such as ups and downs, rotation, etc. Finally, we got a surface defect dataset containing 5 classes (scar, scratch, dirty, cleft) of 2750 images which are all annotated manually. The number of images for each class is about 600, and the size of the image for the input is 300 × 300. The details of the data set are shown in Table 2, and Fig. 3 is an example of some images.

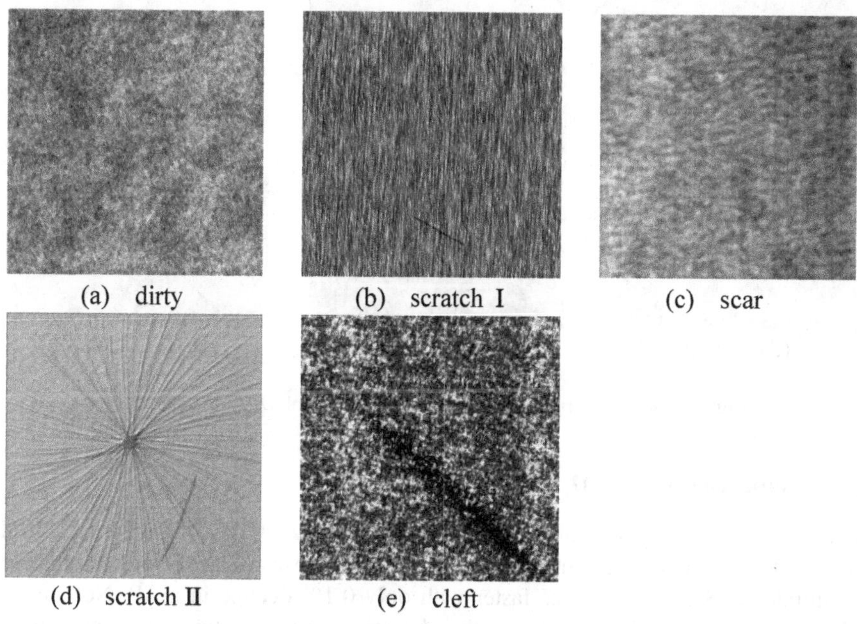

Fig. 3. Samples of the DAGM 2007 dataset.

Table 2. Details of the surface defect dataset.

Data set	Scar	Scratch I	Dirty	Cleft	Scratch II	Amount
Training set	410	400	420	390	430	2050
Test set	140	120	160	100	180	700

4.2 Training Details

We trained our model using Adam with a batch size of 32 samples, epsilon of 1.0, beta1 of 0.9, and beta2 of 0.999. The initial learning rate is 0.004 and is multiplied by 0.94 after every 750 iterations. It took about 7 h (50000 iterations) to train our model with NVIDIA GTX 1080Ti GPU. Our network can not only accurately give the position and category information of surface defects, but also meet the real-time requirements of the actual production in the factory. Some samples of our detection results are shown in Fig. 4.

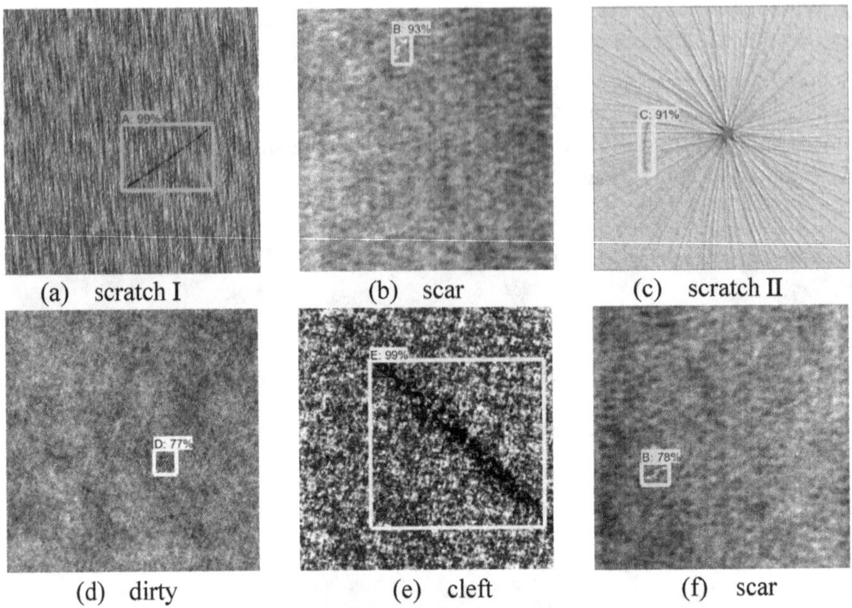

Fig. 4. Detection results of 5 types of defects of DAGM data set.

4.3 Comparison with SSD

Table 3 is the comparison of MobileNet-SSD, ours and the original one. While replacing the standard convolutions in feature extraction conv layers with MobileNet, our MobileNet-SSD is 1.3 times faster with only 0.1% decline in mAP. Not surprisingly, because MobileNet sacrifices the detection accuracy for the computational savings, the scratch I and scratch II reduce by 0.9% and 3.8% in accuracy respectively. The performance of feature extraction network is further improved by replacing optionally an existing feature layer from the base network with Inception which can extract more rich features through multiple convolution combinations of different sizes. So the final mAP and speed for our Inception-based MobileNet-SSD are 96.1% and 73 FPS.

The average speed requirement for reference steel strip production line and mobile phone polarizer inspection is 30 m/s and 5 m/s respectively, a new detection method must be at least 0.033 s for each image. The average inference time of our Inception-based MobileNet-SSD is about 0.014 s, which is satisfied with the real-time requirement for surface defect detection. And the speed of the network can be further improved with better hardware devices or compressing layers behind feature extraction layers. This may be what we will do in the future.

Table 3. Comparison with SSD.

Method	Scar	Scratch I	Dirty	Cleft	Scratch II	mAP	FPS
SSD	98.6%	98.6%	99.9%	84.3%	97.9%	95.9%	59
MobileNet-SSD	98.7%	97.7%	99.9%	88.5%	94.1%	95.8%	**75**
Ours	98.9%	98.3%	99.9%	89.2%	94.2%	**96.1%**	73

4.4 Comparison with Other Methods

We compare our method with others based on deep learning in recent years. As show in Table 4, although the detection accuracy of our network ranks third in the above network, the main advantage of ours is a significant speed gain compared to Faster_rcnn_resnet50 and CNN.

Besides, when using only MobileNet as feature extraction network, the network can detect surface defects faster, up to 75 fps. Although the network is slightly faster than the final version, the performance in terms of accurate and stability for practical application declines. So the network combining with Inception is more suitable.

Table 4. Comparision with other methods.

Inspector	mAP	FPS	Amount of dataset
Faster_rcnn_resnet50	99.01%	29	2750
ViDi [30]	93.70%	50	–
CNN [14]	97.50%	2	1150
FCN [31]	95.99%	50	900
Ours	96.10%	**73**	2750

5 Conclusion

This paper proposes Inception-based MobileNet-SSD, a fast single-shot object detector for multiple categories. Our results yield a solid evidence that the expected real-time requirement by replacing VGG with MobileNet is a viable method for improving neural networks for computer vision. A key feature of our model is the use of Inception attached to multiple feature maps to improve the ability of the network to distinguish between different defects. After training on the surface defect dataset we built, our network achieved 96.1% mAP with a speed of 73 fps. The speed of our method can be further improved by using the latest and more efficient convolution structure. As to further speed up our method, more researches is needed in the future.

Acknowledgments. This work was supported in part by Key Research and Development Plan of Shanxi Province (No. 201703D111023), Key Research and Development Plan of Shanxi Province (No. 201703D111027), Shanxi International Cooperation Project (No. 201803D421039) and Shanxi Scholarship Council of China (No. 2016-044).

References

1. Han, J., Zhang, D., Hu, X., et al.: Background prior-based salient object detection via deep reconstruction residual. IEEE Trans. Circuits Syst. Video Technol. **25**(8), 1309–1321 (2014)
2. Krizhevsky, A., Sutskever, I., Hinton, G.E.: ImageNet classification with deep convolutional neural networks. In: Advances in Neural Information Processing Systems, pp. 1097–1105 (2012)
3. Hu, H., Liu, Y., Liu, M., et al.: Surface defect classification in large-scale strip steel image collection via hybrid chromosome genetic algorithm. Neurocomputing **181**, 86–95 (2016)
4. Yongzhi, M., Biao, Y., Hongfeng, M.A., et al.: Adaptive segmentation algorithm for rail surface defects image. J. Beijing Univ. Technol. **43**(10), 1472–1479 (2017)
5. Yan, P., Zhang, X., Ding, Y.: Vision inspection of metal surface defects based on infrared imaging. Acta Optica Sin. **31**, 0312004 (2011)
6. Xu, K., Wang, L., Wang, J.: Surface defect recognition of hot-rolled steel plates based on Tetrolet transform. J. Mech. Eng. **52**, 13–19 (2016)
7. Zhu, Q., Ren, J., Barclay, D., et al.: Automatic animal detection from kinect sensed images for livestock monitoring and assessment. In: 2015 IEEE International Conference on Computer and Information Technology; Ubiquitous Computing and Communications; Dependable, Autonomic and Secure Computing; Pervasive Intelligence and Computing, pp. 1154–1157. IEEE (2015)
8. Yan, Y., Ren, J., Zhao, H., et al.: Cognitive fusion of thermal and visible imagery for effective detection and tracking of pedestrians in videos. Cogn. Comput. **10**(1), 94–104 (2018)
9. Zheng, J., Liu, Y., Ren, J., et al.: Fusion of block and keypoints based approaches for effective copy-move image forgery detection. Multidimension. Syst. Signal Process. **27**(4), 989–1005 (2016)
10. Swain, M.J., Ballard, D.H.: Indexing via color histograms. In: Sood, A.K., Wechsler, H. (eds.) Active Perception and Robot Vision. NATO ASI Series (Series F: Computer and Systems Sciences), vol. 83, pp. 261–273. Springer, Heidelberg (1992)
11. Conners, R.W., Mcmillin, C.W., Lin, K., et al.: Identifying and locating surface defects in wood: part of an automated lumber processing system. IEEE Trans. Pattern Anal. Mach. Intell. **6**, 573–583 (1983)
12. Jolliffe, I.: Principal Component Analysis. Springer, Heidelberg (2011)
13. Wu, X., Cao, K., Gu, X.: A surface defect detection based on convolutional neural network. In: Liu, M., Chen, H., Vincze, M. (eds.) ICVS 2017. LNCS, vol. 10528, pp. 185–194. Springer, Cham (2017). https://doi.org/10.1007/978-3-319-68345-4_17
14. Wang, Z., Ren, J., Zhang, D., et al.: A deep-learning based feature hybrid framework for spatiotemporal saliency detection inside videos. Neurocomputing **287**, 68–83 (2018)
15. Ren, S., He, K., Girshick, R., et al.: Faster R-CNN: towards real-time object detection with region proposal networks. In: Advances in Neural Information Processing systems, pp. 91–99 (2015)
16. Girshick, R., Donahue, J., Darrell, T., et al.: Rich feature hierarchies for accurate object detection and semantic segmentation. In: Proceedings of the IEEE Conference on Computer Vision and Pattern Recognition, pp. 580–587 (2014)
17. He, K., Zhang, X., Ren, S., et al.: Spatial pyramid pooling in deep convolutional networks for visual recognition. IEEE Trans. Pattern Anal. Mach. Intell. **37**(9), 1904–1916 (2015)
18. Girshick, R.: Fast R-CNN. In: Proceedings of the IEEE International Conference on Computer Vision, pp. 1440–1448 (2015)

19. Redmon, J., Divvala, S., Girshick, R., et al.: You only look once: unified, real-time object detection. In: Proceedings of the IEEE Conference on Computer Vision and Pattern Recognition, pp. 779–788 (2016)
20. Redmon, J., Farhadi, A.: YOLO9000: better, faster, stronger. In: Proceedings of the IEEE Conference on Computer Vision and Pattern Recognition, pp. 7263–7271 (2017)
21. Ren, Q., Geng, J., Li, J.: Slighter faster R-CNN for real-time detection of steel strip surface defects. In: 2018 Chinese Automation Congress (CAC), pp. 2173–2178. IEEE (2018)
22. Li, J., Su, Z., Geng, J., et al.: Real-time detection of steel strip surface defects based on improved YOLO detection network. IFAC-PapersOnLine **51**(21), 76–81 (2018)
23. Liu, W., et al.: SSD: single shot multibox detector. In: Leibe, B., Matas, J., Sebe, N., Welling, M. (eds.) ECCV 2016. LNCS, vol. 9905, pp. 21–37. Springer, Cham (2016). https://doi.org/10.1007/978-3-319-46448-0_2
24. Zhang, A., Sun, G., Ren, J., et al.: A dynamic neighborhood learning-based gravitational search algorithm. IEEE Trans. Cybern. **48**(1), 436–447 (2016)
25. Simonyan, K., Zisserman, A.: Very deep convolutional networks for large-scale image recognition (2014). arXiv preprint arXiv:1409.1556
26. Szegedy, C., Liu, W., Jia, Y., et al.: Going deeper with convolutions. In: Proceedings of the IEEE Conference on Computer Vision and Pattern Recognition, pp. 1–9 (2015)
27. Sifre, L., Mallat, S.: Rigid-motion scattering for image classification. Ph.D. thesis, pp. 1–3 (2014)
28. Howard, A.G., Zhu, M., Chen, B., et al.: MobileNets: efficient convolutional neural networks for mobile vision applications (2017). arXiv preprint arXiv:1704.04861
29. DAGM 2007 Datasets. https://hci.iwr.uni-heidelberg.de/node/3616. Accessed 10 Apr 2017
30. https://www.vidi-systems.com. Accessed 10 Apr 2017
31. Yu, Z., Wu, X., Gu, X.: Fully convolutional networks for surface defect inspection in industrial environment. In: Liu, M., Chen, H., Vincze, M. (eds.) Computer Vision Systems. ICVS 2017. LNCS, vol. 10528. Springer, Cham (2017)

Association Rule Mining for Road Traffic Accident Analysis: A Case Study from UK

Mingchen Feng[1(✉)], Jiangbin Zheng[1], Jinchang Ren[2], and Yue Xi[1]

[1] School of Computer Science, Northwestern Polytechnical University, Xi'an, China
{mingchen, yuexi}@mail.nwpu.edu.cn, zhengjb@nwpu.edu.cn

[2] Department of Electronic and Electrical Engineering, University of Strathclyde, Glasgow, UK
Jinchang.ren@strath.ac.uk

Abstract. Road Traffic Accidents (RTAs) are currently the leading causes of traffic congestion, human death, health problems, environmental pollution, and economic losses. Investigation of the characteristics and patterns of RTAs is one of the high-priority issues in traffic safety analysis. This paper presents our work on mining RTAs using association rule based methods. A case study is conducted using UK traffic accident data from 2005 to 2017. We performed Apriori algorithm on the data set and then explored the rules with high lift and high support respectively. The results show that RTAs have strong correlation with environmental characteristics, speed limit, and location. With the network visualization, we can explain in details the association rules and obtain more understandable insights into the results. The promising outcomes will undoubtedly reduce traffic accident effectively and assist traffic safety department for decision making.

Keywords: Association rules · Data mining · Data visualization · Traffic accident analysis

1 Introduction

Traffic accident analysis continues to be a hot topic in the traffic engineering field. According to global status report on road safety 2018, the number of annual road traffic deaths has reached 1.35 million [1] and around fifty million get injuries or disabilities [2]. Besides, the economic impact is also notable: in a one-year period, the cost of medical care and productivity losses associated with occupant injuries and deaths from motor vehicle traffic crashes exceeded $63 billion [3]. Thus, more research and new models are needed to analyze RTAs in order to discover associated factors and reduce large number of accidents and fatalities. Data mining techniques still need improvement to discover more interesting rules and assist police decision makers in the formulation of new policies and traffic rules from some hidden patterns.

As one of the fundamental algorithms of data mining, association rule mining is an innovative, interdisciplinary, and growing research area, which are used to find all rules in the database satisfying some minimum support and minimum confidence constraints.

J. Ren et al. (Eds.): BICS 2019, LNAI 11691, pp. 520–529, 2020.
https://doi.org/10.1007/978-3-030-39431-8_50

Apriori [4] is a powerful algorithm for mining frequent itemsets for boolean association rules, where two separated steps are performed to generate association rules, i.e. applying minimum support to obtain frequent itemsets and utilizing these itemsets and the minimum confidence constraint to generate rules. Association rules have a unique advantage in discovering frequent patterns with a large dataset.

In this paper, we employ association rule method on UK traffic accident data. Along with some useful rules, we also explored high support and high lift of the rules. With network and other visualization methods, further interpretation of the rules can be obtained.

The major contributions of this paper can be summarized as follows:

(1) By applying association rules, interesting patterns are obtained to investigate the hidden relationship among multi-attributes and factors to RTAs;
(2) With network visualization technique, the association rules obtained above can be easily interpreted, which can provide valuable insights in decision making and in reducing accident risks.

2 Related Work

To date, a number of models have been developed for RTAs analysis. Weng et al. [5] proposed a novel association rules to analyze the characteristics and contributory factors of work zone crash casualties. Montella [6] identified crash characteristics and contributory factors at urban roundabouts and employed the association rule approach to explore their relationships at different crash types. Subasish [7] applied association rules mining method to explore potential patterns of RTAs data under rainy conditions. Gao et al. [8] performed association rules on traffic accidents from Shanghai expressway data and put forward a method to extract strong rules automatically. Priya et al. [9] proposed a technique to categorize the twist of fate information into different classes and carried out apriori algorithm to uncover the semantics of coincidence incidence. Xu [10] used descriptive statistics to illustrate the characteristics of serious casualty crashes in terms of road user behavior, vehicle conditions, geometric characteristics, and environmental conditions and applied association rule mining technique to identify sets of crash contributory factors that often occur together in serious casualty crashes. Das et al. [11] utilized apriori algorithm of supervised association mining technique to discover patterns from the vehicle-pedestrian crash database. Using association rule mining, Gariazzo et al. [12] assessed the relationship between the use of mobile phones at population level and road crash fatalities in large urban areas. Xi et al. [13] utilized association rules to categorize accidental factors and analyze the degree of an accident or the level of influence. Our previous work [14] has visualized and predicted crime trends to discover key factors and patterns related to crimes.

In summary, association rule mining is effective in dealing with datasets which contain large number of attributes. With a proper support and confidence, it can also interpret hidden relationship among them without predetermining the assumptions and functional forms. Moreover, association rule could also reflect the fact that risk factors may exhibit heterogeneous or hidden effects at various circumstances. Thus, we performed association rule mining to explore accident data from UK to uncover more potential patterns.

3 Methodology

3.1 Association Rules

Association rules mining is a well-known data mining algorithm for detecting potential patterns within huge datasets. Among other machine learning methods, association rules mining is flexible due to its no specified function and no dependent variables nature. Guided by the rules, countermeasures can be taken to make quicker decisions and to reduce the risk for accidental incidents. For example, the rules {weather = rainy, light = dark, time = 22–24} ⇒ {accident = rollover} indicates that on rainy days between hours 22 to 24 when the road lights are off, rollover is more likely to happen. Thus, in order to reduce accident we suggest turn on the road lights.

So far, a series of association rules has been put forward, such as apriori and Fp-growth. Apriori was proposed by Agrawal et al. [15] to mine association rules from transaction data. In this paper, we apply Apriori to analyze accident data from UK, the details of this method shown below.

Let $I = \{i_1, i_2, \ldots, i_n\}$ be the set of literals, let $T = \{t_1, t_2, \ldots, t_m\}$ be a set of accident incidents. Each incident in T is a subset of items in I. A rule is defined as $X \Rightarrow Y$ where $X, Y \subseteq I$ and $X \cap Y = \emptyset$. The sets of itemsets X and Y are called antecedent (left-hand-side, LHS) and consequent (right-hand-side, RHS) of the rule.

3.2 Interesting Rule Mining

There are three parameters controlling the number of rules to be generated i.e. Support, Confidence and Lift. Support refers to the proportion of an accident incident, Confidence can be interpreted as an estimate of the probability P(Y|X), and The lift of the rule shows the frequency of co-occurrence of the antecedent and the consequent. They are defined below.

$$Supp(X) = \|\{t \in D|X \subseteq t\}\|/\|t \in D\| \tag{1}$$

$$\mathrm{Conf}(X \Rightarrow Y) = Supp(X \cup Y)/Supp(X) \tag{2}$$

$$\mathrm{lift}(X \Rightarrow Y) = Supp(X \cup Y)/(Supp(X)Supp(Y)) \tag{3}$$

Moreover,

$$Supp(X \cup Y) \geq \sigma \tag{4}$$

$$\mathrm{Conf(X \cup Y)} \geq \delta \tag{5}$$

Where, σ and δ are the minimum of support and confidence.

4 Results and Discussion

4.1 Data

The accident data comes from Department for Transport, UK [16], which amassed traffic data from 2005 to 2017, recording over 2 million incidents in the process. Each record includes two types of information: environmental factors and crash information. Environmental factors refer to factors such as road condition, road type, weather, light condition, junction, and speed limit of the road. Crash information contains the detailed information regarding number of vehicles, time, number of casualties and location. It should be pointed out that these data are real-world data and are high in quality, thus the analysis results based on the collected data are plausible.

4.2 Rules Generation and Visualization

To generate interesting rules from UK traffic accident data, we performed Apriori algorithm using package "arrules" provided by R software. The dataset is first transformed to data-frame, and then converted to transaction for further processing. Besides, the minimum support and minimum confidence are set to be 0.4 and 0.7 respectively. After that a totally 195 rules are obtained. As shown in Fig. 1, by utilizing grouped matrix plot, the column is the LHS items which are grouped into 20 groups while the rows are consequents of the rules. The color stands for the number of the lift, and the size of the circles represents the support values. The plot in the top-left corner also shows that there are 3 rules contain {speed_limit = 30, road_surface = dfry}. Besides, we also noticed that the high lift rules and high support rules are separated. So in order to explore more information about support and lift values, after scatter plot of the 195 rules in Fig. 2, a support >0.6 is determined as high support rules and a lift >1.2 is considered as high lift rules.

With support >0.6 as high support rules, we obtain 20 rules, as shown in Table 1. The high support means high proportion of the items i.e. the high frequent occurrence of accidents. We noticed that Severity = Slight, Weather = Fine no high winds, Number_of_Casualties = 1, RoadType = Single carriageway, Light = Daylight are high frequent rules which are highly related to accident. So in order to get rid of traffic accident, traffic department should pay more attention to these characteristics.

With lift >1.2, we get another 20 rules as shown in Table 2, these are all stronger associations, which tell us that speed_limit = 30, area = urban, road_surface = dry and Weather = Fine no high winds are critical factors that cause accident. These rules remind us that we can reduce speed_limit to 20 or 50 (we can conclude from the data that when speed limit is 20 and 50 the accident rate is 1.8% and 3.4% respectively). For the environmental factors, we can not change them, but traffic safety department can set up warning signs to inform drivers for cautious driving.

Table 1. Association rules with high support.

Rules	LHS	RHS	Support	Confidence	Lift
1	{}	{Severity = Slight}	0.847	0.847	1.00
2	{}	{Weather = Fine no high winds}	0.801	0.801	1.00
3	{}	{Number_of_Casualties = 1}	0.770	0.770	1.00
4	{}	{RoadType = Single carriageway}	0.746	0.746	1.00
5	{}	{Light = Daylight}	0.731	0.731	1.00
6	{Weather = Fine no high winds}	{Severity = Slight}	0.675	0.843	0.99
7	{Severity = Slight}	{Weather = Fine no high winds}	0.675	0.797	0.99
8	{Road_Surface = Dry}	{Weather = Fine no high winds}	0.664	0.958	1.19
9	{Weather = Fine no high winds}	{Road_Surface = Dry}	0.664	0.829	1.01
10	{Number_of_Casualties = 1}	{Severity = Slight}	0.659	0.855	1.01
11	{Severity = Slight}	{Number_of_Casualties = 1}	0.659	0.778	1.01
12	{Light = Daylight}	{Severity = Slight}	0.627	0.858	1.01
13	{Severity = Slight}	{Light = Daylight}	0.627	0.739	1.01
14	{RoadType = Single carriageway}	Severity = Slight}	0.626	0.838	0.99
15	Severity = Slight}	{RoadType = Single carriageway}	0.626	0.738	0.98
16	{Number_of_Casualties = 1}	{Weather = Fine no high winds}	0.619	0.804	1.00
17	{Weather = Fine no high winds}	{Number_of_Casualties = 1}	0.619	0.773	1.00
18	{Light = Daylight}	{Weather = Fine no high winds}	0.609	0.834	1.04
19	{Weather = Fine no high winds}	{Light = Daylight}	0.609	0.761	1.04
20	{RoadType = Single carriageway}	{Weather = Fine no high winds}	0.601	0.805	1.00

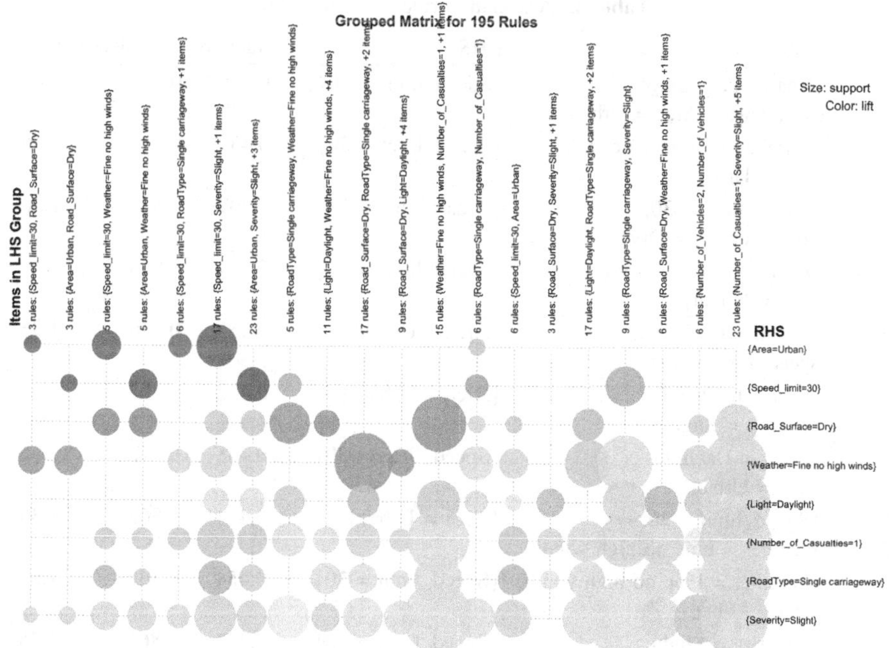

Fig. 1. Grouped matrix plot of the 195 rules. (Color figure online)

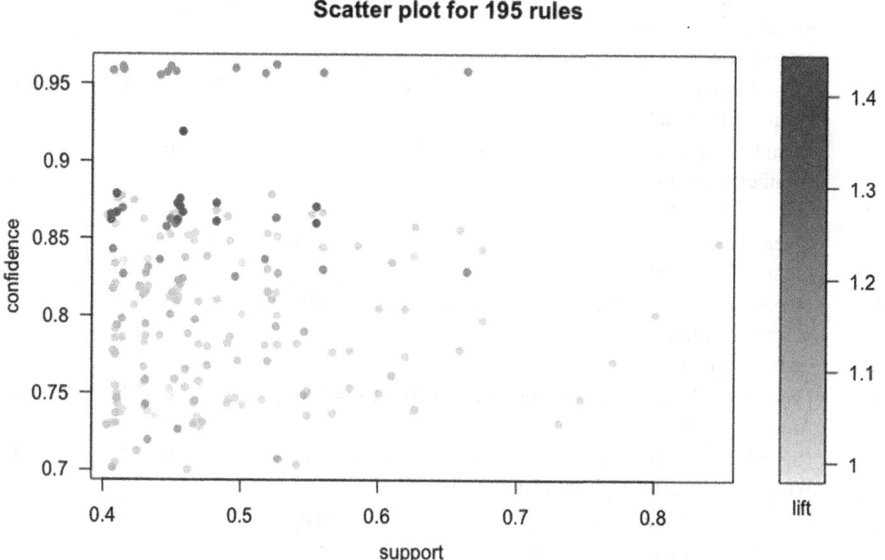

Fig. 2. Scatter plot of the 195 rules. (Color figure online)

Table 2. Association rules with high lift.

Rules	LHS	RHS	Support	Confidence	Lift
1	{RoadType = Single carriageway, Area = Urban}	{Speed_limit = 30}	0.458	0.919	1.44
2	{Number_of_Casualties = 1, Area = Urban}	{Speed_limit = 30}	0.456	0.870	1.36
3	{Speed_limit = 30, Road_Surface = Dry}	{Area = Urban}	0.409	0.878	1.36
4	{Road_Surface = Dry, Area = Urban}	{Speed_limit = 30}	0.409	0.866	1.36
5	{Number_of_Casualties = 1, Speed_limit = 30}	{Area = Urban}	0.455	0.876	1.35
6	{Speed_limit = 30, Severity = Slight}	{Area = Urban}	0.482	0.872	1.35
7	{Light = Daylight, Area = Urban}	{Speed_limit = 30}	0.405	0.862	1.35
8	{Speed_limit = 30, Weather = Fine no high winds}	{Area = Urban}	0.454	0.862	1.35
9	{Weather = Fine no high winds, Area = Urban}	{Speed_limit = 30}	0.454	0.862	1.35
10	{Severity = Slight, Area = Urban}	{Speed_limit = 30}	0.482	0.861	1.35
11	{Area = Urban}	{Speed_limit = 30}	0.555	0.859	1.34
12	{Speed_limit = 30}	{Area = Urban}	0.555	0.870	1.34
13	{Speed_limit = 30, RoadType = Single carriageway}	{Area = Urban}	0.458	0.867	1.34
14	{Speed_limit = 30, Light = Daylight}	{Area = Urban}	0.405	0.865	1.33
15	{Number_of_Casualties = 1, Weather = Fine no high winds, Light = Daylight}	{Road_Surface = Dry}	0.413	0.869	1.25
16	{Weather = Fine no high winds, Light = Daylight}	{Road_Surface = Dry}	0.526	0.863	1.25
17	{Weather = Fine no high winds, Severity = Slight, Light = Daylight}	{Road_Surface = Dry}	0.449	0.862	1.24
18	{Weather = Fine no high winds, Area = Urban}	{Road_Surface = Dry}	0.452	0.859	1.24
19	{Speed_limit = 30, Weather = Fine no high winds}	{Road_Surface = Dry}	0.446	0.857	1.24
20	{Number_of_Vehicles = 2, Weather = Fine no high winds}	{Road_Surface = Dry}	0.407	0.843	1.21

Finally we plot the 100 rules using a network visualization, the plot indicates that road type, light, speed limit and road surface play central roles to accident incidents. Besides, number of vehicles and urban area are also decisive factors for traffic accident. These factors also have some connections, so in order to reduce the risk of traffic accident, we can take proper action to change or eliminate any factors (Fig. 3).

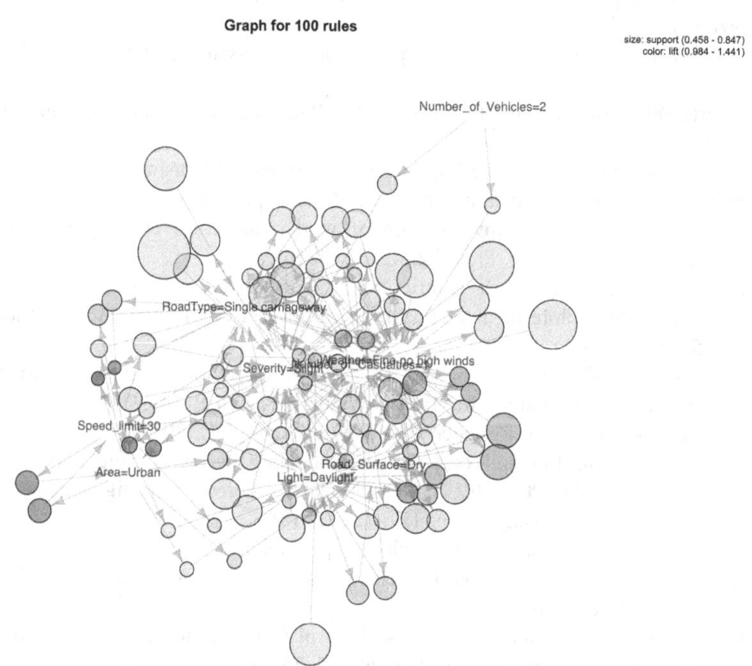

Fig. 3. Network plot of 100 rules.

5 Conclusion and Future Work

In this paper we conduct a study to perform a data mining technique to explore traffic accident data in UK. By mining association rules, we obtain a series of interesting rules and discover critical factors that related to accident. Through using different supports and confidences, we discover the potential reason of the accident. Together with data visualization, a further understanding of the rules and more information are provided.

In the future we will utilize the results to explore more in detail of the accident on how the rules changed in different cities, and whether we can predict or not. Besides, we also want to perform this technique on crime data [17] to mining more interesting rules. Moreover, as Artificial Intelligence [18, 19] and feature selection [20–22] has achieved big success in many field, we also want to seek combination of artificial intelligence algorithms with association rules and add more useful features on our datasets.

Acknowledgement. This work has been supported by HGJ, HJSW and Research & Development plan of Shaanxi Province (Program No. 2017ZDXM-GY-094, 2015KTZDGY04-01).

References

1. World Health Organization: Global status report on road safety 2018. World Health Organization (2018)
2. Road Safety Facts. https://www.asirt.org/safe-travel/road-safety-facts/. Accessed 25 Oct 2018
3. US Department of Health and Human Services, CDC. https://www.cdc.gov/injury/wisqars. Accessed 14 Jan 2018
4. Bhandari, A., Gupta, A., Das, D.: Improvised apriori algorithm using frequent pattern tree for real time applications in data mining. Procedia Comput. Sci. **46**, 644–651 (2015)
5. Weng, J., Zhu, J.Z., et al.: Investigation of work zone crash casualty patterns using association rules. Accid. Anal. Prev. **92**, 43–52 (2016)
6. Montella, A.: Identifying crash contributory factors at urban roundabouts and using association rules to explore their relationships to different crash types. Accid. Anal. Prev. **43**(4), 1451–1463 (2011)
7. Subasish, D., Sun, X.: Investigating the pattern of traffic crashes under rainy weather by association rules in data mining. In: Transportation Research Board 93rd Annual Meeting, No. 14-1540. Transportation Research Board, Washington DC (2014)
8. Gao, Z., Pan, R., et al.: Research on automated modeling algorithm using association rules for traffic accidents. In: 2018 IEEE International Conference on Big Data and Smart Computing (BigComp), Shanghai, pp. 127–132 (2018)
9. Priya, S., Agalya, R.: Association rule mining approach to analyze road accident data. In: 2018 International Conference on Current Trends Towards Converging Technologies (ICCTCT), Coimbatore, pp. 1–5 (2018)
10. Xu, C., Bao, J., et al.: Association rule analysis of factors contributing to extraordinarily severe traffic crashes in China. J. Saf. Res. **67**, 65–75 (2018)
11. Das, S., Dutta, A., et al.: Supervised association rules mining on pedestrian crashes in urban areas: identifying patterns for appropriate countermeasures. Int. J. Urban Sci. **23**(1), 30–48 (2019)
12. Gariazzo, C., Stafoggia, M., et al.: Association between mobile phone traffic volume and road crash fatalities: a population-based case-crossover study. Accid. Anal. Prev. **115**, 25–33 (2018)
13. Deng, X., Zeng, D., Shen, H.: Causation analysis model: based on AHP and hybrid Apriori-Genetic algorithm. J. Intell. Fuzzy Syst. **35**(1), 767–778 (2018)
14. Feng, M., Zheng, J., et al.: Big data analytics and mining for effective visualization and trends forecasting of crime data. IEEE Access **7**(1), 106111–106123 (2019)
15. Agrawal, R., Imieliński, T., Swami, A.: Mining association rules between sets of items in large databases. ACM SIGMOD Rec. **22**(2), 207–216 (1993)
16. UK Road Safety Dataset. https://data.gov.uk/dataset/cb7ae6f0-4be6-4935-9277-47e5ce24a11f/road-safety-data
17. Feng, M., Zheng, J., Han, Y., Ren, J., Liu, Q.: Big data analytics and mining for crime data analysis, visualization and prediction. In: Ren, J., Hussain, A., Zheng, J., Liu, C.-L., Luo, B., Zhao, H., Zhao, X. (eds.) BICS 2018. LNCS (LNAI), vol. 10989, pp. 605–614. Springer, Cham (2018). https://doi.org/10.1007/978-3-030-00563-4_59

18. Yan, Y., Ren, J., et al.: Cognitive fusion of thermal and visible imagery for effective detection and tracking of pedestrians in videos. Cogn. Comput. **10**, 94–104 (2017)
19. Yan, Y., Ren, J., et al.: Unsupervised image saliency detection with Gestalt-laws guided optimization and visual attention based refinement. Pattern Recogn. **79**, 65–78 (2018)
20. Cao, F., Yang, Z., Ren, J., et al.: Local block multilayer sparse extreme learning machine for effective feature extraction and classification of hyperspectral images. IEEE Trans. Geosci. Remote Sens. **57**, 5580–5594 (2019)
21. Sun, H., Ren, J., et al.: Superpixel based feature specific sparse representation for spectral-spatial classification of hyperspectral images. Remote Sens. (MDPI) **11**(5), 536 (2019)
22. Zhang, A., Sun, G., Ren, J., et al.: A dynamic neighborhood learning-based gravitational search algorithm. IEEE Trans. Cybern. **48**, 436–447 (2017)

Automatic Threshold Selection Method for SAR Edge Detection

Pengyi Xie(✉), Jiangbin Zheng, Qianru Wei, and Yuke Wang

Northwestern Polytechnical University, Xi'an, Shaanxi, People's Republic of China
xiepengyi_95@163.com

Abstract. In order to reduce the manual intervention and calculate amount in edge detection processing, an automatic threshold selection method for edge detection of synthetic aperture radar (SAR) images is proposed. The proposed automatic threshold selection (ATS) method determines the optimal thresholds by establishing a relationship between different thresholds and corresponding detection results. The thresholds chosen by the proposed ATS method are very close to the thresholds determined by manual intervention. Comparing with conventional method, ratio-based detectors with ATS obviously reduce the calculate amount and ensure the accuracy of edge detection at the same time, benefiting from less manual intervention and almost the same thresholds. The experimental results on SAR images show that ratio-based detectors combined with the proposed ATS method not only achieve the accurate detection results, but also effectively reduce the time consumption during thresholds selection.

Keywords: Synthetic aperture radar (SAR) · Edge detection · Automatic threshold selection method

1 Introduction

With the increasing number of applications of synthetic aperture radar (SAR) images, more and more tasks, which were hard to be solved in the past, has been dealt with well, such as retrieving the floe size distribution of Arctic sea ice [1] and sea ice image segmentation [2]. The problem of edge detection in various kinds of images, like SAR images, color images [3], hyperspectral images [4] and so on, becomes an important task in image processing and computer vision, since edges contain the most of significant geometry-structural information of an image. Different from the optical images, coherent imaging techniques basically cause severe speckle, which greatly increases the difficulty of SAR edge detection. The speckle, generally modeled as multiplicative noise, makes lots of well-designed optical edge detectors not work well in SAR images [5]. Detectors for optical images, such as Canny [6] and Sobel [7], are generally based on difference-operation. When applied to SAR images, they lose their properties of constant false alarm rate (CFAR). In addition, thresholds of traditional edge detectors need to be manually selected. Although this selection method is quite easy, these thresholds are mainly determined though trial-and-error, which brings a large amount of calculation.

J. Ren et al. (Eds.): BICS 2019, LNAI 11691, pp. 530–539, 2020.
https://doi.org/10.1007/978-3-030-39431-8_51

Due to the influence of speckle, SAR edge detectors are mainly focused on achieving the goal of effectively detecting edges with low false positive rate and high true positive rate. The detectors based on ratio-operation, referred as ratio-based SAR edge detectors, have an advantage of ease of use. The most famous ratio-based detector is named as ratio of average (ROA) edge detector [5]. Based on the idea of ROA, several detectors such as the ratio of exponentially weighted average (ROEWA) edge detector [8], the Gaussian-Gamma-Shaped (GGS) edge detector [9], the Gabor odd filter (GOF) edge detector [10], an efficient ratio-based edge detector (RBED) [11], etc. had been proposed. And there are some other methods for future extraction [12–14]. However, the detection thresholds of these detectors for SAR images with diverse qualities are different. For a large number of detection tasks, the method manually selecting thresholds will consume a large amount of time. So the traditional manual threshold selection method is difficult to meet the existing detection requirements.

Considering the shortcomings of traditional manual threshold selection method, this paper proposes an automatic threshold selection (ATS) method for SAR edge detection. ATS method selects optimal thresholds by establishing a relationship between different thresholds and corresponding detection results for each SAR image to avoid the requirement of manual intervention. Benefiting from the ATS method, several typical ratio-based detectors are able to select thresholds that are close to the ones chosen by manual method in a short period of time and achieve the accurate detection results at the same time.

This paper is organized as follows. Section 2 introduces ratio-based detectors and the proposed ATS method. Section 3 discusses the experimental results on several typical ratio-based detectors with ATS. The conclusion is shown in Sect. 4.

2 Ratio-Based Detectors with Automatic Threshold Selection Method

2.1 Ratio-Based Detectors

Let x and y be the horizontal and vertical coordinates of the SAR image $I(x, y)$, respectively. The ratio-based detector is expressed by:

$$f_A(x, y) = f_L(x, y) + f_R(x, y) \tag{1}$$

where (x, y) denotes the pixel. $f_L(x, y)$ is the left sub-window and $f_R(x, y)$ is the right sub-window.

Let u and v be the Cartesian coordinates of a 2D convolution kernel. We expect that u and v are along and across an edge, respectively. Let θ be the anti-clockwise angle between x and u. Then, we have the following relationships.

$$u = x\cos\theta + y\sin\theta \tag{2}$$

$$v = y\cos\theta - x\sin\theta \tag{3}$$

Rotating (1) yields the sliding window with an orientation angle θ, written by

$$f_{\mathrm{R}}^{\theta}(x,y) = f_R(x,y) \tag{4}$$

$$f_{\mathrm{L}}^{\theta}(x,y) = f_L(x,y) \tag{5}$$

At angle θ, two local weighted averages of pixel $I(x_0, y_0)$ are computed by the following convolutions,

$$m_1(x_0, y_0|\theta) = f_R^{\theta}(x,y) \otimes I(x_0, y_0) \tag{6}$$

$$m_2(x_0, y_0|\theta) = f_L^{\theta}(x,y) \otimes I(x_0, y_0) \tag{7}$$

From the local weighted averages at angle θ_k, the ratio statistic is obtained by

$$\xi^{\theta_k}(x_0, y_0) = min\left\{\frac{m_1(x_0, y_0|\theta_k)}{m_2(x_0, y_0|\theta_k)}, \frac{m_2(x_0, y_0|\theta_k)}{m_1(x_0, y_0|\theta_k)}\right\} \tag{8}$$

where $\theta_k = \pi k/P$, $k = 0, 1, \cdots P-1$ and P is a positive integer. Generally, P is equal to 8 for a good balance between computational complexity and detection precision.

For each pixel $I(x, y)$ and every rotating orientation angle θ_k, the edge strength map (ESM) and the edge direction map (EDM) are computed by

$$ESM(x,y) = 1 - \min_{\theta_k} \xi^{\theta_k}(x,y) \tag{9}$$

$$EDM(x,y) = \operatorname*{argmin}_{\theta_k} \xi^{\theta_k}(x,y) + \frac{\pi}{2} \tag{10}$$

where $ESM(x, y)$ is nonnegative.

2.2 Automatic Threshold Selection Method

To further optimize the detection result, the detector takes use of a post-processing method. As a commonly used post-processing method, non-maximum suppression and hysteretic thresholds (NSHT) [6] is to suppress and extract false and true edge-pixels, respectively. NSHT requires two predefined thresholds, one high threshold T_h and one low threshold T_l. For each SAR image, the two predefined thresholds are usually determined by manual intervention. The thresholds are used to estimate whether an edge-pixel is true by

$$REG(x,y) = \begin{cases} 1, ESM(x,y) \geq T_h \\ ESM(x,y), T_l \leq ESM(x,y) \leq T_h \\ 0, ESM(x,y) \leq T_l \end{cases}. \tag{11}$$

When $ESM(x, y) \geq T_h$, the pixel is considered as a true edge-pixel. And when $ESM(x, y) \leq T_l$, the pixel is supposed to be false. However, if $T_l \leq ESM(x, y) \leq T_h$, it can't be judged directly, which needs to be further considered.

The relationship between connected components of the edge and the threshold is established by performing a threshold processing method on the ESM. In general, as the threshold increases, the number of connected components first increases rapidly and then decreases sharply. After that, it shakes slightly at first and then drops slowly. Figure 1 shows an example of a curve of the number of connected components versus the threshold. According to the relationship between the observed connected components and the change of threshold, an automatic threshold selection method is proposed. Such change law has also been observed and used in other SAR image processing methods, such as image segmentation, to automatically determine the single threshold [15].

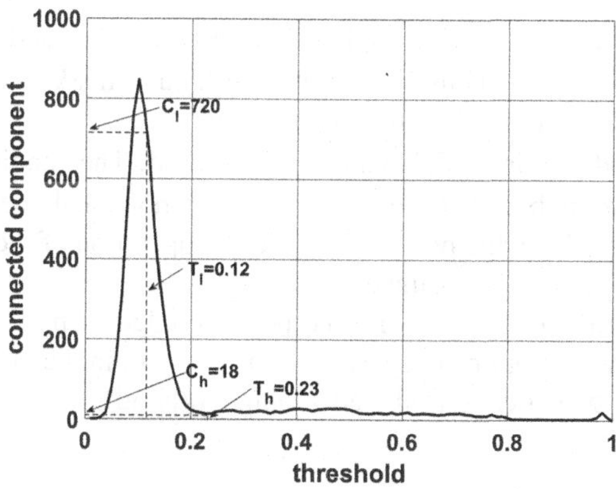

Fig. 1. The number of connected components of edges versus the threshold.

The automatic threshold selection method continuously changes the threshold and records the number of corresponding connected components. Then, plot the 'connected component - threshold' curve. Based on the plotted curve, we find the first minimum of the curve. When the number of connected components rapidly decreases from the global maximum, the local minimum first appearing is recorded as the first minimum. The high threshold T_h corresponds to the first minimum of the curve. The low threshold T_l appears between the global maximum and the first minimum. The number of connect components corresponding to the high threshold is recorded as C_h. The low threshold is fixed as the one corresponding to 40 times of C_h. Figure 1, as an example, marks the locations of the high thresholds and low one.

In traditional post-processing methods, the thresholds are determined by manual experiments. That means, for a SAR image, the way to determine its thresholds is though trial-and-error. Generally, the trial process is very difficult and time-consuming, because the range of the thresholds is too large. On the other hand, even we are lucky enough to find the good thresholds in a very short time. Until the found thresholds have been repeatedly compared with the others, it is difficult to let us know in time the thresholds are good enough. Hence, the traditional method requires a large amount of computation to select optimal thresholds. In the proposed ATS method, the process of building the relationship between the number of connected components and the threshold does take some time. However, comparing with the traditional threshold selection method, the ATS method takes much less time-consuming.

2.3 Typical Algorithm Flow

The formulation of a ratio-based detector with the proposed ATS method is as follows.

(1) Calculate ESM and EDM using the filter $f_A(x, y)$.
(2) Automatically confirm the two thresholds, one high threshold T_h and one low threshold T_l. The automatic threshold selection method shown in Sect. 2.2.
(3) Perform non-maximum suppression. All the maxima form the candidate set of edge-pixels.
(4) Compare candidate edge-pixels with high threshold. The candidate pixel $I(x_i, y_j)$ with edge strength no less than the high threshold is marked as the strong edge-pixel. Finally, the strong edge map is obtained.
(5) Compare candidate edge-pixels with low threshold. The candidate pixel $I(x_i, y_j)$ whose edge strength is between the high threshold and the low threshold is decided as a possible edge-pixel. Similar to the operation of the strong edge map, the possible edge map is obtained.
(6) Connect the strong edge map with the possible edge map. The possible edge is connected to the strong one only when there is a path in the possible edge map to connect it to a strong edge in the edge-neighborhood rule.

3 Experimental Results and Discussion

ATS effectively reduces the time consumption in threshold selection and the ratio-based detector with ATS has good detection capability. In the following, we use three ratio-based detectors, ROA, GGS and RBED, to illustrate the effect of ATS. We record the detectors that incorporate the ATS as A-ROA, A-GGS, A-RBED.

As we known, adjustable parameter setting greatly influences the detection performance of an edge detector. All detectors are first evaluated by the Receiver Operating Characteristic (ROC) curves. ROC curve is an objective evaluator which provides fair evaluations of different detectors at their individual parameter settings. We use simulated SAR images in the experiment. The ROC curve evaluation requires an image and its ground truth (GT) image. The GT image marks edge, non-edge and tolerance regions corresponding to the simulated image. Figure 2 shows an amplitude format 3-look synthetic SAR image and its GT. In Fig. 2(b), black, grey and white color correspond to edge region, non-edge region and tolerance region, respectively. Limited by space, the further detail information of ROC curves is shown in reference [16].

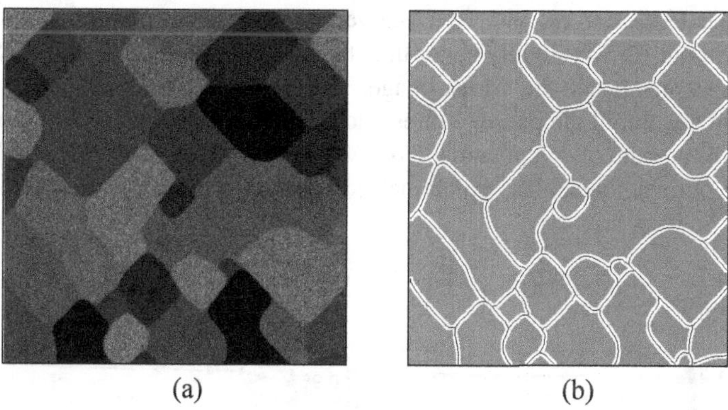

(a) (b)

Fig. 2. (a) A three-look synthetic SAR image and (b) its GT

The parameter spaces of compared detectors are shown as follows. The parameters of ROA detector are chosen from the following space:

$$\begin{cases} r_w = 2 + p_1,\ p_1 = 0, 1, 2, 3, 4, 5 \\ r_l = 5 + p_2,\ p_2 = 0, 2, 4, 6, 8, 10 \end{cases} \tag{12}$$

The parameters of GGS detector and GGS component are chosen from the following space:

$$\begin{cases} \alpha_g = p_1,\ p_1 = 2, 3, 4, 5, 6, 7 \\ \beta_g = 2 + p_2,\ p_2 = 0, 1, 2, 3, 4, 5 \\ \sigma_g = 5 + p_3,\ p_3 = 0, 2, 4, 6, 8, 10 \end{cases} \tag{13}$$

For RBED detector and RBED component, its parameters are chosen from the following parameter space:

$$\begin{cases} \alpha_l = p_1,\ p_1 = 2, 3, 4, 5, 6, 7 \\ \beta_l = 1 + p_2,\ p_2 = 0, 1, 2, 3, 4, 5 \\ \sigma_l = 2 + p_3,\ p_3 = 0, 1, 2, 3, 4, 5 \\ l_r = p_4,\ p_4 = 0, 1, 2, 3, 4, 5 \end{cases} \tag{14}$$

For detectors that do not use ATS, the high and low thresholds (T_l, T_h) of regular NSHT are as follows.

$$\begin{Bmatrix} T_l = 0.06 + 0.02p_1,\ p_1 = 1, 2, \ldots, 14 \\ T_h = T_l + 0.02p_2,\ p_2 = 1, 2, \ldots, (0.4 - T_l)/0.02 \end{Bmatrix} \tag{15}$$

Further expanding the parameter spaces cannot improve the performance of the detectors. Hence, the fixed parameter spaces are considered as a reasonable choice. We compare the detectors on single-look and 3-look synthetic SAR images. Figure 3(a) and

(b) show the ROC curves. The ROC curve shows that the performance of all the detectors without ATS is slightly better than the corresponding ones with ATS on both the single-look image and the 3-look image. The reason is traditional manual selection method searches for all the possible thresholds to include the optimal thresholds at the cost of a huge amount of computation. However, the thresholds selected by ATS is very close to the optimal thresholds, which makes the result of edge detection almost same.

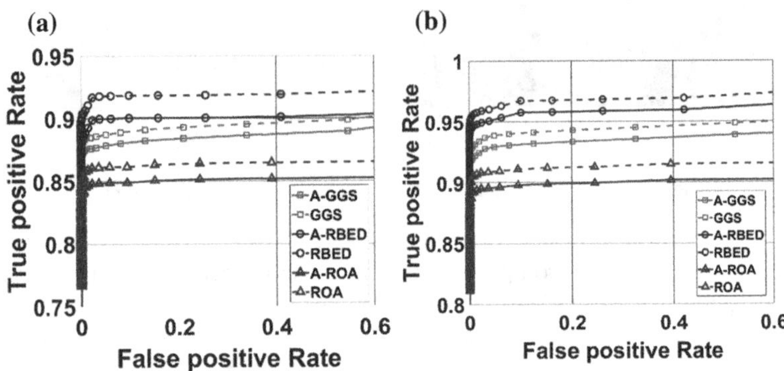

Fig. 3. (a) ROC curves of the single-look image. (b) ROC curves of the 3-look image.

The Pratt's figure of merit (PFOM) [17] fairly evaluates the localization error of detectors. The PFOM is calculated by

$$PFOM = \frac{1}{\max(N_e, N_d)} \sum\nolimits_{k=1}^{N_d} \frac{1}{1 + \alpha d^2(k)} \tag{16}$$

where N_e is the number of true edge pixels in the GT and N_d is the number of edge pixels in the detected result. α is penalization constant, and we take $\alpha = 2$ to severely punish the localization error in this experiment. $d(\cdot)$ is the Euclidean Distance between the kth detected edge pixel and the closest true edge pixel. The larger the PFOM value is, the better localization performance the detector has.

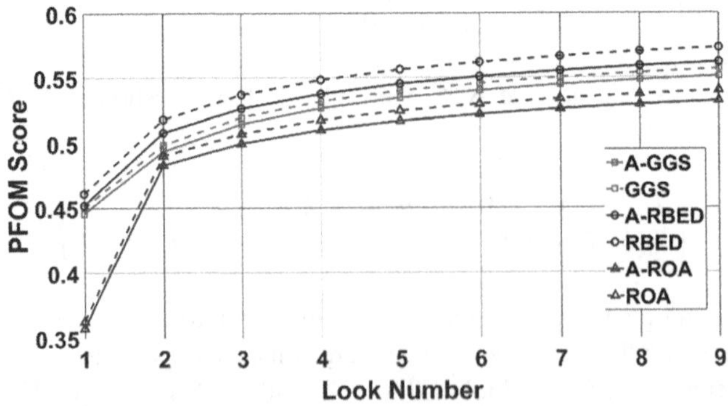

Fig. 4. PFOM score-look number curve

The parameter spaces of the compared detectors take from Eqs. (11)–(14). SAR images with different number of looks are simulated. The simulated image has the same scene with Fig. 2(a). For each number of looks, we record the average PFOM score as the evaluation result for each detector. From Fig. 4, we can see, the scores of all the detectors without ATS are slightly better than the corresponding ones with ATS.

In order to visually compare the influence of the proposed method on the detection results of the detectors. We obtain the binary edge map extracted from the 3-look simulated SAR image through these detectors.

In Fig. 5(a)–(f), we can see, for each detector, the detection results of detectors incorporating ATS are almost the same as those without ATS. This shows that the proposed ATS method finds approximately optimal thresholds.

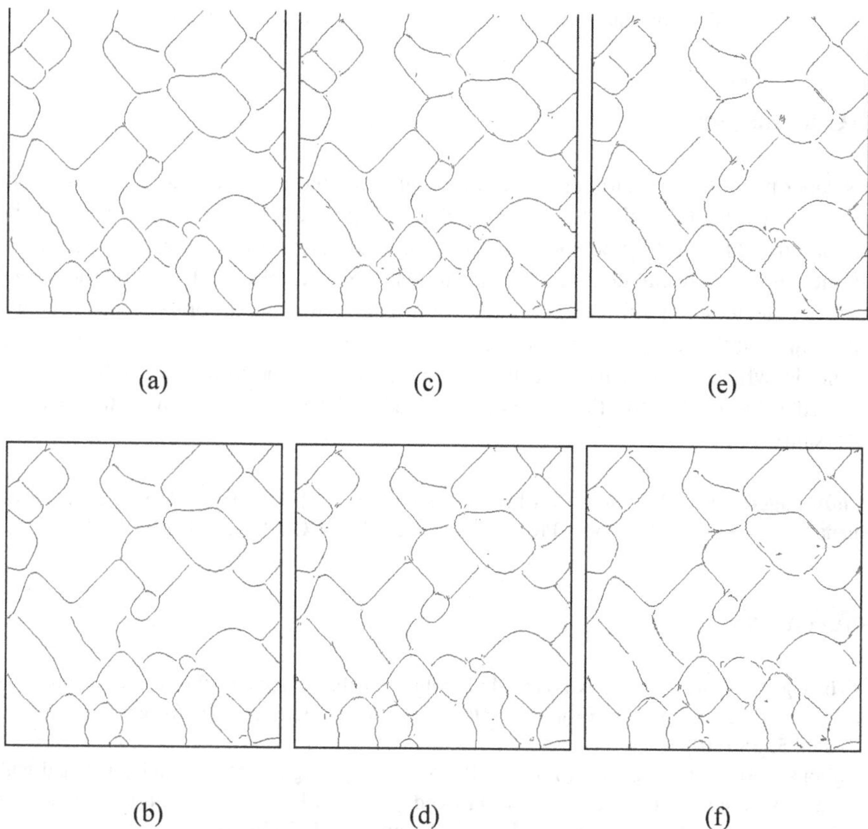

Fig. 5. Edge binary maps obtained by using detectors on the 3-look amplitude-format simulated SAR image. (a) RBED (b) A-RBED (c) GGS (d) A-GGS (e) ROA (f) A-ROA

In order to objectively evaluate the two threshold selection methods, we record the running-time of the two methods on a 3-look synthetic SAR image. Assume the range of low threshold is [0.08, 0.28] and the range of high threshold is [0.1, 0.3]. Then, we perform the ATS method and the traditional method separately on the simulated SAR image. The running time and the selected thresholds are recorded in Table 1. We can see that the high threshold and low threshold obtained by ATS method are very close to the optimal ones which is selected manually. But the ATS method effectively reduces the time consumption. If we make no assumption about the range between the low threshold and high threshold, traditional method based on manual selection will need more time to determine the appropriate thresholds.

Table 1. Comparing the ATS method with the traditional method.

Method	ATS method	Traditional method
Time (s)	0.523	32.814
Two thresholds	$T_l = 0.08\ T_h = 0.12$	$T_l = 0.09\ T_h = 0.14$

4 Conclusions

This paper proposed an automatic threshold selection method for the post-processing of the edge detector. It establishes the close relationship between connected regions of the edge and the threshold by performing threshold processing on the edge intensity map, and then find approximate optimal thresholds. The experimental results show that different detectors can still get good detection results after incorporating this strategy. More importantly, the strategy can greatly reduce the time of selecting excellent thresholds, which makes edge detectors more practical. In the future, we will apply the proposed ATS method to other kinds of SAR edge detectors, like Canny, to verify its universality.

Acknowledgements. This work has been supported by HGJ, HJSW and Research & Development plan of Shaanxi Province (Program No. 2017ZDXM-GY-094, 2015KTZDGY04-01).

References

1. Hwang, B., Ren, J., et al.: A practical algorithm for the retrieval of floe size distribution of Arctic sea ice from high-resolution satellite synthetic aperture radar imagery. Elem. Sci. Anth. **5**, 38 (2017)
2. Ijitona, T.B., Ren, J., Hwang, P.B.: SAR sea ice image segmentation using watershed with intensity-based region merging. In: Proceedings of IEEE International Conference on Computer and Information Technology (CIT), pp. 168–172 (2012)
3. Ren, J., Jiang, J., Wang, D., Ipson, S.S.: Fusion of intensity and inter-component chromatic difference for effective and robust colour edge detection. IET Image Process. **4**(4), 294–301 (2010)
4. Sun, G., Zhang, A., Ren, J., Ma, J., Wang, P., Jia, X.: Gravitationbased edge detection in hyperspectral images. Remote Sens. **9**(6), 592–611 (2017)
5. Touzi, R., Lopes, A., Bousquet, P.: A statistical and geometrical edge detector for SAR images. IEEE Trans. Geosci. Remote Sens. **26**(6), 764–773 (2016)

6. Canny, J.: A computational approach to edge detection. IEEE Trans. Pattern Anal. Mach. Intell. **8**(6), 679–698 (1986)
7. Heath, M.D., Sarker, S., Sanocki, T., Bowyer, K.W.: A robust visual method for assessing the relative performance of edge detection algorithms. IEEE Trans. Pattern Anal. Mach. Intell. **19**(12), 1338–1359 (1997)
8. Fjortoft, R., Lopes, A., Marthon, P., Cubero-Castan, E.: An optimal multiedge detector for SAR image segmentation. IEEE Trans. Geosci. Remote Sens. **36**(3), 793–802 (1998)
9. Shui, P.L., Cheng, D.: Edge detector of SAR images using Gaussian-Gamma-Shaped bi-windows. IEEE Geosci. Remote Sens. Lett. **9**(5), 846–850 (2012)
10. Xiang, Y., Wang, F., Wan, L., et al.: An advanced multiscale edge detector based on Gabor filters for SAR imagery. IEEE Geosci. Remote Sens. Lett. **14**(9), 1522–1526 (2017)
11. Wei, Q.R., Feng, D.Z.: An efficient SAR edge detector with a lower false positive rate. Int. J. Remote Sens. **36**(14), 3773–3797 (2015)
12. Zabalza, J., et al.: Novel segmented stacked AE for effective dimensionality reduction and feature extraction in hyperspectral imaging. Neurocomputing **185**, 1–10 (2016)
13. Zabalza, J., et al.: Novel folded-PCA for improved feature extraction and data reduction with hyperspectral imaging and SAR in remote sensing. ISPRS J. Photogramm. Remote Sens. **93** (7), 112–122 (2014)
14. Zheng, J., Liu, Y., Ren, J., et al.: Fusion of block and keypoints based approaches for effective copy-move image forgery detection. Multidimens. Syst. Signal Process. **27**(4), 989–1005 (2016)
15. Zhu, L., Shui, P.L.: Unsupervised estimation of the equivalent number of looks based on edge strength map in SAR images. J. Electron. Inf. Technol. **35**(5), 1170–1176 (2013)
16. Bowyer, K., Kranenburg, C., Dougherty, S.: Edge detector evaluation using empirical ROC curves. Comput. Vis. Image Underst. **84**(1), 77–103 (1999)
17. Pratt, W.K.: Digital Image Processing. Wiley, New York (1978)

Improving Disentanglement-Based Image-to-Image Translation with Feature Joint Block Fusion

Zhejian Zhang, Rui Zhang, Qiu-Feng Wang, and Kaizhu Huang(✉)

Xi'an Jiaotong-Liverpool University, No. 111 Ren'ai Road, Suzhou 215123, People's Republic of China
Zhejian.Zhang15@student.xjtlu.edu.cn, {rui.zhang02,qiufeng.wang,kaizhu.huang}@xjtlu.edu.cn

Abstract. Image-to-image translation aims to change attributes or domains of images, where the feature disentanglement based method is widely used recently due to its feasibility and effectiveness. In this method, a feature extractor is usually integrated in the encoder-decoder architecture generative adversarial network (GAN), which extracts features from domains and images, respectively. However, the two types of features are not properly combined, resulting in blurry generated images and indistinguishable translated domains. To alleviate this issue, we propose a new feature fusion approach to leverage the ability of the feature disentanglement. Instead of adding the two extracted features directly, we design a joint block fusion that contains integration, concatenation, and squeeze operations, thus allowing the generator to take full advantage of the two features and generate more photo-realistic images. We evaluate both the classification accuracy and Fréchet Inception Distance (FID) of the proposed method on two benchmark datasets of Alps Seasons and CelebA. Extensive experimental results demonstrate that the proposed joint block fusion can improve both the discriminability of domains and the quality of translated image. Specially, the classification accuracies are improved by 1.04% (FID reduced by 1.22) and 1.87% (FID reduced by 4.96) on Alps Seasons and CelebA, respectively.

Keywords: Feature fusion · Image-to-image translation · Generative adversarial networks · Feature disentanglement

1 Introduction

Image-to-image translation can create photo-realistic fake images based on the real images. Using a real image as input, the translation model can change particular styles of the image and output reasonable fake images. StarGAN [2] is the first model to implement multi-domain image-to-image translation with a single generator and discriminator, and it performs well on face images. However, StarGAN does not perform well on some large-scale domain transfer tasks, such as

J. Ren et al. (Eds.): BICS 2019, LNAI 11691, pp. 540–549, 2020.
https://doi.org/10.1007/978-3-030-39431-8_52

changing the season of landscape images. In addition, label supervision makes the model lack the ability of domain control, and some highly relevant attributes such as hair color and gender translations must be learned simultaneously to avoid feature entanglement. Based on the idea of feature disentanglement, domain-supervised GAN (DosGAN) [6] utilizes a pre-trained feature extractor and an encoder to extract the domain features and the background features, respectively. Then, the generator can learn to map the combination of the two extracted features to a target image. The domain-supervised method can disentangle image features in latent space, which makes the model more generalized on different scales translation tasks and reduces dependency between attributes. However, the feature fusion is difficult in the domain-supervised method where the domain feature extractor usually imports noises to the generator.

In this paper, we introduce a new feature joint block for feature disentanglement to overcome issues caused by the domain supervision structure. In order to reduce the irrelevant features in the extracted domain feature, we adopt an embedded neural network to refine the domain feature and learn the high dimensional spatial mapping. Meanwhile, we redesign the fusion strategy of the two extracted features, which guarantees the combination of the domain feature and the background feature can provide sufficient information to the generator with high computation efficiency. Finally, the improved model can learn faster to generate higher quality images, and preserve the advantages of the feature disentanglement.

In summary, our main contribution is to propose a new joint block for the feature fusion in the framework of the DosGAN model, and the proposed method can flexibly implement multi-domain image-to-image translation in a feature disentanglement approach with competitive performance to the state-of-the-art methods. Moreover, we demonstrate both qualitative and quantitative analysis on landscape images' season transfer and face images' hair color translation. The results show the improvement of the training speed, the model robustness, and superiority in comparison with image quality of other baselines.

2 Proposed Method

In this section, we first describe the feature disentanglement in image-to-image translation, which is also the basic idea of DosGAN. Then, we introduce the new joint block of features based on the feature disentanglement framework.

2.1 Feature Disentanglement

An image can be regarded as lying on a high-dimensional manifold $\mathcal{M}_I$ with its attributes as latent features [14]. The nonlinear separability of the manifold allows us to divide the manifold $\mathcal{M}_I$ into two sub-manifolds. One sub-manifold contains the specific domain feature that needs to be changed, and the other one contains the background feature that needs to be preserved. Figure 1 shows the process to translate a given image from original domain A to target domain

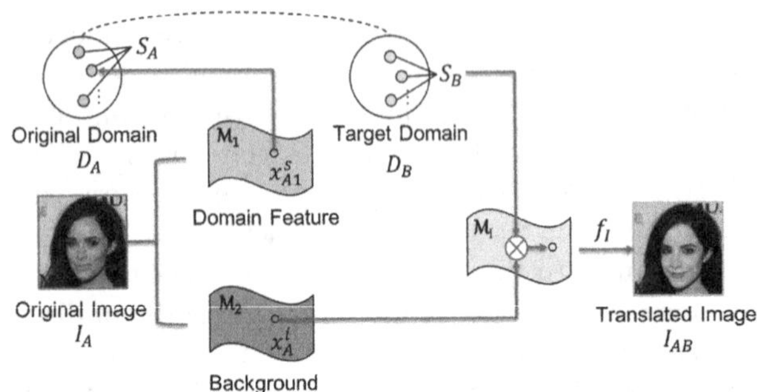

Fig. 1. Domain translation procedure based on the feature disentanglement.

B. For an image input to the model, the domain feature extractor can disentangle the specific domain sub-manifold $\mathcal{M}_1$ where the domain latent features are projected to. Then, a domain feature set of domain A can be obtained after processing all images belonging to this domain. Finally, the average feature of domain A denoted by S_A can be calculated by

$$S_A = \frac{1}{|D_A|} \sum_{x^s_A \in D_A} x^s_A, \tag{1}$$

where D_A is the number of all images that belong to domain A. Therefore, the average feature of target domain B, i.e. S_B, can be obtained in the same way as Eq. (1). Moreover, the background feature extractor is trained to project invariant background latent features x^i_A to another sub-manifold $\mathcal{M}_2$. Then S_B and x^i_A can be combined in the high-dimensional manifold $\mathcal{M}_I$, and be mapped to the image belonging to domain B. This process can be formulated as follows

$$I_{AB} = f_I(S_B \otimes x^i_A). \tag{2}$$

DosGAN adopts a pre-trained domain classifier as the domain feature extractor and a deep convolutional neural network (DCNN) encoder [5] as the background feature extractor. The generator of GAN implements the mapping f_I in Eq. (2), and the model is trained by an adversarial loss and reconstruction losses.

2.2 Feature Joint Block Fusion

To make the generator learn the mapping latent variables from $\mathcal{M}_I$ to the image more effectively, we propose a feature joint block fusion in the DosGAN model as shown in Fig. 2, which includes three parts, i.e., integration, concatenation, and squeeze operation.

Integration. DosGAN utilizes a domain CNN as a domain feature extractor, and the background feature extractor gets the feature by the supervision of the

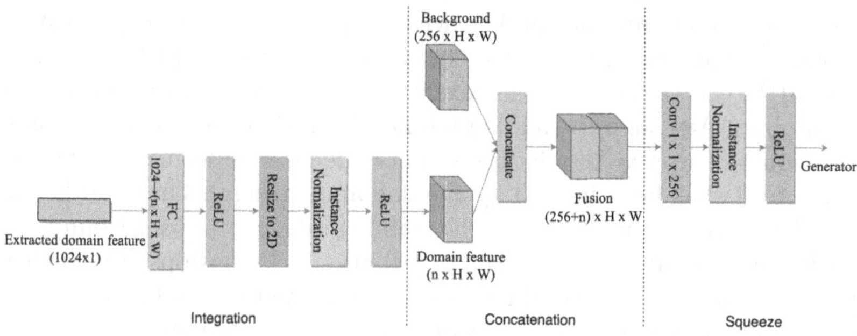

Fig. 2. The overview of feature joint block fusion.

average domain features and the reconstruction loss. However, the domain CNN does not determine which sub-manifold can better harmonize the domain latent variables and merge with the background sub-manifold to form an appropriate $\mathcal{M}_I$. To overcome this issue, a fully connected layer (FC) is used to project domain latent variables to a more precise sub-manifold of $\mathcal{M}_I$. In Fig. 2, n is the channel of the domain feature that can affect the fusion effect in the next concatenation part. We set the channel ratio of the domain feature and the background as 1:1 according to the feature fusion experiment in object detection [1]. An instance normalization layer is used before the activation layer to speed up the model convergence in image translation tasks [12].

Concatenation. The baseline DosGAN model added the two extracted features as follows

$$Z_{add} = \sum_{k=1}^{n}(S_B^k + x_A^{ik}) * C^k, \tag{3}$$

where n is the number of feature channels and C is denoted as the convolution kernels in the subsequent convolution layer. This method has a priori that the corresponding feature maps have similar semantic features [3], and this priori should be learned by the background extractor to match the extracted domain feature, which increases the training difficulty. Instead of the adding two features, we use the concatenation to obtain the feature fusion

$$Z_{concat} = \sum_{k=1}^{m} S_B^k * C^k + \sum_{k=1}^{n} x_A^{ik} * C^{k+m}, \tag{4}$$

where m is the number of domain feature channels and n is the number of background channels. Feature maps of domain feature and background no longer need strict correspondence. Compared with the formula 3 and 4, the adding method combines the domain feature and background features by increasing the amount of information for each extracted feature used to describe an image, while the concatenation method increases the number of features describing an image. Furthermore, the adding method adds the background latent variables in $\mathcal{M}_2$

to the domain latent variables in $\mathcal{M}_1$, which has two requirements: (1) $\mathcal{M}_1$ and $\mathcal{M}_2$ should be linear manifolds with the same structure, and (2) the extracted background latent variables should exactly match the distribution of domain latent variables. Although the adding method is efficient for feature fusion task, the first requirement may restrict the disentanglement performance because the structure of $\mathcal{M}_2$ has been limited by the domain extractor. On the other hand, the second requirement will increase the training difficulty of background extractor and image generator to learn the distribution relationships [13]. Instead of adding the two latent variables directly, the concatenation method concatenates the two extracted features. The tasks of merging two sub-manifolds and combination of latent variables are implemented by the subsequent convolution layers, which reduce the requirements for the extractors and enable the model better consistency with the feature disentanglement because the structure of $\mathcal{M}_2$ is not strictly restricted.

Squeeze. In the squeeze operation, we use a 1×1 kernel size convolution layer [8] to aggregate feature fusion channels, which can add linear transformation before the two kinds of features are summed, and the amount of calculations in the generator is reduced. Meanwhile, the instance normalization layer and the ReLU activation layer [9] are adopted to speed up training and increase nonlinearity, respectively.

In summary, the integration part can refine the domain feature, the concatenation part can retain the details of the background, and the squeeze operation can support the combination of two features. The joint block fusion makes the model disentangle feature well, which can decrease the training difficulty and improve image generation performance.

3 Experiments

In this section, we evaluate the proposed method on two datasets of Alps Seasons and CelebA. Both qualitative and quantitative evaluations are demonstrated. In the experiments, we use DosGAN-concat and DosGAN-add to represent the proposed method and the baseline DosGAN method, respectively.

3.1 Results on Alps Seasons

Qualitative Evaluation. As shown in Fig. 3, all the methods can translate the original image to target domain successfully, but the results of DosGANs based methods have a better vision quality. Furthermore, several improvements can be observed from the comparison of DosGAN-add and DosGAN-concat. First, our join block appear to keeps more detailed information of the background, which makes images smoother and clearer. This effect is more obvious on images that contain fine details. We can see that the wooden lamp in the left-bottom corner of the image retains its original shape by our approach. In comparison, it is blurred by the other methods. Meanwhile, the proposed method provides certain color invariant to prevent the abrupt colors after the transfer, which guarantees more natural colors of grass and snow. Moreover, we can see that there are some noise blocks in the original DosGAN model, which are successfully eliminated by the joint block. One possible reason for these improvements is the joint block fusion enables that the domain feature extractor and the background extractor can map the two different latent variables to two different sub-manifolds, which increases the image to latent space mapping capability and flexibility of $\mathcal{M}_I$.

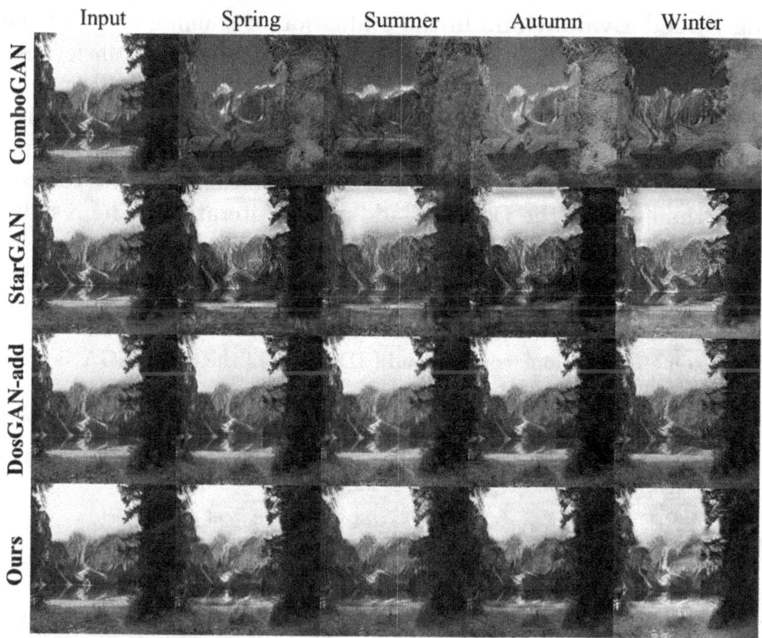

Fig. 3. Season transfer results on Alps Seasons dataset.

Quantitative Evaluation. We implement two different quantitative evaluations for the generated images. In order to verify the domain transfer accuracy of the results, we train a VGG-16 classifier [11] to classify the generated images into the season classes, we also calculate the Fréchet Inception Distance (FID) [4] between the generated images and real images. All results are shown in Table 1, and lower FID score means higher quality of generated images.

We can see DosGAN based methods have a much higher season classification accuracy than other methods, and the proposed method in DosGAN gets the highest accuracy. The possible reason is that the integration operation refines the extracted domain feature and the concatenate method makes full use of this information, which further improved recognition of season features. The last row in Table 1 shows FID scores for different methods, and the proposed method also gets the lowest score which verifies the effectiveness of the proposed method.

Table 1. Top-1 and Top-2 VGG-16 season classification accuracy and FID scores

	ComboGAN	StarGAN	DosGAN-add	DosGAN-concat
Top1	63.44%	79.51%	93.25%	**94.29%**
Top2	82.11%	93.45%	98.44%	**98.70%**
FID	31.61	69.27	25.70	**24.48**

Training Speed Evaluation. In the evaluation of training speed of the proposed method, we show the quantitative evaluation and season transfer results of the two DosGAN methods with different iterations in Table 2 and Fig. 4, respectively. We can see that the baseline model of DosGAN-add performs badly at 200k iterations and the generated image are blurry, while the proposed method DosGAN-Concat performs much better at 200k iterations and the FID score is even better than that of the DosGAN-add at 300k iterations. The results show that the proposed method can speed up the model training because more refined information is obtained for the generator.

Table 2. Season classification accuracy and FID scores of the two DosGANs after 200k and 300k iterations.

	Add-200k	Add-300k	Concat-200k	Concat-300k
Top1	68.03%	93.25%	92.87%	94.29%
FID	33.55	25.70	24.57	24.48

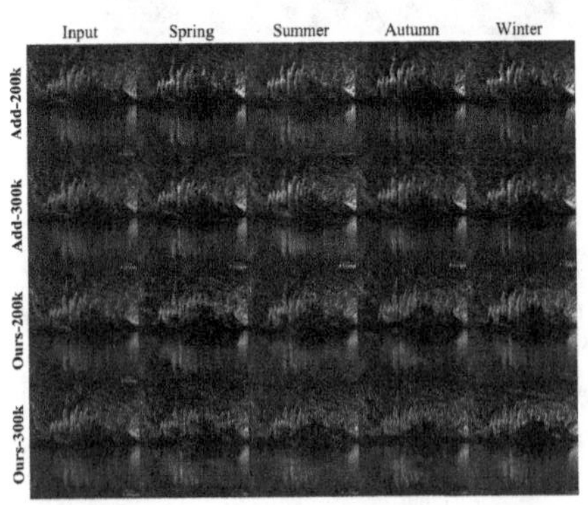

Fig. 4. Season transfer results of two DosGANs for different training iterations.

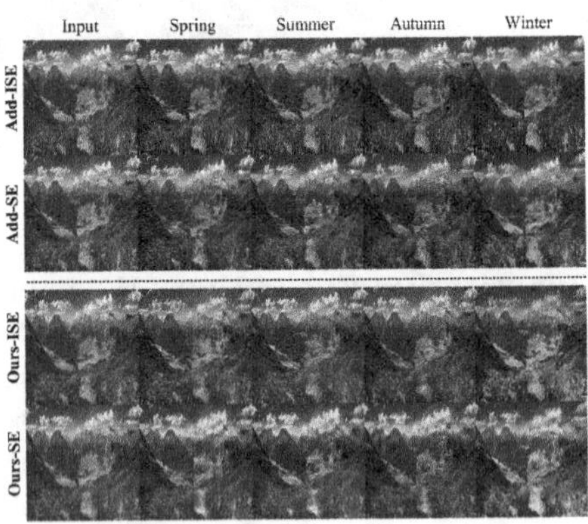

Fig. 5. Season transfer results of two DosGANs under different trained domain feature extractors.

Robustness Evaluation. To evaluate the robustness of the proposed method, we compare two domain feature extractors, which are trained with different iterations. The trained extractor (SE) is trained by 200k iterations, which is sufficient and also used in the aforementioned experiments. Another extractor (ISE) is trained by 100k iterations, which is insufficient. The generated images and classification accuracy of two domain feature extractors in the two methods are shown in Fig. 5 and Table 3, respectively. The top-tight part of Fig. 5 shows that the adding approach is affected by this noise and produces obvious ambiguity especially on the autumn and winter transfers. From Table 3, we can see that the proposed method (Concat) is much less affected by the two feature extractors, especially the top2 accuracy is only reduced by 2.7%. This may be explained in that the domain feature refining in the integration part and the linear transformation in the squeeze part map some irrelevant features to some marginal spaces.

Table 3. Classification accuracy of two DosGANs under different trained domain feature extractors.

	Add-ISE	Add-SE	Concat-ISE	Concat-SE
Top1	56.48%	93.25%	82.63%	94.29%
Top2	76.19%	98.44%	96.02%	98.70%

3.2 Results on CelebA

The second experiment is on the CelebA dataset to learn hair color translation. This is a small-scale translation task since the changes occur in the hair of this small range rather than the overall image of the style. StarGAN is a state-of-the-art model on this task, we hence compare the proposed method with the StarGAN and the baseline DosGAN.

Figure 6 shows the translation results of the three models, where the StarGAN model is more affected by attribute associations, and the age and gender attributes are also changed in this hair color translation. The model can perform better if these two attribute translations are also learned together [7]. The feature disentanglement method provides some background consistency to the DosGAN model to alleviate this attributes entanglement problem. According to the comparison of DosGAN-add and DosGAN-concat, the joint block fusion further promotes the invariance of the background and improves the image resolution, which is more obvious on gray hair translation.

Table 4 shows the hair color classification accuracy and FID score of three models' generated images. We can see that the DosGAN-concat method achieves the highest domain recognition, which shows the effectiveness of the proposed method. Comparing the FID scores in Table 4, we can see that StarGAN gets the best image generation performance in these three models. Nevertheless, the similar attributes association with the original dataset also makes the StarGAN

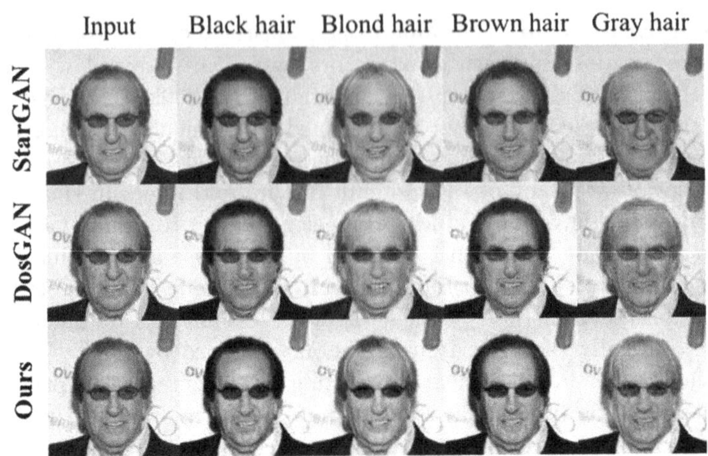

Fig. 6. Hair color translation results on CelebA dataset.

an advantage in this evaluation. Meanwhile, the results show that joint block significantly improves the quality of the generated image for DosGAN and the image translation performance is close to the StarGAN; this means the new feature fusion approach can make the model take full advantage of the feature disentanglement.

Table 4. Top-1 and Top-2 VGG-16 hair color classification accuracy and FID scores.

	StarGAN	DosGAN-add	DosGAN-concat
Top1	70.19%	70.36%	**72.23%**
Top2	88.74%	88.27%	**90.49%**
FID	9.44	16.35	**11.39**

4 Conclusion

In this paper, we propose a new feature joint block fusion method including integration, concatenation and squeeze operation. This method can be easily embedded in the disentanglement-based image-to-image translation model to improve the overall performance. The experimental results on two datasets of Alps Seasons and CelebA show that the proposed method improves remarkably the performance both qualitatively and quantitatively. Moreover, the proposed method also enjoys a higher robustness and training speed compared to the baseline DosGAN method. In the future, we plan to investigate the feature joint block fusion to improve the disentanglement-based image generation models on low-resolution images. Moreover, similar to [10], it is interesting to study how to extend our method to classification.

Acknowledgements. The work was partially supported by National Natural Science Foundation of China under no. 61876155 and 61876154; The Natural Science Foundation of the Jiangsu Higher Education Institutions of China under no. 17KJD520010; Suzhou Science and Technology Program under no. SYG201712, SZS201613; Natural Science Foundation of Jiangsu Province BK20181189 and BK20181190; Key Program Special Fund in XJTLU under no. KSF-A-01, KSF-P-02, KSF-E-26, and KSF-A-10; XJTLU Research Development Fund RDF-16-02-49.

References

1. Cao, G., Xie, X., Yang, W., Liao, Q., Shi, G., Wu, J.: Feature-fused SSD: fast detection for small objects. In: Ninth International Conference on Graphic and Image Processing (ICGIP 2017) (2017)
2. Choi, Y., Choi, M., Kim, M., Ha, J.W., Kim, S., Choo, J.: StarGAN: unified generative adversarial networks for multi-domain image-to-image translation. In: The IEEE Conference on Computer Vision and Pattern Recognition, June 2018
3. He, K., Zhang, X., Ren, S., Sun, J.: Deep residual learning for image recognition. CoRR (2015). http://arxiv.org/abs/1512.03385
4. Heusel, M., Ramsauer, H., Unterthiner, T., Nessler, B., Hochreiter, S.: GANs trained by a two time-scale update rule converge to a local nash equilibrium. In: Advances in Neural Information Processing Systems, pp. 6626–6637 (2017)
5. Huang, K., Hussain, A., Wang, Q., Zhang, R.: Deep Learning: Fundamentals, Theory and Applications. Springer, Cham (2019). https://doi.org/10.1007/978-3-030-06073-2. ISBN 978-3-030-06072-5
6. Lin, J., Xia, Y., Liu, S., et al.: Exploring explicit domain supervision for latent space disentanglement in unpaired image-to-image translation. arXiv 1902.03782 (2019)
7. Liu, M., et al.: STGAN: a unified selective transfer network for arbitrary image attribute editing. In: IEEE Conference on Computer Vision and Pattern Recognition (CVPR) (2019)
8. Long, J., Shelhamer, E., Darrell, T.: Fully convolutional networks for semantic segmentation. In: Proceedings of the IEEE Conference on Computer Vision and Pattern Recognition, pp. 3431–3440 (2015)
9. Nair, V., Hinton, G.E.: Rectified linear units improve restricted Boltzmann machines. In: Proceedings of the 27th International Conference on Machine Learning (ICML 2010), pp. 807–814 (2010)
10. Qian, Z., Huang, K., Wang, Q., Xiao, J., Zhang, R.: Generative adversarial classifier for handwriting characters super-resolution. arXiv:1901.06199 (2019)
11. Simonyan, K., Zisserman, A.: Very deep convolutional networks for large-scale image recognition. arXiv preprint arXiv:1409.1556 (2014)
12. Ulyanov, D., Vedaldi, A., Lempitsky, V.: Improved texture networks: Maximizing quality and diversity in feed-forward stylization and texture synthesis. In: Proceedings of the IEEE Conference on Computer Vision and Pattern Recognition, pp. 6924–6932 (2017)
13. Wang, J., Feng, W., Chen, Y., Yu, H., Huang, M., Yu, P.S.: Visual domain adaptation with manifold embedded distribution alignment. In: 2018 ACM Multimedia, pp. 402–410. ACM (2018)
14. Zhang, Z., Song, Y., Qi, H.: Age progression/regression by conditional adversarial autoencoder. In: Proceedings of the IEEE Conference on Computer Vision and Pattern Recognition, pp. 5810–5818 (2017)

Sequence Similarity Alignment Algorithm in Bioinformatics: Techniques and Challenges

Yuren Liu, Yijun Yan, Jinchang Ren(✉), and Stephen Marshall

Department of Electronic and Electrical Engineering, University of Strathclyde, Glasgow, UK
Jinchang.Ren@strath.ac.uk

Abstract. Sequence similarity alignment is a basic information processing method in bioinformatics. It is very important for discovering the information of function, structure and evolution in biological sequences. The main idea is to use a specific mathematical model or algorithm to find the maximum matching base or residual number between two or more sequences. The results of alignment reflect to what extent the algorithm reflects the similarity relationship between sequences and their biological characteristics. Therefore, the simple and effective algorithm of sequence similarity alignment in bioinformatics has always been a concern of biologists. This paper reviews some widely used sequence alignment algorithms including double-sequence alignment and multi-sequence alignment, simultaneously, introduces a method to call genetic variants from next-generation gene sequence data.

Keywords: Bioinformatics · Longest common subsequence (LCS) · Deoxyribonucleic acid (DNA) · Sequence alignment

1 Introduction

With the successful implementation of the Human Genome Project and the rapid development of information technology, the data volume of the three international nucleic acid sequence databases (Genebank, EMBL and DDBJ) has increased exponentially. Biologists, mathematicians and computer scientists are all facing the same and severe problem, i.e. how to use and express these data to analyse and explain the potential relationship between gene sequences, and to find out the beneficial information for human beings. In order to meet this challenge, bioinformatics emerged as the times require, and has increasingly become one of the core fields of natural science in the 21st century.

In the research of biology, a common method is to obtain useful information through comparative analysis. We analyze the similarities and differences of sequences at the level of nucleic acid and amino acid in order to infer their structure, function and evolutionary relationship. The most commonly used method of comparison is sequence alignment, which provides a very clear map of the relationship between residues of two or more sequences.

One of the purposes of sequence alignment is to enable people to judge whether there is enough similarity between two sequences, so as to determine whether there is

J. Ren et al. (Eds.): BICS 2019, LNAI 11691, pp. 550–560, 2020.
https://doi.org/10.1007/978-3-030-39431-8_53

homology between them. Therefore, sequence alignment is of great significance and practical value in bioinformatics. At present, many classical alignment algorithms have been proposed internationally, and many sequence alignment software have been developed. However, for the same set of sequences, different software uses different sequence alignment algorithms, and their operation speed and alignment results are quite different. Some software takes the comparison results into account and runs for a long time, while others do the opposite. Normally, they can't be achieved both. Therefore, the research of sequence alignment algorithm still needs to be deepened.

The main task of sequence alignment is to use algorithms to compare DNA sequences and discover similarities and differences between them. In bioinformatics, the similarity of DNA sequence or protein sequence is mainly manifested in three aspects: sequence, structure and function. Usually, sequence determines result and structure determines function. Therefore, sequence similarity research is mainly manifested in two aspects. On the one hand, sequence similarity analysis is used to discover the results and functions of sequences, and on the other hand, sequence similarity is used to analyze the evolutionary relationship between sequences.

The aim of this paper is to review a broad selection of sequence alignment algorithms used in bioinformatics with a particular focus on the LCS problem. It also discusses the principle of some classic sequence alignment algorithms. Furthermore, we also summarize the feature of double-sequence and multi-sequence alignment and introduce a method dealing with the compilation issue of many DNA fragmented reads.

The rest of this paper is organized as follows. Section 2 provides an overview of some basic concept of bioinformatics. Section 3 introduces the main frame of dynamic sequence alignment algorithm. Section 4 presents some classic sequence alignment algorithms. Section 5 discusses the main challenges and the future work on gene sequence alignment.

2 Brief of Bioinformatics

The main task of bioinformatics is to analyze, process and study various biological information contained in DNA sequence data. Bioinformatics includes sequence comparison, protein structure comparison and prediction, gene recognition, molecular evolution and comparative genomics, sequence overlap group assembly, structure-based drug design and so on [1].

2.1 Nucleic Acid and Protein

Nucleic acid is a one-dimensional polymer chain, which contains four monomers, each of which is called nucleotide. Nucleic acids carry genetic information, which is mainly expressed in the sequence of nucleotides. According to the different types of nucleotides, nucleic acids are divided DNA and ribonucleic acid (RNA). Nucleotides consist of phosphoric acid, deoxyribose or ribose and bases. The bases that make up nucleotides are divided into purine and pyrimidine. The former mainly refers to adenine (A) and guanine (G), both of which are contained in DNA and RNA. The latter mainly refers to cytosine (C), thymine (T) and uracil (U). Cytosine exists in DNA and RNA, thymine only exists in DNA, and uracil only exists in RNA. Among them, DNA is the main material basis for storing, replicating and transmitting genetic information, and RNA plays an important role in protein synthesis.

2.2 Variation

Variation refers to the alteration of some bases of DNA sequence in the course of biological evolution. Variations can be classified into three categories:

1. Substitution: Substitution of one base in a sequence by another in the course of biological evolution.
2. Insert or delete: Adding or deleting one or more bases in the course of biological evolution.
3. Rearrangement: Some segments of a DNA or protein sequence undergo a change in the sequence of links during synthesis.

Variation plays a very important role in the actual research process. Variation not only causes genetic variation and disease, but also species diversity.

3 Sequence Alignment

3.1 Overview of Sequence Alignment

In scientific research, comparison is one of the most common methods. In order to find the similarities and differences between objects or to discover the possible characteristics of objects, we usually use the method of comparison. In bioinformatics, comparisons are the alignment of multiple and similar sequences. Sequence alignment originated from the theory of evolution. If the two sequences are very similar, it can be inferred that the two sequences may have the same ancestors, which evolved from the compilation process of their ancestors through different gene substitution, addition, deletion and rearrangement. In addition, the structure and function of a given protein sequence can also be inferred by sequence alignment. Therefore, sequence alignment can be applied to secondary structure prediction, functional domain recognition of proteins and gene recognition.

Sequence alignment is to use a specific mathematical model or algorithm to find out the maximum matching base number between sequences, that is, insert a space '-' in two or more string sequences to achieve the maximum number of matched characters. For example, Fig. 1 shows the sequence alignment of two sequences 'AGCTTC-GACCA' and 'AGCTTCGCCA'. Figure 1(a) contains 8 same bases and Fig. 1(b) contains 10 same bases.

Compared with the method of not inserting spaces, it increases the number of matches. It can be seen from this that inserting vacancies is very necessary, and the process also reflects the process of biological evolution. The realization of sequence alignment generally depends on a mathematical model. Different mathematical models may reflect different characteristics of sequence structure, function and evolutionary relationship. It is difficult to judge whether a mathematical model is good or bad, or

A G C T T C G A C C A
| | | | | | | | | |
A G C T T C G C C A
(a)

A G C T T C G A C C A
| | | | | | | | | | |
A G C T T C G - C C A
(b)

Fig. 1. Matching before the insertion of space '-' (a) and after the insertion of space '-' (b).

whether a mathematical model is right or wrong. It only reflects the biological characteristics of a sequence from a certain point of view.

3.2 Multi-sequence Alignment

To sum up, we can use a quintuple to describe the problem of multiple sequence alignment. See Eq. 3:

$$\mathrm{MSA} = (\Sigma, \mathrm{S}, \mathrm{A}, \mathrm{O}, \mathrm{F}) \tag{1}$$

where Σ represents a set of symbols for multiple sequence alignments with a value of $\Sigma 1 \cup \{-\}$; $\Sigma 1$ represents finite set of symbols, while in protein sequence alignment $\Sigma 1 = \{\mathrm{A, C, D, E, F, G, H, I, K, L, M, N, P, Q, R, S, T, V, W, Y}\}$, and while in DNA sequence alignment, $\Sigma 1 = \{\mathrm{A, T, C, G}\}$, - means a space which will be inserted during the process of alignment.

S means the sequence set to be aligned. The unmodulated sequence of protein sequence alignment is composed of amino acids. DNA sequence alignment is that each sequence is composed of bases and the sequence length is different. $S = \{S_i | \mathrm{i} = 1, 2, \ldots, \mathrm{m}\}$,

$S_i = (C_{ij} | j = 1, 2, \ldots, l_i)$, where m equals to the number of sequences, C_{ij} is the jth base in sequence S_i, l_i means the length of the ith sequence.

A represents the result matrix, $A = (a_{ij})_{m \times n}, a_{ij} \in \Sigma$. In the result matrix, line I represents the ith sequence, and each j lists of the matrix represents the result of the comparison of the jth base. The base sequence in the sequence cannot be changed before and after alignment.

O is a set of comparison operations, $O = \{\text{insert\_space}, \text{delete\_space}\}$, which is the operation of insertion and deletion of the gap '-'.

F is the algorithm of alignment in order to figure out the specific position of the insertion and deletion.

3.3 Vacancy Penalty

In the process of sequence alignment, in order to make the results of sequence alignment more in line with certain expectations, the insertion or deletion of sequences is compensated by introducing vacancies. However, we should not introduce vacancies indefinitely, otherwise the results will lack biological significance. In order to limit the insertion of spaces, the usual method is to deduct the total score by inserting spaces. The deduction score is a penalty score, which restricts the insertion of vacancies into the penalty score of vacancies. Therefore, when the result of sequence alignment scored, the total score of matching residues between two sequences and the sum of space penalty scores were obtained [2].

Suppose S_1 and S_2 are used to represent the sequence to be aligned, S_{10} and S_{20} are used to represent the result of alignment, and L is used to represent the length of alignment. Generally, there are three kinds of space penalty rules.

3.3.1 Vacancy Penalty

The simplest penalty rule is the vacancy penalty score. When a vacancy is inserted into a sequence, a fixed penalty score Wg is given. For the whole sequence, the total blank penalty score is equal to the inserted blank Rg multiplied by the penalty score Wg for each vacancy [3].

Vacancy penalty points do not add extra running time, so it is the simplest penalty rules. However, the mutation frequencies of bases in gene sequences are different according to different loci in the actual evolution process, but the penalty scores of each locus in the vacancy penalty score are the same, which is different from its actual biological significance.

3.3.2 Constant Vacancy Penalty

This penalty rule is not for every space, but for every vacancy. Here the connected space is called a vacancy. The penalty score is based on the vacancy inserted in the sequence, and the penalty score of every inserting vacancy is Wg [3]. The specific operation is as follows:

Assuming whether matched or not, the score value is expressed by σ, we have $\forall \mathrm{x}, \sigma(\mathrm{x}, -) = \sigma(-, x) = 0$;

The representation of alignment score becomes:

$$\sum_{i=1}^{L} \sigma(S_{10}[i], S_{20}[i]) + W_g \times gaps \tag{2}$$

where *gaps* represents the number of vacancy.

Constant space penalty can avoid the defect of space length penalty, but when too many connected spaces are inserted, this penalty rule cannot be limited, which may lead to the splitting of sequence segments by connected spaces. This requires a penalty score rule which is closely related to the length of the space. Its penalty score does not only depend on the length of the space, but also does not ignore the length of the space.

3.3.3 Affine Vacancy Penalty

The rule divides the penalty of vacancy into two parts [3]: open vacancy penalty and extended vacancy penalty. If q is the length of the vacancy, W_g is the penalty score of the open vacancy, W_s is the penalty score of the extended vacancy and W is the total penalty score, then: $\mathrm{W} = W_g + \mathrm{q} \times W_s$, so we can have the formula calculating the alignment score:

$$\sum_{i=1}^{L} \sigma(S_{10}[i], S_{20}[i]) + W_g \times gaps + W_s \times spaces \quad (3)$$

where *gaps* is the number of space and spaces represents the number of vacancy.

In practical biology research, the probability of inserting and deleting multiple vacancies connected by a vacancy coin is small, so the affine vacancy penalty score has more biological significance.

3.4 Scoring Matrix

In sequence alignment, a matrix is usually used to record the score of each variation, which becomes the score matrix. The results of sequence alignment will be different if different scoring matrices are chosen. The simplest scoring matrix is a single matrix, also known as a sparse matrix. Using this matrix, we only need to detect whether the bases of corresponding sites between sequences are identical, and the scores of the same bases are 1, and the differences are 0. This matrix, which only considers the identity of bases, has great limitations.

In order to better reflect the biological characteristics, we need to design a more optimized scoring matrix. PAM (point accepted mutation) [4] is the first widely used optimal matrix. A PAM indicates that 1% of the amino acids have changed, that is, the evolutionary unit of variation. Generally, sequences with high similarity use lower PAM matrix, while sequences with low similarity use higher PAM matrix.

Besides PAM matrix, BLOSUM (blocks substitution matrix) [4] matrix is also widely used. BLOSUM matrices also use numbering to distinguish different BLOSUM matrices, where numbering is mainly used to distinguish the similarity of sequences. For example, BLOSUM62 matrix is generally used to align at least 62% of the same proportion of sequences. So the use of BLOSUM matrix is exactly the opposite to that of PAM matrix.

4 Classic Alignment Algorithms

At present, many sequence alignment algorithms are based on dynamic programming algorithm, considering different improvements in computing speed and storage space in Chengdu. Sequence alignment algorithms have several different classification methods. According to the number of alignment sequences, sequence alignment can be divided into double sequence alignment and multiple sequence alignment. According to the range of sequence alignment, sequence alignment can be divided into global sequence alignment and local sequence alignment.

4.1 Global Sequence Alignment and Local Sequence Alignment

Local sequence alignment considers the local similarity of sequences, which is a forehead method to find partial similarity regions of sequences. Local sequence alignment is mainly applied to protein sequence alignment, which is more sensitive and biologically significant than complete sequence alignment. Global sequence alignment is the whole sequence, which considers the similarity of sequences from the global scope. Global sequence alignment is mainly used to predict the homology between sequences and the structure and function of proteins.

4.2 Double-Sequence Alignment

Double sequence alignment is to find the maximum similarity match between two DNA or protein sequences. The search process is based on some algorithm or model. Multiple sequence alignment and sequence database search are based on double sequence alignment. At present, the most classical double sequence alignment algorithms are lattice graph method and dynamic programming algorithm.

4.2.1 Lattice Graph Method

The simplest double sequence alignment algorithm is the lattice graph method. In this method, the sequence to be aligned is placed on a two-dimensional plane, a sequence is placed horizontally on the top of the plane, and a sequence is placed vertically on the left of the plane. A point is marked at the intersection of any two identical bases of the two sequences. Finally, linking the points parallel to the diagonal line constitutes the result of two sequence alignments [5].

The lattice graph method can visually display the insertion and deletion of sequences, and all matched base sequences between two sequences can be visually reflected by lattice graph. However, since the sequence length is counted in thousands, it is unrealistic to use all the lattice computing programs to calculate the real alignment sequence, so other alignment methods will be more used to achieve.

4.2.2 Dynamic Programming Algorithm

Dynamic programming algorithm was first proposed by Needleman and Wunsch and has been widely used and improved. It has gradually become one of the most important theoretical foundations in computational biology. The most classical dynamic programming algorithms are Needleman-Wunsch algorithm [6] and Smith-Waterman algorithm [7]. All global alignment algorithms are based on NW algorithm, while SW algorithm is improved based on NW algorithm, mainly applied to local sequence alignment. The following is a brief introduction to the dynamic programming algorithm.

Given sequence s_1 and s_2, the length of which are m and n correspondingly. $s_1[1...i]$ and $s_2[1...j] (1 \leq i \leq m, 1 \leq j \leq n)$ represent prefix subsequences separately of s_1 and s_2. And the alignment result of s_1 and s_2 contains that of $s_1[1...i]$ and $s_2[1...j]$, which is a recursive relationship.

From this relationship, it can be seen that the optimal solution to its subsequence is the premise of solving the global alignment of two sequences. Through this recursive relation, the optimal value of the whole sequence can be obtained. Then, the optimal alignment result of the sequence is obtained by backtracking the path of the obtained optimal value.

The basic step of dynamic programming algorithm is to use a binary matrix to store the similar scores of two sequences, and then retrieve the optimal alignment of the sequences according to the scores in the matrix. Assume that the sequence s_1 and s_2 are compared by using dynamic programming algorithm, their lengths are m and n, respectively. Firstly, we need to construct a two-dimensional matrix with the size of $(m+1) \times (n+1)$. The element $M[i,j](0 \leq i \leq m, 0 \leq j \leq n)$ in the matrix represents the highest alignment score of its prefix subsequence $s_1[1...i]$ and $s_2[1..j]$. The ratio of prefix subsequence a to vacancy '-' is expressed in both row 0 and column 0 of the matrix. Therefore, the initial values of the elements in the matrix are:

$$M[0,0] = 0 \tag{4}$$

$$M[i,0] = \sum\nolimits_{k=1}^{i} \sigma(s_1[i], -)(1 \leq i \leq m) \tag{5}$$

$$M[0,j] = \sum\nolimits_{k=1}^{j} \sigma(-, s_2[j])(1 \leq i \leq n) \tag{6}$$

By analyzing the prefix subsequence $s_1[1...i]$ and $s_2[1..j]$, there may be three cases to get the optimal score $M[i,j]$:

1. The sum of the alignment score between $s_1[i]$ and $s_2[j]$ and the score between the subsequence $s_1[1...i-1]$ and $s_2[1..j-1]$ which is $M[i-1, j-1]$;
2. The sum of the alignment score between $s_1[i]$ and a space '-' and the score between the subsequence $s_1[1...i-1]$ and $s_2[1..j]$ which is $M[i-1, j]$;
3. The sum of the alignment score between $s_2[j]$ and a space '-' and the score between the subsequence $s_1[1...i]$ and $s_2[1..j-1]$ which is $M[i, j-1]$. And it's shown below (Fig. 2):

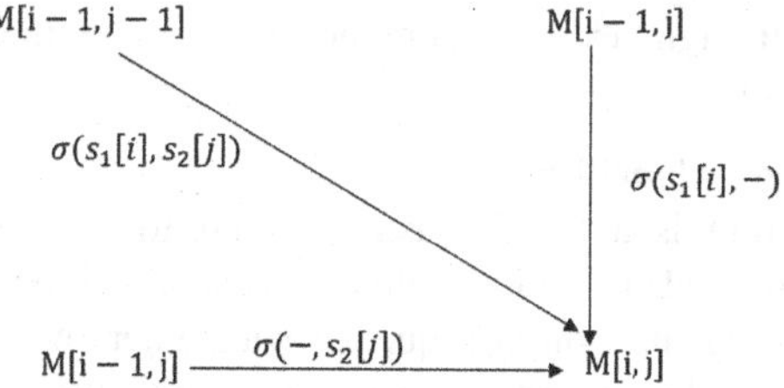

Fig. 2. Source of matrix elements

Thus, the recursive relation is obtained as:

$$M[i,j] = max \begin{cases} M[i-1, j-1] + \sigma(s_1[i], s_2[j]) \\ M[i-1, j] + \sigma(s_1[i], -) \\ M[i, j-1] + \sigma(-, s_2[j]) \end{cases} (1 \leq i \leq m, 1 \leq j \leq n) \tag{7}$$

Using the upper formula, the values of each element in the matrix are calculated in order from left to right and from top to bottom. When the position of the last column in the last row, element M[m, n], is calculated, the best alignment score of two sequences s1 and s2 is obtained.

After obtaining the optimal score, we use the backtracking method to construct the comparison record. That is, starting from the position of the optimal alignment score, i.e. the position of the last column in the last row of the matrix, we retrospect along the path to get the value until reaching column 0 of row 0. At this point, the sequence corresponding to the intersection points in the backtracking process is the alignment result.

When using dynamic programming algorithm for sequence alignment, it is necessary to calculate each element in a two-dimensional array of $(m+1) \times (n+1)$ size. Its time complexity is *O(mn)* and space complexity is *O(mn)*. The backtracking process is from the lower right of the array to the upper left of the array, passing through *(m + n)* elements, so its time complexity is *O(m + n)*, and there is no additional storage overhead. Therefore, the basic dynamic programming algorithm takes a lot of time and space to solve the problem of double sequence alignment, so people put forward various improved algorithms.

4.2.3 Multi-sequence Alignment

The generalization of double sequence alignment in multi-sequence alignment is to extend the alignment problem from two sequences to multiple sequences. Therefore, the method to solve the double sequence problem is also applicable to multiple sequence alignment, but the number of alignments has increased, which makes the problem more complex. Murata has successfully applied dynamic programming algorithm to the alignment of three sequences [8], but because the alignment time is long and the space required is large, it is almost impossible to extend it to more than three sequences alignment. Generally, the dynamic programming algorithm is seldom used in multi-sequence alignment. Basically, heuristic algorithm, random algorithm and partition algorithm are used. Among them, there are many kinds of heuristic algorithms, such as star alignment algorithm, progressive alignment algorithm, iterative thinning method and so on.

4.2.3.1 Star Alignment Algorithm

Star alignment algorithm is a fast heuristic method for solving multiple sequence alignment problems. It needs to find a central sequence, and the result of alignment is established by comparing the central sequence with other sequences. Star alignment algorithm follows a rule, that is, in the alignment process, the space must be added to the central sequence continuously so that the central sequence and alignment sequence can reach the maximum number of matches. Spaces added to the central sequence cannot be removed, and always remain in the central sequence, knowing that the central sequence and the ordered sequence are aligned.

4.2.3.2 Progressive Alignment Algorithm

Another simple and effective heuristic algorithm is the progressive alignment algorithm. The basic idea of progressive alignment algorithm is to use dynamic programming algorithm to iteratively align two sequences. That is to say, the two sequences are aligned first, and then the new sequences are added, until all the sequences are added.

However, different addition order may lead to different comparison results. Therefore, the key of progressive alignment algorithm is how to determine the sequence of alignment. Generally, the alignment begins with the two most similar sequences, and then proceeds to the far alignment to complete all the sequences.

Progressive alignment algorithm mainly consists of three steps:

1. Computation of the distance matrix;
2. Construction of guidance tree;
3. Alignment of the sequences according to the constructed guide tree.

Nowadays, the most widely used progressive comparison procedure is ClustalW. It gives a set of schemes of dynamic selection of comparison parameters, which mainly solves the problem of parameter selection in the process of comparison. Usually, the scoring matrix and reflective blank penalty score are used to solve the selection problem of comparison parameters, and it is hoped that the effective parameters can be set to achieve the desired results.

5 Challenges and Future Directions

Classical similarity analysis of biological sequences is achieved by comparing biological sequences, and sequence alignment is achieved by comparing two or more nucleic acid sequences or protein sequences. By comparing the similarity between the position sequence and the known sequence, we can get their homology to predict the function of the unknown sequence.

At present, the main methods of sequence alignment are: double sequence alignment algorithm, multi-sequence alignment algorithm, knowledge discovery-based alignment algorithm and graphic representation-based alignment algorithm. The first two are based on the idea of dynamic programming, which is realized by mature algorithms and software, but the calculation is quite complicated. However, the method based on knowledge discovery is not yet mature. With the continuous improvement of graphical representation and related theory of biological sequence, there will be a great space for the development of alignment algorithm based on graphical representation.

Therefore, based on the above research, our future work is to improve the current sequence alignment algorithm and try to develop a bio-sequence analysis software based on graphical identification on small-indel variant calling [9], non-human variant calling [10] and high accurate SNP calling [11]. As an interdisciplinary subject of computer science and molecular biology, bioinformatics has become an indispensable and advantageous research tool in genome research [12]. And some advanced feature extraction algorithms [13–15] shall be adopted into a deep learning alignment method, hopefully. It is believed that in the future, improved alignment methods can be used to find genes that may be of research value, or to find out the other side of known genes that have not been discovered.

References

1. Zhang, C.: Current situation and prospect of bioinformatics. World Sci. Technol. Res. Dev. **22**, 17–20 (2000)
2. Parry-Smith, D.J., Attwood, T.K.: Introduction to Bioinformatics, pp. 168–196. Addison Wesley Longman (1999)
3. Xiao, Z.: A Multiple Alignment Approach for DNA Sequence Based on the Maximum Weighed Path Algorithms. Xi'an University of Electronic Science and Technology, pp. 8–9 (2006)
4. Pearson, W.R.: Selecting the right similarity-scoring matrix. Curr. Protoc. Bioinform. **43**, 1–9 (2013)
5. Gibbs, A.J., McIntyre, G.A.: The diagram a method for comparing sequences its use with amino and nucleotide sequences. Eur. J. Biochem. **16**, 1–11 (1970)
6. Wunsh, C.D., Needleman, S.B.: A general method applicable to the search for similarities in the amino acid sequences of two proteins. J. Mol. Biol. **48**, 443–453 (1970)
7. Waterman, M.S., Smith, T.F.: Identification of common molecular subsequences. J. Mol. Biol. **147**, 195–197 (1981)
8. Richardson, J.S., Murata, M., Sussman, J.L.: Simultaneous comparison of three protein sequences. Proc. Natl. Acad. Sci. **93**, 3073–3077 (1985)
9. Chang, P.C., Poplin, R., Alexander, D.: A universal SNP and small-indel variant caller using deep neural networks. Nat. Biotechnol. **36**, 983–987 (2018)
10. McLean, C., Yun, T., Chang, P.C.: Improved Non-human Variant Calling Using Species-specific DeepVariant Models. Google AI DeepVariant Blog (2018)
11. Chang, P.C., Kolesnikov, A.: Highly Accurate SNP and Indel Calling on PacBio CCS with DeepVariant. Google AI DeepVariant Blog (2019)
12. Li, H., Baid, G., Chang, P.C.: Using Nucleus and TenserFlow for DNA Sequencing Error Correction. Google AI DeepVariant Blog (2019)
13. Ren, J., Zabalza, J., et al.: Novel segmented stacked autoencoder for effective dimensionality reduction and feature extraction in hyperspectral imaging. Neurocomputing **185**, 1–10 (2016)
14. Chai, Y., Ren, J., Zhao, H., Li, Y., Ren, J., Murray, P.: Hierarchical and multi-featured fusion for effective gait recognition under variable scenarios. Pattern Anal. Appl. **19**(4), 905–917 (2016)
15. Sun, H., Ren, J., Zhao, H., Yan, Y., Zabalza, J., Marshall, S.: Superpixel based feature specific sparse representation for spectral-spatial classification of hyperspectral images. Remote Sens. **11**(5), 536 (2019)

Effect on Probabilistic Language Model for Cross-Domain Corpus

Ai Zhang(✉)

University of California, San Diego, CA 92093, USA
zhangai1996@sina.com

Abstract. Probabilistic language model has been widely used in the field of natural language processing and it should be based on a suitable data corpus. Limited data is a permanent problem of probabilistic language model. Original data corpus can no longer meet requirements as time goes by, the emergence of new terms and technical terminologies. Therefore, cross-domain training is often needed. In this paper, a probabilistic language model is built with $< UNK >$ filtering and linear interpolation based on N-grams of words. Then, for three different data domain corpus which each has unique word distribution, based on perplexity analysis, data corpus with similar word distribution can be got. With all this information, the accuracy of cross-domain probabilistic model can be promoted.

Keywords: Natural language processing · Probabilistic Language Model · N-grams · Word distribution · Perplexity

1 Introduction

Probabilistic language model has been widely used in machine translation, speech recognition and text abstraction, such as realizing the recognition of the author's article [1], the classification of the article [2,3], analyzing the similarity of sentences [4–6], recommending articles to the new user [2], using N-grams of words for language classification and sentence recognition [7–9].

Probabilistic language model has been widely used in the field of natural language processing and it should be based on a suitable data corpus. Limited data is a permanent problem of probabilistic language model. Original data corpus can no longer meet requirements as time goes by, the emergence of new terms and technical terminologies.

Therefore, cross-domain training is often needed. It is important to build a correct language model based on choosing a suitable data corpus. For this paper, a probabilistic language model is constructed based on three different corpora. Word distribution characteristic is studied and its effect on language model is learned for each corpus so as to choose training data for cross-domain case.

Rest of the paper is organized as follows. Section 2 presents background. Sections 3 and 4 describe methodology, results of experiment and Sect. 5 finally presents the conclusion.

J. Ren et al. (Eds.): BICS 2019, LNAI 11691, pp. 561–569, 2020.
https://doi.org/10.1007/978-3-030-39431-8_54

2 Background

2.1 Language Model

N-gram language model, which computes the probability of a sequence as the product of probabilities of subsequences. They condition on only the past n-1 words. This means that the probability of a sentence $s = < w_1, ..., w_i, ..., w_M >$ can be approximated as formula 1.

$$p(w_1, ..., w_i, ..., w_M) = \prod_{i=1}^{M} p(w_i | w_{i-n+1}, ..., w_{i-1}) \quad (1)$$

This model requires estimating and storing the probability of only V^n events, which is exponential in the order of the N-gram, and not V^M, which is exponential in the length of the sentence. V is the finite set of words in the corpus. The N-gram probabilities can be computed by relative frequency estimation as formula 2.

$$p(w_i | w_{i-n+1}, ..., w_{i-1}) = \frac{count(w_{i-n+1}, ..., w_{i-1}, w_i)}{count(w_{i-n+1}, ..., w_{i-1})} \quad (2)$$

2.2 Smoothing

Back off is one way to combine different order N-gram models. An alternative approach is interpolation: setting the probability of a word in context to a weighted sum of its probabilities across progressively shorter contexts. Instead of choosing a single n for the size of the N-gram, we can take the weighted average across several N-gram probabilities.

$$\hat{p}(w_i | w_{i-n+1}, ..., w_{i-1}) = \sum_{j=1}^{n-1} \lambda_{n-j+1} * p(w_i | w_{i-n+j}, ..., w_{i-1}) + \lambda_1 * p(w_i) \quad (3)$$

where $\sum_{j=1}^{n} \lambda_j = 1$.

2.3 Evaluating a Language Model: Perplexity

A good language model should assign high probability to real language it has not seen before. The goal of probabilistic language models is to accurately measure the probability of sequences of words. Therefore, an intrinsic evaluation metric is the likelihood that the language model assigns to held-out data.

Treating the entire held-out corpus as a single stream of words. Typically, unknown words are mapped to the $< UNK >$ word. This means that we have to estimate some probability for $< UNK >$ on the training data. One way to do this is to fix the vocabulary V to the V-1 words with the highest counts in the training data, and then convert all other words to $< UNK >$.

We have test data consisting of t sentences: $S = s_1, s_2, ..., s_t$. The Log-probability of S is

$$l(S) = \sum_{i=1}^{t} \log_2 p(s_i) \tag{4}$$

Held-out likelihood is usually presented as perplexity, which is a deterministic transformation of the log-likelihood into an information-theoretic quantity,

$$Perplex(S) = 2^{-\frac{l(S)}{M}} = 2^{-\frac{1}{M}\sum_{i=1}^{t} log_2 p(s_i)} \tag{5}$$

Where $M = \sum_{i=1}^{t} |s_i|$ is the total number of words in the held-out corpus.

Lower perplexities correspond to higher likelihoods, so lower scores are better on this metric - it is better to be less perplexed. In practice, language models tend to give perplexities in the range between 1 and V.

3 Methodology

The research process consists of the following steps: Domain corpus selection, corpus preprocessing, N-gram representation, probabilistic language model generation, analysis on In-Domain text, analysis on Out-of-Domain text, adaptation and perplexity evaluation. Figure 1 shows the process.

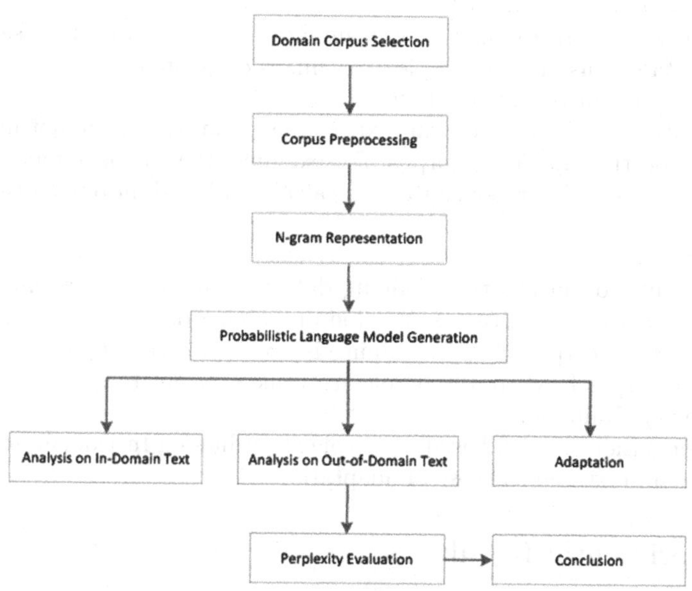

Fig. 1. Research process

(1) Domain Corpus selection
Choose three different domain corpus, Domain A, Domain B and Domain C. Domain A and Domain B have similar word distribution characteristics. The word distribution of Domain C is different from that of Domain A and Domain B.
(2) Corpus Preprocessing
Divide each data corpus into 3 parts, including training set, dev set and test set and the amount of each is accounted for 70% of whole data, 15% of whole data and 15% of whole data respectively.
(3) N-gram Representation
Each training set is represented by using N-gram, including unigram, bigram and trigram.
(4) Probabilistic Language Model Generation
The language model is the linear interpolation of unigram, bigram and trigram models. Three hyper-parameters are used λ_1, λ_2 and λ_3 respectively for the unigram, bigram and trigram where $\lambda_1 + \lambda_2 + \lambda_3 = 1, \lambda_i \geq 0$ for all i. For the bigram and trigram model, Laplace smoothing is applied. Two '*' symbols are appended at the beginning of the sentence and at the end of each sentence, 'STOP' symbol is appended. In order to estimate the term $p(w_i|w_{i-2}, w_{i-1})$, the formula below is applied:

$$p(w_i|w_{i-2}, w_{i-1}) = \lambda_1 * p(w_i|w_{i-2}, w_{i-1}) + \lambda_2 * p(w_i|w_{i-1}) + \lambda_3 * p(w_i) \quad (6)$$

This estimate defines a distribution.
(5) Analysis on In-Domain Text
For analysis on In-Domain text, training and testing are processed inside each data corpus and the perplexity value is calculated.
(6) Analysis on Out-of-Domain Text
For analysis on Out-of-Domain text, training and testing are not limited to process on the same data corpus. For example, the language model can be trained on A and perplexity value is calculated based on testing the model on B.
(7) Adaptation
The adaptation means that training data is transferred between two data corpora. For example, certain portion of training data on corpus B can be added to the corpus C. The training is done on corpus C and the test is done on corpus B where the perplexity value is calculated.
(8) Perplexity Evaluation
The conclusion is given based on perplexity values on In-Domain text, Out-of-Domain text and the case of adaptation.

4 Experimental Results

4.1 Analysis on Corpus

We provide three different corpora from different domains to conduct the evaluation. Table 1 presents the list of the datasets.

Table 1. Datasets summary

Datasets	Description	Size	Train	Dev	Test
Brown	The objective of this corpus is to be the standard corpus to represent the present-day (i.e., 1979) American English [10]	5985 KB	70%	15%	15%
Gutenberg	This corpus contains a selection of text from public domain works by authors including Jane Austen and William Shakespeare [11]	11826 KB	70%	15%	15%
Reuters	A collection of financial news articles that appeared on the Reuters newswire in 1987 [12]	8407 KB	70%	15%	15%

First, the distribution of words in three data corpus should be analyzed. Figure 2 shows frequencies of 25 most frequent words in corpus and Fig. 3 gives word frequency of the training set and test set for three data corpus. For example, inside the brown corpus shown in Fig. 3(a), the most frequent 15 words of training set and test set are the same. If we consider the most frequent 20 words, 19 are the same. If 25 most frequent words are considered, 24 are the same. Figure 4 shows word frequencies on the training set for various data corpus. As shown in Fig. 4(a), for the Brown and Gutenberg corpus, 13 words are the same out of 15 most frequent words (17 words are the same out of 20 most frequent words and 19 words are the same out of 25 most frequent words). This can be explained as these two data corpus have similar characteristics of word distribution. However, as shown in Fig. 4(b), for the Brown and Reuters corpus, only 8 words are the same out of 15 most frequent words (10 are the same out of 20 and 11 are the same out of 25). Similarly, as shown in Fig. 4(c), for the Gutenberg and Reuters data corpus, only 7 words are the same out of 15 most frequent words (9 are the same out of 20 and 10 are the same out of 25). This means that Reuters corpus is different from the Brown and Gutenberg data corpus on word distributions, indicating that Reuters belongs to the field which is quite different from the other two.

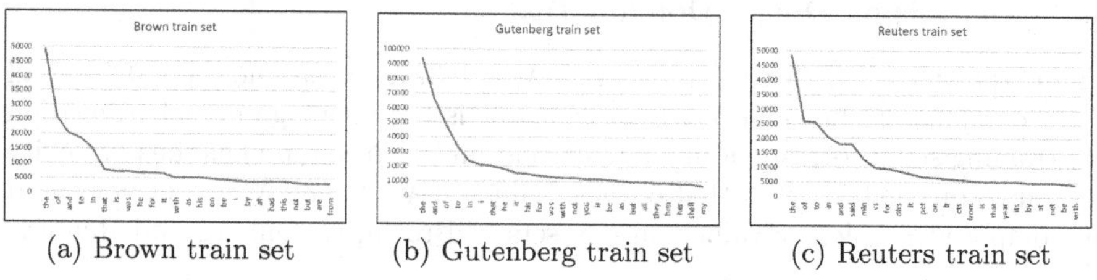

(a) Brown train set (b) Gutenberg train set (c) Reuters train set

Fig. 2. The 25 most frequent word in 3 corpora

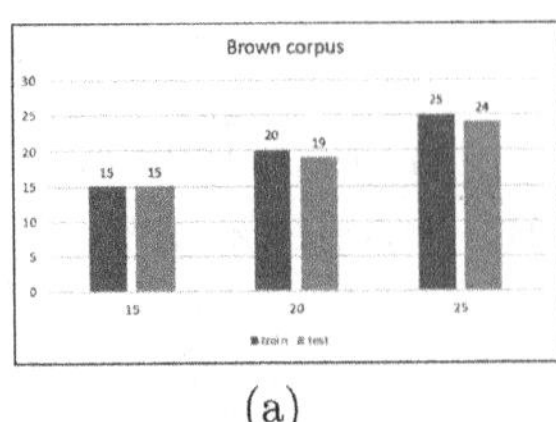

(a)

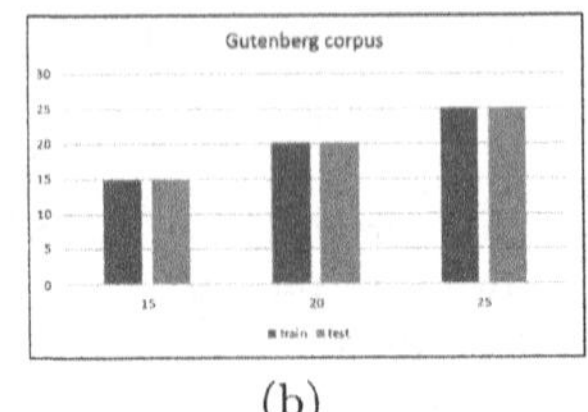

(b)

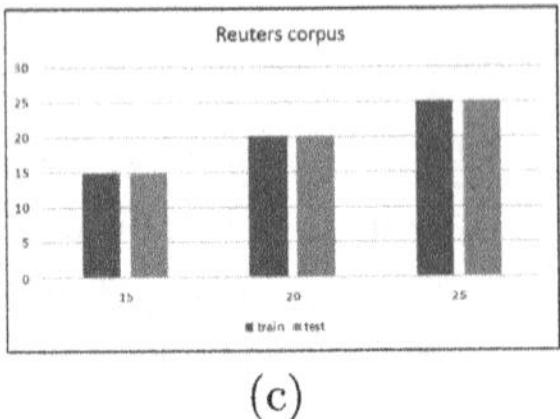

(c)

Fig. 3. Train and test in 3 corpora

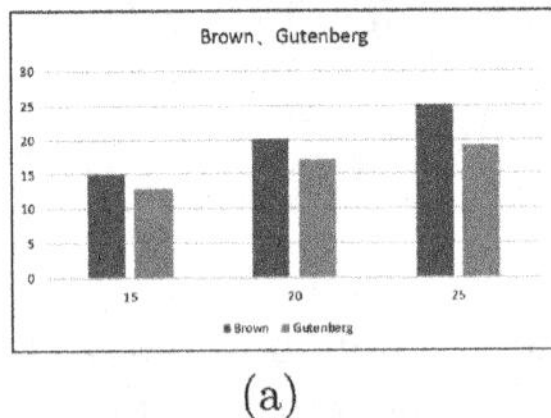

(a)

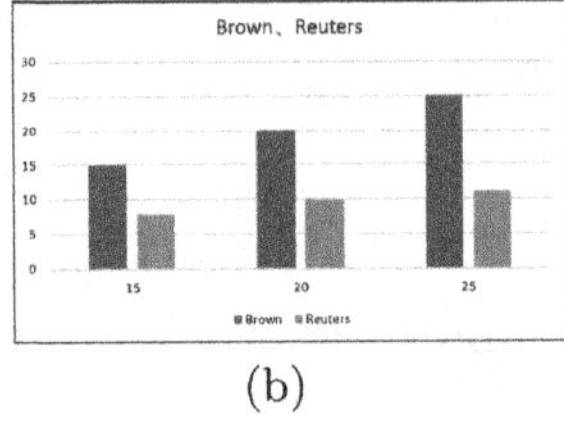

(b)

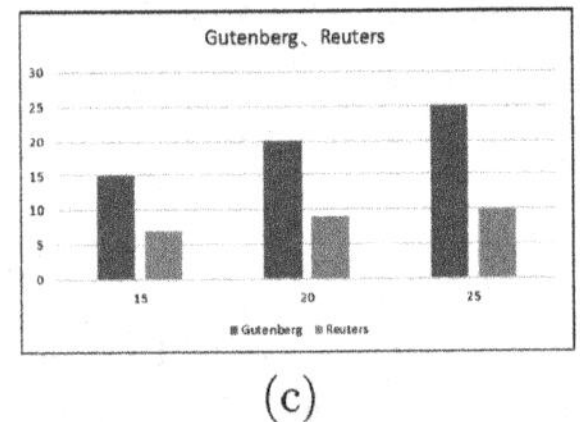

(c)

Fig. 4. Word distribution in different corpora

4.2 Analysis on In-Domain Text

For in-domain text analysis where the model is trained on a domain's training set, and tested on the validation set, the perplexity values for the proposed model, with $\lambda_1 = 0.3$, $\lambda_2 = 0.5$ and $\lambda_3 = 0.2$ are in Table 2.

Table 2. Perplexity values for the unigram and proposed model for In-Domain

	Brown	Gutenberg	Reuters
Unigram model	1513.84	982.57	1471.21
Proposed model	37.66	36.88	25.4

4.3 Analysis on Out-of-Domain Text

The perplexity of all three models, with $\lambda_1 = 0.3$, $\lambda_2 = 0.5$ and $\lambda_3 = 0.2$, on all three domains are in Table 3, where each row is the language model trained on the training set of corresponding data corpus, and each column has the perplexity computed on the test set of that corpus. Values of λ_1, λ_2 and λ_3 can be got based on computed perplexity values on dev sets of Brown, Gutenberg and Reuters.

Different sets of λ_1, λ_2 and λ_3 are used and finally this specific set of values is chosen as perplexity values on dev sets of these three data corpora are relative small compared with that of other combinations of λs.

Table 3. Comparison of perplexity of 3 corpus respectively

		Brown	Gutenberg	Reuters
Unigram model	Brown	1513.8	1758.06	6780.82
	Gutenberg	2616.57	982.57	12420.1
	Reuters	3806.39	4882.8	1471.21
Proposed model	Brown	37.66	538.67	995.92
	Gutenberg	643.79	36.88	1235.58
	Reuters	732.81	783.07	25.4

As Table 3 shown, comparison is between the unigram (the baseline) and our proposed model. Each row denotes the data corpus which the language model is based on. The language model can be trained on the Brown, Gutenberg or the Reuters dataset. Each column denotes the perplexity value calculated on the current test set. Our proposed model achieves better performance. This can be explained as the huge difference exists between the Gutenberg and Reuters data corpus.

4.4 Adaptation

For the huge difference exists between the Gutenberg and Reuters data corpus. Now, I have trained a model on corpus B and wish to test it on the test set for corpus C. Design an approach for using a small fraction of corpus C's training data to adapt the model trained on corpus B. How does it influence performance? Comparisons were done for the Gutenberg and Reuters. The 5, 10, 15 and 20% of data from corpus C is used for adaptation.

As shown in Fig. 5, by adding different proportion of Reuters training corpus to the Gutenberg, the perplexity value decreases significantly. If we add training data reversely which means from Gutenberg to Reuters, same conclusion can be got from Fig. 6. Therefore, language model performance can be promoted by adding the data from target corpus for the out-of-domain training and testing experiments. This strategy is suitable for the case that large amount of training data cannot be obtained. It is really helpful to use the training data which is similar to the dataset we are currently focused on.

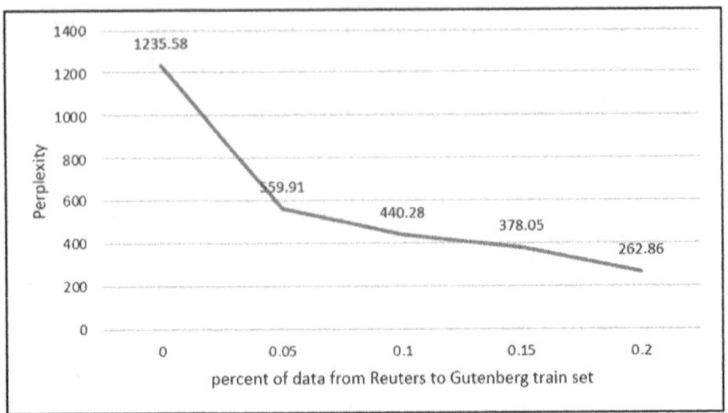

Fig. 5. Perplexity values for the adapted model: Reuters to Gutenberg

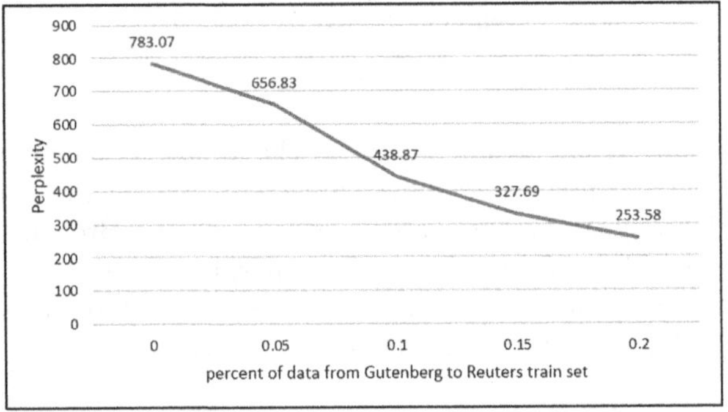

Fig. 6. Perplexity values for the adapted model: Gutenberg to Reuters

5 Conclusion

Probabilistic language model has been widely used in the field of natural language processing and the model should be based on a suitable corpus. In this paper, by constructing a probabilistic language model for each corpus, data corpus with different word distribution is studied and perplexity values between corpus are compared by means of experimental analysis. The conclusion is that training and testing on the same corpus tends to get a good perplexity value. However, if the relationship between training and testing is cross-domain, only improving the language model might not decrease the perplexity value a lot. When we want to build the cross-domain language model, data corpus with similar word distribution should be chosen so as to increase the performance. Moreover, adding similar training data is helpful and beneficial to the language model optimization and this method has important applications in practice, especially the amount of training data is a threshold.

References

1. Raghavan, S., Kovashka, A., Mooney, R.: Authorship attribution using probabilistic context-free grammars. In: Proceedings of the ACL 2010 Conference Short Papers, pp. 38–42 (2010)
2. Bouras, C., Tsogkas, V.: Assisting cluster coherency via n-grams and clustering as a tool to deal with the new user problem. Int. J. Mach. Learn. Cybern. **7**(2), 171–184 (2016)
3. Sohangir, S., Wang, D.: Improved sqrt-cosine similarity measurement. J. Big Data **4**(1), 25–38 (2017)
4. Bisandu, D.B., Prasad, R., Liman, M.M.: Clustering news articles using efficient similarity measure and N-grams. Int. J. Knowl. Eng. Data Min. **5**(4), 333–348 (2018)
5. Islam, A., Milios, E., Kešelj, V.: Text similarity using Google tri-grams. In: Kosseim, L., Inkpen, D. (eds.) AI 2012. LNCS (LNAI), vol. 7310, pp. 312–317. Springer, Heidelberg (2012). https://doi.org/10.1007/978-3-642-30353-1_29
6. Kondrak, G.: *N*-Gram similarity and distance. In: Consens, M., Navarro, G. (eds.) SPIRE 2005. LNCS, vol. 3772, pp. 115–126. Springer, Heidelberg (2005). https://doi.org/10.1007/11575832_13
7. Grefenstette, G.: Comparing two language identification schemes. In: Proceedings of 3rd International Conference on Statistical Analysis of Textual Data, Rome, pp. 1–6 (1995)
8. Damashek, M.: Gauging similarity with n-grams: language-independent categorization of sentence. Science **267**(5199), 843–848 (1995)
9. Biskri, I., Delisle, S.: Les n-grams de caractères pour l'aide à l'extraction de connaissances dans des bases de données sentenceuelles multilingues. In: Proceedings of TALN-2001, pp. 93–102 (2001)
10. http://www.hit.uib.no/icame/brown/bcm.html
11. http://gutenberg.net/
12. https://archive.ics.uci.edu/ml/datasets/Reuters-21578+Text+Categorization+Collection

IoT and Cloud Enabled Evidence-Based Smart Decision-Making Platform for Precision Livestock Farming

Yukang Han[1,2], Jinchang Ren[1(✉)], Qiming Zhu[1,2], David Barclay[2], and James Windmill[1]

[1] Department of Electronic and Electrical Engineering, University of Strathclyde, Glasgow, UK
{yukang.han, jinchang.ren, qzhu, james.windmill}@strath.ac.uk

[2] Innovent Technology Limited, Turriff, UK
{yh, qz, db}@itlscotland.co.uk

Abstract. Precision livestock farming (PLF) refers to utilize sensors and IT management system in cyber-physical farm to introduce more intelligence in farming activities. PLF hardware including sensors as data capturing device and computer as data processing unit. PLF software is for connecting sensors, processing data and visualizing result in real-time. This technology can reduce human error, minimize the number of labours and providing evidence-based decision making. The software which connected to sensors should be flexible and easy to use, able to extend by allowing new type of sensors to be effectively integrated. Although many works have been done for PLF such as object recognition, tracking, weight measuring etc. [4, 5]. however, there still lacks a generic platform which could integrate various algorithms and providing instant information for shareholders. This paper will present the technology stack involved in developing the platform.

Keywords: Precision livestock farming · Animal behaviour · Big data · Smart farming

1 Introduction

Livestock production is one of essential food sources to human, it has a long history in human diet, able to provide rich protein and nutrition for our daily activities. Considering the increasing population worldwide and growing demand for high quality meat and milk, that poses challenging question for government and livestock enterprises: "how to produce enough food to feed the growing population". The growing global demand for animal products, expected to increase by 70% by 2050, calls for expanded and efficient production [1, 2].

At present, we are on a verge of a technological revolution, the Internet of Things (IoT). It represents the future of computing and communication. Combination of IoT and PLF is a key component of sustainable intensification. By gathering data from

J. Ren et al. (Eds.): BICS 2019, LNAI 11691, pp. 570–582, 2020.
https://doi.org/10.1007/978-3-030-39431-8_55

various sensors, a detailed context of the surrounding environment can be presented, where each device contributes specific information for modelling and analysing [3–6].

As for PLF, measuring and assessing behaviour of livestock can be used to indicate their welfare status. Behaviour is formed from an animal's continuous interactions with its environment. It is a response to an internal stimuli(physiological) such as hunger or an external stimulus such as climate. If the goal of the behaviour is not, or cannot be, achieved, the animal may change its behaviour or physiological response. Most observation processes currently used to measure livestock behaviour are subjective, as farm workers perform the welfare assessment. The worker's involvement in these tasks is necessary and thus increases the demand on labours and costs. These have potentially influenced attention levels that each animal receives, and behavioural measurements are open for interpretation and have potential to be overlooked [7].

PLF utilizes cameras in farms as data capturing device, streaming image frame to the software for processing. Valuable feature sets of the target objects can be extracted from frames such as position, gesture, growth and locomotion status. Therefore, a detailed picture of a comprehensive growth cycle of the animals can be drawn upon this integrated system.

1.1 An Overview

Ideally, the platform needs to be running 24 $\times$ 7, not only it can provide sufficient data for processing, but also the data collected in a constant and concentrated manner can be used to build a time-based events model, thus, with more accurate data, we can track down to where and when the event happened and why it happened. A holistic model of the target object will form while the data are accumulating. For animal growth model, we need more than just capturing image frame inside the farm, other external data sources, such as humidity, precipitation, illumination, CO2 concentration and temperature will also need to be considered in this model. Having all the data associated with the animal will play a key role for analysing and making reasonable inferences. The overall method for integration sensors other than camera is the same, one can easily adopt this concept for others, see the diagram in Fig. 1.

Fig. 1. Precision livestock farming concept

2 Hardware

One challenging issue in choosing hardware for animal farms is the severe onsite environmental condition. In order to make devices running 24 × 7, the hardware needs to be able to against liquids, dust or humidity which are common in animal farms. Besides, farms keep regular cleaning protocol by using pressure water. These requirements combined are not suitable for consumer hardware units; however, industrial devices are designed for situation like this, it tested across different environmental condition and obtained a rating degree of its quality to indicate it has higher standards against any entry of moisture or dust. The electronic components themselves are selected for their ability to withstand higher and lower operating temperatures than typical components.

Ingress Protection (IP) ratings, see in Table 1, are assigned using a two-digit code that indicates the degree to which an enclosure prevents the intrusion of solids and liquids. The first digit indicates the level of protection against the ingress of solid foreign objects, and the second digit indicates protection against the harmful ingress of water. The protection from solids rating ranges from no protection at 0 to completely sealed against dust at 6. The protection from liquids rating ranges from no protection at 0 to protected against long periods of immersion under pressure at 8 [8].

Table 1. Ingress protection ratings

Ingress protection (IP) ratings			
Solids		Liquids	
0	No protection	0	No protection
1	Protected against objects greater than 50 mm (large body parts, hands)	1	Protected against dripping water or condensation
2	Protected against objects greater than 12.5 mm (fingers)	2	Protected against dripping water when tilted 15 degrees
3	Protected against objects greater than 2.5 mm (tools/thick wires)	3	Protected against water spray at any angle up to 60 degrees from vertical
4	Protected against objects greater than 1 mm (most wires, screws)	4	Protected against splashing water from any direction
5	Protected against dust, limited ingress	5	Protected against jets of water
6	Dust tight, totally protected against dust	6	Protected against high pressure water jets
		7	Protected against effects of immersion up to 1 m
		8	Protected against immersion beyond 1 m

We use Hikvision IR fixed network camera, model DS-2CD2142FWD. It has up to 4-megapixel high resolution, full HD1080p video, dual stream and IP67 weather-proof protection, operating condition is −30 °C–60 °C (−22 °F–140 °F), humidity is 95% or less [9]. It supports RTSP protocol for video streaming, we need to realize RTSP client to communicate with it. X86 computer can be used as the host machine for our platform. It must have sealed case with minimum IP66 rating to protect the inside components from dust and pressure water.

3 Software

Most farm premises located in rural areas, may lack of stable internet connection. Remote capturing and transferring real-time data often require reliable internet connectivity. For a real-time system, it is impractical to send data to cloud to process. The whole system needs to rely less on cloud computing and work independently. However, for safety and security reasons, generated reports need to send to remote server for further processing and centralized management.

The system will be subjected to large computational pressure, since image processing, the core part of the system normally consumes most of the computing resources. In order to work efficiently, a low-level, close to hardware layer programming language would be suitable for our case. C/C++ is ideal for performance-critical task and computationally intensive application. It has the ability of accessing varies hardware. Moreover, the cross-platform nature of the language would allow deploying the final product in a lower spec hardware which potentially brings more hardware selections as well as reduces running cost.

The general architecture of monitoring systems can be broken into four main stages: initialisation, tracking, pose estimation and recognition [7–10]. We expand this for our case. The diagram below shows the workflow of this system. The green graphs indicate core stages (Fig. 2).

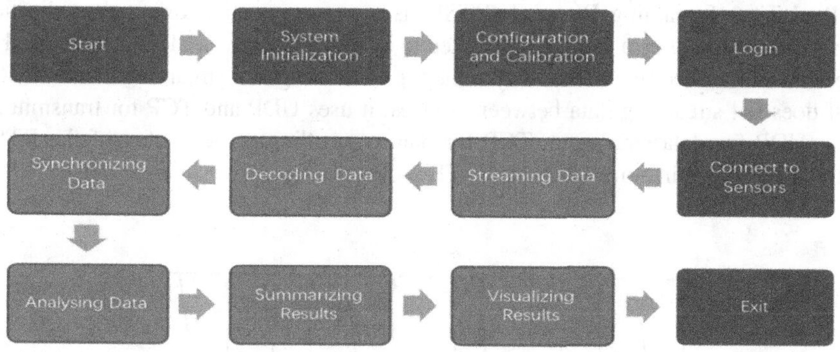

Fig. 2. Platform workflow (Color figure online)

3.1 Streaming

Steaming or retrieving data is a way of communicating between main application and sensors. Communication protocol that uses in transmitting packets often chosen by data type and content. In this proposal, streaming video media is the main objective, the most import point is the guarantee of a low latency, low jitter and efficient transmissions, however, since the system is designed for constantly running, occasional loss of data could be tolerated.

Media streaming protocol is defined considering the structure of the packets and the algorithms used to send real-time media on a network. Different media streaming protocols are available today, which differ in a few implementation details. Two communication categories are: push-based and pull-based protocols [11]. Push-Based Media Streaming Protocols: After establishing the connection between client and server, server side starts sending data to client until the session closed or interrupted. Pull-Based Media Streaming protocols: Client-side works actively requiring data from server when it needs. Therefore, responses depend on how often the client sends out requesting messages (Table 2).

Table 2. Push and Poll protocols

Push and Pull based streaming protocols		
Characteristic	Push-based	Pull-based
Source	Broadcasters and servers like Windows Media, Apple QuickTime, RealNetworks Helix, Cisco CDS/DCM	Web servers such as LAMP, Microsoft IIS, RealNetworks Helix, Cisco CDS
Protocols	RTSP, RTP, UDP, WebSocket	HTTP, AJAX
Bandwidth usage	Likely more efficient	Likely less efficient
Video monitoring	RTCP for RTP transport	Currently proprietary
Multicast support	Yes	No

Real Time Streaming Protocol (RTSP) is a non-connection oriented application layer protocol that uses a session associated to an end point device. It is usually used in entertainment and communication systems for controlling and streaming media. RTSP itself does not streaming data between devices, it uses UDP and TCP for transmitting tasks (UDP for data streaming, TCP for data controlling). The syntax of the RTSP protocol is similar in some ways to HTTP protocol (Fig. 3).

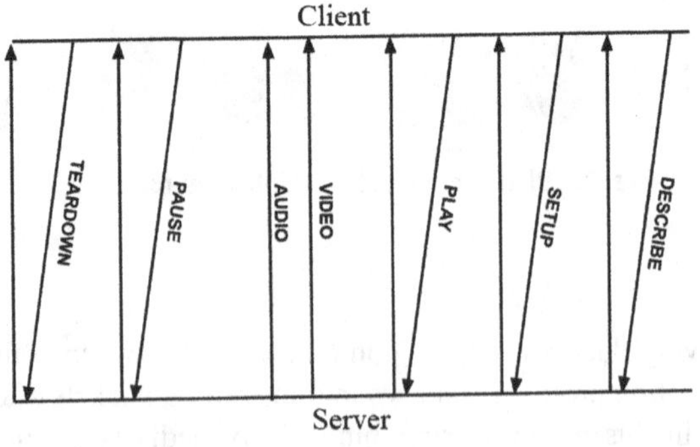

Fig. 3. RTSP protocol

The structure of an URL for RTSP is represented by a "rtps://" header, other than that, it adds new request methods such as DESCRIBE, SETUP, PLAY, PAUSE and TEARDOWN. The DESCRIBE method is used to obtain a description of the presentation or object appointed by the RTSP URL. The server responds to this request with a description of the requested resource. This response corresponds to the initialization phase of RTSP and contains the list of the necessary multimedia streams. On the other hand, the SETUP method is used to establish how is the stream transported the request contains the URL of the multimedia stream and a transport specification that usually includes the port to receive RTP data (video and audio) and another one to the RTCP data(metadata). The server responds confirming the selected parameters and fill the other parts, as they are the ports selected by the server. Every stream must be configured before sending a PLAY request. The PLAY request is used to start the data stream shipment by part of the server using the ports configured with the SETUP request method. Moreover, the PAUSE method stops one or all streams temporarily to resume it later with a PLAY request. Finally, the use of the TEARDOWN request method stops the shipment of data releasing all resources. Note that first of all a TCP connection is established between the client and the server, started by the client and typically over the well-known port of TCP, the 554 port [12].

3.2 Decoding

Decoding or format conversion is the process of converting data from source format to a desirable destination format. In this case, efficient transmitting of video frame often requires encoding source video with good quality and lower bit rates. A broadcast friendly with reasonable compression rate coding technique is required for this task (Fig. 4).

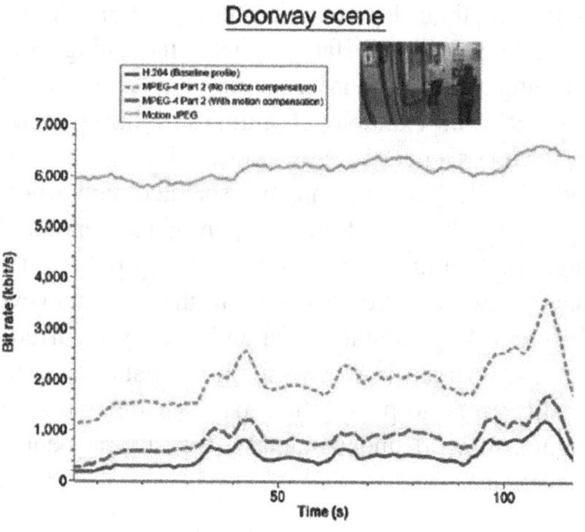

Fig. 4. Bit rate comparison

H.264 coding technique is the modern and most effective video compression standard; high quality video streaming can be achieved with low bit rates. It perhaps best known as being one of the video encoding standards for Blu-ray. The H.264 compressed video stream needs just 10% of an MJPEG compressed in the network bandwidth. It is seen that H.264 video quality was approximately 95% superior when compared to MJPEG video compression method [13]. This coding method has been widely used in many web video-services, such as YouTube, Facebook, and Vimeo. It also can be applied in the field of television broadcast, Blu-ray low-latency video application, surveillance, and web video etc. [14].

An experiment comparison demonstrated bit rate for Motion JPEG, MPEG-4 Part 2 (no motion compensation), MPEG-4 Part 2 (with motion compensation) and H.264 (baseline profile) at the same level of image quality, the result showed that H.264 encoder was at least three times more efficient than an MPEG-4 encoder and at least six times more efficient than with Motion JPEG [15].

FFmpeg usually used to decompress data. It is a multimedia framework for creating video applications or even general purposes utilities. It takes care of all the hard work of video processing by doing all the decoding, encoding, etc. It supports the most format and also highly portable, can compile, run, and pass across Linux, Max OS X, Microsoft Windows, BSDs, etc., under a wide variety of build environment, machine architectures, and configurations [16].

3.3 Synchronizing

In a multiple sensor environment, each sensor represents a node and transmits data to parent node (centre application) constantly. As data generated from different nodes are propagated towards centre application, it is important that centre application fuses data as much as possible for increasing credibility of the report. A fusion or synchronization process is needed at this stage prior to sending out reports to next stage.

The synchronization method depends on data type. For video data, one can combine the very video frame with a time-stamp variable indicating exact time of the frame being generated. Adding this extra information will bring more evidence for the traceability of the scene. For example, if animals fighting each other, the sudden increased volume can trigger an event allows us to analyse the audio and video clip in the same time period. Another variable can be associated with arbitrary data type is the geological information, which can tell the location of the generated data.

Note that, adding more variables on fusion stage may put extra computing pressure on the analysing stage. It would direct us refining the data; however, we still need to balance between fusion of large amount data and latency incurred in the aggregation process to reach our goal of real-time analysis. if the data are unable or unsuitable to fuse at this stage, it still viable to pass on the data as long as it is not corrupted. Since each sensor is designed to work independently, the add-on benefit of data fusion is important but not necessary.

3.4 Analysing

Accurately identify of ROI and target object is the key for modelling in monitoring system. We often define feature representing significant characteristics in images to distinguish with others. These features can be generally classified into temporal, spatial, valued and textural type. Position and velocity are examples of temporal features which can be found between images when motion occurs. Spatial features are shapes of different size and dimensions that represent volume and contour of target objects. Colour information in an image can be classified to valued feature, it can be used to distinguish target object from background scene. Textural features are a group of various features such as colour and shape, it can be seen as a template of features [7].

Identification of features in image frames needs to consider the cost, that includes the cost of time, money and energy, it needs to be practical and capable of meeting the demand on accuracy and computational cost. These processes must capable of locating the target-object such that object referencing and reposition can occur reliably and errors are prevented in subsequent estimation and recognition stages.

Features included in images are the main source for identification, but we should also think of external sources, such as information from different sensors and environment conditions. For example, temperature is a key factor that would affect animal behaviours, animals tend to reduce activities in a less comfortable setting. Combination of temperature feature can be of explanation of current condition to certain behaviours.

Image analysing includes two main processes, segmentation and temporal correspondence. Segmentation is the process of identifying object and generating information by extracting features that describing the target object. Usually, some pre-trained feature sets like shape, colour or height are used to highlight the target object. The result is a group of features that describing the target object. Since image quality is the vital factor for analysing, some techniques might be needed to guarantee of pixel accuracy. For example, in favour of the widest view, some cameras with fisheye lens produce distortion toward edges of every frame, thus, a correcting algorithm needs to apply across each frame prior to analysing [17].

Temporal correspondence is the process of linking features between consecutive images. Features appear in each image can be traced as footprint or evidence for establishing connections in between. Note that in practice, image acquisition time may not be at a fixed interval, packet collision or data corruption can sometime occur during running. To sustain of sudden loss of target object, each feature needs to maintain its own confidence value, i.e. to evaluate credibility of the data. For example, if the location feature has been collecting over 10 times confirming the target object is within the image, sudden 'disappear' of the object in next frame cannot be easily accepted. It could be the animal curls up in an unusual posture that obstructing segmentation procedure. We can reduce location feature's confidence value to note this and still consider the target object is being traced. The true disappearance event could be accepted only after the confidence value is less than a threshold. This flexibility could increase the data credibility and bring more adaption to behaviour recognition process.

The tracking process is very important in animal behaviour studies, because animals' response to stimulus can often reflect to their movement, by recording their position we can draw a detailed picture for helping us better understanding of their behaviour. Responses to stimulus may vary across species of target animal, number of animals, time of day, or other conditions that may associate to. This is a core component of the system for us to understand the welfare and behaviour of animals in farm.

In the segmentation and temporal correspondence processes, four classes of techniques are used to recover a set of features from an image. In general, these are scene-based, motion-based, shape-based and appearance-based techniques [7].

There's no strict order for applying those techniques to an image, any sequence able to speed up the process is preferred. Most farms have limited range of animals, we can pre-define few features in appearance assumption class. For example, Chroma-key is the most welcome and robust method for separating background. If the skin colour of animals different to the ground, we can apply image thresholding to eliminate background, then, apply shape-based technique to extract target objects.

After feature sets are extracted, the intelligence of the system needs to be configured so that postures and behaviours can be recognised. The pose estimation stage determines the correspondence between a pose and feature information such as its orientation, position, appearance and current movement. The word pose should not be associated with only shape and size. For example, a bird may have unique colouring on the underside of its wing that is hidden when it is stationary, hence colour may be used as a cue indicates its posture. The recognition phase is the correct identification and labelling of a sequential combination of poses using a cross-reference to previously obtain data. Similar processes can be used when recognising behaviours from a sequence of poses and when estimating a pose from a given feature-set [7] (Table 3).

Table 3. Feature extraction techniques

Scene-based	Using background image as a reference image, comparing it with updated image, if the background pixel changed, indicating an object has entered the scene
Motion-based	Using temporal correspondence between frames to determine the movement of object within scene, such as velocity, direction, acceleration
Shape-based	Using shapes, edges or points to rebuild the volume information of the object within the image scene
Appearance-based	For RGB camera, we can use the visual properties within the image such as color, saturation, hue, for infrared camera, we can get the temperature readings out of the thermal image, for depth camera, we can measure the distance value of the target object and reconstruct the 3D scene base on Point-Cloud

3.5 Summarizing

Summarization is an optimization approach for reducing noise among feature sets. Due to unexpected interruption occurred during the operation such as dropping frames, illumination changes and shadow which could affect credibility of image frames. It's quite a challenge to match all features within a single frame correctly. However, the combination of a series frames could increase the credibility of the result and reduce the number of false detections. For example, locomotion tracking needs to get target location, orientation, velocity, acceleration features by comparing changes with consecutive frames. We would attach estimated result to those features base on previous trajectory and keep updating them. Comparing the newly observed results with our estimations after the system resumes to determine whether to accept those estimations.

3.6 Visualizing

Visualization as part of the system provides a human friendly way of viewing the analytic results in a diagram fashion. We can use web technology to show results on browsers such as Google Chrome et al. in keeping with the platform independent goal.

There are two approaches for web-based technologies, HTTP pooling and WebSocket. HTTP Polling consists of a serial of request-respond pair messages to communicate between server and client. Since the HTTP is stateless exchange protocol, client needs to actively ask for desired information constantly. One could notice that real-time displaying of information will put enormous pressure on the server side, since the client doesn't know when the data have been updated, thus, it needs to request update constantly, the server responds with a new message, if there is one, or with an empty response if no new message is available for that client. This technology can work well for static webpage but not for real-time information displaying.

Another variation of HTTP Polling is Long Polling, which the server keeps the request open for a set period. If the update message is ready within that period, a response containing the message is sent to client. If the message is not ready within that period, the server sends a response to terminate the open request. This reduce the number of responses to the client when no new messages, however, it isn't believed to provide substantial improvement over traditional polling [18].

WebSocket is a full-duplex, bidirectional communication protocol that operate through a single socket over the Web [19]. It does not involve additional request-respond headers for communication. Besides, the full-duplex connectivity allows transmitting data at the same time from both side without unnecessary overhead. The most significant benefit of WebSocket is it will dramatically reduce network throughput and latency involved in real-time web application.

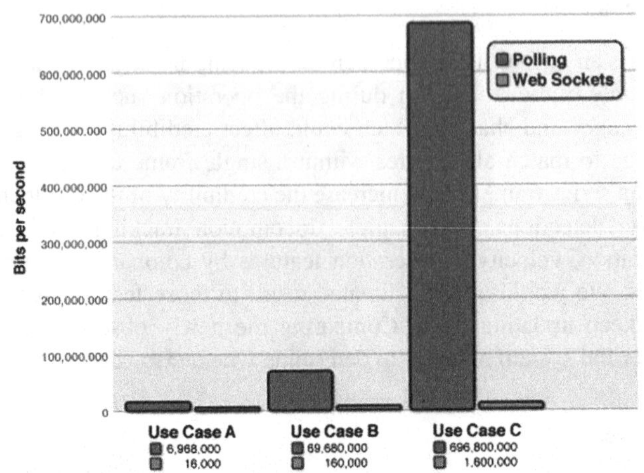

Fig. 5. HTTP polling and WebSocket network throughput comparison

In a comparison for network throughput and latency in HTTP polling and WebSocket, it created two webpages, one for AJAX polling and the other for WebSocket [18] as detailed below. The comparisons are also shown in Figs. 5 and 6.

For AJAX Polling, we have:

- **Use case A**: 1,000 clients polling every second: Network throughput is (871 × 1,000) = 871,000 bytes = 6,968,000 bits per second (bps) (6.6 Mbps)
- **Use case B**: 10,000 clients polling every second: Network throughput is (871 × 10,000) = 8,710,000 bytes = 69,680,000 bps (66 Mbps)
- **Use case C**: 100,000 clients polling every 1 s: Network throughput is (871 × 100,000) = 87,100,000 bytes = 696,800,000 bps (665 Mbps)

Whilst for HTML5 WebSocket, we have:

- **Use case A:** 1,000 clients receive 1 message per second: Network throughput is (2 × 1,000) = 2,000 bytes = 16,000 bps (0.015 Mbps)
- **Use case B:** 10,000 clients receive 1 message per second: Network throughput is (2 × 10,000) = 20,000 bytes = 160,000 bps (0.153 Mbps)
- **Use case C:** 100,000 clients receive 1 message per second: Network throughput is (2 × 100,000) = 200,000 bytes = 1,600,000 bps (1.526 Mbps)

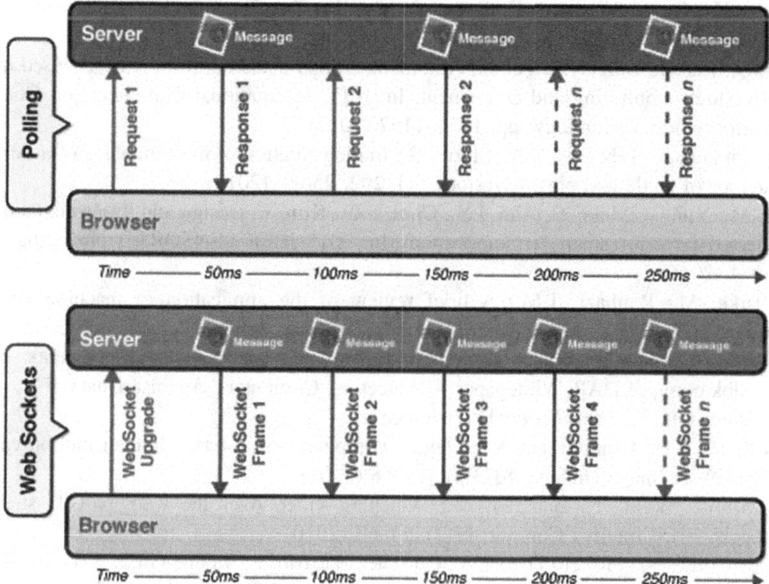

Fig. 6. HTTP Polling and WebSocket latency comparison

4 Conclusions

In conclusion, we have presented technology stacks in developing this platform. Employing modern technology has helped farmers to wisely allocate their time and energy on daily activities. By collecting and analysing vast quantities of data, precision livestock farming can provide shareholders with real-time information of animal's growth and welfare status. A further step would be sharing data to end users of the value chain – consumers, which they will make buying decisions based on farm practice, and farms can optimize production strategies.

Acknowledgment. This study is partially funded by the Knowledge Transfer Partnership (KTP) project (10798) from Innovate UK and Innovent Technology Ltd. in partnership with the University of Strathclyde to redesign the existing precision livestock farming system.

References

1. Morota, G., Ventura, R.V., Silva, F.F., Koyama, M., Fernando, S.C.: Big data analytics and precision animal agriculture symposium: machine learning and data mining advance predictive big data analysis in precision animal agriculture. J. Anim. Sci. **96**(4), 1540–1550 (2018)
2. How to feed the world in 2050. http://www.fao.org/fileadmin/templates/wsfs/docs/expert_paper/How_to_Feed_the_World_in_2050.pdf

3. Wolfert, S., Ge, L., Verdouw, C., Bogaardt, M.J.: Big data in smart farming–a review. Agric. Syst. **153**, 69–80 (2017)
4. Zhu, Q., Ren, J., Barclay, D., et al.: Automatic animal detection from Kinect sensed images for livestock monitoring and assessment. In: IEEE International Conference on Computer and Information Technology, pp. 1154–1157 (2015)
5. Nasirahmadi, A., Edwards, S.A., Sturm, B.: Implementation of machine vision for detecting behaviour of cattle and pigs. Livestock Sci. **202**, 25–38 (2017)
6. Ryu, M., Yun, J., Miao, T., Ahn, I.Y., Choi, S.C., Kim, J.: Design and implementation of a connected farm for smart farming system. In: 2015 IEEE SENSORS 1 November 2015, pp. 1–4 (2015)
7. Tscharke, M., Banhazi, T.M.: A brief review of the application of machine vision in livestock behaviour analysis. Agrárinformatika/J. Agric. Inform. **7**(1), 23–42 (2016)
8. Protecting Computers Against Dust in Industrial and Warehouse Environments. https://www.dbk.com/pdf/DAP_Whitepaper_-_Protecting_Computers_Against_Dust.pdf
9. Hikvision: Official. https://www.hikvision.com
10. Moeslund, T.B., Granum, E.: A survey of computer vision-based human motion capture. Comput. Vis. Image Underst. **81**(3), 231–268 (2001)
11. Begen, A., Akgul, T., Baugher, M.: Watching video over the web: part 1: streaming protocols. IEEE Internet Comput. **15**(2), 54–63 (2010)
12. Santos-González, I., Rivero-García, A., González-Barroso, T., Molina-Gil, J., Caballero-Gil, P.: Real-time streaming: a comparative study between RTSP and WebRTC. In: García, C.R., Caballero-Gil, P., Burmester, M., Quesada-Arencibia, A. (eds.) UCAmI/IWAAL/AmIHEALTH -2016. LNCS, vol. 10070, pp. 313–325. Springer, Cham (2016). https://doi.org/10.1007/978-3-319-48799-1_36
13. Bapayya, K., et al.: RTSP based video surveillance system using IP camera for human detection in OpenCV. Int. J. Comput. Sci. Softw. Eng. **4**(9), 243–247 (2015)
14. Ji, Q., Yu, H., Chen, H.: A smart Android based remote monitoring system. In: 3rd International Conference on Technological Advances in Electrical, Electronics & Computer Engineering (2015)
15. Ponlatha, S., Sabeenian, R.S.: Comparison of video compression standards. Int. J. Comput. Electr. Eng. **5**(6), 549–554 (2013)
16. FFmpeg: Official Web. https://www.ffmpeg.org/
17. Bellas, N., Chai, S.M., Dwyer, M., Linzmeier, D.: Real-time fisheye lens distortion correction using automatically generated streaming accelerators. In: 17th IEEE Symposium on Field Programmable Custom Computing Machines, pp. 149–156 (2009)
18. Lubbers, P.: HTML5 web sockets: a quantum leap in scalability for the web (2011). http://www.websocket.org/quantum.html
19. Pimentel, V., Nickerson, B.G.: Communicating and displaying real-time data with websocket. IEEE Internet Comput. **16**(4), 45–53 (2012)

Partition Compression Flash Translation Layer Based on Data Separation

Xiaochang Li[1(✉)], Zhengjun Zhai[1], Xin Ye[1], and Feiyao Dong[2]

[1] School of Computer Science, Northwestern Polytechnical University, Xi'an, China
{xcli,yexin}@mail.nwpu.edu.cn, zhaizjun@nwpu.edu.cn
[2] PLA Air Force Xi'an Flight Academy, Xi'an, China
254559590@163.com

Abstract. Flash translation layers play an important role in determining the storage performance and lifetime of NAND flash-based electronics devices. And file system designs are undergoing rapid evolution to exploit the potentials of flash memory. Although many compression Flash Translation Layer (FTLs) have been designed, there is serious overhead for the software compression or even hardware compression and decompression process which are inevitable. In this paper, we present a partition FTL which can distinguish the file system metadata and user data. After the division of the mapping table, we add transparent data compression to the user data part, a logical partition compression, called pcFTL, which reduces the amount of data written into NAND flash memory. In addition, no more decrease in (Solid state drive) SSD performance due to no filesystem metadata compression overhead. Transplanting compression on user data part, other than file system data part not only benefit disk performance but also save SDRAM space. pcFTL is one kind of filesystem suited FTL design.

Our evaluations with three real-world workloads show that pcFTL successfully enhances storage performance and lifetime by minimizing the Write Amplification Factor (WAF) by up to 30–40% compared to the case without compression support, for those TXT files. Moreover, pcFTL can improve write performance by up to 10%.

Keywords: SSD · NAND flash · FTL · Filesystem · Metadata · User data

1 Introduction

Solid state drive has been widely adopted across embedded systems to data centers now. It offers several advantages over hard disks: lower and more predictable access latencies for random requests, smaller form factors, lower power consumption, lack of noise, and higher robustness to vibrations and temperature, which has lead it being employed in many embedded and devices. No matter which kind of operation system or file system, solid state drive can replace hard disk transparently. The reason of this equivalent replacement is that Flash Translation Layer (FTL), which performs the virtual-to-physical address translations and hides the erase-before-write characteristics of flash, as a result of SSD core performance factor.

J. Ren et al. (Eds.): BICS 2019, LNAI 11691, pp. 583–592, 2020.
https://doi.org/10.1007/978-3-030-39431-8_56

Here, we list now existing SSD corresponding optimization directions. First, FTL itself optimization technologies. Better garbage collection (GC) algorithm [1] can minimize the serious GC overhead and enhance the SSD lifetime. Some papers have proposed the hot/cold data separation [2] for GC. Wear leveling scheme also plays an important role for disk lifetime. There are many specific technologies for it, such as the classical dual-pool for hot/cold wear leveling [3] and the newest scheme with program error rate statistic information to improve wear leveling efficiency [4]. Compression algorithms are widely used in not only normal page-level mapping [5] but also on-demand FTL [6]. The compression policies are in wide conception, both famous compression algorithms and skillful data structures [6, 14]. The zone partition technology accommodates the limitation size of mapping information [7]. Moreover, Application-oriented optimizations, getting the hint from user application space to design FTL [8]. Application management [9] can be treated as F2FS file system modification SSD interface, keeping compatible with the legacy block device interface that exposes error-free append-only segments through read/write/trim operations. To achieve higher degree of performance, such as key-value storage, KVFTL [10] has been proposed to commercialize that specialized application, KV database. Finally, some papers try to modify the host related components to adapt SSD. For example, ParaFS is a log-structured file system to exploit the internal parallelism of flash device [11]. To deal with inefficient block IO layer, SSD has been developed to simplify block IO layer which now is the bottleneck of flash devices, named as Open Channel SSD [12]. From the above papers, we can find that almost any area has been considered into optimization. What we focus on is new compression FTL adapted to filesystem, which will allow us to use differentiating methods for different kinds of data respectively. The differentiating dealing will lead better performance than that disk with only one kind of treatment. At last, we evaluate our design well under both simulator and prototype. For prototype test, we utilize the specific File Allocation Table (FAT) filesystem [13] as our experiment environment, for it is convenient for almost any well-known operation systems, Linux, Windows and VxWorks.

The rest of the paper is organized as follows. The next section discusses the motivation. The third section introduces the overall design issues of pcFTL. Section 4 presents the experimental results and the last section is conclusion of the paper.

2 Motivation

How to deal with the tradeoff between Write Amplification Factor (WAF) [15] and flash device performance is the key of FTL design. High WAF is the inherent defect from NAND flash physical character (out-of-place update) comparing to the magnetic disk. Out-of-place will lead more write amount than the original write data, which inclines to invoke GC. In fact, the WAF for hard disk is always stationary, value 1. But for flash devices, it will exceed 1. With the compression technology, Sanforce-SSD can reduce WAF to the range of 0.5–0.7 [16]. But if we apply the compression to all the disk data, without the separation of filesystem metadata and user data, there will be high overhead to impact the performance improvement. To minimize that obvious overhead of compression and decompression, we pick out the metadata from user data through partitioning the mapping table into 2 parts. As the design has one 'metadata and user data separator' module in Fig. 1, No any cost for finding the address translation information for disk metadata. The only a little complicated two parts in pcFTL are the light modification for garbage collection and metadata mark, which will be detailed discussed detailedly in Sect. 3.2.

To the best of our knowledge, there is no any FTL now focusing on the differentiating compression now. Those introduced papers above all just use the generous schemes. So, that is reason why we propose one new partition compression FTL to distinguish metadata and user data in disk.

In our test, after the simulator evaluation, we also design the prototype based on FAT. There are 2 reasons for it. First, the classic FAT utilizations now also exist many specific environments. Moreover, our hardware design is fixed on the FAT.

At last, the ideas of mapping table division and differentiating data-compression, can certainly help to improve other filesystems' performance as well for SSD, just a little modification comparing with usual compression FTL [5], with obvious performance improvement.

3 Design

3.1 System Architecture

As shown in Fig. 1, File systems issue read/write requests to block IO layer, organized as 'bio' data structure, which are then fed to SSD disk. The size of each request is a multiple of the logical pages, comprising several disk section size (512B). Logical page size can reach 2 KB/4 KB or 16+ KB, similar to NAND Flash chip page size.

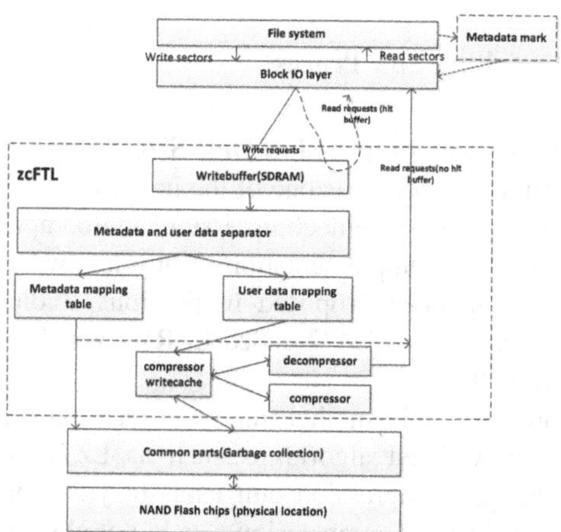

Fig. 1. The overall system architecture of pcFTL. The area enclosed by dotted line is the main part of pcFTL. And 'metadata and user data separator', 'compressor writecache', 'decompressor', 'compressor' are the new parts we add comparing general FTL. (Color figure online)

For write requests, after filtered by writebuffer (SDRAM), the bio requests should be judged by the 'metadata and user data separator' firstly. This data separator will decide which mapping table the incoming request belongs. As the pcFTL aggregates the requested user data in the 'compressor writecache', whose size is equal to compression unit size (we will discuss the selection of compression unit size in Sect. 3.2). If the 'compressor writecache' is full, the user data in 'compressor writecache' module will be compressed and flushed into flash chips. Although the compression unit size is fixed, the resulting chunk is highly variable in size. Hence, we add a lpa_to_chunkid layer, which will be described in Sect. 3.2 as well. If the number of free blocks is below a certain threshold, pcFTL initiates garbage collection to reclaim erase blocks. we will also discuss the garbage collection process later. When write requests for metadata, they are managed by metadata mapping table with no any compression, then no any lpa_to_chunkid layer. Usual mapping table without chunked id will save the mapping table size in SDRAM than usual compression FTL. pcFTL first searches for the requested data in the writebuffer (SDRAM) as it may have the most recent version of the data. When the search fails, pcFTL looks up the metadata mapping table instead of lpa_to_chunkid layer to locate the real page number in physical flash. Finally, fetch the chunk data to 'little compressor writebuffer' or just one uncompressing page for user data or metadata, respectively. If the data are found, then return the data host required.

All the components shown in Fig. 1 can be used without any modification except the 'metadata mark' in red color. Different filesystem contains different metadata structure and size. For the most of file systems, we have to mark the metadata 'bio' structure in kernel from file system layer, and transfer the mark to block IO layer for bio, named as Marked-Bio. With the hints from file system, Marked-Bio can be distinguished by the 'metadata and user data separator'. When it comes to FAT filesystem, the 'metadata mark' will be simplified, as the FAT is designed with a clear size bound between metadata and user data. We will discuss it in Sect. 3.3.

3.2 Compression Algorithm and Process

Compression Algorithm and Compression Unit Size

The choice of compression algorithms is one of the important design issues, because it determines the speed of compression/decompression, the compression ratio, and the complexity of further hardware implementation. Many hardware implementations of LZ77 [17] or variants have been proposed in previous studies. Comparing those algorithms, we choose a variant of LZ77 called LZRW, which is easier to be implemented by hardware as well.

The unit of data compression is another important factor affecting the compression ratio and speed. Dictionary-based algorithms such as LZ77 and LZRW have the characteristic that the bigger compression unit tends to yield the better compression ratio. But for the SSD, the bigger compression size is not always good for small size access in SSD. The inner theory of dictionary compression is utilizing the repeated pattern of strings, longer compression unit size leading better compression ratio, but it will result in higher overhead and space waste as well. There are 2 compression principles, variable-sized [5] or fixed size [18] data compression, in SSD compression.

To balance the tradeoff between compression efficiency and SSD performance, we fix the compression unit size as 4 pages at last.

Address Mapping: pcFTL employs a page-level mapping technique where a per-page mapping entry from the logical page number to the physical flash page number is maintained in the Page Mapping Table (PMT). For the pcFTL, we have partition the mapping information into 2 parts in Fig. 2, 'metadata mapping table' and 'chunk table'. One is for metadata. Another is for user data. This division requires a special garbage collection shown later.

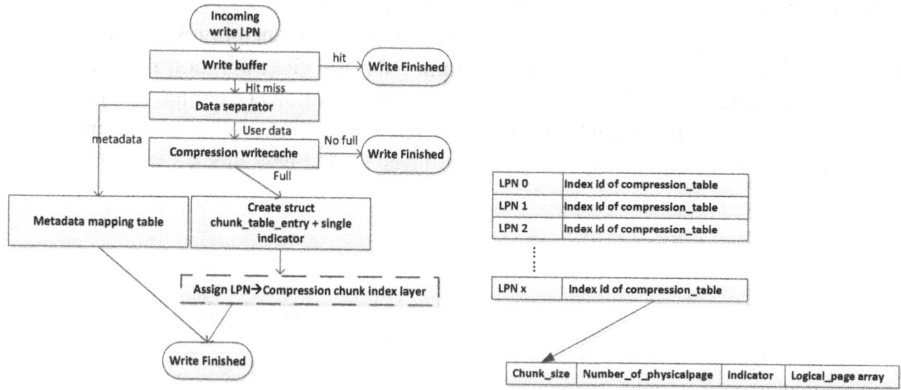

Fig. 2. The write logic process of pcFTL.

Fig. 3. The data structure of chunk layer pcFTL.

Write Process: When write requests come, hit in the write buffer will return request finish. Otherwise, hit miss requests will be classified by data separator as metadata or user data. After data classification, the file system metadata will go through metadata mapping table to arrive flash chip, no compression style mapping information. The compression algorithm only works on user data. Before compressing 4 pages into one chunk, we need to judge whether it is worth compressing them. Only compressed page number is less than our fixed compression unit page number, we compress them and update the logical page address number (LPA) to chunk data mapping information (Fig. 3) in chunk index layer.

General mapping information is the pair of LPA and physical page number (PPN). In our design, for compression mapping table of user data, we change the mapping information as pairs of LPA and chunk information in Fig. 3. The sizes of those four parts of chunk layer in Fig. 3 are flexible in realistic SSD design capacity. Those item concepts are described as follows. Chunk_size is the size after compression. The number of physical page represents the offset position in flash chips. Indicator flag is for compression or not. Logical_page array describes our fixed unit size of page numbers. Their detailed size illustrations in our prototype design part, Sect. 3.3.

To separate the metadata from user data in flash ship, we add the one-bit-size mark in page OOB area for the future GC in Fig. 5 data separator module.

Read Process: Dealing with read is similar to write process. After write buffer filter and data categories classification, we should fetch the flash page according to mapping information. The filesystem metadata lies in left branch of Fig. 4 whereas management of user data lies in right branch, named as lpa_to_chunkid layer, containing decompressing the chunk and picking out our aimed pages.

GC Process: Comparing the classic page-level GC [1], GC in pcFTL is a little different. The first operation is partitioning victim block into the metadata pages and user data pages. As mentioned in introduction part, the mapping table of metadata will save more SDRAM space which will be the most precious source when the SSD capacity increases. Moreover, the smaller size of mapping table, the better anti-power off ability. In our design, we can always merge metadata page in uncompressing state. For compression data in Fig. 5 right branch, chunk data, the GC migration process is the same as decompression, adding compression write operation. Decompress the chunk data and aggregate valid chunk data into compression writecache for migration. After migration, we need to update lpa_to_chunkid layer for the new block's mapping table information.

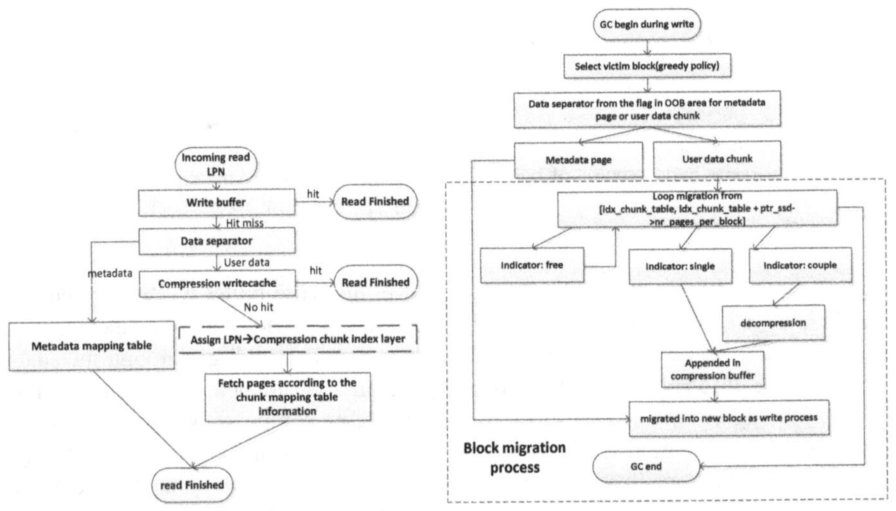

Fig. 4. The read logic process of pcFTL

Fig. 5. The GC logic process of pcFTL

3.3 Our Prototype Board Design

To evaluate the design in realistic SSD, we design a prototype board comprised of Sam3u4e micro control chip and one piece of Samsung NAND Flash chip K9K8G08U0B in 8 Gb size. One Flash chip contains 2 planes with 8192 blocks, which consists of 64 pages per block and 2 KB size per page. We focus our pcFTL prototype evaluation with only one flash chip implemented in FAT file system. The data structure in Fig. 3 should be decided firstly for our fixed Flash chip. The 4 parts in chunk mapping table are set as 12 bytes totally. The detailed sizes illustration is (13 + 11) bits of chunk_size, 13 bits of number_of_physicalpage, 1 bit of indicator and (4 * 13) bits logical_page array. All mapping table size will totally occupy less than 48 blocks according the Eq. 1, containing metadata and user data. Although FAT metadata includes at least 4 parts (DBR, FAT Table 1, FAT Table 2, Root directory) [13], we unify them as metadata.

$$L = (M * U)/(N * O) \tag{1}$$

(L: metadata page number, M: Flash chip page number, U: every mapping entry size, N: page number per block, O: page size).

The number of metadata blocks is less than 60 (DBR, FAT Table 1, FAT Table 2, Root directory) for our fixed Flash chip, according to the FAT character [13]. In fact, these 60 blocks corresponding page mapping table size can be less than 1 blocks, according to 4 bytes per entry. For the mapping table security, we create one redundant backup for mapping table, which costs another 48 blocks and another 1 blocks in physical chip, shown in Fig. 6. At last, with the redundant backup, the total number is 98 blocks. The pcFTL reserves a set of erase blocks (10% of total erase blocks, by default, 820 blocks) to accommodate the running out of available erase blocks.

How to set the metadata mark in Fig. 1 is one complicated module, as this modification is not only related with FTL, but also the kernel file system layer. A little change should be added into kernel to suit our pcFTL. For our now evaluation environment, the data distinction technology in FAT only depends on the LPA scope. The metadata's LPA value stays only in the front part of total size fixedly [13]. This discover helps us to simplify our prototype design without any kernel modification.

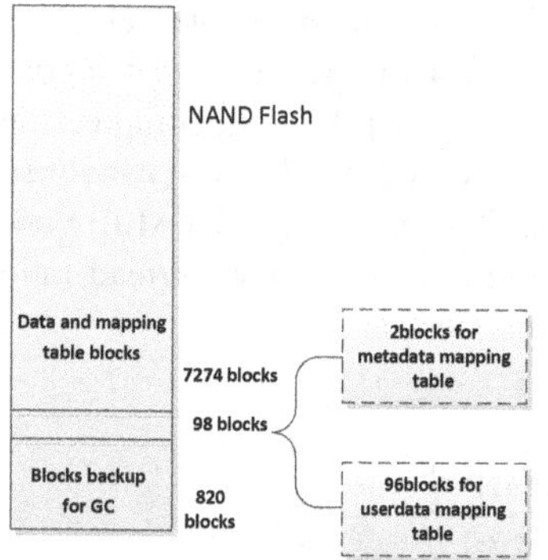

Fig. 6. The physical allocation in prototype design

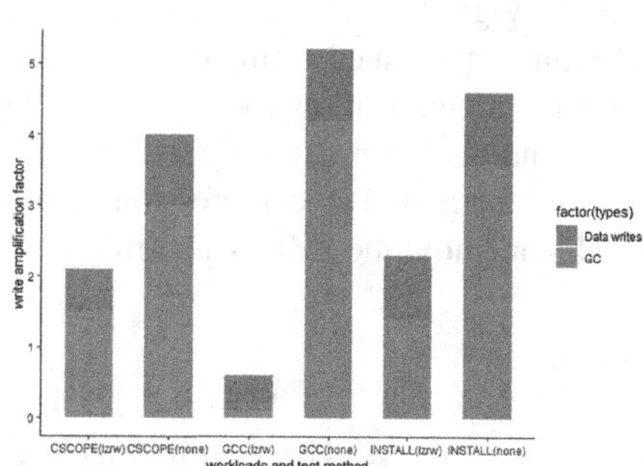

Fig. 7. The real workload WAF result (Color figure online)

4 Evaluation

4.1 Simulator Test

Before the prototype evaluation, we also implemented the design in one software simulator Bluedbm [9] for LZRW algorithm under 3 real workloads test. Table 1 shows the basic information of 3 workloads used in this paper.

Table 1. Workloads used in simulator

Workload	Scenario	Write/read	Write/update
CSCOPE	Linux source code examination	1:2	3:1
GCC	Building Linux Kernel	1:1	1:1
INSTALL	Office productivity software installed	8:1	6:1

CSCOPE is the operation of examination or checking code, with most read requests information. GCC is the workloads executed on the evaluation platform, which compile the source code of a version of open-source operating system. INSTALL workload represents the storage access requests generated while office productivity software is installed in the commercial operating system. And the update operation concept in write/update means update old data already storaged in disk.

Figure 7 compares the Write Amplification Factor (WAF) before and after the compression support is enabled. The WAF breaks down according to the source of writes; it is either for the actual data writes or for the writes issued during garbage collection. The lower bar (in blue color) indicates the amount of additional writes caused by garbage collection, which is as high as about 4 (in GCC) when the compression is not issued, comparing the highly reduction to about 0.3 with compression. Since the amount of data written into chip efficiently, GC will not be easily invoked. This trend has been demonstrated these 3 workloads. CSCOPE and INSTALL workloads perform similar compression results even they are in different write/read ratio, which can show the LZRW algorithm is suited for this design.

Table 2. Workloads used in prototype board

Workload	Size(MB)	Write/read	Source
Txt files	278	150	Txt novels
Office files	230	110	Handbooks
Rar files	311	130	Compression package
Mp3 files	202	32	Music website

4.2 Prototype Board Test

For prototype evaluation, we aggregate common files shown in Table 2. From Fig. 9, the txt and office files' WAF can be better than rar and mp3 files. The reason is clear, as compression will lose efficiency for compressed files. The best compression suited workload is txt files whose WAF can reach almost 46% reduction ratio.

In order to validate our implemented Bluedbm simulator accuracy comparing with prototype, we save the bio requests from test board first, and use simulator to test the bio requests collected from prototype in Table 2. The decreasing page numbers match the prototype WAF very well in Figs. 8 and 9. Txt files perform best and rar files is in worst dealt by pcFTL under the 4 kinds of workloads.

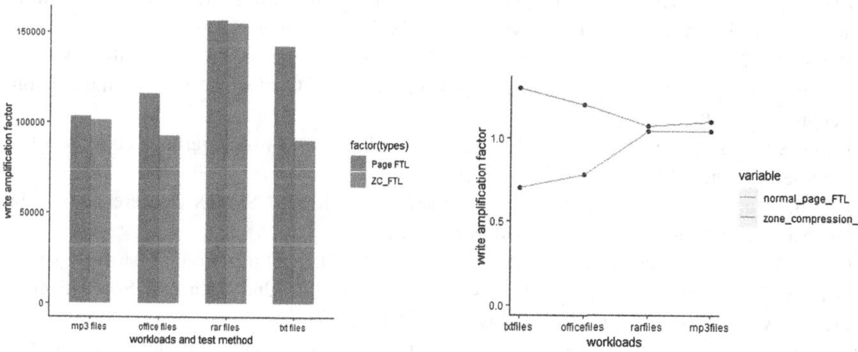

Fig. 8. Compression result in simulator

Fig. 9. WAF result in prototype board

5 Conclusion

Due to inherent characteristics of NAND flash memory which do not allow in-place update and wears out after repeated write/erase cycles, many general researches on flash translation layers have focused on efficient address mapping, wear leveling and garbage collection schemes. But no one tries to discuss the tradeoff between compression and file system for SSD. In this paper, we present pcFTL, a flash translation layer which not only support transparent and partition data compression based on the LRW algorithm, but also distinguish the compression suitable data or not from file system and user data. The data separation technology reduces the compression overhead and power consumption. Through the use of three real-world workloads, we confirm that pcFTL reduces the WAF by up to average 10% compared to the case without compression support. Since the compression FTL with an adding mapping layer between LPA and chunk ID, the mapping table will be enlarged. Our design for the metadata mapping can limit the mapping table magnification in some extent. For the future research, we plan to add the compression predictor by using machine learning methods for user data compression, which will lead further reduction of performance overhead and power consumption. Future work will focus on applications in big data [19] and associated security [20], optimization and machine learning issues [21, 22].

References

1. Nagel, L., Süß, T., et al.: Time-efficient Garbage collection in SSDs (2018)
2. Wei, X., Yong, C.: An adaptive separation-aware FTL for improving the efficiency of garbage collection in SSDs. In: IEEE/ACM International Symposium on Cluster (2014)
3. Chang, L.P.: On efficient wear leveling for large-scale flash-memory storage systems. In: ACM Symposium on Applied Computing. ACM (2007)
4. Shi, X., Wu, F., Wang, S., Xie, C., Lu, Z.: Program error rate-based wear leveling for NAND flash memory. In: 2018 Design, Automation & Test in Europe Conference & Exhibition (DATE), Dresden (2018)
5. Kim, J.S.: zFTL: power-efficient data compression support for NAND flash-based consumer electronics devices. IEEE Trans. Consum. Electron. **57**, 1148–1156 (2011)
6. Zhou, Y., Wu, F., Huang, P., et al.: Understanding and alleviating the impact of the flash address translation on solid state devices. J. ACM Trans. Storage **13**, 14 (2017)
7. Wang, M., Zhang, Y., Kang, W.: ZFTL: a zone-based flash translation layer with a two-tier selective caching mechanism. In: IEEE 14th International Conference on Communication Technology (2012)
8. Hahn, S.S., Kim, J., Lee, S.: To collect or not to collect: just-in-time garbage collection for high-performance SSDs with long lifetimes (2015)
9. Lee, S., Liu, M., Jun, S., et al.: Application-managed flash. In: USENIX Conference on File and Storage Technologies. USENIX Association (2016)
10. Chen, Y.T., Yang, M.C., Chang, Y.H., et al.: KVFTL: optimization of storage space utilization for key-value-specific flash storage devices. In: 22nd Asia and South Pacific Design Automation Conference (ASP-DAC). IEEE (2017)
11. Zhang, J., Shu, J., Lu, Y.: ParaFS: a log-structured file system to exploit the internal parallelism of flash devices. In: USENIX (ATC 2016) (2016)
12. Bjørling, M., Madsen, J., Bonnet, P., Zuck, A., Bandic, Z., Wang, Q.: LightNVM: lightning fast evaluation platform for non-volatile memories (2014)
13. Microsoft-FAT-Specification. http://read.pudn.com/downloads77/ebook/294884/FAT32%20Spec%20%28SDA%20Contribution%29.pdf
14. Jiang, S., Zhang, L., Yuan, X.H., et al.: S-FTL: an efficient address translation for flash memory by exploiting spatial locality (2011)
15. Hu, X., Eleftheriou, E., Haas, R., Iliadis, I., Pletka, R.: Write amplification analysis in flashbased solid state drives. In: Proceedings of the Israeli Experimental Systems Conference (2009)
16. https://www.gamersnexus.net/guides/1157-ssd-controller-technology-overprovisioning-waf
17. Ziv, J., Lempel, A.: A universal algorithm for sequential data compression. IEEE Trans. Inf. Theory **23**(3), 337–343 (1977)
18. Yim, K.S., Bahn, H., Koh, K.: A flash compression layer for SmartMedia card systems. IEEE Trans. Consum. Electron. **50**(1), 192–197 (2004)
19. Feng, M., et al.: Big data analytics and mining for effective visualization and trends forecasting of crime data. IEEE Access **7**, 106111–106123 (2019)
20. Gao, P., Ren, J.: Analysis and realization of Snort-based intrusion detection system. Comput. Appl. Softw. **23**(8), 134–135 (2006)
21. Feng, W., Huang, W., Ren, J.: Class imbalance ensemble learning based on margin theory. Appl. Sci. **8**(5), 815 (2018)
22. Sun, G., Ma, P., et al.: A stability constrained adaptive alpha for gravitational search algorithm. Knowl.-Based Syst. **139**, 200–213 (2018)

Author Index

Printed in the United States
By Bookmasters